"This proposed edited collection will offer a timely updating of the theory and practice of corporate identity, image and reputation to reflect the realities of the contemporary digital era, acknowledging the increasing variety of technology-mediated means by which consumers engage with brands. The breadth of the range of proposed contributions to this volume indicates that it will provide a comprehensive overview of this vitally important aspect of marketing practice".

Professor Gary Warnaby, Marketing Retail & Tourism/
Institute of Place Management

"This excellent book edited by professors Melewar, Dennis and Foroudi is a welcome addition to the corporate branding literature. It provides both academic rigor through systematic analyses and syntheses of literature on a wide range of topics within the area, and practical relevance through in-depth cases that help students and practitioners to apply the concepts in real life".

Guido Berens, Editor in Chief – Corporate Reputation Review

Building Corporate Identity, Image and Reputation in the Digital Era

Brands – corporate, products, service – today are collectively defined by their customers, deriving from personal experiences and word of mouth. This book acts as a forum for examining current and future trends in corporate branding, identity, image and reputation.

Recognising the complexity and plurality at the heart of the corporate branding discipline, this book fills a gap in the literature by posing a number of original research questions on the intrinsic nature of corporate branding ideas from corporate (external) and organisation (internal) identity perspectives as they relate to brand management, corporate reputation, marketing communications, social media, smart technology, experiential and sensory marketing. It incorporates current thinking and developments by both multidisciplinary academics and practitioners, combining a comprehensive theoretical foundation with practical insights. The text will serve as an important resource for the marketing, identity and brand practitioners requiring more than anecdotal evidence on the structure and operation of stakeholders communication in different geographical areas. It determines current practices and researches in diverse areas, regions and commercial and non-commercial sectors across the world.

The book provides scholars, researchers and postgraduate students in business and marketing with a comprehensive treatment of the nature of relationships between companies, brands and stakeholders in different areas and regions of the world.

T C Melewar is Professor of Marketing and Strategy with the Department of Marketing, Branding and Tourism at the Business School, Middlesex University London, UK.

Charles Dennis is Professor of Consumer Behaviour with the Department of Marketing, Branding and Tourism at the Business School, Middlesex University London, UK.

Pantea Foroudi is a Senior Lecturer in Branding with the Department of Marketing, Branding and Tourism at the Business School, Middlesex University London, UK.

Routledge Studies in Marketing

This series welcomes proposals for original research projects that are either single or multi-authored or an edited collection from both established and emerging scholars working on any aspect of marketing theory and practice and provides an outlet for studies dealing with elements of marketing theory, thought, pedagogy and practice.

It aims to reflect the evolving role of marketing and bring together the most innovative work across all aspects of the marketing 'mix' – from product development, consumer behaviour, marketing analysis, branding, and customer relationships, to sustainability, ethics and the new opportunities and challenges presented by digital and online marketing.

13. Internal Marketing
Theories, Perspectives and Stakeholders
David M. Brown

14. Stakeholder Involvement in Social Marketing
Challenges and Approaches to Engagement
Edited by Kathy Knox, Krzysztof Kubacki and Sharyn Rundle-Thiele

15. Decoding Coca-Cola
A Biography of a Global Brand
Edited by Robert Crawford, Linda Brennan and Susie Khamis

16. Luxury and Fashion Marketing
The Global Perspective
Satyendra Singh

17. Building Corporate Identity, Image and Reputation in the Digital Era
Edited by T C Melewar, Charles Dennis and Pantea Foroudi

For more information about this series, please visit: www.routledge.com/Routledge-Studies-in-Marketing/book-series/RMKT

Building Corporate Identity, Image and Reputation in the Digital Era

Edited by T C Melewar, Charles Dennis and Pantea Foroudi

LONDON AND NEW YORK

First published 2022
by Routledge
2 Park Square, Milton Park, Abingdon, Oxon OX14 4RN

and by Routledge
52 Vanderbilt Avenue, New York, NY 10017

Routledge is an imprint of the Taylor & Francis Group, an informa business

© 2022 selection and editorial matter, T C Melewar, Charles Dennis
and Pantea Foroudi; individual chapters, the contributors

The right of T C Melewar, Charles Dennis and Pantea Foroudi to be
identified as the authors of the editorial material, and of the authors for
their individual chapters, has been asserted in accordance with sections
77 and 78 of the Copyright, Designs and Patents Act 1988.

All rights reserved. No part of this book may be reprinted or reproduced
or utilised in any form or by any electronic, mechanical, or other
means, now known or hereafter invented, including photocopying and
recording, or in any information storage or retrieval system, without
permission in writing from the publishers.

Trademark notice: Product or corporate names may be trademarks
or registered trademarks, and are used only for identification and
explanation without intent to infringe.

British Library Cataloguing-in-Publication Data
A catalogue record for this book is available from the British Library

Library of Congress Cataloging-in-Publication Data
Names: Melewar, T. C., editor.
Title: Building corporate identity, image and reputation in the digital
era / edited by TC Melewar, Charles Dennis and Pantea Foroudi.
Description: Abingdon, Oxon ; New York, NY : Routledge, 2021. |
Series: Routledge studies in marketing | Includes bibliographical
references and index.
Identifiers: LCCN 2020051395 (print) | LCCN 2020051396 (ebook)
Subjects: LCSH: Corporate image. | Branding (Marketing) |
Reputation. | Communication in marketing.
Classification: LCC HD59.2 .B85 2021 (print) | LCC HD59.2 (ebook)
| DDC 659.2/85--dc23
LC record available at https://lccn.loc.gov/2020051395
LC ebook record available at https://lccn.loc.gov/2020051396

ISBN: 978-0-367-53123-2 (hbk)
ISBN: 978-0-367-53124-9 (pbk)
ISBN: 978-1-003-08057-2 (ebk)

Typeset in Goudy
By Deanta Global Publishing Services, Chennai, India

Contents

List of figures	x
List of tables	xii
Contributors	xiv

PART I
Introduction   1

1   Introduction: Building corporate identity, image and reputation
    in the digital era   3
    T C MELEWAR, CHARLES DENNIS AND PANTEA FOROUDI

PART II
Building a corporate brand identity   9

2   Corporate identity: Definition and components   11
    MOHAMMAD M. FOROUDI, PANTEA FOROUDI AND JOHN M.T. BALMER

3   Managing marketing competencies: A framework for
    understanding antecedents of marketing capability and its
    relation to the company's core competencies   75
    PANTEA FOROUDI, MOHAMMAD M. FOROUDI, KHALID HAFEEZ AND JAVAD IZADI

4   Reputation: Configuring the symmetrical and asymmetrical
    paths to architecture in a retail setting   113
    MOHAMMAD M. FOROUDI, PANTEA FOROUDI AND ZHONGQI JIN

5   Conceptualising sensory brand experience: Using review of
    knowledge fields to identify potential future research direction   140
    DONGMEI ZHA, PANTEA FOROUDI, ZHONGQI JIN AND T C MELEWAR

viii *Contents*

6 Corporate brand identity: Virtual space 169

MARIA TERESA CUOMO, CINZIA GENOVINO, DEBORA TORTORA AND
ALEX GIORDANO

**7 Aesthetic heritage and corporate branding: Luxury heritage
brands between tradition and modernity** 181

ANGELA BARGENDA

PART III
Building a corporate brand image 203

**8 Corporate multi-channel branding: Platforms for
#CorporateBranding** 205

AWELE ACHI, OGECHI ADEOLA AND FRANCIS CHUKWUEDO ACHI

9 Value co-creation behaviour: Antecedents and consequences 218

YOUSEF ALQAYED, PANTEA FOROUDI, CHARLES DENNIS,
MOHAMMAD M. FOROUDI AND KAOUTHER KOOLI

**10 An assessment of customer experience concept: Looking back to
move forward** 260

DONGMEI ZHA, REZA MARVI, PANTEA FOROUDI, CHARLES DENNIS, AKIKO UENO,
ZHONGQI JIN AND T C MELEWAR

11 Employee occupational identity 289

MARIA J. JEREZ-JEREZ, T C MELEWAR AND PANTEA FOROUDI

**12 Behavioural intentions in the UK fashion industry: The impact
of perceived fashion innovativeness on fashion brand image with
the moderating role of social media marketing and lovemark** 307

HELNAZ AHMADI LARI, PANTEA FOROUDI AND SAHEB IMANI

13 Corporate brand image: Technology and innovation in e-tailing 347

VIRGINIA VANNUCCI AND ELEONORA PANTANO

PART IV
Building a corporate brand reputation 363

**14 Take a new turn: Relationships between corporate identity
management and corporate reputation in a hospitality context** 365

PANTEA FOROUDI, REZA MARVI, JAVAD IZADI, MOHAMMAD M. FOROUDI
AND POUYA PIRZADEH

Contents ix

15 Islamic brand love 401
WALEED YOUSEF AND NAJWA YOUSEF

16 Societal corporate branding and political discourse: where brand
ethics meets with consumers' clicktivism 415
ROSSELLA GAMBETTI, SILVIA BIRAGHI, T C MELEWAR AND ANGELA BECCANULLI

17 Brand knowledge, brand community and brand engagement 444
SURAKSHA GUPTA, DONGMEI CAO AND AISHA ABUELMAATTI

18 Building and sustaining personal brand: Examining the
effectiveness of personal branding in the context of education 467
MARWA TOURKY, PANTEA FOROUDI AND FATMA HAJI AL-ZADJALI

19 How the digital environment and its user experience effects the
customer's perception of luxury brands and co-creation of brand
value 487
NASTARAN NOROUZI RICHARDS-CARPENTER AND THIMO GRANTZ

20 Celebrity endorsement, theories, models, existing literature and
corporate identity, image and reputation 515
SHAHZEB HUSSAIN

Index 535

Figures

2.1 Corporate history and the founder of Brunel Business School with the number of students per year	57
3.1 Conceptual framework	79
4.1 Foundational complex configural model	129
5.1 An integrative framework of sensory brand experience	150
5.2 Brand setting of Alpen Swiss Style Muesli	159
6.1 The process of reputation forming. Source: adapted from Romenti, 2008	173
6.2 The Corporate Brand Identity Matrix. Source: (Urde, 2013)	173
6.3 Think different	176
6.4 Simplicity is the ultimate sophistication	177
9.1 Value co-creation behaviour journey in online community	244
10.1 Customer experience literature intellectual structure pt 1 [1996–2010 (MDS)]	264
10.2 Customer experience literature intellectual structure pt 2 [2011–2016 (MDS)]	265
10.3 Customer experience literature intellectual structure pt 3 [2017–2019 (MDS)]	267
10.4 Customer experience literature intellectual structure pt 1 [1996–2010 (HCA)]	268
10.5 Customer experience literature intellectual structure pt 2 [2011–2016 (HCA)]	269
10.6 Customer experience literature intellectual structure pt 3 [2017–2019 (HCA)]	270
10.7 Customer experience literature intellectual structure pt 1 [1996–2010]	271
10.8 Customer experience literature intellectual structure pt 2 [2011–2016 (EFA)]	272
10.9 Customer experience literature intellectual structure pt 3 [2017–2019 (EFA)]	273
10.10 Longitudinal development of customer experience research	281

Figures xi

11.1	Conceptual framework	298
12.1	Conceptual framework	315
12.2	– Results	333
12.3	Importance-performance map analysis for purchase intention in NorthLondon consumers	334
12.4	Galleria Melissa – New York	337
12.5	A collaboration with Pineapple dance studio held in London; based on Dance Machine Fall/Winter 2016 collection	337
12.6	New York fashion week	338
12.7	Melissa recyclable sandals	339
12.8	The collaboration of Zaha Hadid (architecture) with Melissa extends the portfolio of Zaha Hadid in style	339
13.1	Retailers' competitive advantage creation in the technology-enriched scenario. Source: the authors	353
13.2	A consumer playing with the Gucci app to virtual try-on a certain pair of Gucci sneakers. Source: the authors	357
14.1	The research conceptual model	383
15.1	The major antecedents and consequences of brand love. Source: Albert and Merunka (2013); Batra et al. (2012); Nguyen et al. (2013)	405
16.1	Cucapa's t-shirts in comparison: with calor and sin calor	420
16.2	President Donald Trump's tweet on global warming	422
16.3	"We Accept" manifesto on Airbnb corporate website	423
16.4	"Equality" advertising campaign	425
16.5	Gina Rodriguez and Serena Williams for Nike Equality campaign	425
16.6	Emoji installation at MoMa	426
16.7	Dove Print Campaign #AlternativeFacts	430
16.8	Positive comments on Dove's campaign via Twitter	431
16.9	Green cups featuring an illustration by Shogo Ota showing the faces of more than a hundred people	432
16.10	Examples of positive and negative reactions on Twitter	433
16.11	Nike's first release of advertisement starring Colin Kaepernick	436
16.12	Nike's advertisement "Dream crazy" published on YouTube	436
17.1	Research model	451
17.2	Multigroup comparison: path coefficients, T values and R squares	456
18.1	Building and sustaining personal building	469
18.2	Key dimensions of a personal brand	472
18.3	Personal branding theoretical framework	479

Tables

2.1	Some of the key definitions of corporate identity concept	39
4.1	Demographic profile of the consumers from retailers of international brands compared with the main population figures (N=489)	118
4.2	Cross-tabulations employing the quintiles between the constructs	120
4.3	Exploratory and confirmatory factor analysis	122
4.4	Descriptive statistics and correlations (N=489)	125
4.5	Configurations of physical stimuli, spatial layout/functionality and symbolic artefacts predicting reputation	127
5.1	Overview of main knowledge fields in sensory brand experience research	143
9.1	Brief review of different schools of thought in marketing	222
9.2	Role of operand and operant resources in distinguishing goods-dominance from service-dominant logic	223
9.3	The istorical development of S-D logic	227
12.1	Initial pool of items	323
12.2	Demographic profile of the respondents (N=300)	326
12.3	Fashion innovative shopping experience (N=300)	327
12.4	Summary of GoF indices for the global model	327
12.5	Results of the measurement model	328
12.6	Discriminant validity	330
12.7	Full collinearity VIFs of constructs values for common method bias	331
12.8	Results of hypotheses tests	332
12.9	IPMA for purchase intention in North London consumers	334
14.1	The main scale dimensions, item sources and reliability measures for each construct	377
14.2	Demographic characteristics	379
14.3	Corporate reputation	381
14.4	Results of hypothesis testing	384
15.1	The four sources of *Sharia*	406

		Tables	xiii
17.1	Respondent profile (n=209)		453
17.2	Constructs reliability and validity		455
17.3	Discriminant validity: HTMT criterion		455
17.4	Structural parameter estimates with standardised coefficients		455
17.5	Multiple group analysis (MGA): PLS-MGA and Welch-Satterthwait Test (WST)		458

Contributors

Aisha Abuelmaatti is a Lecturer in Project Management at the Faculty of Business & Law, Coventry University.

Ogechi Adeola is an Associate Professor of Marketing and the Academic Director of the Sales & Marketing Academy at Lagos Business School, Pan-Atlantic University, Nigeria. Ogechi is a prolific academic writer and author of children's books including the Jo and Skippa series and the Miss Wiggy and Makky the Mohawk series.

John M.T. Balmer BA (Hons), MBA (Dunelm), PhD, A.Mus.TCL, Dip.M, PGCE holds a personal chair as Professor of Corporate Marketing in Brunel University London. He is quondam Professor of Corporate Brand/Identity Management at Bradford School of Management where he is also a Visiting Professor. He also pioneered the corporate marketing, corporate heritage brand/identity, total corporate communications, monarchical marketing, ethical corporate identity, corporate marketing notions and, penned the first academic articles in these aforementioned areas. Also co-conceived the corporate heritage brand/corporate brand with a heritage notions and was the originator of the corporate heritage identity and corporate brand orientation notions.

Angela Bargenda is an Associate Professor of Marketing, Communication and Management at ESCE International Business School in Paris.

Angela Beccanulli is a PhD candidate in Management and Innovation at the Università Cattolica del Sacro Cuore in Milan and junior research fellow at LABCOM (Research Lab on Business Communication). Her current research interests are in the areas of consumer relationships with objects, object-oriented sociality, cultural branding, consumer culture and technology.

Silvia Biraghi is Assistant Professor of Management at the Università Cattolica del Sacro Cuore in Milan and Research Associate at LABCOM (Research Lab on Business Communication). Her current research topics include consumer-brand relationships, consumer culture, client-agency relations and consumer connectivity.

Contributors xv

Dongmei Cao is a Lecturer in Business Management and Research Associate with the Faculty of Business & Law at Coventry University, UK. Dongmei's primary research interest is sustainability, which incorporates technology applications, innovation, big data, social media and responsible consumption. Her research has been published in the top domain journals such as *Journal of Business Research*, *Technological Forecasting & Social Change*, *Production Planning & Control*, and *Journal of Cleaner Production*.

Maria Teresa Cuomo is an Associate Professor of Business Economics at the University of Salerno, where she teaches "Management and Innovation" and "Management". She carries out research, consultancy and training for various organisations (both public and private) on finance and performance, investment assessment, market research and marketing.

Mohammad Mahdi Foroudi (PhD, BSc (Honour)) is a founder and managing director of Foroudi Consultancy. He is responsible for managing the firm's worldwide interests and enhancing its strategic and creative global offering to his clients in the UK, including the growth and development of the brand, company's corporate identity and architecture since 2013. He has earned my PhD from Brunel University London. He has published widely in international academic journals such as Journal of Business Research, European Journal of Marketing, and so on.

Rossella Gambetti is Associate Professor of Corporate and Marketing Communication at the Università Cattolica del Sacro Cuore in Milan where she serves as a member of the scientific committee of the Research Lab on Business Communication (LABCOM). Her main research areas are in the field of understanding consumer culture and its influence on communication processes among consumers and between business and society, with a special focus on how technology is shaping consumers' sociality and consumer-brand relationships.

Cinzia Genovino earned a PhD in Management & Information Technology at the University of Salerno, Italy, where she currently teaches management with the Department of Economics and Statistics. She has published national and international chapters in books and articles on raw materials, as well as marketing and corporate finance. Since 1998, she has been working as a financial and marketing consultant for several organizations, especially in the financial sector.

Alex Giordano is currently Researcher in Innovation at the University Federico II of Naples (Italy), where he teaches Innovation and Industry 4.0. His main subjects of interest concern technology and innovation and corporate reputation.

Suraksha Gupta is a Professor of Marketing at Newcastle University, London, UK. In her current work, she has been trying to push boundaries of our knowledge about possible linkages between marketing initiatives of international

xvi *Contributors*

brands and sustainable development goals such as waste management and use of technology to address access-related issues of bottom of the pyramid (BOP) segment.

Khalid Hafeez is Professor of Digital Transformation at the Faculty of Business 7 Law De Montfort university.

Shahzeb Hussain is a Senior Lecturer in Marketing at Northumbria University. His research interests include branding, consumer behaviour, advertising, relationship marketing and ethics.

Saheb Imani is a member of the Department of Business Management, Khorramshahr- Persian Gulf International Branch, Islamic Azad University, Khorramshahr, Iran.

Javad Izadi is a Senior Lecturer in Accounting and Finance at the University of West London. He is a member of the European and Iranian Accounting Association.

Maria J. Jerez-Jerez received her PhD in Business Management from Middlesex University, London, UK. She has a Master of Arts degree in International Hotel and Restaurant Management from London Metropolitan University, UK.

Zhongqi Jin has been involved in teaching and research on innovation and marketing. He has taught both postgraduate and undergraduate students in marketing, marketing research, new product development and innovation management. He has recently completed a 12-country collaborative research project regarding global branding and consumer behaviour including consumers from Brazil, China, Egypt, France, India, Malaysia, Mauritius, South Africa, the UK, the USA and Turkey.

Kaouther Kooli is a Principal Academic in Marketing with the Department of Marketing, Strategy and Innovation at the Faculty of Management, Bournemouth University, UK. She earned a PhD in Marketing. She has over 18 years of higher education teaching experience acquired in Tunisia, the UK and France. Her research interests are in digital B2B marketing, consumer behaviour and digital marketing. She is an expert in both quantitative and qualitative research methods. She is the Associate Editor of the *Journal of Customer Behaviour* and the Chair of the Academy of Marketing B2B Special Interest Group. She has established an annual conference on B2B marketing where academics, students and practitioners get together to debate current issues and challenges facing B2B marketing. She has published in top journals. Kaouther has been invited to give talks at a number of universities both in the UK and abroad.

Helnaz Ahmadi Lari is a PhD student at Middlesex University, UK.

Reza Marvi is an Associate Lecturer of Marketing at Middlesex University, UK. His research interests are mainly customer engagement in the service context.

Contributors xvii

Eleonora Pantano is Senior Lecturer (Associate Professor) of Marketing at University of Bristol.

Nastaran Norouzi Richards-Carpenter is Associate Professor of Marketing-Programme Director of MA Luxury Brand Management at Richmond the American University in London.

Debora Tortora is currently Researcher in Business Management at the University Bicocca of Milan (Italy), where he teaches Management. Her main subjects of interest concern tourism, augmented reality and marketing, consumer behaviour, retail and experience, brand and corporate reputation.

Marwa Tourky is Senior Lecturer of Marketing at Exeter University Business School, UK and Vice-Chair of South West Federation of Museums and Art Galleries, UK. Her research is focused in areas such as corporate brand, identity and reputation, communications and corporate social responsibility (CSR). Marwa is also interested in relationship marketing and networks, both in a business-to-business (B2B) and business-to-customer (B2C) context.

Akiko Ueno joined Middlesex University, UK, in 2013 as a Senior Lecturer in Marketing. She earned an MBA from the University of Exeter, UK, a PhD from the University of Bedfordshire, UK, and a GradDip in Law from the University of Westminster, UK. She is a Fellow of the Higher Education Academy.

Virginia Vannucci is a Post-Doc Research Fellow in Marketing at the University of Florence, Italy. Her research activities explore the impact of digital technologies on consumer behaviour and retailers' strategies, exploring the effects of in-store human and digital touchpoints.

Najwa Yousef is a Dental Intern at Imam Abdulrahman Bin Faisal University. Her research interests include surgery, digital dentistry, business advertisement, private sector marketing and health care awareness.

Waleed Yousef is an Assistant Professor in Marketing at Jubail University College. His research interests include the following areas: consumer behaviour, branding and culture.

Fatma Haji Al-Zadjali is a Joiner Marketing Lecturer at the Higher College of Technology in Muscat, Sultanate of Oman. Her research interests are in branding, advertising and customer relationship management (CRM).

Dongmei Zha is a PhD student at Middlesex University, UK. Her research interests are mainly customer experience and brand sensory experience. She has published in many journals including the *International Journal of Management Reviews*.

Part I
Introduction

1 Introduction

Building corporate identity, image and reputation in the digital era

T C Melewar, Charles Dennis and Pantea Foroudi

Introduction

Corporate branding, identity, image and reputation have become increasingly important in academic research and management practice. The growth has been driven in large part by the prodigious, prestigious research and publication output of researchers in a handful of business schools over a couple of decades. From early work on corporate visual identity published in world-leading journals such as *Journal of International Business Studies*, as far back as the previous millennium, these scholars' works have led to the development of scales for corporate visual identity, progressing to a research agenda encompassing all aspects of corporate branding, identity, image and reputation across a wide spectrum of traditional and new channels.

Over the ensuing decades, this field has been defined and broadened. Previous research published demonstrated that there is a considerable divergence in opinions among practitioners concerning the fundamental components of corporate identity. Over the decades, research has made great strides in unifying the concepts. Further research has progressed beyond the role that visual identity plays in the corporate identity and corporate image literature to encompass non-visual cues. A holistic perspective incorporates all sensory stimuli based on the five human senses (i.e. seeing, hearing, smelling, tasting and touching), proposing the construct of corporate sensory identity. Corporate sensory identity incorporates these five sensory dimensions in a consistent way that reflects all senses by which an organisation can convey its identity to all of its internal and external stakeholders. Other research links corporate logo, image and reputation. The main antecedents of the favourable corporate logo are a corporate name, design and typeface. Logo enhances the corporate image, attitude towards advertisements, recognisability, familiarity and corporate reputation. More recent studies extend understanding of corporate impression formation to online communities and corporate website favourability.

Notwithstanding *extensive study to date, by its very nature, this body of work poses many future research questions*. These include, for example, what are the effects of antecedents such as corporate communication, design, culture, behaviour, strategy, structure, organisation, leadership, financial and social performance

4 T C Melewar, C. Dennis and P. Foroudi

on consequences including customer loyalty, trust and commitment across the whole range of possible contexts? This book thus aims *to bring together researchers addressing research areas such as these in determining what and how customers seek to engage with an organisation and its offerings.* Customers engage with brands through many channels including word of mouth, social networks and mobile apps. As the economic environment becomes more customer-driven, corporate and brand identity become essential aspects of organisation strategy driven by customer demands for value co-creation. Hence brands – corporate, products, service – today are collectively defined by their customers, based on personal or business requirements for economic, emotional or experiential value, deriving from personal experiences and word of mouth.

The book acts as a forum for examining current and future trends in corporate branding, identity, image and reputation. Submissions of chapters are sought to engage with literature and ideas from corporate (external) and organisation (internal) identity perspectives as they relate to brand management, corporate reputation, marketing communications, social media, smart technology, experiential and sensory marketing.

Recognising the complexity and plurality at the heart of the corporate branding discipline, this book will fill a gap in the market, by posing a number of original research questions on the intrinsic nature of corporate branding ideas from corporate (external) and organisation (internal) identity perspectives as they relate to brand management, corporate reputation, marketing communications, social media, smart technology, experiential and sensory marketing. This book incorporates current thinking and developments by both academics and practitioners, combines a comprehensive theoretical foundation with practical insights and provides insights to assist managers in their daily decision-making and long-term brand decisions.

Main focus of the chapter

Issues and perspectives

This book aims to address the following four objectives: (i) to explore the multiple stakeholder audiences that brands of all types must address. Corporate branding encompasses many facets, which are covered throughout the book. Such facets of branding include strategic planning and campaign management, research and measurement, media relations, employee communication, leadership and change communication and crisis branding; (ii) to provide examples from a wide range of industries and firms in order to illustrate the many dimensions of corporate branding and theories; and (iii) to enable readers to understand research studies from different branding points of view. In this sense, they will be able to compare, contrast and comprehend whether "corporate branding" from different lenses are delivered similarly or otherwise in different parts of the world. This enables readers to understand differences and subsequent application towards managing these corporate brands. Readers will be able to acquire knowledge and understanding of (i) the

Introduction 5

key issues in corporate branding theories; (ii) the need for a strategic approach to planning and campaign management; and (iii) new developments in corporate branding theories. In addition, they will be able to (i) analyse the complex web of stakeholder audiences that corporate brands must address; (ii) develop and manage stakeholder strategy and campaigns; and (iii) adapt to the differing demands of stakeholders such as employees, the media and other stakeholder audiences.

Our volume starts from the issues related to corporate branding, identity, internal and external stakeholders, and companies and expands them adding useful insights on legacy, identity and reputation; performance and profit; differentiation and protection; ethics, sustainability and inclusion; aesthetics; sensorium; virtual space; internal stakeholders; external stakeholders; customer experience, customer satisfaction, customer loyalty and business performance. Moreover, our book, proposing a mixture of theory and practice with effective case studies, aims at reaching primarily doctoral, postgraduate, graduate and final year undergraduate students in business and marketing, but it will be suitable for both managers and decision-makers around the world too.

This edited book serves as a core or supplementary text for advanced undergraduates and postgraduates and a key resource for practitioners.

The organisation of the book

There are four main parts to the book – the introduction, which offers the coverage of practical implications for corporate identity, marketing and communication practitioners, and the following paragraphs outline the main parts of the book.

Part I: Introduction "Building corporate identity, image and reputation in the digital era" introduces the book, its goals and briefly summarises the main topics of each part.

Part II: "Building a corporate brand identity" considers interrelationships between corporate identity, marketing assets and capability, architecture, sensorium, virtual space and aesthetic heritage as to whether branding values are delivered similarly in different sectors

Chapter 2 "Corporate identity: definition and components" by Mohammad M. Foroudi, Pantea Foroudi, and John M.T. Balmer provides a systematic review of the identity literature and reviews a range of literature in order to establish the domain of corporate identity and the related concepts. Then, the intrinsic nature of identity and background is shown by examining the growing interest in the evolution of perspectives in the corporate identity field. Also, the chapter examines corporate identity in relation to a number of different strands of established studies and identifies the key concepts related to corporate identity management by drawing insights from the main theoretical paradigms.

Chapter 3 "Managing marketing competencies: a framework for understanding antecedents of marketing capability and its relation to the company's core competencies" by Pantea Foroudi, Mohammad M. Foroudi, Khalid Hafeez and Javad Izadi identifies the key elements of marketing assets and capabilities. The authors state that core competencies are the crown jewels of a company and, therefore,

6 *T C Melewar, C. Dennis and P. Foroudi*

should be carefully identified, nurtured and developed. Based on *resource-based theory*, this study explores how core competence can lead to firms' competitive advantage, and how a *marketing firm* can identify its core competence in the sector to attain competitive advantage.

Chapter 4 "Reputation: configuring the symmetrical and asymmetrical paths to architecture in a retail setting" is written by Mohammad M. Foroudi, Pantea Foroudi and Zhongqi Jin. Grounded in social identity and attribution theories, this chapter focuses on the effect of architecture and its components on reputation. The relationships conceptualised were evaluated using data collected from a survey of 489 online and offline UK retail consumers and employees. To accommodate the equifinality and complexity of these relationships, this study employs fuzzy set qualitative comparative analysis, predictive validity and fit validity check.

Chapter 5 "Conceptualising sensory brand experience: using review of knowledge fields and bibliometric data to identify potential future research direction" by Dongmei Zha, T C Melewar, Pantea Foroudi and Zhongqi Jin proposes a conceptual framework for sensory brand experience. The chapter starts with a review of the seven knowledge fields deemed to have constitutive influences on the development of sensory brand experience literature, followed by two bibliometric methods which cover 151 sensory-related articles and 4,038 citations between 1994 and 2019.

Chapter 6 "Corporate brand identity: virtual space", by Maria Teresa Cuomo, Cinzia Genovino, Debora Tortora and Alex Giordano aims to underline the importance of digital (smart) and social media in corporate branding, identity, image and reputation. Consumers live immersive experiences that enable brand associations, especially in virtual space. By branding the virtual world, businesses can use smart technologies and social media to engage and create relationships with customers, achieving competitive advantages.

Chapter 7 "Aesthetic heritage and corporate branding Luxury heritage brands between tradition and modernity" by Angela Bargenda shows that aesthetic heritage does not oppose digitalisation, but, on the contrary, delivers valuable resources for the construction of a meaningful and value-based corporate identity. Also, in view of the acceleration of digital channels in marketing communication and sales transactions, issues of aesthetics related to heritage brands are becoming ever more pertinent.

Part III: Building a corporate brand image considers interrelationships between branding, design, aesthetics, voice, sensorium and virtual spaces from a wide range of commercial and non-commercial sectors which include business-to-business and business-to-consumers sectors as to whether branding values are delivered similarly in different sectors.

Chapter 8 "Corporate multi-channel branding: platforms for #corporatebranding" by Awele Achi, Ogechi Adeola and Francis Chukwuedo Achi focuses on multi-communication channels for corporate branding. Specifically, this chapter seeks to explicate the various appropriate communication channels open to organisations as they seek to align their overall corporate branding with their internal and external stakeholders, especially, in this digital era of sustainable branding.

Introduction 7

Chapter 9 "Value co-creation behaviour: antecedents and consequences" by Yousef Alqayed, Pantea Foroudi, Charles Dennis, Mohammad M. Foroudi, and Kaouther Kooli emphasises the concept of value co-creation behaviour. The chapter identifies the key factors influencing the favourability of value co-creation behaviour (perceived quality, identification and experience) and the outcomes (satisfaction, passion, corporate brand commitment, brand loyalty and active participation).

Chapter 10 "An assessment of customer experience concept: looking back to move forward" by Dongmei Zha, Reza Marvi, Pantea Foroudi, Charles Dennis, Akiko Ueno, Zhongqi Jin and T C Melewar aims to identify the main knowledge structure of customer experience, to understand how the knowledge structure of customer experience has changed over time, and to build a new customer experience conceptual framework.

Chapter 11 "Employee occupational identity" by Maria J. Jerez-Jerez, T C Melewar and Pantea Foroudi aims to develop a better comprehension of employee's occupational identity concept, its antecedents and consequences (employee turnover and work engagement); the importance of the stimuli and its influence on building corporate identity, image and reputation in the digital era is explained by using salience as a moderator of this relationship.

Chapter 12 "Behavioural intentions in the UK fashion industry: the impact of perceived fashion innovativeness on fashion brand image with the moderating role of social media marketing and lovemark" by Helnaz Ahmadi Lari, Pantea Foroudi and Saheb Imani explores previous literature to (i) evaluate the concept of fashion innovativeness, (ii) identify the aspects that have a significant influence on fashion innovativeness, (iii) develop and assess a conceptual framework concerning the relationships between fashion innovativeness, its antecedents and its consequences and (iv) investigate the impact of fashion innovativeness among British consumers.

Chapter 13 "Corporate brand image: technology and innovation in e-tailing" by Virginia Vannucci and Eleonora Pantano discusses the role of technology (i.e., virtual and augmented reality, social media, etc.) and innovation in improving corporate branding in the context of electronic retailing (e-tailing), with emphasis on the consumer's online interactions with retailers, and on the massive amount of data emerging from these interactions. The chapter proposes a theoretical framework synthesising how retailers would generate a competitive advantage in the new settings enriched with advanced technology. The chapter concludes with a case study of the Gucci App, which merges several innovative features such as augmented reality for users' virtual try-on.

Part IV: Building a corporate brand reputation considers interrelationships between corporate reputation, celebrity endorsement, religiosity, ethics, sustainability and inclusion in the emerging market and developed market.

Chapter 14 "Take a new turn: relationships between corporate identity management and corporate reputation in a hospitality context" by Pantea Foroudi, Reza Marvi, Javad Izadi, Mohammad M. Foroudi, and Pouya Pirzadeh explores what the main factors are that influence corporate identity management? And what are the key factors that influence corporate reputation favourably?

Results demonstrate that philosophy, vision, mission and top management driving force positively influence corporate identity management.

Chapter 15 "Islamic brand love" introduces the concept of corporate religious branding and how beliefs and brand love influence brand loyalty, word of mouth and purchase intention and is written by Waleed Yousef and Najwa Yousef. In this chapter, authors examine religious beliefs as a new antecedent to brand love and propose a new construct, that of Islamic brand love. In addition, this chapter investigates some psychological antecedents to brand love such as cultural identity, religiosity or strongly held values. This chapter aims to address the following objectives: (i) to explore the relationship between religious beliefs and brand love; (ii) to offer a better understanding of Muslim consumer behaviour towards branding; (iii) to explore how *Sharia* sources affect Muslim consumers regarding brand love; (iv) to propose Islamic brand love as a new construct and (v) to offer a new scale for brand love based on religious beliefs.

Chapter 16 "Societal corporate branding and political discourse: where brand ethics meet with consumers' clicktivism" by Rossella Gambetti, Silvia Biraghi, T C Melewar and Angela Beccanulli concentrates on how the current humanistic tension of companies to use the corporate brand as an enabler of political discourses and actions that are felt as cogent in society has become a fundamental embedded dimension of an ethical corporate branding strategy that leverages on consumer clicktivism.

Chapter 17 "Brand knowledge, brand community and brand engagement" by Suraksha Gupta, Aisha Abuelmaatti and Dongmei Cao aims to understand the interactive impact of brand knowledge and brand community engagement on purchase intention with an examination of the Honda car communities in the city of Jakarta.

Chapter 18 "Building and sustaining personal brand: examining the effectiveness of personal branding in the context of education" by Marwa Tourky, Pantea Foroudi and Fatma Haji Al-Zadjali advances theoretical and practical understanding of personal branding strategic use. The chapter presents a unique framework – drawing on social and cultural capital and impression management theories – that should facilitate students, graduates and young professionals to develop their personal brands.

Chapter 19 "How the digital environment and its user experience affect the customer's perception of luxury brands, and co-creation of brand value" by Nastaran Norouzi, Richards-Carpenter and Thimo Grantz focuses on digital sensory branding in luxury marketing. Online engagement has become a primary branding tool, especially in the context of a continuously growing customer audience and its engagement in the luxury industry. This study explores sensory aspects which interact with users to identify the digital relationship, as well as the effects a virtual environment has on brand perception.

Chapter 20 "Celebrity endorsement, theories, models, existing literature and corporate identity, image and reputation" by Shahzeb Hussain describes the concept of celebrity endorsement, models, theories and its impacts on corporate identity, image and reputation.

Part II

Building a corporate brand identity

2 Corporate identity
Definition and components

Mohammad M. Foroudi, Pantea Foroudi and John M.T. Balmer

Introduction

This chapter provides a systematic review of the identity literature and reviews a range of literature in order to establish the domain of corporate identity and the related concepts. Then, the intrinsic nature of identity and background is shown by examining the growing interest in the evolution of perspectives in the corporate identity field. Also, it examines corporate identity in relation to a number of different strands of established studies and identifies the key concepts related to corporate identity management by drawing insights from the main theoretical paradigms

Background to corporate identity

Every organisation has an identity. Corporate identity is the "articulation of what an organisation is, what it stands for, what it does and the way it goes about its business especially the way it relates to its stakeholders and the environment" (Balmer, 2008, p. 899). Research in the corporate identity area demonstrates that the significant purpose of corporate identity management is to achieve a favourable image of the company's internal and external stakeholders (Foroudi et al., 2019, 2020) and reputation (Foroudi, 2019, 2020; Foroudi et al., 2014) that leads to competitive advantage (Balmer and Gray, 2000; Balmer and Stotvig, 1997; Melewar et al., 2006; Van Riel and Balmer, 1997). Corporate identity deals with the experiences, impressions, beliefs, feelings and knowledge that the public has about a corporation (Bernstein, 1986, Foroudi and Marvi, 2021) and demonstrates the bundle of characteristics of the company and displays the company's personality (Cornelissen and Harris, 2001; Markwick and Fill, 1997; Olins, 1978; Van Heerden and Puth, 1995; Van Riel and Balmer, 1995). Furthermore, an effective corporate identity helps employees to have the propensity to work for the company, as well as attracting more investors to buy the company's shares (Van Riel and Balmer, 1997).

It is essential to address the term "identity" when approaching corporate identity studies. Identity has been referred to in various contexts. The most essential of all identity types and the earliest definitions of identity related to individual

12   Foroudi, Foroudi and Balmer

identity (along with gender) can shape corporate identities (Balmer, 2008). Individual identity is determined by corporate identity, which is particularly related to the fields of sociology and ideology (role theory) (Balmer, 2008) and psychoanalysis (Moingeon and Ramanantsoa, 1997). A significant part of identity in psychology is the degree to which an individual views him/herself as a unique person in relation to other people (Moingeon and Ramanantsoa, 1997). The earliest psychologist who was explicitly interested in identity was Erikson (1960). In cognitive psychology, identity is defined as a capacity for self-reflection and the awareness of self (Leary and Tangney, 2003, p. 3). Erikson (1956) states that identity is "a mutual relation in that it connotes both a persistent sameness within oneself (self-sameness) and a persistent sharing of some kind of essential character with others" (p. 102). Analysis of this definition emphasises that the subject of identity is the individual rather than the organisation (He and Balmer, 2007) and the idiosyncratic things that make a person unique.

The notion of identity can also be associated with organisations. More precisely, "the identity goes back to the existence of a system of characteristics which has a pattern which gives the company its specificity, its stability and its coherence" (Moingeon and Ramanantsoa, 1997, p. 385). Identity may be seen as an abstract idea, a distinctive characteristic that suggests each organisation has its own personality, individuality and uniqueness that they express in their dealings with others. As some authors (Balmer, 2001; Bernstein, 1986; Cornelissen et al., 2007) state, organisations have a personality in the same way that people do. Identity can be viewed as the vehicle that expresses an organisation's unique characteristics to audiences (Abratt, 1989; Balmer et al., 2007; Bernstein, 1986; Olins, 1979). Corporate identity is the expression of a company (He and Mukherjee, 2008; Van Riel and Balmer, 1997) and the expression of an identity is a dynamic process so it may change or take different forms over time.

The early management and marketing literature has used corporate identity and corporate image interchangeably (e.g. Bernstein, 1986; Bick et al., 2003; Chajet, 1984; Margulies, 1977; Olins, 1978, 1979, 1989; Schmitt and Simonson, 1997; Selame and Selame, 1975; Simoes et al., 2005; Van Riel and Balmer, 1997). For example, Martineau (1958) stresses the question, "what makes up a store's image in the minds of customers?" (p. 51). Store image elements such as architecture, layout, colour, advertising and salespeople are used as concepts in the development of a retail personality. Marketing researchers have devoted considerable attention to developing the idea that consumers hold images of particular stores in their minds (e.g. Berry, 1969; Chowdhury et al., 1998; Kasulis and Lusch, 1981; Kunkel and Berry, 1968; Marks, 1976; Mazursky and Jacoby, 1986). What makes up a store's image in the minds of customers? Martineau (1958) stressed elements such as layout and architecture (e.g. modernisation of the physical plant), colour schemes, advertising and salespeople. Each of these concepts has its own intellectual roots and practice-based adherents. Plummer (1984) states that corporate image is composed of the functional, physical and emotional characteristics of the organisation. The image is an expression of the corporate personality and co-ordinated and consistent communication with external and internal stakeholders is fundamental to the management of the corporate image (Bernstein, 1986, Foroudi et al., 2020, Olins, 1978, Palazzo et al., 2020). Corporate personality determines the corporate identity. Every corporation has a personality, which can be defined as a set of characteristics – behavioural and intellectual – which serve to distinguish one institution from another (Van Heerden and Puth, 1995). Spector (1961) employs human analogies by citing personality traits when referring to company image.

According to some authors (e.g. Balmer, 1995; Hussain et al., 2020, Van Riel, 1995, 1997; Van Riel and Balmer, 1997) an effective corporate identity management should attempt to influence a favourable corporate image and corporate reputation and vice versa so that the various stakeholders can buy the company's products and services, employees have the inclination to work for the company and so on. The identity of a company is the root and the starting point for a strong corporate reputation and brand building and the tangible benefits of positive corporate reputation and branding champion the importance of identity study (e.g. Balmer and Gray, 2003; Fombrun and Shanley, 1990; Fombrun and Van Riel, 1997, 2004; Schultz and de Chernatory, 2002; Van Riel and van Bruggen, 2002). Favourable corporate reputation management embraces the visibility, distinctiveness, authenticity, transparency and consistency throughout the organisation (Fombrun and Van Riel, 2004). The main concepts used in the marketing literature relating to the notion of identity reveal that they corroborate the idea that the authors incorporate many human metaphors such as personality, identity and character which are concerned with communication or perceptions of a company and its characteristics (Siano et al., 2017).

In marketing, aligning image and identity is important and can be found in both practitioner and academic literature (Balmer, 2009). Some authors have defined corporate identity in two ways: (i) as self-presentation (Birkigt and Stadler, 1986; Margulies, 1977; Markwick and Fill, 1997; Olins, 1989; Van Riel, 1995) and (ii) or as organisational distinctiveness (Ackerman, 1988; Balmer, 2001; Balmer and Wilson, 1998; Dowling, 1986; Gray and Balmer, 1998; Van Rekom, 1997). Furthermore, corporate identity refers to the totality of the self-presentation of an organisation to various stakeholders (mainly customers) which associates with the elements of corporate identity mix which are personality, behaviour, communication and the symbolism to create a favourable image and a good reputation between its internal and external stakeholders (e.g. Balmer and Soenen, 1999; Birkigt and Stadler, 1986; He and Balmer, 2007; Foroudi et al., 2017 ; Olins, 1989; Van Riel, 1995; Van Riel and Balmer, 1997). Balmer (2001) attempts to join corporate identity and organisational identity and offered a more comprehensive definition as,

> An organisation's identity is a summation of those tangible and intangible elements that make any corporate entity distinct. It is shaped by the actions of corporate founders and leaders, by tradition and the environment. At its core is the mix of employees' values which are expressed in terms of their affinities to corporate, professional, national and other identities. It is

14   *Foroudi, Foroudi and Balmer*

multi-disciplinary in scope and is a melding of strategy, structure, communication and culture. It is manifested through multifarious communications channels encapsulating product and organisational performance, employee communication and behaviour, controlled communication and stakeholder and network discourse.

(p. 280).

However, definitions of identity in the early literature are confusing and blurred. Some practitioner and academic studies use the terms "image", "reputation" and "identity" interchangeably. Academics are more concerned with the structure, whereas practitioners take a more process-oriented approach and tend to focus on the more tangible aspects of identity. Markwick and Fill (1997) define corporate identity as the "the organisation's presentation of itself to its various stakeholders and the means by which it distinguishes itself from all other organisations" (p. 397). Corporate identity has an internal foundation in that it represents what is reflected by the company. Some researchers (Balmer, 1995, 2001; Balmer and Gray, 2003; Hatch and Schultz, 2001; Knox and Bickerton, 2003; Schultz and de Chernatory, 2002; Schultz and Hatch, 2003; Van Riel and Maathuis, 1993; Van Riel and Van Bruggen, 2002) state that identity is the starting point for a strong and positive corporate image and corporate reputation. Corporate image has an external perspective since it refers to "the outside world's overall impression of the company" (Mukherjee and Balmer, 2008, p. 10).

According to Karaosmanoglu et al. (2011), in the marketing field there is ambiguity about the concepts of corporate image and corporate reputation. Corporate image is defined similarly to corporate reputation and is defined as the accumulation of the views of external members, other than employees (Alvesson, 1998; Dutton et al., 1994), or the company over time (Dichter, 1985; Dowling, 1993; Ind, 1997; Kennedy, 1977). Some authors acknowledge the similarities between image and reputation and so several distinctions are made. Balmer (2009) introduces a clear-cut definition for reputation and image: "Corporate image represents the immediate mental picture an individual has of an organisation whereas corporate reputation is the result of facts, beliefs, images and experiences encountered by an individual over time" (pp. 558–559).

Intrinsic nature of identity

Identity as a powerful term (Albert et al., 2000) is a central construct of corporate level marketing because of its essential role in the corporate image/reputation formation process. The three major powers of identity and identification were explained by Albert et al. (2000) as first,

they speak to the very definition of an entity – an organisation, a group, a person they have been a subtext of many strategy sessions, organisation development initiatives, team-building exercises, and socialisation efforts.

Identity and identification, in short, are root constructs in organisational phenomena and have been a subtext of many organisational behaviours.

The second part of the power of the constructs, "comes from the need for a situated sense of an entity. Whether an organisation, group, or person, each entity needs at least a preliminary answer to the question 'Who are we?' or 'Who am I?'". Third, the most essential part of the power of identity and identification, "derives from the integrative and generative capacity of these constructs" (p. 13). In terms of integrative capacity, there are terms that travel easily across levels of analysis dealing with an organisation, group, or individual (Albert et al., 2000; Gioia et al., 2000) in the sense of connection between an individual and an organisation (Ahearne et al., 2005; Dutton et al., 1994). Therefore, identity as a fundamental construct with its related concepts explains the direction and persistence of individuals, and more collective behaviours integrated framework in explaining organisational behaviours and strategic actions (Albert et al., 2000). The continuing generative richness of the concepts of organisational identity and identification has generative capacity and "can be used as versatile concepts, frames, or tools that open up possibilities for theoretical development and revelation" (p. 13). The momentum of research identity and identification also comes from a rediscovery of the significance of meaning, motivation and feeling in organisational life.

Identity studies can be attributed to the organisation's internal and external environment. At the organisational level, changes can make identity studies salient. The interrelationship between various organisational functions, such as human resource management, communication, marketing and strategy, manifests the significance of employee behaviours in delivering consistent organisational functions (Schultz et al., 2000). The organisational identity concept is rooted in organisational behaviour (He and Balmer, 2007) and organisational behaviourists have focused on employee behaviour, whereas the marketing scholars have concentrated on customer's behaviour. According to He and Mukherjee (2008), the strong organisational identification is positively associated with more supportive, cooperative and loyal employee behaviour. Organisational members may have a strong identification, or alienation from, a corporate identity (Balmer, 2011). "Corporate identity refers to an organisation's unique characteristics which are rooted in the behaviour of employees" (Balmer and Wilson, 1998, p. 15). The behaviour of employees generates a basis for corporate image formation (Balmer, 1998; Dowling, 1986).

Organisational change is associated with the individual and group behaviour in organisational settings. Managing organisational behaviour challenges individuals to understand and embrace workforce diversity, elements of change, effective communication and performance systems. According to some authors (Ashfort and Mael, 1989; Bergami and Bagozzi, 2000; Elsbach and Kramer, 1996; Gioia and Thomas, 1996) drawing on social identity theory, employees should try to fulfil their self-definitional needs by defining themselves in relation to their own workplaces. Employees' effort to internalise the main characteristics of their

16   *Foroudi, Foroudi and Balmer*

organisations is a form of social identification (Ashfort and Mael, 1989; Dutton et al., 1994). In Dutton et al.'s (1994) own words,

> "The degree to which a member defines him or herself by the same attributes that he or she believes define the organisation"
>
> (p. 239).

Scholars (Kennedy, 1977; Olins, 1991) assert that employees have a vital role in corporate identity management. Balmer (1995) believes that managers need to realise, "that employees are particularly effective spokespersons for any organisation" (p. 40). Balmer (1998) added that,

> The most important audience for any company is its own staff I cannot understand how people can say that the most important audience they have is the consumer. Because if you cannot train your own staff in what you are, in what you think, in how to behave, and in what your mores and precepts are, how the hell can you expect to train your customer?
>
> (p. 974)

Dutton et al. (1994) argued that organisational identification might result in outcomes desirable to the organisation, such as organisational members having a strong identification with, and loyalty to, the organisation by increasing or decreasing competition between sub-groups within the organisation. In addition, it reduces the risk of losing a qualified work force. Organisational identification may lead to greater personal commitment to the organisation and employees positively communicate the intended corporate identity to external parties (Foreman and Whetten, 2002). Senior management should be aware of the gap between its internal reality and external image; according to Dutton and Dukerich (1991), the cultural atmosphere inside an organisation can turn into an undesirable environment. Senior management of an organisation is responsible for creating an organisational climate which nurtures the consensus among employees about their organisation's main purpose to create a favourable organisational identity and favourable organisational identification (Simoes et al., 2005). According to Greyser et al. (2006), institutional and/or individual behaviour which is considered inappropriate might lead to erosion of public support.

Macro environmental factors such as mergers and acquisitions, strategic alliances, spin-offs, outsourcing, increasing frequency of replacement of new technology and the proliferation of new technology companies can contribute to the growth in interest in corporate identity and identification (Balmer, 1988; Balmer and Greyer, 2002). The ultimate purpose of change typologies is usually to provide classifications for different ways that organisational change can occur, for instance, they increase the potential for paying more attention to category definitions and less attention to the dynamics underlying the change event or the process itself (Corley and Gioia, 2004). Albert et al. (2000) state that macro environmental factors offered a simplified approach that encourages

Corporate identity 17

a focus on these important dynamics, and the organisation itself is complex which makes it difficult for members to make sense of who they are as an organisation. The outcome can be the cognitive and emotional bond to organisational members.

Organisational and managerial cognition can contribute to a better, empirically grounded understanding of an issue that is increasingly important to organisational identity as a cognitive schema (Ashforth and Mael, 1996). The association between macro environmental change and organisational change has attracted academics and practitioners to identity study.

Identity study: mapping the terrain

The literature covering the business identity domain refers to the triumvirate of concepts underpinning business identity, which are corporate identity, organisational identity and visual identity, and organisational identification (e.g. Balmer, 1995; Van Riel and Balmer, 1997). Corporate identity is built mainly on corporate visual identity and often used interchangeably. Some researchers have drawn the distinction between corporate identity and visual identity (Abratt, 1989; Albert and Whetten, 1985; Alessandri, 2001; Baker and Balmer, 1997; Balmer, 1994, 1995, 2001; Bernstein, 1986; Birkight and Stadler, 1986; Karaosmanoglu and Melewar, 2006; Leitch and Motion, 1999; Melewar and Jenkins, 2002; Melewar and Saunders, 2000; Melewar and Wooldridge, 2001; Olins, 1978; Pilditch, 1970; Stuart, 1999; Stuart and Muzellec, 2004; Van den Bosch et al., 2006; Van Rekom, 1993; Van Riel, 1995; Van Riel and Balmer, 1997; Van Riel et al., 2001; Van Riel and Van Hasselt, 2002; Wiedmann, 1988).

There has been mutual recognition between corporate identity and organisational identity. For instance, organisational identity is rooted in organisational behaviour (Albert and Whetten, 1985) and is a vital subject in organisational psychology (Dukerich et al., 2002; Elsbach and Bhattacharya, 2001; Mael and Ashforth, 1992; Shamir and Kark, 2004). According to He and Balmer (2007),

> organisational identity can be defined as the degree of salience with which an individual defines himself by his membership of an organisation in given circumstances (for instance, such membership may be mediated by spatial and/or temporal factors). Therefore, organisational identity is socially constructed and situational in nature.
>
> (p. 770)

Hatch and Schultz (2000) attempt building across disciplines from the organisational behaviour to make a bridge between the corporate identity and organisational identity perspectives. Balmer (2008) notices that organisational identity authors such as Cardador and Pratt (2006) believed that the corporate identity/ marketing literature represents an untapped and fertile ground for organisational behaviourists. Organisational identity was created in the corporate identity school of thought (Balmer, 1995).

18 Foroudi, Foroudi and Balmer

Organisational identity has been subdivided into (i) identity of an organisation (organisation's identity) and (ii) identity with an organisation (Ashforth and Mael, 1989; Hatch and Schultz, 2000; Ravasi and Van Rekom, 2003; Whetten and Godfrey, 1998). The three perspectives of identity studies are (i) identity of people in an organisation (organisational identity), (ii) identification with an organisation (organisational identification that is internal identification with organisation) and (iii) identity of an organisation (Gioia et al., 2000).

However, Balmer (2008) introduced the five characteristics of identity and identification as "corporate identity quindrivium", which defined it as "the place where five roads meet" (p. 885). (i) "Identity of a corporation (what are the corporation's distinguishing traits?)", (ii) "Identification from a corporation (what the corporation espouses to be/project via symbolism, especially visual identity?)", (iii) "Stakeholder/s identification with the corporation (who am I/who am I in relation to the corporation?)", (iv) "Stakeholder/s identification to a corporate culture (who am I/who are we (in relation to a corporate culture?)" and (v) "envisioned identities and identifications (envisioned identity of another corporation towards us; envisioned identification with our corporation by a stakeholder group and envisioned identification of another corporate culture to our corporate culture) by underlying question of (what do envision to be our identity traits as perceived by another corporation?)" (pp. 886–892).

Corporate identity (in broader sense)

Perspective 1: visual identity: visual and verbal cues

Corporate visual identity (CVI) is one of the principal means whereby the company's corporate identities are manifested visually (Olins 1978, 1989; Selame and Selame, 1988) in order to develop a strong corporate image and reputation. Corporate identity has its origin in graphic design in the 1930s and 1940s (Steiner, 2003). The term "corporate identity" was used by Margulies to differentiate his work from American designers in the 1950s (Steiner, 2003). Topalian (1984) states that visual identity is the face of the company. The early authors in the field of graphic design were practitioners until the main emphasis of corporate identity research conducted in the 1980s (Balmer, 1995; Carter, 1982; Simoes et al., 2005). The visual identity paradigm focuses on organisational nomenclature, company name, logos, buildings, company's architecture and the design and the decor of the corporate retail outlets' architecture and exterior design, interior design and so on; in fact, anything that can be related to graphic design (Bernstein, 1986; Carter, 1982; Hatch and Schultz, 2000; Ind, 1990; Margulies, 1977; Olins, 1989, 1991; Pilditch, 1970; Selame and Selame, 1988).

Kennedy (1977) demonstrated that an organisation's employees play a role in creating an organisational identity and in its communication to external stakeholders. Kennedy's (1977) study shows that corporate identity impacts beliefs and behaviours of organisational members on which the corporate culture is built (Balmer, 1995; Downey, 1986). Therefore, the characteristics of organisational culture may be reflected through corporate symbolism (Balmer, 1995; Van Riel and Balmer, 1997). Corporate symbols that transmit the strategic, visual dimensions of corporate identity to various audiences require management (Hatch and Schultz, 1997; Van Riel and Balmer, 1997). According to the authors (Balmer, 1995; Foroudi, 2018; Van Riel and Balmer, 1997), the focus of study in this field has shifted to the assessment of how visual expressions of an organisation were designed to reflect its core values and principles. Identity should be communicated by all corporate features, visible (e.g. buildings, communication material) and invisible (e.g. organisational behaviours towards internal and external audiences). All the features should communicate to internal audiences (Margulies, 1977) and external audiences, which introduce the concept of corporate image (Gioia et al., 2000). Corporate identity and corporate image must be coherent (Carter, 1982). Visual identity has been generally praised as a way of transmitting a company's identity through visual and tangible aspects, which impact its image in the eyes of different stakeholders. Identity facilitates clarifying the organisation's structure. The major conceptual development of the visual/graphic school was introduced by Olins (1978, 1991).

Balmer (1995, 1996, 2009) identified seven corporate identity schools of thought: strategic, strategic visual, behavioural, visual behavioural, corporate communications, strategic communications and design-as-fashion. The three schools of corporate identity, which are non-graphic design concentrates on strategic, cultural (behavioural) or promotional (corporate) communications in nature and are related to social identity, organisational identity and visual identity/corporate identity (Balmer, 2009). The remaining schools (strategic visual, visual behavioural, strategic communications and design-as-fashion) related graphic design to the organisation's strategy, culture and communications. Graphic design incorporates strategic change. It can be achieved through visual means, the integrated corporate communication and the multi-disciplinary perspectives (Van Riel and Balmer, 1997). Visual identity is the face of the company (Topalian, 1984) used consistently across all possible forms of a company's physical identification (e.g. advertisements, letterheads, business cards, buildings and logos) (Carter, 1982; Margulies, 1977; Olins, 1991, 1978; Pilditch, 1970). It brings visibility to a company and should be kept modern (Balmer, 2001; Karaosmanoglu et al., 2011; Van Riel and Balmer, 1997) in order to create a favourable corporate image. The visual school focuses on a corporate visual identity.

The strategic school focuses on corporate strategy, corporate communications and organisational behaviour which articulate the corporate vision, mission and philosophy (Olins, 1995) and are related to corporate communication, public relations and reputation management communication. The strategic visual school focuses on strategic change, which can be achieved through visual means and is rooted in graphic design (Ageeva et al., 2018, 2019). Integrated corporate communication is focused on the integration of marketing communications and public relations, marketing communications functions and integration of all communications functions (Balmer, 2009, Foroudi et al., 2019). The integrated corporate communication school of thought is focused on the need

20 *Foroudi, Foroudi and Balmer*

for effective communication with various stakeholders (Bernstein, 1986). Some studies (Balmer, 2001; Balmer and Gray, 2000) have stated that the total corporate communications consist of primary (the communication effects of products and of corporate behaviour) and secondary, as well as tertiary communications (word of mouth and messages imparted about the organisation from third parties). Corporate communications (what we claim we are) relates to the totality of a company's controlled messages to stakeholders (Balmer et al., 2011).

From the visual identity perspective, Olins (1978, 1991) proposed that organisations express their corporate culture and corporate strategy mainly by employing three visual identity styles, namely (i) monolithic, for example, authors (Melewar et al., 2005; Olins, 1989, 1995; Van Riel, 1995) refer to monolithic identity where the organisation consistently uses its name and style across the organisation, (ii) endorsed identity where the organisation has several activities or companies which are endorsed by the group name and identity and the brand is associated with subsidiaries (e.g. Holiday Inn Express), (iii) branded identity where products are differentially branded and may be unrelated to each other or the company (e.g. Pantene and Wella at the Procter and Gamble Corporation).

Baker and Balmer (1997) have described the adoption of a new visual identity for a UK university and discussed how the role of visual identity assessment and audit would be helpful in terms of spotting the organisation's weaknesses and malaises. The results of the study suggested that visual identity should be integrated into a holistic approach to organisational repositioning. The visual treatment and quality of an organisation's output makes up its visual identity.

Perspective 2: *corporate identity: integrated communication approach*

The integrated communications approach was realised by marketers and graphic designers' knowledge of the efficacy of overall consistency in formal visual and marketing communications led to a number of authors arguing that there should be consistency in formal corporate communication (Bernstein, 1986, 1986; Keller, 1993; Schultz et al., 1994; Van Riel, 1995, 1997; Van Riel and Balmer, 1997). This approach links communication and marketing theory. According to Van Riel (1995, 1997), the integrated communication approach to corporate identity as self-presentation has shifted towards a multi-disciplinary approach.

The integrated marketing communications is defined by Duncan and Everett (1993, p. 33) as "the strategic co-ordination of all messages and media used by an organisation to influence its perceived brand value". By integrating the companies' communication strategies, they can generate synergies between their different forms of communication. Furthermore, companies should place more stress on internal communications. According to Kennedy (1977), looking at the formal communication activities suggested that employees' interactions with external audiences are influences on corporate image. Authors (e.g. Abratt, 1989; Barich and Kotler, 1991; Bernstein, 1986; Dowling, 1986; Gray and Smeltzer, 1987; Schmitt et al., 1995; Wells and Spinks, 1999) researched how company's corporate identity should be communicated internally and externally.

Corporate identity   21

It is important that organisations harmonise their internal and external communications to facilitate the generation of a favourable image of company for the stakeholders (Gilly and Wolfinbarger, 1998; Van Riel, 1995). Moreover, Abratt (1989) states that there is interface consistency among the projected identities and the perceived image. Corporate communication embraces marketing, organisational and management communication (Van Riel, 1995). Corporate image can be communicated through nomenclature, formal statements, organisational communication, imagery and graphics, permanent media (e.g. stationery, buildings) and promotional media (e.g. advertising, public relations) (Gray and Smeltzer, 1985). These forms of communication should be consistent and coherent to external audiences in the environment (Gilly and Wolfinbarger, 1998). Total corporate communications include primary, secondary, as well as tertiary communications (Balmer and Gray, 2000). Bick et al. (2003) argued that it is vital to understand the company's corporate identity and whether it is communicated efficiently in order to make sure that the stakeholders of an organisation perceive it as projected. Bernstein's (1986) study states that the integrated communication paradigm emphasises the need for effective communication with all the company's stakeholders. Stakeholders can include employees or even competitors (Hatch and Schultz, 1997; Olins, 2000; Schultz and Ervolder, 1998). The integrated communication approach is related to corporate identity as total corporate communication and is necessary for managing associations with stakeholders.

Perspective 3: corporate identity: marketing approach

The corporate identity concept has strong practitioner roots and has a notable marketing presence (He and Balmer, 2007). Within this perspective, corporate identity is grounded in corporate-level concepts such as corporate branding, corporate communications, corporate image and corporate reputation (Balmer and Greyser, 2003; He and Balmer, 2007). Connecting the notion of identity and marketing philosophy is related to the company (Balmer, 2008). The early literature of marketing scholarship (e.g. Bolger, 1959; Easton, 1966; Hill, 1962; Martineau, 1958; Nelson, 1962; Newman, 1953; Spector, 1961; Tucker, 1961) focuses on customers and stakeholders' perception of corporate identity and its advantage to organisations and stakeholders (Balmer, 2011).

The complicated perceptions of stakeholders and the complex markets have required companies to position their product brands by distinguishing their companies (Hatch and Schultz, 2003). Balmer (2011) asserts that authors in the marketing field have focused on product brands. The significance of outcome of corporate brands is to consider the relationship between institutional and product brands. Corporate identity may be viewed as branding at the corporate level (Schmitt and Pan, 1994). Ind (1997) states that "a corporate brand is more than just the outward manifestation of an organisation its name, logo, visual presentation. Rather it is the core of values that defines it" (p. 13). Some authors (Balmer, 2001; Balmer and Gray, 2003; Knox and Bickerton, 2003; McDonald et al., 2001,

22 Foroudi, Foroudi and Balmer

Simoes et al., 2005) acknowledged the organisation as a brand in its entirety and organisation as a strategic element in branding which presents an opportunity to include a company's core values among its strategic selling points (Hatch and Schultz, 2000, 2003; Urde, 2003) and organisations should avoid unclear core values (Urde, 1999, 2009). The branding concept can be directly applied at the corporate level (Aaker, 1996; Ind, 1997). Berry (2000) describes,

> Branding plays a special role in service companies because strong brands increase customers' trust of the invisible purchase. Strong brands enable customers to better visualise and understand intangible products. They reduce customers' perceived monetary, social, or safety risk in buying services, which are difficult to evaluate prior to purchase. Strong brands are the surrogates when the company offers no fabric to touch, no trousers to try on, no watermelons or apples to scrutinise, no automobile on test-drive.
>
> (p. 128)

He and Balmer (2007) argued that in terms of addressing some fundamental marketing issues, corporate identity can be explanatory. Institutional brands (corporate brand) are part of corporate marketing (Balmer, 2008) which conveys the corporate identity characteristics of an organisation, and works as a means for establishing the desired identity perception in the minds of both an organisation's internal and external stakeholders (Van Riel and Balmer, 1997). This assumption asserts that the main purpose of marketing communications is to develop a desired corporate image with the audience and unsuccessful communications "may result in key groups holding erroneous and negative perceptions of the corporate brand" (Balmer, 1995, p. 35). From a behavioural perspective, brand orientation emphasises the significance of brand identity which contains three elements (mission, vision and values) as a guiding light and hub for organisational culture, behaviour and strategy (Urde et al., 2013).

Marketing scholars have focused on customers and believe that all stakeholders' perceptions as primary receivers of corporate communications should be investigated to analyse the link between visual identification and customer/stakeholder perceptions of the corporation. Brown (1998) states the particular relations that consumers have with a company's core values are on the basis of their beliefs, feelings and experiences about the company (Zha et al., 2020). For example, Nguyen (2006) identified the information, which was employed by credit union members in evaluating the image of their service organisations. The results show that the physical environment, countries' cooperative value, organisational culture and identity, and contact personnel are significant factors affecting internal-stakeholders' perceptions of corporate image.

Communication has a relationship with both external and internal stakeholders' perceptions (Aaker and Joachimsthaler, 2000, Brown et al., 2019). Adopting this perspective means looking at the contributions of employees to the external perception of an organisation. Aaker and Joachimsthaler (2000) stressed how "internal communication programs to employees and firm partners, can be vital

Corporate identity   23

to creating the clarity and culture needed to deliver on the identity" (p. 317). According to the literature (Balmer, 1998; Barich and Kotler, 1991; Dowling, 1986; Keller, 1999; Kennedy, 1977; Van Riel, 1995) employees transmit the company's values to customers and they have an influence on employee behaviour in communicating organisational messages externally.

Perspective 4: corporate identity: organisational approach

The organisational literature centres on organisational members' perceptions (member identification) and identity (Kennedy, 1977) and organisational behaviour, (e.g. Albert and Whetten, 1985; Ashfort and Mael, 1989; Bergami and Bagozzi, 2000; Dutton and Dukerich, 1991; Dutton et al., 1994; Elsbach and Kramer, 1996; Foreman and Whetten, 2002; Gioia and Thomas, 1996; Gioia et al., 2000; Whetten and Godfrey, 1998; Whetten and Mackey, 2002) which are connected to organisational identity by focusing on the association between employees and organisations (Balmer, 1998; Hatch and Schultz, 1997). Scholars (Dutton and Dukerich, 1991; Dutton et al., 1994) have argued that companies' employees should perceive their own organisation and understand how they interpret external views of their organisation to influence their attachment to their own organisations by perceiving the importance of the organisation's identity (what the organisation stands for and where the organisation intends to go) and internalising a cognitive structure. According to He and Balmer (2007), the organisational perspective on the organisation's identity is connected to organisational and managerial cognition. Cognitive connection with the organisation and the employees' behaviours suggests the concept of organisational identification as defined by Dutton et al. (1994) as "when a person's self-concept contains the same attributes as those in the perceived organisational identity, we define this cognitive connection as organisational identification" (p. 239). It may be that the strong emphasis on cognition in organisational identity theory and research merely reflected the "cognitive revolution" in psychological research.

Research on organisational behaviour constituted by corporate identity management primarily draws on organisational culture studies (Balmer, 1998; Hatch and Schultz, 1997). The related terms to this approach are organisation identity (identity of an organisation), image, reputation and organisational identification. Corporate identity has an overlap with the multi-disciplinary approach to organisational identity (Balmer, 2001; Balmer and Wilson, 1998; Van Riel and Balmer, 1997). The organisation's identity is the organisation's self-perception from the organisational perspective (He and Balmer, 2007).

Organisational identity has been defined by scholars (Albert and Whetten, 1985; Balmer, 2001) as what are an organisation's central (i.e. the character), distinctive and enduring characteristics which are of interest to corporate identity management. Ashforth and Mael (1989) identified the identity in organisation and identity with organisation as two perspectives of identity studies. Gioia et al. (2000) comment that,

24 *Foroudi, Foroudi and Balmer*

> We might characterise extant approaches to studying identity as involving three ways of thinking about the concept: (1) concern with the identity of organisations, (2) concern with the identity of people within organisations, and (3) concern with people's identification with organisations. The first of these related domains is the area most in need of innovative thinking and also is the area with the most potential for becoming a definitive area for organisational study, rather than another eclectic handmaiden of psychology and sociology.
>
> (p. 146)

Organisational identity is related to a special form of the individual's social identity, which highlights the salience of organisational membership to the individual (Marin and de Maya, 2013; Pratt, 1998). Employees' perceived organisational identity and their construed external image of organisations reflect the extent to which the insiders' experience of that organisation is perceived as positive/negative by outsiders (Dutton et al., 1994; Foroudi et al., 2016). Organisational members use images such as a gauge to assess how external people judge organisations. Dutton and Dukerich (1991, p. 518) clarified the matter: "our interpretation is that some organisational actions are tied to sets of concerns that we call issues. Issues are events, developments, and trends that an organisation's members collectively recognise as having some consequence to the organisation". Dutton and Dukerich (1991) defined organisational identity, image and reputation as:

> An organisation's identity describes what its members believe to be its character; an organisation's image describes attributes members believe people outside the organisation use to distinguish it. Organisational image is different from reputation: reputation describes the actual attributes outsiders ascribe to an organisation, but image describes insiders' assessments of what outsiders think. Both organisational image and identity are constructs held in organisation members' minds.
>
> (p. 547)

Authors (Dutton et al., 1994; Ashfort and Mael, 1989) argue that employees' efforts to internalise the main characteristics of their organisations is a form of social identification, drawing on social identity theory authors (Ashfort and Mael, 1989; Bergami and Bagozzi, 2000; Elsbach and Kramer, 1996; Gioia and Thomas, 1996; Marin and de Maya, 2013) who state that an organisation's employees define themselves in relation to their own workplaces (Ashfort and Mael, 1989; Bergami and Bagozzi, 2000; Elsbach and Kramer, 1996; Gioia and Thomas, 1996). Employees try to internalise the main characteristics of their organisations as a form of social identification (Ashfort and Mael, 1989; Dutton et al., 1994). Dutton et al. (1994) "The degree to which a member defines him- or herself by the same attributes that he or she believes define the organisation" (p. 239). Organisational studies underlie social identity theory (Ashforth and Mael, 1989; Dutton and Dukerich, 1991; Dutton et al., 1994; Elsbach and Kramer, 1996; Gioia and Thomas, 1996). According to social identity theory, there is

Corporate identity   25

a psychological link between organisational and social identities and the way employees try to identify with the workplace. Ashforth and Mael (1989) have confirmed that organisational identification is a form of social identification and there are multiple identities inside the organisation. Organisational identification is related to the process of depersonalisation and incorporates organisational identity into self-definition (Pratt, 1998).

Ashforth and Mael (1989) have noted that employees' behaviour and employee's identification could have an influential power on the identity of the company for the external stakeholders. They assert that social identification can create the initialisation of beliefs of employees, group values and norms and homogeneity in attitudes and behaviour. Ashforth and Mael (1989) addressed social identification as,

> Distinguishable from internalisation. Whereas identification refers to self in terms of social categories (I am), internalisation refers to the incorporation of values, attitudes, and so forth within the self as guiding principles (I believe). Although certain values and attitudes typically are associated with members of a given social category, acceptance of the category as a definition of self does not necessarily mean acceptance of those values and attitudes. An individual may define herself in terms of the organisation she works for, yet she can disagree with the prevailing values, strategy, system of authority, and so on.
>
> (p. 21–22)

Corporate identity and organisational identity are complex concepts and three perspectives can be recognised on organisational and identity studies which are (i) identity of organisation (organisation's identity) which is related to individual's identity and represents the essence of that identity which can answer the questions about "who we are and what we are", (ii) identity (of people) in the organisation (individual's organisational identity) is a metaphor coming from an organisational identity or social identity (Ashforth and Mael, 1989) which an individual defines him/herself by resorting to their membership of the focal organisation either spatially or temporally. Individuals have personal identity (who I am), as well as social identity (Ashforth and Mael, 1989; Marin and de Maya, 2013; Tajfel and Turner, 1985), (iii) identity with the organisation (organisational identification). Organisational identification is used interchangeably with organisational identity. Organisational identity is used to describe a state and organisational identification to describe a process (Ashforth and Johnson, 2001). Organisational identification occurs when an individual's beliefs about his or her organisation become self-referential or self-defining (Pratt, 1998, p. 172).

Top managers play a fundamental role in influencing internal and external stakeholders' identification with the organisation. In order to differentiate organisations in the eyes of managers and stakeholders, they aim for the promotion of favourable organisational images to achieve organisational goals, mission, organisational practices, values and action which contributes to shaping organisational identity (Scott and Lane, 2000). According to Sutton and Callahan (1987), a damaged managerial image influences the trust of target audiences in the organisation. Regarding the

26   Foroudi, Foroudi and Balmer

artefacts of identity, managers are responsible for creating and managing symbols such as physical settings to express an organisation's identity. The expression of behaviours and artefacts should be consistent in all internal and external forms in order to convey the desired identity. Ashforth and Mael (1989) assert that,

> It is tacitly understood by managers that a positive and distinctive organisational identity attracts the recognition, support, and loyalty of not only organisational members but other key constituents (e.g. stakeholders, customers, job seekers), and it is this search for a distinctive identity that induces organisations to focus so intensely on advertising, names and logos, jargon, leaders and mascots, and so forth.
>
> (p. 28)

Accordingly, corporate identity management should be conceived within multiple disciplines and should be seen to represent three major dimensions: (i) visual identity/symbolism (Carter, 1982; Melewar and Saunders, 1998, 1999, 2000; Melewar et al., 2001; Olins, 1991; Pilditch, 1970), (ii) communication (Van Riel, 1995) and (iii) philosophy, mission and values (Abratt, 1989; Balmer, 1994).

Visual identity as a hard tangible fundamental of corporate identity forms the physical symbols and generates physical recognition of the organisation (Carter, 1982; Melewar and Saunders, 1998; Pilditch, 1970; Olins, 1991). However, the intangibility of services exacerbates the difficulty of managing the visual components. For instance, architecture (physical evidence, environmental design and decor), with employee presentation help to convey the tangible hints that impact customer behaviour (Bitner, 1990). The visual identity of an organisation can be viewed as identification (Downey, 1986). Furthermore, the design components indicate the company's culture and values and should be recognised by the organisation's employees (Berry, 2000). According to Bitner (1990) and Foroudi et al. (2020) in a service encounter context, the physical environment can influence how consumers perceive service failure and should be used to differentiate services from competitors.

From the marketing perspective, everything in and about a company is communication. According to some authors (Foroudi et al., 2019, Van Riel, 1995), communication is the touchstone for presenting an image. Marketing messages should be consistent and coherent in all forms of communication to create a cohesive corporate identity and corporate image. The company's philosophy, mission and values dimension gives the organisation a consistency and attempts to bring a strategic basis to the corporate identity construct. Corporate philosophy is an important step in the process of creating an identity. The key element of philosophy is the corporate mission. Balmer (1996) states,

> the acquisition of a favourable corporate image is dependent upon and understanding of, and, where appropriate, the nurturing by management of a distinct corporate culture which reflects the corporate mission and philosophy and as such becomes one of the dominant cultures within the organisation (i.e. the desired corporate personality) which results in the desired corporate

Corporate identity 27

identity (i.e. where the innate character of the organisation mirrors the corporate strategy and philosophy).

(p. 254)

Corporate identity is related to corporate values and sharing them with organisational members. The company's philosophy indicates the company's decisions, policies and actions (Melewar et al., 2020). Every organisation has a vision and a mission statement (Dowling, 1994), which transmit the company's purpose and aspirations. Levin (2000) defined the vision and mission statements in the following way: mission is an explanation of what the organisation is and does – the business and beliefs about how it ought to be conducted and its contribution in general and usually last over time. However, vision is "a high lucid story of an organisation's preferred future in action. A future that describes what life will be like for employees, customers, and other key stakeholders" (Levin, 2000, p. 93).

Perspective 5: corporate identity: interdisciplinary/multi-disciplinary approach

Corporate identity is a multifaceted phenomenon (Balmer, 1995, 1998). There is a large and distinctive body of knowledge on corporate identity which is one of an organisation's most important assets and, therefore, is worthy of constant management likely to benefit from a multi-disciplinary/interdisciplinary approach (Balmer, 2001, 2008; Balmer and Greyser, 2002; Balmer and Wilson, 1998; Brown et al., 2006; Cornelissen et al., 2007; Van Riel and Balmer, 1997).

From the multi-disciplinary approach, corporate identity management relates to corporate values and principles which constitute its personality (Balmer, 1995; Tourky et al., 2020; Olins, 1978), the organisation's historical roots, its corporate strategy (Wiedmann, 1988). The corporate identity mix within the multi-disciplinary approach consists of the following four elements: behaviour/communications/ symbolism, mind/soul/voice, communication/visual identity and behaviour/ corporate culture/market conditions (He and Balmer, 2007, p. 768), and employees' sense making about their organisation's identity in order to bring about a favourable corporate reputation (Fombrun, 1996). Some authors (Balmer, 2009; Brown et al., 2006; Hatch and Schultz, 1997, He and Balmer, 2007; Foroudi et al., 2020) have highlighted the important role of a corporate behaviour which begins to dissipate in relation to identity as people judge the corporation by its actions. Communications as integrated to corporate identity is based on the sum of the ways (verbal and visual) a corporation decides to be recognised by its public (Balmer and Greyser, 2003; He and Balmer, 2007). Symbolism, as shown in the visual audit, provides useful insights into a corporate identity, which includes all sorts of visual cues to increase corporate visibility and helps to distinguish the organisation (Balmer, 2001; He and Balmer, 2007; Van Riel and Balmer, 1997).

Mind is the conscious decisions made by the companies, which relate to managerial vision, strategy and product performance, corporate philosophy and corporate history (Balmer, 2001; Balmer and Soenen, 1999; He and Balmer, 2007).

28 Foroudi, Foroudi and Balmer

Soul is a subjective element of corporate identity that consists of values held by personnel and is influenced by the mix of sub-cultures, and the mix of identity types present within organisations (Balmer, 2001; Urde, 2003). Balmer (2001) has employed the term "voice", which refers to the total corporate communication. Balmer (2001) maintains,

> Every organisation has an identity. It articulates the corporate ethos, aims and values and presents the sense of individuality that can help to differentiate the organisation within its competitive environment. When well managed, corporate identity can be a powerful means of integrating the many disciplines and activities essential to an organisation's success. It can also provide the visual cohesion necessary to ensure that all corporate communications are coherent with each other and result in an image consistent with the organisation's defining ethos and character.
>
> By effectively managing its corporate identity an organisation can build understanding and commitment among its diverse stakeholders. This can be manifested in an ability to attract and retain customers and employees, achieve strategic alliances, gain the support of financial markets and generate a sense of direction and purpose. Corporate identity is a strategic issue. Corporate identity differs from traditional brand marketing since it is concerned with all of an organisation's stakeholders and the multifaceted way in which an organisation communicates.
>
> (Balmer, 2001, p. 291)

The corporate identity is reflected by the existence of multiple versions of corporate identity within an organisation. The actual, conceived, communicated, ideal, and desired (ACID) test is a sophisticated model which has undergone a number of developments and refinements of corporate identity management (Balmer, 2009). The variations of the ACID test related to multiple categorisations of corporate identity are ACID, AC2ID and AC3ID (Balmer and Greyser, 2003; He and Balmer, 2007). Corporate identity management requires alignment between identity types. There are six identity types: actual identity, communicated identity, ideal identity, desired identity, conceived identity (Balmer, 2001; Balmer et al., 2009; Balmer and Gray, 2003; Balmer and Greyser, 2002; He and Balmer, 2007), and covenanted or corporate brand identity (He and Balmer, 2007). Corporate brand identity "in turn describes a distillation of corporate identity" (Urde, 2013, p. 744).

Actual identity (what we really are) as unique attributes of the corporation can be shaped by a number of elements consisting of purposes, leadership style of management, organisational structure, business activities, corporate style and ethos, markets covered and overall business performance. Actual identity includes the set of values held by those who "make" the company (management and employees) (Balmer and Greyser, 2002; Balmer et al., 2009).

Communicated identity (what we say we are) includes controlled (advertising, sponsorship and public relations) and non-controlled communications (word of mouth, media commentary) and total corporate communications (primary,

Corporate identity 29

secondary and tertiary communications) (Balmer, 2009; Balmer and Gray, 2000; Balmer and Greyser, 2002; Balmer et al., 2009).

Ideal identity (what we ought to be) is the optimum strategic (future-oriented) positioning of the corporation in the market. The ideal identity includes organisational competencies and prospects assets, the competition and changes in the political, economic, ethical, social and technological environment. It refers to strategic planning leadership, environmental and corporate analysis and the corporate structure's actual identity (Balmer, 2001; Balmer and Gray, 2003; Balmer and Greyser, 2002; Balmer et al., 2009; He and Balmer, 2007).

Desired identity (what we wish to be) is often misunderstood to be almost indistinguishable from ideal identity (Balmer and Greyser, 2002). Desired identity lives in the hearts and minds of the company's CEO; it is the vision, personality and ego of the corporate leader. Desired identity is cognitive/aspirational in character, whereas ideal identity usually emerges by following a rational assessment of the organisation's research and analysis in a particular time and is strategic in nature (Balmer, 2009; Balmer and Greyser, 2002; Balmer et al., 2009, Mellower et al., 2017).

Conceived identity (what we are seen to be) refers to corporate image, the corporate reputation of the organisation (which is held by customers and other stakeholder groups), and corporate branding. Management must make a judgement as to which external publics' perceptions are most important to the organisation (Balmer, 2009; Balmer and Greyser, 2002; Balmer et al., 2009).

Covenanted or corporate brand identity (what the brand stands for) underpins a corporate brand and is associated with the architecture. It is "owing to the power and strength of association with a corporate brand by customers, employees and others (which sometimes has a religious-like fervour), the term covenant appears to be appropriate" (Balmer et al., 2009, p. 20). The brand identity in turn serves as a "bridge" between the internal identity and the identity that the customers perceive (Urde, 2009). According to Van Riel and Balmer (1997), the interdisciplinary perspective draws on marketing, and this includes those undertaking research in human resources, organisational studies, graphic design, public relations and communication studies. Van Riel and Balmer (1997) formulated the following statement:

> Academics acknowledge that corporate identity refers to an organisation's unique characteristics which are rooted in the behaviour of members of the organisation ... management of an organisation's identity is of strategic importance and requires a multi-disciplinary approach.
>
> (p. 341)

A multi-disciplinary approach (Van Riel and Balmer, 1997) addresses the question of "what are we as an organisation", and the characteristics which make the corporate identity distinctive (He and Balmer, 2007, p. 772). This approach draws heavily on organisational behaviour (Balmer and Wilson, 1998; Van Riel and Balmer, 1997). Some authors (Olins, 1978; Van Riel, 1995; Van Riel and Balmer, 1997) have proposed that the understanding of corporate identity has gradually broadened and is now taken to indicate the way in which an organisation's identity is revealed through

30 Foroudi, Foroudi and Balmer

communicative and behavioural activities, as well as through strategically planned symbolism for internal and external audiences.

According to He and Balmer (2007), corporate identities and corporate brands are inseparable and should be aligned. Corporate branding can be related to multiple stakeholders and management of corporate identity requires formal communication with them internally and externally (Balmer, 1998; Balmer and Gray, 2003, Hatch and Schultz, 2003, Palazzo et al., 2020). Some authors (Balmer, 2001; Bick et al., 2003; Christensen and Askegaard, 2001; Dacin and Brown, 2002; Melewar and Karaosmanoglu, 2005; Melewar et al., 2003; Simoes et al., 2005; Van Riel and Balmer, 1997) emphasise corporate identity management, which needs to follow a multi-disciplinary approach. For instance, Bhattacharya and Sen (2003) included social identity theory in marketing-oriented studies and developed a framework in order to understand how the corporate identity can influence internal-stakeholders' identification with their companies and, furthermore, they introduced the new term of "stakeholders' identification".

Having broadly recognised the breadth across which corporate identity can be conceptualised, following the interdisciplinary approach, multiple inputs are considered in the discussion.

The corporate identity management construct

Corporate identity is the holistic, multi-disciplinary and integrated approach to corporate identity management (Bernstein, 1986). Corporate identity management is a multifaceted phenomenon (Balmer, 1995, 1998). The corporate identity management construct aims to recognise aspects of identity that are manageable and that are used to develop corporate identity. The domain of the corporate identity construct is concerned with the controllable aspects of corporate identity.

Discussion in the literature about the components of corporate identity is widespread. Corporate identity is made up of the features, characteristics, traits or attributes of a company that are presumed to be central, distinctive and enduring (Albert and Whetten, 1985; Balmer, 2001, 2007, 2008; Bick et al., 2003; Balmer and Stotvig, 1997; Barnett et al., 2006; Gray and Balmer, 1998; He and Balmer, 2007; Mukherjee and He, 2008; Fombrun and Van Riel, 2004; Markwick and Fill, 1997; Van Riel and Balmer, 1997) and serves as a vehicle for the expression of the company's philosophy (Abratt, 1989; Balmer, 1994; Bernstein, 1986; Bhattacharya and Sen, 2003), values, beliefs and mission (Ashforth and Mael, 1989; Balmer, 1996; Gray and Balmer, 1997; Simoes et al., 2005), communications (Balmer, 1996; Van Riel, 1995) and corporate visual identity (Carter, 1982; Dowling, 2001; Melewar and Saunders, 1998, 1999, 2000; Melewar et al., 2001; Olins, 1991; Pilditch, 1970) to all its audience (Van Riel, 1995).

Philosophy, mission and value

Corporate identity management captures and serves as a vehicle for the expression of the company's philosophy (Abratt, 1989; Balmer, 1994; Bernstein, 1986;

Corporate identity 31

Bhattacharya and Sen, 2003), values, beliefs and mission (Ashforth and Mael, 1989; Balmer, 1996; Gray and Balmer, 1997; Simoes et al., 2005). "The creation of a corporate identity often begins with the articulation of a business philosophy" (Simoes et al., 2005, p. 158). The term "corporate philosophy" has become popular since the 1980s (Ledford et al., 1995; Peters and Waterman, 1982) and is critical for coordinating the company's activities. Many publications have described the concept of management philosophy as referring to company culture (Athos and Pascale, 1981; Ouchi, 1981; Wright, 1984). According to Abratt (1989), corporate philosophy is an element of corporate culture and embodies the core values and assumptions of a corporation (Kono, 1990).

A corporation's philosophy is defined as the set of guideline principles that help communicate goals, plans, and policies and behaviour to all employees at all levels of a company (Wright, 1984). The philosophy establishes the context of day-to-day operating decisions and guides the organisation in making trade-offs among competing performances for short-term and long-term goals (Ledford et al., 1995; Wright, 1984), and the performance and all activities of the organisation tend to be linked directly to the philosophy (Wright, 1984). The company's philosophy "directs decisions, policies, and actions and entails core motivating assumptions, principles, values, and tenets" (Simoes et al., 2005, p. 158).

According to Van Rekom (1997), there has been a proliferation of statements of corporate beliefs through corporate philosophies and statements of corporate principles. O'Gorman and Doran's (1999) corporate philosophy and mission statements motivate employees. A philosophy statement can help channel employee attention in a direction, share goals and expectations, in order to understand how their individual roles fit within a larger picture (Ledford et al., 1995). According to Ledford et al. (1995), philosophy describes the "right thing" in the minds of employees and managers alike, and philosophy is a key to business success (Ledford et al., 1995). The philosophy, mission and values dimension impacts upon the organisation's strategy and organisational culture (Dowling, 1986). According to Balmer (1994), "the emerging alternative theory on corporate identity emphasises the importance of strategy; the articulation of a corporate philosophy and the acquisition of a corporate culture" (p. 43).

Corporate philosophy can be expressed in the corporate mission statement (Collins and Porras, 1991; Simoes et al., 2005). A corporate mission is a corporation purpose for the existence of the company and is the most important part of the corporate philosophy (Abratt, 1989; De Witt and Meyer, 1998; Melewar and Karaosmanglu, 2006). The corporate mission is "vital to the corporate identity, in explaining why the corporation exists and what engages and motivates it, beyond the aim of making money" (Urde, 2013, p. 751). According to Swales and Rogers (1995), a mission statement emerges and collaborates in response to crises. Most are designed as displayable single page documents, which deal with abstractions possessing a strategic level of generality and ambiguity (Fairhurst, 1993). Mission statements are very different and tend to stress value, positive behaviour and guiding principles within the company's belief and ideology, in order to promote corporate culture and philosophy. Corporate mission statements are engendered

32 Foroudi, Foroudi and Balmer

by senior management or the CEO (Swales and Rogers, 1995). A company's mission statement functions as a principle of order (Primeaux, 1992, p. 78) and organises the company's principles (Fritz et al., 1999). According to Gray and Balmer (1997), this feature is very important and corporate culture (i.e. common values and beliefs held by organisational members) should impact organisational philosophy. Balmer (1996) asserts,

> the acquisition of a favourable corporate image is dependent upon and understanding of, and, where appropriate, the nurturing by management of a distinct corporate culture which reflects the corporate mission and philosophy and as such becomes one of the dominant cultures within the organisation (i.e. the desired corporate personality) which results in the desired corporate identity (i.e. where the innate character of the organisation mirrors the corporate strategy and philosophy).
>
> (p. 254)

Therefore, to manage corporate identity, decision-makers need to communicate the organisation's values and beliefs to employees and employees should be "aware of what they are doing to enforce their ethical standards and that reward managers' adherence to standards are acting wisely, reinforcing the organisation's identity and strengthening employee commitment to that identity" (Fritz et al., 1999, p. 297). It is vital that the whole company understands the meaning of the corporate core values. If they do so, it is possible for the core values to become transformed into a way of acting that influences the behaviour of the whole corporation. Thus, the values can serve as a relationship between the soul of the corporation and the identity of the customers (Urde, 2003). In addition, core values can be viewed as dynamic entities and the only way for a corporation to achieve them is through action (Urde, 2003) which involves the core values having to be proven over and over again (Urde, 2009).

The starting point for a company's philosophy is the company's vision (Collins and Porras, 1991). A company's vision "extends the mission by formalising its view of where it is heading and what inspires it to move forward" (p. 751). There is some confusion between corporate vision and mission. Corporate mission is the basic point of departure, whereas a corporate vision is the desired future at which the company hopes to arrive. Levin (2000) explains vision as "a high lucid story of an organisation's preferred future in action. A future that describes what life will be like for employees, customers, and other key stakeholders" (p. 93). Cummings and Davies (1994) elucidate that "the value of any statement of corporate mission or vision lies in fusing together a corporation's many elements by providing some commonality of purpose" (p. 150) and are sources of commitment (Urde, 2013).

Corporate vision can be defined as the signature of a company, which helps it to stand out from its competition (Hatch and Schultz, 2001). According to Kissler (1991), effective change requires a formal communication strategy and captivating vision to help the essential consensus building. Most identity change programmes reflect the vision of the CEO (Balmer, 2001). Corporate vision is typically expressed by the corporation founder and/or the chief executive and management board (Balmer, 2001). Hatch and Schultz (2001) state that the gaps between strategic vision, organisational culture and corporate image serve to identify key dilemma areas for corporate brands.

Corporate vision is the desired future at which the company hopes to arrive (Collins and Porras, 1994; Hatch and Schultz, 2003; Hatch and Schultz, 2003), which is the corporate direction and inspiration (Urde, 2013), and which impacts upon the organisation's strategy (Dowling, 1986). The role of strategic vision requires top managers to reflect on what the company is and what it wants to become in the future (Hatch and Schultz, 2003). Balmer and Soenen (1999) argued that corporate identity is driven by relating vision to changes in corporate strategy. However, there is a relationship between vision and the values embedded in the organisational culture (Collins and Porras, 1994; Balmer and Soenen, 1999). Vision has a connection to external stakeholders' images, who need information about the organisation that goes beyond what the corporation provides. Every organisation has a vision, which is formalised in a document that contains the company's values (Akarsu et al., 2019; Hatch and Schultz, 2003).

According to Urde (2003), core values are dynamic, but need to be long lasting to create value. Some authors (Urde, 2009) state that corporate values play a significant role in the formation of the corporate identity and are the beliefs and ethical principles that lie behind the company's culture, and compose a major system of beliefs within a company that include daily language and ideologies (Van Riel and Balmer, 1997). More particularly, Balmer et al. (2006) state that "the organisational values answer in principle the question of what the organisation stands for and "what makes us who we are?" (p. 147). According to Ledford et al. (1995), organisational values are fundamental to organisational culture, that values need to be understood and they are, necessarily, actively shaped. The concept of core values is well recognised from the brand management perspective (Urde, 1999, 2003, 2009), in practice by high-performing organisations (Kotter and Heskett, 1992, p. 56).

Corporate core values have an external meaning, and it is recommended that they not be used for slogans or something similar because that might undermine their significance (Urde, 2003). Hence, in other words, it is significant for organisations to have a clear picture of the internal corporate identity when selecting core values. Urde (2003) states that if organisations just choose core values that are catchy or serve as good slogans, there is a big risk of developing hollow and unfavourable corporate core values, which harm the identity and culture of the organisation. Urde (2009) emphasised that the main success of core values is based on how well they bridge the internal values with the stakeholders' perception of credibility in the long run. According to Urde (2009), an organisation's core values should be linked internally and externally and that decides whether core values will be successful or not. The customers' identity is related to the perceived values that convey the organisation's core values externally which could

34 Foroudi, Foroudi and Balmer

be a way for the organisation to position itself and attract customers and stakeholders (Urde, 2009). Organisational values are translated into core values that guide the organisation's efforts (Balmer et al., 2006, p. 148).

According to Melewar and Karaosmanoglu (2006), there is an emphasis on ethical and cultural values, and organisational history and philosophy. A company develops the values to develop a positive image, which is reflected in the outside world (Melewar and Karaosmanoglu, 2006). Furthermore, it is espoused by the managers or the founder (Balmer, 1995; Kono, 1990).

A corporate mission, corporate philosophy, and value are articulated through corporate visual identity to the company's audiences and employees (Alessandrini, 2001; Baker and Balmer, 1997; Henderson and Cote, 1998; Gorman, 1994; Otubanjo and Melewar, 2007; Melewar et al., 2005; Melewar and Jenkins, 2002; Melewar and Karaosmanoglu, 2006; Van Riel et al., 2001). Wilson (1997) believes that the company's visual identity component is easier to control than its behavioural aspects.

Philosophy is defined as the core values and assumptions that constitute the corporate culture, along with the business mission and values espoused by the management board or founder of the company (Abratt, 1989; Collins and Porras, 1991; Ledford et al., 1995; Simoes et al., 2005; Wright, 1984). Mission is the company's purpose, the reason for which a company exists or its objectives (De Witt and Meyer, 1998). Values are the dominant system of beliefs and moral principles that lie within the organisation that comprise the everyday language, ideologies, rituals and beliefs of personnel (Balmer, 1995; Kono, 1990).

Communication

Corporate identity is the expression as manifested in the communications of the organisation (Balmer, 1995, 1998; Balmer and Wilson, 1998; Balmer and Soenen, 1999; Baker and Balmer, 1997; Bernstein, 1986; Birkigt and Stadler, 1986; Comelissen and Harris, 2001; Ind, 1990; Markwick and Fill, 1997; Van Riel and Balmer, 1997). Communication is the touchstone for presenting an image and, therefore, it is recognised in the image formation process (Balmer, 1996; Cornelissen, 2000; Van Riel, 1995). Everything in and about a company is communication and it has a wide spectrum of influence. Research on consumer behaviour has widely accepted that communication from annual reports to advertising and internal communications impacts individuals' behaviours and attitudes (Brown and Reingen, 1987; Cristiansen and Tax, 2000; Lau and Ng, 2001). According to Fombrun and Rindova (2000), clear communication can have an impact on trust and enhance the commitment of stakeholders to an organisation.

It is essential for an organisation's managers to understand which communication tools, channels and marketing messages are more influential on internal-stakeholders' perception (Abratt, 1989). Furthermore, managing corporate identity and its communication should be grounded in a company's consumers' reception of messages; therefore, it is essential to study communication from a receiver's perspective in order to reveal how organisational cues are gathered and interpreted. Stakeholders not only are passive receivers of company communication, but also shape what organisations should be.

Brand core is supposed to be something lasting that supports internal and external brand building (Urde, 2009). According to Duncan and Moriarty (1998),

> brand messages originate at the corporate, marketing, and marketing communication levels. In other words, all corporate activities, marketing mix activities, and marketing communications have communication dimensions. At the corporate level, messages sent by the company's overall business practices and philosophies have communications dimensions. For example, its mission, hiring practices, philanthropies, corporate culture, and practice of responding or not responding to inquiries send messages that reconfirm, strengthen, or weaken brand relationships.
>
> (p. 6)

The marketing communication mix should be used to convey the distinctive qualities of an organisation (Van Riel, 1995). Some authors (29Balmer, 2001; Van Riel and Balmer, 1997) claim that anything a company does communicates its identity in the stakeholders' context.

Brown and Dacin (1997) stated that management put considerable effort into managing the company's identities; however, it is not easy to know whether it is the planned communication or external response to their efforts that impacts on internal-stakeholders' perception. Some authors have emphasised the significance of consistency between the corporate identity and the company's communication (Bernstein, 1986; Gray and Smeltzer, 1985; Van Riel and Balmer, 1997). The strategic coordination of all messages and media used by an organisation influences its "perceived brand value" (Duncan and Everett, 1993, p. 33). Integrated marketing communications (IMC) is a concept of marketing communications planning that recognises the added value of a comprehensive plan that evaluates the strategic roles of a variety of communications disciplines (for example, general advertising, direct response, sales promotion and public relations) and combines these disciplines to provide clarity, consistency and maximum communications impact (Schultz, 1993, p. 17; Schultz and Kitchen, 1997, p. 9).

Communication has a wide impact on how a company presents its image visually as well as verbally. The main dimensions of how communications are managed in a company are marketing communications (e.g. advertising, sponsorship, public relations activities, corporate advertising), corporate communications (e.g. annual report, internal publications) (Balmer and Gray, 2003; Van Riel, 1995) and consistency among all communication vehicles and messages. Communication is defined as the aggregate of messages from both official and informal sources, through a variety of media, by which a company conveys its identity to its multiple audiences or stakeholders (Gray and Balmer, 1998).

Visual identity

Corporate visual identity is arguably the most tangible facet of corporate identity, which reflects the company culture and values and that creates physical recognition for the organisation (Carter, 1982; Cornelissen and Elving, 2003; Dowling, 2001; Melewar and Saunders, 1999, 2000; Stuart, 1999; Olins, 1991; Pilditch, 1970; Van Riel and Balmer, 1997). Corporate visual identity has received the attention of marketing researchers (Henderson et al., 2004; Tavassoli, 2001; Childers and Jass, 2002; Henderson and Cote, 1998; Veryzer and Hutchinson, 1998) who feel that it needs to be supported by consistent marketing communications and clear corporate visual identity.

Corporate visual identity, graphic design, and corporate identity are often used interchangeably. Researchers have drawn the distinction between corporate identity and corporate visual identity, and their coordination (Abratt, 1989; Albert and Whetten, 1985; Alessandri, 2001; Baker and Balmer, 1997; Balmer, 1994, 1995; Bernstein, 1986; Van den Bosch et al., 2006; Childers and Jass, 2002; Henderson and Cote, 1998; Henderson et al., 2004; Olins, 1978; Melewar and Jenkins, 2002; Melewar and Saunders, 2000; Melewar and Wooldridge, 2001; Pilditch, 1970; Stuart, 1999; Stuart and Muzellec, 2004; Tavassoli, 2001; Van Riel, 1995; Van Riel et al., 2001; Van Riel and Van Hasselt, 2002; Van Rekom, 1993; Veryzer and Hutchinson, 1998; Wiedmann, 1988). According to Melewar and Saunders (2000), corporate visual identity is essential for well-being and communications mix to express the organisation's identity (Cornelissen and Elving, 2003) in serving as a reminder of the corporation's real purpose (Abratt, 1989).

In addition, the intangibility of services exacerbates the need for management of visual components. The visibility and consistency should emphasise the physical dimensions of service delivery (Bharadwaj et al., 1993), which impacts on the corporate identity. For instance, staff appearance, colour and architecture are essential to the brand awareness and transmitted image in the service context (Berry, 2000). Furthermore, physical evidence such as environmental design, architecture, interior design, decor, signage and stationery convey tangible hints that impact on employee and customer behaviour (Bitner, 1990). Visual identity management has significant business implications (Schmitt et al., 1995). According to Bitner (1990), in a service encounter context, the physical environment can have an influence on how consumers perceive service failure. Corporate visual identity uses tangible clues to differentiate services (Onkvisit and Shaw, 1989).

Furthermore, corporate awareness and visual identification support the utility of corporate visual identity. Identification tools are important in modern marketing such as the architecture of the corporation, as it gives the corporation identity and symbolises its purpose. Identification is important to employees (Bromley, 2001; Dutton et al., 1994; Kiriakidou and Millward, 2000) and corporate visual identity plays a symbolic role in generating such identification. Furthermore, the internal purpose of corporate visual identity relates to employees' identification with the organisation. Thus, managers must ensure that they create a reliable belief to communicate in the market (Van den Bosch et al., 2005; Gray and

Balmer, 1998). Employees need to be aware of corporate visual identity and its meaning (Berry, 2000). Furthermore, the visibility and physical consistency of visual identity underlies the numerous physical dimensions, which are used to deliver the service, such as ground transportation vehicles and name on airplanes (Bharadwaj et al., 1993). For all these reasons, managers need to understand the design process to communicate with designers using a common language from a similar point of view (Kohli et al., 2002; Henderson et al., 2003).

Conceptualising the management of corporate visual identity in terms of specific dimensions is essential as it involves generating and implementing guidelines for the use of symbolism within the company. A corporate visual identity consists of architecture, corporate name, corporate symbol/logo, typeface, colour, building, interior design, symbolism, understanding and staff appearance which express organisational characteristics (Carter, 1982; Dowling, 1994; Margulies, 1977; Melewar and Saunders, 1999, 2000; Melewar et al., 2001; Olins, 1991, Pilditch, 1970; Schultz et al., 2000; Van Riel et al., 2001) as well as providing recognisability (Balmer and Gray, 2000).

Corporate visual identity is defined as an assembly of visual cues which express the identity of the organisation (Cornelissen and Elving, 2003) by which an audience can recognise the company and distinguish it from others (Bernstein, 1984) in serving to remind the audience of the corporation's real purpose (Abratt, 1989).

The next section proposes a definition for corporate identity by merging the three dimensions (visual identity, communications, and philosophy, mission and values), which are discussed in this section.

Defining the corporate identity concept

As mentioned before, corporate identity has been defined using different metaphors (Cornelissen and Harris, 2001). Abratt (1989) says "corporate identity is about appearance" (p. 66). Some design authors (Bernstein, 1986; Carter, 1982; Lippincott and Margulies, 1957; Margulies, 1977; Olins, 1989, 1991; Pilditch, 1970; Selame and Selame, 1988) assert that corporate identity is about corporate visual design to present the company to internal and external audiences via visible artefacts such as buildings, communication material, advertisements, exterior design, interior design, symbols, colours and so on and also the invisible such as organisational behaviours. After the shift towards recognising the significance of its influences on behaviour (Abratt, 1989; Balmer, 1995, 2004, 2007, 2008; Christensen and Askegaard, 2001; Mukherjee and He, 2008; Dutton et al., 1994; Kottasz et al., 2008; Melewar and Karaosmanoglu, 2005; Olins, 1989; Powell et al., 2009; Pratt, 1998; Simoes et al., 2005; Van Riel, 1995; Van Riel and Balmer, 1997), marketing and design authors suggest that the corporate identity concept reflects this sense of the essential character which deals with the impressions, image, uniqueness, personality and individuality that an organisation presents to internal and external stakeholders (Abratt, 1989; Balmer, 1995, 1998; Balmer and Soenen, 1999; Downey, 1986; Hatch and Schultz, 1997; He and

38 Foroudi, Foroudi and Balmer

Balmer, 2007; Markwick and Fill, 1997; Melewar and Jenkins, 2002; Olins, 1978; Pilditch, 1970; Schmitt and Pan, 1994; Stuart, 2003; Simoes et al., 2005; Van Heerden, 1999; Van Riel, 1995; Van Riel and Balmer, 1997). The stability and coherence must exist between customers, employees and managers' behaviour, and all should be adjusted to the company's philosophy, values and personality.

The personality of an organisation has been described thus

> the corporate identity is the 'personality' and 'soul' of the corporation. ... Every company has a personality, which is defined as the sum total of the characteristics of the organisation. These characteristics – behavioural and intellectual – serve to distinguish one organisation from another. This personality is projected by means of conscious cues which constitute an identity.
>
> (Abratt, 1989, pp. 66–67)

The behavioural and intellectual characteristics have been recognised by some authors (Baker and Balmer, 1997; Balmer, 1995, 1998; Balmer and Wilson, 1998; Bernstein, 1986; Markwick and Fill, 1997) as the product of the beliefs and attitudes shared by organisation's employees. Corporate identity is a phenomenon that expresses the corporate personality of a company and refers to "what the company is", "what the company stands for" (Pilditch, 1970) and "where the company is going" (Olins, 1978). Cornelissen and Harris (2001) defined corporate identity as the "tangible representation of the personality, the expression as manifest in the behaviour and communication of the organisation. Corporate identity efforts are undertaken strictly reflecting the personality of the organisation" (p. 56).

The organisation's personality has been described using a metaphor of company as human being to explain corporate identity (Cornelissen and Harris, 2001). Corporate identity is an indirect expression of a corporate personality. Therefore, the organisation must "balance internal preoccupations of organisational identity with external imperatives" (Cornelissen and Harris, 2001, p. 57). In other words, marketing scholars (Balmer and Soenen, 1999; Birkigt and Stadler, 1986; He and Balmer, 2007; Melewar and Jenkins, 2002; Van Riel, 1995; Van Riel and Balmer, 1997) have argued that corporate identity refers to the totality of the self-presentation of an organisation to various stakeholders (mainly customers) which correspond to the elements of corporate identity mix which are personality, behaviour, communication and the symbolism to create a favourable image and a good reputation between its internal and external stakeholders.

Corporate identity requires consistency across visible and invisible forms of communication to represent the company (Balmer, 2001; Gioia et al., 2000; Markwick and Fill, 1997; Olins, 1989; Simoes et al., 2005; Van Heerden, 1999; Van Riel and Balmer, 1997). Corporate identity should be embedded throughout the organisation to clearly articulate the company's philosophy and mission and its organisational values (Baker and Balmer, 1997; Balmer, 2008; Dowling, 1994; Mukherjee and He, 2008; Olins, 1995; Pondar, 2005; Simoes et al., 2005). Drawing on the arguments above (see Table 2.1 which presents a chronology of

Corporate identity 39

Table 2.1 Some of the key definitions of corporate identity concept

Authors	Definitions
Powell, 2011	Corporate identity is the values and ethos of an organisation that reflects the foundations around which the corporate brand is built (Balmer and Gray, 2003).
	Corporate identity (not to be confused with the graphic design paradigm of identity): What are the corporation's distinctive attributes? (p. 1368).
Balmer et al., 2009	Corporate identity is what we really are (p. 7).
	Corporate identity is actual Identity (p. 7).
Mukherjee and He, 2008	Corporate identity (CI) "refers to the features, characteristics, traits or attributes of a company that are presumed to be central, distinctive and enduring" (p. 2).
	Corporate identity is "constituted of core values (e.g. operating philosophy, vision and mission, leadership) and demographics (e.g. business, size, age, competitive position, country of origin, location) of the company" (p. 1).
	Corporate identity is "important for consumer marketing, because: (a) it defines the essence of a company and accords economic, social and symbolic meanings to a company in the perception of the consumer; (b) it situates the company at the fundamental level among the social and economic exchange networks of other organisations, e.g. competitors, suppliers, distributors, buyers, governmental agents; (c) it represents the basic subject for evaluation by consumers, which in turn has cognitive, affective and behavioural consequences by those consumers, such as consumers' perceptions, images, identifications and action for/ against the focal company (e.g. Dutton, Dukerich, and Harquail, 1994; Pratt, 1998); and (d) consumers with more positive perception of corporate identity will, through association, have more positive attitude toward the company's products, i.e. there will be a positive consumer response (be it cognitive, affective or behavioural) to the company's products" (p. 2).
	Corporate identity is "increasingly important for contemporary consumer marketing due to the post-modern levity resulting from globalisation of consumer markets, technologically savvy consumers" (p. 2).
	"Corporate identity mainly refers to the organisation's communication" (p. 3).
	Corporate identity "forms a central and integrative function within the corporate and competitive strategy and that corporate identity forms a pivotal role which can influence the strategy content as well as providing a corporate communication system to stakeholders" (p. 3).
	"Corporate identity is translated into consumer responses through a variety of mechanisms, which can originate from the company (e.g. corporate communications, corporate branding, and other identity communicators), from cultural environments, from the consumers themselves, and from the interaction between the consumers and the company. In this paper, we only focus on the final one: the interaction between the consumers and the company" (p. 5).
	"Corporate identity influences consumers to develop identification with a company" (p. 13).
	Corporate identity is "central to marketing thought as it shapes consumer attitudes and behaviour towards marketing activities of companies" (p. 13).

(*Continued*)

40 Foroudi, Foroudi and Balmer

Table 2.1 (Continued)

Authors	Definitions
Powell et al., 2009	Corporate identity refers to an organisation's unique characteristics which are rooted in the behaviour of members of the organisation" (p. 422).
Elsbach, 2009	Corporate identity "is seen not just as involving the visible outward presentation of a company [through corporate logos and products], but also the set of intrinsic characteristics or 'traits' that give the company its specificity, stability, and coherence" (p. 1047).
Van den Bosch et al., 2008	Most research on managing corporate identity deals with the strategic development of corporate identity and the design and effects of specific elements of the CVI.
Kottasz et al., 2008	Corporate identity "is a presentation to the outside world of the core values, philosophy, products and strategies of an organisation".
	Corporate identity involves the projection of "who you are, what you do, and how you do it".
	"The planned self-presentation of an organisation normally involved the transmission of cues via its behaviour, communications and symbolism, and that the regulation of these transmissions constituted 'corporate identity management' (p. 237). Successful corporate identity management results in an enhanced corporate image and, over time, an improved corporate reputation."
	The "characterisation of corporate identity management as comprising three components (behaviour, communication and symbolism), the potential contributions of a CAC to corporate identity management can be summarised as follows" (p. 237).
Balmer, 2008 Identity based	The characterisation of identity should be adapted so that an institution's corporate identity is characterised by its central, distinctive and evolving nature (p. 888).
	Corporate identity is as follows: "Articulation of what an organisation is, what it stands for, what it does and the way it goes about its business especially the way it relates to its stakeholders and the environment" (p. 899).
	"Corporate identity management is concerned with the conception, development, and communication of an organisation's mission, philosophy and ethos. Its orientation is strategic and is based on a company's values, cultures and behaviours". "The management of corporate identity draws on many disciplines, including strategic management, marketing, corporate communications, organisational behaviour, public relations and design" (p. 899).
Balmer, 2008	Corporate identity as the central platform upon stakeholder identifications/associations with the corporation.
	Corporate identity is "articulation of what an organisation is, what it stands for, what it does and the way it goes about its business especially the way it relates to its stakeholders and the environment" (p. 899).
	Corporate identity (the distinctive attributes of an organisation) (pp. 29–30).
	Corporate identity (identity here being defined as the distinct and defining characteristics of the organisation) (p. 37).

(Continued)

Corporate identity 41

Table 2.1 (Continued)

Authors	Definitions
Balmer et al., 2007, 2006 nature	Corporate identity is the signature that runs through the core of all a corporation does and communicates (p. 8).
Cornelissen et al., 2007	The distinctive public image that a corporate entity communicates that structures people (p. 3).
He and Balmer, 2007	Corporate identity is an organisation's distinctive attributes addressing "what the organisation is" (p. 771).
Balmer and Liao, 2006	Corporate identity was conceptualised in terms of visual identification (p. 6). Corporate identity as distinctive attributes (p. 10). Corporate identity was originally conceptualised in terms of visual identification (p. 9).
Barnett et al., 2006	Corporate identity is "the set of values and principles employees and managers associate with the company" (p. 29). Fombrun and van Riel (2004, pp. 165–166), who state that it consists of "(a) features that employees consider central to the company, (b) features that make the company distinctive from other companies (in the eyes of employees) and (c) features that are enduring or continuing, linking the present and the past to the future". The idea of enduring, central features of organisations that makes them distinctive from others (p. 32).
Melewar and Karaos-manoglu, 2005	The behaviour is an intangible part of corporate identity, corporate behaviour includes employee behaviour and management behaviour and corporate behaviour can affect the organisational identity in the long run. Moreover, employee behaviour can influence customers and other stakeholders.
Simoes et al., 2005	Corporate identity and image are ways for companies to encourage positive attitudes towards their organisation. The effective corporate identity management (CIM) provides a potential route to competitive advantage. Corporate identity deals with the impressions, image and personality that an organisation presents to its stakeholders. Consumers' and other audiences' perceptions of organisations are key in determining their response to the companies' products and services (p. 153). The corporate identity concept reflects this sense of "essential character" and suggests that each company has its own personality, uniqueness and individuality. From an organisational perspective, identity can be viewed as a vehicle by wh ich a company's character is conveyed to different audiences. Corporate identity is an expression of identity and is also an inherently dynamic process that tends to evolve over time as the organisational context changes. Corporate identity refers to image or personality rather than to identity, or they interchange the terms image and identity (p. 154).

(Continued)

42 Foroudi, Foroudi and Balmer

Table 2.1 (Continued)

Authors	Definitions
	Corporate identity refers to "the way in which an organisation's identity is revealed through behaviour, communications as well as through symbolism to internal and external audiences" (p. 341).
	Corporate identity comprises symbols (visual identity and design aspects, such as corporate name and house style) and communications (both internal and external corporate communications) (p. 157).
	Corporate identity refers to soul (e.g. values, culture), voice (e.g. communication, symbolism), and mind (e.g. vision, philosophy), and core values (e.g. organisational mission) (p. 158).
	Corporate identity extends beyond visual symbols and how they are communicated to the articulation of a company's philosophy, mission and values.
	The creation of a corporate identity often begins with the articulation of a business philosophy. The business philosophy
	can be expressed in the mission statement to convey a sense of commonality and purpose.
	Corporate identity is the implementation, support and maintenance of visual systems, the expression and pursuit of brand and image consistency through global organisational symbols and forms of communication and the endorsement of consistent behaviour through the diffusion of a company's mission, values and goals.
	Corporate identity is a form of communication that conveys an image and seeks an integrated approach to articulate identity in coherent and harmonised messages through internal and external forms of communication.
	Corporate identity articulates what is intrinsic and unique to the organisation. Through the clear articulation of the company's philosophy and mission, organisational values and norms are unified (p. 158).
He and Balmer, 2007	"Corporate identity tells the world – whether actively or by default- just what the corporate strategy is".
	Corporate identity addresses four questions: "who you are, what you do, how you do it and where you want to go" (p. 6).
	"Corporate identity forms a central and integrative function within the corporate and competitive strategy and that corporate identity forms a pivotal role which can influence the strategy content as well as providing a corporate communication system to stakeholders" (p. 6).
Pondar, 2005	Corporate identity is the "Expression of culture, values, philosophy/ strategy, vision, mission" and "Distinctiveness, recognition, diversification" (p. 74).
	The managing of corporate identity is of great importance for company success. Although there is no general definition of corporate identity the understanding of corporate identity is quite homogenous – the most common definition, according to the research, is corporate identity is a mix of characteristics that an organisation possesses as a subject (p. 79).
	Corporate identity refers to the internal as well as external communications (p. 80).

(Continued)

Corporate identity 43

Table 2.1 (Continued)

Authors	Definitions
Suvatjis and de Cherna- tony, 2005	Corporate identity is "the set of meanings by which an object allows itself to be known and through which it allows people to describe, remember and relate to it". "Corporate identity is a multidimensional area requiring a multidimensional model" (p. 822).
He and Balmer, 2004	Corporate identity is "the distinct characteristics of the organisation" (p. 5). Corporate identity is graphic design (as corporate logo, and/or company name). Corporate identity is self-presentation via symbolism, behaviour and communication (p. 6). Corporate identity "refers to those critical attributes and traits that make us distinctive and which defines who we are and what we are as an organisation" (p. 6).
Topalian, 2003	Corporate identity is the articulation of what an organisation is, what it stands for, what it does and how it goes about its business (especially the way it relates to its stakeholders and the environment) (p. 1119). Corporate identity as visual identification (p. 1121).
Steiner, 2003	Corporate identity is "the body" of a company, thus the viewing of the company as a living thing (p. 181). Corporate identity is connected to corporate culture and core competence and in many cases it survives structural changes, because it is retained in employees' knowledge (p. 182).
Stuart, 2003	Corporate identity is "the planned and operational self-presentation of a company, both internal; and external, based on an agreed company philosophy" (p. 32). Corporate identity is an action or expression of a company that could be classified under the headings of behaviour, communication and symbolism, and these media are the means by which the personality of a company manifests itself. Corporate identity is often erroneously used when referring to the visual identity, and this incorrect terminology persists among practitioners (pp. 30–31). Corporate identity is the tangible representation of the organisational identity, and that efforts to manage corporate identity should reflect the organisational identity of the company, that is, members' beliefs about its existing character (p. 32).
Balmer and Gray, 2000, 2003	Corporate identity is a powerful tool to communicate strategy and facilitating the realisation of strategy.
Dacin and Brown, 2002	Corporate identity refers to those intended characteristics of an organisation that decision-makers and marketers within the group choose to promote to their internal and external constituents (p. 254). Corporate identity is "inextricably linked to understanding how and why various constituents form corporate associations and the specific corporate associations that they hold" (p. 254). Corporate identity of an "organisation, along with understanding how organisational constituent groups interpret and respond to corporate information, are critical areas for continued research by researchers who study marketing-related Phenomena" (p. 255).

(*Continued*)

44 *Foroudi, Foroudi and Balmer*

Table 2.1 (Continued)

Authors	Definitions
	"The concept corporate identity, as used here, refers to the desired set of corporate associations that decision-makers in an organisation would like their various constituencies to hold – the attributes of the organisation that the decision-makers wish to promote" (p. 256).
	Develop and "manage corporate identity is inextricably linked to understanding how and why various constituents form corporate associations and the specific corporate associations that they hold" (pp. 254–255).
Balmer and Gray, 2002	Corporate identity refers to the distinct attributes of an organisation and as such addresses the questions "What are we?" and "Who are we?" (p. 10).
Melewar and Jenkins, 2002	Corporate identity is the firm's actions, as far as these actions and is "the degree to which the firm has achieved a distinct and coherent image in its aesthetic output".
	Corporate identity is the firm's presentation of itself to its different stakeholders mine.
Abratt, 1989; Christensen and Askegaard, 2001; Balmer, 1995; Olins, 1989; Van Riel and Balmer, 1997.	"Corporate identity is a set of symbolic representations including graphic designs and, sometimes, organisational behaviour". The "notion of corporate identity is generally seen as belonging to the sender side of the communication process" (p. 295).
Balmer, 1995; Balmer, 2001; van Rekom, 1997; Balmer and Wilson, 1998	Corporate identity is defined as what the organisation is.
Balmer, 2001	Corporate identity is (a) the mix of elements which gives organisations their distinctiveness: the foundation of business identities; (b) Although there is still a lack of consensus as to the characteristics of a corporate identity, authors do, for the main, emphasise the importance of several elements including culture (with staff seen to have an affinity to multiple forms of identity), strategy, structure, history, business activities and market scope.
	Corporate identity is erroneously used when referring to visual identity (p. 254).
	Corporate identity is "What are we?" It also involves addressing a series of questions including "What is our business/structure/strategy/ethos/market/performance/history and reputation/relationships to other identities?" (p. 257).
Alessandri, 2001	Corporate identity is the outward presentation of the company and pleasing corporate identity can produce positive corporate image.

(Continued)

Corporate identity 45

Table 2.1 (Continued)

Authors	Definitions
Melewar et al., 2001	The act of building corporate identity and visual identity into the strategic management equation provides companies with a dimension of difference that is impossible for competition to duplicate (p. 417).
Zinkhan et al., 2001	Corporate identity represents "the ways a company chooses to identity itself to all the publics" (p. 154).
Melewar and Wooldridge, 2001	Corporate identity originated from the positive and negative influences of communication between planned and perceived image.
Urde, 2003	The values can serve as a connection between the soul of the organisation and the identity of the customers.
Balmer and Gray, 1999, 2000	Corporate identity is the reality and uniqueness of an organisation which is integrally related to its external and internal image and reputation through corporate communication (p. 256).
Kiriakidou and Millward, 2000	The notion of corporate identity addresses the question "Who are we?". Corporate identity is the vision and aims of the top management board and reflects the organisation's identity which the management board wishes to acquire, that is, the desired identity of the organisation. This desired identity is communicated mainly through streamlining organisational symbolism and corporate communications on an external basis in order to achieve a favourable market image and to promote competitive advantage (p. 50). Corporate identity is the tangible representation of the organisational identity, the expression as manifest in the behaviour and communication of the organisation (p. 51). Corporate identity is based on the vision and aims of the top management (p. 57).
Fombrun and Shanley, 1990; Dowling, 1993; Cornelissen, 2000; Hatch and Shultz, 1997	Corporate identity influences corporate image through the constant interplay of information.
Gioia et al., 2000	The corporate identity field is most concerned with "visual representations of the corporation emphasised through the design and management of corporate symbols". Corporate identity is a projected image, in recent work on corporate identity (p. 66). Corporate identity is a consistent and targeted representation of the corporation emphasised through the management of corporate symbols and logos; strategically planned and operationally applied internal and external self-representation (p. 67). Expressing corporate identity is a dynamic process.

(Continued)

46   *Foroudi, Foroudi and Balmer*

Table 2.1 (Continued)

Authors	Definitions
	Shell's initial response to the negative publicity, for instance, involved numerous corporate identity efforts aimed at helping outsiders see who the "real Shell" was (p. 70).
	Corporate identity is composed of three things; who you are, what you do and how you do it.
	Corporate identity is a planned visual element that distinguishes the firm from all others.
	Corporate identity is a representation of the firm with emphasis on the firm's symbolic elements and logos. It is a strategy applied both internally and externally.
Melewar and Saunders, 2000	A corporate identity programme is aimed at influencing outsiders' perceptions to be better aligned with self definitions.
	The corporate identity is the meaning of an object which allows itself to be recognised allowing a group to explain, remember and communicate as it is a fusion of strategy, behaviour, culture, design, market conditions, products and services.
Van Heerden, 1999	Corporate identity consists solely of visual identity cues.
	Corporate identity consists of both visual and behavioural cues.
	Corporate identity consists of both visual elements and the way that the corporation behaves (p. 493).
	Every corporation is unique; it is essential that the corporate identity should spring from its roots, personality, strengths and weaknesses.
	Corporate identity is all about values – corporate values, societal values and living values (p. 493).
	Corporate identity aims to create coherence, symbolism and positioning (p. 494)
	Corporate identity creates corporate image (p. 494).
	A well-managed corporate identity is one of a company's most valuable marketing assets (p. 495).
Balmer and Soenen, 1999	Corporate identity is conceptualised as a function of leadership and by its focus on the visual (p. 77).
	Corporate identity is defined as encompassing the "Soul", "Mind" and "Voice" of an organisation and delineates "what an organisation is", or "is a set of interdependent characteristics of the organisation which gives it specificity, stability and coherence".
Melewar and Saunders, 1999	Corporate visual identity is a main part of the corporate identity that a company can use to project their quality, prestige and style to stakeholders.
Gregory, 1999	Corporate identity is what the firm is and how the firm is perceived.
	Corporate identity is the distinct characteristics of the firm.
	Corporate identity is a planned visual element.
Balmer and Soenen, 1998	Corporate identity distinguishes the company from the other competitors and articulates what the firm is, what it does and how it does it and is made up of the strategies it adopts.
	Corporate identity is the mind, soul and voice of an organisation.
Balmer, 1995, 1998	Corporate identity and its management are multifaceted phenomena.

(Continued)

Corporate identity   47

Table 2.1 (Continued)

Authors	Definitions
Balmer, 1998	Corporate identity is formed by the aggregate of messages and experiences received about an organisation's products and services by an individual, group or groups over a period of time (p. 970). Corporate identity is about behaviour as much as appearance. Corporate identity is the source of the corporate culture. He asserted that culture is the "what" of a company and concluded that identity is the "why"; "corporate culture – which has been described as a company's shared values, beliefs and behaviour – in fact flows from and is the consequence of corporate identity (p. 976). Corporate identity is fundamentally concerned with reality, "what an organisation is", i.e. its strategy, philosophy, history, business scope, the range and type of products and services offered and its communication both formal and informal (p. 979). Corporate identity is multifaceted and draws on several disciplines. A number of writers support this proposition. The elements of corporate identity mix as personality traits (a predisposition to act in a particular way), acts of behaviour, communications and symbols. The mix comprises five elements: corporate culture, corporate behaviour, products and services, communication and design as well as market conditions and strategies. It has also been postulated that corporate identity is eclectic in that it draws on many management and non-management disciplines and may in fact be regarded as an emerging philosophy or approach to management. Third, corporate identity is based on the corporate personality, i.e. it is based on the values present within the organisation. A number of authors hold this to be the most important of all the concepts associated with the area (p. 980).
Gray and Balmer, 1998	Corporate identity is the distinct characteristic of the company. Corporate identity is distinctiveness and centrality. Corporate identity is the reality of the corporation. Corporate identity refers to the distinct characteristics of the organisation or, stated very simply, "what the organisation is" (p. 4) The management of a corporate identity involves the dynamic interplay among the company's business strategy, the philosophy of its key executives, its corporate culture and its organisational design. The interaction of these factors results in differentiating the firm from all others, making, to use a marketing metaphor, its "corporate brand" distinct (p. 696).
Abratt, 1989; Balmer, 1998, Olins, 1990; Van Riel, 1997	Corporate identity is referred to as the distinct characteristics of a firm. Corporate identity focuses on culture, strategy, structure, history, business activity and business scope. Corporate identity is the mix of elements, which give the organisation their distinctiveness. And the key questions are who are we and what are structure, strategy, business, reputation, performance, business and history?

(*Continued*)

48 Foroudi, Foroudi and Balmer

Table 2.1 (Continued)

Authors	Definitions
Balmer and Wilson, 1998	"Corporate identity refers to an organisation's unique characteristics which are rooted in the behaviour of employees" (p. 15).
Baker and Balmer, 1997	Corporate identity summarises the mission, purpose or positioning of the organisation or a product or service (p. 366).
	Corporate identity is the explicit management of all the ways in which the organisation presents itself through experiences and perceptions to all of its audiences (p. 373).
Balmer and Stotvig, 1997	Corporate identity is now seen to refer to the distinct attributes of an organisation, i.e. "What it is". The distinguishing features of corporate identity may be described as follows (p. 169).
	Corporate identity is concerned with reality, and encompasses corporate strategy, philosophy, history, business scope and the range and type of products and services offered. Second, corporate identity is multifaceted and draws on several disciplines. Third, corporate identity is based on the corporate personality; in other words, the values held by staff within the organisation.
	Managing and evaluating an organisation's identity is complicated. It involves understanding the company's philosophy, personality, identity, image and reputation; examining key internal-external-environment interfaces for signs of inconsistency and incompatibility; ongoing management by senior management, with the chief executive taking a particular interest.
	The main objective of corporate identity management is to ensure that an organisation's key stakeholders and stakeholder groups are favourably disposed towards the organisation (p. 170).
	Corporate identity refers to "what an organisation is", or explained slightly differently, it may also be seen to refer to an organisation's distinct characteristics.
	An organisation's identity should be central, distinctive and enduring. An identity is experienced through everything an organisation says, makes or does. The elements comprising the corporate identity mix have been variously described as strategy, culture and communications, symbolism, behaviour and communication and culture, behaviour, market, communication design, products and services (p. 170).
Hatch and Schultz, 1997	Corporate identity is a very important business concept because it demonstrates corporate ethos, aims and values and presents a sense of individuality that can help to differentiate an organisation from its competitors.
Van Riel and Balmer, 1997	Corporate identity refers to an organisation's unique characteristics which are rooted in the behaviour of members of the organisation (p. 341).
	Corporate identity sees corporate identity management as taking into account an organisation's historical roots, its personality, its corporate strategy and the three parts of the corporate identity mix (behaviour of organisational members, communication and symbolism) in order to acquire a favourable corporate reputation which results in improved organisational performance (p. 342).

(Continued)

Corporate identity 49

Table 2.1 (Continued)

Authors	Definitions
Markwick and Fill, 1997	Corporate identity is made up of individual characteristics by which a person or thing is recognised. In this sense, identity refers to individuality, a means by which others can differentiate one person from another. This differentiation can be influenced by the use of visual cues, for example the choice of clothes, gestures and hairstyle, to name but a few. However, the use of visual cues alone can be misleading and, in order that we understand the individual at a deeper level, we rely on other cues such as speech, behaviour and mannerisms. Identity at the individual level is concerned with aspects of identification and recognition. Just as individuals have an identity, so do organisations. Corporate identity is the organisation's presentation of itself to its various stakeholders and the means by which it distinguishes itself from all other organisations. Corporate identity is the articulation of what the organisation is, what it does and how it does it and is linked to the way an organisation goes about its business and the strategies it adopts. Corporate identity is projected to stakeholders using a variety of cues and represents how the organisation would like to be perceived. These cues can be orchestrated so that deliberately planned messages are delivered to specific target audiences to achieve particular objectives. Typical of these planned communications are the use of corporate identity programmes, consistent content in advertising messages (Perrier, British Airways), dress codes and operating procedures (McDonald's) and policies towards customer contact (answering the telephone at TNT Overnight). Some of these planned cues will constitute the organisation's visual identity, that is the design and graphics associated with an organisation's symbols and elements of self-expression (p. 239). Corporate identity focuses on behaviour, the actions of the organisation and other forms of communication (397). The management of corporate identity is the corporate personality (399). Corporate identity forms a central and integrative function within the corporate and competitive strategy and that corporate identity forms a pivotal role which can influence the strategy content as well as providing a corporate communication system to stakeholders (401).
Hatch and Schultz, 1997	Corporate identity "differs from organisational identity in the degree to which it is conceptualised as a function of leadership and by its focus on the visual. Although both concepts build on an idea of what the organisation is, strong links with company vision and strategy emphasise the explicit role of top management in the formulation of corporate identity. The marketing approach has specified more fully the ways in which management expresses this key idea to external audiences (e.g. through products, communications, behaviour and environment), while the organisational literature has been more concerned with the relationship between employees and their organisation (e.g. studies of organisational commitment and identification)" (p. 357).

(Continued)

50 Foroudi, Foroudi and Balmer

Table 2.1 (Continued)

Authors	Definitions
	"The symbolic construction of corporate identity is communicated to organisational members by top management, but is interpreted and enacted by organisational members based on the cultural patterns of the organisation, work experiences and social influence from external relations with the environment" (p. 358).
	Corporate identity does "focus on how these material aspects express the key idea of the organisation to external constituencies, studies of organisational culture address how they are realised and interpreted by organisational members" (p. 360).
	Corporate identity is used "as any other device top managers use to influence what employees and other constituencies perceive, feel and think about the organisation" (p. 363).
	"Corporate identity management involves formulating and communicating organisational vision and strategy in reference to external Constituencies" (p. 363).
Stuart, 1997	"Identity is formed by an organisation's history, its beliefs and philosophy, the nature of its technology, its ownership, its people, the personality of its leaders, its ethical and cultural values and its strategies" (p. 360).
Baker and Balmer, 1997; Van Rekom 1997	Corporate identity is one basis for achieving this and can be defined as "what an organisation is".
Baker and Balmer, 1997	Corporate identity is "what an organisation is". Corporate identity can be viewed as a vehicle by which a company's character is conveyed to different audiences.
Van Rekom, 1997	"What an organisation is" (p. 411).
	Corporate identity is "the set of meanings by which an object allows itself to be known and through which it allows people to describe, remember and relate to it" (p. 411).
	Corporate identity is a set of meanings by which an object allows people to describe, remember and relate to it.
	Corporate identity is a set of meaning by which the object allows itself to be known and through which it allows people to describe, remember and relate to it.
Leuthesser and Kohli, 1997	Corporate identity is the way a company reveals its philosophy and strategy through communication, behaviour and symbolism.
Van Riel and Balmer, 1997	Corporate identity is a way the company represents itself through behaviour and symbolism to internal and external audiences. It is rooted in the individual behaviour of the firm members expressing the firm's sameness overtime.
	Corporate identity as "the self presentation of an organisation, rooted in the behaviour of individual organisational members, expressing the organisation's sameness over time or continuity, distinctiveness, and centrality" (p. 290).
	Three paradigms of corporate identity are graphic design, integrated corporate communications and interdisciplinary.

(Continued)

Corporate identity 51

Table 2.1 (Continued)

Authors	Definitions
	Corporate identity refers to the characteristics of an organisation and works as a means for establishing the desired identity perception in the minds of an organisation's both internal and external stakeholders.
	Corporate identity indicates the way a company presents itself though behaviour and symbols to internal and external audiences and expresses the firm's sameness and distinctiveness over time.
Schmitt and Simonson, 1997	The visual school of thought focuses on the visual and tangible manifestations of what the firm is.
Markwick and Fill, 1997	Corporate identity is something that symbolises the organisation as a whole identity.
	Corporate identity is who a person is or what a thing is.
	Corporate identity is the instrument of management by means of which all consciously used forms of internal and external communication are harmonised as effectively and efficiently as possible, so as to create a favourable basis for relationships with the groups upon which the company is dependent (p. 411).
	Corporate identity has been defined above as "what an organisation is" (p. 411).
	Corporate identity is a crucial factor determining the effectiveness of communication (p. 413).
	Corporate identity is the domain of the signals which can be sent to stakeholders. The organisation's central value orientations, which permeate all its behaviour and are consciously or unconsciously present in the minds of an organisation's employees, can form an excellent source of inspiration, especially if they are unique for the organisation in question (p. 413).
	Corporate identity establishes the elements that constitute the "centrality" within the organisation (p. 416).
	Corporate identity is the "the organisation's presentation of itself to its various stakeholders and the means by which it distinguishes itself from all other organisations" (p. 397).
	Corporate identity is obtained through understanding an organisation's personality and its corporate values.
Van Heerden and Puth, 1995	Corporate identity creates a set of beliefs, experiences, feelings, knowledge, attitudes and perceptions about the institution in the minds of different stakeholders. This interaction creates overall impressions which constitute a corporate image.
	Corporate identity consists of both visual elements and the way in which the corporation behaves (p. 12).
	Corporate identity is a major means of achieving a unique positioning, which may lead to increased profits and improved business relationships with customers, suppliers, intermediaries, subsidiaries, the authorities, the media and international contacts (p. 13).
Van Riel, 1995	Corporate identity has been too little understood.
	Corporate identity demonstrates the bundle of characteristics of the company and displays the company's personality.

(*Continued*)

52   Foroudi, Foroudi and Balmer

Table 2.1 (Continued)

Authors	Definitions
Balmer, 1995; Downey, 1986	Corporate identity impacts beliefs and behaviours of organisational members on which the corporate culture is built.
Balmer, 1995	Corporate identity has many ways to communicate to create organisation distinctiveness. Corporate identity is defined as what the organisation is.
Moingeon and Ramanant- soa, 1995	"Corporate identity is the existence of a system of characteristics which has a pattern which gives the company its specificity, its stability and its coherence" (p. 253). Corporate identity is a set of interdependent characteristics of the firm that provide the firm specificity, stability, and coherence and thus make the firm also identifiable.
Olins, 1995	Corporate identity refers to the ways the company presents itself through experiences and perceptions to all people. Corporate identity is part of the strategic process, which consists of the vision, mission and philosophy of the firm.
Bernstein, 1984; Schmitt and Pan, 1994	Corporate identity reflects the sense of "essential character", since each company has its own personality, uniqueness and individuality.
Dowling, 1994	Corporate identity of an organisation as "the symbols an organisation uses to identify itself to people". Corporate identity is related to corporate values and sharing them with organisational members. A company's philosophy indicates the company's decisions, policies and actions. Every organisation has a vision and mission statement.
Balmer, 1993	Corporate identity is a fusion of strategy, communication and behaviour and it come in to being when there is a common ownership of organisation's philosophy. Corporate identity is a fusion of strategy and behavioural communications.
Olin, 1990	Corporate identity projects three things; who you are, what you do and how you do it.
Abratt, 1989	Corporate identity is a set of visual cues, physical and behavioural, that make the firm different and distinguish it from others and these cues are used to symbolise and represent the firm. Corporate identity is a set of visual cues which include physical and behavioural; that make a firm identifiable from other firms and these cues are used to represent the firm. Corporate identity strongly emphasises the key requirement of integrated corporate communications for both internal and external audiences. An organisation's corporate identity articulates what the organisation is, what it stands for and what it does … (and) … will include details of size; products manufactured and/or services offered; markets and industries served; organisational structure; geographical spread; and so on. Corporate identity is the fundamental style, quality, character and personality of an organisation, those forces which define, motivate and embody it.

(Continued)

Corporate identity 53

Table 2.1 (Continued)

Authors	Definitions
	Corporate identity is about appearance.
	Corporate identity is the "impression of the overall corporation held by (its) various publics" (Gray and Smeltzer, 1985).
	Corporate identity is the sum of the visual cues by which the public recognises the company and differentiates it from others (p. 67).
	Corporate identity is a set of visual cues-physical and behavioural – that makes a company recognisable and distinguishes it from other companies. These cues are used to represent and symbolise the company.
Lambert, 1989	Corporate identity is all distinctive manifestations of the firm.
Ackeman, 1988	Corporate identity is a firm's unique capabilities.
Bernstein, 1986	Corporate identity is the holistic and multi-disciplinary approach to corporate identity management.
Albert and Whetten, 1985	Corporate identity is that which is central, continuing and different about an organisation's character.
Bernstein, 1984	Corporate identity is the visible expression of the corporate image, which can be result of the interaction of all experiences, impressions, beliefs, feelings and knowledge that the public have about a corporation.
	Corporate identity deals with the experiences, impressions, beliefs, feelings and knowledge that the public have about a corporation.
Marguilies, 1977	Corporate identity management is concerned with the terms of graphic design and visual identity and could shape or influence externally held perceptions of companies.
	Corporate identity is all the ways a firm should identify itself to its entire stakeholder community; customers, employees, stockholder and investment bankers.
Selame and Selame, 1975	Corporate identity is who and what the firm is and how it views itself in the world. Corporate identity is the company' visual statement to the world of who and what the company is – of how the company views itself – and therefore has a great deal to do with how the world views the company.
Pilditch, 1970	Corporate identity can identify and communicate the corporate personality.
Abratt, 1989; Alessandri, 2001; Balmer, 1995; Balmer, 2001; Balmer and Gray, 2000;	Corporate identity management is used to achieve a favourable image between company's internal and external stakeholders.

(*Continued*)

54 Foroudi, Foroudi and Balmer

Table 2.1 (Continued)

Authors	Definitions
Olins, 1989; Simoes et al., 2005; Van Riel and Balmer, 1997; Van Rekom, 1997	
He and Mukherjee, 2009; Van Riel and Balmer, 1997	Corporate identity is the expression of a company.
Birkigt and Stadler, 1986; Margulies, 1977; Markwick and Fill, 1997; Olins, 1989; Van Riel, 1995	Corporate identity as self-presentation.
Ackerman, 1988; Balmer, 2001; Balmer and Wilson, 1998; Dowling, 1986; Gray and Balmer, 1998; Van Rekom, 1997	Corporate identity as organisational distinctiveness.
Balmer and Soenen, 1998; Birkigt and Stadler, 1986; He and Balmer, 2007; Melewar and Jenkins, 2002;	Corporate identity refers to the totality of the self-presentation of an organisation to various stakeholders (mainly customers) which associates with the elements of corporate identity mix which are personality, behaviour, communication and the symbolism to create a favourable image and a good reputation between its internal and external stakeholders.

(*Continued*)

Table 2.1 (Continued)

Authors	Definitions
Olins, 1989; Van Riel, 1995; Van Riel and Balmer, 1997	
Balmer, 1995; Olins, 1978	Corporate identity management relates to a corporation's values and principles which constitute its personality.

some of the key definitions of the concept of corporate identity), corporate identity is defined as the following:

Corporate identity is made up of the features, characteristics, traits or attributes of a company that are presumed to be central, distinctive and enduring (Albert and Whetten, 1985; Balmer, 2001, 2007, 2008; Bick et al., 2003; Balmer and Stotvig, 1997; Barnett et al., 2006; Gray and Balmer, 1998; He and Balmer, 2007; Mukherjee and He, 2008; Fombrun and Van Riel, 2004; Markwick and Fill, 1997; Van Riel and Balmer, 1997) and serves as a vehicle for the expression of the company's philosophy (Abratt, 1989; Balmer, 1994; Bernstein, 1986; Bhattacharya and Sen, 2003), values, beliefs and mission (Ashforth and Mael, 1989; Balmer, 1996; Gray and Balmer, 1997; Simoes et al., 2005), communications (Balmer, 1996; Van Riel, 1995) and corporate visual identity (Carter, 1982; Dowling, 2001; Melewar and Saunders, 1998, 1999, 2000; Melewar et al., 2001; Olins, 1991; Pilditch, 1970) to all its audience (Van Riel, 1995).

Conclusion

Corporate identity requires visibility, tangibility and consistency with other aspects of corporate identity that can be dictated by their aesthetic attractiveness. However, the aesthetic aspect of architecture is essential for organisations, since it expresses an increase in desire among corporate managers to promote the physical expression of the building as a means of enhancing corporate image and identification. The structure and design of its buildings influence the image of the organisation and creates a feeling of identification among stakeholders.

CASE STUDY: POSITIONING AND BRANDING OF A LONDON-BASED BUSINESS SCHOOL

Along with the expansion at undergraduate and postgraduate levels, the number of the international students studying at UK universities has increased rapidly. The UK is a popular international destination for students and is well established in the history of higher education with an international reputation. The higher education industry has been identified by governments as a strategic sector to attract more foreign students. For two decades or so, the provision of education for international students has emerged as a prominent growth area in the service sector. To improve performance and budget allocations, university ranking tables are used by universities to improve performance and budget allocations.

Given the significance of UK higher education, the history of Brunel University is a story of exponential growth and consistent academic development. Corporate identities are informed by history and can be shaped by past strategies. The history of Brunel University dates back to 1798; however, the first Department of Management Studies was launched by Professor A. Woods as the Head of Department in 1994 with 15 Students. In 2007, Professor Z. Irani was the Head of School with 686 students. Due to a lack of documentary material from the library, or from the school or on the web regarding the history of the Brunel Business School (BBS), the researcher interviewed *Professor Keith Dickson*, the main founder of the Brunel Business School, the head of the department and those who were involved (15 participants) in corporate identity changes. Figure 2.1 illustrates the corporate history and the founder of Brunel Business School.

The Brunel Business School (Eastern Gateway Building) is located on the north side of the campus and "creates a stunning entrance to the University Campus". This "£32m building has state of the art facilities with 7,000m over four floors to house the Business School Faculty, students and leading-edge research activities as well as an art gallery" (brunel.ac.uk/bbs, 2014). The Beldam Gallery, which is the university's art gallery and regularly displays exhibitions of local and national artists, as well as the work produced by members of the Brunel Art Centre in the cafeteria and in the building atrium ((brunel.ac.uk/bbs, 2014). The main outcome from the new building was to improve the BBS rankings and its competitive position. Brunel Business School moved to a new building in 2012.

Brunel University's mission is

> to create knowledge and advance understanding, and equip versatile graduates with the confidence to apply what they have learnt for the benefit of society. Brunel University's vision is to be a world-class creative community that is inspired to work, think and learn together to meet the challenges of the future.
>
> (brunel.ac.uk/about/strategic-plan/introduction, 2014)

As "a research-intensive university", Brunel places

> great value on the usefulness of the research, which improves the understanding of the world around Brunel and informs up to the

Corporate identity 57

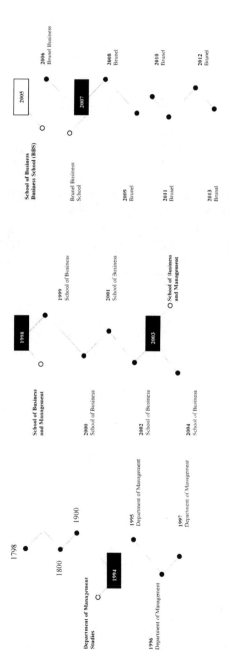

Source: The Researcher based on the Degree Congregation and award Ceremony booklets from 1994 to 2013.

Figure 2.1 Corporate history and the founder of Brunel Business School with the number of students per year. *Source*: designed by the researcher based on the degree congregation and award ceremony booklets from 1994 to 2013.

minute teaching. Research is responsible for much of the collaborative work with business, industry and the public sector, providing opportunities for work experience, and demonstrates the commitment to producing professionally-minded graduates that employers want to recruit. The 2008 Research Assessment Exercise (RAE) judged 82% of our research to be of international standing, leading to a 54.5% increase in its research funding from the Higher Education Funding Council, compared to the sector average increase of 7.8% in 2014.

Brunel has always had a strong sense of self-determination and autonomy, which has enabled it to develop and grow from its early beginnings into a highly respected research-intensive university, with a broad portfolio of undergraduate and postgraduate programmes attracting staff and students from across the world and to increase the attractiveness of the institutions in the international markets.

Corporate strategy and positioning are enormously significant in today's corporations to keep loyal customers, establish a competitive edge and increase the establishment image, especially to sustain a competitive advantage in today's competitive global market. A high-quality corporate strategy was reported in the participants' comments as a contributing factor towards a favourable corporate image. For instance,

> we've got an idea of where we really want to be and how we're going to get there, and I think it's taken a long time to get to top ranking personally. And, for a long time, we were asking what our strategy was. I feel now, we've made a decision and we know where we are going and I do feel it is quite clear to anyone.

Another participant added, "our school's corporate strategy is summarised in our school plan and outsiders are clear as to what our strategy is and where we are going in the future, what we are still working on".

> BBS corporate branding has a consistent short and long time strategic framework, which I think includes the school's activities and was designed by the top management at the school, and I think was aligned based on the school's brand identity. It presents the company's values, both emotional and functional by building the clear connection among strategic vision, organisational culture and stakeholder image, consumers, customers, and government, etc. We should consider the difficulties, such as aligning the internal and external stakeholders, and create credible and authentic identity.
>
> (Professor)

> I think the school changed its strategy and for this reason they needed to revise the School's visual identity. Our new name and logo provides

the clues to distinguish the changes in the school. I think all the changes appear in our communication to the students and staff. I think our name and logo are the main expression of Brunel, through which people can identify us and differentiate us from others.

(School Manager)

From the participants' comments, it is recognisable that BBS can help the brand by having a well-designed building that is distinctive and that this is critical in creating a brand that provides a favourable image. The above statements are consistent with the covenanted identity concept (or corporate brand identity), which is defined as what the school stands for. The covenanted identity refers to the covenant that underpins a corporate brand. It illustrates indicative character rather than comprehensive in character. The exhibit can be adapted so that its primary focus is on corporate brand identity.

The findings from the qualitative study indicate that positioning is a key element of the company in the market, which is wedded to customer decisions when choosing what to purchase. Additionally, the textual analysis of interviewees reveals a focus on defining the school's position in the market. The following comments illustrate a manager's assessment:

Our competitors are well known. We always look at league tables as the main source I would say, statistics and benchmark alongside our competitors. We look at NSS results … I think we're a market leader. We are famous and have enough experience in doing this.

(Senior Lecturer)

The comments made by the interviewees also emphasised that the NSS (National Student Survey) has a major impact on league tables. This can be illustrated in the description provided by one Lecturer:

in the UK, there is a clear categorisation of universities, the top six or seven and then you have the Russell group, middling group and then modern universities; then at the bottom of the line are the new universities that are struggling to be seen as universities. We're in the group of middle ranking university, and not far to the Russell group, hopefully, a realistic aspiration is that we are pushing ourselves up to the top, whereas now we're currently in the middle.

This case study presented the findings from qualitative research to better understand the contextualisation of the study, namely, to place the case of the business school in context in terms of its history, positioning and branding to answer "where does a business school come from?" "Where would a business school like to go?" and "what is needed as a more precise description of BBS identity, the position it aspires to and its strategic intent?".

60 *Foroudi, Foroudi and Balmer*

Case questions

Conduct research on the Brunel Business School website (https://www.brunel.ac
.uk/business-school) and answer the following questions.

How does the school carry the past over to the present and makes itself valuable
to contemporary internal and external stakeholders?

Identify the key identity elements of the Brunel Business School and how it
impacts on the school's reputation

Discuss the strategies employed by the school and how it impacts on its future
vision and philosophy?

Key terms and definitions

Corporate identity is made up of the features, characteristics, traits or attributes
of a company that are presumed to be central, distinctive and enduring and
serves as a vehicle for expression of the company's philosophy, values and
mission, communications and corporate visual identity to all its audience.

Corporate visual identity is an assembly of visual cues used to make an expression of the organisation by which an audience can recognise the company
and distinguish it from others by serving to remind an audience of the real
purpose of the corporation.

Communication is the aggregate of messages from both official and informal
sources, through a variety of media, by which a company conveys its identity
to its multiple audiences or stakeholders.

Philosophy is made up of the core values and assumptions that constitute the
corporate culture, business mission and values espoused by the management
board or founder of the company.

Mission is the company purpose, the reason for which a company exists.

Value is the dominant system of beliefs and moral principles that lie within the
organisation that comprise everyday language, ideologies, rituals and beliefs
of personnel.

Architecture is a visual presentation of a company encapsulating a company's
purpose and identity, set of elements (physical structure/spatial layout and
functionality, ambient conditions/physical stimuli of an environment, and
symbolic artefacts/decor and artefacts) which have an influence on internal-stakeholders' attitude, and behaviour. It can be decisive in facilitating
employees and internal-stakeholders' identification.

Physical structure/spatial layout and functionality refers to the architectural
design and physical placement of furnishings in a building, the arrangement
of objects (e.g. arrangement of buildings, machinery, furniture and equipment), the spatial relationships among them and the physical location and
physical layout of the workplace which are particularly pertinent to the service industry and can symbolise something.

Physical stimuli/ambient conditions of an environment in service settings
encourage stakeholders to pursue the service consumptions and subsequently,

can affect employees' behaviours, attitudes, satisfaction with and performance relating to the service provider.

Symbolic artefacts/decor and artefacts are aspects of the physical setting that individually or collectively guide the interpretation of the social setting, can be related to the aesthetics and attractiveness of the physical features of the environment, develop a complex representation of workplace identity and are mainly relevant to the service industry.

References

Aaker, D. (1996) *Building Strong Brands*, Free Press, New York.

Aaker, D. and Joachimsthaler, E. (2000) *Brand Leadership*, Free Press, London.

Abratt, R. (1989) "A new approach to the corporate image management process", *Journal of Marketing Management*, Vol. 5, No. 1, pp. 63–76.

Ackerman, L. D. (1988) "Identity strategies that make a difference", *Journal of Business Strategy*, Vol. 3, pp. 28–32.

Ageeva, E. and Foroudi, P. (2019) "Tourists' destination image through regional tourism: from supply and demand sides perspectives", *Journal of Business Research*, Vol. 101 (Aug), pp. 334–348.

Ageeva, E., Foroudi, P., Melewar, T. C., Nguyen, B. and Dennis, C. (2019) "A holistic framework of corporate website favourability", *Corporate Reputation Review*, Vol. 21 (Sep), pp. 1–14.

Ageeva, E., Melewar, T. C., Foroudi, P. and Dennis, C. (2019) "Evaluating the factors of corporate website favorability: a case of UK and Russia", *Qualitative Market Research: An International Journal*, Vol. 22, No. 5, pp. 687–715.

Ageeva, E., Melewar, T. C., Foroudi, P. and Dennis, C. (2019) "Cues adopted by consumers in examining corporate website favorability: an empirical study of financial institutions in the UK and Russia", *Journal of Business Research*, Vol. 98 (May), pp. 15–32.

Ageeva, E., Melewar, T. C., Foroudi, P., Dennis, C. and Jin, Z. (2018) "Examining the influence of corporate website favorability on corporate image and corporate reputation: findings from fsQCA", *Journal of Business Research*, Vol. 89 (Aug), pp. 287–304.

Ahearne, M., Bhattacharya, C. B. and Gruen, T. (2005) "Antecedents and consequences of customer-company identification: expanding the scope of relationship marketing", *Journal of Applied Psychology*, Vol. 90, No. 3, pp. 574–585.

Akarsu, T. N., Foroudi, P. and Melewar, T. C. (2019) "Rethinking the nexus of TV series/movies and destination image: changing perceptions through sensorial cues and authentic identity of a city", in Foroudi, P., Mauri, C., Dennis, C. and Melewar, T. C. (Eds.), *Place Branding: Connecting Tourist Experiences to Places*. Routledge, UK.

Albert, A., Ashforth, B. E. and Dutton, J. E. (2000) "Organisational identity and identification: charting new waters and building new bridges", *Academy of Management Review*, Vol. 25. No. 1, pp. 13–17.

Albert, S. and Whetten, D. A. (1985) "Organisational identity", *Research in Organisational Behavior*, Vol. 7. pp. 263–295.

Alessandri, S. W. (2001) "Modelling corporate identity: a concept explication and theoretical explanation", *Corporate Communications: An International Journal*, Vol. 6, No. 4, pp. 173–182.

62   Foroudi, Foroudi and Balmer

Alvesson, M. (1998) "The business concept as a symbol", *International Studies of Management and Organization*, Vol. 28, No. 3, pp. 86–108.

Ashforth, B. E. and Johnson, S. A. (2001) "Which hat to wear? The relative salience of multiple identities in organisational contexts", in M. A. Hogg and D. J. Terry (Eds.), *Social Identity Processes in Organisational Contexts*, pp. 31–48. Psychology Press, Philadelphia.

Ashforth, B. E. and Mael, F. A. (1989) "Social identity theory and the organisation", *Academy of Management Review*, Vol. 14, No. 1, pp. 20–39.

Ashforth, B. E. and Mael, F. A. (1996) "Organisational identity and strategy as a context for the individual", *Advances in Strategic Management*, Vol. 13, pp. 19–64.

Athos, A. G. and Pascale, R. (1981) *The Art of Japanese Management*, Warner Books, New York.

Baker, M. J. and Balmer, J. M. T. (1997) "Visual identity: trappings or substance?", *European Journal of Marketing*, Vol. 31, No. 5, pp. 366–382.

Balmer, J. M. T. (1993) "Corporate identity: the power and the paradox", *Design Management Journal*, Vol. 6, pp. 39–44.

Balmer, J. M. T. (1994) "The BBC's corporate identity: myth, paradox and reality", *Journal of General Management*", Vol. 19, No. 3, pp. 33–49.

Balmer, J. M. T. (1995) "Corporate branding and connoisseurship", *Journal of General Management*, Vol. 21, No. 1, pp. 22–46.

Balmer, J. M. T. (1996) *The Nature of Corporate Identity: An Explanatory Study Undertaken Within BBC Scotland*, unpublished PhD thesis, University of Strathclyde, Glasgow, UK.

Balmer, J. M. T. (1997) *Corporate Identity: Past, Present and Future*. Department of Marketing, Working Paper Series, University of Strathclyde, England.

Balmer, J. M. T. (1998) "Corporate identity and the advent of corporate marketing", *Journal of Marketing Management*, Vol. 14, No. 8, pp. 963–996.

Balmer, J. M. T. (2001) "Corporate identity, corporate branding and corporate marketing seeing through the fog", *European Journal of Marketing*, Vol. 35, No. 3/4, pp. 248–291.

Balmer, J. M. T. (2008) "An epiphany of three: corporate identity, corporate brand management, and corporate marketing", in T. C. Melewar (Ed.), *Facets of Corporate Identity, Communication and Reputation*, pp. 35–54. Routledge, Abingdon.

Balmer, J. M. T. (2009) "Corporate marketing: apocalypse, advent and epiphany", *Management Decision*, Vol. 47, No. 4, pp. 544–572.

Balmer, J. M. T. (2011) "Corporate heritage identities, corporate heritage brands and the multiple heritage identities of the British Monarchy", *European Journal of Marketing*, Vol. 45, No. 9/10, pp. 1380–1398.

Balmer, J. M. T. and Gray, E. R. (1999) "Corporate identity and corporate communications: creating a competitive advantage", *Corporate Communications: An International Journal*, Vol. 4, No. 4, pp. 171–176.

Balmer, J. M. T. and Gray, E. R. (2000) "Corporate identity and corporate communications: creating a competitive advantage", *Industrial and Commercial Training*, Vol. 32, No. 7, pp. 256–262.

Balmer, J. M. T. and Gray, E. R. (2003) "Corporate brands: what are they? What of them?", *European Journal of Marketing*, Vol. 37, No. 7/8, pp. 972–997.

Balmer, J. M. T. and Greyser, S. A. (2002) "Managing the multiple identities of the corporation", *California Management Review*, Vol. 44, No. 3, pp. 72–86.

Balmer, J. M. T. and Greyser, S. A. (2003) *Revealing the Corporation*, Routledge, London.

Corporate identity 63

Balmer, J. M. T. and Liao, M. N. (2006) "Shifting loyalties and identition to corporate brand: an exploratory case-study of students identification in higher education", Working Paper, Bradford University School of Management.

Balmer, J. M. T. and Soenen, G. (1998) "A new approach to corporate identity management. International Centre for Corporate Identity Studies", *European Journal of Marketing*, Vol. 40, No. 7–8, pp. 846–869.

Balmer, J. M. T. and Soenen, G. B. (1999) "The acid test of corporate identity management", *Journal of Marketing Management*, Vol. 15, No. 1/3, pp. 69–92.

Balmer, J. M. T. and Stotvig, S. (1997) "Corporate identity and private banking; a review and case study", *International Journal of Banking, Special Edition on Corporate Identity in Financial Services*, Vol. 15, No. 5, pp. 169–184.

Balmer, J. M. T. and Wilson, A. (1998) "Corporate identity: there is more to it than meets the eye", *International Studies of Management and Organization*, Vol. 28, No. 3, pp. 12–31.

Balmer, J. M. T., Greyser, S. A. and Urde, M. (2006) "The crown as a corporate brand: insights from monarchies", *Brand Management*, Vol. 14, No. 1/2, pp. 137–161.

Balmer, J. M. T., Fukukawa, K. and Grey, E. (2007) "The nature and management of ethical corporate identity: a commentary on corporate identity, corporate social responsibility and ethics", *Journal of Business Ethics*, Vol. 76, No. 1, pp. 7–15.

Balmer, J. M. T., Stuart, H. and Greyser, S. A. (2009) "Aligning identity and strategy: corporate branding at British Airways in the late 20th century", *California Management Review*, Vol. 51, No. 3, pp. 6–23.

Balmer, J. M. T., Powell, S. M. and Greyser, S. A. (2011) "Explicating ethical corporate marketing. Insights from the BP Deepwater horizon catastrophe: the ethical brand that exploded and then imploded explicating ethical corporate marketing insights from the BP deepwater horizon catastrophe: the ethical brand that exploded and then imploded", *Journal of Business Ethics*, Vol. 102, No. 1, pp. 1–14.

Barich, H. and Kotler, P. (1991) "A framework for image management", *Sloan Management Review*, Vol. 32, No. 2, pp. 94–104.

Barnett, M. L. L., Jermier, J. M. and Lafferty, B. A. (2006) "Corporate reputation: the definitional landscape", *Corporate Reputation Review*, Vol. 9, No. 1, pp. 26–38.

Bergami, M. and Bagozzi, R. P. (2000) "Self-categorization, affective commitment and group self-esteem as distinct aspects of social identity in the organisation", *British Journal of Social Psychology*, Vol. 39, pp. 555–557.

Bernstein, D. (1984) *Company Image and Reality: A Critique of Corporate Communications*. Taylor & Francis, London.

Bernstein, D. J. (1986) *Company Image and Reality: A Critique of Corporate Communications*, Cassell Educational Ltd, London.

Berry, L. L. (1969) "The components of department store image: a theoretical and empirical analysis", *Journal of Retailing*, Vol. 45, pp. 3–20.

Berry, L. L. (2000) "Cultivating service brand equity", *Journal of the Academy of Marketing Science*, Vol. 28, No. 1, pp. 128–137.

Bharadwaj, S., Varadarajan, R. and Fay, J. (1993) "Sustainable competitive advantage in service industries", *Journal of Marketing*, Vol. 57, No. 4, pp. 83–99.

Bhattacharya, C. B. and Sen, S. (2003) "Consumer-company identification: a framework for understanding consumers' relationships with companies", *Journal of Marketing*, Vol. 67, No. 2, pp. 76–88.

Bick, G., Jacobson, M. C. and Abratt, R. (2003) "The corporate identity management process revisited", *Journal of Marketing Management*, Vol. 19, No. 7/8, pp. 835–855.

64 Foroudi, Foroudi and Balmer

Birkigt, K. and Stadler, M. M. (1986) *Corporate Identity, Grundlagen, Funktionen, Fallspielen*, Verlag Moderne Industrie, Landsberg an Lech.

Bitner, M. J. (1990) "Evaluating service encounters: the effects of physical surrounding and employee responses", *Journal of Marketing*, Vol. 54, No. 2, pp. 69–82.

Bolger, J. F. Jr. (1959) "How to evaluate your company image", *Journal of Marketing*, Vol. 24 (October), pp. 7–10.

Bromley, D. B. (2001) "Relationships between personal and corporate reputation", *European Journal of Marketing*, Vol. 35, No. 3/4, pp. 316–334.

Brown, D., Foroudi, P. and Hafeez, K. (2019) "Marketing management capability: the construct, and its dimensions: an examination of managers and entrepreneurs' perception in the retail setting", *Qualitative Market Research: An International Journal*, Vol. 22, No. 5, pp. 609–637.

Brown, T. J. (1998) "Corporate associations in marketing: antecedents and consequences", *Corporate Reputation Review*, Vol. 1, No. 3, pp. 215–233.

Brown, T. J. and Dacin, P. A. (1997) "The company and the product: corporate associations and consumer product responses", *Journal of Marketing*, Vol. 61, No. 1, pp. 68–84.

Brown, J. J. and Reingen, P. H. (1987) "Social ties and word-of-mouth referral behaviour", *Journal of Consumer Research*, Vol. 14, No. 3, pp. 350–362.

Brown, T. J., Dacin, P. A., Pratt, M. G. and Whetten, D. A. (2006) "Identity, intended image, construed image, and reputation: an inter-disciplinary framework and suggested terminology", *Journal of the Academy of Marketing Science*, Vol. 34, No. 2, pp. 99–106.

Cardador, M. T. and Pratt, M. G. (2006) *Occupational Identity and Meaning of Work: Toward an Expanded Understanding of Work Orientation*, Academy of Management, Atlanta, GA.

Carter, D. E. (1982) *Designing Corporate Identity Programs for Small Corporations*, Art Direction Book Company, New York.

Chajet, C. (1984) "Communicating corporate identity", *Bankers' Magazine*, Vol. 167, No. 6, pp. 53–58.

Childers, T. L. and Jass, J. (2002) "All dressed up with something to say: effects of typeface semantic associations on brand perception and consumer memory", *Journal of Consumer Psychology*, Vol. 12, No. 2, pp. 93–106.

Chowdhury, J., Reardon, J. and Srivastava, R. (1998) "Alternative modes of measuring store image: an empirical assessment of structured versus unstructured measures", *Journal of Marketing Theory and Practice*, Vol. 6 (Spring), pp. 72–86.

Christensen, L. T. and Askegaard, S. (2001) "Corporate identity and corporate image revisited: a semiotic perspective", *European Journal of Marketing*, Vol. 35, No. 3/4, pp. 292–315.

Christiansen, T. and Tax, S. (2000) "Measuring word of mouth: the questions of who and when?", *Journal of Marketing Communications*, Vol. 6, No. 3, pp. 185–199.

Collins, J. C. and Porras, J. I. (1991) "Organisational vision and visionary organisations", *California Management Review*, Vol. 34, No. 1, pp. 30–52.

Collins, J. C. and Porras, J. I. (1994) *Built to Last: Successful Habits of Visionary Companies*, Harper Business, New York.

Corley, K. G. and Gioia, D. A. (2004) "Identity ambiguity and change in the wake of a corporate spin-off", *Administrative Science Quarterly*, Vol. 49, pp. 173–208.

Cornelissen, J. P. (2000) "Corporate image: an audience centred model", *Corporate Communications: An International Journal*, Vol. 5, No. 2, pp. 119–125.

Corporate identity 65

Cornelissen, J. P. and Elving, W. J. L. (2003) "Managing corporate identity: an integrative framework of dimensions and determinants", *Corporate Communications: An International Journal*, Vol. 8, No. 2, pp. 114–120.

Cornelissen, J. P. and Harris, P. (2001) "The corporate identity metaphor: perspectives, problems, and prospects", *Journal of Marketing Management*, Vol. 17, pp. 49–71.

Cornelissen, J. P., Haslam, S. A. and Balmer, J. M. T. (2007) "Social identity, organisational identity and corporate identity: towards an integrated understanding of processes, patternings and products", *British Journal of Management*, Vol. 18, pp. 1–16.

Cummings, E. M. and Davies, P. T. (1994) *Children and Marital Conflict: The Impact of Family Dispute and Resolution*, Guilford, New York.

Dacin, P. and Brown, T. (2002) "Corporate identity and corporate associations: a framework for future research", *Corporate Reputation Review*, Vol. 5, No. 2/3, pp. 254–253.

De Wit, B., and Meyer, R. (1998) *Strategy, Process, Content and Context*, 2nd ed. Thomson Learning, London.

Dichter, E. (1985) "What's in an image?", *Journal of Consumer Marketing*, Vol. 2 (Winter), pp. 75–81.

Dowling, G. R. (1986) "Managing your corporate image", *Industrial Marketing Management*, Vol.15, pp. 109–115.

Dowling, G. R. (1993) "Developing your company image into a corporate asset", *Long Range Planning*, Vol. 26, No. 2, pp. 101–109.

Dowling, G. R. (1994) *Corporate Reputation: Strategies For Developing the Corporate Brand*, Kogan Page, London.

Dowling, G. R. (2001) *Creating Corporate Reputations ± Identity Image, and Performance*, Oxford University Press, Oxford.

Downey, S. M. (1986) "The relationship between corporate culture and corporate identity", *Public Relations Quarterly*, Vol. 31, No. 4, pp. 7–12.

Dukerich, J. M., Golden, B. R. and Shortell, S. M. (2002) "Beauty is in the eye of the beholder: the impact of organisational identification, identity, and image on the cooperative behaviour of physicians", *Administrative Science Quarterly*, Vol. 47, pp. 507–533.

Duncan, T. and Everett, S. (1993) "Client perceptions of integrated marketing communications", *Journal of Advertising Research*, Vol. 33, No. 3, pp. 30–39.

Duncan, T. and Moriarty, S. E. (1998) "A communication-based marketing model for managing relationships", *Journal of Marketing*, Vol. 62, No. 2, pp. 1–13.

Dutton, J. E. and Dukerich, J. M. (1991) "Keeping an eye on the mirror: image and identity in organisational adaptation", *Academy of Management Journal*, Vol. 34, No. 3, pp. 517–554.

Dutton, J. E., Dukerich, L M. and Harquail, C. V. (1994) "Organisational images and member identification", *Administrative Science Quarterly*, Vol. 39, No. 2, pp. 239–263.

Easton, A. (1966) "Corporate style versus corporate image", *Journal of Marketing Research*, Vol. 3 (May), pp. 168–174.

Elsbach, K. D. (2009) "Identity affirmation through 'signature style': a study of toy car designers", *Human Relations*, Vol. 62, pp. 1041–1072.

Elsbach, K. D. and Bhattacharya, C. B. (2001) "Defining who you are by what you're not: organisational disidentification and the National Rifle Association", *Organization Science*, Vol. 12, No. 4, pp. 393–413.

Elsbach, K. D. and Kramer, R. M. (1996) "Members' responses to organisational identity threats: encountering and countering the business week rankings", *Administrative Science Quarterly*, Vol. 41, No. 3, pp. 442–476.

Erikson, E. (1956) "The problem of ego identity", *Psychoanalytic Association*, Vol. 4, pp. 56–121.

Erikson, E. (1960) "The problem of ego Identity", in Stein, M., Vidich, J. and White, D. (Eds.), *Identity and Anxiety: Survival of the Person in Mass Society*. The Free Press of Glencoe, Illinois.

Fairhurst, G. T. (1993) "Echoes of the vision: when the rest of the organisation talks total quality", *Management Communication Quarterly*, Vol. 6, pp. 331–371.

Fombrun, C. J. (1996) *Reputation: Realizing Value from the Corporate Image*. Harvard Business School Press, Boston.

Fombrun, C. J. and Rindova, V. P. (2000) "The road to transparency: reputation management at Royal Dutch/Shell", *The Expressive Organization*, Vol. 7, pp. 7–96.

Fombrun, C. J. and Shanley, M. (1990) "What is in a name? Reputation building and corporate strategy", *Academy of Management Journal*, Vol. 33, No. 2, pp. 233–258.

Fombrun, C. J. and Van Riel, C. B. M. (1997) "The reputational landscape", *Corporate Reputation Review*, Vol. 1, No. 1/2, pp. 5–13.

Fombrun, C. J. and Van Riel, C. B. M. (2004) *Fame and Fortune: How Successful Companies Build Winning Reputation*, Financial Times Prentice Hall, New Jersey.

Foreman, P. and Whetten, D. A. (2002) "Members' identification with multiple-identity organisations", *Organization Science*, Vol. 13, No. 6, pp. 618–635.

Foroudi, M. M., Balmer, M. T., Chen, W. and Foroudi, P. (2019) Corporate identity, place architecture, and identification: an exploratory case study. *Qualitative Market Research An International Journal*, Vol. 22 (5), pp. 638–668.

Foroudi, M. M., Balmer, J. M., Chen, W., Foroudi, P. and Patsala, P. (2020) Explicating place identity attitudes, place architecture attitudes, and identification triad theory. *Journal of Business Research*, Vol. 109 (March), pp. 321–336.

Foroudi, P. (2018) "Corporate design: what makes a favorable university logo"? in Bang Nguyen, T. C. Melewar and Jane Hemsley-Brown (Eds.), *Strategic Brand Management in Higher Education*. Routledge, UK.

Foroudi, P. (2019) Influence of brand signature, brand awareness, brand attitude, brand reputation on hotel industry's brand performance, *International Journal of Hospitality Management*, Vol. 76 (Jan), pp. 271–285.

Foroudi, P. (2020) "Corporate brand strategy: drivers and outcomes of corporate brand orientation in international marketing", *International Journal of Hospitality Management*, Vol. 88 (July), pp. 102519.

Foroudi, P., Akarsu, T. N., Ageeva, E., Foroudi, M. M., Dennis, C. and Melewar, T. C. (2018) Promising the dream: the changing destination image of London through the effect of website place", *Journal of Business Research*, Vol. 83 (Feb), pp. 97–110.

Foroudi, P., Jin, Z., Gupta, S., Melewar, T. C. and Foroudi, M. M. (2016) "Influence of innovation capability and customer experience on reputation and loyalty", *Journal of Business Research*, Vol. 69, No. 11, pp. 4882–4889.

Fouroudi, P., Kitchen, P. J., Marvi, R., Akarsu, T. N. and Uddin, H. (2020) "A bibliometric investigation of service failure literature and a research agenda", *European Journal of Marketing*, Vol. 54, No. 10, pp. 2575–2619.

Foroudi, P., Marvi, R., Izadi, J., Izadi, J. and Pirzadeh, P. (2020) "Take a new turn: relationships between corporate identity management, antecedents and corporate reputation in hospitality context", in Melewar, T. C., Dennis, C. and Foroudi, P. (Eds.), Building Corporate Identity, Image and Reputation in Digital Era. Routledge, UK.

Foroudi, P. and Marvi, R. (2021) "SOME LIKE IT HOT: the role of identity, website, co-creation behavior on identification and love", *European Journal of International Management* (Just published).

Foroudi, P., Melewar, T. C. and Gupta, S. (2014) Linking corporate logo, corporate image, and reputation: an examination of consumer perceptions in the financial setting, *Journal of Business Research*, Vol. 67, No. 11, pp. 2269–2281.

Foroudi, P., Nazarian, A., Ziyadin, S., Kitchen, P., Hafeez, K., Priporas, C. and Pantano, E. (2020) "Co-creating brand image and reputation through stakeholder's social network", *Journal of Business Research*, Vol. 114 (June), pp. 42–59.

Foroudi, P., Yu, Q., Gupta, S. and Foroudi, M. M. (2019) "Enhancing university brand image and reputation through customer value co-creation behaviour", *Technological Forecasting and Social Change*, Vol. 138 (Jan), pp. 218–227.

Fritz, J. M. H., Arnett, R. C. and Conkel, M. (1999) "Organisational ethical standards and organisational commitment", *Journal of Business Ethics*, Vol. 20, No. 4, pp. 289–299.

Fukukawa, K., Balmer, J. M. T. and Gray, E. R. (2007) "Mapping the interface between corporate identity, ethics, and corporate social responsibility", *Journal of Business Ethics*, Vol. 76, No. 1, pp. 1–5.

Gilly, M. C. and Wolfinbarger, M. (1998) "Advertising's internal audience", *Journal of Marketing*, Vol. 62, No. 1, pp. 69–88.

Gioia, D. A. and Thomas, J. B. (1996) "Identity, image, and issue interpretation: sensemaking during strategic change in academia", *Administrative Science Quarterly*, Vol. 41, pp. 370–403.

Gioia, D. A., Majken, S. and Corley, K. G. (2000) "Organisational identity, image, and adaptive instability", *Academy of Management Review*, Vol. 25 No. 1, pp. 63–81.

Gorman, C. (1994) "Developing an effective corporate identity program", *Public Relations Journal*, Vol. 50, No. 7, pp. 40–42.

Gray, E. R. and Balmer, J. M. T. (1997) *Corporate Identity: A Vital Component of Strategy*, Working Paper, University of Strathclyde International Centre for Corporate Identity Studies, Glasgow.

Gray, E. R. and Balmer, J. M. T. (1998) "Managing corporate image and corporate reputation", *Long Range Planning*, Vol. 31, No. 5, pp. 695–702.

Gray, E. R. and Smeltzer, L. R. (1985) "Corporate image: an integral part of strategy", *Sloan Management Review*, Vol. 26, No. 4, pp. 73–77.

Gray, E. R. and Smeltzer, L. R. (1987) "Planning a face-lift: implementing a corporate image program", *The Journal of Business Strategy*, Vol. 1, No. 1, pp. 4–10.

Gregory, J. R. (1999) *Marketing Corporate Image: Your Company as Your Number One Product*, Second edition, Lincolnwood, IL.

Greyser, S. A., Balmer, J. M. T. and Urde, M. (2006) "The monarchy as a corporate brand: some corporate communications dimensions", *European Journal of Marketing*, Vol. 40, No. 7/8, pp. 902–908.

Grunig, J. M. (1993) "Image and substance: from symbolic to behavioural relationships", *Public Relations Review*, Vol. 19, No. 2, pp. 121–39.

Hatch, M. J. and Schultz, M. (1997) "Relations between organisational culture, identity, and image", *European Journal of Marketing*, Vol. 31, No. 5/6, pp. 356–365.

Hatch, M. J. and Schultz, M. (2000) "Scaling the tower of babel: relational differences between identity, image and culture in organisations", in M. Schultz, M. J. Hatch and M. H. Larsen (Eds.), *The Expressive Organisation: Linking Identity, Reputation, and the Corporate Brand*, pp. 13–35. Oxford University Press, Oxford.

68   *Foroudi, Foroudi and Balmer*

Hatch, M. J. and Schultz, M. (2001) "Are the strategic stars aligned for your corporate brand", *Harvard Business Review*, Vol. 69 (February) pp. 128–134.

Hatch, M. J. and Schultz, M. (2003) "Bringing the corporation into corporate branding", *European Journal of Marketing*, Vol. 3, No. 7/8, pp. 1041–1064.

He, H. W. and Balmer, J. M. T. (2007) "Identity studies: multiple perspectives and implications for corporate-level marketing", *European Journal of Marketing*, Vol. 41, No 7/8, pp. 765–785.

He, H. W. and Mukherjee, A. (2009) "Corporate identity and consumer marketing: a process model and research Agenda", *Journal of Marketing Communications*, Vol. 15, No. 1, pp. 1–16.

Henderson, P. W. and Cote, J. A. (1998) "Guidelines for selecting or modifying logos", *Journal of Marketing*, Vol. 62, No. 2, pp. 14–30.

Henderson, P. W., Cote, J. A., Meng, L. S. and Schmitt, B. (2003) "Building strong brands in Asia: selecting the visual components of image to maximize brand strength", *International Journal of Research in Marketing*, Vol. 20, No. 4, pp. 297–313.

Henderson, P. W., Giese, J. and Cote, J. A. (2004) "Impression management using typeface design", *Journal of Marketing*, Vol. 68, No. 4, pp. 60–83.

Hill, E. W. (1962) "Corporate images are not stereotypes", *Journal of Marketing*, Vol. 26, No. 1, pp. 72–75.

Hussain, S., Melewar, T. C., Priporas, C. and Foroudi, P. (2020) "Examining the effects of advertising credibility on brand credibility, corporate credibility and corporate image: a qualitative approach", *Qualitative Market Research: An International Journal*, Vol. 23, No. 4, pp. 549–573.

Ind, N. (1990) *The Corporate Image*, Kogan Page, London.

Ind, N. (1997) *The Corporate Brand*, New York University Press, New York.

Karaosmanoglu, E. and Melewar, T. (2006) "Corporate communications, identity and image: a research agenda', *Journal of Brand Management*, Vol. 14, No. 1/2, pp. 196–206.

Karaosmanoglu, E., Bas, A. B. E. and Zhang, J. (2011) "The role of other customer effect in corporate marketing its impact on corporate image and consumer-company identification", *European Journal of Marketing*, Vol. 45, No. 9/10, pp. 1416–1445.

Kasulis, J. J. and Lusch, R. F. (1981) "Validating the retail store image concept", *Journal of the Academy of Marketing Science*, Vol. 9, No. 4, pp. 419–435.

Keller, K. L. (1993) "Conceptualizing, measuring, and managing customer-based brand equity2", *Journal of Marketing*, Vol. 57 (January) pp. 1–22.

Keller, K. L. (1999) "Brand mantras: rationale, criteria and examples", *Journal of Marketing Management*, Vol. 15, No. 1/3, pp. 43–51.

Kennedy, S. H. (1977) "Nurturing corporate images", *European Journal of Marketing*, Vol. 11, No. 3, pp. 120–164.

Kiriakidou, O. and Millward, L. J. (2000) "Corporate identity: external reality or internal fit", *Corporate Communications: An International Journal*, Vol. 5, No. 1, pp. 49–58.

Kissler, G. D. (1991) *The Change Riders: Managing the Power of Change*, Addison-Wesley, Reading.

Knox, S. and Bickerton, D. (2003) "The six conventions of corporate branding", *European Journal of Marketing*, Vol. 37 No 7/8, pp. 998–1016.

Kohli, C., Suri, R. and Thakor, M. (2002) "Creating effective logos: insights from theory and practice", *Business Horizons*, Vol. 45, No. 3, pp. 58–64.

Kono, T. (1990) "Changing a company's strategy and culture", *Long Range Planning*, Vol. 27, No. 5, pp. 85–97.

Kottasz, R., Bennett, R., Savani, S. and Ali-Choudhury, A. (2008) "The role of corporate art in the management of corporate identity", *Corporate Communications: An International Journal*, Vol. 13, No. 3, pp. 235–254.

Kotter, J. and Heskett, J. L. (1992) *Corporate Culture and Performance*, The Free Press, New York.

Kunkel, J. H. and Berry, L. L. (1968) "A behavioural conception of retail image", *Journal of Marketing*, Vol. 32, pp. 21–27.

Lambert, A. (1989) "Corporate identity and facilities management", *Facilities* (December), pp. 7–12.

Lau, G. T. and Ng, S. (2001) "Individual and situational factors influencing negative word- of-mouth behaviour" *Canadian Journal of Administrative Sciences*, Vol. 18, No. 3, pp. 163–178.

Leary, M. and Tangney, J. (2003) *Handbook of Self and Identity*, Guilford Press, New York.

Ledford, J., Wendenhof, J. and Strahley, J. (1995) "Realising a corporate philosophy", *Organisational Dynamics*, Vol. 23, pp. 5–19.

Leitch, S. and Motion, J. (1999) "Miplicity in corporate identity strategy", *Corporate Communications: An International Journal*, Vol. 4, No. 4, pp. 193–200.

Leuthesser, L. and Kohli, C. (1997) "Corporate identity: the role of mission statements", *Business Horizons*, Vol. 40, No. 3, pp. 59–66.

Levin, M. L. (2000) "Vision revisited", *Journal of Applied Behavioral Science*, Vol. 36, No. 1, pp. 91–107.

Lippincott, J. G. and Margulies, W. (1957) "The corporate look: a problem in design", *Public Relations Journal*, Vol. 13, p. 27.

Mael, F. and Ashfort, B. E. (1992) "Alumni and their Alma Mater: a partial test of the reformulated model of organisational identification", *Journal of Organisational Behavior*, Vol. 13, No. 2, pp. 103–123.

Margulies, W. P. (1977) "Make the most of your corporate image", *Harvard Business Review*, Vol. 55, No. 4, pp. 66–74.

Marin, L. and Riuz de Maya, S. (2013) "The role of affiliation, attractiveness and personal connection in consumer-company identification", *European Journal of Marketing*, Vol. 47, No 3–4, pp. 655–673.

Marks, R. B. (1976) "Operationalising the concept of store image", *Journal of Retailing*, Vol. 52, pp. 37–46.

Markwick, N. and Fill, C. (1997) "Towards a framework for managing corporate identity", *European Journal of Marketing*, Vol. 31, No. 5/6, pp. 396–409.

Martineau, P. (1958) "Sharper focus for the corporate image", *Harvard Business Review*, Vol. 36 (Nov/Dec) pp. 49–58.

Mazursky, D. and Jacoby, J. (1986) "Exploring the development of store images", *Journal of Retailing*, Vol. 62, pp. 145–165.

Mcdonald, M., de Chernatony, L. and Harris, F. (2001) "Corporate marketing and service brands: moving beyond the fast-moving consumer goods model", *European Journal of Marketing*, Vol. 35, pp. 335–353.

Melewar, T. C. and Jenkins, E. (2002) "Defining the corporate identity construct", *Corporate Reputation Review*, Vol. 5, No. 1, pp. 76–90.

Melewar, T. C. and Karaosmanoglu, E. (2005) "Corporate identity: concept, components and contribution", *Journal of General Management*, Vol. 31, No. 1, pp. 59–81.

Melewar, T. C. and Karaosmanglu, E. (2006) "Seven dimensions of corporate identity A categorisation from the practitioners' perspectives", *European Journal of Marketing* Vol. 40, No. 7/8, pp. 846–869.

Melewar, T. C. and Saunders, J. (1998) "Global corporate visual identity systems: standardization, control and benefits", *International Marketing Review*, Vol. 15, No. 4, pp. 291–308.

Melewar, T. C. and Saunders, J. (1999) "International corporate visual identity: standardisation or localisation?", *Journal of International Business Studies*, Vol. 30, No. 3, pp. 583–598.

Melewar, T. C. and Saunders, J. (2000) "Global corporate visual identity systems: using an extended marketing mix", *European Journal of Marketing*, Vol. 34, No. 5, pp. 538–550.

Melewar, T. C. and Wooldridge, A. (2001) "The dynamics of corporate identity", *Journal of Communication Management: An International Journal*, Vol. 5, No. 4, pp. 327–340.

Melewar, T. C., Foroudi, P., Dinnie, K. and Nguyen, B. (2018) "The role of corporate identity management in the higher education sector: an exploratory case study", *Journal of Marketing Communications*, Vol. 24, No. 4, pp. 337–359.

Melewar, T. C., Foroudi, P. and Jin, Z. (2020) "Corporate branding, identity, image and reputation: current and future trends, developments and challenges (Editorial Notes)", *Journal of Business Research* (Just published).

Melewar, T. C., Saunders, J. and Balmer, J. M. T. (2001) "Cause, effect and benefits of a standardised corporate visual identity system of UK companies operating in Malaysia", *European Journal of Marketing*, Vol. 35, No. 3/4, pp. 414–427.

Melewar, T. C., Karaosmanoglu, E. and Paterson, D. (2003) "Resolving the corporate identity conundrum: an exploratory study of the concept and its contribution", in C. Veloutsou (Ed.), *Communicating With Customers: Trends and Developments.* ATINER, Athens.

Melewar, T. C., Karaosmanoglu, E. and Patterson, D. (2005) "Corporate identity: concept, components and contribution", *Journal of General Management*, Vol. 31, No. 1, pp. 59–82.

Melewar, T. C., Bassett, K. and Simoes, C. (2006) "The role of communication and visual identity in modern organisations", *Corporate Communications: An International Journal*, Vol. 11, No. 2, pp. 138–147.

Moingeon, B. and Ramanantsoa, B. (1995) "An identity study of firm mergers: the case of a French Savings Bank", in Klein, H. E. (Ed.), *Case Method Research and Application.* WACRA, Needham, MA, Volume VII.

Moingeon, B. and Ramanantsoa, B. (1997) "Understanding corporate identity: the French school of thought", *European Journal of Marketing*, Vol. 3, No. 5/6, pp. 383–395.

Mukherjee, A. and He, H. (2008) "Company identity and marketing: an integrative framework", *Journal of Marketing Theory and Practice*, Vol. 16, No. 2, pp. 111–125.

Nelson, B. H. (1962) "Seven principles in image formation", *Journal of Marketing*, Vol. 26, No. 1, pp. 67–71.

Newman, W. H. (1953) "Basic objectives which shape the character of a company", *Journal of Business*, Vol. 26, No. 4, pp. 211–223.

Nguyen, N. (2006) "The perceived image of service cooperatives: an investigation in Canada and Mexico", *Corporate Reputation Review*, Vol. 9, No. 1, pp. 62–78.

O'Gorman, C. and Doran, R. (1999) "Mission statements in small- and medium-sized businesses", *Journal of Small Business Management*, Vol. 37, No. 4, pp. 59–66.

Olins, W. (1978) *The Corporate Personality: An Inquiry into The Nature of Corporate Identity*, Kynoch Press, UK.

Olins, W. (1979) "Corporate identity: the myth and the reality", *Journal of the Royal Society of Arts*, Vol. 127, No. 5272, pp. 208–223.

Olins, W. (1989) *Corporate Entity: Making Business Strategy Visible Through Design*, Thames and Hudson, London.

Olins, W. (1990) *The Wolf Olins Guide to Corporate Identity*. Black Bear Press, Cambridge.

Olins, W. (1991) *Corporate Identity*, Toledo, Thames and Hudson, Spain.

Olins, W. (1995) *The New Guide to Corporate Identity*. Gower, Aldershot.

Olins, W. (2000) "How brands are taking over the corporation", in Schultz, M., Hatch, M.J. and Larsen, M.H. (Eds.), *The Expressive Organisation: Linking Identity, Reputation, and the Corporate Brand* (pp. 77–96). Oxford University Press, New York.

Onkvisit, S. and Shaw, J. J. (1989) "Service marketing: image, branding, and competition", *Business Horizons*, Vol. 32, No. 1, pp. 13–18.

Otubanjo, B. O. and Melewar, T. C. (2007) "Understanding the meaning of corporate identity: a conceptual and semiological approach", *Corporate Communications: An International Journal*, Vol. 12, No. 4, pp. 414–432.

Ouchi, W. G. (1981) *Theory Z: How American Business Can Meet the Japanese Challenge*, Avon Books, New York.

Palazzo, M., Foroudi, P., Kitchen, P. J. and Siano, A. (2020) "Developing corporate communications in Italian firms: an exploratory study", *Qualitative Market Research: An International Journal*, Vol. 23, No. 3, p. 5.

Palazzo, M., Vollero, A., Siano, A. and Foroudi, P. (2020) "From fragmentation to collaboration in tourism promotion: an analysis of the adoption of IMC in the Amalfi Coast", *Current Issues in Tourism*, June, 567–589.

Peters, T. and Waterman, R. (1982) *In Search of Excellence*, Harper and Row, New York.

Pilditch, J. (1970) *Communication by Design: A Study in Corporate Identity*. McGraw-Hill, London.

Pittard, N., Ewing, M. and Jevons, C. (2007) "Aesthetic theory and logo design: examining consumer response to proportion across cultures", *International Marketing Review*, Vol. 24, No. 4, pp. 457–473.

Plummer, J. T. (1984) "How personality makes a difference", *Journal of Advertising Research*, Vol. 24 (Dec/Jan), pp. 27–31.

Pondar, K. (2005) "Corporate identity in Slovenia", *Corporate Communications: An International*, Vol. 10, No. 1, pp. 69–82.

Powell, S. M. (2011) "The nexus between ethical corporate marketing, ethical corporate identity and corporate social responsibility An internal organisational perspective", *European Journal of Marketing*, Vol. 45, Nos. 9/10, pp. 1365–1379.

Powell, S. M., Elving, W., Dodd, C. and Sloan, J. (2009) "Explicating ethical corporate identity in the financial sector", *Corporate Communications: An International Journal*, Vol. 14 No. 4, pp. 440–455.

Pratt, M. G. (1998) "To be or not to be? Central questions in organisational identification", in D. A. Whetten and P. C. Godfrey (Eds.), *Identity in Organisations: Building Theory Through conversations*, pp. 171–207. SAGE, Thousand Oaks, CA.

Primeaux, P. (1992) "Experiential ethics: a blueprint for personal and corporate ethics", *Journal of Business Ethics*, Vol. 11, pp. 779–788.

Ravasi, D. and Van Rekom, J. (2003) "Key issues in organisational identity and identification theory", *Corporate Reputation Review*, Vol. 6, pp. 118–132.

Schmitt, B. H. and Pan, Y. (1994) "Managing corporate and brand identities in the Asia Pacific region", *California Management Review*, Vol. 36, No. 4, pp. 32–48.

Schmitt, B. H. and Simonson, A. (1997) *Marketing Aesthetics*, The Free Press, New York.

Schmitt, B. H., Simonson, A. and Marcus, J. (1995) "Managing corporate image and identity", *Long Range Planning*, Vol. 28, No. 5, pp. 82–92.

72 *Foroudi, Foroudi and Balmer*

Schultz, D. E. (1993) "Integrated marketing communications: maybe definition is in the point of view", *MarketingNews*, January 18.

Schultz, D. E. and Kitchen, P. J. (1997) "Integrated marketing communications in US advertising agencies: an exploratory study", *Journal of Advertising Research*, Vol. 37, No. 5, pp. 7–17.

Schultz, D. E., Tannenbaum, S. and Lauterborn, R. (1994) *The New Marketing Paradigm: Integrated Marketing Communications*, NTC Business Books, Lincolnwood, IL.

Schultz, M. and de Chernatory, L. (2002) "Introduction, the challenges of corporate branding", *Corporate Reputation Review*, Vol. 5, No. 2/3, pp. 105–114.

Schulz, M. and Ervolder, L. (1998) "Culture: identity and image consultancy: crossing boundaries between management, advertising, public relations and design", *Corporate Reputation Review*, Vol. 2, No. 1, pp. 19–50.

Schultz, M. and Hatch, M. J. (2003) "Cycles of corporate branding: the case of LEGO company", *California Management Review*, Vol. 46, No. 1, pp. 6–26.

Schultz, M., Hatch M. J. and Larsen, M. H. (2000) *Introduction: Why the Expressive Organisation?*, *The Expressive Organisation*, Oxford University Press, Oxford.

Scott, S. G. and Lane, V. R. (2000) "A stakeholder approach to organisational identity", *Academy of Management Review*, Vol. 25, No. 1, pp. 43–62.

Selame, E. and Selame, J. (1975) *The Company Image*, John Wiley and Sons, New York.

Selame, E. and Selame, J. (1988) *The Company Image: Building Your Identity and Influence in the Marketplace*, John Wiley and Sons, New York.

Shamir, B. and Kark, R. (2004) "A simple graphic scale for the measurement of organisational identification", *Journal of Occupational and Organisational Psychology*, Vol. 77, pp. 115–123.

Siano, A., Palazzo, M. and Foroudi, P. (2017) "Rethinking bernstein communication wheel: a re-visitation of a communication tool", *The Bottom Line*, Vol. 30, No. 3, pp. 186–194.

Siano, A., Vollero, A., Volpe, M. D., Confetto, M. G., Foroudi, P. and Palazzo, M. (2017). "The role of physical metaphors for decision-making in integrated corporate communication", *The Bottom Line*, Vol. 31, No. 1, pp. 42–55.

Simoes, C., Dibb, S. and Fisk, R. (2005) "Managing corporate identity: an internal perspective", *Journal of the Academy of Marketing Science*, Vol. 33, No. 2, pp. 153–168.

Spector, A. J. (1961) "Basic dimensions of the corporate image", *Journal of Marketing*, Vol. 25, No. 6, pp. 47–51.

Steiner, L. (2003) "Roots of identity in real estate industry", *Corporate Reputation Review*, Vol. 6, No. 2, pp. 178–196.

Stuart, F. I. (1997) "The influence of organisational culture and internal politics on new service design and introduction", *International Journal of Service Industry Management*, Vol. 9, No. 5, pp. 469–485.

Stuart, H. (1999) "Towards a definitive model of the corporate identity management process", *Corporate Communications: An International Journal*, Vol. 4, No. 4, pp. 200–207.

Stuart, H. (2003) "The effect of organisational structure on corporate identity management", in J. M. T. Balmer and S. A. Greyser (Eds.), *Revealing the Corporation: Perspectives on Identity, Image, Reputation, Corporate Branding and Corporate-Level Marketing*, pp. 106–123. Routledge, London.

Stuart, H. and Muzellec, L. (2004) "Corporate makeovers: can a Hyena be rebranded?", *Journal of Brand Management*, Vol. 11, No. 6, pp. 472–484.

Sutton, R. I. and Callahan, A. L. (1987) "The stigma of bankruptcy: spoiled organisational image and its management", *Academy of Management Journal*, Vol. 30, pp. 405–436.

Suvatjis, J. Y. and de Chernatony, L. (2005) "Corporate identity modelling: a review and presentation of a new multi-dimensional model", *Journal of Marketing Management*, Vol. 21, No. 7, pp. 809–834.

Swales, J. M. and Rogers, P. S. (1995) "Discourse and the projection of corporate culture", *Discourse and Society*, Vol. 6, pp. 225–244.

Tajfel, H. and Turner, J. C. (1985) "The social identity theory of intergroup behaviour", in S. Worchel and W. G. Austin (Eds.), *Psychology of Intergroup Relations*, pp. 2–6. Nelson-Hall, Chicago.

Tavassoli, N. T. (2001) "Colour memory and evaluations for alphabetic and logographic brand names", *Journal of Experimental Psychology: Applied*, Vol. 7, No. 2, pp. 104–111.

Topalian, A. (1984) "Corporate identity: beyond the visual overstatements", *International Journal of Advertising*, Vol. 3, No. 1, pp. 55–62.

Tourky, M., Foroudi, P., Gupta, S. and Shaalan, A. (2020) "Conceptualising corporate identity in a dynamic environment", *Qualitative Market Research: An International Journal* (Just published).

Tucker, W. T. (1961) "How much of the corporate image is stereotype?", *Journal of Marketing*, Vol. 25, No. 3, pp. 61–65.

Urde, M. (1999) "Brand orientation: a mindset for building brands into strategic resources", *Journal of Marketing Management*, Vol. 15, pp. 117–133.

Urde, M. (2003) "Core value-based corporate brand building", *European Journal of Marketing*, Vol. 37, No 7/8, pp. 1017–1040.

Urde, M. (2009) "Uncovering the corporate brands core values", *Management Decision*, Vol. 47, No. 4, pp. 616–638.

Urde, M. (2013) "The corporate brand identity matrix", *Journal of Brand Management*, Vol. 20, No. 9, pp. 742–761.

Urde, M., Baumgarth, C. and Merrilees, B. (2013) "Brand orientation and market orientation from alternatives to synergy", *Journal of Business Research*, Vol. 66, pp. 13–20.

Van den Bosch, A. L. M., De Jong, M. D. T. and Elving, W. J. L. (2005) "How corporate visual identity supports reputation", *Corporate Communications: An International Journal*, Vol. 10, No. 2, pp. 108–116.

Van den Bosch, A. L. M., Elving, W. J. L. and De Jong, M. D. T. (2006) "The impact of organisational characteristics on corporate visual identity", *European Journal of Marketing*, Vol. 40, No. 7/8, pp. 870–885.

Van den Bosch, A. L. M., De Jong, M. D. T. and Elving, W. J. L. (2008) "Managing corporate visual identity: exploring the differences between manufacturing and service, and profit-making and nonprofit organisations", *Journal of Business Communication*, Vol. 43, No. 2, pp. 138–157.

Van Heerden, C. H. (1999) "Developing a corporate image model", *South African Journal of Economic and Management Sciences*, Vol. 2, No. 3, pp. 492–508.

Van Heerden, C. H. and Puth, G. (1995) "Factors that determine the corporate image of South African banking institutions: an exploratory investigation", *International Journal of Bank Marketing*, Vol. 13, No. 3, pp. 12–17.

Van Rekom, J. (1993) "Corporate identity: the operationalization of a broad concept", *Tinbergen Institute Research Bulletin*, Vol. 5, No. 1, pp. 49–55.

Van Rekom, J. (1997) "Deriving an operational measure of corporate identity", *European Journal of Marketing*, Vol. 31, No. 5/6, pp. 410–422.

Van Riel, C. B. M. (1995) *Principles of Corporate Communication*, Prentice Hall, London.

Van Riel, C. B. M. (1997) "Protecting the corporate brand by orchestrated communication", *Journal of Brand Management*, Vol. 4, No. 6, pp. 409–418.

Van Riel, C. B. M. and Balmer, J. M. T. (1997) "Corporate identity, concept, its measurement and management", *European Journal of Marketing*, Vol. 31, No. 5/6, pp. 340–355.

Van Riel, C. B. M. and Maathuis, O. J. M. (1993) *Corporate Branding*, Working Paper, Erasmus University Rotterdam.

Van Riel, C. B. M. and Van Bruggen, G. H. (2002) "Incorporating business unit managers' perspectives in corporate-branding strategy decision making", *Corporate Reputation Review*, Vol. 5, No. 2/3, pp. 241–251.

Van Riel, C. B. M. and van Hasselt, J. J. (2002) "Conversion of organisational identity research findings into action", in G. Soenen and B. Moingeon (Eds.), *Corporate and Organisational Identities: Integrating Strategy, Marketing, Communication and Organisational Perspectives*, pp. 156–174. Routledge, London.

Van Riel, C. B. M., Van den Ban, A. and Heijmans, E. J. (2001) "The added value of corporate logos: an empirical study", *European Journal of Marketing*, Vol. 35, No. 3/4, pp. 428–440.

Veryzer, R. W. and Hutchinson, J. W. (1998) "The influence of unity and prototypicality on aesthetic responses to new product designs", *Journal of Consumer Research*, Vol. 24, No. 4, pp. 374–394.

Wells, B. and Spinks, N. (1999) "Communicating with the community", *Career Development International*, Vol. 4, No. 2, pp. 108–116.

Whetten, D. A. and Godfrey, P. C. (1998) *Identity in Organisations, Building Theory Through Conversations*, SAGE, United States and America.

Whetten, D. A. and Mackey, A. (2002) "A social actor conception of organisational identity and its implications for the study of organisational reputation", *Business and Society*, Vol. 41, No. 4, pp. 393–414.

Wiedmann, K. P. (1988) "Corporate identity als unternehmensstrategie weist", *Wirtschaftswissenschaftliches Studium*, Vol. 5, pp. 236–242.

Wilson, A. (1997) "The culture of the branch team and its impact on service delivery and corporate identity", *International Journal of Bank Marketing*, Vol. 15, No. 5, pp. 163–168.

Wright, G. N. (1984) *Behavioural Decision Theory: An Introduction*, SAGE, Beverly Hills, CA.

Zha, D., Melewar, T. C., Foroudi, P. and Jin, Z. (2020) "An assessment of brand experience knowledge literature: using bibliometric to identify future research direction", *International Journal of Management Reviews* (Just published).

Zinkhan, G. M., Jaiskankur, G., Anumpam J. and Hayes, L. (2001) *Corporate Image: A Conceptual Framework for Strategic Planning, Enhancing Knowledge Development in Marketing*, Vol. 12. American Marketing Association, Chicago.

3 Managing marketing competencies

A framework for understanding antecedents of marketing capability and its relation to the company's core competencies

*Pantea Foroudi, Mohammad M. Foroudi,
Khalid Hafeez and Javad Izadi*

Introduction

Core competencies are the crown jewels of a company and, therefore, should be carefully identified, nurtured and developed. Based on the *resource-based theory*, this study explores how core competence can lead to firms' competitive advantage, and how a *marketing firm* can identify its core: competence in the sector to attain competitive advantage.

Keywords – capability; competence; emotional assets; cultural and intangible assets; resources.

Background to marketing capability

During the last two decades the theory of core competence has attracted substantial attention from researchers and practitioners (Foroudi, 2021; Hafeez et al., 2019; 2002a, 2002b; Ljungquist, 2013). The theory declares that the corporate and business strategies must be constructed upon the strengths of the core competencies of a firm (Hamel and Prahalad, 1990) to strengthen competition in the marketplace. Core competence is frequently acknowledged in the arrangement of tangible and intangible assets (Hafeez and Essmail, 2007; Ljungquist, 2013). In some researchers' view, core competencies can be recognised from firm-specific, dynamic capabilities (Drejer, 2000).

According to Wang (2013), the development of the knowledge economy has changed the main value perception of businesses from traditional physical tangible assets to intellectual and emotional intangible assets. There are two types of intangible assets – intellectual assets – that can be divided into internal, external and human assets and – emotional assets – where the consumer perceives emotional value of the organisation such as trust and commitment. Within the competitive market, organisations should acquire and utilise intellectual assets to produce profitable innovations (Bismuth and Tojo, 2008). Intellectual assets are significant through capabilities of human resources, organisational power, leadership, technology know-how, and reputational, knowledge, trust, and perceived quality brand power (Sumita, 2008). However, Cohen (2010) states that physical and tangible *assets* are a valuable strategic resource that can significantly affect financial and organisational outcomes. Examples of such assets include visual identity (logo, name, colour, design etc.) physical environmental design, its components (physical structure/spatial layout and functionality, physical stimuli/ambient conditions, and symbolic artefacts/decor and artefacts) and digital technology.

Technological advances can also influence the core competence of firms that are taking initiatives to promote the creating and implementation of the place's digital infrastructure; however, such initiatives will need to place an emphasis on providing the favourable assets for the organisation (Hafeez et al., 2016). It is fair to say that technology can have direct impacts on a company's marketing capability. *Marketing capability* highlights a superior method of utilising company knowledge and resources in order to reply successfully to shifting market requirements (Foroudi et al., 2020; Gupta et al., 2016; Imani et al., 2020ab). Greater marketing capability can be combined with company's assets and resources such as technology allowing companies to employ a more innovative orientation and at the same time influence performance of the business (Fahy et al., 2000). It is important to realise the importance of the core competence valuation progression and how organisational intangible assets composite with tangible assets to develop a core competence at the organisational level (Hafeez et al., 2002a). Also, organisations should have more concern about an organisation's cultural and intangible assets which can be described as the knowledge that internal stakeholders recieved from the company (Grasenick and Low, 2004), which are applied to the business through cultural background and intangible assets. According to Hofstede (1991), culture is often conceptualised as a collective programming of the company's employees that is important to employment growth, disseminating innovation, and throughout the economy, it also creates economic enforcement in local areas (Anyadike-Danes et al., 2009).

Previous authors have recognised the importance of resource-based theory in the area of marketing, explaining related terminologies. However, most of the efforts are faded with trying to explain terminologies. In addition, there were no systematic procedures developed in order to benefit marketing organisations and to identify marketing capabilities and core competence. In this chapter, we summarise salient features of recent marketing and management theories to answer the following questions: what are the factors that make up the key marketing assets (i) intellectual and emotional assets, (ii) physical/tangible assets and (iii) cultural/intangible assets?, what are the key components of organisations' marketing capability?, what is the nature of the relationships of organisation's marketing assets with organisations' marketing capability?, how do we isolate competencies from marketing capabilities by evaluating the "collectiveness" and "unique" attributes of marketing capabilities? and how do we further determine core competencies by evaluating the "strategic flexibility" of competencies?

There is a body of marketing literature that espouses the related concepts such as a company's assets (Kozlenkova et al., 2014), intellectual and emotional assets (Bismuth and Tojo, 2008; Cohen, 2010), physical/tangible assets (REF), and cultural/intangible assets (Bick et al., 2003; Cornelissen and Harris, 1999), marketing capability (Gupta et al., 2016; O'Cass and Weerawardena, 2009), competence and core competence (Hamel and Heena, 1994). However, this all provides a confusing picture for academics and practitioners alike, as little attempts are made to understand and delineate how organisational intangible assets are weaved in with tangible assets to develop marketing capabilities, and how these capabilities can turn into company's competencies and core competence. Therefore, this leave managers and marketers without any understanding of when and how a company can create a favourable marketing capability which can impact on a company's performance (Fakhreddin et al., 2021).

This chapter contributes to the growing research on employee-company relationships by proffering the notion of marketing capability management as the primary psychological substrate for the kind of deep, committed and meaningful relationships that marketers are increasingly seeking to build with their employees. Moreover, it draws on theories of resource-based view (Barney, 1991; Wernerfelt, 1984), a resource-conscious view (Kumar, 2015) and resource-advantage theory (Hunt and Morgan, 1995) intending to demonstrate a new approach to the dynamics of competition (Rossi and Mafud, 2014) to provide a coherent, comprehensive articulation of the bundle of assets and capabilities in creating competitive advantage for a firm.

Earlier concepts proposed how to evaluate core competence (Hafeez et al., 2002a); we propose a linking mechanism specific to the marketing domain that develops a relationship in between assets, resources, marketing capabilities, marketing competencies and core competence. This chapter helps marketing and branding managers to make more informed strategic management decisions regarding capability development, outsourcing, focusing or diversification, with regards to new products, services or markets. The developed framework is generic in nature and is applicable to benchmark a business, public or service sector organisation. The research will conclude with a discussion of the managerial and customer implications for Small and medium-sized enterprises (SMEs).

Background and propositions development

Understanding the factors of a firm's superior performance is a theme of consistent discussion and of significant interest to both researchers and practitioners (Fahy et al., 2000; Tsai and Shih, 2004; Vorhies and Morgan, 2005). The view of core competence was presented by Hamel and Prahalad (1990) as what the company can do particularly well. However, an earlier paper by Ansoff (1965) who portrays core competence in a rich discussion of its meaning which referred to it as "common thread" (p. 105). Ansoff (1965) signifies the business competencies as "a relationship between present and future product markets which would enable outsiders to perceive where the firm is heading, and the inside management to give it guidance" (p. 105). Previous findings presented by Prahalad and Hamel (1990) illustrated core competence as the core system that "provides nourishment, sustenance, and stability" (p. 82).

Marketing capabilities employ a substantial and positive result on internal and external stakeholders' satisfaction, which eventually lead to superior organisational performance in terms of sales, profit and competence (Santos-Vijande et al., 2012). In order to guide the following discussion, Figure 3.1 demonstrates the research conceptual framework which recognises the key research constructs. The model has been used in this study to scrutinise a number of relationships that are identified in the literature and qualitative study. Generating an organisational-level conceptual framework established on resource-based and resource-advantage theory demonstrates: (1) the relationship between the organisations' marketing capability concept and its elements that foster or discourage capability; (2) its benefits or outcomes for corporations; and (3) the associations between other theoretically and empirically identified variables. The literature discussed below determines that organisation resources are an embodiment of three assets, namely (1) intellectual and emotional assets, (2) physical/tangible assets and (3) cultural/intangible assets. In addition, to identify an organisation's core competitiveness, the organisation needs to identify and nurture six types of marketing capabilities, viz. market-sensing, corporate/brand identity management, customer relationship, social media/communication, design/innovation management and performance management capability. This chapter deliberates on the antecedents and consequences of organisations' marketing capability and develops propositions based on the literature and the qualitative field.

Antecedents to marketing capability

Hafeez et al. (2002a, 2002b) define organisation resource as the essential input to make up organisational capability. Also, organisation resources are made up of three different type of assets: (intellectual and emotional assets, physical/tangible assets, and cultural/intangible assets). This study first explores four antecedents to marketing intellectual and emotional assets, five antecedents to marketing physical assets and five antecedents to marketing cultural assets.

Intellectual and emotional assets

We identify four antecedents to marketing intellectual and emotional (intangible) assets as described in the following subsection.

Corporate reputation → intellectual and emotional assets

The first set of factors, which is positively related and influences intellectual and emotional assets pertains to corporate reputation. *Corporate reputation* is a subjective and collective opinion (Van Der Merwe and Puth, 2014) and overall evaluation (Foroudi et al., 2014, 2016) based on the stakeholder's direct experiences with the company. Corporate reputation is the representation of a company's past actions and future prospects (Alniacik et al., 2011) and consists of the knowledge and the emotions held by individuals. Based on a resource-based view,

Managing marketing competencies 79

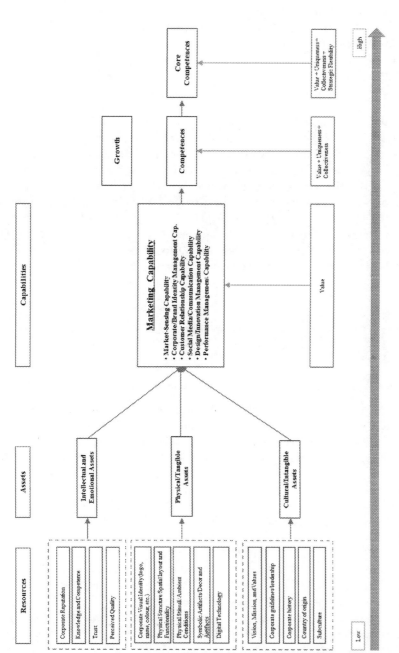

Figure 3.1 Conceptual framework.

80   P. Foroudi, M. M. Foroudi, K. Hafeez and J. Izadi

corporate reputation is the key element of intellectual and emotional assets and is a mechanism to maintain competitive advantage (Abratt and Kleyn, 2012). However, company reputation is categorised as wise use of assets, quality of management and value as a long-term investment (Sur and Sirsly, 2013). Literature (Flatt and Kowalczyk, 2008) suggests that corporate reputation emerges from multiple constituent groups or stakeholders. A firm's reputation is a key element of intangible resources of many SMEs and is an intangible asset that contributes to SMEs' competitive advantage and performance (Hall, 1992, 1993; Flatt and Kowalczyk, 2008).

According to resource-based view and resource-advantage theory, corporate reputation is categorised as an intangible asset – unobservable and thus difficult to imitate (Flatt and Kowalczyk, 2008; Hunt and Morgan, 1995). However, Fombrun (2000) states that reputation is just one of many intangible assets to which stakeholders impute value creation. Intangible resources are classified as creation of capability or assets (Hall, 1992). The asset of corporate reputation has strong characteristics of belongingness (Hall, 1992). Hall (1993) argues that reputation represents emotions held by people about a product and services range. Fombrun (2000) asserts that people possess feeling, the emotional appeal towards firms. However, the human asset has the ability to cause supportive behaviour towards corporate reputation. Corporate reputations are strategic assets that build on distinctiveness, focus, consistency, identity and transparency (Fombrun, 2000). Accordingly, the following proposition is incorporated into the framework:

> *P1a: The higher the level of a company's corporate reputation, the higher the level of a company's intellectual and emotional assets.*

Knowledge and skills→intellectual and emotional assets

A second element of intellectual and emotional assets relates to knowledge and skills. Knowledge is defined as a set of organised statements of facts or ideas, and complex process which build through continuous learning (Hafeez et al., 2006). It can be transmitted to others through some communication medium and creates value that is sustainable over time. Knowledge and skills as experience, information or expertise are essential ingredients for developing individual and corporate competencies (Hafeez et al., 2007) and they can be used for organisational development to generate greater performance. According to Moustaghfir (2009), knowledge includes organisational intellectual assets, employee's skills and know-how. However, knowledge is a result of interaction between people and groups (Knight, 1999). Intellectual capital can be defined as knowledge, people's intelligence and their actions. However, knowledge is the major asset for SMEs and drivers remaining competitive in the market. Therefore, SMEs rely on intellectual capital to generate revenues (Kavida and Sivakoumar, 2009). Knowledge has been recognised as an intellectual asset and refers to intangible resources, which are difficult to imitate. Though Kavida and Sivakoumur (2009)

Managing marketing competencies 81

agree broadly with previous studies (Bismuth and Tojo, 2008; Huggins and Weir, 2007a; Knight, 1999), that knowledge is an attribute of human capital and their distinctive features are "tacit" subjective and "explicit" objective knowledge. Knowledge is acquired from employees, which are part of the human capital of SMEs. However, intellectual capital is one of the characteristics of human capital. According to Kavida and Sivakoumar (2009), human assets include work-related knowledge and competencies. Knowledge is recognised as a potential value enhancer; however, knowledge does not directly impact profitability or confer competitive advantage. Although, knowledge is seen as an intangible resource or stock controlled by an organisation, which supports its competencies. Therefore, based on the above discussion that highlights the importance of knowledge and skills and its ambiguous relationship with intellectual and emotional asset research, we propose:

P1b: The higher the level of knowledge and skills, the higher the level of a company's intellectual and emotional assets.

Trust → intellectual and emotional assets

Trust has very strong links with intellectual and emotional capital and it is regarded as subjective attitude, belief and optimistic expectation the emotional bond that stakeholders feel towards an organisation taking morally correct decisions and actions (Van Der Merwe and Puth, 2014) works to establish a company's reputation or image (Kim et al., 2015). Suciu et al. (2012) state that the key part of the relational capital is trust that is established between SMEs and its stakeholders. Trust is an intangible asset built, maintained, sustained, broken and restored between people through communication (Palazzo et al., 2019). Suciu et al. (2012) also assert that trust is a liaison between organisational and social capital, which is a form of intangible asset such as culture, rules and norms, which in turn form organisational competencies. Trust has become more and more important as a means of sustaining relationships between people (Savolainen and Lopez-Frenso, 2013).

It plays multiple roles in SMEs with regard to relationships – interpersonal interactions between individuals, and within groups and within SMEs (Allee, 2008). However, trust is embedded in the classification of intellectual capital (Allee, 2008; Ikonen, 2012; Savolainen and Häkkinen, 2011; Savolainen and Lopez-Frenso, 2013). According to Allee (2008), trust is a part of social capital both within SMEs and externally as reputation and brand. It is seen as skills in human capital and as intangible asset within structural capital. Thus, it is important to know that trust generates and renews intangible capital (Savolainen and Lopez-Frenso, 2013; Allee, 2008; Ikonen, 2012; Savolainen and Häkkinen, 2011).

Ikonen (2012) believes that trust exists in interpersonal relations and is a key element of cooperation and communication within SMEs. However, it is classified as intellectual capital building leadership skills within human capital.

82   P. Foroudi, M. M. Foroudi, K. Hafeez and J. Izadi

There is a fair degree of consensus among researchers that trust is important as an intangible asset for building and maintaining relationships with stakeholders and provides vitality of competitiveness (Ikonen, 2012; Savolainen and Häkkinen, 2011; Savolainen and Lopez-Frenso, 2013). Commitment and trust – although not recognised by all SMEs – are categorised as emotional assets. This means that trust builds emotional and intellectual assets. However, SMEs, which are rich in emotional intelligence raise their organisations trust, enthusiasm, positive attitude and quality of relationship with stakeholders (Yadav, 2014). Therefore, based on the above discussion, we formulate the following proposition:

P1c: The higher the level of trust, the higher the level of a company's intellectual and emotional assets.

Perceived quality → intellectual and emotional assets

The last element investigated in the current study related to intellectual and emotional assets is perceived quality. The literature on the subject suggests that quality is a key factor of competitiveness and capabilities of human capital (Çolakoğlu and Ayrancı, 2013; Huggins and Weir, 2007ab; Olmedo-Cifuentes and Martínez-León, 2015; Hafeez et al., 2006). Attitudes can reflect a perception of reliability or durability of a brand can directly affect corporate performance. However, according to Çolakoğlu and Ayrancı (2013), perceived quality has strong links with human capital. In addition, the characteristics of human capital are made of quality and commitment of employees (Çolakoğlu and Ayrancı, 2013). Human capital in SMEs represents knowledge and competencies . That is why intellectual capital has an effect on SME's customer perception. In service organisations, customers interact with employees, who play crucial roles in delivering exceptional service quality (Olmedo-Cifuentes and Martínez-León, 2015).

In essence, customer-perceived quality refers to service quality provided by employees – human capital of an organisation or reliability or durability of products (Olmedo-Cifuentes and Martínez-León, 2015). Interestingly, Steenkamp and Kashyap (2010) perceive quality as the most valuable driver for value creation. Sumita (2008) also embrace the concept of emotional asset because of its high importance to enhancing the overall quality of service or work or interpersonal relationships, which are based on trust. Employees with greater emotional assets are referred to as having more solid quality in their relationships (Kavida and Sivakoumar, 2009). Development, and maintaining and sustaining that quality relationship are associated with emotional assets – employees and their abilities to provide high-quality customer service (Kavida and Sivakoumar, 2009; Hafeez et al., 2006; Hafeez and Aburawi, 2013). In light of the above, we propose that all of the antecedents of intellectual and emotional assets are engaged in the creation of perceived quality, and therefore we postulate:

P1d: The higher the level of perceived quality, the higher the level of company's intellectual and emotional assets.

Physical assets

This study has identified five antecedents to marketing physical (tangible) assets as described in the following subsection.

Corporate visual identity → physical (tangible assets)

Corporate visual identity (known as corporate design) is a term used to define the vast amount of visual cues which are linked with a specific organisation. This corporate visual identity system is created by five elements, namely, organisation's name, symbol/logotype, slogan, typography and colour (Dowling, 1994; Foroudi, 2018; 2019; Melewar et al., 2002; Melewar and Saunders, 1998; Topalian, 1984). Corporate visual identity has received the attention of marketing researchers (Henderson et al., 2004; Foroudi et al., 2014, 2016; Tavassoli, 2001; Childers and Jass, 2002) who feel that it is part of an organisation's physical and tangible assets which impact on core competence at the organisational level. In addition, the intangibility of services exacerbates the need for management of visual components. The visibility and consistency should emphasise the physical dimensions of service delivery (Bharadwaj et al., 1993), which impact on the corporate identity. For instance, staff appearance, colour and logo are essential to the brand awareness and transmitted image in the service context (Berry, 2000; Foroudi et al., 2020; Foroudi and Marvi, 2020; Tourky et al., 2020). Visual identity management has significant business implications (Foroudi, 2020; Foroudi et al., 2019; 2017; 2016; 2014; Montes and Foroudi, P., 2017; Schmitt et al., 1995). According to Bitner (1990), in a service encounter context, the physical environment can have an influence on how consumers perceive service failure. Corporate visual identity uses tangible clues to differentiate services (Onkvisit and Shaw, 1989).

P2a: The higher the level of corporate visual identity, the higher the level of a company's physical (tangible) assets.

Physical structure/spatial layout and functionality → physical/tangible assets

Physical structure/spatial layout and functionality, as the second components of an organisation's physical and tangible assets, can be defined as the architectural design and physical placement of furnishings in a building, the arrangement of objects (e.g. arrangement of the layout, machinery, furniture and equipment), the spatial relationships among them, physical location and physical appearance of the workplace which are particularly pertinent to the service industry (Bitner, 1992; Foroudi et al., 2019; 2020; Han and Ryu, 2009; McElroy and Morrow, 2010; Nguyen, 2006). Spatial layout influences or regulates social interaction (Davis, 1984, p. 272), intends to affect perceptions of culture (McElroy and Morrow, 2010, p. 614) and influences customer satisfaction (Brennan et al., 2002, p. 288; Han and Ryu, 2009, p. 505; Fischer et al., 2004, p. 132; Oldham and Brass, 1979, p. 282), productivity (Ayoko et al., 2003, p. 386; Kamarulzaman et al., 2011, p. 265)

84 P. Foroudi, M. M. Foroudi, K. Hafeez and J. Izadi

and motivation (Oldham and Brass, 1979, p. 282). Moreover, the structure of an organisation can affect the behaviour of organisational members and employees' comfort (Davis, 1984, p. 273). Comfort, overall layout and table/seating arrangements are the main elements of physical structure (Han and Ryu, 2009, p. 496). The physical structure of a workplace is expected by managers to impact on how people behave and interact (Davis, 1984, p. 272). The physical structure is essential in service settings and is the purposeful environment that exists to aid the work of employees' and fulfil customers' specific needs and wants (Bitner, 1992; Han and Ryu, 2009; Nguyen, 2006). Physical structure/spatial layout and functionality is one of the best tools a firm can possess (a physical and tangible asset) that can be transmitted/processed in order to gain organisational competencies.

> P2b: The higher the level of physical structure/spatial layout and functionality, the higher the level of a company's physical and tangible assets.

Physical stimuli/ambient conditions → physical/tangible assets

Ambient conditions/physical stimuli are those aspects of the physical setting which are intangible background characteristics that intrude into the managers' or organisation members' awareness and are likely to have a pervasive effect on his/her behaviour (Davis, 1984, p. 274). The physical stimuli are important factors of the physical and tangible assets (Bitner, 1992). Environmental psychology research suggests that employees need to have the opportunity to control task-relevant dimensions of their workplace environment (Elsbach and Pratt, 2007, p. 196) because employees spend long hours in their workplace (Bitner, 1992). The physical stimuli have a direct influence on employees' attitudes, behaviours and satisfaction (Brennan et al., 2002) that, in turn, improve job performance (Brennan et al., 2002; Elsbach and Pratt, 2007; Kamarulzaman et al., 2011) and productivity (Parish et al., 2008, p. 222).

In addition, ambient conditions may need to be a major priority for many managers (Davis, 1984). Managers regularly introduce ambient conditions into the workplace environment to counteract negative influence as well as to remind themselves "of what needs to be accomplished" (Davis, 1984, p. 275). Ambient conditions/physical stimuli act as tangible hints that impact on physiological reactions, which can cause comfort or discomfort during the service encounter (Bitner, 1992; Nguyen, 2006). Importantly, managers need to be aware of employee's preferences which must be balanced against customers' and employee's needs (Bitner, 1992).

> P2c: The higher the level of physical stimuli/ambient conditions, the higher the level of company's physical and tangible assets.

Symbolic artefacts/decor and artefacts → physical/tangible assets

Symbolic artefacts as a valuable component of company's physical asset can be defined as "aspects of the physical setting that individually or collectively guide the interpretation of the social setting" (Davis, 1984, p. 279) which particularly contribute to the attractiveness of the physical environment (Han and Ryu, 2009). Symbolic artefacts can be related to the aesthetics of the environment, which are intended to affect perceptions of culture as well as have an effect on customer satisfaction (Han and Ryu, 2009). According to some authors (Han and Ryu, 2009; Wakefield and Blodgett, 1994), symbolic artefacts/decor and artefacts not only contribute to the attractiveness of the physical environment but also affect customer satisfaction and customer loyalty (Han and Ryu, 2009). Furthermore, physical artefacts impact professional creative identities and personalities (Elsbach, 2009, p. 1065) and develop a complex representation of workplace identity (Elsbach, 2004, p. 99). However, there has been limited research on "how employees perceive the specific dimensions of workplace identities in work environments that limit the display of personal identity markers" (Elsbach, 2003, p. 623).

Corporations try to communicate status differentiation between employees by assigning higher ranked individuals better offices than their colleagues (McElroy and Morrow, 2010, p. 619). Employees feel a loss of workplace identity because of their restricted ability to show uniqueness and status through the display of their personal artefacts (Varlander, 2012). Furthermore, employees build their own alternative means of signalling status through other physical markers, for instance, the number of personal artefacts shows the different levels of managers (Elsbach, 2003, p. 262). Employees personally select and display artefacts even though they are not related to work; however, these types of uniqueness categorisations are essential to an employee's core sense of self (Elsbach, 2003, p. 235). According to Elsbach (2004), a variety of "physical artefacts are examined and compared to specific managerial exemplars to develop a complex representation of workplace identity" (p. 99). Symbolic artefacts are "aspects of the physical setting that individually or collectively guide the interpretation of the social setting" (Davis, 1984, p. 276) which is mainly relevant to the service industry (Han and Ryu, 2009). Furthermore, decor and artefacts influence, "the degree of overall customer satisfaction and subsequent customer behaviour" (Han and Ryu, 2009, p. 489). It is essential to understand the core competence valuation progression and how organisational physical and tangible assets develop a core competence at the organisational level.

P2d: The higher the level of symbolic artefacts/decor and artefacts, the higher the level of a company's physical and tangible assets.

Digital technology → physical/tangible assets

Digital technology effectively adapted by tangible/intangible assets contribute to information quality and service convenience which leads to the company's core competence. Digital technology enhances learning, and it is one of the most critical elements of design innovation. Digital technology focuses on developing new products and market segments, it plays an important role in the marketing department where constant interaction and exchange of information with customers are fed back to the design department (Setia et al., 2013). Digital technology and devices provide entry to innovative information. As claimed by Dewett (2003), technologies deliver workers direct entry to original information by permitting them to link up with acquaintances' repositories and with information experts (Hussain and Hafeez, 2008a).

Service convenience links to the speed and ease with which consumers can obtain appropriate information as well as identify and select the products or services. Information quality relates to the quality of information that are valuable for business customers, significant for decision making and easy to understand (Gorla et al., 2010; Mahmood and Hafeez, 2013). The literature in view of competence adoption delivers an understanding of how dynamic processes including digital technology, tangible/intangible assets and marketing capability could help firms to enhance the ability to achieve core competence in the market (Brown et al., 2019). The firm's capability to learn and acquire knowledge will prepare them for advance steps of competence, which ultimately determines whether the firm is able to progress to the next stage of development. In particular, this links to knowledge of management capabilities and technology (Hafeez et al., 2010). According to Fruhling and Siau (2007), the human capital accessible within the organisation is likely to be a fundamental factor in core competence. Consequently, management strengths should be focused on nurturing and exploiting these strategic resources (Wernerfelt, 1984).

Technology can also influence the core competence of firms who are already taking initiatives to promote the creating and implementation of the place's digital infrastructure; however, such initiatives will need to place an emphasis on providing the favourable assets for the organisation, delivering relevant training courses. Marketing capability highlights a superior method of utilising company knowledge and recourses in order to reply successfully to shifting market requirements (Gupta et al., 2016). Greater marketing capability combined with technology allows companies to employ a more innovative orientation and at the same time influence the performance of the business (Fahy et al., 2000). Digital technology is one of the best techniques/tools and through using it well a firm's possessed knowledge (intangible asset) is transmitted/ processed in order to gain organisational competencies. A firm's assets strongly focus on developing new product and market segments, by monitoring market trends and seeking market opportunities. In addition, firms with stronger tangible/intangible assets capability will be relative to firms with lesser tangible/intangible assets capability.

P2e: The higher the level of digital technology, the higher the level of a company's intellectual and emotional assets.

Cultural assets

Five antecedents have been recognised as important to marketing cultural (intangible) assets as described in the following subsection.

Vision, mission, and values → cultural

Many researchers have identified a strong relationship between vision, mission, values and cultural (intangible) assets (Bick et al., 2003; Cornelissen and Harris, 1999; Melewar and Karaosmanoglu, 2006). The vision, mission and values are the key components of a company's corporate strategy that helps organisations to realise how to react in terms of differentiation and positioning in the market (Melewar and Karaosmanoglu, 2006). Corporate mission is defined as the reason for the existence of a company. According to Abratt (1989), corporate mission is the most important part of the corporate philosophy that defines company purpose and paves the way to differentiate against all other organisations. According to Melewar (2003), the corporate mission summarises the basic points of the start. On the other hand, the corporate vision summarises the desired future which the organisation hopes to achieve. Corporate values can be described as the beliefs and moral principles held behind a company's culture. In addition, Van Riel and Balmer (1997) defined "corporate values as dominant systems of beliefs within an organization that comprise everyday language, ideologies and rituals of personnel and form the corporate identity" (Melewar, 2003, p. 203). Vision, mission and values of a company are the cultural and intangible assets which are controlled resources which subsidise towards potential benefits of the firm and make an enormous contribution in the business success (Hussain and Hafeez, 2008a).

> P3a: The stronger a company's vision, mission and values, the stronger the impact of a company's cultural assets.

Corporate guidelines/leadership → cultural assets

Corporate guidelines are a key component of cultural assets in articulation and interpretation of corporate principles for individual areas of business activity and functions that guide the behaviour of individuals in an organisation (Melewar, 2003). These play an important role in communicating and reinforcing the company's values (Oliveira and Roth, 2012). Previous research has stated that leaders must cultivate an internal culture of honesty and integrity in order to avoid uncontrolled communication (Moingeon and Ramanantsoa, 1997). A relationship between culture and communication must be recognised as positive communication by leadership helps in the attainment of employee commitment of core corporate values (Melewar and Karaosmanoglu, 2006). Corporate guidelines and leadership also help to design and innovate management capability. Corporate guidelines can change management strategies as it enables a business to find areas for improvement.

> P3b: The stronger a company's corporate guidelines/leadership, the stronger the impact of a company's cultural assets

Corporate history → cultural assets

Corporate history – is not something only in the passive sense of having a past, or its members having memories (Akarsu et al., 2021; Delahaye et al., 2009; Foroudi et al., 2020; Mellower et al., 2018; 2017), or a source of memory for reproducing useful activities (Booth and Rowlinson, 2006; Walsh and Ungson, 1991). The relationship between corporate history and culture in undeniable, as culture progresses through individual's interactions over time (Melewar and Karaosmanoglu, 2006). Moingeon and Ramanantsoa (1997) suggested that although history is contributory in defining corporate identity, the identity itself is contributory in guiding history by its influence on the development of cultural norms mentioned in perceptions and members' actions. Studies argue that there is a strong link between the national culture from which an organisation originated and its corporate identity (Check-Teck and Lowe, 1999; Melewar and Karaosmanoglu, 2006; Rowlinson and Procter, 1999; Varey and Lewis, 2000). Many researchers posit that a company is an amalgamation of subcultures (Balmer and Wilson, 1998; Deal and Kennedy, 1982). This is because corporate culture is vastly inter-meshed with behavioural and historical characteristics of the company and its employees, and the point that each employee interprets management communication and history differently suggests that the progression of unitary corporate culture is almost impossible.

P3c: The stronger the company's corporate history, the stronger the impact of the company's cultural assets

Country of origin and subculture → cultural assets

Country of origin can be defined as "the picture, the reputation, and the stereotype that employees and consumers attach to products of a specific country" (Piron, 2000, p. 308). When a national emphasis brings benefits, companies often promote their national identities together with their corporate identities. Cultural and other intangible assets, particularly, employee know-how and organisational knowledge, are repeatedly regarded as the most significant component of the core competence. Management capabilities highlight the importance of cultural and intangible assets which enhance firms to obtain core competence. Assets are resource endowments that a firm has accrued over time, and that can be deployed for forming a competitive advantage (Amit and Schoemaker, 1993; Fahy and Smithee, 1999; Grant, 1991).

Balmer (1995) argued that an organisation is a combination of multiple cultures and refers to the different cultures belonging to different divisions or departments in an organisation (Melewar, 2003; Van Maanen, 1979). Therefore, according to different perspectives, consensus, instead of being organisation wide, happens only within the limitations of a subculture. For example, in the study of Disneyland by Van Maanen (1979) and Balmer (1995), groups of staff were found to identify with precise groups rather than the whole organisation. These precise groups or subcultures were related to different roles and levels of organisational status, class and gender. This discussion leads to propose:

P3d: The stronger the company's country of origin effect, the stronger the impact of the company's cultural assets

P3e: The higher the level of company's subculture, the stronger the impact of the company's cultural assets

Intellectual and emotional assets and marketing capability

Intellectual and emotional assets include organisational philosophy and the system of leveraging the SME's capability (Kavida and Sivakoumar, 2009). What is commonly referred to as intellectual capital or knowledge capital (Kavida and Sivakoumar, 2009) is also referred to as output, in an intangible form (Kavida and Sivakoumar, 2009). When legally protected, it becomes intellectual property (Kavida and Sivakoumar, 2009) and those knowledge-based items have diverse components (Kavida and Sivakoumar, 2009) that includes things such as the organisation's image (Kavida and Sivakoumar, 2009) brand, reputation, trademarks, software, research and development, patents, staff skills, strategy, process quality, supplier and customer relationships (Bismuth and Tojo, 2008) such as R&D and human capital, which have the capacity to produce a future stream of benefits for the organisation (Bismuth and Tojo, 2008). Marketing capability may be defined as complex skill and accumulated knowledge, which through organisational process coordinate activities and make use of organisational assets including tangible and intangible resources.

Capability is a dynamic mix of tangible and intangible assets (Hafeez et al., 2007). Thus, marketing capabilities are firm-specific activities and they provide market-sensing, corporate brand identity management and customer relationship management. Marketing capability is the process of integrating a company's resources and capabilities for use in marketing operation that comprises knowledge, experience, skills and resources of the organisation (Mohammed et al., 2014). Organisations make use of their tangible and intangible resources and capabilities of brand, sales, channel, product and services to meet the needs of customers and build a market opportunity that is better than that of their competitors. Marketing capability has become the major asset in the modern world for SMEs which helps to retain competitiveness. Marketing capabilities are transformed into a company's competencies to produce goods or services or ensure its renewal and development (Hou and Chien, 2010).

P4: The higher the value added of intellectual and emotional assets in a company's portfolio, the more likely the chance is that it will qualify as a company's marketing capability.

Physical/tangible assets → marketing capability

Physical and tangible assets are the conceivable foundation of competitive advantage (Argote and Ingram, 2000, Dyer and Singh, 1998; Flamholtz and Hua, 2003). Since the company's assets impact on competitive advantage, they are much more critical and influential (Hafeez and Abdelmeguid, 2003); therefore, the organisation must focus on their physical and tangible assets such as the company's logo and brands to build competitive advantage. Rossen (2011) underlined a few groupings of tangible (trademarks, trade names, service marks, certification marks, internet domain), customer-related intangible assets (customer lists, order or production backlog, customer contracts and the related customer relationships), contract-based intangible assets (licensing, royalties, management, service or supply contracts, lease agreements, franchise agreements, broadcast rights), technology-based intangible assets (patented technology and unpatented technology, software, databases, trade secrets such as formulae and processes). These are the best example of where marketing capability holds these items in order to deny other parties access to them (Wang and Feng, 2012).

Assets are resource endowments that a firm has accrued over time, and that can be deployed for forming a competitive advantage (Amit and Schoemaker, 1993; Fahy and Smithee, 1999; Grant, 1991). If marketing capabilities including customer relationship capabilities and assets are successfully deployed to build greater customer value, then competitive advantage is formed (Fahy and Smithee, 1999). Hooley et al. (2005) emphasised that building customer satisfaction and loyalty enrich superior market performance. The customer relationship capabilities merging with a firm's assets expose company success (Setia et al., 2013).

P5: *The higher the value added of physical and tangible assets in a company's portfolio, the more likely the chance that it will qualify as company's marketing capability*

Cultural/intangible assets → marketing capability

The market orientation literature has highlighted that a company's cultural and intangible assets can be the key factor for business performance, as by tracing and replying to customers' preferences and needs, market-oriented organisations can fulfil customers' requirements better while performing at a higher level of marketing capability (Foroudi et al., 2016) and organisation performance (Kohli et al., 1993; Olavarrieta and Friedmann, 1999).

According to previous studies (Barney, 1986; Fombrun and Van Riel, 1997), a company's cultural assets encourage managers and employees' motivations and views. Mutual cultural values and a powerful sense of identity give the employees the guidance to define the reasons that their firms exist; it also justifies their strategies for cooperating with important stakeholders (Fombrun and Van Riel, 1997). Strong cultures regulate views inside the companies, therefore increasing the probability that managers will provide more reliable self-presentation to external participants. By building the main principle, which is general knowledge of the correct way of achieving things in an organisation, culture adds to the consistency of organisations' images with stakeholders (Camerer and Vepsalainen, 1988; Fombrun and Van Riel, 1997). Culture and identity are linked as identity defines core, enduring and unique features of an organisation that provides mutual interpretations between managers about ways which they should accommodate to external situations (Albert and Whetten, 1985; Fombrun and Van Riel, 1997). Furthermore, a supplier's behavioural performance and cultural values such as the manifestations of an organisation market marketing capability, may impact a purchasing organisation's perceptions of a seller or any other related task performance as well as in turn, the buying organisation's future objectives towards the supplier.

P6. The higher the "value added" of cultural and intangible assets in a company's portfolio, the more likely the chance that it will qualify as a company's marketing capability.

Marketing capability and competencies

The elementary postulation of the competence theory highlights that capabilities and assets of a firm govern a countless value-creating strategy in competition. These internal dynamics (capabilities and assets) generate core competencies throughout the path of "collective learning" (Hafeez and Essmail, 2007). Marketing capabilities are integrative processes designed to apply the collective knowledge, skills and resources of the firm to the market-related needs of the business, adding value to goods and services in meeting competitive demands (O'Cass and Weerawardena, 2009). Besides, marketing capabilities are an imperative feature of business strategy as these may increase the proficiency of a firm to sense and react to a shifting business environment (Haeckel, 1999; Roberts and Grover, 2012).

Firm competencies are prized capabilities in terms of "enabling the firm to deliver some fundamental consumer benefits" (Hamel, 1994, p. 11). Competencies involve generally a complex of capabilities rather than being single activity based. Many authors have highlighted that to develop a competence, a capability must be unique in the marketplace and collective in nature (Hafeez et al., 2002b). Competencies are the podium of numerous lines of businesses within a corporation and are the most significant constituents of cross-functional business processes (O'Cass and Weerawardena, 2009). Competencies supply a firm with new patterns of product competition. The business environment is progressively portrayed by competition, constant technological change and constrained resources. The power to innovate is a crucial factor of firm success (Shieh and Wang, 2010). Fahy et al. (2000), Tsai and Shih (2004), and Vorhies and Morgan (2003) and establishes an encouraging link among marketing capabilities and competence.

According to resource-based view theory, an organisation is a bundle of assets and capabilities. SMEs can determine future business directions based on the competencies. Organisations accumulate unique assets and competencies, also known as strategic resources, create competitive advantage. Companies develop competencies for the long-term success of a firm. Marketing capability is recognised as company competence. Therefore, marketing capability is created by a number of value-added key capabilities that comprise tangible and intangible assets (Hafeez and Essmail, 2007). According to Hafeez et al. (2002a, 2002b), competencies are those key (value-added) capabilities that have the characteristics of being "unique" in competition and "collective" in terms of its widespread use that entails being across products, across business functions and across business units. Being unique is defined as something that is "rare", "inimitable" and "non-substitutable" (see Figure 3.1). We propose that the marketing competence is formed by a number of (value added) key capabilities that lead us to postulate the following:

> *P7a. The more "unique" a company's marketing key capability is in competition, the more likely it will qualify to become marketing competence.*

> *P7b. The more "collective" a company's marketing key capability in its company-wide operation is, the more likely it will qualify to become marketing competence.*

From our analysis of the literature, we identify the key capabilities that are likely to aid candidates to improve their marketing competence. These include improving market sensing, corporate/brand identity management, customer relationship management, social media/communication capability, design/innovation management and performance management key capabilities.

Market sensing key capability

As noted earlier, several scholars suggested that intellectual and emotional assets are positively related and influenced by market-sensing capability and competencies. Hawke (1993) distinguishes four functions, namely (i) sensing (ii) intuition, (iii) thinking and (iv) feeling, which in psychological types can be thought of as competencies. Skilled human capital with sensing competence will use their sense to pick up concrete data and factors or sense events. This competence is concerned with experience, facts and detail (Hawke, 1993). The literature on the subject suggests that competencies are valuable capabilities, which enable a company to deliver customer benefit. According to Ljungquist (2013), sensing components are: R&D, process in innovation, development. However, according to Hafeez et al. (2002a), capabilities are deeply embedded in organisational practices and routines and business activities. Market sensing is a business activity of learning about the external environment on demand, customers and competitors while using knowledge to guide operations of the market (Sukdej and Ussahawanitchakit, 2015).

Teece (2007) argued that R&D, marketing, market search, production and distribution capabilities are highly valuable, rare, unique, inimitable and non-substitutable and these capabilities form competencies. Market-sensing capability requires pursuit and examination throughout technologies and markets (Teece, 2007), as it exposes the organisational capability to determine about customers, competitors and the broader market environment (Akarsu et al., 2020). Market-sensing capability can be implemented by utilising a variety of

Managing marketing competencies 93

processes, including sustaining relationships with customers and suppliers as well as participating in professional associations and perceiving best practices. These processes require greater use of intangible assets of a firm. Particularly, market-sensing processes generate inputs for the requirements of reconfigured operational capabilities (Eisenhardt and Martin, 2000). Competencies involve a network of capability or activity for example, R&D as part of market sensing involves research and product development (Hafeez et al., 2002b; Hafeez et al., 2007). Accordingly, the following discussion research proposes that:

P8a. The more "unique" a company's market-sensing key capability is, the more likely it will qualify as marketing competence.

P8b. The more "collective" a company's market-sensing key capability is, the more likely it will qualify as marketing competence.

Corporate brand identity management key capability

A corporate brand is frequently used to improve a company's brand trust competence and quality attributes. However, Gammoh (2006) recognised collaborative alliances which create competencies as the organisational ability to build relationship between people, groups or joined-together states for benefits or to achieve a common purpose. The brand competence is to create, maintain and manage brand image in order to create relationship with people. Management capabilities highlight the importance of the learning processes that are essential parts of corporate brand identity (Pittaway and Rose, 2006). In addition, brand competencies are closely linked to the knowledge creation by organisational learning, skills, experience, relationship and output, which provide superior performance that competitors are unlikely to acquire (Zha et al., 2020). However, rights to knowledge, patents brand image, employee know-how etc., are very often seen as elements of organisational competencies (Hafeez et al., 2006). Strong brand identity communicates unique characteristics, initiating relationship with channel members and consumers. Accordingly, the above discussion leads to the following proposals:

P9a. The more "unique" a company's corporate brand identify management key capability is, the more likely it will qualify as marketing competence.

P9b. The more "collective" a company's corporate brand identify management key capability is, the more likely it will qualify as marketing competence.

Customer relationship management key capability

Communication capability is a procedure that reflects a firm's ability to apply knowledge and in finding combined and adapt tangible assets (e.g., billboards, point of sale) and intangible assets (e.g., brand identity, slogans) into direct and indirect performance outcomes (e.g., brand equity, sales, return on investment) (Luxton et al., 2015). Social media can be professionally employed by tangible/

94 *P. Foroudi, M. M. Foroudi, K. Hafeez and J. Izadi*

intangible assets in effective ways which allow organisation to have more open and distributed communication. Communication capabilities exemplify a complex set of abilities to accomplish a firm's processes cost-effectively and systematically utilising a variety of organisational assets co-ordinately (Santos-Vijande et al., 2012).

Customer relationship capability has two underlying assumptions. The first is the understanding that relationships with customers are far more than a sequence of discrete transactions, with a relationship level viewed as more likely to create profitable outcomes for suppliers and bigger need satisfaction for customers (Dwyer et al., 1987; Verhoef, 2003). The second is an understanding that current customers are equally drawn from the perspective of an organisation's capacity to profitably fulfil their needs and requirements (Morgan et al., 2009). Therefore, customer relationship capabilities can be defined as an organisation's capability to recognise attractive customers including prospects, to start and maintain relationships with attractive customers and to influence these relationships into customer level profit (Boulding et al., 2005; Morgan et al., 2009).

Competence is defined by Ndubisi et al. (2007) as the buyer's perception, or refers to the ability of the company to serve customers well. As has been mentioned before by Hafeez et al. (2002a), integrated capabilities from business activities turn into competencies. The competence in the business can be described as that a company can give special unique service, and according to Hafeez et al. (2002a), the company can easily differentiate themselves against competitors. However, customer relationship is a part of relational capital, and relational capital is a resource which forms capability. In addition, customer relationship is the hardest capital to retain because it requires a lot of time and trust which in this case are recourses. Accordingly, the following discussion research proposes that:

P10a. The more "unique" a company's customer relationship management key capability is, the more likely it will qualify as marketing competence.

P10b. The more "collective" a company's customer relationship management key capability is, the more likely it will qualify as marketing competence.

Social media/communication key capability

According to Bradley and McDonald (2011), social media is "an evolution to expand organizational capabilities and it becomes part of company's culture" (p. 5). Assets itself are outlined with a wide variety of meanings. Grant's portrayal that "assets are inputs into the production process – they are the basic unit of analysis", where a capability is identified as "the capacity for a team of resources to perform some task or activity" (Hafeez et al., 2006, p. 3594). Capabilities upshot commencing an intricate pattern of actions and a positive synergy between numerous assets. Social media and communication capability have been described as the extent to which organisations are able to effectively manage marketing communication programmes and use marketing skills to approach customers in the market. Murray (2011) suggested that social media and communication capability characterises the organisation's competence in using technologies such as the internet and others to facilitate the interactions with customers. These interactions enable customers to have access to organisation resources and add value by facilitating employees to optimise their focus on the customer by synchronising information and activities throughout the organisation.

P11a. The more "unique" a company's social media/communication management key capability is, the more likely it will qualify as marketing competence.

P11b. The more "collective" a company's social media/communication management key capability is, the more likely it will qualify as marketing competence.

Design/innovation management key capability

Corporate design, also known as visual identity, is a term used to define the vast amount of visual cues which are linked with a specific organisation. Corporate visual identity (CVI) is an outcome of five elements, namely symbol/logotype, slogan, typography and colour (Dowling, 1994; Melewar and Saunders, 1998; Topalian, 1984). CVI can be conveyed through products, location, vehicle and architecture of its buildings. On the other hand, the interior design of a building may symbolise aspects of the corporate culture. According to Melewar (2003), there is an undeniable relationship between design and culture, as corporate slogan and mission are regularly seen as key factors of cultures and design.

Oliveira and Roth (2012) argue that innovation is a market-driven phenomenon and leadership is a driver which affects innovation (Foroudi et al., 2014; Gupta et al., 2016; Jaskyte, 2004). Leaders are able to build and manage an organisational culture which promotes innovation, that may be to do with product or process or its implementation to build organisational structure which encourages innovativeness (Jaskyte, 2004; Peters and Waterman, 1982; Van de Ven, 1986). Transformational leadership can increase an organisation's capacity to innovate by directing energy and resources in order to implement new programmes (Jaskyte, 2004).

P12a. The more "unique" a company's design/innovation management key capability is, the more likely it will qualify as marketing competence.

P12b. The more "collective" a company's social design/innovation management key capability is, the more likely it will qualify as marketing competence.

Performance management key capability

Magee (2002) posits that organisational culture and performance management are interdependent, and variation in one will have an impact in the other. According to Mujeeb and Ahmad (2011), good performance depends on strong culture. It is the organisational culture that differentiates the outcome of business

96   P. Foroudi, M. M. Foroudi, K. Hafeez and J. Izadi

strategies for two organisations in the same location and in the same industry (Kandula, 2006; Mujeeb and Ahmad, 2011). A strong and positive culture can even make an average employee outperform and achieve whereas a weak culture can demotivate an outstanding employee to underperform and end up underachieving (Mujeeb and Ahmad, 2011; Murphy and Cleveland, 1995).

Performance management capabilities render the organisation's ability to create and manage an effective performance measurement and analysis system (Hafeez et al., 2006), which includes the selection of suitable metrics, gathering and analysis of data from suitable sources to support managerial decision-making, communication of performance to appropriate stakeholders and association of the performance management system with present and future business directions (Mithas et al., 2011).

P13a. The more "unique" a company's performance management key capability is, the more likely it will qualify as marketing competence.

P13b. The more "collective" a company's performance management key capability is, the more likely it will qualify as marketing competence.

Competencies and core competencies

Competencies are assortments of knowledge, skills and performance, where performance is the ability to apply the knowledge and skills. The Project Management Institute defines competence as "a cluster of related knowledge, attitudes, skills, and other personal characteristics that affect a major part of one's job" (Project Management Institute, 2007, p. 73). Competence can be measured in contradiction of predefined norms and improved by training and development. In addition, competencies are extents of behaviour which are connected to superior job performance (Hafeez et al., 2002a).

Core competence is defined as organisational routines manifested in business activities and processes that bring assets together and enable them to be deployed advantageously (Hamel and Prahalad, 1990; Drejer, 2000). Core competencies are those competencies that are flexible to meet the strategic needs of the organisation (Hafeez, et al. 2002a, 2007). Strategic flexibility is manifested by two determinants (i) ability of a firm to "redeploy its resources" to meet future needs of the company (ii) ability of the firm to be able to re-organise its routines to meet a company's future needs to develop new products and/or services (Hafeez et al., 2002b). Appropriate management of a competence portfolio complements value to an organisation as well as strengthening core competence and its chance of survival in the business environment (Shieh and Wang, 2010).

P14a. The more flexible the "re-deployment" of a marketing competence to meet its future product/service needs is, the more likely it will qualify as a company's core competence.

P14b. The more flexible the "routine re-organisation" of a marketing competence to meet its future product/service needs is, the more likely it will qualify as a marketing company's core competence.

Model testing

An empirical examination is the logical next stage in establishing the reliability and validity of the research framework and its propositions. Such examining must be constructed on several organisations and industries, with methods ranging from experimental research, qualitative study to surveys. Due to the number of constructs in the model, it is suggested to examine only a portion of the framework in the first phase. In addition, it is recommended to adopt Churchill's (1979) paradigm, which integrates a qualitative paradigm (in-depth interviews and focus groups) to gather information in the first phase of the study. To increase the validity of findings as well as the richness of the conclusion, in-depth interviews with key informants and focus group discussions with employees and customers should be carried out. Such study helps one obtain the necessary information and further understanding about the phenomenon in addition to purifying measures for the questionnaire. The data triangulation boosts the validity of findings as well as the fullness of the study conclusion (Churchill, 1979; Deshpande, 1983; Saunders et al., 2007).

Multi-item Likert scales can be obtained or (re)adapted from previous studies in the domain for every concept (Churchill, 1979). The constructs can be operationalised by means of either objective or subjective measures or a combination thereof. After the measurement items are confirmed, we recommend distinct examinations of the three submodels that establish the research conceptual model (i.e. (i) intellectual and emotional assets and its antecedents, (ii) physical/tangible assets and its antecedents and (iii) cultural/intangible assets and its antecedents → marketing capability and its components → competencies → core competencies). Due to the moderately time-independent nature of the company's assets on marketing capability, it is predominantly amenable to experimental examination. Furthermore, it can be examined by means of questionnaire administered to a pertinent setting concerning the research associations with companies. These relationships can be tested by fsQCA (fuzzy set/Qualitative Comparative Analysis), SEM (structural equation modelling) or path analysis.

Discussion

This chapter contributes to several study streams. The current commentary builds on the growing body of research on the subject of core competence. With deeper engagement in competence observable uniqueness and companywide learning (collectiveness) accomplishments, firms can exploit company's resources more frequently by utilising company assets, marketing capability and core competence. This chapter delivers a combined conceptualisation that points to company's assets and marketing capability as being at the centre of the firm's determinations to generate competence and core competence.

This study expounds theoretical and managerial suggestions to boost the comprehending and supervision of marketing core competencies. In particular, our framework suggests that in harnessing the power of marketing capability in their own company–consumer contexts, managers must realise the following questions: what are the factors that have an influence on (i) intellectual and emotional (intangible) assets, (ii) physical (tangible) assets and (iii) cultural (intangible) assets?, what are the key components of organisations' marketing capability?, what is the nature of the relationships of the organisation's assets with the organisations' marketing capability?, how to isolate competencies from marketing capabilities by evaluating the collectiveness and unique attributes of marketing capabilities?, and how to further determine core competencies by evaluating the strategic flexibility of competencies? Before formulating and implementing core competencies, their organisations must ascertain whether they actually want their employees and consumers to identify with their company. The creation of a unique model for core competence is a fundamental provision of the current investigation. The major task in here is the creation of (multi-disciplinary) unique comprehensions into interactions, which can be transformed into outcomes with functioning applicability in the study (Palmer and Bejou, 2006).

Organisations that develop the variables of organisations' assets can achieve marketing capability accomplishing greater business competencies. The designed conceptualisation places marketing capability as central based on variables that establish and support the direction of marketing management capability to ultimately achieve superior business core competencies (Bismuth and Tojo, 2008; Kavida and Sivakoumar, 2009; Lim and Dallimore, 2004; Suciu et al., 2012; Sukdej and Ussahawanitchakit, 2015).

The most important aspect of the study is to extend knowledge by examining consumers and employees' evaluation of effect of company's assets and capabilities on competencies within the performance settings for providing competitive advantage (Hafeez et al., 2002a, b; Johnson, 2002; Kavida and Sivakoumar, 2009; Perunovic et al., 2012; Steenkamp and Kashyap, 2010). Some researchers (Bismuth and Tojo, 2008; Hafeez et al., 2007; Huggins and Weir, 2007ab; Kavida and Sivakoumar, 2009) suggested that a company's assets relate to capabilities. However, the current study provides a validated framework that investigates the relationship between the construct of (i) intellectual and emotional assets, (ii) physical/tangible assets and (iii) cultural/intangible assets with marketing capability, the factors which influence them (its antecedences) and the relationship between marketing capability and its factors which influence competencies and its consequences. It attempts to fulfil the research gap and responds to previous investigations from the perspective of different marketers (Kavida and Sivakoumar, 2009; Knight, 1999; Perunovic et al., 2012). The multi-disciplinary paradigm for the intellectual and emotional assets is a major contribution to the present research. However, many researchers believe that intangible, intellectual and emotional resources which result in distinctive capabilities are more influential because they are more likely to create value and meet attributes of the resource-based view such as valuable, rare, inimitable and non-substitutable (Flatt and Kowalczyk, 2008; Hall, 1992; Omil et al., 2011).

This study seeks to explain in a more holistic manner the relationship between organisations' assets, marketing capability and competencies in the eyes of consumers and employees within performance settings for providing competitive advantage. An organisation's substantial assets are very important for any organisation because of its growing importance in innovation, productivity, growth, enterprise competitiveness and economic performance; also, it is very costly (Lim and Dallimore, 2004). Besides, additional supposition can be delivered since this investigation related to the managers' and "decision-makers" approaches (Sedera and Gable, 2010). Firms command a lifecycle-wide knowledge obtaining strategy. It is these authors' confidence that each of the nine components of core competence should be adopted in all management plans for organisational competence. Nevertheless, a firm's tangible/intangible assets' creativities have naturally sought to increase exploration of digital technology and exploitation of marketing capabilities (Cuomo et al., 2020; Foroudi et al., 2017; Levinthal and March, 1993). The present study establishes an exceptional significance of all the dynamics of competence; each component delivering a distinct and significant contribution to organisational core competence.

Emphasising the perceived constructive relationship among core competence dynamics and a firm's success, we anticipate that the outcomes of this research will aid managers practice successfully and efficiently to develop their organisational-related competence, thus improving levels of competitive advantage and firm success for exploiting its strategic assets and tangible assets (Sedera and Gable, 2010; Foroudi et al., 2017).

Future research directions

This marketing research presents a preliminary initiation into the conceptualisation of the company's resources, assets, addressing their role in marketing capabilities and competencies. Nevertheless, this research should be interpreted in the light of some important limitations that are relevant for future research related to the need for empirical testing as well as its measurement. As a pioneering study in the area of marketing, this is a first attempt to investigate the topic of organisations' assets, its antecedents and consequences on marketing capability and competencies. Further research should be undertaken to increase validity of the study. Because again this study represents a first attempt to investigate the concept of organisation's assets, its antecedents and consequences on marketing capability and competencies, the existing literature was limited. The results from quantitative studies would help to develop a new scale adapted from previous studies.

Conclusion

This study reviewed how marketing capability can lead to firms' competitive advantage; however, there was no work on how a *marketing firm* can identify

100 *P. Foroudi, M. M. Foroudi, K. Hafeez and J. Izadi*

its core competence in the sector to attain competitive advantage. By revisiting the resource-based theory, we present an integrated framework to identify and determine the antecedents of marketing capability and its relation to company's core competencies. We undertook an extant literature review to identify, fuse and systhesise the marketing and strategic management literature to provide a framework for core capability identification. We used the *resource-based theory* to develop a core competence identification mechanism. We employed the *marketing theory* to identify the antecedents (under tangible and intangible assets) that are input to the marketing capability and core competence. This study is the first attempt to identify antecedents of marketing competence by exploiting tangible and intangible assets in terms of *intellectual, emotional* and *cultural* assets, and their relation to company's capability and core competence. This chapter articulates a theoretical framework that makes a significant contribution to the marketing and strategic management literature.

CASE STUDY

Next Plc is one of the main retailers of clothes, apparels, footwear, home products and related accessories in the UK. It is the third largest clothing retailer after Primark and Marks & Spenser. Next Plc. is listed on the London Stok Exchange (LSE). From 700 Next Plc stores, 500 hinderers are located in the UK and the rest of them are active across Europe, Middel East and Asia. In 1864, it was founded by Joseph Hepworh & Son as a tailor in Leeds. At the beginning, Hepworth was in partnership with James Rhodes but in 1872 the partnership was dissolved. After that, Hepworth extended the business and became an innovator to develop a chain of stores in Britain and the company had 100 outlets at the end of the1884 across the UK. In 1984, Davies as the new chief executive converted 50 Hepworth stores across the UK to the Next format. This helped the company to develop a small department store. After several years in 2008, Next bought the brand Lipsy. In 2009, for the first time, Next created an online catalogue for offering shoes, clothes and accessories.

According to (Distance Selling) Regulations 2000, BBC had an investigation in 2010 and found that there was a breaking of the consumer right agreements for its delivery costs. They had been charging customers for three years but assured that they would comply by 2010. Before 2007, Next usually used TV and newspapers to advertise their products. However, Next, after facing a 7.2% fall in sales, decided to invest £17 million over the next three years to resuscitate its existing stores and also, to offer new products and an additional £10m for marketing. Next celebrated its 25th anniversary in September 2007. At this time, Next produced "Ali's Party" with the song "Suddenly I See" which was the first television campaign it had run in 12e years.

Case questions

1. Can Next Plc. manage the market competencies?
2. What are the main features of the Next Plc approach to marketing?
3. Is there any framework for understanding the Next Plc. marketing capability and its relation to the company's core competencies?

Key terms and definitions

Marketing capability: highlights a superior method of utilising company knowledge and resources in order to reply successfully to shifting market requirements.

Corporate reputation is endowed with a judgement and is the overall evaluation of a company over time.

Knowledge management is a complex undertaking involving the development of structures that allow the firm to recognise, create, transform and distribute knowledge.

Trust has been defined as "a feeling of security held by the consumer in his/her interaction with the brand, such that it is based on the perceptions that the brand is reliable and responsible for the interests and welfare of the consumer".

Perceived quality is defined as a consumer's judgement about an entity's overall excellence or superiority. Perceived service quality is also defined as the discrepancy between a customer's expectations and their perceptions of the service performance. In other words, perceived service quality is the disparity between the consumer's expectations and their experiences.

Corporate visual identity is an assembly of visual cues to make an expression of the organisation by which an audience can recognise the company and distinguish it from others in serving to remind them of the corporation's real purpose.

Physical structure/spatial layout and functionality is the architectural design and physical placement of furnishings in a building, the arrangement of objects (e.g. arrangement of buildings, machinery, furniture and equipment), the spatial relationships among them, physical location and physical layout of the workplace which are particularly pertinent to the service industry and can symbolise something.

Ambient conditions/physical stimuli of an environment in service settings encourage stakeholders to pursue the service consumptions and subsequently affect on employees' behaviours, attitudes, satisfaction and performance towards the service provider.

Symbolic artefacts/decor and artefacts are aspects of the physical setting that individually or collectively guide the interpretation of the social setting, can be related to the aesthetics and attractiveness of the physical features of the environment, develop a complex representation of workplace identity and are mainly relevant to the service industry.

Digital technology builds and sustains present and future business applications resources and supports the critical internal processes.

Vision is the top management's aspirations for the company (Mukherjee and Balmer, 2007) and provides guidance about what core to preserve and what future to stimulate progress towards

Mission is the company purpose, the reason for which a company exists or its objectives.

Value is the dominant system of beliefs and moral principles that lie within the organisation that comprise everyday language, ideologies, rituals and beliefs of personnel.

Corporate guidelines are the articulation and interpretation of corporate principles by CEO vision/leadership for individual areas of business activity and functions and are used to guide the behaviour of individuals in an organisation.

Corporate history is history of the company and its ownership.

Country of origin is the picture, reputation and the stereotype that consumers attach to products of a specific country.

Subculture refers to the different cultures belonging to different divisions or departments in an organisation.

Market-sensing capability concerns a firm's ability to learn about customers, competitors, channel members and the broader market environment in which it operates.

Customer relationship capability is the firm's ability to identify attractive customers and prospects, initiate and maintain relationships with attractive customers and leverage these relationships into customer-level profits.

Social media and communication capability is the extent to which companies can effectively manage marketing communication programmes and use marketing skills to reach customers in the market. Social media and communication capability represents a firm's competence in using the internet and other information technologies to facilitate rich interactions with customers. These interactions provide customers with access to firm resources and create value by enabling employees to improve their focus on the customer by synchronising activities and information throughout the organisation.

Market-sensing capability concerns a firm's ability to learn about customers, competitors, channel members and the broader market environment in which it operates.

Corporate brand identity communicates to customers the differential qualities of their products, which in turn help firms improve their shareholder value. It assists organisations in communicating their differential advantage to the marketplace; however, all such organisation-specific attributes are signalled through the brand rather than other means of corporate communications.

Customer relationship capability is the firm's ability to identify attractive customers and prospects, initiate and maintain relationships with attractive customers and leverage these relationships into customer-level profits.

Core competencies are those competencies that are flexible to meet the strategic needs of the organisation.

References

Abratt, R. (1989). A new approach to the corporate image management process. *Journal of Marketing Management*, 5(1), 63–76.

Abratt, R. and Kleyn, N. (2012). Corporate identity, corporate branding and corporate reputations: reconciliation and integration. *European Journal of Marketing*, 46(7/8), 1048–1063.

Akarsu, T., Marvi, R. and Foroudi, P. (2021). History, past themes and future trends of corporate heritage: its evolution from 1970 and 2019 and an agenda for future inquiry. *European Journal of International Management* (Just accepted).

Albert, S. and Whetten, D. A. (1985). Organizational identity. *Research in Organizational Behavior*. Sage. 263–285.

Allee, V. (2008). Value network analysis and value conversion of tangible and intangible assets. *Journal of Intellectual Capital*, 9(1), 5–24.

Alniacik, U., Alniacik, E. and Genc, N. (2011). How corporate social responsibility information influences stakeholders' intentions. *Corporate Social Responsibility and Environmental Management*, 18(4), 234–245.

Amit, R. and Schoemaker, P. J. (1993). Strategic assets and organizational rent. *Strategic Management Journal*, 14(1), 33–46.

Ansoff, H. I. (1965). *Corporate Strategy: Business Policy for Growth and Expansion*. McGraw-Hill Book.

Anyadike-Danes, M., Bonner, K., Hart, M. and Mason, C. (2009). *Measuring Business Growth: High Growth Firms and Their Contribution to Employment in the UK*. Aston University, Birmingham.

Argote, L. and Ingram, P. (2000). Knowledge transfer: a basis for competitive advantage in firms. *Organizational Behavior and Human Decision Processes*, 82(1), 150–169.

Ayoko, O. B., Härtel, J. and Charmine, E. (2003). The role of space as both a conflict trigger and a conflict control mechanism in culturally heterogeneous workgroups. *Applied Psychology*, 52(3), 383–412.

Ayranci, E. and Çolakoğlu, N. (2014). An empirical study on the nexus between the emotional intelligence of top managers and their assessment of intellectual capital. *Quality & Quantity*, 48(4), 2023–2052.

Balmer, J. M. (1995). Corporate identity: the power and the paradox. *Design Management Review*, 6(1), 39–44.

Balmer, J. M. and Wilson, A. (1998). Corporate identity: there is more to it than meets the eye. *International Studies of Management & Organization*, 28(3), 12–31.

Barney, J. B. (1986). Organizational culture: can it be a source of sustained competitive advantage?. *Academy of Management Review*, 11(3), 656–665.

Barney, J. B. (1991). Firm resources and sustained competitive advantage. *Journal of Management*, 17(1), 99–120.

Berry, L. L. (2000). Cultivating service brand equity. *Journal of the Academy of Marketing Science*, 28(1), 128–137.

Bharadwaj, S. G., Varadarajan, P. R. and Fahy, J. (1993). Sustainable competitive advantage in service industries: a conceptual model and research propositions. *Journal of Marketing*, 83–99.

Bick, G., Jacobson, M. C. and Abratt, R. (2003). The corporate identity management process revisited. *Journal of Marketing Management*, 19(7–8), 835–855.

Bismuth, A. and Tojo, Y. (2008). Creating value from intellectual assets. *Journal of Intellectual Capital*, 9(2), 228–245.

Bitner, M. J. (1990). Evaluating service encounters: the effects of physical surroundings and employee responses. *Journal of Marketing*, 54(2), 69–82.

Bitner, M. J. (1992). Servicescapes: the impact of physical surroundings on customers and employees. *Journal of Marketing*, 56(2), 57–71.

Booth, C. and Rowlinson, M. (2006). Management and organizational history: prospects. *Management & Organizational History*, 1(1), 5–30.

Boulding, W., Staelin, R., Ehret, M. and Johnston, W. J. (2005). A customer relationship management roadmap: what is known, potential pitfalls, and where to go. *Journal of Marketing*, 69(4), 155–166.

Bradley, A. J. and McDonald, M. P. (2011). *The Social Organization: How to Use Social Media to Tap the Collective Genius of Your Customers and Employees*. Boston, MA: Harvard Business Press.

Brennan, A., Chugh, J. S. and Kline, T. (2002). Traditional versus open office design: a longitudinal field study. *Environment and Behavior*, 34(3), 279–299.

Brown, D., Foroudi, P. and Hafeez, K. (2019). Marketing management capability: the construct and its dimensions. *Qualitative Market Research: An International Journal*, 22(5), 609–637.

Camerer, C. and Vepsalainen, A. (1988). The economic efficiency of corporate culture. *Strategic Management Journal*, 9(S1), 115–126.

Check-Teck, F. and Lowe, A. (1999). Modelling for corporate identity studies: case of identity as communications strategy. *Corporate Communications: An International Journal*, 4(2), 89–92.

Childers, T. L. and Jass, J. (2002). All dressed up with something to say: effects of typeface semantic associations on brand perceptions and consumer memory. *Journal of Consumer Psychology*, 12(2), 93–106.

Churchill Jr, G. A. (1979). A paradigm for developing better measures of marketing constructs. *Journal of Marketing Research*, 64–73.

Cohen, L. M. (2010). Physical assets in the M&A mix: a strategic option. *Journal of Business Strategy*, 31(6), 28–36.

Çolakoğlu, N. and Ayrancı, E. (2013). An empirical study on the nexus between the emotional intelligence of top managers and their assessment of intellectual capital. *Quality & Quantity*, 48(4), 2023–2052.

Cornelissen, J. and Harris, P. (1999). *Two Perspectives on Corporate Identity: As the Expression of the Corporate Personality and as the Essential Self*. International Centre for Corporate Identity Studies, University of Strathclyde.

Cuomo, M. T., Tortora, D., Foroudi, P., Giordano, A., Festa, G. and Metallo, G. (2020). Digital transformation and tourist experience co-design: big social data for planning cultural tourism. *Technological Forecasting and Social Change*, 162(Sep), 120345.

Davis, T. R. (1984). The influence of the physical environment in offices. *Academy of Management Review*, 9(2), 271–283.

Deal, T. E. and Kennedy, A. A. (1982). *Corporate Cultures: The Rites and Rituals of Organizational Life. Reading/T. Deal, A. Kennedy.–Mass.* Addison-Wesley, 2, 98–103.

Delahaye, A., Booth, C., Clark, P., Procter, S. and Rowlinson, M. (2009). The genre of corporate history. *Journal of Organizational Change Management*, 22(1), 27–48.

Deshpande, R. (1983). "Paradigms Lost": on theory and method in research in marketing. *Journal of Marketing*, 47(4), 101–110.

Dewett, T. (2003). Understanding the relationship between information technology and creativity in organizations. *Creativity Research Journal*, 15(2–3), 167–182.

Dowling, G. R. (1994). *Corporate Reputations: Strategies for Developing the Corporate Brand*. Kogan Page.

Drejer, A. (2000). Organizational learning and competence development. *The Learning Organization*, 7(4), 206–220.

Dwyer, F. R., Schurr, P. H. and Oh, S. (1987). Developing buyer-seller relationships. *Journal of Marketing*, 51(2), 11–27.

Dyer, J. H. and Singh, H. (1998). The relational view: cooperative strategy and sources of interorganizational competitive advantage. *Academy of Management Review*, 23(4), 660–679.

Eisenhardt, K. M. and Martin, J. A. (2000). Dynamic capabilities: what are they?. *Strategic Management Journal*, 21(10–11), 1105–1121.

Elsbach, K. D. (2003). Relating physical environment to self-categorizations: identity threat and affirmation in a non-territorial office space. *Administrative Science Quarterly*, 48(4), 622–654.

Elsbach, K. D. (2004). Interpreting workplace identities: the role of office décor. *Journal of Organizational Behavior*, 25(1), 99–128.

Elsbach, K. D. (2009). Identity affirmation through signature style: A study of toy car designers. *Human Relations*, 62(7), 1041–1072.

Elsbach, K. D. and Pratt, M. G. (2007). 4 the physical environment in organizations. *Academy of Management Annals*, 1(1), 181–224.

Fahy, J. and Smithee, A. (1999). Strategic marketing and the resource based view of the firm. *Academy of Marketing Science Review*, 1999, 1.

Fahy, J., Hooley, G., Cox, T., Beracs, J., Fonfara, K. and Snoj, B. (2000). The development and impact of marketing capabilities in Central Europe. *Journal of International Business Studies*, 31(1), 63–81.

Fakhreddin, F., Foroudi, P. and Rasouli Ghahroudi, M. (2021). The bidirectional complementarity between market orientation and launch proficiency affecting new product performance. *Journal of Product and Brand Management* (Just accepted).

Fischer, G. N., Tarquinio, C. and Vischer, J. C. (2004). Effects of the self-schema on perception of space at work. *Journal of Environmental Psychology*, 24(1), 131–140.

Flamholtz, E. and Hua, W. (2003). Searching for competitive advantage in the black box. *European Management Journal*, 21(2), 222–236.

Flatt, S. J. and Kowalczyk, S. J. (2008). Creating competitive advantage through intangible assets: the direct and indirect effects of corporate culture and reputation. *Journal of Competitiveness Studies*, 16(1/2), 13.

Fombrun, C. (2000). The value to be found in corporate reputation. *Financial Times*, 4(2).

Foroudi, M. M., Balmer, J. M., Chen, W., Foroudi, P. and Patsala, P. (2020). Explicating place identity attitudes, place architecture attitudes, and identification triad theory. *Journal of Business Research*, 109(March), 321–336.

Foroudi, M. M., Balmer, M. T., Chen, W. and Foroudi, P. (2019). Corporate identity, place architecture, and identification: an exploratory case study, *Qualitative Market Research: An International Journal*, 109(May), 321–336.

Foroudi, P. (2018). *CORPORATE DESIGN: What Makes a Favorable University Logo?*, *Strategic Brand Management in Higher Education* (edited by Bang Nguyen, TC Melewar and Jane Hemsley-Brown), Routledge, UK.

Foroudi, P. (2019). Influence of brand signature, brand awareness, brand attitude, brand reputation on hotel industry's brand performance. *International Journal of Hospitality Management*, 76(Jan), 271–285.

Foroudi, P. (2020). Corporate brand strategy: drivers and outcomes of corporate brand orientation in international marketing. *International Journal of Hospitality Management*, 88(July), 1–14.

Foroudi, P. (2021). Relationship between marketing-assets and marketing capability. *European Journal of International Management* (Just accepted).

Foroudi, P., Cuomo, M. T., Foroudi, M. M., Katsikeas, C. S. and Gupta, S. (2020). Linking identity and heritage with image and a reputation for competition. *Journal of Business Research*, 113(May), 317–325.

Foroudi, P., Foroudi, M. M., Nguyen, B. and Gupta, S. (2019). Conceptualising and managing corporate logo: a qualitative study from stakeholders perspectives. *Qualitative Market Research: An International Journal*. 22(3), 381–404.

Foroudi, P., Gupta, S. and Melewar, T. C. (2017). Corporate logo: history, definition, and component. *International Studies of Management and Organization*, 47(2), 176–196.

Foroudi, P., Gupta, S., Nazarian, A. and Duda, M. (2017). Digital technology and marketing management capability: achieving growth in SMEs. *Qualitative Market Research: An International Journal*, 20(2), 230–246.

Foroudi, P., Gupta, S., Nazarian, A. and Duda, M. (2017). Digital technology and marketing management capability: achieving growth in SMEs. *Qualitative Market Research: An International Journal*, 20(2), 230–246.

Foroudi, P., Hafeez, K. and Foroudi, M. M. (2016). Evaluating the impact of corporate logos towards corporate reputation: a case of Persia and Mexico. *Qualitative Market Research: An International Journal*, 20(2), 158–180.

Foroudi, P., Jin, Z., Gupta, S., Melewar, T. C. and Foroudi, M. M. (2016). Influence of innovation capability and customer experience on reputation and loyalty. *Journal of Business Research*, 69(11), 4882–4889.

Foroudi, P. and Marvi, R. (2020). SOME LIKE IT HOT: the role of identity, website, co-creation behavior on identification and love. *European Journal of International Management*.

Foroudi, P., Marvi, R. and Imani, S. (2020). The impact of internal marketing on knowledge sharing capability. *European Journal of International Management* (Just accepted).

Foroudi, P., Melewar, T. C. and Gupta, S. (2014). Linking corporate logo, corporate image, and reputation: an examination of consumer perceptions in the financial setting. *Journal of Business Research*, 67(11), 2269–2281.

Fombrun, C. and Van Riel, C. (1997). The reputational landscape. *Corporate Reputation Review*, 1–16.

Fruhling, A. L. and Siau, K. (2007). Assessing organizational innovation capability and its effect on e-commerce initiatives. *Journal of Computer Information Systems*, 48(1), 133–145.

Gammoh, B. S. (2006). *Propensity to Participate in Brand Alliances: A Managerial Perspective*. Doctoral dissertation, Oklahoma State University.

Gorla, N., Somers, T. M. and Wong, B. (2010). Organizational impact of system quality, information quality, and service quality. *The Journal of Strategic Information Systems*, 19(3), 207–228.

Grant, R. M. (1991). The resource-based theory of competitive advantage: implications for strategy formulation. *California Management Review*, 33(3), 114–135.

Grasenick, K. and Low, J. (2004). Shaken, not stirred: defining and connecting indicators for the measurement and valuation of intangibles. *Journal of Intellectual Capital*, 5(2), 268–281.

Gupta, S., Malhotra, N. K., Czinkota, M. and Foroudi, P. (2016). Marketing innovation: a consequence of competitiveness. *Journal of Business Research*, 69(12), 5671–5681.

Haeckel, S. H. (1999). *Adaptive Enterprise*. Harvard Business School Press.

Hafeez, K. and Abdelmeguid, H. (2003). Dynamics of human resource and knowledge management. *Journal of the Operational Research Society*, 54(2), 153–164.

Hafeez, K. and Aburawi, I. (2013). Planning human resource requirements to meet target customer service levels. *International Journal of Quality and Service Sciences*, 5(2), 230–252.

Hafeez, K. and Essmail, E. A. (2007). Evaluating organisation core competences and associated personal competencies using analytical hierarchy process. *Management Research News*, 30(8), 530–547.

Hafeez, K., Foroudi, P. and Nguyen, B. (2019). An integrated core competence evaluation framework for portfolio management in the oil industry. *International Journal of Management and Decision Making*, 18(3), 229–256.

Hafeez, K., Zhang, Y. and Malak, N. (2002a). Core competence for sustainable competitive advantage: a structured methodology for identifying core competence. *IEEE Transactions on Engineering Management*, 49(1), 28–35.

Hafeez, K., Zhang, Y. and Malak, N. (2002b). Determining key capabilities of a firm using analytic hierarchy process. *International Journal of Production Economics*, 76(1), 39–51.

Hafeez, K., Malak, N. and Abdelmeguid, H. (2006). A framework for TQM to achieve business excellence. *Total Quality Management and Business Excellence*, 17(9), 1213–1229.

Hafeez, K., Malak, N. and Zhang, Y. (2007). Outsourcing non-core assets and competences of a firm using analytic hierarchy process. *Computers & Operations Research*, 34(12), 3592–3608.

Hafeez, K., Keoy, K. H. A., Zairi, M., Hanneman, R. and Koh, S. L. (2010). E-supply chain operational and behavioural perspectives: an empirical study of Malaysian SMEs. *International Journal of Production Research*, 48(2), 525–546.

Hafeez, K., Foroudi, P., Dinnie, K., Nguyen, B. and Parahoo, S. K. (2016). The role of place branding and image in the development of sectoral clusters: the case of Dubai. *Journal of Brand Management*, 23(4), 383–402.

Hall, R. (1992). The strategic analysis of intangible resources. *Strategic Management Journal*, 13(2), 135–144.

Hall, R. (1993). A framework linking intangible resources and capabilities to sustainable competitive advantage. *Strategic Management Journal*, 14(8), 607–618.

Hamel, G. and Heene, A. (1994). *Competence-based Competition*. Wiley.

Hamel, G. and Prahalad, C. K. (1990). Corporate imagination and expeditionary marketing. *Harvard Business Review*, 69(4), 81–92.

Han, H. and Ryu, K. (2009). The roles of the physical environment, price perception, and customer satisfaction in determining customer loyalty in the restaurant industry. *Journal of Hospitality & Tourism Research*, 33(4), 487–510.

Hawke, R. (1993). A Jungian guide to competences. *Journal of Managerial Psychology*, 8(1), 29–32.

Henderson, P. W., Giese, J. and Cote, J. A. (2004). Impression management using typeface design. *Journal of Marketing*, 68(4), 60–83.

Hofstede, G. (1991). *Cultures and Organizations: Software of the Mind London*. McGraw-Hill Book.

Hooley, G. J., Greenley, G. E., Cadogan, J. W. and Fahy, J. (2005). The performance impact of marketing resources. *Journal of Business Research*, 58(1), 18–27.

Hou, J. J. and Chien, Y. T. (2010). The effect of market knowledge management competence on business performance: a dynamic capabilities perspective. *International Journal of Electronic Business Management*, 8(2), 96.

Huggins, R. and Weir, M. (2007a). Intellectual assets and public policy. *Journal of Intellectual Capital*, 8(4), 708–720.

Huggins, R. and Weir, M. (2007b). Managing intellectual assets in SMEs: evaluating the scope for policy intervention. *International Journal of Learning and Intellectual Capital*, 4(4), 412–429.

Hunt, S. D. and Morgan, R. M. (1995). The comparative advantage theory of competition. *Journal of Marketing*, 59(2), 1–15.

Hussain, Z. and Hafeez, K. (2008). Changing attitudes and behavior of stakeholders during an information systems-led organizational change. *The Journal of Applied Behavioral Science*, 44(4), 490–513.

Ikonen, M. (2012, October). Dynamics between trust in interpersonal work relations and intellectual capital. In *Proceedings of the 9th International Conference on Intellectual Capital, Knowledge Management & Organizational Learning* (pp. 335–341).

Imani, S., Foroudi, P., Amiri, N. S. and Dehghani, N. (2020). Improving employees' performance through internal marketing and organizational learning: mediating role of organizational innovation in an emerging market. *Cogent Business and Management*, 7(1), 1–23.

Imani, S., Foroudi, P. and Marvi, R. (2020). Praise of intra-organizational social capital and knowledge sharing behaviors in MNCs. *European Journal of International Management* (Just accepted).

Jaskyte, K. (2004). Transformational leadership, organizational culture, and innovativeness in nonprofit organizations. *Nonprofit Management and Leadership*, 15(2), 153–168.

Johnson, W. H. (2002). Leveraging intellectual capital through product and process management of human capital. *Journal of Intellectual Capital*, 3(4), 415–429.

Kamarulzaman, N., Saleh, A. A., Hashim, S. Z., Hashim, H. and Abdul-Ghani, A. A. (2011). An overview of the influence of physical office environments towards employee. *Procedia Engineering*, 20, 262–268.

Kandula, S. R. (2006). *Performance Management: Strategies, Interventions, Drivers*. PHI Learning Pvt, Ltd.

Karaosmanoglu, E. and Melewar, T. C. (2006). Corporate communications, identity and image: a research agenda. *Journal of Brand Management*, 14(1–2), 196–206.

Kavida, V. and Sivakoumar, N. (2009). Intellectual capital: a strategic management perspective. *IUP Journal of Knowledge Management*, 7(5/6), 55.

Kim, H., Hur, W. M. and Yeo, J. (2015). Corporate brand trust as a mediator in the relationship between consumer perception of CSR, corporate hypocrisy, and corporate reputation. *Sustainability*, 7(4), 3683–3694.

Knight, D. J. (1999). Performance measures for increasing intellectual capital. *Strategy & Leadership*, 27(2), 22–27.

Kohli, A. K., Jaworski, B. J. and Kumar, A. (1993). MARKOR: a measure of market orientation. *Journal of Marketing Research*, 467–477.

Kozlenkova, I. V., Samaha, S. A. and Palmatier, R. W. (2014). Resource-based theory in marketing. *Journal of the Academy of Marketing Science*, 42(1), pp.1–21.

Kumar, V. (2015). Evolution of marketing as a discipline: what has happened and what to look out for. *Journal of Marketing*, 79(1), 1–9.

Levinthal, D. A. and March, J. G. (1993). The myopia of learning. *Strategic Management Journal*, 14(S2), 95–112.

Lim, L. L. and Dallimore, P. (2004). Intellectual capital: management attitudes in service industries. *Journal of Intellectual Capital*, 5(1), 181–194.

Ljungquist, U. (2013). Adding dynamics to core competence concept applications. *European Business Review*, 25(5), 453–465.

Luxton, S., Reid, M. and Mavondo, F. (2015). Integrated marketing communication capability and brand performance. *Journal of Advertising*, 44(1), 37–46.

Magee, K. C. (2002). The impact of organizational culture on the implementation of performance management. *Academy of Management Review*, 29(3), 388–403.

Mahmood, T. and Hafeez, K. (2013). Performance assessment of an e-learning software system for sustainability. *International Journal of Quality and Service Sciences*, 5(2), 208–229.

McElroy, J. C. and Morrow, P. C. (2010). Employee reactions to office redesign: a naturally occurring quasi-field experiment in a multi-generational setting. *Human Relations*, 63(5), 609–636.

Melewar, T. C. (2003). Determinants of the corporate identity construct: a review of the literature. *Journal of Marketing Communications*, 9(4), 195–220.

Melewar, T. C., Foroudi, P., Dinnie, K. and Nguyen, B. (2018). The role of corporate identity management in the higher education sector: an exploratory case study. *Journal of Marketing Communications*, 24(4), 337–359.

Melewar, T. C., Foroudi, P., Kitchen, P., Gupta, S. and Foroudi, M. M. (2017). Integrating identity, strategy and communications for trust, loyalty and commitment. *European Journal of Marketing*, 51(3), 572–604.

Melewar, TC., Foroudi, P. and Jin, Z. (2020). Corporate branding, identity, image and reputation: current and future trends, developments and challenges. *Journal of Business Research*, 117, 672–674.

Melewar, T. C. and Karaosmanoglu, E. (2006). Seven dimensions of corporate identity: a categorisation from the practitioners' perspectives. *European Journal of Marketing*, 40(7/8), 846–869.

Melewar, T. C. and Saunders, J. (1998). Global corporate visual identity systems: standardization, control and benefits. *International Marketing Review*, 15(4), 291–308.

Mithas, S., Ramasubbu, N. and Sambamurthy, V. (2011). How information management capability influences firm performance. *MIS Quarterly*, 35(1), 237–256.

Mohammed, A. A., Rashid, B. B. and Tahir, S. B. (2014). Customer relationship management (CRM) technology and organization performance: is marketing capability a missing link? an empirical study in the Malaysian hotel industry. *Asian Social Science*, 10(9), 197.

Moingeon, B. and Ramanantsoa, B. (1997). Understanding corporate identity: the French school of thought. *European Journal of Marketing*, 31(5/6), 383–395.

Montes, E. and Foroudi, P. (2017). Corporate e-communication: its relationship with the corporate logo in the construction of the consumers online interaction. *The Bottom Line*, 30(3), 201–215.

Morgan, N. A., Vorhies, D. W. and Mason, C. H. (2009). Market orientation, marketing capabilities, and firm performance. *Strategic Management Journal*, 30(8), 909–920.

Moustaghfir, K. (2009). How knowledge assets lead to a sustainable competitive advantage: are organizational capabilities a missing link?. *Knowledge Management Research & Practice*, 7(4), 339–355.

Mukherjee, A. and Balmer, J. M. (2007). Preface: new frontiers and perspectives in corporate brand management: in search of a theory. *International Studies of Management & Organization*, 37(4), 3–19.

Mujeeb, E. M., Masood, M. M. and Ahmad, M. A. (2011). Relationship between organizational culture and performance management practices: a case of university in Pakistan. *Journal of Competitiveness*, 3(4), 78–86.

Murphy, K. R. and Cleveland, J. (1995). *Understanding Performance Appraisal: Social, Organizational, and Goal-based Perspectives*. SAGE.

Murray, J. H. (2011). *Inventing the Medium: Principles of Interaction Design as a Cultural Practice*. MIT Press.

Nguyen, N. (2006). The perceived image of service cooperatives: an investigation in Canada and Mexico. *Corporate Reputation Review*, 9(1), 62–78.

O'Cass, A. and Weerawardena, J. (2009). Examining the role of international entrepreneurship, innovation and international market performance in SME internationalisation. *European Journal of Marketing*, 43(11/12), 1325–1348.

Olavarrieta, S. and Friedmann, R. (1999). Market-oriented culture, knowledge-related resources, reputational assets and superior performance: a conceptual framework. *Journal of Strategic Marketing*, 7(4), 215–228.

Oldham, G. R. and Brass, D. J. (1979). Employee reactions to an open-plan office: a naturally occurring quasi-experiment. *Administrative Science Quarterly*, 24(2), 267–284.

Oliveira, P. and Roth, A. V. (2012). Service orientation: the derivation of underlying constructs and measures. *International Journal of Operations & Production Management*, 32(2), 156–190.

Olmedo-Cifuentes, I. and Martínez-León, I. (2015). Reputation as an outcome of human capital. In *European Conference on Intellectual Capital* (p. 245). Academic Conferences.

Oly Ndubisi, N., Kok Wah, C. and Ndubisi, G. C. (2007). Supplier-customer relationship management and customer loyalty: the banking industry perspective. *Journal of Enterprise Information Management*, 20(2), 222–236.

Omil, J. C., Lorenzo, P. C. and Liste, A. V. (2011). The power of intangibles in high-profitability firms. *Total Quality Management*, 22(1), 29–42.

Onkvisit, S. and Shaw, J. J. (1989). The international dimension of branding: strategic considerations and decisions. *International Marketing Review*, 6(3).

Palazzo, M., Vollero, A., Foroudi, P. and Siano, A. (2019). Evaluating constitutive dimensions of CSR E-communication: a comparison between 'business-to-business' and 'close-to-market'companies. *Journal of Business-to-Business Marketing*, 26(3–4), 341–355.

Palmer, A. and Bejou, D. (2006). The future of relationship marketing. *Journal of Relationship Marketing*, 4(3–4), 1–10.

Parish, J. T., Berry, L. L. and Lam, S. Y. (2008). The effect of the servicescape on service workers. *Journal of Service Research*, 10(3), 220–238.

Perunovic, Z., Christoffersen, M. and Mefford, R. N. (2012). Deployment of vendor capabilities and competences throughout the outsourcing process. *International Journal of Operations & Production Management*, 32(3), 351–374.

Peters, T. J., Waterman, R. H. and Jones, I. (1982). *In Search of Excellence: Lessons from America's Best-Run Companies*. NY: Harper & Row, Publishers Inc.

Piron, F. (2000). Consumers' perceptions of the country-of-origin effect on purchasing intentions of (in) conspicuous products. *Journal of Consumer Marketing*, 17(4), 308–321.

Pittaway, L. and Rose, M. (2006). Learning and relationships in small firms: introduction to the special issue. *International Small Business Journal*, 24(3), 227–231.

Prahalad, C. K. and Hamel, G. (1990). The core competencies of the corporation. *Harvard Business Review*, (3), 79–91.

Managing marketing competencies 111

Project Management Institute (2007). https://www.pmi.org (Assessed on 16 Jun 2016).

Roberts, N. and Grover, V. (2012). Leveraging information technology infrastructure to facilitate a firm's customer agility and competitive activity: an empirical investigation. *Journal of Management Information Systems*, 28(4), 231–270.

Rossen, P. E. T. (2011). Initial identification of internally generated intangible assets in the context of the definitions of an asset and an intangible asset. *The Journal of Theoretical Accounting Research*, 6(2), 1–9.

Rossi, R. M. and Mafud, M. D. (2014). Resource-advantage theory: O Estado Da ARTE/resource-advantage theory: state of art. *Revista Pensamento Contemporâneo em Administração*, 8(2), 35.

Rowlinson, M. and Procter, S. (1999). Organizational culture and business history. *Organization Studies*, 20(3), 369–396.

Santos-Vijande, M. L., López-Sánchez, J. Á. and Trespalacios, J. A. (2012). How organizational learning affects a firm's flexibility, competitive strategy, and performance. *Journal of Business Research*, 65(8), 1079–1089.

Saunders, M., Lewis, P. and Thornhill, A. (2007). *Research Methods for Business Students*. 4th ed. Harlow, UK: Financial Times Prentice Hall.

Savolainen, T. and Häkkinen, S. (2011). *Trusted to Lead: Trustworthiness and its Impact on Leadership*. Open Source Business Resource, March.

Savolainen, T. and Lopez-Fresno, P. (2013). Trust as intangible asset-enabling intellectual capital development by leadership for vitality and innovativeness. *Electronic Journal of Knowledge Management*, 11(2), 244–255.

Schmitt, B. H., Simonson, A. and Marcus, J. (1995). Managing corporate image and identity. *Long Range Planning*, 28(5), 82–92.

Sedera, D. and Gable, G. G. (2010). Knowledge management competence for enterprise system success. *The Journal of Strategic Information Systems*, 19(4), 296–306.

Setia, P., Venkatesh, V. and Joglekar, S. (2013). Leveraging digital technologies: how information quality leads to localized capabilities and customer service performance. *Mis Quarterly*, 37(2), 565–590.

Shieh, C. J. and Wang, I. M. (2010). A study of the relationships between corporate core competence, management innovation and corporate culture. *International Journal of Organizational Innovation (Online)*, 2(3), 395.

Steenkamp, N. and Kashyap, V. (2010). Importance and contribution of intangible assets: SME managers' perceptions. *Journal of Intellectual Capital*, 11(3), 368–390.

Suciu, M. C., Picioruş, L. and Imbrişcă, C. (2012). Trust, cultural traits and reputation: key-elements for an efficient intellectual capital formation process in the Romanian education system. In *ePub-Proceedings of the 4th European Conference on Intellectual Capital: ECIC 2012* (p. 444). Academic Conferences Limited.

Sukdej, S. and Ussahawanitchakit, P. (2015). Dynamic marketing capability and marketing survival: evidence from auto parts businesses in Thailand. *Business Management Review*, 7(1), 177.

Sumita, T. (2008). Intellectual assets based management for innovation: lessons from experiences in Japan. *Journal of Intellectual Capital*, 9(2), 206–227.

Sur, S. and Sirsly, C. A. T. (2013). What's in a name? Decomposing corporate reputation to assess the relative impact of temporal, firm and industry level factors. *Journal of Management & Governance*, 17(4), 1047–1072.

Tavassoli, N. T. (2001). Color memory and evaluations for alphabetical and logographic brand names. *Journal of Experimental Psychology: Applied*, 7(2), 104.

Teece, D. J. (2007). Explicating dynamic capabilities: the nature and microfoundations of (sustainable) enterprise performance. *Strategic Management Journal*, 28(13), 1319–1350.

Topalian, A. (1984). Corporate identity: beyond the visual overstatements. *International Journal of Advertising*, 3(1), 55–62.

Tourky, M., Foroudi, P., Gupta, S. and Shaalan, A. (2020). Conceptualising corporate identity in a dynamic environment. *Qualitative Market Research: An International Journal* (Just accepted).

Tsai, M. T. and Shih, C. M. (2004). The impact of marketing knowledge among managers on marketing capabilities and business performance. *International Journal of Management*, 21(4), 524.

Van de Ven, A. H. (1986). Central problems in the management of innovation. *Management Science*, 32(5), 590–607.

Van den Bosch, A. L., Elving, W. J. and de Jong, M. D. (2006). The impact of organizational characteristics on corporate visual identity. *European Journal of Marketing*, 40(7/8), 870–885.

Van Der Merwe, A. W. and Puth, G. (2014). Towards a conceptual model of the relationship between corporate trust and corporate reputation. *Corporate Reputation Review*, 17(2), 138–156.

Van Maanen, J. (1979). The fact of fiction in organizational ethnography. *Administrative Science Quarterly*, 24(4), 539–550.

Van Riel, C. B. and Balmer, J. M. (1997). Corporate identity: the concept, its measurement and management. *European Journal of Marketing*, 31(5/6), 340–355.

Varey, R. J. and Lewis, B. R. (2000). *Internal Marketing: Directions for Management*. Psychology Press.

Värlander, S. (2012). Individual flexibility in the workplace: a spatial perspective. *The Journal of Applied Behavioral Science*, 48(1), 33–61.

Verhoef, P. C. (2003). Understanding the effect of customer relationship management efforts on customer retention and customer share development. *Journal of Marketing*, 67(4), 30–45.

Vorhies, D. W. and Morgan, N. A. (2003). A configuration theory assessment of marketing organization fit with business strategy and its relationship with marketing performance. *Journal of Marketing*, 67(1), 100–115.

Vorhies, D. W. and Morgan, N. A. (2005). Benchmarking marketing capabilities for sustainable competitive advantage. *Journal of Marketing*, 69(1), 80–94.

Wakefield, K. L. and Blodgett, J. G. (1994). The importance of servicescapes in leisure service settings. *Journal of Services Marketing*, 8(3), 66–76.

Walsh, J. P. and Ungson, G. R. (1991). Organizational memory. *Academy of Management Review*, 16(1), 57–91.

Wang, M. C. (2013). Value relevance on intellectual capital valuation methods: the role of corporate governance. *Quality & Quantity*, 47(2), 1–11.

Wang, Y. and Feng, H. (2012). Customer relationship management capabilities: measurement, antecedents and consequences. *Management Decision*, 50(1), 115–129.

Wernerfelt, B. (1984). A resource-based view of the firm. *Strategic Management Journal*, 5(2), 171–180.

Yadav, S. (2014). The role of emotional intelligence in organization development. *IUP Journal of Knowledge Management*, 12(4), 49.

Zha, D., Melewar, T. C., Foroudi, P. and Jin, Z. (2020). An assessment of brand experience knowledge literature: using bibliometric to identify future research direction. *International Journal of Management Reviews* (Just accepted).

4 Reputation

Configuring the symmetrical and asymmetrical paths to architecture in a retail setting

Mohammad M. Foroudi, Pantea Foroudi and Zhongqi Jin

Introduction

Grounded in social identity and attribution theories, this study focuses on the effect of architecture and its components on reputation. The relationships conceptualised were evaluated using data collected from a survey of 489 online and offline UK retail consumers and employees. To accommodate the equifinality and complexity of these relationships, this study employs fuzzy set qualitative comparative analysis, predictive validity and fit validity check.

Background to architecture in a retail setting

Recent research has demonstrated that a favourable architecture can help customers focus on what an organisation stands for and what it aspires to communicate. Modern architecture integrates industry attributes with art and contemporary social needs, while architecture in general expresses the emotional stance of a company's purpose and position (Vischer, 2007). Architectural design is, therefore, defined as the preparation of instructions for the manufacturer of artefacts to create an image of corporate identity (Alessandri, 2001; Akarsu et al., 2019). Surprisingly, the majority of academic studies have focused on the design aspects of architecture, neglecting the relevant strategic elements. Since the visual character of architectural design transcends geographical and cultural barriers, organisations spend substantially on the design and construction of effective building (Ellis and Duffy, 1980; Forodui, 2018). This is mainly because the concept of architecture is not only related to the physical, but also to the social and cultural aspects of buildings (Saleh, 1998).

A large body of research conducted in research domains pertinent to disciplines such as design, management, organisations, psychology and social identity (Bonaiuto et al., 1996; Marin and de Maya, 2013; Speller et al., 2002; Stedman, 2002; Tajfel, 1981, 1982; Twigger-Ross and Uzzell, 1996; Twigger-Ross et al., 2003) have tried to explain whether, and how, architecture can influence corporate identity (Melewar and Jenkins, 2002). Other scholars have investigated how a favourable architecture could influence identification, employee attachment,

114   M. M. Foroudi, P. Foroudi and Z. Jin

job satisfaction, well-being and feelings of comfort (Knight and Haslam, 2010). Several scholars (see, for example, Balmer, 2001, 2005, 2006; Melewar, 2003; Pittard et al., 2007; Van den Bosch et al., 2005) have identified a strong relationship between architecture and consumer perception. Some authors examined architecture and the physical environment (Bernard and Bitner, 1982; Bitner, 1992a, b; Davis et al., 2010; Elsbach and Bechky, 2007; Foroudi et al., 2019; 2020; Han and Ryu, 2009; Laing, 2006; McElroy and Morrow, 2010; Nguyen, 2006); however, those studies were not conducted in relation to (the construct/concept of) reputation. Although some previous studies (Davis et al., 2010; Elsbach, 2003; Han and Ryu, 2009; McElroy and Morrow, 2010; Rooney et al., 2010) attempt to contribute to the field, contrary to the present study, they did not evaluate reputation. It should be, thus, highlighted that the current research extends knowledge in the field by investigating the relationship between corporate identity, architecture and reputation constructs.

This chapter contributes to the growing literature on interest in architecture by extending the notion of reputation defined as the chief psychological substrate for the kind of deep, committed and meaningful relationships that retailers, marketers and designers are progressively looking for. In addition, this research encompasses elements of/is also grounded in social identity theory whereby people define themselves using/with the same attributes as organisations (Ashfort and Mael, 1989; Bergami and Bagozzi, 2000; Elsbach and Kramer, 1996; Gioia and Thomas, 1996; Marin and de Maya, 2013). Within this context/along these lines, attribution theory relates to how people make sense of their own world (Graham, 1991; Jones et al., 1972) in order to describe a "sense of place" (Foroudi et al., 2016; Hafeez et al., 2016; Stedman, 2002; Zomerdijk and Voss, 2010), which is also associated with the reputation of an organisation (Hoeken and Ruikes, 2005; Foroudi et al., 2016; 2019; 2020; Walsh et al., 2008) that, in turn, communicates the company's identity, internally and externally (Melewar techmeaning of buildings; Sadalla and Sheets, 1993). In addition, the theory of complexity was also exploited to clear/enrich the authors' reflection of non-linearity among the relationships under examination in a competitive marketplace and under a situation of uncertainty. In terms of research design/methodology, this chapter employs confirmatory factor analysis (CFA), structural equation modelling (SEM) and fuzzy set qualitative comparative analysis (fsQCA) (Gupta et al., 2016; Ragin, 2006, 2008). It becomes evident that the resulting (more profound) perspective works well with complexity theory (Foroudi et al., 2016; Gupta et al., 2016; Mikalef et al., 2015; Ordanini et al., 2013; Woodside, 2014; Wu et al., 2014).

In the following sections, the paper draws on existing studies from a multi-disciplinary approach in order to develop a consumer/employees level conceptual model, which will offer research propositions regarding the main determinants and consequences of retail architecture. We then present the method implemented, the results retrieved and the data analysis conducted. We then conclude with the managerial, theoretical and research implications of this work.

Conceptual model and research propositions

The physical environment has a strong influence on customer behaviour by creating an overall aesthetic impression and corporate reputation, especially pertinent to a service industry (Han and Ryu, 2009). The three main components of architecture are (i) symbolic artefacts/decor and artefacts in general, (ii) physical structure/spatial layout and functionality as well as (iii) ambient conditions/physical stimuli, which will be explained in the following sections (Bitner, 1992a; Han and Ryu, 2009; McElroy and Morrow, 2010; Nguyen and Leblanc, 2002; Wakefield and Blodgett, 1999). These factors are the main sufficient factors of the physical environment for customer behaviour research in a service context (Edvardsson et al., 2005; Han and Ryu, 2009; Nguyen and Leblanc, 2002).

More precisely, symbolic artefacts represent "aspects of the physical setting that individually or collectively guide the interpretation of the social setting" (Davis, 1984, p. 279). Apart from contributing to the attractiveness of the physical environment, symbolic artefacts enhance customer satisfaction and loyalty as well (Han and Ryu, 2009; Wakefield and Blodgett, 1994). Furthermore, physical artefacts impact professional creative identities and personalities (Elsbach, 2009, p. 1065) and they develop a complex representation of workplace identity (Elsbach, 2004, p. 99). However, there has been limited research on "how employees perceive specific dimensions of workplace identities in work environments that limit the display of personal identity markers" (Elsbach, 2003, p. 623).

Symbolic artefacts consist of certain features of the physical setting, which can be described as the quality of the environment for a company's employees (Davis, 1984, p. 278). Elsbach (2004) states that in corporate settings "office decor sits on the front lines of social judgment processes" (p. 119). A company's artefacts are the visible display of an organisation that may induce employees to express organisational attachment (Elsbach and Pratt, 2007, p. 201), employee thought processes, behaviours and feelings (McElroy and Morrow, 2010, p. 613). Elsbach's (2004) study indicates how corporate employees may interpret office decor as clues from the workplace in a corporation.

In addition, symbolic artefacts also refer to the aesthetics of the office environment: the colours of the walls, the type of flooring, the pictures, flowers, floor, furniture style and overall the office decor which may differentiate the company and place from its competitors' (Han and Ryu, 2009). Davis (1984) states that the physical structure and symbolic artefacts, "all tend to communicate information about the organisation and the people who work there" (p. 277). The physical structure, physical stimuli and symbolic artefacts are all involved in the office re-design effort (Davis, 1984). Any changes made in the symbolic artefacts can improve users' positive reaction; for instance, the natural lighting and the use of bright colours cause/lead to a more pleasant work atmosphere (McElroy and Morrow, 2010).

116 M. M. Foroudi, P. Foroudi and Z. Jin

T1: No single best configuration of factors such as décor and symbolic artefacts lead to a favourable reputation towards retail store, but there exists
multiple, equally effective configurations of causal factors.

Physical structure/spatial layout and functionality, on the other hand, can be
defined as the architectural design and physical placement of furnishings in a
building. The spatial relationships among them, the physical location and
appearance are particularly pertinent to the service industry (Bitner, 1992a;
Han and Ryu, 2009; McElroy and Morrow, 2010; Nguyen, 2006). The spatial
layout can also influence or regulate social interaction (Davis, 1984, p. 272),
affect perceptions of culture (McElroy and Morrow, 2010, p. 614) and influence
customer satisfaction as well (Brennan et al., 2002, p. 288; Han and Ryu, 2009,
p. 505; Fischer et al., 2004, p. 132; Oldham and Brass, 1979, p. 282), productivity (Ayoko and Hartel, 2003, p. 386; Kamarulzaman et al., 2011, p. 265) and
motivation (Oldham and Brass, 1979, p. 282). Moreover, the structure of an
organisation can affect the behaviour of its organisational members and employees' comfort (Davis, 1984, p. 273). Based on the relevant literature, the physical
structure of a workplace not only influences how people behave and interact
(Davis, 1984, p. 272), but it is also critical in service settings; in other words, it
is the purposeful environment that exists to aid the work of employees' and to
fulfil customers' specific needs and desires (Bitner, 1992ab; Han and Ryu, 2009;
Nguyen, 2006; Völckner et al., 2010).

According to Varlander (2012), the physical structure is significant for a better understanding and conceptualisation of organisational flexibility and individuality which is mandated from top management to suitably design organisational
structures that increase flexibility (p. 36). It should be highlighted that achieving
long-term flexibility is "more costly than delivering short-term functionality, and
planners are now more pragmatic, seeking an appropriate balance between cost
and adaptability requirements" (McDonald, 2006, p. 4). Designers, for instance,
create open offices as flexible spaces; such a layout is a more sensitive approach
and results in changes to the organisational structure and size, since it is more
easily reconfigured at minimal cost to meet changing needs (Ageeva and Foroudi,
2019; Brennan et al., 2002, p. 280).

According to Davis (1984), ambient conditions or physical stimuli are the
intangible physical background settings that intrude into the managers' or organisation members' awareness and are likely to affect their behaviours (p. 274).
The physical stimuli are extremely important factors in many interpersonal service-oriented businesses, such as banks, hospitals and hotels (Bitner, 1992ab).
Environmental psychology research suggests that employees need to have the
opportunity to control task-relevant dimensions of their workplace environment (Elsbach and Pratt, 2007, p. 196), as employees spend long hours in their
workplace (Bitner, 1992a). Undoubtedly, the physical stimuli directly influence
employees' attitudes, behaviours and satisfaction (Brennan et al., 2002) which,
in turn, improve job performance and staff productivity (Brennan et al., 2002;
Elsbach and Pratt, 2007; Kamarulzaman et al., 2011).

Reputation 117

In addition, surrounding conditions need to be a major priority for many managers (Davis, 1984); managers regularly introduce ambient conditions into their workplace environment to counteract negative influences, as well as to function as a reminder "of what needs to be accomplished" (Davis, 1984, p. 275). Ambient conditions or physical stimuli impact on physiological reactions, which can cause comfort or discomfort during the service encounter (Bitner, 1992ab; Nguyen, 2006). This is the reason why, more importantly, managers need to balance employee preferences with customer needs (Bitner, 1992b).

Research method

Data collection

The present study sought to examine how store physical stimuli, spatial layout and functionality, as well as symbolic artefacts may influence the management of corporate reputation. The questions addressed related to respondents' perceptions of these influences on reputation (Foroudi et al., 2020). Conceptualised relationships were evaluated using data collected through a survey of a convenience sample of 489 online and offline UK retail consumers and employees, which was conducted during a four-month period. The retail stores enjoy a favourable reputation from their association with its retailers' brand names (Dennis et al., 2014; Foroudi, 2019; 2020; Foroudi et al., 2016). Therefore, to increase the sample size a non-probability sample was employed, rendering some units in the population more likely to be selected than others (Bryman and Bell, 2007).

To be more specific, 345 face-to-face questionnaires were collected, with questionnaires being considered the most used sampling method in large-scale surveys. Furthermore, one of the researchers approached the shop managers who agreed to help with collecting the data from their employees and customers. The samples were deemed representative of the majority of shoppers in the retail store (Foroudi et al., 2019). According to Stevens (1996), for a rigorous statistical analysis the data sample should consist of more than 300 respondents. Furthermore, Bentler and Chou (1987) state that five cases per parameter are an acceptable sample when the data are perfectly distributed and have no missing or outlying cases. Following the above approach, a total of 523 questionnaires were collected, with 34 being excluded due to large amounts of missing data. Taking into account all the above aspects, the sample size targeted/achieved/reached in this study was 489 respondents. Out of the 489 usable responses, 37.8% came from the 30–39 age group, while 27.2% were completed by respondents of 20 to 29 years old. Moreover, 51.7% of the whole sample were retrieved from men and 48.3% from women. The results also demonstrated that the majority of the participants tend to visit the stores "a few times a year" (34.6%), whereas 27.2% visit stores "a few times a month". In terms of educational background, 65.4% of the respondents held a postgraduate degree and above. Among the sample, a high percentage (29.9%) of the respondents were students, while 14.9% were owners

118 M. M. Foroudi, P. Foroudi and Z. Jin

Table 4.1 Demographic profile of the consumers from retailers of international brands compared with the main population figures (N=489).

	Frequency	%		Frequency	%
Gender			**Degree**		
Female	236	48.3	High school	7	1.4
Male	253	51.7	Undergraduate	162	33.1
Age			Postgraduate and above	320	65.4
19 years old or less	58	11.9	**Job**		
20 to 29 years	133	27.2	Top executive or manager	61	12.5
30 to 39 years	185	37.8	Owner of a company	73	14.9
40 to 49 years	63	12.9	Lawyer, dentist, architect, etc.	65	13.3
50 to 59 years	34	7.0	Office/clerical staff	35	7.2
60 years old or more	16	3.3	Worker	19	3.9
How often do you visit the place?			Civil servant	15	3.1
Five times a week	70	14.3	Craftsman	17	3.5
A few times a week	117	23.9	Student	146	29.9
A few times a month	133	27.2	Housewife	35	7.2
A few times a year	169	34.6	Retired	23	4.7

of a company. More details about the respondents' profile and characteristics are illustrated in Table 4.1.

Survey instrument

The concept of architecture and the three components (physical stimuli, spatial layout and functionality and symbolic artefacts) were adopted from previous studies and validated by Foroudi et al. (2020). Physical stimuli were measured using two constructs: (i) light/aroma/music/temperature/noise (following Bernard and Bitner, 1982a; Bitner, 1992; Brennan et al., 2002; Danielsson and Bodin, 2008; Davis et al., 2010; Davis, 1984) and (ii) security/privacy (based on Ayoko and Hartel, 2003; Booms and Bitner, 1982ab; Davis et al., 2010; Davis, 1984; Knight and Haslam, 2010; Knight and Haslam, 2010; McDonald, 2006; McElroy and Morrow, 2010). On the other hand, spatial layout and functionality was measured through four constructs: (i) layout (Bitner, 1992ab; Booms and Bitner, 1982ab; Brennan et al., 2002; Danielsson and Bodin, 2008; Davis et al., 2010); (ii) location (outdoor) (Brennan et al., 2002; Brown et al., 2005; Davis et al., 2010; Davis, 1984; Duffy and Tanis, 1993; Elsbach and Bechky, 2007); (iii) location entrance (Bitner, 1992a; Davis, 1984; Fayard and Weeks, 2007; McDonald, 2006) and (iv) special comfort (Ayoko and Hartel, 2003; Bitner, 1992a; Booms and Bitner, 1982; Brennan et al., 2002; Davis, 1984; Elsbach and Bechky, 2007). Moreover, two constructs were used to measure symbolic artefacts: (i) art (Baker et al., 1994; Bitner, 1992; Turley and Milliman, 2000; Wakefield and Blodgett,

1999; Wakfield and Baker, 1998) and (ii) interior design/plants/flowers/paintings/pictures/wall/floor/colour/technology (see Ayoko and Hartel, 2003; Bitner, 1992; Brennan et al., 2002; Brown et al., 2005; Davis et al., 2010; Davis, 1984; Duffy and Tanis, 1993; Elsbach and Bechky, 2007; Elsbach and Pratt, 2007; Fayard and Weeks, 2007). At the same time, in order to measure reputation, we employed five items: *I admire and respect the retailer; I trust the retailer; The retailer offers products and services that are good value for money; The retailer is environmentally responsible;* and *The retailer offers high-quality services and products* (Foroudi et al., 2014, 2016).

Content/face validity was examined with the contribution of seven Retail and Marketing academics, who were asked to provide an indication of the adequacy of the questionnaire (DeVellis, 2003) and to ensure that the items were representative of the scale's domain (De Vaus, 2002; DeVellis, 2003). Based on the results of the content/face adequacy assessment retrieved, measurement items were modified and submitted to a scale refinement stage/phase through the actual administration of the questionnaire. The questionnaire contained 7-point Likert scale responses and it was developed to measure the research constructs. Subjects were invited to rate their agreement with each item on a 7-point Likert scale ranging from (1) *Strongly disagree* to (7) *Strongly agree*.

Data analysis methods – fsQCA

Based on complexity theory, this chapter used fuzzy and fsQCA set to adopt a richer perspective regarding the data collected (Foroudi et al., 2016; Gupta et al., 2016; Leischnig and Kasper-Brauer, 2015; Mikalef et al., 2015; Woodside, 2014). Fuzzy set qualitative comparative analysis is a set-theoretic approach employed for/towards obtaining linguistic summarisations/summaries from data that are associated with cases; this is conducted by recognising causal configurations of elements leading to a consequence which develops a set of empirical cases among independent and dependent constructs (Foroudi et al., 2016, 2017). Previous studies ignored contrarian cases when examining data, predicting fit validity and formulating theory (Woodside, 2014). Yet, for this chapter, cross-tabulations were performed by using the quintiles between the research constructs, also employing contrarian case analysis. Table 4.2, which illustrates an example among/related to the location (entrance) and reputation, displays that the correlation coefficients between the two constructs are significant ($p < 0.001$). In addition, Table 4.2 reveals a functional asymmetric association among entrance, location and reputation. The eight cells in the top right and bottom left of the cross-tabulation reveal $14 + 19 + 16 + 7 = 56$; therefore, when reputation is high, entrance location is low. On the other hand, there are $17 + 21 + 17 + 13 = 68$ cases where entrance location is high and reputation is low. Hypotheses are supported statistically; however, there are $56 + 68 = 124$ cases strongly against them, which in fact illustrates the existence of causal asymmetric relationships.

Based on a suggestion made by Lambert and Harrington (1990), we employed the Mann-Whitney U-test to examine the existence of any potential non-response

120   M. M. Foroudi, P. Foroudi and Z. Jin

Table 4.2 **Cross-tabulations employing the quintiles between the constructs**

| | | | \multicolumn{5}{c}{*Percentile group of reputation*} | *Total* |
			1	2	3	4	5	
Percentile group of loclay (location)	1	Count	24	25	15	14	19	97
		% within percentile group of loclay	24.7%	25.8%	15.5%	14.4%	19.6%	100.0%
	2	Count	17	30	17	16	7	87
		% within percentile group of loclay	19.5%	34.5%	19.5%	18.4%	8.0%	100.0%
	3	Count	16	15	12	20	17	80
		% within percentile group of loclay	20.0%	18.8%	15.0%	25.0%	21.3%	100.0%
	4	Count	17	21	10	30	20	98
		% within percentile group of loclay	17.3%	21.4%	10.2%	30.6%	20.4%	100.0%
	5	Count	17	13	10	36	51	127
		% within percentile group of loclay	13.4%	10.2%	7.9%	28.3%	40.2%	100.0%
Total		Count	91	104	64	116	114	489
		% within percentile group of loclay	18.6%	21.3%	13.1%	23.7%	23.3%	100.0%

bias. We collected the first 50 observations, which were taken as early respondents, and the last 50 taken as late respondents. The results demonstrated that the significance value in any variable is not less than, or equal to, 0.5 probability value, thus being insignificant; therefore, there is no statistically major difference between early and late respondents. As a result, in this research non-response bias does not constitute a concern.

Results

Construct validity

A confirmatory factor analysis was conducted to confirm the factor structure of the reflective constructs. The preliminary measurement items underwent a series of factor and reliability analyses as a preliminary investigation of their performance within the entire sample (Melewar, 2001). In brief, all a priori scales demonstrated acceptable reliability (Cronbach's alpha 0.928 > 0.70) and were highly appropriate for the study aims (De Vaus, 2002; Hair et al., 2006). It should be noted that reliability constitutes an essential requirement of validity.

Reputation 121

The two techniques of factor analysis that based on literature support researchers in discovering the variable of interest from a set of coherent subsets, which are relatively independent from each other, are (i) the exploratory factor analysis (EFA) and (ii) the confirmatory factor analysis (CFA) (Hair et al., 2006; Tabachnick and Fidell, 2007). Both of them can be used for structuring groups of variables or data reduction. EFA was employed in our pilot study to help us recognise any pattern in the data (De Vaus, 2002). In the current research, exploratory factor analysis was performed for the items derived from the literature. Initially, the items associated with the architecture and reputation were examined using exploratory factor analysis to contribute to ten theoretically established constructs. Moreover/within that context, Kaiser-Meyer-Olkin (KMO) was tested for appropriateness and truthfulness of the collected data (0.889 > 0.6); also, the Bartlett's test of sphericity (BTS) was significant (BTS = <0.001) and satisfied the required criteria (Tabachnick and Fidell, 2007).

At the same time, CFA was carried out to assess the measurement properties of the existing scales' validity (Churchill, 1979; Gerbing and Anderson, 1988; Hair et al., 2006). According to Hair et al. (2006), CFA is useful towards confirming the theory of the latent variables. Composite reliability is a principal measure used in assessing the overall reliability of the measurement model for every latent construct in the model. In this study, composite reliability measured how well constructs were assessed/evaluated by its assigned items (Fornell and Larcker, 1981). Composite reliability and Cronbach's alpha were calculated to examine the construct level reliability. Results indicate that all measures consistently represent the same latent construct (0.72 > (greater than) 0.7) (Foroudi et al., 2014; Hair et al., 2006). Table 4.3 presents descriptive statistics and correlation coefficients of all variables.

Convergent validity, which is interwoven with the homogeneity of the constructs, was tested in order to identify which independent measures of the same construct converge or are highly correlated. The average variance extracted (AVE) for each construct ranged from 86.48 to 91.43. A good rule of thumb is that an AVE of 0.5 or higher indicates adequate convergent validity. Discriminant validity, on the other hand, can be measured by the AVE for each construct, and compared with the square correlation between them (Fornell and Larcker, 1981 and Hair et al., 2006). Various scholars (see, for example, Anderson and Gerbing, 1988; Bagozzi et al., 1991) state that discriminant validity is present when the relationship between two constructs is significantly lower than 1.00. Discriminant validity, which is the complementary concept to convergent validity, can be used to identify the extent to which measures diverge from other operationalisations whereby the construct is truly distinct from other constructs (Peter and Churchill, 1986; Steenkamp and Van Trijp, 1991). The results of the present research unveiled that the estimated correlations among factors were less than the recommended value of 0.92. In addition, Cronbach's alpha of all measures (0.957 > 0.70) confirmed the internal consistency in each factor (De Vaus, 2002).

Table 4.3 Exploratory and confirmatory factor analysis

Construct	Item code	CFA loading	Mean	STD	AVE	Construct reliability	Square root of AVE	Cronbach @
Spatial layout and functionality (Foroudi et al., 2020)								
Layout								
Table/seating arrangement gives me enough space.		0.817	5.89	1.257	91.43%	0.77	0.96	0.950
The retailer area is located close to people I need to talk to with my shopping.		0.851	5.83	1.215				
The physical layout of the retailer helps make this a nice place to come to shop.		0.802	5.75	1.303				
I like the way rooms are configured.		0.838	5.82	1.301				
Location (outdoor)					82.48%	0.76	0.91	0.910
Outdoor space is attractive.		0.831	5.68	1.265				
The retailer is well located.		0.795	5.33	1.410				
Outdoor space is attractive.		0.731	5.69	1.308				
Outdoor space is suitable.		0.832	5.61	1.292				
Location (entrance)					88.63%	0.95	0.94	0.890
The entrance of the building is convenient.		0.849	5.76	1.474				
The entrance of the building is safe.		0.845	5.77	1.456				
Attractive interior decor and pleasant atmosphere.		0.777	5.68	1.375				
Spatial comfort					89.87%	0.96	0.95	0.854
The size of rooms corresponds to their brand position in the retailer hierarchy.		0.763	5.42	1.533				

(Continued)

Table 4.3 (Continued)

Construct		Item code	CFAloading	Mean	STD	AVE	Construct reliability	Square root of AVE	Cronbach @
	Conditions at the place are appropriate to my shopping.		0.921	5.55	1.575				
	I have enough shopping surface area at the retailer place.		0.912	5.45	1.483				
Physical stimuli									
Light/music/noise/temperature						90.90%	0.96	0.95	0.879
	Temperature is comfortable.		0.909	5.66	1.510				
	Background music is pleasing.		0.882	5.56	1.481				
	Lighting creates a warm atmosphere.		0.814	5.45	1.551				
Privacy/security						89.50%	0.97	0.95	0.949
	I find it hard to concentrate on my shopping.		0.904	5.59	1.328				
	I can talk privately and not be overheard.		0.913	5.59	1.357				
	I feel personally safe and secure coming to and going from retailer.		0.920	5.59	1.361				
	The visual privacy I need to do my shopping is favourable.		0.896	5.65	1.323				
Symbolic artefacts									
Art						88.83%	0.72	0.94	0.918
	The overall design of the retailer building is interesting.		0.776	5.21	1.355				

(Continued)

Table 4.3 (Continued)

Construct		Item code	CFA loading	Mean	STD	AVE	Construct reliability	Square root of AVE	Cronbach @
	Appearance of building and ground are attractive.		0.865	5.15	1.395				
	I like the material the retailer is made off.		0.881	5.29	1.354				
	The design of retailer is functional.		0.866	5.24	1.388				
Interior design plants/flowers/paintings/pictures/wall/floor/colour/technology						87.58%	0.81	0.94	0.957
	Wall decor is visually attractive.		0.863	5.58	1.359				
	Colours used in the wall or ceiling create a warm atmosphere.		0.855	5.57	1.338				
	Floor is of high quality.		0.853	5.57	1.427				
	Colours used in the building create a warm atmosphere.		0.849	5.61	1.306				
	Tables and décor used in the building are of high quality.		0.851	5.56	1.325				
Reputation (Foroudi, 2019; Foroudi et al., 2014, 2016)						90.55%	0.77	0.95	0.918
	I admire and respect the retailer.		0.883	5.59	1.309				
	I trust the retailer.		0.892	5.44	1.443				
	The retailer offers products and services that are good value for money.		0.885	5.40	1.431				
	The retailer is environmentally responsible.		0.781	5.84	1.228				

Table 4.4 Descriptive statistics and correlations (N=489)

	LAYOT	OUTLAY	COMLAY	LOCLAY	PHS	PHSPRCY	ART	INART	CR	Visit	Gender	Age	Degree	Job
LAYOT	1													
OUTLAY	0.496**	1												
COMLAY	0.135**	0.188**	1											
LOCLAY	0.421**	0.315**	0.130**	1										
PHS	0.248**	0.232**	0.113**	0.252**	1									
PHSPRCY	0.221**	0.187**	−0.032	0.148**	0.238**	1								
ART	0.386**	0.477**	0.162**	0.205**	0.194**	0.098*	1							
INART	0.467**	0.399**	0.164**	0.464**	0.183**	0.197**	0.277**	1						
CR	0.361**	0.303**	−0.034	0.183**	0.167**	0.221**	0.243**	0.274**	1					
Visit the place	0.073	0.023	0.100*	0.060	0.053	0.051	0.020	0.090*	−0.052	1				
Gender	−0.054	−0.132**	−0.036	−0.039	−0.050	−0.042	−0.057	0.026	−0.089*	0.087*	1			
Age	−0.031	−0.021	−0.083*	−0.023	−0.027	0.011	0.014	−0.084*	0.076*	0.036	0.056	1		
Degree	−0.088*	−0.049	0.002	-0.124**	0.040	−0.078*	−0.060	−0.067	−0.042	0.009	−0.209**	0.033	1	
Job	0.036	−0.023	−0.061	0.032	0.013	−0.010	−0.017	−0.084*	0.031	−0.043	0.054	0.048	0.075*	1

** Correlation is significant at the 0.01 level (2-tailed).

* Correlation is significant at the 0.05 level (2-tailed).

Note: LAYOUT (physical structure/spatial layout and functionality); OUTLAY (outdoor location); COMLAY (comfort); LOCLAY (location); PHS (physical stimuli/ambient conditions); PHSPRCY (Privacy); ART (symbolic artifacts/decor and artifacts); INART (Interior Design); CR (Corporate reputation).

126   M. M. Foroudi, P. Foroudi and Z. Jin

Fit indices calculate "how well a specified model fits relative to some alternative baseline model" (Hair et al., 2006, p. 749). Attaining "a good fit to observations does not necessarily mean we have found a good model, and choosing the model with the best fit is likely to result in poor predictions" (Wu et al., 2014, p. 1667). Therefore, the "favourable" fit values provide a satisfactory fit to the data: that is, the results of the proposed conceptual model attest that root mean square error of approximation (RMSEA) reveals a value of 0.067 (below 0.08) (Hair et al., 2006); the comparative fit index (CFI) of 0.914, incremental fit index (IFI) of 0.915, Tucker-Lewis (TLI) of 0.907 (Byrne, 2001; Hair et al., 2006), verifying that they are within the acceptable limits and fit is only marginal (Byrne, 2001; Hair et al., 2006; Tabachnick and Fidell, 2007). A normed fit index (NFI) score of 0.880 and relative fit index (RFI) score of 0.870 confirm that the hypothesised model offers an adequate fit for the research empirical data, thus indicating the uni-dimensionality of the measures (Anderson and Gerbing, 1988; Foroudi et al., 2014). According to Gerbing and Anderson (1993), due to a lack of agreement among researchers about the best goodness-of-fit index and because some indices are sensitive to sample size, the best strategy is to adopt several different goodness-of-fit indices.

Findings from fsQCA

In order to examine the data through a fsQCA, in this study authors transformed the conventional variables into fuzzy-set membership scores. Based on Wu et al.'s (2014) recommendations, the principle of calibration was used to adjust extreme scores which were ignored by the respondents. However, only a few cases out of the 489 respondents scored less than 3 on a 7-point Likert scale. Therefore, we set 7 as the threshold for full membership (fuzzy score = 0.95), 4 as the threshold for full non-membership (fuzzy score = 0.50), and 5 as the cross-over point (fuzzy score = 0.50). In an attempt to identify which configurations exhibit high scores in the outcome, we used fsQCA 3.0. In alignment with Wu et al. (2014), we set 2 as the minimum for frequency and 0.85 as the cut-off point for consistency, and then we compared the intermediate solution with a parsimonious solution to find out the peripheral conditions, necessary conditions and core conditions. Table 4.5:

Table 4.5 presents the findings of fsQCA through three types of solutions: (i) a complex solution, (ii) an intermediate solution and (iii) a parsimonious solution. This study employs intermediate solutions, and it calibrated the index of reputation and its negation as outcomes correspondingly, while it employed physical stimuli, spatial layout/functionality and symbolic artefacts as predictor variables. The results yielded support Tenet 2 (Table 4.5). The configurations that lead to high reputation need the presence of at least one architecture causal condition. Along these lines, Table 4.5 presents 13 solutions that have a total of 0.49 in solution coverage and a consistency of 0.81. We thus recommend that the combination of physical stimuli, spatial layout/functionality and symbolic artefacts accounts for a substantive proportion of reputation. Solution 1, for example, suggests that high scores of

Table 4.5 Configurations of physical stimuli, spatial layout/functionality and symbolic artefacts predicting reputation

Model 1 Reputation as outcomes

Configuration Variables	1	2	3	4	5	6	7	8	9	10	11	12	13
Layout	●	●	●	⊗	●	●	●	●	●	●	●	●	⊗
Location (outdoor)		⊗	●	●	⊗	●	●	⊗	●	●	●	●	●
Location (entrance)	●	●		⊗	⊗	●	●	●	●	⊗	⊗	⊗	⊗
Spatial comfort	⊗	⊗	⊗		⊗	⊗	⊗		⊗		⊗	⊗	⊗
Light/music/noise/temperature	⊗			⊗	●	⊗	●	●	⊗	●	●	⊗	●
Privacy/security	●	●	●	●	●	●		●		⊗	⊗	⊗	●
Art	●		●	⊗	●	⊗	●	⊗	●	●	⊗	⊗	●
Interior design		●	●	⊗		●	⊗	●	●	●	⊗	⊗	⊗
Raw coverage	0.21	0.21	0.25	0.14	0.16	0.16	0.16	0.17	0.20	0.15	0.13	0.15	0.14
Unique coverage	0.01	0.01	0.05	0.01	0.02	0.01	0.01	0.02	0.01	0.02	0.01	0.01	0.01
Consistency	0.84	0.87	0.85	0.88	0.89	0.89	0.91	0.86	0.86	0.86	0.91	0.89	0.87
Overall solution coverage	**0.49**												
Overall solution consistency	**0.81**												

Model 2 Negation of reputation as outcomes*

Configuration Variables	1	2	3	4	5	6	7	8	9
Layout	⊗	⊗	⊗	⊗	⊗	●	⊗	●	●
Location (outdoor)	⊗	⊗	⊗	⊗	●	⊗	●	●	●
Location (entrance)	⊗	⊗	⊗	⊗	⊗	●	●	●	⊗
Spatial comfort			⊗	⊗	⊗	⊗	●	●	●
Light/music/noise/temperature	⊗	⊗		⊗	⊗	⊗	⊗	⊗	●
Privacy/security	⊗	⊗	●	⊗	●	⊗	⊗	⊗	⊗
Art		⊗	⊗	●	●	⊗	●	●	●
Interior design	⊗		⊗	⊗		●	⊗	●	●
Raw coverage	0.37	0.27	0.21	0.22	0.13	0.14	0.13	0.14	0.11
Unique coverage	0.06	0.01	0.04	0.00	0.01	0.02	0.00	0.02	0.01
Consistency	0.92	0.97	0.91	0.93	0.94	0.89	0.97	0.89	0.89
Overall solution coverage	**0.51**								
Overall solution consistency	**0.85**								

Note: Black circles indicate the presence of a condition, and circles with "X" indicate its absence. Blank spaces indicate "neither presence nor absence".

layout, location (outdoor), privacy/security, and art, coupled with low scores of spatial comfort and light/music/noise/temperature are sufficient conditions predicting reputation. Solution 2 recommends that joint scores of layout, location (entrance), privacy/security and interior design are sufficient conditions predicting reputation. Moreover, solution 3 suggests that joint high scores of layout, location (outdoor), privacy/security, art and interior design are sufficient conditions predicting reputation. The first solution in model 2 indicates that joint low scores of layout, location (outdoor), location (entrance), location (entrance), light/music/noise/ temperature, privacy/security and interior design can/do predict the non-occurrence of reputation. Solution 2, model 2 provides a similar recipe; yet, it also stresses that joint low scores of layout, location (outdoor), location (entrance), location (entrance), light/music/noise/temperature privacy/security, art and interior design predict the non-occurrence of reputation. The latter result provides a far richer picture compared to the results retrieved from a SEM analysis.

Discussion and implications

The fundamental aim of this research study is to advance the design, retail and marketing literature; it also wishes to address research gaps mostly by providing insights into the potential aspects of architecture (i.e. the physical stimuli, spatial layout/functionality, and symbolic artefacts) as well as its main consequences to reputation from consumers' perspective, examining also theories in a service setting/retail sector to increase a company's external validity.

Theoretical contribution

With respect to the theoretical contributions of the current study, this research aspires to have contributed to the corresponding literature in multiple ways: the findings advance current knowledge by adding alternative insights into service industry views on possible antecedent factors of corporate architecture. Moreover, it offers an empirically validated conceptual model framework (see Figure 4.1) which confirms that the more favourable the architecture is perceived by customers to be, the more favourable the reputation of a company becomes (Elsbach, 2003, 2004; Kioussi and Smyth, 2009; Rooney et al., 2010).

In addition, the present study has acknowledged the following literature gaps in the existing body of knowledge: (i) research on employees and the open-offices phenomenon within the more modern office environment (McElroy and Morrow, 2010, p. 615) is absent in the literature; (ii) a lack of empirical research into how architecture might be defined is also attested; (iii) furthermore, little is known about contemporary changes in office environments (McElroy and Morrow, 2010 p. 612); (iv) there is scarcity of empirical findings on how the introduction of new or re-designed offices may be successfully managed (Davis et al., 2010, p. 221); (v) limited research has been also conducted on the connections between place and the formation of

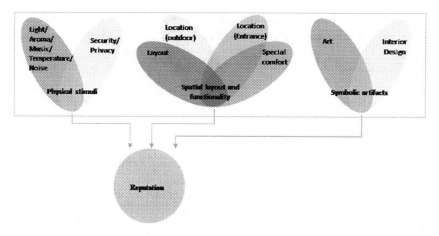

Figure 4.1 Foundational complex configural model.

identities, or how a connection to a place can influence responses to organisational change (Rooney et al., 2010); (vi) there is a small number of studies related to the different levels of significance among the components of the physical environment in predicting outcome variables (Han and Ryu, 2009); (vii) almost no research has explored how employees perceive specific dimensions of workplace identity in work environments that limit the display of personal identity markers (Elsbach, 2003, p. 623); (viii) moreover, in marketing literature there is a total absence of a systematic examination of the relationship between architecture and reputation; and lastly, (ix) literature is lacking in explanatory models and theory building studies in the area of architecture. Against this context, this study constitutes a major empirical examination and has successfully addressed the above research gaps.

It should be highlighted that this research is one of the first studies which examined the configural analysis of architecture based on individual-level data, and which has used the application of complexity theory in individual-level phenomena for theory building (Ageeva et al., 2017; Leischnig and Kasper-Brauer, 2015), exhibiting predictive validity and fit validity. This chapter used CFA and fsQCA analyses to highlight interdependencies and interconnected causal structures between the research constructs (Woodside, 2014) by using complexity theory from a configurational approach (Gunawan and Huarng, 2015; Leischnig and Kasper-Brauer, 2015; Ordanini et al., 2013; Woodside, 2014; Wu et al., 2014).

Managerial contribution

In light of the findings retrieved, this study provides management recommendations to managers dealing with multiple substantive areas, such as design/ architecture, communication, retail, as well as to senior managers whose role is instrumental in planning and delivering the changes that supported the new policy and strategic agenda (Rooney et al., 2010).

Specifically, under the management implications from this research one may find the following: (i) an entity's architecture should be managed strategically and should be in alignment with other visual identity elements (decor and artefacts/symbolic artefacts, spatial layout and functionality/physical structure, and ambient conditions/physical stimuli); (ii) the architecture/image/reputation gap should be constantly and carefully managed; (iii) the architecture/identification (emotional attachment) gap should be regularly monitored. Moreover, this study provides policy/management recommendations for multiple substantive areas in retail settings in the UK. In other words, a clear understanding of the dimensions of the relevant concepts can assist managers in policy development/shaping towards developing a coherent policy for managing favourable architecture which can influence stakeholders' image, reputation and identification. In addition, the findings of this study may also support and shape business policy.

The policy makers, or decision makers, usually define the set of written rules and entitlements to an informal set of standards, according to which organisation members tend to follow each other's example and bargain over who gets what. For instance, furniture selection, placement and seating arrangements may be determined partly by the place's administrative staff, or partly by the individual manager. The control over physical stimuli in the immediate environment, such as over piles of paper, is likely to be more under the control of the individual manager. Symbolic artefacts (such as carpeting and what is put on the walls) may be partially under the control of the manager, and partly determined by the place administrator. Therefore, providing a pleasant and innovative atmosphere and high quality of spaces to customers is required in order to develop and improve stakeholders' perception. Theoretical and empirical insights derived from this research bear several implications for policy makers and managers with regard to architecture, which assists the insights managers have to improve the place. Consequently, policy makers and managers should express a greater concern/ interest in developing a favourable architecture for the retail place which could, in turn, generate a truly positive feeling of the/a place.

Future research directions

The present work represents a preliminary foray into the conceptualisation of *architecture* and *reputation*. Notwithstanding the support that it lends to the research theoretical framework, there are a number of limitations related to this research. To begin with, it is limited in terms of its sole focus on stakeholders' perspective, i.e. its sole focus on a single distinctive sector. Nonetheless/secondly/ additionally, there is certainly a need for future research to scrutinise the variables that have been investigated in the current study. Another limitation of the current research refers to the fact that due to the size of the survey, the empirical study was conducted entirely within a single industry, which inevitably limits the generalisability of the research findings. Another research stream could help

Reputation   131

replicate this study in an additional sector or country in order to examine the generalisability of the findings extracted.

In terms of the research setting, the current research was carried out in a single setting that was limited to the UK context. Although conducting the study in a single setting provides/equips the researcher with better control over market and environmental differences, it does limit the external validity (namely the generalisability of the findings). Another limitation of the current research is that data were collected from convenient samples of customers of a retail store based in London. As such, the study does not allow for the generalisation of the findings. Given the importance and dynamic nature of architecture, future studies should attempt to understand how customers experience service organisations over time, assessing, for instance, customers' perception throughout a variety of consumption stages.

Conclusion

Based on social identity and attribution theories, this study examined the effect of architecture and its components on reputation based on the survey of 489 online and offline UK retail consumers and employees. To accommodate the equifinality and complexity of these relationships, this study employs fuzzy set qualitative comparative analysis (fsQCA), predictive validity and fit validity check. By using such a complexity theory-based configurational approach, the findings highlight interdependencies and interconnected causal structures between the research constructs. The study identifies and confirms key elements of architecture, which influence retailing reputation. It suggests that high scores of layout, location (outdoor), privacy/security and art, coupled with low scores of spatial comfort and light/music/noise/temperature are sufficient conditions predicting reputation. Furthermore, it recommends that joint scores of layout, location (entrance), privacy/security and interior design are sufficient conditions predicting reputation. It also suggests that joint high scores of layout, location (outdoor), privacy/security, art and interior design are sufficient conditions predicting reputation. More importantly, the study indicates that joint low scores of layout, location (outdoor), location (entrance), location (entrance), light/music/ noise/temperature privacy/security and interior design predict the non-occurrence of reputation. These results provide a far richer picture/depiction than the results retrieved via the regression-based approach. The results contribute to managers and academic literature on architecture/design/marketing/place brand management. It also results in/encompasses guidelines for managers on how to create customer value by organising physical stimuli, spatial layout/functionality and symbolic artefacts together in a retail environment. The research makes two key contributions. Firstly, we make a theoretical contribution by recognising the main elements of architecture and their influence on reputation of retailers, and from this to extrapolating key directions for future research. Secondly, this study specifies a number of managerial implications intended to help in/towards the formulation of improved professional practice(s).

CASE STUDY

London Heathrow Terminal 5 is an iconic part of London with a capacity of 30 million passengers a year. Terminal 5 is the busiest and largest free-standing building in the United Kingdom (UK) opened on 27 March 2008 by Queen Elizabeth II. Terminal 5 is owned by British Airways Airline Ltd. The building construction took around four years. Terminal 5 involved the longest public inquiry in British history. It won Skytrax's "World's Best Airport Terminal" prize in 2014 and became an industry-leading building. The building was designed by Rogers, Stirk Harbour & Partners. Rogers structured the building to perfectly combine functionality with its aesthetics. The design was based on the travellers' journey and experience, environmental issues, architectural merit, and maintainability. Terminal 5 is 40m high, 176m wide and 396m long. The building has a single span wave-roof held up by 22 huge steel legs and nodes. It was developed to be an airy and open space with great light and its design features an elegant, curved "floating roof" the size of five football pitches, fantastic views of the airfield and unique structures. The place has a facade which is fully glazed with over 30,000sq metres of 5,500 glass panels or glass (which is coated with a film which controls the amount of sunlight entering the building). Also, the temperature is managed by the interior brise soleil panels (fixed aluminium louvres that act like sun shades, deflecting glare) which were fitted to the exterior (https://www.e-architect.co.uk/london/heathrow-terminal-5, 2020).

Case questions

Please visit website of Terminal 5

1. Can you identify the key components of terminal physical structure/spatial layout and functionality?
2. Can you describe the key components of terminal physical stimuli/ambient conditions?
3. Can you classify the key components of terminal symbolic artefacts/decor and artefacts?
4. To what extent do you think the architectural design of Terminal 5 can impact on travellers' experience?

Key terms and definitions

Architecture is a visual presentation of a company encapsulating a company's purpose and identity, set of elements (physical structure/spatial layout and functionality, ambient conditions/physical stimuli of an environment, and symbolic artefacts/decor and artefacts) which have an influence on internal-stakeholders' attitude and behaviour. It can be decisive in facilitating employees and internal-stakeholders' identification.

Physical structure/spatial layout and functionality is the architectural design and physical placement of furnishings in a building, the arrangement of objects (e.g. arrangement of buildings, machinery, furniture and equipment), the spatial relationships among them, and the physical location and physical layout of the workplace which is particularly pertinent to the service industry and can symbolise something.

Physical stimuli/ambient conditions of an environment in service settings encourage stakeholders to pursue the service consumptions and subsequently can affect employees' behaviours, attitudes, satisfaction with and performance relating to the service provider.

Symbolic artefacts/decor and artefacts are aspects of the physical setting that individually or collectively guide the interpretation of the social setting, can be related to the aesthetics and attractiveness of the physical features of the environment, develop a complex representation of workplace identity and are mainly relevant to the service industry.

Corporate reputation is endowed with a judgement and is the overall evaluation of a company over time.

References

Ageeva, E. and Foroudi, P. (2019) "Examining the destination website: a case of visit Tatarstan", in Foroudi, P., Mauri, C., Dennis, C. and Melewar, T. C. (Eds.), *Place Branding: Connecting Tourist Experiences to Places*, Routledge, UK.

Ageeva, E., Melewar, T. C., Foroudi, P., Dennis, C. and Jin, Z. (2017) "Examining the influence of corporate website favourability on corporate image, corporate reputation, consumer-company identification and loyalty: finding from AMOS-SEM and fsQCA", *Journal of Business Research*, (Just Published).

Akarsu, T. N., Foroudi, P. and Melewar, T. C. (2019) "Rethinking the nexus of TV series/movies and destination image: changing perceptions through sensorial cues and authentic identity of a city", in Foroudi, P., Mauri, C., Dennis, C. and Melewar, T. C. (Eds.), *Place Branding: Connecting Tourist Experiences to Places*, Routledge, UK.

Alessandri, S. W. (2001) "Modelling corporate identity: a concept explication and theoretical explanation", *Corporate Communications: An International Journal*, Vol. 6, No. 4, pp. 173–182.

Anderson, J. C. and Gerbing, D. W. (1988) "Structural equation modelling in practice: a review and recommended two-step approach", *Psychological Bulletin*, Vol. 103, No. 3, pp. 411–423.

Ashforth, B. and Mael, F. (1989) "Social identity theory and the organisation", *Academy of Management Review*, Vol. 14, No. 1, pp. 20–39.

Ayoko, O. B and Hartel, C. E. J. (2003) "The role of space as both a conflict trigger and a conflict control mechanism in culturally heterogeneous workgroups", *Applied Psychology*, Vol. 52, pp. 383–412.

134 M. M. Foroudi, P. Foroudi and Z. Jin

Baker, J., Grewal, D. and Parasuraman, A. (1994) "The influence of store environment on quality inferences and store image". *Journal of the Academy of Marketing Science*, Vol. 22, No. 4, pp. 328–339.

Balmer, J. M. T. (2001) "Corporate identity, corporate branding and corporate marketing seeing through the fog", *European Journal of Marketing*, Vol. 35, No. 3/4, pp. 248–291.

Balmer, J. M. T. (2005) "Corporate brand cultures and communities", in Schroeder, J. E. and SalzerMorling, M. (Eds.), *Brand Culture*, Routledge, London, pp. 34–49.

Balmer, J. M. T. (2006) *Comprehending Corporate Marketing and the Corporate Marketing Mix*, Working Paper, Bradford School of Management, Bradford.

Bagozzi, R. P., Yi, Y. and Phillips, L. W. (1991) "Assessing construct validity in organisational research", *Administrative Science Quarterly*, Vol. 36, No. 3, pp. 21–58.

Bentler, P. M. and Chou, C. P. (1987) "Practical issues in structural modeling", *Sociological Methods and Research*, Vol. 16, No. 1, pp. 78–117.

Bergami, M. and Bagozzi, R. P. (2000) "Self-categorization, affective commitment and group self-esteem as distinct aspects of social identity in the organisation", *British Journal of Social Psychology*, Vol. 39, pp. 555–557.

Bernard, H. B. and Bitner, M. J. (1982) "Marketing services by managing the environment", *Cornell Hotel and Restaurant Administration Quarterly*, (May), pp. 23–35.

Bitner, M. J. (1992a) "Servicescapes: the impact of physical surroundings on customers and employees", *Journal of Marketing*, Vol. 56, pp. 57–71.

Bitner, M. J. (1992b) "The impact of physical surroundings on customers and employees", *Journal of Marketing*, Vol. 56, No. 2, pp. 57–71.

Bonaiuto, M., Breakwell, G. and Canto, L. (1996) "Identity processes and environmental threat: the effects of nationalism and local identity upon perception of beach pollution", *Journal of Community and Applied Social Psychology*, Vol. 6, pp. 157–175.

Booms, B. H. and Bitner, M. J. (1982) "Marketing services by managing the environment", *Cornell Hotel and Restaurant Administration Quarterly*, (May), pp. 23–35.

Brennan, A., Chugh, J. and Kline, T. (2002) "Traditional versus open office design: a longitudinal field study", *Environment and Behavior*, Vol. 34, pp. 279–299.

Brown, G., Lawrence, T. B. and Robinson, S. L. (2005) "Territoriality in organisations", *Academy of Management Review*, Vol. 30, pp. 577–594.

Bryman, A. and Bell, E. (2007) *Business Research Methods*, Second Edition, Oxford University Press, Oxford.

Byrne, B. M. (2001) *Structural Equation Modeling with Amos*, Lawrence Erlbaum Associates, New Jersey.

Churchill, G. A. (1979) "A paradigm for developing better measures of marketing constructs", *Journal of Marketing Research*, Vol. 16, No. 1, pp. 64–74.

Danielsson, C. B. and Bodin, L. (2008) "Office type in relation to health, well-being and job satisfaction among employees', *Environment and Behavior*, Vol. 40, pp. 636–668.

Davis, M. C., Leach, D. J. and Clegg, C. W. (2010) "The physical environment of the office: contemporary and emerging issues", *International Review of Industrial and Organisational Psychology*, Vol. 26, No. 29, pp. 193–237.

Davis, T. R. V. (1984) "The influence of the physical environment in offices", *Academy of Management Journal*, Vol. 9, No. 2, pp. 271–283.

De Vaus, D. (2002) *Surveys in Social Research*, Routledge, London.

Dennis, C., Brakus, J. J., Gupta, S. and Alamanos, E. (2014) "The effect of digital signage on shoppers' behavior: the role of the evoked experience", *Journal of Business Research*, Vol. 67, No. 11, pp. 2250–2257.

DeVellis, R. F. (2003) *Scale Development: Theory and Application*, Second Edition. SAGE, California.

Duffy, F. and Tanis, J. (1993) "A Vision of the New Workplace", *Industrial Development Section*, Vol. 162, No. 2, pp. 1–6.

Edvardsson, B., Enquist, B. and Johnston, R. (2005) "Cocreating customer value through hyperreality in the prepurchase service experience", *Journal of Service Research*, Vol. 8, No. 2, pp. 149–161.

Ellis, P. and Duffy, F. (1980) "Lost office: landscapes", *Management Today*, May, pp. 47–51.

Elsbach, K. D. (2003) "Relating physical environment to self- categorizations: identity threat and affirmation in a non- territorial office space", *Administrative Science Quarterly*, Vol. 48, pp. 622–654.

Elsbach, K. D. (2004) "Interpreting workplace identities: the role of office décor", *Journal of Organisational Behavior*, Vol. 25, pp. 99–128.

Elsbach, K. D. (2009) "Identity affirmation through 'signature style': a study of toy car designers", *Human Relations*, Vol. 62, 1041–1072.

Elsbach, K. D. and Bechky, B. A. (2007) "It's more than a desk: Working smarter through leveraged office design", *California Management Review*, Vol. 49, No. 2, pp. 80–101.

Elsbach, K. D. and Kramer, R. M. (1996) "Members' responses to organisational identity threats: encountering and countering the Business Week rankings", *Administrative Science Quarterly*, Vol. 41, No. 3, pp. 442–476.

Elsbach, K. D. and Pratt, M. G. (2007) "The physical environment in organizations". *Academy of Management Annals*, Vol. 1, No. 1, pp. 181–224.

Fayard, A. L. and Weeks, J. (2007) "Photocopiers and water-coolers: the affordances of informal interaction", *Organization Studies*, Vol. 28, No. 5, pp. 605–634.

Fischer, G. N., Tarquinio, C. and Vischer, J. C. (2004) "Effects of the self-schema on perception of space at work", *Journal of Environmental Psychology*, Vol. 24, pp. 131–140.

Fornell, C. and Larcker, D. (1981) "Structural equation models with unobservable variables and measurement error", *Journal of Marketing Research*, Vol. 18, No. 1, pp. 39–50.

Foroudi, M. M., Balmer, J. M., Chen, W., Foroudi, P. and Patsala, P. (2020) "Explicating place identity attitudes, place architecture attitudes, and identification triad theory", *Journal of Business Research*, Vol. 109 (March), pp. 321–336.

Foroudi, P. (2018) "CORPORATE DESIGN: what makes a favorable university logo?", in Bang Nguyen, TC Melewar and Jane Hemsley-Brown (Eds.), *Strategic Brand Management in Higher Education*, Routledge, UK.

Foroudi, P. (2019) "Influence of brand signature, brand awareness, brand attitude, brand reputation on hotel industry's brand performance", *International Journal of Hospitality Management*, Vol. 76(Jan), pp. 271–285.

Foroudi, P. (2019) "Influence of brand signature, brand awareness, brand attitude, brand reputation on hotel industry's brand performance", *International Journal of Hospitality Management*, Vol. 76, pp. 271–285.

Foroudi, P. (2020) "Corporate brand strategy: drivers and outcomes of corporate brand orientation in international marketing", *International Journal of Hospitality Management*, Vol. 88(July), pp. 1–14.

Foroudi, P., Melewar, T. C. and Gupta, S. (2014) "Linking corporate logo, corporate image, and reputation: an examination of consumer perceptions in the financial setting", *Journal of Business Research (JBR)*, Vol. 67, No. 11, pp. 2269–2281.

Foroudi, P., Gupta, S., Kitchen, P., Foroudi, M. M. and Nguyen, B. (2016) "A framework of place branding, place image, and place reputation: antecedents and moderators", *Qualitative Market Research: An International Journal*, Vol. 19, No. 2, pp. 241–264.

Foroudi, P., Hafeez, K. and Foroudi, M. M. (2016) "Evaluating the impact of corporate logos towards corporate reputation: a case of Persia and Mexico", *Qualitative Market Research: An International Journal*, Vol. 20, No. 2, pp. 158–180.

Foroudi, P., Jin, Z., Gupta, S., Melewar, T. C. and Foroudi, M. M. (2016) "Influence of innovation capability and customer experience on reputation and loyalty", *Journal of Business Research*, Vol.69, No. 11, pp. 4882–4889.

Foroudi, P., Jin, Z., Gupta, S., Foroudi, M. M. and Kitchen, P. J. (2017) "Perceptional components of brand equity: configuring the symmetrical and asymmetrical paths to brand loyalty and brand purchase intention from Latin America", *Journal of Business Research*, (Just Published).

Foroudi, P., Cuomo, M. and Foroudi, M. M. (2019) "Continuance interaction intention in retailing: relations between customer values, satisfaction, loyalty, and identification", *Information Technology and People*, Vol. 33, No. 4, pp. 1303–1326.

Foroudi, P., Yu, Q., Gupta, S. and Foroudi, M. M. (2019) "Enhancing university brand image and reputation through customer value co-creation behaviour", *Technological Forecasting and Social Change*, Vol. 138 (Jan), pp. 218–227.

Foroudi, P., Nazarian, A., Ziyadin, S., Kitchen, P., Hafeez, K., Priporas, C. and Pantano, E. (2020) "Co-creating brand image and reputation through stakeholder's social network", *Journal of Business Research*, Vol. 114 (Jun), pp. 42–59.

Foroudi, P., Stone, M. and Palazzo, M. (2020) "Why and how use mixed-method research?", in Len Tiu Wright (Ed.), *Companion for Marketing Research*, Routledge, UK.

Gioia, D. A. and Thomas, J. B. (1996) "Identity, image, and issue interpretation: sensemaking during strategic change in academia", *Administrative Science Quarterly*, Vol. 41, pp. 370–403.

Graham, S. (1991) "A review of attribution theory in achievement contexts", *Educational Psychology Review*, Vol. 3, No. 1, pp. 5–39.

Gerbing, D. W. and Anderson, J. C. (1988) "An updated paradigm for scale development incorporating unidimensionality and its assessment", *Journal of Marketing Research*, Vol. 25, No. 2, pp. 186–192.

Gerbing, D. W. and Anderson, J. C. (1993) "Monte Carlo evaluation of goodness of fit indices for structural equation models", in K. A. Bollen and J. S. Long (Eds.), *Testing Structural Equation Modems* (pp. 40–65), Sage Publications, CA.

Gupta, S., Malhotra, N. K., Czinkota, M. and Foroudi, P. (2016) "The local brand representative in reseller networks", *Journal of Business Research*, Vol.69, No. 12, pp. 5712–5723.

Hafeez, K., Foroudi, P., Dinnie, K., Nguyen, B. and Parahoo, S. K. (2016) "The role of place branding and image in the development of sectoral clusters: The case of Dubai", *Journal of Brand Management*, Vol. 23, No. 4, pp. 383–402.

Hair, J. F., William, C. B., Barry, B., Rolph, J., Anderson, E. and Tatham, R. L. (2006) *Multivariate Data Analysis*, Pearson, New Jersey.

Han, H. and Ryu, K. (2009) "The roles of the physical environment, price perception, and customer satisfaction in determining customer loyalty in the restaurant industry", *Journal of Hospitality and Tourism Research*, Vol. 33, No. 4, pp. 487–510.

Hoeken, H. and Ruikes, L. (2005) "Art for art's sake?: an exploratory study of the possibility to align works of art with an organisation's identity", *Journal of Business Communication*, Vol. 42, pp. 233–246.

Jones, E. E., Kanouse, D. E., Kelley, H. H., Nisbett, R. E., Valins, S. and Weiner, B. (1972) *Attribution: Perceiving the Causes of Behaviour*, General Learning Press, Morristown, NJ.

Kamarulzaman, N., Saleh, A. A., Hashim, S. Z., Hashim, H. and Abdul-Ghan, A. A. (2011) "An overview of the influence of physical office environments towards employees", *Procedia Engineering*, Vol. 20, pp. 262–268.

Kioussi, S. and Smyth, H. (2009) "Client identification with design and the architecture firm: scoping identification through design-led visualisation", In *Proceedings Proceedings of International Conference Changing Roles: New Roles; New Challenges*, 5–9 October, Delft University of Technology, Rotterdam.

Knight, C. and Haslam, S. A. (2010) "Your place or mine? Organisational Identification and comfort as mediators of relationships between the managerial control of workspace and employees' satisfaction and well-being", *British Journal of Management*, Vol. 21, pp. 717–735.

Laing, A. (2006) "New patterns of work: the design of the office", In Worthington, J. (Ed.), *Reinventing the Workplace* (50–70), second edition, Architectural Press, Oxford.

Lambert, D. M. and Harrington, T. C. (1990) "Measuring nonresponse bias in customer service mail surveys", *Journal of Business Logistics*, Vol. 11, No. 2, pp. 5–25.

Leischnig, A. and Kasper-Brauer, K. (2015) "Employee adaptive behavior in service enactments", *Journal of Business Research*, Vol. 68, No. 2, pp. 273–280.

Marin, L. and Riuz de Maya, S. (2013) "The role of affiliation, attractiveness and personal connection in consumer-company identification", *European Journal of Marketing*, Vol. 47, No 3–4, pp. 655–673.

McDonald, A. (2006) "The ten commandments revisited: the qualities of good library space", *Liber Quarterly*, Vol. 16, No. 2, pp. 2–10.

McElroy, J. C. and Morrow, P. C. (2010) "Employee reactions to office re-design: a naturally occurring quasi-field experiment in a multi-generational setting", *Human Relations*, Vol. 63, No. 5, pp. 609–636.

Melewar, T. C. (2001) "Measuring visual identity: a multi-construct study", *Corporate Communications An International Journal*, Vol. 6, No. 1, pp. 36–41.

Melewar, T. C. (2003) "Determinants of the corporate identity construct: a review of the literature", *Journal of Marketing Communications*, Vol. 9, No. 4, pp. 195–220.

Melewar, T. C. and Jenkins, E. (2002) "Defining the corporate identity construct", *Corporate Reputation Review*, Vol. 5 No. 1, pp. 76–90.

Mikalef, P., Pateli, A., Batenburg, R. S. and Wetering, R. V. D. (2015) "Purchasing alignment under multiple contingencies: a configuration theory approach", *Industrial Management & Data Systems*, Vol. 115, No. 4, pp. 625–645.

Nguyen, N. (2006) "The perceived image of service cooperatives: an investigation in Canada and Mexico", *Corporate Reputation Review*, Vol. 9, No. 1, pp. 62–78.

Nguyen, N. and LeBlanc, G. (2002) "Contact personnel, physical environment and the perceived corporate image of intangible services by new clients", *International Journal of Service Industry Management*, Vol. 13, No, 3/4, pp. 242–262.

Oldham, G. R. and Brass, D. (1979) "Employee reactions to an open-plan office: a naturally occurring quasi-experiment", *Administrative Science Quarterly*, Vol. 24, No. 2, pp. 267–284.

Ordanini, A., Parasuraman, A. and Rubera, G. (2013) "When the recipe is more important than the ingredients a Qualitative Comparative Analysis (QCA) of service innovation configurations", *Journal of Service Research*, Vol. 17, No. 2, pp. 134–149.

Peter, J. P. and Churchill Jr, G. A. (1986) "Relationships among research design choices and psychometric properties of rating scales: A meta-analysis", *Journal of Marketing Research*, Vol. 23, No. 1, pp. 1–10.

Pittard, N., Ewing, M. and Jevons, C. (2007) "Aesthetic theory and logo design: examining consumer response to proportion across cultures", *International Marketing Review*, Vol. 24, No. 4, pp. 457–473.

Ragin, C. C. (2006) "Set relations in social research: evaluating their consistency and coverage", *Political Analysis*, Vol. 14, No. 3, pp. 291–310.

Ragin, C. C. (2008) *Redesigning Social Inquiry: Fuzzy Sets and Beyond*, Chicago University Press, Chicago.

Rooney, D., Paulsen, N., Callan, V. J., Brabant, M., Gallois, C. and Jones, E. (2010) "A new role for place identity in managing organisational change", *Management Communication Quarterly*, Vol. 24, No. 1, pp. 44–73.

Sadalla, E. K. and Sheets, V. L. (1993) "Symbolism in building materials: self-representational and cognitive components", *Environment and Behavior*, Vol. 25, No. 2, pp. 155–180.

Saleh, M. A. E. (1998) "Place identity: the visual image of Saudi Arabian cities", *Habitatitnl*, Vol. 22, No. 2, pp. 149–164.

Speller, G. M., Lyons, E. and Twigger-Ross, C. L. (2002) "A community in transition: the relationship between spatial change and identity process", *Social Psychology Review*, Vol. 4, No. 2, pp. 39–58.

Stedman, R. C. (2002) "Towards a social psychology of place: predicting behaviour from place-based cognitions, attitude and identity", *Environment and Behavior*, Vol. 34, pp. 561–581.

Steenkamp, J. B. E. and Van Trijp, H. C. (1991) "The use of LISREL in validating marketing constructs", *International Journal of Research in Marketing*, Vol. 8, No. 4, pp. 283–299.

Stevens, J. (1996) *Applied Multivariate Statistics for the Social Sciences*, Lawrence Erlbaum, New Jersey.

Tabachnick, B. G. and Fidell, L. S. (2007) *Using Multivariate Statistics* (5th ed.), Allyn and Bacon, New York.

Tajfel, H. (1981) *Human Groups and Social Categories*, Cambridge University Press, Cambridge.

Tajfel, H. (1982) *Social Identity and Intergroup Relations*, Cambridge University Press, Cambridge.

Turley, L. W. and Milliman, R. E. (2000) "Atmospheric effects on shopping behaviour: a review of the experimental evidence", *Journal of Business Research*, Vol. 49, No. 1990, pp. 193–211.

Twigger-Ross, C. L. and Uzzell, D. L. (1996) "Place and identity processes", *Journal of Environmental Psychology*, Vol. 16, pp. 205–220.

Twigger-Ross, C. L., Bonaiuto, M. and Breakwell, G. M. (2003) "Identity theories and environmental psychology", in Bonnes, M., Lee, T. and Bonaiuto, M. (Eds.), *Psycho-Logical Theories for Environmental Issues*, Ashgate, Aldershot, pp. 203–234.

Van den Bosch, A. L. M., De Jong, M. D. T. and Elving, W. J. L. (2005) "How corporate visual identity supports reputation", *Corporate Communications: An International Journal*, Vol. 10, No. 2, pp. 108–116.

Varlander, S. (2012) "Individual flexibility in the workplace: a spatial perspective", *Journal of Applied Behavioral Science*, Vol. 48, No. 1, pp. 33–61.

Vischer, J. C. (2007) "The effects of the physical environment on job performance: towards a theoretical model of workplace stress", *Stress and Health*, Vol. 23, pp. 175–184.

Völckner, F., Sattler, H., Hennig-Thurau, T. and Ringle, C. M. (2010) "The role of parent brand quality for service brand extension success", *Journal of Service Research*, Vol. 13, No. 4, pp. 379–396.

Wakefield, K. L. and Baker, J. (1998) "Excitement at the mall: determinants and effects on shopping response", *Journal of Retailing*, Vol. 74, No. 4, pp. 515–539.

Wakefield, K. L. and Blodgett, J. G. (1994) "The importance of servicescapes in leisure service settings", *Journal of Services Marketing*, Vol. 8, No. 3, pp. 66–76.

Wakefield, K. L. and Blodgett, J. G. (1999) "Customer response to intangible and tangible service factors", *Psychology and Marketing*, Vol. 16, No.1, pp. 51–68.

Walsh, K., Enz, C. A. and Canina, L. (2008) "The impact of strategic orientation on intellectual capital investments in customer service firms", *Journal of Service Research*, Vol. 10, No. 4, pp. 300–317.

Woodside, A. G. (2014) "Embrace perform model: complexity theory, contrarian case analysis, and multiple realities", *Journal of Business Research*, Vol. 67, No. 12, pp. 2495–2503.

Wu, P. L., Yeh, S. S. and Woodside, A. G. (2014) "Applying complexity theory to deepen service dominant logic: configural analysis of customer experience-and-outcome assessments of professional services for personal transformations", *Journal of Business Research*, Vol. 67, No. 8, pp. 1647–1670.

Zomerdijk, L. G. and Voss, C. A. (2010) "Service design for experience-centric services", *Journal of Service Research*, Vol. 13, No. 1, pp. 67–68.

5 Conceptualising sensory brand experience

Using review of knowledge fields to identify potential future research direction

Dongmei Zha, Pantea Foroudi, Zhongqi Jin and T C Melewar

Introduction

This chapter aims to propose a conceptual framework for sensory brand experience. We will start with a review of the seven knowledge fields deemed to have constitutive influences on the development of sensory brand experience literature, followed by a discussion based on a two-dimensional integrative framework which also serves as a research template for future research.

Background

The contemporary business environment has become highly competitive as firms search for new ways to connect consumers with their brands. The use of sensory brand experiences (SBE) represents an increasingly important means for firms to differentiate themselves from competitors in the crowded market space. From the Mini car museum in Oxford offering a multisensory 360-degree experience with a full complement of smells and sounds of vintage Minis to craft beer brands offering virtual SBE tours of their heritage breweries, companies are fast discovering the effectiveness of SBE. However, in spite of the prevalence of these SBE ideas at both practitioner and applied levels, some of the most fundamental questions remained unanswered.

(i) What are the factors contributing to a positive SBE? (ii) What is the impact of SBE on consumption behaviour? (iii) What moderates the impact of SBE on consumer behaviour? Bringing a conceptual framework to this ubiquitous marketing phenomenon is the purpose of this study. Conceptualising a *cocktail* concept – SBE presents many challenges. First, the roots of SBE research can be traced back to a diversity of domains including atmospherics (e.g. Foroudi et al., 2019), information processing theory (e.g. Mollen and Wilson, 2010), experiential marketing (e.g. Schmitt, 2011), hedonic consumption (e.g. Yoganathan, Osburg and Akhtar, 2019), service experience (e.g. Iglesias, Markovic and Rialp, 2019), brand experience (e.g. Foroudi et al., 2016) and is composed of four distinct dimensions: sensory, affective, intellectual and behavioual. Sensory brand experience has mainly been examined as a dimension of

Conceptualising sensory brand experience 141

brand experience (e.g. Barnes et al., 2014) that can create an impressive experience for consumers and then generate satisfaction and loyalty, and sensory marketing (e.g. Krishna, 2012). The broad spectrum of knowledge that underlies the SBE concept implies that the design of a framework needs to incorporate the many strands of thought and research traditions that make up its intellectual structure.

Conceptualising a compound concept inevitably leads to questions of core and peripherality. For decades, theses domains have seen their pathways intersect and interface (Lindstrom, 2005), but never purposefully investigated as a unified stand-alone concept. The first signs of this theoretical convergence emerged when Brakus et al. (2009) injected branding as an integral component into the study of consumption experience conceptualising brand experience as a subjective response evoked by brand-related stimuli embedded in the external environment. Based on this parent concept, this chapter defines SBE as *a transfer of affective brand meaning, from the meaning maker to the consumer via a multisensory setting to characterise the meaning of the brand in the consumer's mind.* Only when we recognise the transfer of affective brand meaning as the unifying logic, can we find the thread to link the multivariate antecedents, processing and outcomes of SBE to build a meaningful and cohesive theoretical infrastructure (Deshpande, 1983).

The objectives of this chapter are the following: (1) to examine SBE intellectual structure showing the diversity of intellectual inputs; (2) to highlight and investigate gaps and inconsistencies in the SBE intellectual structure with the goal of building sound SBE theoretical infrastructure; and (3) to present an integrative framework for future undertakings bringing into focus the outstanding knowledge gaps that need research attention. Specifically, this study provides four essential contributions. First, this study makes an important contribution to the SBE theory by providing a knowledge guide on how one can meaningfully access SBE literature. Second, this chapter advances branding theory by asserting the primacy of SBE in shaping brand relationship, brand preference and brand favourability through a multisensory characterisation of brand meaning (Batra, 2019; Möller and Herm, 2013). While much research work has been focused on the role of the affective and cognitive dimensions of brand experience (e.g. Hepola, Karjaluoto and Hintikka, 2017; Morrison and Crane, 2007), this study shows it is in the early stages of the consumer environment interface where the important groundwork for brand experience has been laid. Finally, although our primary purpose is to advance theory, it is also our intent to provide managerial inputs by articulating SBE for marketers in the experience economy. Peter and Olson (1983) suggested that a good way to assess the value of a theory is to check whether the theory made sense when its core principles were simulated based on an actual event. At the end of this chapter, a section is dedicated to managerial implications highlighting three areas of managerial applications: (1) the implications of SBE logic for marketers; (2) implications of a multisensory environment; and (3) generalisability of SBE application.

Sensory brand experience: *a review of knowledge fields*

Previous attempts at conceptualising SBE have assumed a single paradigm approach; the sensory marketing (SM) framework proposed by Hultén (2011) is anchored in sensory marketing's multimodality model of visual, audio, olfactory, taste and haptic cues. The hypothesised structural model in Iglesias et al. (2019) is grounded in the brand experience framework; whereas the consumer environment paradigm describes the interaction between an external stimulus and the organismic response evoked, the same environment reframed in a branding paradigm becomes a firm-based *brand setting*, staged, manipulated and encoded to characterise the meaning of a brand. Whereas sensory marketing focuses on how information processed at the sensorimotor level (visual, auditory, olfactory, taste and haptic) has perception-altering qualities, hedonic consumption describing the same multisensory processes, adds an overlay of interoceptive psychological states into the processing of product and brand information. As Table 5.1 shows, these emphasise specific facets of SBE in seven knowledge fields, including brand experience, experiential marketing, consumption studies, information processing theory, sensory marketing, consumer environment studies and service marketing. Among the studies in these seven knowledge areas, some are paradigms, some are approaches, some are established domains; as a general rule, in this study we label each as a knowledge field.

Brand experience

The conceptual foundation of SBE is the brand experience. SBE first appeared in Brakus et al. (2009) as one dimension of the brand experience construct. To understand the nature of SBE, to first understand the concept of brand experience, Brakus et al. (2009) conceptualised brand experience as "subjective, internal consumer responses (sensations, feelings, and cognitions) and behavioural responses evoked by brand related stimuli that are part of a brand's design and identity, packaging, communications, and environments" (p. 53). The authors identified the instantiation of these brand-related sensations, feelings and cognitions as taking place in locations where the symbols of brands are visible. Visibility of a brand image should include salient features such as brand name, company logo, brand-specific colours, choice of typeface and also include peripheral features such as design backdrop, mascots and characters, product packaging, brochures, advertisements, websites and environments where brand symbols are present (Morrison and Crane, 2007).

The authors (Brakus, Schmitt and Zarantonello, 2009) differentiated the brand experience from other consumer experiences by defining it as "experiences provided by brands" (p. 53). An SBE then is a sensory experience provided by a brand. This idea, simple as it might appear, has profound implications. For decades, consumption studies (Akaka and Schau, 2019; Carù and Cova, 2003; Skandalis, Byrom and Banister, 2016) assumed a brand-neutral approach. The assumption was that consumer behaviour theory would be better served without

Knowledge field	Theoretical contributions	Implications for SBE research	Exemplars
Brand experience	• A subjective response to brand-related stimuli • 4 dimensions: sensory, affective, intellectual, behavioural • Outcome variables • Moderated by brand personality	• Brand experience is the conceptual foundation of SBE • SBE is a brand-driven approach • SBE is a subjective internalised response involving sensation, perception and feeling states • SBE instantiations take place at different levels of consumer-brand interaction	Brakus et al., 2009Iglesias et al., 2011Dolbec and Chebat, 2013Dennis et al., 2014Ding and Tseng, 2015Das et al., 2019
Experiential marketing	• A managerial firm-driven approach • Experience marketing's logic is engaging transactions • Sees symbols as resources • Value to customer: memorable customer experiences	• A brand meaning-driven approach • Marketer as manufacturer of brand meaning and manipulator of meaning-encoded brand symbols • Value to customer: co-created brand meaning	Pine et al., 1998 Schmitt, 1999Zarantonello and Schmitt, 2010, 2013 Lanier and Hampton, 2009
Consumption studies	• Includes both explicit and implicit psycho-physical processes • Hedonic experience is multisensory and imaginal • Exteroception and interoception	• Conceptual foundations for the nature of experience • Implications of implicit processing for SBE-derived information • SBE conceived as a multisensory interoceptive feeling state	Hirschman and Holbrook, 1982Holbrook and Hirschman, 1982Arnould and Price, 1993 Cova and Cova, 2012
Information processing	• Consumer learning through direct product experiences • The hypothesis testing model • Haptics-derived information and product judgements • Aesthetic evaluation	• Product-based stimuli as antecedent • The moderating effect of aesthetics on SBE instantiation and information processing	MacInnis and Price, 1987Peck and Childers, 2003b; Peck and Wiggins, 2006; Petit et al., 2019; Yoganathan et al., 2019; Jin and Phua, 2015

(*Continued*)

Table 5.1 (Continued)

Knowledge field	Theoretical contributions	Implications for SBE research	Exemplars
Consumer environment	• Store atmospherics' impact on consumption behaviour • Application of the S-O-R model in retail setting • The influence of the transactional environment • Sense of place and intangible influences	• Transfer of atmospheric stimuli onto perceptions of products and brands • S-O-R model demonstrates the relationship between the environment and behaviour • The intangible influence of ecosystems on SBE	Donovan et al., 1994Mattilaa and Wirtz, 2001 Puccinelli et al., 2009
Sensory marketing	• Sensation and perception • Understanding the psycho-physical process underlying consumption experience • Characterising of abstract notions of product	• Psychological boundaries of SBE • The product-based stimuli antecedent to SBE • Purpose of SBE – to characterise the brand meaning in the customer's mind	Hultén et al., 2009 Krishna and Schwarz, 2014Peck and Johnson 2011 Hultén, 2011Krishna, 2012
Service marketing	• Customer-centric perspective • The human dimensions in a service setting • The concept of servicescape • Co-creativity	• Customer-centric perspective of the environment • The different levels of social dynamics at work in a retail environment • SBE outcomes are co-created	Bitner et al., 1990Nysveen et al., 2013Vargo and Lush, 2008

Conceptualising sensory brand experience   145

the encumbrance of commercialism that came with the brand variable (Belk, 1987; Holbrook, 1987). With the brand variables taken into consideration in the consumption experience, the dynamics changed. A brand contains two basic functions, identity and differentiation (Davis and Chun, 2003). When a product is given an identity, no matter how rudimentary, it is turned into a brand. A brand is differentiated by articulating its uniqueness and presenting it as an offering that is widely valued by buyers (Porter, 1985). The articulation of a product's uniqueness, its individuality and its special character (Alderson, 1957), constitutes the essence of brand meaning.

Experiential marketing

Brakus et al.'s (2009) paper is an ideational derivative, a theoretical extension as it were (Schmitt, 2009) of the experiential marketing concept presented by Schmitt (1999) a decade earlier. Experiential marketing's important contribution to the SBE concept is the articulation of a managerial, firm-driven approach. In the experiential marketing paradigm, the firm is the source of brand origination (McCracken, 1988). The experience providers are marketers with communication, design and marketing expertise (Schmitt, 1999). They decide on the brand meanings they wish to portray and build a set of symbols around them (Lanier and Hampton, 2009). These symbols are carriers of brand meanings. Marketers are responsible for the manipulation of these brand symbols so that they become a consortium of sensory cues (visual, auditory, tactile, taste and olfactory), to evoke brand-related sensations, feelings and cognitions in the customer's mind.

Experiential marketing's managerial approach broadly corresponds with Pine and Gilmore's (1999) economy experience model, where the emphasis is also on the manipulation of symbolic resources to stage a memorable customer experience. While the prevailing description used in their study is *themed experiences*, the different dimensions of a customer experience broadly correlate with the types of experience in experiential marketing. The two typologies (experiential marketing and economy experience), articulated as four dimensions in Brakus et al.'s (2009) paper, would eventually become the ideational seedbed for the emergence of the SBE concept.

Consumption studies

In spite of the nescience regarding SBE, its roots are deep, going back to the consumption literature of the early 1980s. Consumption experience, to which brand experience and SBE are conceptually related, can be conceived as a managerial response to a sea-change in the marketing landscape occasioned by the growing focus on experience in consumer behaviour studies (Cova and Cova, 2012). This swing towards the experiential has been widely credited to the work of the two co-authors (Holbrook and Hirschman, 1982; Hirschman and Holbrook, 1982) who were among the first to advocate the study of experience as an integral part of consumer research. In the first, on the nature of experience, Holbrook and

146 *Zha, Foroudi, Jin and Melewar*

Hirschman (1982) suggested that, to understand the nature of experience, it was crucial for researchers to recognise the role of implicit processes in the human psyche, including unconscious thoughts, automatic responses and imaginal representations. In a later reflection and summary (Holbrook, 2018), the author reiterated that the purpose of the paper was to make the case that the various states of feeling, including amazement, curiosity, shock, anger, anxiety and disgust, influence our consumption behaviour more than we would like to admit.

In the second, Hirschman and Holbrook (1982) defined hedonic experiences as consumer behaviour facets related to multisensory product experiences, where *multisensory* refers to receiving experiences in *multiple sensory modalities*, this definition of hedonic experience has all the hallmarks of an SBE – a subjective product-use response, or a multisensorial experience. From this perspective, hedonic consumption can be perceived as a precursor to SBE. But there is a fundamental difference. Whereas hedonic consumption is product-evoked, SBE is brand-evoked. One is a consumer-centred view; the other a firm-centred view. One looks at the fun, *feeling and fantasy* aspects of hedonic experience; the other examines the experience of fun, feeling and fantasy derived from *brand meanings*.

Information processing theory

In contrast to the multisensorial nature of hedonic experience, early information processing models in consumer research were basically *non-modal* and assumed vision to be the primary receptor (Childers and Houston, 1984; MacInnis and Price, 1987). Interest in the multisensory dimensions of product experience came to the fore when researchers started looking at how consumers processed, encoded and integrated information at the product experience level to arrive at product judgements (Bloch and Richins, 1983). Hoegg and Alba (2011) examined how perceptions of product form had an impact on product judgements, while Hoch and Ha (1986) investigated the relationship between advertising and direct product experiences.

Research in product experiences paved the way for a multimodal research approach incorporating the five senses (Hoch and Deighton, 1989). McCabe and Nowlis (2003) were the first to point out and examine the fact that besides product aesthetics, which are essentially visual, the material properties of products. For instance, roughness, hardness, temperature and weight provided an important source of product information not available through other sensual modalities (Grohmann, Spangenberg and Sprott, 2007). Furthermore, McCabe and Nowlis (2003) compared decision-making in a remote consumption environment with decision-making in an in-store environment and found that the availability of tactile information was the prime differentiator. Research into tactile information, also called sensory attributes, led to Peck and Childers's (2003a) development of the *need for touch* scale.

In addition to product information, the sense of touch provides consumers with brand-related information. For some brands, unique tactile features have become brand identifiers. For example, for decades millions of consumers have

Conceptualising sensory brand experience   147

used the tactile recipe provided by the grooves on the iconic CocaCola's coke bottle to distinguish it from other drinks. Another example is McDonald's choice of potato, which gives its chips a unique masticating quality that consumers worldwide instinctively identify with the fast-food brand. Most recently, studies (Jin and Phua, 2015; Petit, Velasco and Spence, 2019; Yoganathan, Osburgand and Akhtar, 2019) have also demonstrated how new technology provided through the sense of touch has an impact on brand evaluation in the online environment.

Sensory marketing

The changes taking place in consumer behaviour research led to the emergence of the sensory marketing approach in the mid-1990s. While the focus of the information processing model is on processes that take place at higher cognitive levels, sensory marketing concentrates its investigations on a level lower, in areas involving sensation and perception (Spence et al., 2014). By taking an experimental approach, the work of sensory marketing at the microscopic level has created a valuable knowledge base cataloguing the psycho-physical processes underlying the more subtle aspects of consumer behaviour (for a taxonomic review, see Krishna, 2012). For example, this approach has elucidated how our preference for certain products may be biased by perceptions of elongated packaging. Other studies have focused on how scenting improves brand recall (Krishna, Lwin and Morrin, 2010), how the size of labels, large or small, influences levels of consumption (Aydinoğlu and Krishna, 2012), and how oral haptics, mastication and orosensory perception influence food choice and consumption volume (Biswas et al., 2014). This accrual of micro-level knowledge provides a crucial empirical and psychological undergirding for SBE research.

While most of these studies (e.g. Krishna et al., 2017; Krishna, Elder and Caldara, 2010; Kwon and Adaval, 2017) are product based, sensory marketing has also looked at the influences of indirect product experiences. An understanding of how advertising copy influences sensory thoughts and taste (Elder and Krishna, 2009), the effects of visual depiction (Elder and Krishna, 2011) and the impact of imagined odours on consumer response have profound implications for SBE research. Observing the ability of unimodal reception (e.g. watching a KFC advertisement) to stimulate a multimodal internalised response – gustative, olfactory or even auditory sensations – changes the way we think of a multisensory experience. This ability to generate internalised multisensory stimulation at the response level opens up multiple possibilities into how sensory cues can be manipulated to achieve the desired effects (Stein et al., 2010).

Although sensory marketing's theoretical contribution has been limited, the few published works have contributed immensely to SBE knowledge by addressing some of the most elemental issues of the field. For example, Krishna's (2012) incisive comment on the unique capability of multisensory experiences "to create subconscious triggers that can characterize consumer perceptions of abstract notions of the product" (p. 2) has far-reaching implications for research into the nature and role of SBE. While the roots of sensory marketing are in information

148 Zha, Foroudi, Jin and Melewar

processing, grounded cognition theories are an important theoretical substrate of the domain (for a full review, see Krishna and Schwarz, 2014). Although references to grounded cognitive studies in the SBE literature have been scattered and sparse, their inputs have been crucial in key areas of research such as inter-conception processes, mental simulation and the reenactment of perpetual experiences in multisensory dimensions.

Consumer environment studies

The atmospherics taxonomic approach provides a much-needed matrix for analysing environmental factors antecedent to SBE. Although Kotler (1973) might not have been the first to come up with the term *atmospherics* (Kotzan and Evanson, 1969; Martineau, 1958; Smith and Curnow, 1966), the coining of the term stirred the imagination of the marketing community (Turley and Milliman, 2000). By noting the subtle ability of perceived sensory qualities emanating from the environment to modify buyers' information and emotions, Kotler (1973) ignited the conversation on environmental stimuli. Taking inspiration from Kotler (1973), Donovan and Rossiter (1982) provided the *meat and flesh* to the study of atmospherics by applying the Stimulant-Organism-Response (S-O-R) model borrowed from environmental psychology (Mehrabian and Russell, 1974) to a retail store setting. The S-O-R approach, rooted in Barker's (1968) ecological theories, sees the interaction of an organism with its environment as a loop, originating in distal objects in the environment, extending via sensation events at the sensory surfaces, being processed at the organismic level and directing behavioural responses to the distal object in the environment (Gibson, 1966). In the intervening years, many studies have used Donavan and Rossiter's (1982) approach to study different types of music (Yalch and Spangenberg, 1990), colours (Bellizzi and Hite, 1992) and the personality and emotional state of shoppers. These findings were further reinforced by the work of Wakefield and Baker (1998), whose field study of shopping malls gave empirical grounding for the observation that environmental variables such as shop mix, ambience and interior decor are linked to excitement and repeat mall visits.

We also note the contribution of Baker et al. (2002), whose retailing studies model showed a deeper integrative effort. Retail marketing literature has traditionally been more focused on the improvement of store atmosphere through the manipulation of sensory cues like scents, music, tactile and visual inputs to enhance affective customer response. Baker (1998) articulated the need for a concurrent examination of the factors that contribute to the functional and transactional elements in the store environment, including the influence of price, assortment and the perceived value of the store. While Sherry and McGrath's (1989) concept of *sense of place* brought an embodied perspective to the study of atmospherics, and also provided the conceptual background for recognising the impact of socio-cultural factors antecedent to SBE.

At the meta-analytical level, Turley and Milliman's (2000) taxonomy of "facility-based environmental cues" represents the most comprehensive to date. The

Conceptualising sensory brand experience   149

structure of their taxonomic exercise is premised on the work of Berman and Evans (1995), who provided a schema to classify different types of stimuli, differentiating the store exterior from the general interior, general design and overall layout, point-of-purchase counters and interior decor variables. Turley and Milliman (2000) also included human variables in the revised typology; while Spence et al.'s (2014) application of sensory marketing's multisensory approach to the study of store atmospherics provided an alternative checklist with a typology based on visual atmospherics, auditory atmospherics, olfactory atmospherics, taste atmospherics, tactile atmospherics and multisensory atmospherics. Most recently, a meta-analysis of store atmospherics gives us an overview of the outcome variables prevalently tested in the store atmospherics literature (Roschk, Loureiro and Breitsohl, 2017).

Service marketing

In addition to the inputs from store atmospherics, the contributions from service marketing have provided a customer perspective to the study of environment-based influences on consumption behaviour. In the late 1980s, service marketing experienced explosive growth (Berry, 2000; Fisk et al., 1993; Vargo and Lush, 2008) as it entered a period of new assertiveness, prompting researchers to extend their scope beyond the confines of the service industry (Vargo and Lush, 2004). It was within the historical context that Bitner's (1992) concept of *servicescapes* redefined the conversation on consumers' interaction with the environment. But the concept advanced on the existing environmental psychology model by integrating both the physical and social aspects of a service environment. Bitner's (1992) framework, taken from a customer service perspective, saw customers and employees, and their interactions within the service environment, as one integrated *servicescapes*. Building on Bitner's (1992) model, Tombs and McColl-Kennedy's (2003) social *servicescapes* included the physical and social components in the environment. The social component was later broken down into various types of social interactions in the consumption environment including customer-to-customer (Nicholls, 2010), employee-to-customer (Venkatraman and Nelson, 2008), human density (Ardley et al., 2012), dyadic (Sosa, 2011), and customers' perception of service personnel, including compatibility of looks, appearance and behaviour. Some studies have emphasised the moderating role of the prototypical employee (Liao and Chuang, 2004). In addition to executing core tasks such as the knowledge of products, providing service for customer needs and providing customer support to help them achieve their goals, the employee also plays a critical role in shaping customers' perception of the brand (Spiro and Weitz, 1990; Bitner et al., 1990). Building on this incremental accrual of service-driven knowledge, Verhoef et al. (2009) developed a model of customer experience that included the following factors: retail brand and customer experiences.

Discussion and future research directions

From the discussion above, the proposed framework (see Figure. 5.1) offers a two-dimensional perspective, indicating where and how the contributions from each

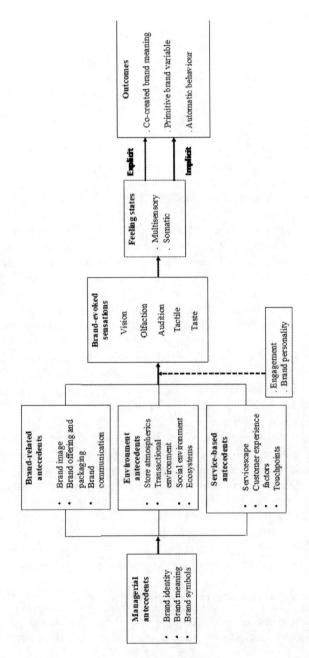

Figure 5.1 An integrative framework of sensory brand experience.

Conceptualising sensory brand experience 151

knowledge field fit into the anatomy of the SBE intellectual structure, antecedents, processes and outcomes. At the same time, the framework also serves as a template to highlight research priorities, identify gaps and provide portals of relevant theories pertinent to these research concerns, with the goal of facilitating future undertakings in SBE research.

The discussion is organised into the following categories: (1) the antecedents of SBE, (2) the nature of SBE, (3) the processing of SBE information and (4) the outcomes of SBE. At the end of each discussion, research gap suggestions and prompters are provided.

Antecedents of SBE: *managerial, brand-related symbols, environmental, service-based*

We propose three antecedents that have a causal effect on SBE: (1) managerial antecedents, (2) brand-related antecedents, (3) environmental antecedents and (4) service-driven antecedents. Expressing the theoretical causality between them, we see managerial antecedents as first order (brand identity, brand symbols, brand meaning) and the other three knowledge fields as second order; these are brand-related antecedents (brand image, brand offering and packaging, brand communication), environment antecedences (store atmospherics, transactional environment, social environment, ecosystems) and service-drive antecedents (servicescapes, customer experience factors, touchpoints).

From an SBE perspective, managerial antecedents are a priori. SBE favourability is contingent on the marketer's ability to deliver a meaning-driven multisensory experience. In our model, the marketer is first and foremost a generator of brand meaning, a *meaning maker*. From a firm-based perspective, SBE can be conceived as a transfer of brand meaning, from the meaning maker to the consumer. For example, Weetabix, a UK-based company, markets the Alpen brand of muesli as a Swiss-style product, which can be safely assumed to have an intended brand meaning that it offers a *taste of Swiss lifestyle*. To that end, the marketer goes about developing a set of symbols with multisensory qualities: the sound symbolism of the brand name *Alpen* evokes the *Swiss Alps*; the visual image of the rustic curvy typeface on the logo evokes traditional Swiss culture; the gustative stimulation from images of muesli descending into a bowl evokes a Swiss family breakfast; the backdrop of pristine snow-covered mountains on the packaging evokes an aspirational Swiss lifestyle. The effectiveness of this consortium of sensory cues in characterising the brand meaning is contingent on the marketer's ability to manipulate and manage these meaning-encoded symbols.

From this managerial perspective, items from the next three knowledge fields – brand-related, environmental and service-driven antecedents – become resources that the marketer actively conscripts to characterise brand meaning. Items from Brakus et al.'s (2009) study include brand symbols such as brand name, brand-identifying colours, shapes and typefaces, product and packaging, websites, digital signage etc. In addition to symbols, items drawn from store atmospherics or consumer environment studies represent sensory cues that the marketer can harness

152   *Zha, Foroudi, Jin and Melewar*

from the environment, including the brand's soundscapes (e.g. in-store music and sounds), ambient scent (e.g. a smell or fragrance), touch (e.g. temperature) and taste (e.g. in-store tastings). Service-driven sensory cues derived from services-capes and customer experience theories include customer/employee interactions, customer/customer interactions, employees' appearance and disposition, human density and crowds.

The challenge for SBE research in the next phase of its development is the integration of the variables drawn from each knowledge field into an SBE-specific antecedent framework. At the local level, some integrative and cross-domain work has already started (Spence et al., 2014; Turley and Milliman, 2000; Verhoef et al., 2009). For example, Turley and Milliman (2000) integrated ideas from the atmospherics literature into a services marketing context, and Verhoef et al's (2009) study offered an integrated model based on the customer experience perspective, while Spence et al.'s (2014) paper applied the principles of sensory marketing into a store atmospherics context.

Among other urgent tasks is the integration of product-based antecedents. A taxonomic review to systematise the research findings from sensory marketing will be very helpful. The integration of intangible factors in the brand environment is another potential research area. As a result of technology, brands today are exposed to the influences of a host of socio-cultural and technological ecosystems, including social media, payment ecosystems (e.g. credit cards, Apple Pay), merchandising ecosystems (e.g. Groupon, Star Alliance loyalty programme), country-of-original effects, terroir influences (Melewar and Skinner, 2018) and sense of place influences. The integration of these factors represents a research gap.

Finally, developing a SBE-specific taxonomy of antecedents will take more than just the amalgamation of items from the existing taxonomies: an SBE-based taxonomy needs a new SBE logic. One way of reframing the scatter of items is to identify the levels where SBE instantiation takes place. These might include brand signature level, product level, value proposition level, environment level, social dynamics level and ecosystem level.

Research gap 1a: Research on SBE should examine the creation of a taxonomic framework to categorise product-based and brand-related stimuli.

Research gap 1b: Research on SBE should examine the antecedents drawn from different knowledge fields.

The nature of SBE: *sensation, perception and feeling states*

To the best of our knowledge, *no published paper has yet offered a fresh definition* of SBE: all have chosen to extrapolate on the *brand experience* definition and see their work as an extension of the parent construct. Hultén (2011) is the only scholar to offer a definition as "an individual's perception of goods or services or other elements in a service process as an image that challenges the human mind

Conceptualising sensory brand experience 153

and senses" (p. 258). However, on closer inspection, this appears to be more an elaboration than a theoretical proposition.

It would seem that in the interests of expediency, SBE researchers have simply transcribed features and characteristics of the parent concept onto the SBE concept without re-visiting the ontological architecture of the construct. In our view, this methodology is inadequate for the task. To conceptualise SBE as an independent and differentiated variable, researchers need to revisit the psychological processes underlying the SBE construct.

To achieve this research goal, sensory marketing offers us a solution through the use of a processual perspective. Krishna (2012) identified that the concept of sensation and perception is essentially processual, the author saw sensation and perception as stages in the processing of product or brand information. Besides consumer psychology, this processual view of experience has another anecdotal precedence. Behavioural economics examining the impact of changes in intensity over time on experience (Ariely, 1998; Varey and Kahneman, 1992) have segmented overall experience into experience episodes, or what are known as *hedonic profiles*, to track the difference between segmented response (e.g. every ten minutes) and overall evaluation of the experience (Ariely and Zauberman, 2003).

In addition to sensation and perception, Hirschman and Holbrook's (1982) paper on the nature of hedonic experience expanded on the processual view by highlighting the interaction-dominant nature of SBE processes as having both afferent (inward effect) and efferent (outward effect) qualities. According to the paper, hedonico-sensory stimuli not only evoke sensations, but they set off a chain of interoceptive events resulting in "feeling states". These interoceptive body-mind processes are essentially autonomic and preconscious, resulting in feeling states that are imaginal in representation. This paper posits that the resultant feeling states comprising "multisensory images, fantasies and emotional arousal" (p. 93) provides the co-ordinates for a multisensory characterisation of the meaning of the brand.

This processual view of experience provides us with a vocabulary enabling us to speculate where SBE begins and where it ends. We suggest that the circumspect of SBE's psychological boundaries should be somewhere within the bounds of sensations, perceptions and interoceptive feeling states. Therefore, conceptualisation of the nature of SBE should include the following: (1) a multisensory response to meaning-encoded cues in the environment; (2) interoceptive processing of brand-evoked information resulting in feeling states and (3) the characterisation of the intended brand meaning based on the visceral and implicit inputs from these feeling states. Therefore, we conceptualise SBE as the transfer of an intended brand meaning, from the meaning maker to the consumer, via a multisensory and interoceptive processing of meaning-encoded cues in the environment, with the goal of characterising the meaning of the brand in the consumer's mind. This psychological profile of SBE broadly corresponds with the *hedonic response* in hedonic consumption, the subjective brand-evoked response in the brand experience (BE) literature and the characterising of abstract notions described in the sensory marketing model.

154   *Zha, Foroudi, Jin and Melewar*

Research gap 2: The investigation into the interoceptive processes underlying SBE represents a research gap.

Information processing: *explicit and implicit processing*

We suggest that three types of information processing mechanisms are operative in the knowledge fields: the consumer learning model, the associative network theory (ANT) of memory (Keller, 1993), and the S-O-R model. The influence of the consumer learning model is expressed as a research group (Group 3), while the workings of the ANT model are implied in the BE literature, where the authors predicated the BE framework on Aaker's (1997) brand personality theory, which is basically ANT-denominated. Hoch and Deighton's (1989) paper, from Group 3, conceptualised consumer learning as a hypothesis testing process whereby new brand information appeared constantly to challenge the veracity of one's existing brand beliefs and described them as a kind of information "hypotheses". The source of these hypotheses can be the media, the internet, word of mouth or product experiences which obviously include SBEs. For example, if a regular customer of Costa is invited to Starbucks and finds its SBE more positive than anticipated, this new hypothesis challenges their existing beliefs about their choice of cafe. Erdem et al.'s (1999) comparative review of the consumer learning model and the brand equity model showed that the concept of hypotheses largely corresponded with the concept of *brand nodes* in Keller's (1993) brand equity model, where a brand's cognitive and affective attributes are gradually assimilated through a process of association. Both models provide a theoretical basis for the processing of SBE-prompted information at the explicit cognitive level.

However, many studies have now shown that consumer learning and information retention form a two-track process, incorporating both conscious and unconscious modes of processing (Krishnan and Chakravarti, 1999). Two types of implicit processing have been distinguished in the cognitive psychology literature (Bargh, 1997): intuitive learning and preconscious processing. Both forms can operate without conscious effort and cognitive directives, but intuitive learning requires intention to act while preconscious processing does not (Bargh and Chartrand, 1999). Alba and Hutchinson's (1987) paper on the dimensions of consumer expertise refers to the learned mental skill model, describing automaticity as the "overlearning of very specific skills" (p. 413). According to the authors, the automatic response happens through the repeat learning of tasks with minimum variation. With practice, these tasks become more efficient over time, until they can operate without conscious monitor (Anderson, 1983; Shiffrin and Schneider, 1977; Smith and Lerner, 1986). However, research on preconscious processing has shown that these processes are not just effortless but take place in the absence of any level of awareness (Treisman, 1960). This implicit processing of information, and its influence on consumer behaviour and preferences, has been well-documented in many of the experimental studies on sensory marketing. In particular, studies have shown that the acquisition of brand knowledge may occur through automatic, unconscious mechanisms, for example how

Conceptualising sensory brand experience 155

scenting influences automatic brand recall (Krishna et al., 2010). Since SBE's characterisation of brand meaning is primarily implicit, a deeper level of understanding in this area represents a vital research gap in the SBE literature.

> *Research gap 3: Research on SBE should examine the integrative work between the consumer learning model, association memory network model and S-O-R environment psychology model as they relate to the processing of brand-evoked meaning.*

> *Research gap 4: Research on SBE should understanding the implicit processing of SBE-derived information.*

Outcomes of SBE: *co-created meaning, primitive brand variables and automatic behaviour*

Each knowledge field has a choice set of outcome variables tested and operationalised by researchers in their own respective fields. A meta-analysis of 256 quantitative BE studies in 73 papers published between 2009 and 2015 (de Oliveira Santini et al., 2018) showed a positive influence of BE on the following outcomes: brand satisfaction, brand trust, brand loyalty and word of mouth. Roschk et al.'s (2017) meta-analysis of the store atmospherics literature identified four frequently studied shopping outcomes: arousal, pleasure, satisfaction and behavioural intentions. The question therefore arises as to what some of the outcome variables are specific to the SBE model. Based on inputs from the three processing mechanisms, we list three criteria for consideration.

Firstly, when determining SBE outcomes, candidate variables should show a level of automaticity. In one sensory marketing study investigating how touch interface affected choice of food, Shen et al. (2016) found a correlation between affective response and sensorimotor mechanism: in other words, elements of the affect had a direct physiological impact on behaviour. Other studies have shown a proclivity for automatic behavioural response when the stimulus is affective and hedonic denominated. The automaticity of behavioural response is also an important feature of Mehrabian and Russell's (1974) S-O-R model, while Holbrook et al.'s (1984) study exploring compatibility levels between the hedonic experience and S-O-R models found automaticity as a feature linking the variables in both. Environmental psychology theory sees the stimulant (S), organismic states (O) and behavioural response (R) as a continuum (Holbrook et al., 1984). These continuous processes are autonomic, one setting off another, without the need for higher cognitive processing and representation. Depending on the temporal proximity of the outcome to the point of instantiation, the levels of automaticity may vary in intensity. Vargas et al.'s (2008) three types of implicit cognition can be conceived as three levels of automaticity: (1) consumers may be unaware that the stimulus in the environment is biasing their behaviour; (2) they may be unaware of the intermediary processes between the stimulus and outcome; and (3) they may be unaware of the outcome. For SBE studies, this represents a new frontier of research.

156   *Zha, Foroudi, Jin and Melewar*

Secondly, in determining SBE outcome variables, we looked for the early prototypes of existing brand variables. One solution may be to review the choice sets of variables in the BE literature and work backwards to locate these primitives (Fletcher et al., 2000). For example, Brakus et al. (2009) identified satisfaction and loyalty as two outcome variables of BE. Satisfaction is a post-consumption evaluative based on a hedonic scale starting with the feeling state of *pleasant* (see Oliver and Swan, 1989; Westbrook and Oliver, 1991). While both cognitive and emotional components are present in the formation of satisfaction responses, we can assume that, in the early stages, the emotive content exceeds the cognitive content. Researchers have noted that the regularity with which respondents in studies have used the adjective "satisfied" to assess pleasantness or other positive emotions gives grounds to promote the variable "pleasant" as a "primitive" precursor of satisfaction. Wirtz et al. (2000) saw pleasure as the basic organismic strata in the S-O-R model, and arousal as having an amplifying effect on pleasure. Studies have shown that when consumers experience pleasure, they intend to become more loyal, and have a greater intent to recommend (Chitturi et al., 2008). *Pleasure* may therefore be another candidate variable. In brand equity models, favourability is a valenced variable detected early in the brand association process (Keller, 1993). Dacin and Smith (1994) further explained that consumers' favourability towards a brand was "the most basic of all brand associations" (p. 230) and was at the centre of "conceptualizations of brand equity" (p. 230). Favourability can therefore also be conceived as a primitive brand variable. Like the pleasure variable, it is also valenced and represents a kind of early organismic response to external cues (Amato and McInnes, 1983; Mehrabian and Russell, 1974). Other variables include brand preference, identified in previous studies as a precursor of brand choice (Louviere et al., 2000).

Thirdly and finally, SBE outcome variables should show early signs of co-creativity. In Keller's (1993) brand association model, uniqueness is identified as one of the most important qualities of association. Unique associations are important because they differentiate the brand from competitors (Broniarczyk and Alba, 1994; Farquhar, 1989; Keller, 1993). However, this uniqueness is realised only when the unique value of a brand or its brand meaning are co-created in the consumer's mind (Sayin and Gürhan-Canlı, 2015). Marketers instil meaning into brands, but it is consumers who creatively reinterpret and infuse aspects of the self into the brand meaning (Ligas and Cotte, 1999). We speculate that for most people, this co-created brand meaning will remain implicit because of the inherent viscerality of SBEs. The eventual emergence from imaginal representation to ideational may signal the transition of an SBE to brand experience.

Research gap 5a: Research on SBE should examine the relationship between automaticity and SBE brand variables..

Research gap 5b: Research on SBE should examine the operationalisation of the outcome variable co-created brand meaning.

Moderators: brand personality and engagement

In extant literature, two variables have been identified by researchers and deemed to have a moderating effect on SBE – brand personality and engagement. In Brakus et al. (2009), the authors deliberated on the role of brand personality as a moderator in the brand experience model and found sufficient empirical evidence to support their choice of moderator. Engagement is a well-attested psychological feature of a hedonic experience. In an interpretative study of 20 experiential marketing offerings, once a consumer feels or senses the relevance of a brand, it provides a motive to know more about the brand (Celsi and Olson, 1988; Greenwald and Leavitt, 1984). In the interpretive study of ten experiential products (Lanier and Hampton, 2009) such as amusement parks, concerts, parks, concerts, cruises and zoo, data consistently show *engagement* as having a moderating influence on experiential offerings.

Managerial implications

In addition to the chapter's conceptual contributions to SBE theory and research, as set out in the discussion above, the SBE model has significant implications for the marketing practitioner in the field.

Firstly, this chapter underscores the important role of the marketer in the SBE process. By providing the end-to-end conceptual framework of the SBE process from managerial antecedents to brand outcome, we enable the marketer to understand his or her role, and to see how all parts of the process fit together to achieve the company's objectives. Whether it is Ikea's *Scandinavian lifestyle* or Alpen cereal's *taste of Swiss lifestyle*, a dream, an aspiration or a fantasy, it is the marketer who decides on the intended meaning of the brand. As this manager of brand meaning, the marketer is responsible for mobilising and organising a host of symbols into a consortium of sensory cues with the goal of instantiating SBEs at every possible level of customer interaction (Chattopadhyay and Laborie, 2005; Meyer and Schwager, 2007). Brand meaning is not the result of natural occurrence or happenstance, but of clear purpose, obsession with details and execution.

Secondly, the study contributes to managerial knowledge by highlighting the immeasurable possibilities and potential of a multisensory approach (Lindstrom, 2005). The SBE approach sees a transaction environment as a multisensory environment. In an SBE environment, nothing is left to chance: every single item in the store is sensorially primed to produce the optimal SBE effect. For example, when customers walk into a Starbucks cafe, they are entering an artificial environment surrounded by a host of brand-encoded sensory cues: the logo, based on a 16th-century seafarers' symbol, is there to intimate a desire for world travel; the ambience, lighting and colour cues are not only for aesthetics, but are signals pregnant with meaning; the background jazz music and the haptic information from the texture of the sofas have been carefully designed to simulate a certain feel; the coffee from Guatemala, Ethiopia and Bali connects you to a globalist culture. This consortium of cues is hard at work to instantiate an SBE in consumers' minds: *You are a member of a global fraternity, a cool jazz elite with a globalist outlook.* By understanding the inner workings of a multisensory process, the practitioner becomes better informed and better equipped to exploit the spectrum of sensory cues to project the intended meaning of the brand.

Thirdly and finally, this chapter contributes to managerial knowledge through the application of SBE logic. The application of a method may be limited to the context of its use. Logic, on the other hand, is the abstraction of a methodology and therefore can be adapted to different kinds of business circumstance (Prahalad and Ramaswamy, 2004). SBE logic works equally well with all types of product offerings, experiential product offerings and experiential offerings. It is equally effective in different types of consumption environments, from large corporations to small- and medium-sized enterprises and even to individuals, including in digital environments. For example, wearing an "SBE hat" reveals the logic behind the design of a successful website like *booking.com* which has designed brand instantiations at every level of interaction: the brand signature is blue, inferring reliability and efficiency; the hotel ambience captured in the photos is intended to induce a sense of pleasure; the pop-up message "Last 2 rooms" is meant to generate excitement and a psycho-physical reaction; the information "viewed by 49 people" creates the feeling that there are "other customers" in the digital vicinity; descriptions of London link consumers to the city's ecosystem; information on what other guests like links them to the world traveller ecosystem. These sensory cues did not occur by chance. They are part of a carefully planned digital environment where the cues work in concert to instantiate a unique SBE in the customer's mind: "You are a member of a trusted hotel booking network".

Conclusion

As research interest in SBE continues to grow, this study makes a unique contribution to theory as the first comprehensive review of the SBE literature and related knowledge fields. First, in line with our goal of presenting an anatomy of the intellectual structure of SBE, articulating its antecedents, processes and outcomes, we have delineated the prior knowledge fields, determining what is core and what is peripheral. This means we now have an anatomical view of SBE's theoretical infrastructure. However, an anatomical view is not a functional view: a functional view perceives the structure as the whole, its role and dynamic. Therefore, secondly, by providing an end-to-end vision of SBE, from managerial antecedents to brand outcomes, we have been able to articulate its function clearly. Finally, this study has differentiated SBE as a construct from other related constructs. While experiential marketing is experience-driven, motivated by the goal of producing engaging and memorable transactions (Lanier and Hampton, 2009), SBE is brand meaning-driven. While service marketing is customer-centric, with a worldview that pivots on the question "what value can the customer realize from the transaction?" (Vargo and Lush, 2008), SBE is brand

Conceptualising sensory brand experience 159

meaning-centric, with a worldview that pivots on the question of what they want the customer to sense about the brand. The differences are not simply perceptual but essential. SBE is not simply the juxtaposition of three separate concepts, sensory, brand and experience: it is a new logic (Merz et al., 2009).

While we recognise brand experience as the foundation of the SBE concept, SBE must move beyond its reliance on BE theories and work towards its own theoretical infrastructure, in order to better capture the nuances and issues specific to SBE phenomena. We see this chapter as part of this exciting initiative. For a concept to be given its proper place in the field of study, it must undergo the rigours of conceptualisation and the burnishing of its assumptions in the court of academic inquiry (Smith, 2003). This chapter has taken one step in that direction, but much more work needs to be done.

CASE STUDY

When you pick up a pack of *Alpen Swiss Style Muesli*, you are *walking* into a defined brand setting (see Figure 5.2). This consortium of sensory cues (auditory, visual, tactile, gustative, olfactory), also called the brand gestalt is designed to generate an affect map in your mind to characterise the intended meaning of the brand.

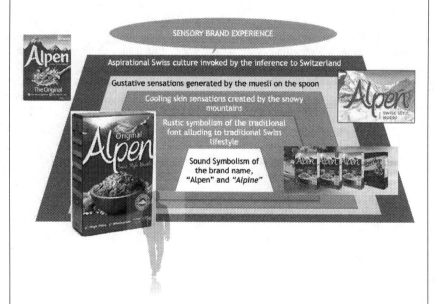

Figure 5.2. Brand setting of Alpen Swiss Style Muesli.

Concerning the sound symbolism of the brand, the name *Alpen* evokes images of the iconic Swiss Alps through the auditory correlate, *alpine*. The font used to illustrate the brand name is cursive and traditional, a visual cue alluding to the pastoral fantasies of isolated Alpine hamlets and villages. The image of the snowy peaks in the background transports you to the tranquillity of the pristine Swiss mountains. This world evoked by the packaging generates a cross-modal cooling sensation across the surface of your dermatological system. The sight of muesli cereal descending on a spoon and spilling over evokes a gustative sensation of plenitude and abundance. All the sensory cues work together to instantiate a sensory brand experience in your mind and in the process transfer a consortium of affects to simulate a virtual world of Continental lifestyle skiing and Alpine lodges. This packaging implies that if you consume Alpen muesli, you are ingesting aspirational Swiss culture. This intended meaning of the brand, however, is not created by a Swiss company; it is actually created by a UK-based food manufacturing company, Weetabix.

Case questions

1. How does the visual cue of the fruits behind the bowl of muesli add to the intended meaning of the brand?
2. Why you do think the marketer choose "Swiss lifestyle" as the intended meaning of the muesli brand?
3. Based on the above illustration, identify and illustrate the brand setting of another product using this multisensory affect map as a guide.

Key terms and definitions

Sensory brand experience: a response to the transfer of affects via a brand setting characterising the meaning of the brand in the consumer's mind (Brakus et al., 2009; Hulten, 2011; Schmitt, 1999).

Visual stimuli: aesthetic elements relating to store design including space design, lighting, colour, displays, placement of merchandise, furniture and decoration variables which are part of an overallstore's sensorial expression including design, packaging, style, colour, light, theme, graphics, exterior and interior (Brakus et al., 2009; Hulten, 2011).

Auditory stimuli: hearing and listening stimuli present in retail settings realised in the context of music, words or voices and ambient background sounds (noise, service or product sounds, noise levels by talking consumers or environmentally naturally occurring retail sounds) which are part of a store's overall sensorial expression including jingles, voice and music atmosphere, attentiveness and thematic and signature sounds and sound brand (Bartholmé and Melewar, 2011; Hulten, 2011).

Conceptualising sensory brand experience 161

Olfactory stimuli: the application of pleasure odours through ambient scenting techniques with sensorial expressions including product congruence, intensity and sex atmosphere, advertency and theme and signature brand scent (Spangenberg et al., 2005)

Tactile stimuli: the sense of touch which enables the perceptual differentiation of material, surface temperature, weight and steadiness. Touch is also defined as sensations aroused through the stimulation of receptors in the skin, as one of the first of our human senses to develop and the largest sensory organ it is often regarded as one of our most intimate senses, involving physical contact with the skin, with the hands playing a major role as our "principal source of input to the touch perceptual system" (Peck and Childers, 2003a).

Taste stimuli: taste attraction or taste aversion involving multisensory inputs. A single negative reaction to something eaten can lead to consistent long-term avoidance while a positive reaction can recall highly positive experiences of food consumption perhaps more rich and vivid than a single auditory, visual, olfactory or tactile experience (Spence et al., 2014).

Corporate sensory identity: the totality of sensory cues by which an audience can recognise the company and distinguish it from others (Bartholmé and Melewar, 2011)

Brand meaning: a complete network of brand associations in the consumer's mind produced by the consumer's interactions with the brand and communications about it (Batra, 2019; Keller, 2003)

References

Aaker, J. L. (1997). Dimensions of brand personality. *Journal of Marketing Research*, 34(3), 347–356.

Akaka, M. A. and Schau, H. J. (2019). Value creation in consumption journeys: recursive reflexivity and practice continuity. *Journal of the Academy of Marketing Science*, 47(3), 499–515.

Alba, J. W. & Hutchinson, J. W. (1987). Dimensions of consumer expertise. *Journal of Consumer Research*, 13(4), 411–454.

Alderson, W. (1957). *Marketing Behavior and Executive Action*, Richard D. Irwin, Homewood, IL.

Amato, P. R. & McInnes, I. R. (1983). Affiliative behavior in diverse environments: a consideration of pleasantness, information rate, and the arousal-eliciting quality of settings. *Basic and Applied Social Psychology*, 4(2), 109–122.

Anderson, J. R. (1983). A spreading activation theory of memory. *Journal of Verbal Learning and Verbal Behavior*, 22(3), 261–295.

Ardley, B., Taylor, N., McLintock, E., Martin, F. & Leonard, G. (2012). Marketing a memory of the world: Magna Carta and the experiential servicescape. *Marketing Intelligence & Planning*, 30(6), 653–665.

Ariely, D. (1998). Combining experiences over time: the effects of duration, intensity changes and on-line measurements on retrospective pain evaluations. *Journal of Behavioral Decision Making*, 11(1), 19–45.

Ariely, D. & Zauberman, G. (2003). Differential partitioning of extended experiences. *Organizational Behavior and Human Decision Processes*, 91(2), 128–139.

Aydinoğlu, N. Z. & Krishna, A. (2012). Imagining thin: why vanity sizing works. *Journal of Consumer Psychology*, 22(4), 565–572.

Baker, J. (1998). Examining the informational value of store environments. *Servicescapes: The Concept of Place in Contemporary Markets*, 3(4), 55–79.

Baker, J., Parasuraman, A., Grewal, D. & Voss, G. B. (2002). The influence of multiple store environment cues on perceived merchandise value and patronage intentions. *Journal of Marketing*, 66(2), 120–141.

Bargh, J. A. (1997). Automaticity in social psychology. In E. T. Higgins & A. W. Kruglanski (Eds.), *Social Psychology: Handbook of Basic Principles*, Guilford Press, New York, pp. 109–183.

Bargh, J. A. & Chartrand, T. L. (1999). The unbearable automaticity of being. *American Psychologist*, 54(7), 462.

Barker, R. G. (1968). *Ecological Psychology: Concepts and Methods for Studying the Environment of Human Behavior*, Standford University Press, Stanford, CA

Barnes, S. J., Mattsson, J. & Sørensen, F. (2014). Destination brand experience and visitor behavior: testing a scale in the tourism context. *Annals of Tourism Research*, 48, 121–139.

Bartholmé, Roland H. & Melewar, T. C. (2011). Remodelling the corporate visual identity construct. *Corporate Communications: An International Journal*, 16, 53–64.

Batra, R. (2019). Creating brand meaning: a review and research agenda. *Journal of Consumer Psychology*, 29, 535–546.

Belk, R. W. (1987). Material values in the comics: a content analysis of comic books featuring themes of wealth. *Journal of Consumer Research*, 14(1), 26–42.

Bellizzi, J. A. & Hite, R. E. (1992). Environmental color, consumer feelings, and purchase likelihood. *Psychology & Marketing*, 9(5), 347–363.

Berman, B. & Evans, J. R. (1995). *Retail Management: A Strategic Changes to the Retail Environment are All That Is Required to Approach*, 6th Edition, Prentice-Hall, Inc., Englewood Cliffs, NJ. Change how shoppers behave inside a store.

Berry, L. L. (2000). Cultivating service brand equity. *Journal of the Academy of Marketing Science*, 28(1), 128–137.

Biswas, D., Labrecque, L. I., Lehmann, D. R. & Markos, E. (2014). Making choices while smelling, tasting, and listening: the role of sensory (dis) similarity when sequentially sampling products. *Journal of Marketing*, 78(1), 112–126.

Bitner, M. J. (1990). Evaluating service encounters: the effects of physical surroundings and employee responses. *Journal of Marketing*, 54(2), 69–82.

Bitner, M. J. (1992). Servicescapes: the impact of physical surroundings on customers and employees. *Journal of Marketing*, 56(2), 57–71.

Bitner, M. J., Booms, B. H. & Tetreault, M. S. (1990). The service encounter: diagnosing favorable and unfavorable incidents. *Journal of Marketing*, 54(1), 71–84.

Bloch, P. H. & Richins, M. L. (1983). A theoretical model for the study of product importance perceptions. *Journal of Marketing*, 47(3), 69–81.

Brakus, J. J., Schmitt, B. H. & Zarantello, L (2009). Brand experience: what is it? How is it measured? Does it affect loyalty? *Journal of Marketing*, 73(3), 52–68.

Broniarczyk, S. M. & Alba, J. W. (1994). The importance of the brand in brand extension. *Journal of Marketing Research*, 31(2), 214–228.

Celsi, R. L. & Olson, J. C. (1988). The role of involvement in attention and comprehension processes. *Journal of Consumer Research*, 15(2), 210–224.

Chattopadhyay, A. & Laborie, J. L. (2005). Managing brand experience: the market contact audit™. *Journal of Advertising Research*, 45(1), 9–16.

Childers, T. L. & Houston, M. J. (1984). Conditions for a picture-superiority effect on consumer memory. *Journal of Consumer Research*, 11(2), 643–654.

Chitturi, R., Raghunathan, R. & Mahajan, V. (2008). Delight by design: the role of hedonic versus utilitarian benefits. *Journal of Marketing*, 72(3), 48–63.

Carù, A. & Cova, B. (2003). Revisiting consumption experience: a more humble but complete view of the concept. *Marketing Theory*, 3(2), 267–286.

Cova, B. & Cova, V. (2012). On the road to prosumption: marketing discourse and the development of consumer competencies. *Consumption Markets & Culture*, 15(2), 149–168.

Dacin, P. A. & Smith, D. C. (1994). The effect of brand portfolio characteristics on consumer evaluations of brand extensions. *Journal of Marketing Research*, 31(2), 229–242.

Das, G., Agarwal, J., Malhotra, N. K. & Varshneya, G. (2019). Does brand experience translate into brand commitment?: a mediated-moderation model of brand passion and perceived brand ethicality. *Journal of Business Research*, 95(2), 479–490.

Davies, G. & Chun, R. (2003). The use of metaphor in the exploration of the brand concept. *Journal of Marketing Management*, 19(1–2), 45–71.

de Oliveira Santini, F., Ladeira, W. J., Sampaio, C. H. & Pinto, D. C. (2018). The brand experience extended model: a meta-analysis. *Journal of Brand Management*, 25(6), 519–535.

Dennis, C., Brakus, J. J., Gupta, S. & Alamanos, E. (2014). The effect of digital signage on shoppers' behavior: the role of the evoked experience. *Journal of Business Research*, 67(11), 2250–2257.

Deshpande, R. (1983). Paradigms lost: on theory and method in research in marketing. *Journal of Marketing*, 47(9), 101–110.

Ding, C. G. &Tseng, T. H. (2015). On the relationships among brand experience, hedonic emotions, and brand equity. *European Journal of Marketing*, 49, 994–1015.

Dolbec, P. Y. & Chebat, J. C. (2013). The impact of a flagship vs. a brand store on brand attitude, brand attachment and brand equity. *Journal of Retailing*, 89(4), 460–466.

Donovan, R. & Rossiter, J. (1982). Store atmosphere: an environmental psychology approach. *Journal of Retailing*, 58, 34–57.

Donovan, R. J., Rossiter, J. R., Marcoolyn, G. & Nesdale, A. (1994). Store atmosphere and purchasing behavior. *Journal of Retailing*, 70(3), 283–294.

Elder, R. S. & Krishna, A. (2009). The effects of advertising copy on sensory thoughts and perceived taste. *Journal of Consumer Research*, 36(5), 748–756.

Elder, R. S. & Krishna, A. (2011). The "visual depiction effect" in advertising: facilitating embodied mental simulation through product orientation. *Journal of Consumer Research*, 38(6), 988–1003.

Erdem, O., Ben Oumlil, A. & Tuncalp, S. (1999). Consumer values and the importance of store attributes. *International Journal of Retail & Distribution Management*, 27(4), 137–144.

Farquhar, P. H. (1989). Managing brand equity. *Marketing Research*, 1(9), 24–33.

Fisk, R. P., Brown, S. W. & Bitner, M. J. (1993). Tracking the evolution of the services marketing literature. *Journal of Retailing*, 69(1), 61–103.

Fletcher, G. J., Simpson, J. A. & Thomas, G. (2000). Ideals, perceptions, and evaluations in early relationship development. *Journal of Personality and Social Psychology*, 79(6), 933.

164 Zha, Foroudi, Jin and Melewar

Foroudi, M. M., Balmer, M. T., Chen, W. & Foroudi, P. (2019). Corporate identity, place architecture, and identification: an exploratory case study. *Qualitative Market Research: An International Journal*, (Just Accepted).

Foroudi, P., Jin, Z., Gupta, S., Melewar, T. C. & Foroudi, M. M. (2016). Influence of innovation capability and customer experience on reputation and loyalty. *Journal of Business Research*, 69(11), 4882–4889.

Gibson, J. J. (1966). *The Senses Considered as Perceptual Systems*, Houghton Mifflin, Boston.

Greenwald, A. G. & Leavitt, C. (1984). Audience involvement in advertising: four levels. *Journal of Consumer Research*, 11(1), 581–592.

Grohmann, B., Spangenberg, E. R. & Sprott, D. E. (2007). The influence of tactile input on the evaluation of retail product offerings. *Journal of Retailing*, 83(2), 237–245.

Hepola, J., Karjaluoto, H. & Hintikka, A. (2017). The effect of sensory brand experience and involvement on brand equity directly and indirectly through consumer brand engagement. *Journal of Product & Brand Management*, 26(3), 282–293.

Hirschman, E. C. & Holbrook, M. B. (1982). Hedonic consumption: emerging concepts, methods and propositions. *Journal of Marketing*, 46(3), 92–101.

Hoch, S. J. & Deighton, J. (1989). Managing what consumers learn from experience. *Journal of Marketing*, 53(2), 1–20.

Hoch, S. J. & Ha, Y. W. (1986). Consumer learning: advertising and the ambiguity of product experience. *Journal of Consumer Research*, 13(2), 221–233.

Hoegg, J. & Alba, J. W. (2011). Seeing is believing (too much): the influence of product form on perceptions of functional performance. *Journal of Product Innovation Management*, 28(3), 346–359.

Holbrook, M. B. (1987). What is consumer research? *Journal of Consumer Research*, 14(1), 128–132.

Holbrook, M. B. (2018). Essay on the origins, development and future of the consumption experience as a concept in marketing and consumer research. *Qualitative Market Research: An International Journal*, 21, 421–444.

Holbrook, M. B., Chestnut, R. W., Oliva, T. A. & Greenleaf, E. A. (1984). Play as a consumption experience: the roles of emotions, performance, and personality in the enjoyment of games. *Journal of Consumer Research*, 11(2), 728–739.

Holbrook, M. B. & Hirschman, E. C. (1982). The experiential aspects of consumption: consumer fantasies, feelings, and fun. *Journal of Consumer Research*, 9(2), 132–140.

Hultén, B. (2011). Sensory marketing: the multi-sensory brand-experience concept. *European Business Review*, 23(3), 256–273.

Hultén, B., Broweus, N. & Van Dijk, M. (2009). What is sensory marketing?. In *Sensory Marketing*, Palgrave Macmillan, London, pp. 1–23.

Iglesias, O., Markovic, S. & Rialp, J. (2019). How does sensory brand experience influence brand equity? Considering the roles of customer satisfaction, customer affective commitment, and employee empathy. *Journal of Business Research*, 96(3), 343–354.

Iglesias, O., Singh, J. J. & Batista-Foguet, J. M. (2011). The role of brand experience and affective commitment in determining brand loyalty. *Journal of Brand Management*, 18, 570–582.

Japutra, A., Ekinci, Y. & Simkin, L. (2018). Tie the knot: building stronger consumers' attachment toward a brand. *Journal of Strategic Marketing*, 26(3), 223–240.

Jin, S. V. & Phua, J. (2015). The moderating effect of computer users' autotelic need for touch on brand trust, perceived brand excitement, and brand placement awareness in haptic games and in-game advertising (IGA). *Computers in Human Behavior*, 43(2), 58–67.

Keller, K. L. (1993). Conceptualizing, measuring, and managing customer-based brand equity. *Journal of Marketing*, 57(1), 1–22.

Kotler, P. (1973). Atmospherics as a marketing tool. *Journal of Retailing*, 49(4), 48–64.

Kotzan, J. A. & Evanson, R. V. (1969). Responsiveness of drug store sales to shelf space allocations. *Journal of Marketing Research*, 6(4), 465–469.

Krishna, A. (2012). An integrative review of sensory marketing: engaging the senses to affect perception, judgment and behavior. *Journal of Consumer Psychology*, 22(3), 332–351.

Krishna, A. & Schwarz, N. (2014). Sensory marketing, embodiment, and grounded cognition: a review and introduction. *Journal of Consumer Psychology*, 24(2), 159–168.

Krishna, A., Elder, R. S. & Caldara, C. (2010). Feminine to smell but masculine to touch? Multisensory congruence and its effect on the aesthetic experience. *Journal of Consumer Psychology*, 20(4), 410–418.

Krishna, A., Lwin, M. O. & Morrin, M. (2010). Product scent and memory. *Journal of Consumer Research*, 37(1), 57–67.

Krishnan, H. S. & Chakravarti, D. (1999). Memory measures for pretesting advertisements: an integrative conceptual framework and a diagnostic template. *Journal of Consumer Psychology*, 8(1), 1–37.

Krishna, R., Zhu, Y., Groth, O., Johnson, J., Hata, K., Kravitz, J., ... & Fei-Fei, L. (2017). Visual genome: connecting language and vision using crowdsourced dense image annotations. *International Journal of Computer Vision*, 123(1), 32–73.

Kwon, M. & Adaval, R. (2017). Going against the flow: the effects of dynamic sensorimotor experiences on consumer choice. *Journal of Consumer Research*, 44(6), 1358–1378.

Lanier Jr, C. D. & Hampton, R. D. (2009). Experiential marketing: understanding the logic of memorable customer experiences. In A. Lindgreen, J. Vanhamme & M. B. Beverland (Eds.), *Memorable Customer Experiences: A Research Anthology*, Gower Publishing Company, England, pp. 9–24.

Liao, H. & Chuang, A. (2004). A multilevel investigation of factors influencing employee service performance and customer outcomes. *Academy of Management Journal*, 47(1), 41–58.

Ligas, M. & Cotte, J. (1999). The process of negotiating brand meaning: a symbolic interactionist perspective. *Advances in Consumer Research. Association for Consumer Research (U. S.)*, 26, 609–614.

Lindström, M. (2005). *Brand Sense: Build Powerful Brands Through Touch, Taste, Smell, Sight, and Sound*, Free Press, New York.

Louviere, J. J., Hensher, D. A. & Swait, J. D. (2000). *Stated Choice Methods: Analysis and Applications*, Cambridge University Press, Cambridge.

MacInnis, D. J. & Price, L. L. (1987). The role of imagery in information processing: review and extensions. *Journal of Consumer Research*, 13(4), 473–491.

Martineau, P. (1958). The personality of the retail store. *Harvard Business Review*, 36 (1–2), 47–55.

Mattila, A. S. & Wirtz, J. (2001). Congruency of scent and music as a driver of in-store evaluations and behavior. *Journal of Retailing*, 77(2), 273–289.

McCabe, D. B. & Nowlis, S. M. (2003). The effect of examining actual products or product descriptions on consumer preference. *Journal of Consumer Psychology*, 13(4), 431–439.

166 *Zha, Foroudi, Jin and Melewar*

McCracken, G. (1988). *Culture and Consumption*, Indiana University Press, Bloomington, IN.

Mehrabian, A. & Russell, J. A. (1974). *An Approach to Environmental Psychology*, MIT, Cambridge, MA.

Melewar, T. C. & Skinner, H. (2018). Territorial brand management: beer, authenticity, and sense of place. *Journal of Business Research*, 116(7), 680–689.

Merz, M. A., He, Y. & Vargo, S. L. (2009). The evolving brand logic: a service-dominant logic perspective. *Journal of the Academy of Marketing Science*, 37, 328–344.

Meyer, C. & Schwager, A. (2007). Understanding customer experience. *Harvard Business Review*, 85(2), 116.

Mollen, A. & Wilson, H. (2010). Engagement, telepresence and interactivity in online consumer experience: reconciling scholastic and managerial perspectives. *Journal of Business Research*, 63(9–10), 919–925.

Möller, J. & Herm, S. (2013). Shaping retail brand personality perceptions by bodily experiences. *Journal of Retailing*, 89(4), 438–446

Morrison, S. & Crane, F. G. (2007). Building the service brand by creating and managing an emotional brand experience. *Journal of Brand Management*, 14(5), 410–421.

Nicholls, R. (2010). New directions for customer-to-customer interaction research. *Journal of Services Marketing*, 24(1), 87–97.

Nysveen, H., Pedersen, P. E. & Skard, S. (2013). Brand experiences in service organizations: exploring the individual effects of brand experience dimensions. *Journal of Brand Management*, 20(5), 404–423.

Oliver, R. L. & Swan, J. E. (1989). Consumer perceptions of interpersonal equity and satisfaction in transactions: a field survey approach. *Journal of Marketing*, 53(2), 21–35.

Peck, J. & Childers, T. L. (2003a). Individual differences in haptic information processing: the "need for touch" scale. *Journal of Consumer Research*, 30(3), 430–442.

Peck, J. & Childers, T. L. (2003b). To have and to hold: the influence of haptic information on product judgments. *Journal of Marketing*, 67(2), 35–48.

Peck, J. & Wiggins, J. (2006). It just feels good: customers' affective response to touch and its influence on persuasion. *Journal of Marketing*, 70(4), 56–69.

Peck, J. & Johnson, J. W. (2011). Autotelic need for touch, haptics, and persuasion: the role of involvement. *Psychology & Marketing*, 28(3), 222–239.

Peter, J. P. & Olson, J. C. (1983). Is science marketing? *Journal of Marketing*, 47(4), 111–125.

Petit, O., Velasco, C. & Spence, C. (2019). Digital sensory marketing: integrating new technologies into multisensory online experience. *Journal of Interactive Marketing*, 45(2), 42–61.

Pine, B. J., Pine, J. & Gilmore, J. H. (1998). Welcome to the experience economy. *Harvard Business Review*, 76, 97–105.

Pine, J. B. & Gilmore, J. H. (1999). *The Experience Economy: Work Is Theatre and Every Business a Stage*, Harvard Business School, Cambridge.

Porter, M (1985). *Competitive Advantage*, Free Press, New York.

Prahalad, C. K. & Ramaswamy, V. (2004). *The Future of Competition: Co-creating Unique Value with Customers*. Harvard Business Press.

Puccinelli, N. M., Goodstein, R. C., Grewal, D., Price, R., Raghubir, P. & Stewart, D. (2009). Customer experience management in retailing: understanding the buying process. *Journal of Retailing*, 85(1), 15–30.

Roschk, H., Loureiro, S. M. C. & Breitsohl, J. (2017). Calibrating 30 years of experimental research: a meta-analysis of the atmospheric effects of music, scent, and color. *Journal of Retailing*, 93(2), 228–240.

Sayin, E. & Gürhan-Canli, A. (2015). Feeling attached to symbolic brands within the context of brand transgressions. *Brand Meaning Management: Review of Marketing Research*, 12(5), 233–256.

Schmitt, B. (1999). Experiential marketing. *Journal of Marketing Management*, 15(1–3), 53–67.

Schmitt, B. (2009). The concept of brand experience. *Journal of Brand Management*, 16, 417–441.

Schmitt, B. (2011). Experience marketing: concepts, frameworks and consumer insights. *Foundations and Trends® in Marketing*, 5(2), 55–112.

Shen, H., Zhang, M. & Krishna, A. (2016). Computer interfaces and the "Direct-Touch" effect: can iPads increase the choice of hedonic food? *Journal of Marketing Research*, 53(5), 745–758.

Sherry, J. F. Jr. & McGrath, M. A. (1989). Unpacking the holiday presence: a comparative ethnography of two gift stores. In E. C. Hirschman (Ed.), *Interpretive Consumer Research*, Association for Consumer Research, Provo, UT, pp. 148–167.

Shiffrin, R. M. & Schneider, W. (1977). Controlled and automatic human information processing: II. Perceptual learning, automatic attending and a general theory. *Psychological Review*, 84(2), 127.

Skandalis, A., Byrom, J. & Banister, E. (2016). Paradox, tribalism, and the transitional consumption experience: in light of post-postmodernism. *European Journal of Marketing*, 50(7/8), 1308–1325.

Smith, E. R. & Lerner, M. (1986). Development of automatism of social judgments. *Journal of Personality and Social Psychology*, 50(2), 246.

Smith, G. M. (2003). *Film Structure and the Emotion System*, Cambridge University Press.

Smith, P. C. & Curnow, R. (1966). Arousal hypothesis and the effects of music on purchasing behavior. *Journal of Applied Psychology*, 50(3), 255.

Sosa, M. E. (2011). Where do creative interactions come from? The role of tie content and social networks. *Organization Science*, 22(1), 1–21.

Spangenberg, E. R., Grohmann, B. & Sprott, D. E. (2005). It's beginning to smell (and sound) a lot like Christmas: the interactive effects of ambient scent and music in a retail setting. *Journal of Business Research*, 58(11), 1583–1589.

Spence, C., Puccinelli, N. M., Grewal, D. & Roggeveen, A. L. (2014). Store atmospherics: a multisensory perspective. *Psychology & Marketing*, 31(7), 472–488.

Spiro, R. L. & Weitz, B. A. (1990). Adaptive selling: conceptualization, measurement, and nomological validity. *Journal of Marketing Research*, 27(1), 61–69.

Stein, B. E., Burr, D., Constantinidis, C., Laurienti, P. J., Alex Meredith, M., Perrault Jr, T. J., … Schroeder, C. E. (2010). Semantic confusion regarding the development of multisensory integration: a practical solution. *European Journal of Neuroscience*, 31(10), 1713–1720.

Tombs, A. & McColl-Kennedy, J. R. (2003). Social-servicescape conceptual model. *Marketing Theory*, 3(4), 447–475.

Treisman, A. M. (1960). Contextual cues in selective listening. *Quarterly Journal of Experimental Psychology*, 12(4), 242–248.

Turley, L. & Milliman, R. (2000). Atmospheric effects on shopping behaviour: a review of the experimental evidence. *Journal of Business Research*, 49(2), 193–211.

Varey, C. & Kahneman, D. (1992). Experiences extended across time: evaluation of moments and episodes. *Journal of Behavioral Decision Making*, 5(3), 169–185.

Vargas, M., Cháfer, M., Albors, A., Chiralt, A. & González-Martínez, C. (2008). Physicochemical and sensory characteristics of yoghurt produced from mixtures of cows' and goats' milk. *International Dairy Journal*, 18(12), 1146–1152.

Vargo, S. L. & Lusch, R. F. (2008). Service-dominant logic: continuing the evolution. *Journal of the Academy of Marketing Science*, 36(1), 1–10.

Venkatraman, M. & Nelson, T. (2008). From servicescape to consumptionscape: a photo-elicitation study of starbucks in the New China. *Journal of International Business Studies*, 39(6), 1010–1026.

Verhoef, P. C., Lemon, K. N., Parasuraman, A., Roggeveen, A., Tsiros, M. & Schlesinger, L. A. (2009). Customer experience creation: determinants, dynamics and management strategies. *Journal of Retailing*, 85(1), 31–41.

Wakefield, K. & Baker, J. (1998). Excitement at the mall: determinants and effects on shopping response. *Journal of Retailing*, 74(4), 15–539.

Westbrook, R. A. & Oliver, R. L. (1991). The dimensionality of consumption emotion patterns and consumer satisfaction. *Journal of Consumer Research*, 18(1), 84–91.

Wirtz, J., Mattila, A. S. & Tan, R. L. (2000). The moderating role of target-arousal on the impact of affect on satisfaction – an examination in the context of service experiences. *Journal of Retailing*, 76(3), 347–365.

Yalch, R. & Spangenberg, E. (1990). Effects of store music on shopping behavior. *Journal of Consumer Marketing*, 7(2), 55–63.

Yoganathan, V., Osburg, V. S. & Akhtar, P. (2019). Sensory stimulation for sensible consumption: multisensory marketing for e-tailing of ethical brands. *Journal of Business Research*, 96(3), 386–396.

Zarantonello, L. & Schmitt, B. H. (2010). Using the brand experience scale to profile consumers and predict consumer behaviour. *Journal of Brand Management*, 17(7), 532–540.

Zarantonello, L. & Schmitt, B. H. (2013). The impact of event marketing on brand equity: the mediating roles of brand experience and brand attitude. *International Journal of Advertising*, 32(2), 255–280.

6 Corporate brand identity

Virtual space

Maria Teresa Cuomo, Cinzia Genovino, Debora Tortora and Alex Giordano

Introduction

Consumers live immersive experiences that enable brand associations, especially in virtual space. By branding the virtual world, businesses can use smart technologies and social media to engage and create relationships with customers, achieving competitive advantages. This chapter aims to underline the importance of digital (smart) and social media in corporate branding, identity, image and reputation. Key terms include virtual space, corporate brand identity, digital and smart technologies, social media, image and reputation.

Background

As we know, branding is a potent tool that business can adopt to reinforce the way consumers perceive their products achieving competitive advantages. According to Keller (2003, p. 8), branding generates "mental structures and helping consumers organise their knowledge about products and services in a way that clarifies their decision making and, in the process, provide value to the firm".

Nowadays, it is clear that the world has gone through a radical shift, moving from the sphere of a traditional branding strategy to the realm of digital, where smart and new media technologies are very relevant. Thus, with the rapid development of new technologies and social media, the need for virtual spaces has increased as an undeniable and participatory context where businesses can create and promote their brands; and in turn, users can experience brands in a unique and immersive mode (Berthon et al., 2009; Pitt et al., 2006).

Furthermore, managerial studies have attempted to explain whether and how companies and real brands can exploit virtual worlds and to investigate issues related to consumer behaviour in virtual worlds. However, virtual spaces are considered as a valid alternative to the physical world (i.e. fictional worlds) – where business can communicate their brands or to get useful data respecting customer requirements and emotions.

Hence, this chapter investigates the opportunities offered by virtual spaces for creating and managing successful corporate brand strategies, exploring in particular the importance of smart technologies and social media in branding identity, image and reputation. In the following sections, relevant concepts are discussed,

170 *Cuomo, Genovino, Tortora and Giordano*

and several propositions are developed on that basis, thereby opening up opportunities for future research and clarifying potential managerial implications.

Virtual space in corporate branding

The term "virtual space" refers to a virtual world that can be conceived as persistent online social spaces – or virtual environments – where people experience others as being there with companies, and where they can interact with each other. This conceptualisation suggests that virtual spaces provide users with the experience of being present, together with other users with the opportunity to generate relationships with others, with business and with the environment itself (Schroeder, 2008, p. 1).

In other words, then, virtual space has been defined as a persistent and computer-mediated online social environment that offers the opportunity for real-time interactions among users and between users and the virtual space itself, and that is populated by a virtual representation of users, namely by avatars.

The managerial literature has investigated virtual spaces in depth to capture the multifaceted nature of this complex phenomenon. In particular, some studies have defined virtual spaces as simulated environments where users can interact not only with each other but also with products and services or with companies, and as an important new channel for brand-building (Barnes and Mattsson, 2011). Other empirical studies have highlighted the importance of virtual spaces as immersive or absorptive, active or passive alternative worlds that business can enhance to boost their products and brands offering innovative and engaging marketing experiences (Barnes, 2007; Vernuccio, 2014).

Corporate brand identity, image and reputation in a virtual world

Traditionally, brand identity is defined as "a unique set of brand associations that the brand strategist aspires to create and maintain" (Aaker, 1996, p. 68). This classic definition has been integrated with one that considers "brand identity as a continually evolving constellation of meanings, constructed through a dialectical process among a multitude of stakeholders in relation to their individual and collective identities" (Essamri et al., 2019). This process of social negotiations among different stakeholders results in "a nested system of identities" (Kornum et al., 2017, p. 432), where different identities are related in complementary or contradictory ways (Essamri et al., 2019). This interpretation finds strong evidence especially in the virtual world where community members – or users – tend to express their perceptions and opinions about the brand to others in terms of (i) consciousness of kind, (ii) evidence of the rituals and traditions and (iii) a sense of obligation to the community and its members (Muñiz and O'Guinn, 2001). Thus, in the virtual world brand community members play an active role, both as providers and beneficiaries (Essamri et al., 2019), creating value for individuals, brand communities (Cova and White, 2009) and for companies (Pongsakornrungsilp and Schroeder, 2011). In this regard, this implies a new company attitude towards online consumers: they can also co-create brand

Corporate brand identity 171

identity with community members and other users (Vallaster and von Wallpach, 2013; Gyrd-Jones and Kornum, 2013).

Expanding the analysis at the corporate level (Melewar and Jenkins, 2002; Balmer, 2010, 2008), corporate brand identity is related to any organisation expressing, according to Balmer (2010, p. 186), a "distillation of corporate identity". In particular, the virtual context implies that the corporate brand identity could reinforce taking into account the relationships with the most relevant stakeholders. Stakeholders become powerful only when they integrate their resources and skills to interact with one another and with firms, and to represent themselves, share in participatory marketing programmes or challenge corporate communication (Cova and Dalli, 2009; Cova et al., 2015). These understandings suggest that companies can attract such stakeholders, particularly consumers (i.e. users in the virtual space) and offer them resources and value (co-created).

From an analytical perspective moreover, reputation is represented by numerous variables, it is based on a series of past experiences both in the macro- and micro-environment and established stakeholder relations that however need constant nurturing and consolidating (Blombäck and Ramirez 2012; Winn et al., 2008). In this regard, thus, a strong relationship of trust concurs in improving the business relational ability with its stakeholders (i.e. users), especially in the virtual space, both within (corresponding to inside knowledge) and outside the firm (in terms of knowledge relative to the firm). Inside the firm, trust refers to the cohesion and motivation on the part of the human resource capital, founded on shared ideas, values, beliefs and convictions that make up the corporate culture. Trust contributes to the system maintaining balance and guaranteeing dynamism, favouring efficient managerial processes. From an external perspective on the other hand, trust concerns credibility and corporate image (Pruzan, 2001; Furman, 2010; Otubanjo et al., 2010) perceived by the wide range of effective and potential interlocutors and the manner and outcome of relations (trade or otherwise) the organisation interweaves with them, not to mention the processes of communication expressly finalised at shaping and maintaining corporate reputation (Pastore and Vernuccio, 2008).

Hence, reputation constitutes the alternative, based on trust, to the recipient verifying corporate activity at first hand (Gili, 2005). Accordingly, reputation constitutes a vector which is capable of "encapsulating" trust, spreading and defending it in the digital era (Syed Alwi et al., 2020).

In this perspective, corporate brand reputation is acknowledged as directly contributing to the generating of economic value for the firm seeing as by enhancing the status of branding strategy in the market; furthermore, fixing a premium price for the firm's offer is acknowledged (Fombrun and Shanley, 1990) increasing the firm's credibility in the eyes of the users. Finally, corporate brand reputation contributes to strengthening inter-sector competitive barriers as it acts as a deterrent to the entry of new competitors, at the same time, limiting the risk of aggressive reactions in relation to strategic corporate decision-making. In short, empirical studies have shown how positive corporate performance acts as active support for the production of factors critical for success, provided they are effectively consistent and superior to the results obtained by competitors and

172 Cuomo, Genovino, Tortora and Giordano

rejecting the short-sightedness of strategies based on the mere analysis of the reserve of intangibles:

> In other words, reputation is not absolute but relative; thus firms cannot ignore the reputation of their competitors when building and enhancing their own. More importantly, although firm performance has an effect on reputation, it is the consistency in firm performance that makes a difference between competitors' reputations.
>
> (Ang and Wight, 2009)

Therefore, public acknowledgement of the corporate behaviour of a specific organisation i.e. reputation, even as concerns attention addressed to its stakeholders or interest groups (in terms of evidence of the construct) is considered one of the most important resources for the viability of the firm. As concerns the "widely acknowledged, established judgement that different interlocutors attribute to a firm's credibility relative to the quality and reliability of its products and corporate social responsibility" (Ravasi and Gabbioneta, 2004), reputation is the product of unique, symmetrical relations between organisations the protection of which represents a strategic element for success in the marketplace. In terms of output of the process of socialisation for the construction of shared opinions and social consensus, corporate reputation, based on a close network of information exchanges is in effect the product of a process of attribution of sense to a firm's action on a social level (Gardberg and Fombrum, 2002) nurtured, shared and socialised in terms of consensus in the new virtual space. The parties concerned, in relation to direct experience with the firm or in conformity with information and value signals received/transmitted, by means of official channels and informal virtual networks, attribute significance to the business' message, its visual and symbolic identity, culture and image held in the marketplace (Figure 6.1).

This dynamic process of sensemaking, seeing as it occurs over time, has retrospective collective consistency, referring as it does, to past events (Romenti, 2008). In sum, potential processes of sensemaking can be put in place by addressing attention to future business opportunities as a decisional platform for orienting strategic choice.

So that the formulation in prospect may occur, involvement on the part of the interested parties in decision-making processes is fundamental especially in co-creation approach. Smart technologies and social media as a vector for activating cooperation become an essential element of the creating of organisational settings in which such reputational expectations are generated (Syed Alwi et al., 2020; Yannopoulou et al., 2013). In shaping corporate brand reputation, communication is given the key role of divulging input for decision-making processes and diffusion of results (communication of information) not to mention the transfer to the outside of a firm's intrinsic values (narrative-symbolic function). Added to these elements is the role played by the process of the nurturing sensemaking in prospect, in terms of expected future reputation. In this vision, corporate reputation is people-dependent, "viewed differently by different stakeholder groups" (Ang and Wight, 2009).

Corporate brand identity

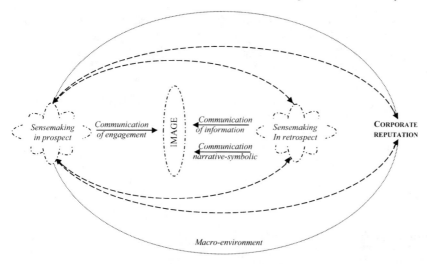

Figure 6.1 The process of reputation forming. Source: adapted from Romenti, 2008.

Solutions and recommendations

Many studies tried to give managerial solutions to understand the corporate brand identity. According to Urde (2013), corporate brand identity is composed of nine elements, as shown in Figure 6.2.

The centrality of the "core" – both internal and external elements – is evident. It radiates all other elements that are part of a matrix, namely the Corporate Brand Identity Matrix (CBIM.). Furthermore, it allows for a market-oriented, brand-oriented or combined approach to the process of defining and aligning corporate

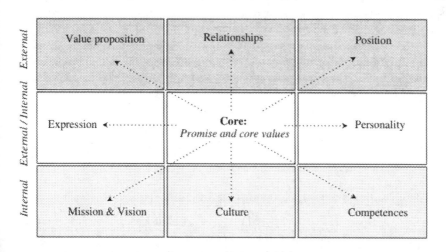

Figure 6.2 The Corporate Brand Identity Matrix. Source: (Urde, 2013).

174 *Cuomo, Genovino, Tortora and Giordano*

brand identity. Typically, a market-oriented approach is started by considering the external elements, such as the value propositions that have proper characteristics in the virtual world. In a brand-oriented approach, the internal elements and the core itself constitute the foundation and the starting point (Urde, 2013). As a managerial tool, the CBIM and its "indicative questions" (Urde, 2013) are conceptualised to support all those working operationally or strategically with the corporate brand identity, but it could reveal as a powerful managerial solution to monitor the corporate brand identity in the complexity of the virtual world (Syed Alwi et al., 2020). In this regard, the recommendation is to check the activation of the virtuous mechanism (Foroudi et al., 2014) of corporate branding, identity, image and reputation, as displayed in Figure 6.1. The positive circle appears vulnerable due to the high complexity of virtual space and thus could be easily compromised.

Future research directions and conclusions

The investigation of the opportunities offered by virtual spaces for generating and managing successful corporate brand strategies could be achieved by exploring the importance of smart technologies and social media to enhance branding, identity, image and reputation.

Furthermore, the effect produced by informational gaps leads to the over-exposing of a few specific firms capable of "hogging the stage" thanks to a conspicuous supply of resources which generates greater notoriety in the minds of the public. In polarising corporate behaviour dynamics between "knowing how to" (i.e. being good in reputational terms) and "letting others know" (i.e. being known), the latter seems to assume more relevance. Consequently, reputation can be defined even in function of the particular dimension of prominence, or in other words, with reference to the extent to which an organisation is both acknowledged collectively and is distinguished at firm level, in a competitive context (Rindova et al., 2005). In any event, the cognitive representation of corporate reputation constitutes, accordingly, a meta-concept which is constructed and governed in the long term.

In this regard, the centrality of corporate branding strategies in terms of identity, image and reputation should orientate future research directions to avoid losing the competitive advantages and fronting thus, this new challenge to select the most efficacious and useful digital technologies and social media. (Yannopolou et al., 2013).

CASE STUDY

Think different! Apple corporate brand identity

Today, companies need to invest in innovation. Innovative ideas, tools and processes are the main way to keep up with the times achieving a leading position in a given area of their business. Furthermore, there are companies that in order to see their brand known by the market have to use technology to convey it in the minds of consumers, and companies instead – like Apple – where technology has been able to strengthen the brand in the minds of consumers. For all these reasons, companies that do not have a recognisable brand identity must invest in technological and social media solutions because they can easily know and predict the new habits of consumers anticipating the market trends.

Therefore, it is interesting to understand the impact of technology on the competitiveness of the branding strategies and in particular the brand identity of companies on the Web. As illustrated before (Figure 6.2), corporate brand identity reflects the values of the company, what it is. In this regard, a company's logo and its variations, colours, fonts, image style and graphics are the main elements of brand identity and it is through them that a business may transfer its values, entering into users' minds. Hence, branding is the process of creating, managing and developing a brand. It is used to create awareness and recognition, raise awareness of potential customers and create the loyalty of existing customers, so the impression that customers, potential or acquired, have of a business is positive and as faithful as possible to what you intend to suggest. In this respect, what a company should do is to create a strong sense of brand membership and engagement encouraging the sharing of brand values (Cova and White, 2010).

Being present online via a web site, offering users interesting content to make their business more human (sharing images, videos with social media) are all decisive steps towards a substantial improvement of their corporate identity that almost always leads to an improvement of contacts and revenues. Using the platforms provided by digital technologies, setting up virtual environments where discussions around the brand can be generated might be a valid solution to generate and maintain competitive advantages. Thus, users can become opinion leaders, bearers of the value of the brand, helping to spread the image of a company and influencing opinions and perceptions. A bitten apple is a symbol of innovation, creativity and irreverence but also it is evidence of minimalism and simplicity. In 1997, one of the commercials that best describes the company's vision aired, with the slogan "Think Different". Apple targets mavericks, those who "think differently" than others, and Steve Jobs commented:

> We dedicate this commercial to the fools, the mavericks, the rebels, the troublemakers, all those who see things differently. They don't like the rules and have no respect for the status quo. […] And while some might call them crazy, we see the genius. Because only those who are crazy enough to think they can change the world really change it.
>
> (Beahm, 2019)

The "us vs. others" dichotomy is very much present in Apple's marketing and communication strategies. In the wake of a philosophy of counterculture, the company has worked over the years to build a community and the sense of belonging that not only purchases but it is also ready to defend the brand and its values and products.

The Apple ecosystem is often described as a "closed system", to the extent that each product involves the use of the iOS operating system, but the company has also focused on other elements that reinforce its "diversity".

Consumers, however, know and love the benefits and advantages of this system depending on it, becoming as well as loyal customers of brand advocates. With the aim of increasing brand loyalty, Apple is still going beyond key elements such as product quality and innovation, exemplary customer experience and well-researched marketing strategies. In actual fact, Apple has virtually created a kind of "common enemy" to members of its community: the PC and its users, as Roger Dooley points out in an article published in *Forbes* magazine.

According to the expert, this element would be the basis of the success of Apple's strategy and would serve to strengthen its fan base. It is a matter of social identity and the definition of one's personal identity based on that of the group to which you belong. As Roger Dooley explains, it's about "making your customers feel different from people who use a brand competitor" (https://www.insidemarketing.it/strategie-di-marketing-e-comunicazione-di-apple/).

The concepts of simplicity and minimalism, however, have also shaped Apple strategies for almost forever. In actual fact, at the launch of the Apple II, a new commercial with a red apple and the inscription on a white background read: "Simplicity is supreme sophistication".

The principle of minimalism, stated by Steve Jobs, is identified in all business practices: "the way we manage the company, the design of the

Figure 6.3 Think different.

Corporate brand identity 177

Figure 6.4 Simplicity is the ultimate sophistication.

products, the advertising, everything is summed up as follows: we make everything simple. Very simple" (Beahm, 2019). Another commercial in 2003 that became very popular is that focusing the new shape launched in 2003, which combined minimalism with another element deeply linked to the corporate brand identity.

As regards social media, the company has a strong presence on the three social networks with other accounts, such as: @AppleSupport and @AppleMusic; the company decided to open a proprietary account only in 2017. It is clear that such a strategy can work exclusively for Apple.

On the minimalist and simplicity imprint that seems to accompany the business model as a whole, a clarification must be made, quoting Steve Jobs:

> Simplicity can be more difficult than complexity. You have to work hard to be able to think clearly in order to make everything simple. But it's worth it in the end, because once you get there, you can move the mountains.
>
> (Beahm, 2019)

In this regard, if the Mac was a revolution for the sector, the launch of the smart phone (the first iPhone), changed the world as well. Several Apple products were initially welcomed with much criticism (often for highly innovative features), ending up later to become market successes such as the iPod and the launch of Apple Air Pods, the wireless headphones that were a huge success. From the beginning, Apple's vision of the future would prove prophetic: the idea was that of a device similar to an iPad (which would be launched in 2010). Watching the video, however, you can identify other technologies that would come out on the market many years later. Among them, we see the use of a touch screen, the making of a FaceTime or Skype-style video call and, perhaps the most amazing element such as Siri's predecessor.

The identity of the company from Cupertino will always remain tied to that of its co-founder, Steve Jobs. After his demise, many questioned about what the company's future prospects would be, but Apple remains firmly at the top of the companies with the largest capitalisation in terms of brand equity (https://www.forbes.com).

Expectations for the newly launched products are so high that it becomes a "tradition" among customers to queue at the entrance of Apple stores, sometimes even all night, to buy the product on launch day. Apple stores remain a key element of the company's strategy and the biggest marketing success. It is a way to give even more concreteness to the community experience, creating a physical point that allows immersion in the Apple world.

Furthermore, branding strategies based on the anthropomorphisation of the Mac, as described above, end up increasing emotional involvement with a brand already so loved and admired by consumers. In this direction, the principle of minimalism is also applied to Apple's social strategy that only in 2017 opened the Instagram account, while on other social networks the activity of the company remains quite passive. No post has ever been posted on the Twitter account (@apple), and the company is not active even on the Facebook page (@apple).

It is clear that the Apple limited usage of social media does not have implications on the branding processes in terms of identity, image and reputation; conversely and despite this strategic option, Apple is in first place among the ten most recognised brands in the world. Hence and in conclusion, the strategies are not standardised and capable of giving a competitive advantage to all companies. But perhaps this may exclusively work for a giant like Apple!

Case study questions

1. Can digital technologies and social media be useful in improving the corporate brand identity in virtual environments?

2. How much do Apple digital technologies and social media enhance corporate branding?
3. What are the key factors of the successful Apple corporate branding, identity, image and reputation?

References

Aaker, D. A. (1996). *Building Strong Brands*. New York: Free Press.

Ang, S. H. and Wight, M.-M. (2009). Building intangible resources: the stickiness of reputation. *Corporate Reputation Review*, 12(1), 21–32.

Balmer, J. M. T. (2008). Identity based view of the corporation: insights from corporate identity, organisational identity, social identity, visual identity, corporate brand identity and corporate image. *European Journal of Marketing*, 42(9–10), 879–906.

Balmer, J. M. T. (2010). Explicating corporate brands and their management: reflections and directions from 1995. *Journal of Brand Management*, 18(3), 180–196.

Barnes, S. (2007). Virtual worlds as a medium for advertising. *ACM SIGMIS Database: The DATABASE for Advances in Information Systems*, 38(4), 45–55.

Barnes, S. J. and Mattsson, J. (2011). Exploring the fit of real brands in the second life 1 virtual world. *Journal of Marketing Management*, 27(9–10), 934–958.

Beahm, G. (2019). I, Steve: Steve jobs in his own words. *B2 Books*.

Blombäck, A. and Ramírez-Pasillas, M. (2012). Exploring the logics of corporate brand identity formation. *Corporate Communications: An International Journal*, 17(1).

Cova, B., Dalli, D. (2009). Working consumers: the next step in marketing theory? *Marketing Theory*, 9(3), 315–339.

Cova, B., Pace, S. and Skalen, P. (2015). Marketing with consumers: the case of a carmaker and its brand community. *Organization*, 22(5), 682–701.

Essamri, A., McKechnie, S., & Winklhofer, H. (2019). Co-creating corporate brand identity with online brand communities: a managerial perspective. *Journal of Business Research*, 96, 366–375.

Fombrun C. and Shanley, M. (1990). What's in a name? Reputation building and corporate strategy. *Academy of Management Journal*, 33(2), 233–258.

Foroudi, P., Melewar, T. C. and Gupta, S. (2014). Linking corporate logo, corporate image, and reputation: an examination of consumer perceptions in the financial setting. *Journal of Business Research*, 67(11), 2269–2281.

Furman, D. M. (2010). The development of corporate image: a historiographic approach to a marketing concept. *Corporate Reputation Review*, 13(1), 63–75.

Gardberg, N. A. and Fombrun, C. J. (2002). The global reputation quotient project: first steps towards a cross-nationally valid measure of corporate reputation. *Corporate Reputation Review*, 4(4), 303–307.

Gili, C. (2005). *La credibilità. Quando e perché la comunicazione ha successo*. Soneria Mannelli (CZ): Rubbettino.

Gyrd-Jones, R. and Kornum, N. (2013). Managing the co-created brand: value and cultural complementarity in online and offline multi-stakeholder ecosystems. *Journal of Business Research*, 66(9), 1484–1493.

https://www.forbes.com/sites/martyswant/2020/07/27/apple-microsoft-and-other-tech-gia nts-top-forbes-2020-most-valuable-brands-list/#36917aa33ada

https://www.insidemarketing.it/strategie-di-marketing-e-comunicazione-di-apple/

Keller, K. L. (2003). Understanding brands, branding and brand equity. *Interactive Marketing*, 5(1), 7–20.

180 *Cuomo, Genovino, Tortora and Giordano*

Kornum, N., Gyrd-Jones, R., Al Zagir, N. and Brandis, K. A. (2017). Interplay between intended brand identity and identities in a Nike related brand community: co-existing synergies and tensions in a nested system. *Journal of Business Research*, 70, 432–440.

Melewar, T. C. and Jenkins, J. (2002). Defining the corporate identity construct. *Corporate Reputation Review*, 5(1), 76–90.

Muñiz, A. M. and O'Guinn, T. C. (2001). Brand community. *Journal of Consumer Research*, 27(4), 412–432.

Otubanjo, O., Amujo, O. C. and Cornelius, N. (2010). The informal corporate identity communication process. *Corporate Reputation Review*, 13(3), 157–171.

Pastore, A. and Vernuccio, M. (2008). *Impresa e comunicazione. Principi e strumenti per il management*. Milano: Apogeo.

Pongsakornrungsilp, S. and Schroeder, J. E. (2011). Understanding value co-creation in a co- consuming brand community. *Marketing Theory*,11(3), 303–324.

Pruzan, P. (2001). Corporate reputation: image and identity. *Corporate Reputation Review*, 4(1), 50–64.

Ravasi, D. and Gabbioneta, C. (2004). Le componenti della reputazione aziendale. Indicazioni dalla ricerca RQ Italy. *Economia: Management*, 3, 35–48.

Rindova, V. P., Williamson, I. O., Petkova, A. P. and Sever, J. M. (2005). Being good or being known: an empirical examination of the dimensions, antecedents, and consequences of organizational reputation. *Academy of Management Journal*, 48(6), 1033–1049.

Romenti, S. (2008). Corporate governance e reputazione: dallo stakeholder relationship management allo stakeholder engagement. *Impresa Progetto-Electronic Journal of Management*, (2).

Schroeder, R. (2008). Defining virtual worlds and virtual environments. *Journal for Virtual Worlds Research*, 1(1), 1–5.

Syed Alwi, S. F., Melewar, T. C., Cuomo, M. T. and Schwaiger, M. (2020). Digital society and corporate reputation: towards the next generation of insights. 23, 129–132.

Urde, M. (2013). The corporate brand identity matrix. *Journal of Brand Management*, 20(9), 742–761.

Vallaster, C. and von Wallpach, S. (2013). An online discursive inquiry into the social dynamics of multi-stakeholder brand meaning co-creation. *Journal of Business Research*, 66(9), 1505–1515.

Vernuccio, M. (2014). Communicating corporate brands through social media: an exploratory study. *International Journal of Business Communication*, 51(3), 211–233.

Winn, M. I., MacDonald, P. and Zietsma, C. (2008). Managing industry reputation: the dynamic tension between collective and competitive reputation management strategies. *Corporate Reputation Review*, 11(1), 35–55.

7 Aesthetic heritage and corporate branding

Luxury heritage brands between tradition and modernity

Angela Bargenda

Introduction

In view of the acceleration of digital channels in marketing communication and sales transactions, issues of aesthetics related to heritage brands are becoming ever more pertinent. The chapter shows that aesthetic heritage does not oppose digitalisation, but, on the contrary, delivers valuable resources for the construction of a meaningful and value-based corporate identity. *Key points* include corporate heritage, aesthetics, corporate branding, sensory marketing, atmospherics and luxury brands.

Background

With the rapid rise of digital communication and trade channels, especially in the aftermath of the coronavirus pandemic, brands are facing new challenges to maintain their attractiveness in the marketplace. This is particularly the case for high-end luxury brands, which have long drawn their seductive power from aesthetically captivating store environments. In the past, high-end brands have considered the codes of luxury incompatible with digital channels and therefore only recently espoused viral modes of communication. New marketing communications mediated through social networks, influencer marketing, posts and podcasts, augmented reality pages and viral buzzes, have profoundly transformed formerly mono-channel into multi-channel and cross-channel means of brand communications. Brands now seek to reach consumers both through exclusive traditional brick-and-mortar environments and innovative digital strategies.

Main focus of the chapter

Expressing heritage values and identity issues through aesthetic branding warrants awareness of the technical constraints and opportunities of each medium. Whilst an in-store experience offers a physical relationship with the brand through the materials used, the lighting, music, smell and ergonomics of the customer itinerary etc., digital interfaces are mainly perceived through visual and auditory modes. Thus, the chapter first outlines strategies of visual identity

182 Angela Bargenda

building, before presenting the potential of aesthetics and atmospherics to generate positive image and reputation. The ensuing case study will illustrate how aesthetic heritage contributes to the identity construct of an ultra-luxury brand.

Visual brand identity

Corporate visual identity systems (CVIS) represent a major part of corporate identity (Melewar and Karaosmanoglu 2006; Baker and Balmer 1997). The visual vocabulary of brands includes the logo, signage, packaging, product design, advertisements, web sites, but also architectural elements, such as interior decoration and building style. Balmer et al. (2006b) apply Gestalt theory to claim the competitive advantages of a harmonious congruence of visual elements. If packaging and product design have become prominent corporate visual identity (CVI) research topics, the contribution of corporate architecture to the CVI mix has only recently gained momentum in marketing literature (Foroudi et al. 2019; Bargenda 2018, 2015a, 2015b, 2014; Kirby and Kent 2010; Berg and Kreiner 1990).

As a symbolic resource, architecture lies at the heart of corporate identity (Balmer 2006) and significantly affects the perception of corporate identity (Melewar and Jenkins 2002). Consequently, Knight and Haslam (2010) show that a positively perceived architecture allows for identification.

Centrally located at the core of CVI, the logo represents a door of entry to the brand (Van den Bosch et al. 2006; Heilbrunn 2006; Melewar and Saunders 1998; Balmer 1998, 1995). Foroudi et al. (2014) show that cues of corporate logos pertaining to name, colour, design and typeface have an impact on corporate image and reputation.

Colour is a predominantly aesthetic feature of logos, eliciting reactions from consumers and communicating brand personality (Van den Bosch et al. 2005; Melewar and Saunders 2000). As a symbolic vector of communication, colour induces emotions, affects consumer behaviour and increases brand differentiation (Aslam 2006; Wheeler 2003). Colours enhance visual recognition, create competitive advantage and support brand image (Balmer and Gray 2000), given the fact that brand image is "what comes to mind when one hears the name or sees the logo" (Gray and Balmer 1998, 696). Given that the colours of the logo impact on the perception of brand image and behaviour (Balmer et al. 2011; Karaosmanoglu et al. 2011), choosing the right colour potentially increases reputational capital, as a positive brand image improves its reputation (Walsh et al. 2009).

Purposely employing repertoires of visual branding favours product differentiation, enhances customer loyalty, allows for premium pricing, cuts through clutter and protects against competition (Henderson et al. 2003; Schmitt and Simonson 1997; Schmitt 2009). Melewar and Saunders (2000, 1999) hold that a standardised CVI positively impacts on recruitment, organisational communication, product and service information, recognition of advertising messages, profit and market share.

Aesthetic heritage and corporate branding 183

Kress and Van Leeuwen (1996) argue that visual elements can be decoded using the grammatical rules of verbal texts. The compositional structure of logos or advertising images, for instance, creates a narrative through socially constructed knowledge. Thus, figurative or abstract logos, their colours, shapes and text-image combination, generate distinct brand identity, meaning and reputation. These visual components of brand identity enact aesthetic experiences, as they are perceived through the senses and relate brands to external cultural, social and historical environments.

Aesthetics and cultural artefacts

The aesthetic experience is derived from sensory and emotional perception, following its etymology (*aisthētikos*, from *aisthesthai*, to perceive). Gagliardi (1990) considered aesthetics essential for the assessments of cultural artefacts. Strati (2009, 2006, 1999) has shown the importance of aesthetics to organisational life. He argues that the aesthetic perception through the senses of vision, smell, touch and taste does not allow for intellectual and rational understanding. If aesthetic legitimation is more intuitive, and largely subliminal, it derives from a holistic, phenomenological experience based on sentiments.

Given the qualitative nature of aesthetics, it is impossible to determine a unique account of the aesthetic experience. It can be explained solely in dimensions of feeling and perceptive labels of aesthetic categories, such as beautiful, ugly, sublime, gracious etc. (Strati 1999). But the perceptive-sensory faculties that lead to a sensitive-aesthetic judgement are always subjective, yielding multiple interpretations of identity (Rafaeli 2013).

Thus, aesthetic branding aims to elicit affective responses from consumers through brand experiences, defined as "subjective, internal consumer responses (sensations, feelings, and cognitions) and behavioural responses evoked by brand-related stimuli that are part of a brand's design and identity, packaging, communications, and environments" (Brakus et al., 2009, p. 53). The multi-sensory brand experience is related to customer value, experiences and the perception of brand as image (Hultén 2011), embodying cultural and iconic brand meaning (Holt 2004).

Traditionally, brand management concerns the communication of messages, in line with the brand's intention (Kapferer 2004), but contextual effects, including cultural processes, are not included (Schroeder, 2009). Cultural codes are mobilised when commercial branding initiatives interact with cultural, ideological and sociological phenomena. In this perspective, brand meaning and value are not only derived from economic exchanges in the marketplace, but also determined by culture, aesthetics, ideology and history (Schroeder and Salzer-Mörling 2006). The concept of brand culture incorporates the understanding of brands in their cultural, historical and political context. As cultural phenomena, brands communicate messages within a representational system of traditional and historic references. The aesthetic value of a brand, subjectively experienced by consumers, produces cultural meaning (McCracken 1988, 1986), with aesthetic and

184   *Angela Bargenda*

stylistic considerations "taking precedence over utilitarian ones" (McCracken 1988, 19). Moreover, brands not only mediate cultural meaning, but become cultural references in and of themselves, establishing brand meaning and value in the marketplace beyond brand identity and brand image (Askegaard 2006; Heilbrunn 2006).

The prevalence of aesthetics over function also determines strategies of aesthetic marketing (Schmitt and Simonson 1997). The aesthetic output of a brand in terms of how a brand feels and looks provides a competitive edge for identity building. Schmitt and Simonson (1997) consider that the management of brand aesthetics through logos, brochures, packages and advertisements, but also sensory perceptions such as sounds, scents and lighting, create memorable experiences. According to the context, specific themes and styles convey symbolic meanings that affect customer satisfaction and loyalty by creating irresistible appeal and lasting impressions of the brand's personality. In the global context, aesthetically pleasing retail spaces and environments, but also aesthetic digital management, allow for the development of a differentiated brand identity.

Aesthetics and atmospherics

A particularly important element of brand aesthetics concerns the customer touchpoints on the point of sale. Kotler (1973) introduced the concept of "atmospherics" to marketing literature, emphasising the critical role of the store environment as a sales tool. He established that store atmospheres are created through sensory factors, especially the visual, auditory, olfactory and tactile dimensions (Kotler 1973, p. 51). This sensory repertoire is purposely used by management to create an intended store atmosphere and to enhance purchase probability. Store atmospheres serve to arouse interest and attention, as well as to create messages and affect (Kotler 1973, p. 54).

On the consumer's end, the perceived atmosphere includes partly learned reactions to colours, sounds and noises, which connect consumers to their own emotions and cognitive state of mind. The atmosphere of a store makes an immediate impact, instantly impregnating consumers in a holistic and all-encompassing way (Biehl-Missal and Saren 2012). This observation is based on the premise that atmospheres are totalities, pervading the entire sales venue. As atmospheres are experienced by the sentient subject through emotional states, their floating character cannot be fully expressed through words.

Bonn et al. (2007) show that in the tourism sector, the atmospheric environment of a heritage attraction can trigger either approach or avoidance behaviour. Applied to museums, for example, visitors may be encouraged or discouraged to remain in the museum due to the perceived atmospherics.

Böhme (2011) distinguishes between reception aesthetics and production aesthetics, with the perception of atmospheres originating in reception aesthetics. Due to the fact that atmospheres are irrational and induce in the subject a characteristic mood, their properties contrast with those of production aesthetics.

Aesthetic heritage and corporate branding   185

In the latter case, aesthetics is purposely used to produce a certain reaction in the consumer. One application of production aesthetics is the servicescape, where marketers produce atmospheres in retail outlets aiming to enhance the attractiveness of the shopping experience.

Aesthetics and servicescape

Aesthetics of store environments have been largely discussed in marketing literature (Mari and Poggesi 2013; Mazzalovo 2012; Bitner 1992, 1990; Donovan and Rossiter 1982). In particular, the concept of the "servicescape" has served as a conceptual framework for research. Coined by Bitner (1992, 1990), it denotes a physical setting in which a marketplace exchange is performed, delivered and consumed. Bitner (1992) analysed the effects of the servicescape on customer responses such as approach/avoidance behaviours, money spent and repatronage intentions. The servicescape impacts directly or indirectly on customers' sense of well-being through the sensory appreciation of place related to the expectation of the service. The aesthetic and atmospheric conditions of the sales venue positively or negatively determine customers' attitudes and decision-making. For instance, background music, lighting options, display materials and colours, wall decoration and fragrances create a distinct brand atmosphere and elicit responses from customers (Dijksterhuis et al. 2005). Bitner (1992) notes that interactions within servicescapes are based on individual behaviours, but also result from social interactions between customers and employees.

In addition to the functional features of the servicescape, such as spatial layout and ambient conditions, signs, symbols and artefacts determine the way consumers perceive the brand (Bitner 1992). Customer responses to the servicescape environment can be cognitive, emotional or physiological. For example, when customers' attitudes are changed as a result of an aestheticised retail experience, the response is cognitive. When customers enjoy themselves in the store, the response is emotional, and when the temperature, lighting and spatial experience are pleasant, the response is physiological.

More recent scholarship shows that "a servicescape not only influences customer perceptions of service functions and service quality, but more subtly, also influences the meanings a customer draws from the many intangible, contextual and symbolic elements of a service" (Nilsson and Ballantyne 2014, pp. 374–375). Thus, the social and cultural dimensions, created through the aesthetic design of place, are critical facets of brand identity. Customers derive meaning from aestheticised value propositions, thereby actively participating in the creation of brand value.

Service-dominant (S-D) logic

This co-creation of the brand's value proposition is at the centre of the service-dominant (S-D) Logic, which replaces the former product-dominant (P-D) approach to marketing. The S-D perspective considers value co-creation as a

186   *Angela Bargenda*

reciprocal process perspective on exchange (Vargo and Lusch 2012, 2004; Vargo et al. 2020). The S-D ecosystem has been applied to branding by Merz et al. (2009). The authors stipulate that the customer is an operant resource, rather than a target. The S-D logic embraces a process-oriented conceptualisation, based on value-in-use, in contrast to traditional output-oriented models. Therefore, S-D models acknowledge that "value is always uniquely and phenomenologically determined by the beneficiary" (Merz et al., 2009, 330). This relationship focus was prominently established by Fournier (1998), who argued that "consumer-brand relationships are valid at the level of lived experience" (Fournier, 1998, p. 344). Fournier viewed the consumer-brand relationship as a holistic concept of self and the brand. Consumers do not choose "brands, they choose lives", adding that "consumers' experience with brands are often phenomenologically distinct from those assumed by the managers" (Fournier, 1998, p. 367).

This *Customer-Brand Relationship Focus* has been extended, in the years 2000 and beyond, by the *Stakeholder-Focus Brand Era*, characterised by dynamic and social processes (Merz et al., 2009; Ind and Bjerke, 2007; Jones, 2005; McAlexander et al., 2002; Muniz et al., 2001). In this most recent research stream, not only individual consumers, but larger brand communities and all other stakeholders co-create value in a continuous and dynamic process. The stakeholder perspective denotes that brands are co-created within stakeholder-based ecosystems, that stakeholders form networks, rather than only one-to-one relationships with brands, and that value is dynamically constructed through social interactions among different stakeholders (Merz et al., 2009, p. 337). In this logic, the focus of brand value creation is on the stakeholders, given that brands are dynamically constructed through social interactions within brand communities and within the minds of consumers. Thus, all stakeholders are resources for the building of brand identity through processes of symbolic interpretations and personal narratives based on network relationships between stakeholders and brands (Muniz et al., 2001). The social interactions among stakeholder ecosystems lie at the heart of the most recent theorisations in brand literature (Iansiti and Levien, 2004). Consistent with the S-D paradigm, it is assumed that all stakeholders mutually create value through phenomenological perception, i.e. in context.

Therefore, aesthetic branding initiatives, which address stakeholders through personal and phenomenological experiences, lend themselves ideally to the process of co-creation of brand identity. Heritage-rich brands could benefit particularly from creating aesthetically engaging environments to create competitive advantage and differentiation.

Corporate brand heritage

The concept of (corporate) brand heritage is defined as

> all the traits and aspects of an organisation [and/or brand] that link its past, present, and future in a meaningful and relevant way…it refers to some aspect of an organisation's [and/or brand's] past that is still deemed by current

Aesthetic heritage and corporate branding   187

customers and/or other stakeholders to be relevant and meaningful for contemporary concerns and purposes but concurrently perceived as worth to be maintained and nurtured for future generations.

(Burghausen and Balmer, 2014a, pp. 394–395)

Pecot and De Barnier (2017) elucidate brand heritage from a multidisciplinary perspective and distinguish different approaches to heritage branding, such as retro, nostalgia and authenticity. Based on the assumption that brands seek a compromise between tradition and modernity, the authors distinguish two types of brands. On the one hand, the group of familiar, customer-oriented, omni-temporal and pioneering brands and on the other hand, the group of aristocratic, past, product-oriented and prestigious brands. The authors define brand heritage as a dynamic construct based on an inherited or borrowed past, with a view to supporting and transmitting brand identity.

Most heritage scholarship focuses on corporate heritage brands, whilst some literature also discusses heritage from a product brand perspective, stressing the importance of heritage in the marketing mix (Dion and Borraz, 2015; Joy et al., 2014; Dion and Arnould, 2011; Balmer, 2010). Whilst the product brand level focuses on product marketing and the relations between product manager and consumers, the corporate brand level considers the whole organisation, including its multiple stakeholders, as a brand (Balmer and Gray 2003). Corporate heritage brands are distinct from brands with a heritage, which may have a rich past but do not mobilise it at an organisational level (Urde et al. 2007).

At the echelon of corporate heritage brands, five characteristics are common to the corporations: longevity, track records, core values, the use of symbols and an organisational belief that history is important (Urde et al., 2007). Balmer (2013) defines corporate heritage identity as the institutional traits remaining meaningful and invariant over time, identifying six fundamental criteria of corporate heritage identities: omni-temporality, institutional trait consistency, tri-generational heredity, augmented role identities, ceaseless multigenerational stakeholder utility and unremitting management tenacity. Burghausen and Balmer (2014a) further observe that corporate heritage brands operate a selective appropriation of the past relevant to internal and external stakeholders.

Research has also focused on the management of corporate heritage over time (Burghausen and Balmer, 2015; Miller, 2014). In particular, the concept of ambidexterity, designating a brand's capability to remain both relevant and consistent over time, has been discussed (Moussa and De Barnier, 2020; Beverland et al., 2015; Melewar and Nguyen, 2014). Ambidextrous strategies have been approached from a design thinking perspective (Beverland et al., 2015), but also from a brand-based approach to identify managerial activities relative to corporate heritage identity stewardship (CHIS), a particular managerial mindset characterised by awareness of positionality, heritage and custodianship (Burghausen and Balmer, 2015). More recently, Moussa and De Barnier (2020) presented a model linking CHIS to the concept of ambidexterity, arguing that the enactment of corporate heritage identity is optimally derived from internal resources to

188 *Angela Bargenda*

foster stakeholder support and adhesion over time, rather than external concepts, such as design thinking.

Other areas of corporate heritage research include the communication of heritage to stakeholders (Burghausen and Balmer, 2014a; Blombäck and Brunninge, 2009). Santos et al. (2016) investigated the relationship between the corporate and the product brand levels, whilst Pecot and Barnier (2017) and Pecot et al. (2018) further explored heritage brands from a consumer perspective, following the findings that consumers may not define brand heritage in the same way as managers (Rindell et al., 2015). Rose et al. (2016) found that brand heritage positively impacts purchase intention, inspires positive emotions, engenders trust and facilitates brand attachment and commitment, whilst Balmer and Chen (2017) showed that heritage brands positively impact consumer satisfaction.

In the tourism sector, the identity impact of heritage experiences on consumers concerns both the individual level, as consumers redefine themselves after the experience, for example after visiting a heritage site or a museum (Gonzalez, 2008; Poria et al., 2009), and the collective level, since heritage experiences inscribe cohesion and solidarity within communities (Park, 2010). Goulding (2000) explored the perception of authenticity of touristic heritage sites with a special focus on the commodification of the past. Chen and Chen (2010) suggested that heritage aesthetics can have a notable impact in terms of attachment and loyalty with the heritage site.

Consumers connect with heritage brands through an immersive experience of history, expertise and know-how (Urde et al., 2007). But consumers also refer to distinct features of socially constituted patrimony through heritage artefacts that are external to market relationships. Otnes and Maclaren (2007) argue that heritage objects are at the core of identity transmission and construction mechanisms, as they are built on a set of commonly accepted values. Heritage-related artefacts physically embody history, thereby building a bridge between the past and the present (McDonald, 2011).

Thus, a brand's aesthetic heritage can be employed to make the brand relevant and meaningful for contemporary stakeholders (Mencarelli et al., 2020; Spielmann et al., 2020; Maier and Andersen, 2017; Santos et al., 2016; Bargenda, 2015a, b; Balmer, 2011a, 2011b, 2013; Burghausen and Balmer, 2014b; Hudson, 2011; Balmer et al., 2006). In particular, the literature highlights that aesthetic experience offers a more palpable and embodied relationship between the stakeholder ecosystem and the brand than merely rational processing.

Through the aesthetic mediation of heritage, brands are appreciated for their visual and sensory appeal. Pecot et al. (2018) showed that these positive outcomes apply to both established companies and new entrants.

Issues, controversies, problems: the promotion of aesthetic heritage in the digital age

As heritage invariably emanates from a reference system of shared cultural values, heritage aesthetics translate these values into a sensory repertoire, which

Aesthetic heritage and corporate branding 189

materialises the past and makes it palpable and relevant for today's audiences. In the digital age, however, the continued use of major aesthetic attributes, such as the atmospherics of a place, generated by sound, smell, olfactory and tactile experiences, presents challenges to marketers. In cyberspace, the five senses are mainly subsumed under the visual and auditory experiences. In view of the fast-growing importance of digital spaces at the detriment of physical places, it is essential for heritage brands to understand and mobilise appropriate resources to promote brand identity, image and reputation on digital platforms. In the digital market environment, computer and mobile screens replace the physical context of the servicescape. Thus, the all-encompassing, phenomenological interaction between customers and brands in the retail environment is reduced to a digital experience on a computer or mobile screen.

Solutions and recommendations

Servicescape scholarship has only recently integrated the digital service spaces as branding resources, conceptualised previously as mere sales tools and information platforms. In light of the service-dominant) logic, Nilsson and Ballantyne (2014, p. 377) argue that digital platforms can support "customer interaction and dialogue and pay attention to the likely symbolic meanings derived from website design". They note that the terminology of physical places is metaphorically integrated in digital communication, such as "check-out" and "shopping cart". Concerning aesthetic elements in particular, the authors argue that the décor of a sales venue can be digitally transcribed by colour and artistic spatial arrangements, music and sound. They infer that the shifts of representational design between the physical place of the servicescape and virtual space follow the same underlying forms of symbolic interaction with customers (Morrison et al., 2011; Bitner, 1990; Booms and Bitner, 1981).

Conversely, in brick-and-mortar settings, the customer journey could be enhanced by supplementing engaging interactive digital resources. Nilsson and Ballantyne (2014) claim that servicescape design logic applies in a physical place or virtual space, a retail store or on a website and thus, the integration of resources could prove influential in pursuing the brand's value proposition and customer experience. By establishing multiple service interaction zones (Ballantyne et al., 1995), together with other engagement platforms, value co-creation could be facilitated by opening up additional options for customers, such as web-stores, social network forums, applications etc. Nilsson and Ballantyne (2014) view this digital interaction as a world of episodic engagements, where each click brings up customer experiences. This extended understanding of the servicescape from physical places to virtual spaces requires a process-oriented design, where click-through stages mark the customer itinerary and continuous customer engagement.

The adaptation of aesthetic heritage branding to the context of the digital era, therefore, offers innovative strategies to build brand identity and image. In particular, the stakeholder-focus approach to branding allows benefits from the

190   *Angela Bargenda*

potential of digital channels, as consumers can be addressed within specific communities through forums, flash mobs, contests, crowd-sourcing initiatives etc.

Digital spaces should not be viewed in contrast to traditional servicescapes, but as extensions of the traditional service model towards a multi-dimensional, integrated and process-oriented articulation of heritage. The case study of this chapter seeks to illustrate the valorisation of brand heritage through aesthetics, both in the physical and the digital settings.

Future research directions

There are multiple directions for research in the field of the aesthetic management of corporate heritage brands.

First, it could be investigated to what extent corporate heritage brands should remain past-oriented and to which degree they should espouse innovative technologies and future-oriented designs. For example, heritage brands can dilute their core identity by disrupting their aesthetic repertoire. If heritage brands intend to modernise their image to keep abreast with market developments, they might lose brand value, competitive advantage and credibility. However, if they fail to modernise, they might seem antiquated. It could be researched to what extent heritage is (in-)compatible with a contemporary image and in which sectors a pronounced retro-orientation would favourably align with modern consumer trends.

A second direction for future research concerns the fact that not all international markets place value on heritage. Therefore, it might be advisable for heritage brands to pursue a differentiated approach. According to data indicating the valorisation of heritage by consumers, brands could adapt their heritage-driven marketing and communication strategies to international market environments, rather than pursuing a standardised approach.

Third, studies could be conducted along the lines of integrated strategies. In today's connected marketplace, the interaction of physical, digital and phygital channels could achieve valuable synergies and bring heritage branding to the next level of expression.

A fourth research venue could consist in the exploration of marketing opportunities that arise from sponsorship programmes with the non-profit sector. When commercial heritage brands associate with prestigious arts institutions, such as museums, theatres, music halls and national monuments, they draw on the aesthetic power of these venues. Therefore, it could be investigated to what extent philanthropic initiatives offer opportunities in terms of image and reputation management for corporate heritage brands.

Conclusion

Corporate identity, especially corporate visual identity, has become a prominent topic in marketing research. If managers must be cognizant of the type of identity projected by their brand, the past is a relevant identity component for

Aesthetic heritage and corporate branding 191

heritage-rich corporate brands. Thus, the valorisation of tradition, know-how and expertise can translate into positive image and reputational capital, differentiating heritage brands from new market entrants.

However, the materialisation of corporate heritage through sensory marketing tools, which enable consumers to see, feel, smell and touch various manifestations of brand heritage, presents challenges to marketers. On the one hand, heritage is always past-oriented; on the other hand, it needs to be made relevant to contemporary audiences in order not to be perceived as outdated. The awareness and preservation of the value of heritage need to be instilled in the stakeholder ecosystem, ideally by an internal process of corporate heritage identity stewardship. This process is optimally achieved by managerial techniques located within internal company resources. Aesthetic features, such as logo design, retail architecture, servicescapes etc., are part of the toolkit that managers can mobilise to project a heritage-rich brand identity.

For instance, a 19th-century logo confers a sense of longevity and tradition but could also be negatively perceived by some consumers as outdated if the brand fails to update it to modern taste. Thus, the chapter has shown that the essential feature of corporate heritage management consists in bridging the perceived dichotomy between corporate heritage as a phenomenon relegated to the past and corporate heritage as a feature relevant to contemporary and future audiences. The update of visual cues, for example, needs to accommodate the brand's anchorage in the past with modern features of design and lifestyle.

Brand atmospherics represent another vector of heritage communication. Contrary to quantifiable brand identifiers, however, the atmosphere created by a brand can only be perceived by the sentient subject, and therefore represents a unique and personal experience. Atmospherics do not transcribe heritage cognitively, such as for example an iconographic logo design, a symbolically charged colour or any other explicit reference to culture, history or ideology. Atmospherics create an emotional state in the consumer, derived from the phenomenological brand experience in a sensory environment, where aesthetic elements such as lighting, material of display cases, floor plan, wall decoration, furniture etc. contribute to generating an affective response. This form of lived brand experience is invariably based on the co-creation of meaning, as the consumer is actively involved in the process of value creation. In light of the service-dominant logic, the process of heritage identity building through atmospherics oscillates between purposely employed design features and intuitively perceived atmospheres that vary from one individual to the other. Thus, the brand image drawn from these experiences emanates from a holistic approach, where meaning is created through the interaction between members of the organisation and external audiences.

The translation of identity-building aesthetics into cyberspace is critically important for the survival of heritage brands. In digital environments, the repertoire of sensory clues is drastically reduced to sound and design, even though there are some technological forays into olfactory transmissions through digital channels. Therefore, creativity, imagination and a sense of artistic composition

192   Angela Bargenda

are needed to render heritage palpable through digital networks. Constructing heritage identity through novel digital designs and creative reputation and image remains a central task for corporate heritage brand managers.

Due to the fast-moving digital transitions in the marketplace, ultra-luxury heritage brands, which have long been reluctant to espouse digital communication channels, have begun to invest in cyberspace. To illustrate these transformations, the following case study discusses the French heritage brand Hermès. It first provides an outline of the brand's history, before presenting heritage-related brand strategies. Finally, it raises the question of the brand's positioning in the digital space.

CASE STUDY

The valorisation of aesthetic heritage in the luxury sector: the case of Hermès

Hermès International S.A. is a French high-end luxury goods manufacturer established as a business in 1837. It specialises in ready-to-wear fashion, leather goods, accessories, home furnishings, perfumery, jewellery and watches. The flagship store is located on 24 Rue du Faubourg Saint-Honoré in Paris.

Like most prestigious fashion brands, Hermès is steeped in history and tradition. Company founder Thierry Hermès was born in 1801 in Germany to a French father and a German mother. His birthplace, Krefeld, is known as the "City of Velvet and Silk", due to its strong textile history. Thus, the very foundation of the brand is related to the industrial and cultural heritage of the textile sector.

When the Hermès family moved to France in 1828, they settled in a small town in Normandy, Pont Audemer, where Thierry learned the trade of leather making. At this time, he also started to craft harnesses. In 1837, Thierry Hermès established the house of Hermès as a harness workshop in Paris, counting among his clientele the members of the European aristocracy. Hermès also sold wrought iron harnesses and bridles for carriage trade, which won him several awards at the Universal Expositions in Paris in 1855 and 1867.

In 1880, Hermès's son, Charles-Emile Hermès, took over his father's business and opened the current location in Paris. Whilst he continued as a saddler artisan, he expanded the retail sales to international audiences, catering to the upper class of Europe, Russia, North Africa, Asia and the Americas. At the turn of the century, he launched the *Haut à courroies* bag, which allowed riders to carry their boots and saddles with them. This bag encountered unprecedented success and its design served as inspiration for iconic handbags, such as the Birkin bag.

In 1902, the Hermès brothers Adolphe and Emile-Maurice took over the business from their father Charles-Emile. When Emile-Maurice began furnishing the czar of Russia in 1914, he gained exclusive rights to use the zipper on leather goods and clothing. Thus, Hermès introduced the device in France and subsequently created the first leather golf jacket with a zipper for Edward, Prince of Wales. In France, the zipper became known as the *fermeture Hermès* (*Hermès fastener*).

In the aftermath of the First World War (WWI), the horse harnesses and equipment business declined and was replaced by new products. Handbags for women were especially high in demand, and Hermès launched a smaller version of the *Haut à courroies* bag in 1922, before introducing the first women's apparel collection in 1929. In 1935, Hermès launched one of the most iconic products, the *Sac à dépêches*, which became later known as the *Kelly bag*. When the silk scarf was introduced in 1937, it immediately became fashionable with celebrities. The perfumery division was established in 1950. At this time, Hermès began using the signature orange boxes and the duc-carriage-with-horse logo based on a drawing by French painter Alfred de Dreux, which Emile Hermès had used as his ex-libris since 1923.

Today, the brand ranks as one of the most valuable brands in the ultra-luxury segment in the world, combining its rich heritage of over a century with long-term orientated creativity and craftsmanship, where the product always occupies the central place. To this day, Hermès products are almost entirely made in France and manufactured by hand by a single craftsman. This not only guarantees the quality and uniqueness of the product, but also the human imprint inscribed in each product.

The company projects an aura of exclusivity, which is very strongly based on its heritage. For example, new employees receive a three-day training to become familiarised with the brand's values, history, culture and identity. The brand strategy is standardised at the global level, as the same product collections are sold all over the world, with a significant amount of limited editions to warrant the scarcity of its products. Consistent with the principles of heritage and exclusivity, the brand communication is based on its core identity. Likewise, Hermès sponsors events that directly relate to its image and legacy. For instance, in relation to the company's founding association with horses and saddlery manufacturing, Hermès sponsors horse racing events around the world, and teams such as the U.S. Show Jumping Team.

When developing new products, Hermès mobilises its rich heritage, which lies at the core of its brand identity and differentiates the brand from competitors. Iconic product designs from the past have recently been relaunched. For example, the ring bag created in 1958 inspired the icon belt launched in 2014. The Piano belt from 1954 was relaunched in 2014.

To this day, designers mostly draw inspiration from objects assembled by Emile Hermès (1871–1951), which are exhibited in the private museum

194 *Angela Bargenda*

above the flagship store and revolve around the basic theme of movement. Emile started to collect in 1883, at the age of 12, when he acquired a walking stick containing a little parasol inside. This walking stick served as an object of gallantry, providing shade to a lady when the sun was shining. The collection is a source of inspiration and innovation for designers, but also connects the history of the brand to the present through sensory objects, thus keeping memory alive. The main aesthetic artefact of the collection is the horse, literally and metaphorically transcribing the idea of movement and travel, with the oldest object going back to 2500 BC and representing the statue of a horse from the Indus Valley between Pakistan and India.

The collection includes books, paintings and prints from all around the world, telling stories of movement: movement of lifestyle and human beings, bridging the gap between the past and modernity, history and innovation. Following Emile Hermès, Hermès designers today, mainly the scarf and tie designers, but also the jewellery designers, browse through the objects to find something new and learn more about the roots of Hermès. The Emile Hermès collection is a unique place where heritage is materialised through sensory artefacts that reflect the identity of the brand through historic references and human values. It transcends historical ages and serves as a timeless treasure trove, which ensures the aesthetic and inspirational continuity of the brand.

In addition to the private collection of Emile Hermès, the sales floor itself is very richly decorated with paintings and artwork, so as to provide an almost museum-like atmosphere, where commercial activities are enhanced through cultural artefacts and artistic creativity.

In the transition to the digital age, the brand has continued to promote its rich heritage on its corporate website (www.hermes.com]). For example, the painting by Alfred de Dreux (1810–1860), which inspired the duc-carriage-with-horse logo, is prominently reproduced.

Case questions

Conduct research on the Hermès website (www.hermes.com) and answer the following questions.

1. Analyse the key identity elements of the company's digital representation (Hermes.com – About Hermès). How does the brand carry the past over to the present and makes its heritage valuable to contemporary consumers?
2. Show how Hermès has implemented an integrated aesthetic branding strategy, combining various resources, such as the point of sale (windows design, in-store visual merchandising, art collection, exterior and interior

architecture etc.) and the aesthetics of its website (typescript, layout, visuals, colours, shapes etc.).

3. Discuss the strategies employed by Hermès, including sponsorship and philanthropy, to cultivate a positive identity, image and reputation.
4. Do you consider that the aesthetic heritage of Hermès is sufficiently valorised on the Hermès apps *Silk Knots* and *Tie Break?* Consider the graphic design, gamification strategies, Gen Y digital culture, web-to-store feature etc.

Key terms and definitions

Aesthetics: in philosophy, aesthetics concerns the natural and artificial sources of beauty and taste, as well as the philosophy of art. Founded by the philosopher Alexander Baumgarten in 1735, it raises questions about the experience of aesthetic objects through the senses, for example artwork, music, literature etc. It explores our reaction to art in a sensory and emotional way, and in relation to the physical, social and cultural context.

Ambidexterity: etymologically derived from ambi- ("both") and dexter ("right"), the term means "both right". In the context of business studies, it designates an organisation's capacity to conduct business efficiently today whilst remaining agile and adaptable to cope with future challenges. In the case of heritage brands, traditional and successful strategies from the past need to be constantly evaluated for their performance. To remain in phase with the developments in the marketplace, innovation, flexibility and learning have become organisational imperatives.

Atmospherics: the term designates a qualitative construct through which consumers experience commercial space in terms of architecture, including exterior structure, interior design and window displays. A pleasantly experienced atmosphere creates attention, communicates messages and triggers affect. Architectural space design impacts on the way people perceive a sales outlet. Thus, the sensory qualities of atmospherics enhance purchase probability through the consumer's perception. Kotler considers atmospherics as key elements in the positioning of the value offering.

Brand culture discusses brands from a multidisciplinary angle, extending the traditionally positivistic and quantitative approach to brands by a broader qualitative analysis of brands in their historical, social, political and ideological context. Therefore, brand culture research incorporates findings from e.g. sociology, history, anthropology and cultural studies to gain a wider understanding of the brand's interaction with consumers and society. As cultural phenomena, brands communicate messages within a representational system of traditional and historic references.

Corporate heritage brand: the corporate brand level considers the whole organisation, including its multiple stakeholders, as a brand, as opposed to the product brand, which focuses on product marketing and the relations between product manager and consumers. Corporate heritage brands intentionally

196 Angela Bargenda

mobilise resources from their corporate past to make them relevant for contemporary consumers. In doing so, they use symbols, representational artefacts and aesthetic tools that signal the importance placed on the brand's history.

Service-Dominant (S-D) logic replaces the former product-dominant (P-D) approach to marketing. The S-D perspective considers value co-creation as a reciprocal process perspective on exchange, where the customer is an operant resource, rather than a target. S-D models acknowledge that value creation is always subjective, as value is uniquely and phenomenologically created by the consumer through lived experience.

Corporate heritage identity stewardship (CHIS) is a mindset held by top management that supports the valorisation of heritage. Managers are aware that the promotion of brand heritage represents a meaningful contribution to the identity construct and positioning strategies.

References

Askegaard, S. (2006). Brands as a global ideoscape. In J. E. Schroeder and M. Salzer Mörling (Eds.), *Brand culture* (pp. 91–102). London: Routledge.

Aslam, M. (2006). Are you selling the right colour? A cross-cultural review of colour as a marketing cue. *Journal of Marketing Communications, 12*(1), 15–30.

Baker, M. J. and Balmer, J. M. T. (1997). Visual identity: Trappings or substance. *European Journal of Marketing, 31*(5), 366–382.

Ballantyne, D., Christopher, M. and Payne, A. (1995). Improving the quality of services marketing: Service (re)design is the critical link. *Journal of Marketing Management, 11*(1/3), 7–24.

Balmer, J. M. T. (1995). Corporate identity: The power and the paradox. *Design Management Journal (Former Series), 6*(1), 39–44.

Balmer, J. M. T. (1998). Corporate identity and the advent of corporate marketing. *Journal of Marketing Management, 14*(8), 963–996.

Balmer, J. M. T. (2006). Corporate brand cultures and communities. In J. E. Schroeder and M. Salzer Mörling (Eds.), *Brand culture* (pp. 34–49). London: Routledge.

Balmer, J. M. T. (2010). Explicating corporate brands and their management: Reflections and directions from 1995. *Journal of Brand Management, 18*(3), 180–196.

Balmer, J. M. T. (2011a). Corporate heritage identities, corporate heritage brands and the multiple heritage identities of the British Monarchy. *European Journal of Marketing, 45*(9–10), 1380–1398.

Balmer, J. M. T. (2011b). Corporate heritage brands and the precepts of corporate heritage brand management: Insights from the British monarchy and the eve of the royal wedding of Prince William (April 2011) and Queen Elizabeth's Diamond Jubilee (1952–2012). *Journal of Brand Management, 18*(8), 517–544.

Balmer, J. M. T. (2013). Corporate heritage, corporate heritage marketing, and total corporate heritage communications: What are they? What of them? *Corporate Communications: An International Journal, 18*(3), 290–326.

Balmer, J. M. T. and Chen, W. (2017). China's brands, China's brand development strategies and corporate brand communications in China. In: J. M. T. Balmer, Chen W. (Eds.), *Advances in Chinese brand management* (pp.19–47). London: Palgrave Macmillan.

Balmer, J. M. T. and Gray, E. R. (2000). Corporate identity and corporate communications: Creating a competitive advantage. *Industrial and Commercial Training, 32*(7), 256–262.

Balmer, J. M. T. and Gray, E. (2003). Corporate brands: What are they? What of them? *European Journal of Marketing, 37*(7/8), 972–997.

Balmer, J. M. T., Greyser, S. A. and Urde, M. (2006a). The Crown as a corporate brand: Insights from monarchies. *Journal of Brand Management, 14*(1–2), 137–161.

Balmer, J. M. T., Mukherjee, A., Greyser, S. A., Jenster, P., van den Bosch, A. L., Elving, W. J. and de Jong, M. D. (2006b). The impact of organisational characteristics on corporate visual identity. *European Journal of Marketing, 40*(7/8), 870–885.

Balmer, J. M. T., Powell, S. M. and Greyser, S. A. (2011). Explicating ethical corporate marketing. Insights from the BP Deepwater Horizon catastrophe: The ethical brand that exploded and then imploded. *Journal of Business Ethics, 102*(1), 1–14.

Bargenda, A. (2014). *Communication visuelle dans le secteur bancaire Européen: L'esthétique de la finance*. Paris: Collection Questions contemporaines/Questions de communication, L'Harmattan.

Bargenda, A. (2015a). Corporate heritage brands in the financial sector: The role of corporate architecture. *Journal of Brand Management, 22*(5), 431–447.

Bargenda, A. (2015b). Space design as an expressive device in ambient marketing: Case studies of Deutsche Bank and Banca Monte dei Paschi di Siena. *Journal of Marketing Communications, 21*(1), 78–90.

Bargenda, A. (2018). Building meaning: Architectural dialectic in spatial marketing systems. *Journal of Macromarketing, 38*(3), 262–277.

Berg, P. O. and Kreiner, K. (1990). Corporate architecture: Turning physical settings into symbolic resources. In: P. Gagliardi (Ed.), *Symbols and artifacts: Views of the corporate landscape* (pp. 41–67). New York: de Gruyter.

Beverland, M. B., Wilner, S. J. and Micheli, P. (2015). Reconciling the tension between consistency and relevance: Design thinking as a mechanism for brand ambidexterity. *Journal of the Academy of Marketing Science, 43*(5), 589–609.

Biehl-Missal, B. and Saren, M. (2012). Atmospheres of seduction: A critique of aesthetic marketing practices. *Journal of Macromarketing, 32*(2), 168–180.

Bitner, M. J. (1990). Evaluating service encounters: The effects of physical surroundings and employee responses. *Journal of Marketing, 54*(2), 69–82.

Bitner, M. J. (1992). Servicescapes: The impact of physical surroundings on customers and employees. *Journal of Marketing, 56*(2), 57–71.

Blombäck, A. and Brunninge, O. (2009). Corporate identity manifested through historical references. *Corporate Communications: An International Journal, 14*(4), 404–419.

Böhme, G. (2011). Un paradigme pour une esthétique des ambiances: L'art de la scénographie. In J.-F. Augoyard (Ed.), *Faire une ambiance = creating an atmosphere* (pp. 221–228). Grenoble: A la croisée.

Bonn, M. A., Joseph-Mathews, S. M., Dai, M., Hayes, S. and Cave, J. (2007). Heritage/cultural attraction atmospherics: Creating the right environment for the heritage/cultural visitor. *Journal of Travel Research, 45*(3), 345–354.

Booms, B. H. and Bitner, M. J. (1981). Marketing strategies and organizational structures for service firms. In J. H. Donnelly and W. R. George (Eds), *Marketing of services* (pp. 47–51). Chicago, IL: American Marketing Association.

Brakus, J. J., Schmitt, B. H. and Zarantonello, L. (2009). Brand experience: What is it? How is it measured? Does it affect loyalty?. *Journal of Marketing, 73*(3), 52–68.

198 *Angela Bargenda*

Burghausen, M. and Balmer, J. M. T. (2014a). Repertoires of the corporate past: Explanation and framework. Introducing an integrated and dynamic perspective. *Corporate Communications: An International Journal, 19*(4), 384–402.

Burghausen, M. and Balmer, J. M. T. (2014b). Corporate heritage identity management and the multi-modal implementation of a corporate heritage identity. *Journal of Business Research, 67*(11), 2311–2323.

Burghausen, M. and Balmer, J. M. T. (2015). Corporate heritage identity stewardship: A corporate marketing perspective. *European Journal of Marketing, 49*(1–2), 22–61.

Chen, C. F. and Chen, F. S. (2010). Experience quality, perceived value, satisfaction and behavioral intentions for heritage tourists. *Tourism Management, 31*(1), 29–35.

Dijksterhuis, A., Smith, P. K., Van Baaren, R. B. and Wigboldus, D. H. (2005). The unconscious consumer: Effects of environment on consumer behavior. *Journal of Consumer Psychology, 15*(3), 193–202.

Dion, D. and Arnould, E. (2011). Retail luxury strategy: Assembling charisma through art and magic. *Journal of Retailing, 87*(4), 502–520.

Dion, D. and Borraz, S. (2015). Managing heritage brands: A study of the sacralization of heritage stores in the luxury industry. *Journal of Retailing and Consumer Services, 22*, 77–84.

Donovan, R. J. and Rossiter, J. R. (1982). Store atmosphere: An environmental psychology approach. *Journal of Retailing, 58*(1), 34–57.

Foroudi, M. M., Balmer, J. M., Chen, W. and Foroudi, P. (2019). Relationship between corporate identity, place architecture and identification. *Qualitative Market Research: An International Journal, 22*(5), 638–668.

Foroudi, P., Melewar, T. C. and Gupta, S. (2014). Linking corporate logo, corporate image, and reputation: An examination of consumer perceptions in the financial setting. *Journal of Business Research, 67*(11), 2269–2281.

Fournier, S. (1998). Consumers and their brands: Developing relationship theory in consumer research. *Journal of Consumer Research, 24*(4), 343–373.

Gagliardi, P. (Ed.). (1990). *Symbols and artifacts: Views of the corporate landscape.* Berlin: de Gruyter.

González, M. V. (2008). Intangible heritage tourism and identity. *Tourism Management, 29*(4), 807–810.

Goulding, C. (2000). The commodification of the past, postmodern pastiche, and the search for authentic experiences at contemporary heritage attractions. *European Journal of Marketing, 34*(7), 835–853.

Gray, E. R. and Balmer, J. M. (1998). Managing corporate image and corporate reputation. *Long Range Planning, 31*(5), 695–702.

Heilbrunn, B. (2006). Brave new brands: Cultural branding between utopia and atopia. In J. E. Schroeder and M. Salzer Mörling (Eds.), *Brand culture* (pp. 103–117). London: Routledge.

Henderson, P. W., Cote, J. A., Leong, S. M. and Schmitt, B. (2003). Building strong brands in Asia: Selecting the visual components of image to maximize brand strength. *International Journal of Research in Marketing, 20*(4), 297–313.

Holt, D. B. (2004). *How brands become icons: The principles of cultural branding.* Boston: Harvard Business School Press.

Hudson, B. T. (2011). Brand heritage and the renaissance of Cunard. *European Journal of Marketing, 45*(9/10), 1538–1556.

Hultén, B. (2011). Sensory marketing: The multisensory brand experience concept. *European Business Review, 23*(3), 256–273.

Iansiti, M. and Levien, R. (2004). Strategy as ecology. *Harvard Business Review*, 82(3), 68–78.

Ind, N. and Bjerke, R. (2007). The concept of participatory market orientation: An organisation-wide approach to enhancing brand equity. *Journal of Brand Management*, 15(2), 135–145.

Jones, R. (2005). Finding sources of brand value: Developing a stakeholder model of brand equity. *Journal of Brand Management*, 13(1), 10–32.

Joy, A., Wang, J. J., Chan, T. S., Sherry, Jr, J. F. and Cui, G. (2014). M (Art) worlds: Consumer perceptions of how luxury brand stores become art institutions. *Journal of Retailing*, 90(3), 347–364.

Kapferer, J.-N. (2004). *Strategic brand management: Creating and sustaining brand equity long term*. London: Kogan Page.

Karaosmanoglu, E., Bas, A. B. E. and Zhang, J. K. (2011). The role of other customer effect in corporate marketing: Its impact on corporate image and consumer-company identification. *European Journal of Marketing*, 45(9–10), 1416–1445.

Kirby, A. E. and Kent, A. M. (2010). Architecture as brand: Store design and brand identity. *Journal of Product and Brand Management*, 19(6), 432–439.

Knight, C. and Haslam, S. A. (2010). Your place or mine? Organizational identification and comfort as mediators of relationships between the managerial control of workspace and employees' satisfaction and well-being. *British Journal of Management*, 21(3), 717–735.

Kotler, P. (1973). Atmospherics as a marketing tool. *Journal of Retailing*, 49(4), 48–64.

Kress, G. R. and Van Leeuwen, T. (1996). *Reading images: The grammar of visual design*. London: Routledge.

Maier, C. D. and Andersen, M. A. (2017). Strategic internal communication of corporate heritage identity in a hypermodal context. *Corporate Communications: An International Journal*, 22(1), 36–59.

Mari, M. and Poggesi, S. (2013). Servicescape cues and customer behavior: A systematic literature review and research agenda. *The Service Industries Journal*, 33(2), 171–199.

Mazzalovo, G. (2012). *Brand aesthetics*. Basingstoke: Palgrave Macmillan.

McAlexander, J. H., Schouten, J. W. and Koenig, H. F. (2002). Building brand community. *Journal of Marketing*, 66(1), 38–54.

McCracken, G. (1986). Culture and consumption: A theoretical account of the structure and movement of the cultural meaning of consumer goods. *Journal of Consumer Research*, 13(June), 71–84.

McCracken, G. (1988). *Culture and consumption*. Bloomington: Indiana University Press.

McDonald, H. (2011). Understanding the antecedents to public interest and engagement with heritage. *European Journal of Marketing*, 45(5), 780–804.

Melewar, T. C. and Jenkins, E. (2002). Defining the corporate identity construct. *Corporate Reputation Review*, 5(1), 76–90.

Melewar, T. C. and Karaosmanoglu, E. (2006). Seven dimensions of corporate identity, A categorisation from the practitioners' perspectives. *European Journal of Marketing*, 40(7/8), 846–869.

Melewar, T. C. and Nguyen, B. (2014). Five areas to advance branding theory and practice. *Journal of Brand Management*, 21(4), 1–12.

Melewar, T. C. and Saunders, J. (1998). Global corporate visual identity systems: Standardization, control and benefits. *International Marketing Review*, 15(4), 291–308.

Melewar, T. C. and Saunders, J. (1999). International corporate visual identity: Standardization or localization? *Journal of International Business Studies*, 30(3), 583–598.

Melewar, T. C. and Saunders, J. (2000). Global corporate visual identity systems: Using an extended marketing mix. *European Journal of Marketing*, 34(5), 538–550.

Mencarelli, R., Chaney, D. and Pulh, M. (2020). Consumers' brand heritage experience: Between acceptance and resistance. *Journal of Marketing Management*, 36(1–2), 30–50.

Merz, M. A., He, Y. and Vargo, S. L. (2009). The evolving brand logic: A service-dominant logic perspective. *Journal of the Academy of Marketing Science*, 37(3), 328–344.

Miller, D. (2014). Brand-building and the elements of success: Discoveries using historical analyses. *Qualitative Market Research: An International Journal*, 17(2), 92–111.

Morrison, M., Gan, S., Dubelaar, C. and Oppewal, H. (2011). In-store music and aroma influences on shopper behaviour and satisfaction. *Journal of Business Research*, 64(6), 558–564.

Moussa, A. and de Barnier, V. (2020). How can corporate heritage identity stewardship lead to brand ambidexterity?. *Journal of Strategic Marketing*, 1–16.

Muniz, A. M., Jr., Albert, M. and O'Guinn, T. C. (2001). Brand community. *Journal of Consumer Research*, 27(4), 412–432.

Nilsson, E. and Ballantyne, D. (2014). Reexamining the place of servicescape in marketing: A service-dominant logic perspective. *Journal of Services Marketing*, 28(5), 374–379.

Otnes, C. and Maclaren, P. (2007). The consumption of cultural heritage among a British Royal family brand tribe. In B. Cova, R. Kozinets and A. Shankar (Eds.), *Consumer tribes*. Oxford: Elsevier, 51–66.

Park, H. Y. (2010). Heritage tourism: Emotional journeys into nationhood. *Annals of Tourism Research*, 37(1), 116–135.

Pecot, F. and De Barnier, V. (2017). Brand heritage: The past in the service of brand management. *Recherche et Applications en Marketing (English Edition)*, 32(4), 72–90.

Pecot, F., Merchant, A., Valette-Florence, P. and De Barnier, V. (2018). Cognitive outcomes of brand heritage: A signaling perspective. *Journal of Business Research*, 85(April), 304–316.

Poria, Y., Biran, A. and Reichel, A. (2009). Visitors' preferences for interpretation at heritage sites. *Journal of Travel Research*, 48(1), 92–105.

Rafaeli, A. (2013). *Artifacts and organisations*. London: Routledge.

Rindell, A., Santos, F. P. and de Lima, A. P. (2015). Two sides of a coin: Connecting corporate brand heritage to consumers' corporate image heritage. *Journal of Brand Management*, 22(5), 467–484.

Rose, G. M., Merchant, A., Orth, U. R. and Horstmann, F. (2016). Emphasizing brand heritage: Does it work? And how? *Journal of Business Research*, 69(2), 936–943.

Santos, F. P., Burghausen, M. and Balmer, J. M. (2016). Heritage branding orientation: The case of Ach. Brito and the dynamics between corporate and product heritage brands. *Journal of Brand Management*, 23(1), 67–88.

Schmitt, B. H. (2009). The concept of brand experience. *Journal of Brand Management*, 16(7), 417–419.

Schmitt, B. H. and Simonson, A. (1997). *Marketing aesthetics: The strategic management of brands, identity, and image*. New York: Free Press.

Schroeder, J. E. (2009). The cultural codes of branding. *Marketing Theory*, 9(1), 123–126.

Schroeder, J. E. and Salzer-Mörling, M. (2006). Introduction: The cultural codes of branding. In J. E. Schroeder and M. Salzer Mörling (Eds.), *Brand culture* (pp. 1–12). London: Routledge.

Spielmann, N., Cruz, A. D., Tyler, B. B. and Beukel, K. (2020). Place as a nexus for corporate heritage identity: An international study of family-owned wineries. *Journal of Business Research*. https://doi.org/10.1016/j.jbusres.2019.05.024.

Strati, A. (1999). *Organization and aesthetics*. London: SAGE.

Strati, A. (2006). Organizational artifacts and the aesthetic approach. In A. Rafaeli and M. G. Pratt (Eds.), *Artifacts and organizations. Beyond mere symbolism* (pp. 23–39). London: SAGE.

Strati, A. (2009). Do you do beautiful things? Aesthetics and art in qualitative methods of organization studies. In A. Bryman (Ed.), *The Sage handbook of organizational research methods* (pp. 230–245). London: SAGE.

Urde, M., Greyser, S. A. and Balmer, J. M. (2007). Corporate brands with a heritage. *Journal of Brand Management*, 15(1), 4–19.

Van den Bosch, A. L., De Jong, M. D. and Elving, W. J. (2006). Managing corporate visual identity: Exploring the differences between manufacturing and service, and profit-making and nonprofit organizations. *The Journal of Business Communication*, 43(2), 138–157.

Van den Bosch, A. L., De Jong, M. D. and Elving, W. J. (2005). How corporate visual identity supports reputation. *Corporate Communications: An International Journal*, 10(2), 108–116.

Vargo, S. L. and Lusch, R. F. (2004). Evolving to a new dominant logic for marketing. *Journal of Marketing*, 68(1), 1–17.

Vargo, S. L. and Lusch, R. F. (2012). The nature and understanding of value: A service-dominant logic perspective. *Review of Marketing Research*, 9(1), 1–12.

Vargo, S. L., Lusch, R. F., Akaka, M. A. and He, Y. (2020). Service-dominant logic. In: E. Bridges and K. Fowler, *The Routledge handbook of service research insights and ideas* (pp. 3–23). London: Routledge.

Walsh, G., Mitchell, V. W., Jackson, P. R. and Beatty, S. E. (2009). Examining the antecedents and consequences of corporate reputation: A customer perspective. *British Journal of Management*, 20(2), 187–203.

Wheeler, A. (2003). *Designing brand identity: A complete guide to creating, building and maintaining strong brands*. Hoboken, NJ: John Wiley.

Part III

Building a corporate brand image

8 Corporate multi-channel branding

Platforms for #CorporateBranding

Awele Achi, Ogechi Adeola and Francis Chukwuedo Achi

Introduction

The digital environment has accelerated the branding dynamics of organisations as they are constantly on the lookout for modern ways of *genuinely connecting* with the passion and values of the target audience and stakeholders – customers, employees, suppliers, investors, partners, government institutions, the general public and media houses. This chapter focuses on the multi-communication channels for corporate branding. Specifically, our chapter seeks to explicate the various appropriate communication channels open to organisations as they seek to align their overall corporate branding with their internal and external stakeholders, especially, in this digital era of sustainable branding. Then, we highlight the implications of the central points raised in the chapter.

Background

Over the past four decades, the notions of corporate branding (Balmer, 2017; Rindell, 2017), corporate image (Pongpiachan, 2019; Horng et al., 2018; Dowling, 1986) and corporate reputation (Chun et al., 2019; Bundy and Pfarrer, 2015, Chun, 2005; Fombrun, 1996) have received attention from academics, practitioners and policymakers. Just as studies focusing on corporate branding have become mainstream, research focusing on communication platforms is growing as the media has become fragmented and it is vital to create and consolidate corporate brands to achieve competitive advantage (Vinuales and Sheinin, 2020; Otubanjo and Epie, 2017; Forman and Argenti, 2005; Gray and Balmer, 1998). The interest in corporate branding has been heightened by two key elements. First, organisations are keen on utilising their corporate heritage and identity as a core aspect of their value proposition in the marketplace (Hatch and Schultz, 2008). Second, there is an increasing need to manage and coordinate corporate brands separately from product brands by leveraging on the corporate image, formed by external stakeholders to build a strong corporate heritage.

Further, senior management are confronted with the major issue of determining how to actualise corporate plans, as soon as corporate branding is integrated with the strategy formulation process of organisations (Schultz and Hatch,

206 A. Achi, O. Adeola and F. C. Achi

2003). Due to drastic changes in global economic activities and the impact of the COVID-19 pandemic, organisations are faced with crucial transformations that these issues have brought as more business activities are shifting towards digital platforms. As a result, maintaining and reinforcing organisations' corporate image, reputation and overall corporate brand with the *right* communication platforms have become imperative to the survival of organisations.

Rindell (2017) noted that corporate reputation and corporate image appear as similar notions as shown in some studies (Walker, 2010); however, the two are not the same thing, as corporate reputation operates at the collective stakeholder level, whereas corporate image is formed by an individual. This distinction is discussed in much detail in the sections that follow. The overall corporate branding, including corporate image and corporate reputation are heavily shaped by an organisation's corporate heritage, its total corporate communications efforts, as well as the perception of the internal and external stakeholders about corporate activities over a period of time (Lin-Hi and Blumberg, 2018; Balmer, 2017; Ellen et al., 2006).

From this context, our chapter seeks to explore the necessity of corporate branding efforts in this era of sustainability challenges, by explicating the different communication channels and platforms available to maintain and reinforce corporate branding, corporate image and reputation of an organisation. For this purpose, first, we review the current discussions on corporate branding, corporate image, corporate reputation and the linkages between corporate image and corporate reputation; next, we present the different communication channels and platforms for corporate branding efforts. Based on this background, we provide a discussion of the implication of these diverse communication platforms and make necessary recommendations. The chapter concludes with a case study.

The need for corporate image

Over the years, scholars have argued that there is no universally accepted meaning to the concept of corporate image (Manzaneres, 2019; Abratt and Kleyn, 2012). With the growing societal expectations from actions of organisations because of changes in the business and general environment, building a favourable corporate impression in the eyes of stakeholders has taken a forefront role for differentiating among corporate brands (Liat et al., 2017).

Corporate image describes the aggregation of individual experiences and information processed, based on the physical/tangible and affective cues of the organisation – the mental picture; Kennedy (1977) ascribed the physical cues as the functional image and the affective aspect as the emotional image of corporate image construct. Consequently, for organisations, identifying with a specific corporate image is difficult because different individuals in diverse stakeholder groups have various pictures they paint in their minds (Nguyen and Leblanc, 2001). For instance, staff are concerned with work environment conditions and salaries/wages; investors worry about profitability and financial stability, while customers focus on product features and reliability of the organisation. Corporate image, hence, occupies a key position in the evaluation of an organisation's corporate strategy (Manzanares, 2019; Liat et al., 2017).

Corporate image appears to be fluid and inconsistent, as it can quickly move from being good, bad or even ordinary in the mind of individuals, based on the activities of an organisation. Subsequently, while it is difficult for organisations to influence how the personal experience of individuals determine the perceptual outcome of their corporate image, however, they do possess some form of control over the organisational culture, information and messages released out to the public in their marketing and corporate communications' channels (Hatch and Schulz, 2002; Zhang et al., 2019).

Why build a corporate reputation?

Corporate reputation has long been considered as an essential intangible asset that determines the performance of organisations (Bergh et al., 2010) and a vital tool for managing crisis (Wei et al., 2017; Tucker and Melewar, 2005).

In this present day, a day does not pass by where questions about the reputation of an organisation are not raised in the news media as it is the most intangible asset of any business entity. Corporate reputation is defined as "a perceptual representation of a company's past actions and future prospects that describes the firm's overall appeal to its key constituents" (Wei et al., 2017, p. 2103). This implies that corporate reputation is the collective impression of an organisation as held by its stakeholders; hence it falls on an organisation to work tirelessly and effectively in framing positive perceptions and emotions in the minds of stakeholders.

Prior studies suggest that organisations that dedicate resources to the management of its corporate reputation reap several benefits, which include improved relationships with stakeholders (Forman and Argenti, 2005), strategic positioning for the brand (De Chernatony, 1999), sustainable competitive advantage (Roberts and Dowling, 2002), better financial performance (Liu et al., 2019) and generalised favourability (Wei et al., 2017).

Corporate reputation plays a strategic role in an organisation, such as ensuring customer satisfaction and loyalty, as well as staff retention (Chun, 2005). Hence the need to effectively coordinate it, as it can determine if an organisation is perceived as either "doing good" or "being bad" (Chun et al., 2019; Roberts and Dowling, 2002).

Multiple platforms for strengthening corporate image and corporate reputation in this digital era

The physical separation of an organisation from its markets prompts immense complexity in effectively communicating the corporate image and reputation of the corporate brand to its various internal and external stakeholders. Previously, organisations relied mainly on their own corporate websites to provide corporate communication for most of their stakeholder groups. Nowadays, however, there is a greater need for effective planning, usage and integration of different multi-channel communication tools that can influence the perceptions on the organisation's image in the minds of the stakeholders. This should aid the organisation to achieve various objectives, such as building the brand (corporate and product), product or service awareness, gaining new audiences, brand loyalty and increased sales as well as concrete and honest feedback from customers.

Social media

The term "social media" has been used extensively to describe different web-based application activities, such as electronic media, internet and online-based web 2.0 means for social interaction and collaboration (Kaplan and Haenlein, 2010). It is sometimes wrongly denoted as "social networks" which is just one form of social media (Fill, 2013). There is, however, no unanimity in the definition of this concept, despite the prevalent usage of the word. According to Larson and Watson (2011, p. 3), social media is "the set of connectivity-enabled applications that facilitate interaction and co-creation, exchange and publication of information among firms and their networked communities of customers". The use of social media as a marketing communication tool for maintaining corporate reputation is increasingly assuming a crucial role in online communication and interaction (Fill, 2013; Singh et al., 2020). This has been driven by the democratisation of communication, leading to customer engagement and user-generated content (Kaplan and Haenlein, 2010). Consequently, Fill (2013) posited that the most visible feature of social media, as a marketing communication tool, is the management of this interaction/relationship which then engenders a change from one-way to two-way models. It can be assumed that the influence of social media is accentuated by this two-way interactive communication (Hansen et al., 2011).

Social media platforms such as the popular Facebook, Twitter and Instagram have led to the decline of online (including offline) expert opinion and the rise of opinion leaders because consumers now greatly rely on them (Smith, 2009). Recent findings by Oksiutycz and Kunene (2017) indicate that social media when used appropriately by organisations, especially, with high levels of interactivity, visual appeal and timeliness, has an impact on their corporate reputation.

Celebrity endorsement

The continual rise of online business activities and organisations' awareness of the influence of social media on their target audience have led to the engagement of celebrities to endorse brands in a bid to positively influence the perceptions of stakeholders, especially customers towards their products (Singh et al., 2020). The use of celebrity endorsement for communications purposes and marketing objectives of corporations has come a long way. Surprisingly, it appears the trend will go on even more in this current digital era since they (celebrities) are seen as instrumental and effective in imparting cultural meaning of corporate brands, to their stakeholders. The earned recognition of these celebrities, hence, is utilised by the organisations to draw the attention of their stakeholders.

Moreover, organisations cannot afford to be faceless in this era. Transparency and authenticity are key indicators that stakeholders utilise in their evaluation of a corporate image and reputation. The use of celebrities to endorse a corporate brand, hence, should be done as just one aspect of an integrated communications strategy, in a dynamic online world. Presently, the challenge is no longer communication's usefulness in projecting the image and reputation of the business, but how to optimise the practice to serve as a cutting-edge strategy. For example, Nike has, over the years, been able to use celebrities to project its corporate image and reputation. Nike has consistently been successful at this, from its positive collaboration with Michael Jordan, although it has also had some downsides, such as some negative publicity from Tiger Woods. These oscillations, however, have been professionally managed by the company and, as a result, the corporate image and reputation of Nike have been maintained and reinforced; both Jordan and Woods still endorse the Nike brand.

In the light of this, we argue that organisations need to ponder on the following three key questions when evaluating the impact of such collaborations with celebrities on their corporate image and reputation:

- What are the potential benefits and downsides of using celebrities?
- In what ways can such celebrities reinforce a corporate image?
- What is the attraction of these celebrities that will positively impact on a corporate reputation?

Online stakeholder (customer) engagement

The challenges of today's business practices have been extended considerably with the development of online activities of customers and businesses. It is no longer enough for corporations to provide products and services to their target markets through traditional means and online platforms, but now corporations require consistent engagement with their customers, in this digital era where communication is a vital aspect in the present "economy of attention".

There exist several benefits of online communication, although one element of its outstanding value is the ease of measuring customers actions and responses it provides, as the marketing metrics are more reliable and accurate. The features of online communications provide the means for dialogue, engagement and interaction between organisations and their customers; a process which also conveys the organisation's corporate identity. Nonetheless, there are reputational risks involved with online communications, due to the capacity of customers to generate contents that can adversely affect the brand; these are usually outside the control of the firm (Linke and Zerfass, 2013). According to Gulbrandsen and Just (2016), customers, among the various stakeholders of organisations, are usually at the forefront of spreading negative messages about a brand, especially in this digital era; this indicates a shift in the balance of power.

210   A. Achi, O. Adeola and F. C. Achi

The effects of multidirectional complexity of online communication mean that organisations must continuously be engaging with their customers, providing feedback and updating contents. It is through this means of engaging with stakeholders (customers) in dialogues, through different platforms, that organisations gain insights into customers' anticipations and areas to improve on (Martin and Grub, 2016); these interactions also provide opportunities to reinforce corporate reputation (Oksiutycz and Kunene, 2017).

Online corporate communication

The digital environment has changed how organisations create and manage the foundation of its relationship with stakeholders. According to Van Riel and Fombrun (2007), "corporate communication consists of the dissemination of information by a variety of specialists and generalists in an organization, with the common goal of enhancing the organization's ability to retain its license to operate" (p. 25). Online corporate communication captures the diverse internal and external ways organisations can favourably communicate and engage with its targeted audience. Examples of internal online communication tools include online forums, internal group emails, online newsletters, online social intranets, etc. External online communications range from online advertising, organising online conferences, presentations, email marketing campaigns, online press releases, corporate websites, etc. These diverse online corporate communication tools have become crucial to corporate brands, especially in situations where remote working/living is the norm, e.g. lockdown during the COVID-19 (coronavirus) pandemic.

Online corporate communication, thus, can influence the perceptions stakeholders have about the corporate reputation as it is mostly aimed at increasing the stakeholders' trust of the firm (Brønn, 2010), and understanding of its activities, judging from their messages (Floreddu and Cabiddu, 2016).

One of the main goals of corporate communication is to achieve a favourable corporate image and reputation in the minds of their stakeholders, to build their trust, as well as provide an explanation of the corporate strategy. It is expected that organisations should focus more on communicating their corporate brand online (Will and Porak, 2000), particularly, in this dispensation, where the boundaries between organisations and their stakeholders are increasingly becoming blurred because of changes in the socio-economic and environmental contexts.

Online corporate communication acts as a bridge between an organisation and its stakeholders since corporate reputation and corporate image are the results of the perceptions of internal and external stakeholder groups, which are heavily shaped by the actions and identity of the organisation. Online corporate communication acts as a nexus between branding elements of corporate reputation, corporate image and corporate identity of the organisation. Subsequently, the integration of the online corporate communication functions that harmonise the organisations' operations will ensure a strong alignment necessary for effective management of the corporate reputation. The need for synergy by the numerous

Corporate multi-channel branding   211

managers within the organisations is essential and guides the online communications put out by the organisation; hence, it should be done strategically to support and strengthen corporate reputation (Floreddu et al., 2014).

Discussion

In an era where corporate brand management and corporate branding efforts have been on the steady increase (Balmer, 2001; Otubanjo and Epie, 2017; Yakimova et al., 2017; Yang and Tan, 2017), it has become imperative to appreciate the various communication channels corporations and business organisations can use to conduct their corporate branding campaigns.

Organisations have several communication platforms at their disposal in their quest to create favourable corporate image and to manage crises that can affect their business operations. For instance, Public Health England employed its corporate websites, and corporate social media handles to serve as a means for stakeholders to understand the vision, mission, heritage and future direction of the organisation as a health institution during the COVID-19 pandemic, while also using the opportunity to favourably enhance its corporate image, corporate reputation and overall corporate brand.

Further, the use of multiple communication channels ensures that narratives about the corporate values and identity are enshrined in the various messages put out. This strategy ensures more visibility for the corporate brand that can meet the different expectations of their in-house parties and external groups. The building of a strong corporate image and reputation to enhance the value of a brand to stakeholders, in recent times, has been accelerated by the advancement of online-based communication technology using multiple platforms.

Solutions and recommendations

From the discussions we have put forward in this chapter, we provide the following recommendations.

First, we suggest that irrespective of the number of communication platforms utilised by organisations towards their corporate branding efforts, corporate brand managers have to ensure that there is consistency in the *fit* of the message as it relates to the what the organisation was (*past*), what the organisation is currently at (*present*) and what it hopes to be, going forward (*future*). Such an alignment of messages can boost the overall corporate brand, as they can help reflect the values of management, employees, customers and other stakeholder groups of the organisation.

Second, we contend that continually strengthening and reinforcing the corporate brand, including corporate image and corporate reputation are long-term projects for organisations. We suggest, therefore, that organisations make considerable investments into their communication platforms and strategies, so that these are adaptable towards unforeseen changes in the overall business environment. This is vital as we have now organisations, such as universities which

212   A. Achi, O. Adeola and F. C. Achi

have to adjust their overall corporate activities and communications during the COVID-19 pandemic.

Finally, we argue that organisations must identify their specific niche audience and make use of interactive communication platforms which offer these stakeholders (internal and external) the avenue for successful engagements that can align with corporate objectives. As Forman and Argenti (2005), posit that "corporate branding is … focused on the corporation itself as it relates to a variety of constituencies and derives, at least in part, from an alignment between strategy and communication" (p. 247). This implies that it is essential for corporate brand managers to take a critical look at their multiple stakeholders; how they can be reached through cost-minimising communications channels that align with the overall corporate strategy which, at the same time, yields optimal results for the organisation.

Future research directions

The discussions in this chapter were based on a review of existing literature; hence, no empirical data were exploited; this offers potential for future research. By conducting, for example, a case study, data-based research can be conducted on communication platforms used by organisations and their effect on corporate branding constructs such as corporate reputation and corporate image. In the light of recent happenings, like the COVID-19 pandemic, such research could produce results which identify the most potent of these communication platforms. Additionally, future research can investigate the factors influencing corporate brand managers' decisions to utilise specific communication platforms for their corporate branding activities.

Conclusion

In this chapter, we have attempted to explore the key communication channels open to corporate brand managers, in coordinating the corporate brand of an organisation, especially, given the present era's need for sustainable marketing practices. Specifically, our chapter explicated the four key channels of communication (social media, celebrities, stakeholders' empowerment and corporate communications) for establishing and managing corporate brands that best speak to their market audience, in a bid to enhance the corporate image and reputation of organisations. The decision by organisations to engage in corporate branding is fuelled by the need to build a strong corporate culture (Balmer, 2013) and create a powerful brand that aligns with the internal and external environments (Pranjar and Sarkar, 2020; Yakimova et al., 2017) on the three key tenets of passion, vision and values. We conclude by remarking that in this digital era, effective corporate branding efforts are crucial to creating and sustaining corporate symbols, values and heritage of organisations such that it connects authentically to the minds of the internal and external stakeholders of an organisation.

CASE STUDY

FirstBank launches … "Life is a Movie"

September 28, 2015

Ever wondered … if your life was a movie, what would you like it to be? Would you play a protagonist? Would it be a comedy or a thriller? First Bank of Nigeria Limited, Nigeria's most valuable banking brand, is offering its customers and consumers a unique opportunity to participate in a onetime blockbuster titled "Life is a Movie" featuring our customers. That includes YOU.

The Bank is again living up to its brand promise to put YOU first, through a series of consumer experience. Moments in our lives play out like scenes from a movie which could fit into the genres of romance, adventure, comedy and definitely drama. Whatever this moment is, FirstBank is requesting you to share this moment with us so we can begin to see the world from our customers' point of view.

With the "Life is a Movie Campaign", the Bank is requesting its customers to share experiences of exciting moments and adventures in their lives. Customers can take on characteristics they want exemplified in a movie and send video recordings of not more than one minute to the Bank. To participate, upload your video on your Facebook page and tag FirstBank's Facebook page –www.facebook.com/firstbankofnigeria or upload your video on your Instagram Page and tag FirstBank's Instagram Page – www.instagram.com/firstbanknigeria using the hashtag #LifeisaMovie.

The best entries will be pulled together to make the first ever customer focused television commercial in Nigeria starring YOU. In a statement by the Bank's spokesperson, Folake Ani-Mumuney, FirstBank has chosen its customers to run its new "YOU FIRST" advertising campaign in movie style. "Having the faces of our customers used as part of our advertising campaign represents not only what we do for our customers, but what our customers do with us". "With this campaign, we want you, our customers assured that even when life feels like a movie, FirstBank will be part of the script with lifestyle-fit products and services you need to make sure your life follows the script you planned", she stated.

This campaign demonstrates how the Bank puts its customers first. Whether it is getting them to do something new, putting them in line for something special or taking their business to the next level, FirstBank would support its customers, and ensure that they enjoy the different moments of their lives. Having been around for over 120 years, FirstBank has become the trusted and dependable partner throughout the journey of life – experiencing many moments right along with its customers and thus, playing a major role in the movie of their lives.

According to FirstBank's GMD/CEO, Bisi Onasanya, the Bank has become more than a financial institution. "Our new proposition goes beyond banking and dovetails into various aspects of the lives of the people who matter the most to us – YOU. To our customers, we are a trusted partner. A partner who you can trust to take you places, elevate your personal and professional position, and expose you to new experiences and adventures", he said.

This campaign demonstrates FirstBank's readiness to stand behind every dream, every new experience and every accomplishment and much more to better serve customers and truly put them first. Whether it is FirstBank cards to make sure you have an enjoyable holiday, or even experience another country for the first time, or its Premium banking lounges to make sure you never have to wait in line for anything or its home mortgage to make the dream of owning your first home a reality – FirstBank offers a solution designed to suit all your needs.

About First Bank

First Bank of Nigeria Limited, a subsidiary of FBN Holdings Plc, is Nigeria's leading financial services institution by total assets and gross earnings and one of the largest corporate and retail banking financial institutions in sub-Saharan Africa (excluding South Africa). Since its establishment in 1894, the Bank has consistently built relationships with customers focusing on fundamentals of good corporate governance, strong liquidity, risk management and strong capitalisation.

FirstBank operates an extensive distribution network with over 750 business locations (623 branches, 61 quick service points and 69 cash centres/ agencies), over 2,464 ATMs and over 10 million customer accounts. The Bank provides a comprehensive range of financial services and has international presence through its subsidiaries, FBN Bank (UK) Limited in London and Paris, FBNBank DRC Congo, FBNBank Ghana, International Commercial Bank (ICB) The Gambia, Guinea, Sierra-Leone and Senegal as well as its Representative Offices in Johannesburg, Beijing and Abu Dhabi.

Source: First Bank of Nigeria Limited (2015)
(reproduced with permission).

Case questions

1. How is FirstBank utilising social media to project its corporate brand and which image does the brand seek to project in the mind of its target audience?
2. What are the possible marketing outcomes of this **#LifeisaMovie** campaign?
3. Discuss how the online stakeholder (customer) engagement was utilised by the FirstBank to reinforce its brand image.

Corporate multi-channel branding   215

4. Are there challenges to the use of this corporate branding strategy by FirstBank?
5. What is the role of online corporate communication as a brand strategy?

Definitions for the key constructs

- Celebrity endorsement: the use of a well-known individual to promote a brand.
- Communication channels: these are platforms or media utilised by organisations to pass across messages about their corporate brand.
- Corporate branding: these are activities or sets of activities designed to build a favourable corporate brand.
- Corporate image: these are individually held perceptions of an organisation's corporate brand.
- Corporate reputation: an organisation's overall appeal in the minds of its entire group of stakeholders.

References

Abratt, R. and Kleyn, N. (2012). Corporate identity, corporate branding and corporate reputations: Reconciliation and integration. *European Journal of Marketing*, 46(7/8), 1048–1063.

Balmer, J. M. T. (2001). Corporate identity, corporate branding and corporate marketing: Seeing through the fog. *European Journal of Marketing*, 35(3/4), 248–291.

Balmer, J. M. T. (2013). Corporate brand orientation: What is it? What of it? *Journal of Brand Management*, 37(7–8), 723–741.

Balmer, J. M. T. (2017). The corporate identity, total corporate communications, stakeholders' attributed identities, identifications and behaviours continuum. *European Journal of Marketing*, 51(9/10), 1472–1502.

Bergh, D. D., Ketchen, D. J. Jr., Boyd, B. K. and Bergh, J. (2010). New frontiers of the reputation—Performance relationship: Insights from multiple theories. *Journal of Management*, 36(3), 620–632.

Brønn, P. S. (2010). Reputation, communication, and the corporate brand. *The Sage Handbook of Public Relations*, 307–320.

Bundy, J. and Pfarrer, M. D. (2015). A burden of responsibility: The role of social approval at the onset of a crisis. *Academy of Management Review*, 40(3), 345–369.

Chun, R. (2005). Corporate reputation: Meaning and measurement. *International Journal of Management Reviews*, 7(2), 91–109.

Chun, R., Argandoña, A., Choirat, C. and Siegel, D. S. (2019). Corporate reputation: Being good and looking good. *Business & Society*, 58(6), 1132–1142.

De Chernatony, L. (1999). Brand management through narrowing the gap between brand identity and brand reputation. *Journal of Marketing Management*, 15(1–3), 157–179.

Dowling, G. R. (1986). Managing your corporate images. *Industrial Marketing Management*, 15(2), 109–115.

Ellen, P. S., Webb, D. J. and Mohr, L. A. (2006). Building corporate associations: Consumer attributions for corporate socially responsible programs. *Journal of the Academy of Marketing Science*, 34(2), 147–157.

216   A. Achi, O. Adeola and F. C. Achi

Fill, C. (2013). *Marketing Communications: Brands Experience and Participation* (6th ed.). Harlow, UK: Pearson Education Limited.

First Bank of Nigeria Limited (2015). *FirstBank Launches…Life is a Movie* (Press release). Retrieved from https://www.firstbanknigeria.com/firstbank-launcheslife-is-a-movie/

Floreddu, P. B. and Cabiddu, F. (2016). Social media communication strategies. *Journal of Services Marketing, 30*(5), 490–503.

Floreddu, P. B., Cabiddu, F. and Evaristo, R. (2014). Inside your social media ring: How to optimize online corporate reputation. *Business Horizons, 57*(6), 737–745.

Fombrun, C. J. (1996). *Reputation: Realizing Value from the Corporate Image.* Boston, MA: Harvard University Press.

Foreman, J. and Argenti, P. A. (2005). How corporate communication influences strategy implementation, reputation and the corporate brand: An exploratory qualitative study. *Corporate Reputation Review, 8*(3), 245–264.

Gray, E. R. and Balmer, J. M. (1998). Managing corporate image and corporate reputation. *Long Range Planning, 31*(5), 695–702.

Gulbrandsen, I. T. and Just, S. N. (2016). In the wake of new media: Connecting the who with the how of strategizing communication. *International Journal of Strategic Communication, 10*(4), 223–237.

Hansen, D., Shneiderman, B. and Smith, M. A. (2011) *Analyzing Social Media Networks with NodeXL: Insights from a Connected World.* Burlington, MA: Morgan Kaufmann.

Hatch, M. J. and Schultz, M. (2002). The dynamics of organizational identity. *Human Relations, 55*(8), 989–1018.

Hatch, M. J. and Schultz, M. (2008). *Taking Brand Initiative: How Companies Can Align Strategy, Culture, and Identity through Corporate Branding?* San Francisco, CA: Jossey-Bass.

Horng, J. S., Liu, C. H., Chou, S. F., Tsai, C. Y. and Hu, D. C. (2018). Does corporate image really enhance consumer's behavioural intentions? *Asia Pacific Journal of Tourism Research, 23*(10), 1008–1020.

Kaplan, A. M. and Haenlein, M. (2010). Users of the world, unite! The challenges and opportunities of social media. *Business Horizons, 53*(1), 59–68.

Kennedy, S. H. (1977). Nurturing corporate images: Total communication or ego trip? *European Journal of Marketing, 11*(3), 120–164.

Liat, C. B., Mansori, S., Chuan, G. C. and Imrie, B. C. (2017). Hotel service recovery and service quality: Influences of corporate image and generational differences in the relationship between customer satisfaction and loyalty. *Journal of Global Marketing, 30*(1), 42–51.

Lin-Hi, N. and Blumberg, I. (2018). The link between (not) practicing CSR and corporate reputation: Psychological foundations and managerial implications. *Journal of Business Ethics, 150*(1), 185–198.

Linke, A. and Zerfass, A. (2013). Social media governance: Regulatory frameworks for successful online communications. *Journal of Communication Management, 17*(3), 270–286.

Liu, X., Vredenburg, H. and Steel, P. (2019, July). Exploring the mechanisms of corporate reputation and financial performance: A meta-analysis. In *Academy of Management Proceedings* (Vol. 2019, No. 1, p. 17903). Briarcliff Manor, NY: Academy of Management.

Manzanares, F. V. (2019). Export performance of SMEs: An empirical analysis of the mediating role of corporate image. *Journal of Small Business Management, 57*(2), 386–399.

Corporate multi-channel branding   217

Martin, S. and Grüb, B. (2016). Towards a process of agenda setting driven by social media. *International Journal of Energy Sector Management*, 10(1), 38–55.

Nguyen, N. and Leblanc, G. (2001). Corporate image and corporate reputation in customers' retention decisions in services. *Journal of retailing and Consumer Services*, 8(4), 227–236.

Oksiutycz, A. and Kunene, S. (2017). Contribution of online corporate communication to brand reputation among Millennials in the Vaal region. *Communicatio*, 43(3–4), 74–94.

Otubanjo, O. and Epie, C. (2017). Re-examining the meaning of corporate branding: Does corporate advertising give useful insights? *IUP Journal of Brand Management*, 14(4), 7–32.

Pongpiachan, S. (2019). Variables that influence stakeholder satisfaction with the creation of corporate images of Thailand's National Housing Authority. *Journal of Human Behavior in the Social Environment*, 29(3), 346–371.

Pranjal, P. and Sarkar, S. (2020). Corporate brand alignment in business markets: A practice perspective. *Marketing Intelligence & Planning*, 38(7), 907–920.

Rindell, A. (2017). Corporate image heritage. In J. M. T. Balmer (Ed)., *Foundations of Corporate Heritage* (pp. 275–287). Abingdon, UK: Routledge.

Roberts, P. W. and Dowling, G. R. (2002). Corporate reputation and sustained superior financial performance. *Strategic Management Journal*, 23(12), 1077–1093.

Schultz, M. and Hatch, M. J. (2003). The cycles of corporate branding: The case of the LEGO company. *California Management Review*, 46(1), 6–26.

Singh, J., Crisafulli, B. and Xue, M. T. (2020). 'To trust or not to trust': The impact of social media influencers on the reputation of corporate brands in crisis. *Journal of Business Research*, 119(2020), 464–480.

Smith, T. (2009). The social media revolution. *International Journal of Market Research*, 51(4), 559–561.

Tucker, L. and Melewar, T. C. (2005). Corporate reputation and crisis management: The threat and manageability of anti-corporatism. *Corporate Reputation Review*, 7(4), 377–387.

Van Riel, C. B. and Fombrun, C. J. (2007). *Essentials of Corporate Communication: Implementing Practices for Effective Reputation Management*. Abingdon: Routledge.

Vinuales, G. and Sheinin, D. A. (2020). Comparing blogs with print ads for corporate branding. The role of source credibility. *International Journal of Internet Marketing and Advertising*, 14(2), 168–183.

Walker, K. (2010). A systematic review of the corporate reputation literature: Definition, measurement, and theory. *Corporate Reputation Review*, 12(4), 357–387.

Wei, J., Ouyang, Z. and Chen, H. (2017). Well known or well liked? The effects of corporate reputation on firm value at the onset of a corporate crisis. *Strategic Management Journal*, 38(10), 2103–2120.

Will, M. and Porak, V. (2000). Corporate communication in the new media environment: A survey of 150 corporate communication web sites. *International Journal on Media Management*, 2(3–4), 195–201.

Yakimova, R., Mavondo, F., Freeman, S. and Stuart, H. (2017). Brand champion behaviour: Its role in corporate branding. *Journal of Brand Management*, 24(6), 575–591.

Yang, F. X. and Tan, S. X. (2017). Event innovation induced corporate branding. *International Journal of Contemporary Hospitality Management*, 29(3), 862–882.

Zhang, J., He, X., Zhou, C. and van Gorp, D. (2019). Antecedents of corporate image: The case of Chinese multinational enterprises in the Netherlands. *Journal of Business Research*, 101, 389–401.

9 Value co-creation behaviour
Antecedents and consequences

Yousef Alqayed, Pantea Foroudi,
Charles Dennis, Mohammad M. Foroudi
and Kaouther Kooli

Introduction

The chapter focuses on the concept of value co-creation behaviour. It identifies the key factors that have influences on favourability of value co-creation behaviour (perceived quality, identification and experience) and the outcomes (satisfaction, passion, corporate c/b commitment, brand loyalty and active participation).

Background to value co-creation and development

Value co-creation's origin goes back to the marketing orientation era of the 1960s when customers started to decide what they wanted of products (Wikstrom, 1996; Dholakia and Firat, 1998). The concept thrived as a result of the technological evolution (Tim, 2005) in the digital era, which was characterised by the rapid evolution of information technologies, Web 2.0, decentralised organisations and online communities (Fuller et al., 2009). Value co-creation is mostly studied in business-to-customer/business-to-business (B2C/B) contexts and there is limited research in the peer-to-peer (P2P) context, despite the rising need for businesses to manage value co-creation (Merz et al., 2018; Wirtz et al., 2013). Value co-creation provides organisations with access to creative and valuable ideas from different stakeholders about many aspects in the value chain including raw material use, product packaging and distribution channels (Payne et al., 2008). Value co-creation also generates brand loyalty as customer engagement in product and service design establishes and strengthens the bond between the organisation and the customer (Payne et al., 2008; Gummesson and Mele, 2010). In addition, value co-creation makes a contribution to reducing marketing and product innovation costs (Payne et al., 2008). Hence, value co-creation fosters brand loyalty, organisations' innovativeness and creativity, cost reduction, the creation of more customer-centric products and, at the same time, it contributes to their competitiveness (Payne et al., 2008; Gummesson and Mele, 2010). Moreover, value co-creation mitigates the risks associated with product design because different stakeholders participate in product idea generation, which translates into a better rate of new product success (Payne et al., 2008).

Value co-creation behaviour has become an extensively investigated concept, predominantly since Vargo and Lusch (2004) observed it as "evolving into a novel dominant logic for marketing". A service-dominant logic approach has suggested that customers (businesses) are co-creators of value (Vargo and Lush, 2008) and are involved in the procedure of value co-creation where customers' and sellers' roles are not clearly specified (Gronroos, 2008). The service-dominant logic

> is firm-centric and managerially oriented" (Vargo and Lush, 2008, p. 2) and has its origin in the foundational propositions that create value among organisations and stakeholders "in every aspect of the value chain (**foundational** premises – FP6) and that it is the beneficiary who always uniquely and phenomenologically determines this value through value-in-use perceptions (FP10).
>
> (Merz et al., 2018, p. 79)

Various studies ranging from co-creation (Gronroos, 2008; Payne et al., 2008; Simula and Ahola, 2014; Vargo and Lush, 2008) and service-dominant logic (Merz et al., 2009; Ramaswamy and Ozcan, 2016; Vargo and Lusch, 2016) have tried to understand how brand value can be co-created (Fournier, 1998; Harmeling et al., 2017; Merz et al., 2018). However, as Merz et al. (2018) pointed out, co-creation in peer platforms is likely to remain indefinable for marketers without a more particular understanding of when and how peers can co-create value and how that value can be evaluated via a peer platform.

There is a growing interest in value co-creation in different business contexts (e.g., B2C and B2B). According to Foroudi et al. (2019), value co-creation is an emerging business concept, in which customers' participation involves personalised experiences, goods and services, by being involved in the design and development procedure and through their participation in the brand community. Value co-creation is regarded as a tool for developing services and products through interaction with employees (e.g. internal), customers (e.g. external) and stakeholders (Ramaswamy and Gouvillart, 2010) as a collective, highly dynamic continuous process among all the actors participating in the network of relationships (Iansiti and Levien, 2004). Value co-creation is the future of innovation (Prahalad and Ramaswamy, 2003). However, there is limited empirical study on how the concept of peer value co-creation behaviour might be defined. Furthermore, previous research (e.g. Gronroos, 2011; Merz et al., 2018; Vargo and Lusch, 2004, 2008, 2011) *did not address the cause-and-effect relationship between peer value co-creation behaviour and its consequences.*

The importance of value co-creation – Value co-creation provides organisations with access to creative and valuable ideas from different stakeholders about many aspects in the value chain including raw material use, product packaging and distribution channels (Payne et al., 2008). Value co-creation also generates brand loyalty because customer participation in product design establishes and strengthens the bond between the organisation and the customer (Gummesson and Mele, 2010; Payne et al., 2008). In addition, value co-creation contributes to reducing marketing and product innovation costs (Payne et al., 2008).

According to Vargo and Lush (2004), all stakeholders are co-creators of value. This value can only be determined by customers themselves (Vargo and Lusch, 2008). Gronroos and Voima (2013) argued that customers and organisations directly or indirectly interact to generate value. Indirect interaction between customers and organisations implies that organisations manufacture products, and, hence, act as value facilitators, and customers create this value through the use of the offering (Gronroos and Voima, 2013; Prahalad and Ramaswamy, 2004). Consequently, this value is a "value in use" because it is only created when the consumer uses the product (Ballantyne and Varey, 2008; Gronroos, 2008). In direct interaction, customers co-create value with the organisation (Gronroos and Voima, 2013) through different stages of value co-creation (VCC) (Bonsu and Darmody, 2008).

VCC has mainly been conceptualised from the direct interaction between the organisation and the customers (Vargo and Lusch, 2004). Little attention has been given to VCC indirect interaction. Iglesias et al. (2013) argued that multiple economic and social actors within networks contribute to VCC. Organisations'/customers' direct interaction is leveraged by online social network. However, even though research addressed the direct customer/organisation interaction on social media (Michaelidou et al., 2011), it did not emphasise the role of different online platforms, i.e. peer platforms, compared to the indirect interaction between them in VCC.

The rise of the sharing economy context, or as it is also known, collaborative consumption, has had a drastically significant influence on economic growth and has attracted both academic and practitioner interest. Completely dissimilar to the common B2B model, the concept of a sharing economy represents a new peer-to-peer business model in which separate individuals (also known as peers) play an active role in delivering a service. Individuals who transact directly with other individuals in an online platform that is managed and run by a third party. The best examples in this regard include Airbnb, Eatwith and Uber. The sharing economy business model is managed by "the value in taking under-utilised assets and making them accessible online to a community, leading to a reduced need for ownership" (Stephany, 2015, p. 205). Having access to and using other resources instead of owning them can facilitate the consumption of goods and services (Schor and Fitzmaurice, 2015) and allows peer consumers (peers who purchase and employ other peer resources in the platform) to purchase and use other goods and services with the lower process (Leismann et al., 2013). The P2P business model rooted in the sharing economy context suggests that the essence of the customer-firm relationship and brand-focused relationship, which are built upon traditional business contexts (B2C and B2B), can no longer hold. What makes VCC different as a result of P2P interaction in a peer platform, has not been adequately discussed. In order to better manage and enhance VCC, P2P platforms have to understand how value is created through the peer interaction in their platforms.

Three spheres of value co-creation – According to Vargo and Lush (2004), all stakeholders are value co-creators. In addition, customers can assess value themselves (Vargo and Lusch, 2008). However, Gronroos and Voima (2013) claimed that there are three spheres for value co-creation: (i) the provider value creation sphere – in this sphere, the organisation acts as a value facilitator because production is done in the organisation without direct relationship between the organisation and the customers. However, the value cannot be created with the organisation alone in the absence of customers (Gronroos and Voima, 2013). (ii) The customer value creation sphere – in this sphere, value is created while the consumer uses the product. This is why it is called the "value-in-use" approach (Gronroos, 2008; Ballantyne and Varey, 2008). In this sphere, the organisation is a facilitator of the potential value, and the customer creates this value through the use of the offering (Gronroos and Voima, 2013; Prahalad and Ramaswamy, 2004). (iii) The joint value creation sphere – in this sphere, value is the result of the direct communication between the organisation and the customers through different stages of value co-creation (Bonsu and Darmody, 2008) and, thus, customers co-create value with the organisation (Gronroos and Voima, 2013). The concept of value co-creation has mainly been conceptualised from the dynamic relationship between the organisation and customers in the joint value creation sphere point of view (Gronroos and Voima, 2013). The literature highlights that multiple social and economic actors within networks contribute to value co-creation (Iglesias et al., 2013; Vargo and Lusch, 2004).

The notion of value co-creation has gained considerable attention from both business and management researchers (e.g. Grönroos et al., 2013; Schau et al., 2009). Over the preceding years, different researchers have analysed a wide range of value co-creation related concepts including co-creation behaviour (Hatch and Schultz, 2010; Yi and Gong, 2013), co-creation ecosystems (Pitelis, 2012) and co-innovation (Lee et al., 2012), all of which have received substantial attention. This body of knowledge remains disjointed and indicates very few normative and prescriptive approaches to value co-creation. To develop more relevant research on the concept of value co-creation, a valid intellectual, structural analysis is needed.

The concept of service

During the early 1960s, scholars (e.g. Fuchs, 1965; Judd, 1964) argued that the business discipline and, more specifically, marketing, should be mainly product-centric and should mainly concentrate on the quality of products/services. The service sectors, such as insurance or transportation, were mainly considered as aiding in making higher quality products (Converse, 1921). Subsequently, in a long debate between the service and goods paradigms, there were some arguments suggesting that the study of marketing cannot be solely based on the simple axiom that services and goods are two different concepts and, as Wyckham et al. (1975) pointed out, it is more likely to be *dysfunctional*.

222 Alqayed, Foroudi, Dennis, Foroudi and Kooli

As the different sectors (e.g. bank industry, transportation) contribute profoundly to the GDP of different industrialised countries, different scholars (e.g. Carman and Langeard, 1980; Morris and Johnston, 1987) realised the importance of the service provision as a separate paradigm from goods. The study by Shostack (1977) highlighted the importance of understanding services more succinctly, as there were no prior and practical knowledge and terminology relevant to service (Table 9.1 presents a brief review of various schools of thought in marketing literature).

There has been a fundamental shift in the marketing perspective from what is called "good dominant"'(G-D logic) to the term "service-dominant logic" (S-D logic). Different scholars (e.g. Lusch et al., 2007; Merz et al., 2009) have underpinned six main differences between each of these approaches, which are summarised in Table 9.2.

Service science is a disciplinary method that mainly concentrates on studying systems that comprise resources, processes and participants. Researchers (e.g. Barile and Polese, 2010; Vargo and Lusch, 2008) suggest that the main purpose of service science is for creating value and improving the relationship in the service system. Maglio and Spohrer (2008) stated that the service system is studying the dynamics of the configuration of resources (e.g. technology, shared information and organisations). Besides, the service system can comprise methods that are helpful for clarification and a better understanding of value co-creation for both practitioners and researchers.

In addition, the work of Vargo and Lusch (2004) provides the basis of value co-creation in the service system. scholars (e.g. Alves et al., 2016; Hietanen

Table 9.1 Brief review of different schools of thought in marketing

Timeline	The main focus of the literature	Fundamental ideas of the proposition
1800–1920	**Classic and neoclassic economics**	• Value is only generated through manufacturing. • Goods can become commodities. • Wealth in society is generated through the acquisition of stuff.
1920–1950	**Formative marketing**	• Products/functions. • Focus on process and output. • Adding value to products. • Marketing can only provide utility.
1950–1980	**Marketing management**	• 4Ps (Product/price/place/promotion). • Sales can be "determined" and 'embedded". • Focus on customer satisfaction.
1980– Present	**Marketing as economic and social process**	• Relationship marketing. • Market orientation. • Quality management. • Values and supply chain management. • Network analysis.

Source: adopted from Vargo and Lusch (2004, p. 3).

Value co-creation behaviour   223

Table 9.2 Role of operand and operant resources in distinguishing goods-dominance from service-dominant logic

Goods-dominant logic	Resources	Service-dominant logic
Wealth is generated by obtaining tangible goods and resources. In this regard, wealth is referred to as controlling, owing to producing operand resources.	Source of economic growth	Wealth is made through the integration and application of specific knowledge and skill, which represent the right to use operant resources.
Value is only determined by the producers. It is embedded in goods and refers to the term "exchange value".	Meaning and determining of value	Value is perceived and can be determined on the basis of value in use. Firms can only make "propositions".
The customers are considered to act as an *operand resource*. They also act in a way to make a transaction with resources.	Firm-customer relationship	Customers actively participate in relational co-production and exchange.
The customer is the recipient of products. Marketers do things to customers (segmentation, distribution, penetration, promotion). In this respect, customers are operand resources.	Role of customer	The customer can co-create with service. Marketing is the process of interaction with customers. Customers are mainly operant resources.
Products are considered to be operand resources. Marketers take matter and change its form, place time, and possession.	Role of goods	People exchange to acquire the benefits of specific competencies (skills and knowledge) or services. *Operant resources.*
People exchange for goods. These goods serve primarily as operand resources.	The primary unit of exchange	People exchange to acquire the benefits of specialised competences (knowledge and skill) or services. *Operant resources*

Source: developed based on Vargo and Lusch (2004a, p. 7).

et al., 2018; Maglio and Spohrer, 2008, 2013; Pohlmann and Kaartemo, 2017; Skålén and Edvardsson, 2016; Wilden et al., 2017) who stated that S-D logic shifted the marketing paradigm from good-dominant logic centred in marketing towards service-dominant logic. Noteworthily, Lusch and Vargo (2006) pointed out that S-D logic is an approach for having a better insight into service (or process) instead of services (plural) and goods as outcomes of customer transactions with firms. However, as Osborne (2013) pointed out, S-D logic can be applied in generating new and novel perspectives in service system configurations. What is more, Maglio and Spohrer (2008) added that S-D conceptualisation could largely be used in generating new perspectives in service-systems. Service science needs

224 Alqayed, Foroudi, Dennis, Foroudi and Kooli

the integration and application of a wide range of theories from different perspectives, such as psychology, marketing and information systems.

The first and most fundamental difference between the S-D logic and G-D logic is the service conceptualisation of service and a shift concerning the important role of value co-creation (Vargo and Lusch, 2008). Vargo and Lusch (2004) suggested that service is the integration of different competencies (e.g. knowledge and skill) to benefit others and themselves. In this respect, service is conceptualised as the process of doing something for a third party, instead of the units of the tangible outcome. Vargo and Akaka (2009) suggested that service can be provided either directly or indirectly through social and economic exchange. In the S-D logic, the value co-creation refers to the process of service-for-service perspectives (Maglio and Spohrer, 2008). In this vein, Vargo and Akaka referred to value co-creation as a dynamic process in a social system in which "service is provided, resources are integrated, and value is co-created" (p. 207).

Service-dominant logic

The service-dominant logic is the solid foundation of all exchanges in the complex configuration of resources (e.g. institutions, money, goods) (Vargo et al., 2008). Additionally, the service-dominant-logic is described as being more of a marketing perspective than a marketing offering (Grönroos, 2008). Customers are not so much interested in what they purchase and use, but the positive results rooted in the service activities they peruse (Grönroos and Ravald, 2011). What is more, S-D logic has been seen as a perspective that integrates different segments of marketing together in a new marketing configuration. The Nordic school service management perspective (Grönroos, 2008) expresses similar views on S-D logic. The very basis of these approaches is that the value is not purely generated in the customer and companies exchange, but instead, it is generated in the value co-creation between different stakeholders (Grönroos, 2008). Similar to the system approach in the information system, S-D logic can be seen discussed with similar traits in the visible system approach (VSA) that argues that every business and company is a system in a related context aiming to make actions visible through interaction with other actors in a system configuration. Similarly, S-D logic shares some similarities with group approaches in industrial marketing and purchasing (IMP), which focuses on the actor-resources activities model.

Service-dominant logic is the outcome of the Vargo and Lusch article in 2004 in the *Journal of Marketing* and a related book published in 2006. Service-dominant logic suggests that "The fundamental purpose of economic exchange and marketing that is, service is exchanged for service. We believe this logic is applicable not only to markets and marketing but also to society" (Lusch and Vargo, 2006a, p. 17). S-D logic tries to offer customised services to customers to increase their satisfaction. S-D logic states that the process of consumption and production of goods is a continuous process and not a distinctive activity. In this vein, Lusch et al. (2007) stated that consumption and production are "superordinate service (the process of providing benefit) to products (units of output that

Value co-creation behaviour 225

are sometimes used in the process)" (p. 6). Customers are not merely the recipient of firm value, but they are also involved in the process of value co-creation (Etgar, 2008) and can act as a source of the operand and operant resources (Vargo and Lusch, 2004) for companies.

The historical development of S-D logic

The S-D logic has profoundly contributed to marketing and has raised international scholars to a new "perspective on business and marketing" (Grönroos and Gummerus, 2014, p. 210). While some scholars (Edvardsson et al., 2011; Harris et al., 2010; Skålén and Edvardsson, 2016) refer to it as a theory, Vargo and Lusch (2014) referred to service pre-theoretic, which provides a theoretical foundation for marketing (p. 211).

The fundamental premises of S-D logic make upan alternative perspective to good-dominant logic, in which value is generated through the process of exchange (Akakka and Vargo, 2015) between the customer and firms (Harris et al., 2010; Uusitalo and Grønhaug, 2012). Initially, service marketing emerged as a sub-discipline in marketing literature and gradually became distinctive from good marketing. This distinction between these two categories took place due to the main difference in the essence of goods and services (Zeithaml et al., 1985). The findings of Zeithaml et al. (1985) revealed that there are archetypal characteristics in service, which distinguish it from goods. These distinctions are (1) services are not tangible (contrary to goods, services are mainly the performance and lack the quality of goods), (2) heterogeneity (services can be different from one producer to another producer), (3) inseparability between consumption and production (the process of consumption and production occur simultaneously) and, finally, perishability (services cannot be inventoried or be generated in advance).

Vargo and Lusch (2004b) proposed, contrary to the discussed distinctions, "goods are distribution mechanisms for service provision", and that "economic exchange is fundamentally about service provision" (p. 326). Service is common in all kinds of exchanges regardless of being services or goods. In this vein, Gummesson (1994) suggested that customers do not buy goods or services: they buy offerings that "render services which create value" (p. 250). By primarily focusing on the value-in-exchange or the price of goods or services, the S-D logic shifts the attention to the contextual and phenomenological aspect of value (known as the value-in-use). Additionally, S-D logic proposes that customers are in the centre of generating and identifying the value (Akaka and Vargo, 2015; Grönroos, 2011; Skålén and Edvardsson, 2016).

Although S-D logic refers to service as the foundation of different exchanges, both economic and social exchanges, its fundamental notion of this perspective is not primarily new (Vargo and Lusch, 2016). Basiat was the first one who proposed that "services are exchanged for services" (Grönroos and Gummerus, 2014). In a similar vein, different scholars (e.g. Bowman and Ambrosini, 2000; Prahalad and Ramaswamy, 2003; Ramirez, 1999) applied the value co-creation concept for several years before the initial article of Vargo and Lusch was published in 2004.

226   Alqayed, Foroudi, Dennis, Foroudi and Kooli

Furthermore, to some extent, the notion of S-D logic has been used in marketing literature since 1970 (Grönroos, 2011) and is combined with a newer perspective of "service reciprocity" in the marketing literature. As stated by Vargo and Lusch (2008),

> In fact, S-D logic was, from its beginning, more about the identification and extension of apparent coalescence in the ongoing development of marketing thought...than a radically new idea. That is, it has been grounded on a foundation built by many others, as has been its progress.
>
> (p. 2)

Furthermore, S-D logic has continuously evolved and has undergone a series of changes since its emergence (Table 9.3 illustrates these changes). In this chapter, the researcher's attention was mainly on the revision of S-D logic, which is mainly relevant for the focus of this research instead of all the modifications made to this perspective.

The service-dominant logic and value co-creation

As discussed earlier, S-D logic is regarded as the basis of all exchanges through a complicated combination of resources (e.g. knowledge, money) (Saarijärvi et al., 2013). In addition, S-D logic is a perspective in the marketing literature instead of a marketing literature offering (Grönroos, 2008). In this vein, Grönroos and Ravald (2011) stated that customers are not primarily keen on the service/products a firm can offer to them, and are, on the contrary, mainly eager for positive outcomes and value as a result of the service activities. Additionally, the results of Edvardsson et al. (2005) support the same view in which the service is mainly considered to be an activity. Their findings suggest that a service is an approach to value co-creation instead of the categorising of the market. Vargo et al. (2008) suggested that service should be seen as an integration of resources for benefiting the other actor or the actor in a service ecosystem. Vargo and Lusch (2013) also noted that service should not be interpreted as units of intangible outputs (e.g. transportation) and should be regarded as a unit of intangible output that can refer to all business companies.

As Ramaswamy and Gouilart (2010) stated, value co-creation can influence the strategies of companies and the way they operate. Payne et al. (2008) stated that, usually, a business strategy of one actor is considered to conduct the decisions of which the core product or business can operate in. However, according to Payne et al. (2008), based on the S-D logic, business strategies commence with realising the value co-creation and deciding what part the supplier would be in it in order to provide better support for value co-creation. To find a more comprehensive understanding of how value can be co-created, and also to gain a more integrated and detailed understanding of value co-creation, it is vital to realise who co-creates value (e.g. customers, employees), what type of resources are needed in the value co-creation process and, ultimately, what kind of mechanism is value co-created.

Value co-creation behaviour 227

Table 9.3 The istorical development of S-D logic

	Vargo and Lusch, 2004a	*Vargo and Lusch, 2004a*	*Lusch and Vargo, 2014/ Vargo and Lusch, 2016a update*
FP1	The application of specialised skill(s) and knowledge is the fundamental unit of exchange	Service is the fundamental basis of exchange	*Remains the same but given* AXIOM STATUS-Axiom 1
FP2	Indirect exchange masks the fundamental basis of exchange	*Remains the same*	*Remains the same*
FP3	Goods are distribution mechanisms for service provision	Goods are a distribution mechanism for service provision	*Remains the same*
FP4	Knowledge (operant resources) is the fundamental source of competitive advantage	Operant resources are the fundamental source of competitive advantage	Operant resources are a fundamental source of strategic benefit
FP5	All economies are services economies	All economies are service economies	*Remains the same*
FP6	The customer is always a co-producer	The customer is always a co-creator of value	Value is co-created by multiple actors always including the service beneficiary. AXIOM STATUS-Axiom 2
FP7	The enterprise cannot deliver value, but only offer value propositions	The enterprise cannot deliver value, but only offer value propositions	Actors cannot deliver value but can participate in the creation and the offering of value propositions
FP8	A service-centred view is customer oriented and relational	A service-centred view is inherently customer oriented and relational	*Remains the same*
FP9	N/A	All social and economic actors are resource integrators	*Remains the same but given* AXIOM STATUS-Axiom 3
FP10	N/A	Value is always uniquely and phenomenologically determined by the beneficiary	*Remains the same but given* AXIOM STATUS-Axiom 4
FP11	N/A	N/A	Value co-creation is coordinated through actor-generated institutions and institutional arrangements. AXIOM STATUS-Axiom 5

Actors

All economic and social actors can take part in integrating the resources. In this respect, value co-creation is an interactive process; involving different actors (e.g. employees, customers) (Macdonald et al., 2011; Vargo and Lusch, 2008). Actors who participate in value co-creation should be able to identify and recognise such incentives. These incentives can be either intrinsic benefits or monetary rewards (Saarijärvi et al., 2013). As customers play an important role in co-creating value with different actors, companies are under the pressure of customer intrinsic, social and extrinsic motivation for taking part in the joint process of value co-creation (Antikainen, 2011). Additionally, firms should be able to take into account the partner requirement in their value networks.

Firms can not solely create or offer value to their customers, but they can offer the advantages of service, which can be created collaboratively. As a matter of fact, Vargo and Lusch (2008) suggested that the role of the firm is facilitating the value co-creation with customers, instead of designing and providing value to the peers. Based on the S-D logic, value proposition is the main and the key fundamental premise in S-D logic. A value proposition can be considered as forming a relationship, network and connection and, in some cases, opportunities (Vargo et al., 2008). Additionally, Grönroos (2008) stated that through the process of interaction between the customer and the company, the company could also be engaged in co-creating value. Companies can, in both a direct and indirect manner, have an impact on the process of value co-creation by being involved in the joint process of value co-creation and collaboratively create value with their customers. Hence, firms can no longer be considered to be value co-creation propositions but able to engage themselves in the customers' value fulfilment (Grönroos, 2008). Consequently, firms can benefit from the value in terms of customer referral, revenue and higher profit margin. The results of Payne and Frow (2005) suggested that when firms manage to co-create the value successfully, customers are highly likely to stay loyal to them.

What is more, firms can also expand market offers when they include firm interaction (Grönroos, 2008). For instance, firm employees can be seen participating in a dialogue with customers (Payne et al., 2008). Ballantyne and Varey (2008) conducted research about the importance of the communication, suggesting that communication and, more importantly, dialogue, is an interactive process of learning in any marketing relationship. What is more, the results of Payne et al. (2008) suggested that both customers and service providers have this chance to co-create value with customised offerings (Payne et al., 2008).

As for companies, only certain customers are considered to be more valuable than others; the surplus of unprofitable customers is not interested in joining the value co-creation. The output of value co-creation is mainly based on customer economic value. Customers are considered to be valuable for companies as long as they offer value to them. S-D logic stresses that customers are the source of value co-creation (Prahalad and Ramaswamy, 2004). Customers should acquire knowledge, utilise and adapt to what firms offer them based on their usage situation, individual needs and behaviour (Vargo and Lusch, 2004). In such cases, Payne et al. (2008) suggested that customers mainly represent the role of a quality controller, co-marketer and co-producer. According to Rifkin (2000), customers are mainly interested in forming a relationship with firms that can satisfy their needs over an extended period of time. At the same time, customers have a chance to influence the activities of the firms. Such activities have an essential and necessary impact on the value co-creation (Grönroos, 2008).

To begin with, customers use services. Otherwise, they purchase products and services (Vargo and Lusch, 2004). By using these services, customers can create value through a dynamic process. Additionally, they can identify the value for themselves through the dynamic process (Grönroos and Ravald, 2011). Consequently, the process of value co-creation cannot occur in the manufacturing process but is rooted in the process that the customer actually uses to consume the products/services (this process is also known as the value in use) (Grönroos, 2008). As Tapscott and Williams (2006) stated, customers are no longer a passive target of the marketing segmentation, but they have shifted their roles from that of mere consumers to creators and contributors in value co-creation. This view implies the fact that value is only created when different actors in a service ecosystem actually use and utilise the products/services (Grönroos and Voima, 2013).

Value can range from an economic strategy to a behavioural dimension. Customer perception about value is dependent on their ability to achieve and satisfy their needs in certain usage situations. Customers are mainly interested in maximising their perceived benefits while decreasing the resources they possess (e.g. customers are mainly interested in paying less for the same quality product/service). In order to engage different actors (e.g. customers, employees) in value co-creation, customers should have the necessary resources (e.g. mental and physical resources/tools). Firms can develop a highly competitive advantage through the process of consumption and using (Vargo and Lusch, 2004) the products/services. When firms engage themselves in the process of consumption and the use of products and services (Grönroos, 2008), firms can learn the customers' needs, which, consequently, results in developing more varied products/services (Grönroos, 2008) that can satisfy customer needs more easily.

Resources

S-D logic argues that services are the fundamental basis of the exchange. Customers not only require goods, but, additionally, they need them to perform physical and mental resources for satisfying their needs (Vargo and Lusch, 2004). From this point of view, value co-creation is a change in the traditional role of firms that are considered customers as consumers of product/services and the customers as not only the providers of the source of income for firms (Saarijärvi et al., 2013).

Based on the S-D logic, all social and economic parties can participate in integrating resources (Vargo and Lusch, 2008; Saarijärvi et al., 2013). The application and integration of unique resources can constitute and motivate exchange (Vargo and Lusch, 2006). Customers follow activities that support their own resources or other resources that are acquired from external resources. In order to be involved in the process of value co-creation, some customers have to acquire a certain type of resource, while other resources are the ones that the customer possesses. Additionally, customers need the required skill for being able to develop the value potential of resources in the value in use. If customers do not have the necessary resources and skills that are needed by other actors, the value in use cannot exist or be co-created. In other words, the value for the company is then dependent on the value that resources present for the customer (Grönroos, 2008).

Dynamic resources are the sources that are fundamental for achieving a sustainable competitive advantage for firms (Vargo and Lusch, 2004, 2008) for value co-creation and are categorised into operand and operant resources. The first type of resources, operand resources, are those that act or in which the operation is done to generate an effect. The second category, operant, should be employed on operand resources (Constantin and Lusch, 1994). For instance, mental competencies and knowledge can be referred to as operant resources. Additionally, operand resources can be considered as physical materials and raw materials. Additionally, customers can be an operand resource (Vargo and Lusch, 2004) and also be considered as an operant resource for a firm. Grönroos (2008) stated that customers can be considered as value co-creators and can create value for the firms and themselves by applying skills that are held together by using the resources provided by the company.

Mechanisms

The S-D logic emphasises the important role of the resources and process that firms seek to create value propositions (Vargo and Lusch, 2004). It needs actors to be able to interact directly with each other and apply their expertise by working on a resolution (Ramaswamy and Gouillart, 2010). The process comprises mechanisms, such as tasks, interaction and activities that support value co-creation. Grönroos (2008) suggested that value co-creation is a process of activities and interaction in which actors are a part.

Firms need to manage their resources in an effective way. This can be necessary for determining the value proposition and providing a total customer offering to satisfy customer needs (Grönroos, 2008). In order to be successful in the value co-creation, companies should provide a platform that mainly focuses on gathering the experiences of the main key actors (Ramaswamy and Gouillart, 2010). Such a platform should allow actors to interact and share their knowledge. Different purposes for sharing information can be, for example, gathering customer requirements for new product development, identifying unknown customer needs and trying to accommodate those needs (Ramaswamy and Gouillart, 2010). Customers follow activities and process (e.g. manufacturing, advertising, accounting) that might be supportive of their own resources and the resources that are acquired from outside resources (Grönroos, 2008).

Customers and firms should have a dynamic, interactive and longitudinal relationship (Payne et al., 2008) with each other for successful value co-creation. However, finding such a mechanism in which all actors (e.g. operator employees and customers) are involved is difficult (Ramaswamy and Gouillart, 2010). As value can be created in such customer's practices, firms should primarily focus on this process (Grönroos, 2008). Vargo and Lusch (2004) suggested that the success/failure of a firm in value co-creation is mainly dependent on offering an efficient and standardised solution that makes it easier for customers to participate in the value co-creation process (Vargo and Lusch, 2004).

Co-production and co-creation

Based on the S-D logic framework, co-production is the "creation of the value proposition – essentially design, definition, production, etc.", and value co-creation is "the actions of multiple actors, often unaware of each other, that contribute to each other's well-being" (Vargo and Lusch, 2016a, p. 8). In contrast, co-production comprises those activities in which customers are engaged in developing and improving the service (e.g. new service development). Similarly, Chathoth et al. (2013) stated that co-creation and co-production are two separate concepts that "can be adopted by organisations in their attempts to respond to customer expectations" (p. 11). Their findings suggest that co-production and co-creation are different in respect of "whether value creation is derived through a production or consumption process" (p. 13). Their study suggests that the difference "between co-creation and co-production is a continuum rather than a dichotomy" (p. 11).

The difference between co-production and value co-creation extends beyond the S-D logic framework. The study by Ranjan and Read (2016) on 149 articles suggested two distinctive dimensions: value in use and co-production. In this respect, co-production is mainly found to be concerned with the aspect of "exchange" in the customer-firm interaction, while "value in use" is more aligned with the view that suggests that value is always created in use. Additionally, their study suggests that value co-creation comprises two primary elements (co-production and value in use) that have their own unique dimensions. These dimensions include personalisation, knowledge, relationship, experience, communication and equity. To some extent, the first five elements are reflected in the S-D logic framework. However, it is more ambiguous how equity can be reflected within the S-D logic. According to the S-D logic (Lusch and Vargo, 2014) customers "themselves are operant resources" (p. 119) and consider that all the actors involved in value co-creation can take part in integrating resources. Concerning the capacity of being able to be involved in the value co-creation process in relation to the process of value co-destruction. On the other hand, Vargo and Lusch (2016) stated that "generic actors" in S-D logic could not "be confused with a position that all actors are identical" (p. 7).

The differences between co-creation and co-production in S-D logic have been emphasised to some extent. However, it is noteworthy, that as the term is

232 *Alqayed, Foroudi, Dennis, Foroudi and Kooli*

shared by different disciplines (e.g. public management and service marketing), it cannot be assumed that these two terms are identical. According to Vargo and Lusch (2016b), this is mainly because these terms have been used for describing quite a similar phenomenon

Value co-creation

According to S-D logic, the concentration of value co-creation has moved from the company output to value in use, and, ultimately, value in context (Vargo et al., 2008). Lusch and Vargo (2006) suggested that the main purpose of value co-creation is the collaborative effort in which different actors reciprocally and jointly take part in creating value. Vargo et al. (2008) claimed that value co-creation goes through different processes, such as resource integration and the application of competencies to create sustainable value for others and also themselves.

According to the second axiom, Vargo and Lusch (2016) suggested that the nature of value co-creation is made by multiple and different actors who try to maximise their value and benefits. In this respect, value co-creation does not happen through an individual actor who provides different resources, as it requires customers to contribute to value co-creation. The main difference of value in use and value co-creation is that, while value co-creation occurs through multi-actor interaction, the value in use does not require multiple parties (Kuzgun and Asugman, 2015). Although there has been extensive literature on value as being co-created, another researcher believed that value is the judgement of an individual perspective. However, S-D logic argues that value can be co-created by parties instead of being the mere outcome of service co-creation.

Value in a multi-actor relationship is conceptualised as the value in context. According to Chandler and Vargo (2011), context is "a set of unique actors with unique reciprocal links among them" (p. 40). Consequently, instead of the value being embedded through service/products. Value in use should be captured while customers are experiencing the co-creation of products and services (Woodruff and Flint, 2006). The co-created value consequences can contain subjective beneficial outcomes for the customers instead of state benefit, which can be perceived in a negative way. In other words, as Vargo and Lusch (2016) stated in their Axiom Four (A4) "value is always uniquely and phenomenologically determined by the beneficiary" (p. 10).

According to Ballantyne and Varey (2006), value is a difficult perception in its nature. According to Zeithaml (1988), value is the individual's evaluation of supplier offering, which includes the benefits and costs. Similarly, Khalifa (2004) defined value as the weight given by consumers to diverse benefits when they are evaluating a service/product. While benefits mainly comprise intangible and tangible features, costs mainly include non-monetary and monetary factors like effort and time (Gale et al., 1994; Gronroos, 1997). Consequently, the value can be conceptualised as the perception and preference of the actor (Echeverri and Skålén, 2011). Value is always determined by perception and is always assessed by experiencing and using service outcomes (Vargo and Lusch,

2008). Consequently, value is considered to be a multi-dimensional factor that can change through customer experiences (Vafeas et al., 2016).

Previous studies highlighted the importance of value as a cognitive concept that can have a direct influence on customer behaviour (Babin et al., 2019; Cossío-Silva et al., 2016; Gallarza et al., 2016; Han et al., 2017; Karjaluoto et al., 2016). Other researchers (e.g. Fornell et al., 2016; Hamilton et al., 2016; Iniesta-Bonillo et al., 2016; Lam et al., 2012; Oh and Kim, 2017) have stated that value is the main predictor of customer satisfaction and behavioural outcome. Consequently, value is defined in terms of context and is realised by the subjective judgement of actors in the co-creation system. This study defines value as the "value in context" in the multiple customer and firms' interactions. Additionally, this study is in line with the result of Vafeas et al. (2016) who suggested that "service is co-created, while the value is realised by the individual as an evaluative judgement of the benefit or worth against criteria derived from personal values (plural)" (p. 480).

Customer value co-creation behaviour

The results of Yi and Gong (2013) suggested that there are two main components for value co-creation behaviour. The first one, or customer participation behaviour, refers to the required customer behaviour for participating in the value co-creation. Participation behaviour provides sustainable value for the firms, but it is not necessary for the value co-creation (Yi and Gong, 2008; Yi et al., 2011) process. Empirical research indicates that extra-role and in-role behaviour have distinctive antecedents and consequences (Yi et al., 2011). Consequently, researchers have to apply different and separate scales for evaluating customer participation behaviour and customer citizenship behaviour.

This chapter conceptualised the customer value co-creation behaviour as a multi-dimensional concept; comprising higher-order factors each of which include different and multiple dimensions. Based on the results of Yi and Gong (2013), this chapter suggests that participation behaviour has many dimensions, including information sharing, information seeking, personal interaction and responsible behaviour. Additionally, based on the findings of Yi and Gong (2013), this chapter suggests that citizenship behaviour comprises four sub-constructs – tolerance, advocacy, feedback and help.

The following sections discuss each of these constructs and sub-constructs in detail.

Participation behaviour

Participation behaviour refers to the behaviour that is vital for creating a successful service by customers. According to Yi et al. (2011), participation behaviour is customers' involvement in the process of value co-creation. Wilson (2012) highlighted the important role of customers in generating successful service outcomes. For instance, companies, such as fitness training, can benefit from the participation behaviour of individuals (Yi et al., 2011).

Information seeking refers to the individuals' eagerness for finding information that clarifies the service requirement and helps them to understand their expected role in the value co-creation (Elsharnouby, 2015; Yi and Gong, 2013). The methods through which customers used to have access to such information has altered drastically in recent years (Hennig-Thurau et al., 2010). In this regard, customers are actively seeking new information and do not rely solely on the firm-released information. Customers not only seek a new and reliable source of information but also prefer to rely on such sources instead of the formal sources (Fagerstrøm and Ghinea, 2013).

Customers are mainly involved in exchanging information for the purpose of clarity in the service and accommodating their cognitive needs. Additionally, according to Kellogg et al. (1997), newly hired employees demonstrate the same behaviour to understand their position in service delivery as a participant in the value co-creation process. The provision of this information aids in decreasing the level of uncertainty when customers are involved in the value co-creation process.

Information sharing plays a vivid role in providing essential information to the firm to aid it to accommodate customer needs more efficiently (Elsharnouby, 2015; Yi and Gong, 2013). Information sharing plays a vital and important role in service firms for creating value co-creation. What is more, it is essential for companies to realise how their resources have been spent and how effective they were (Lengnick-Hall, 1996). In this regard, if the information provided by customers is not accurate, companies cannot accommodate customers' needs efficiently (Ennew and Binks, 1999). Consequently, sharing accurate and precise information with firms can result in a higher level of value co-creation with the service. Therefore, information sharing plays an undeniable role in the success of value co-creation behaviour.

Responsible behaviour refers to when a customer perceives that they have the same responsibilities and duties (Ennew and Bink, 1999) similar to a partial employee. In this respect, co-operative behaviour can be refered to the extent to which individuals conform to the role expected of them by the firms. Additionally, as proposed by Ennew and Brinks (1999), responsible behaviour is one of the most important dimensions of participation behaviour as it sheds light on the important role of the customer in generating successful service delivery. The results of Bettencourt (1997) suggested that in order for value co-creation to be successful, customers should act cooperatively and follow the platform guidelines, which can result in successful value co-creation (Yi and Gong, 2013).

Personal interaction is the interpersonal relationship between different stakeholders for achieving successful value co-creation. In the service setting, customer encounters with firms can result in a customer-firm relationship. This relationship can be either close or can be more distant. Such interaction between customers and firms is essential for creating value (Ennew and Binks, 1999). According to Kelley et al. (1990), and Yi and Gong (2013), customer functional quality is considered to be one of the most important components that increase the quality of value co-creation.

Citizenship behaviour

According to Yi et al. (2011), citizenship behaviour is a voluntary behaviour that individuals have towards the firms. The results of Groth (2005) suggested that this behaviour is mainly due to the customer's own discretion.

Feedback refers to the voluntary act in which the customers in the platforms take part in providing constructive suggestions and recommendations for improving the firm performance (Podsakoff et al., 2000). Different firms can benefit from the feedback provided by customers through different touchpoints. According to Bettencourt (1997), feedback is one of the most important constructs of citizenship behaviour that results in the development and governance of the major contribution of firm performance of customers. In addition, Groth et al. (2005) also considered feedback as being one of the most important dimensions of citizenship behaviour that results in improving the service development. What is more, the results of Yi and Gong (2013) suggested that customers who are receiving and purchasing the service/products of a firm are the ones that can benefit firms by their feedback and suggestions.

Advocacy is recommending the firm and the firm's offering (friends, family member) (Groth et al., 2004). Advocacy is considered to be a voluntary behaviour that shows the customer's commitment to the firm and is beyond individual promotion (Bettencourt, 1997). Recommendations and referrals are important for the service setting as, through them, firms can promote their services/products and enhance their positive image. Such behaviour, which is a dimension of citizenship behaviour, is considered to be voluntary and plays a vital role in the success of value co-creation (Yi and Gong, 2013).

Helping comprises the activities that voluntarily benefit others (Podsakoff et al., 2000). Groth et al. (2004) defined helping as the process of customers helping other customers. According to Groth et al. (2004), it is close to the concept of altruism in organisational citizenship behaviour. Altruism is the directed behaviour and helping of specific individuals with a clear purpose of helping. Additionally, the results of Rosenbaum and Massiah (2011) suggested that customers help other customers voluntarily due to their social responsibility.

Tolerance is a willingness to tolerate the inevitable inconveniences and impositions of work without complaining (Organ, 1990, p. 96). According to Lengnick-Hall et al. (2000) tolerance refers to the willingness and patience during a mishap and any shortages by the firms, such as not providing adequate and sufficient services at the promised point in time. This willingness and patience refer to tolerance (Yi and Gong, 2013), which is helpful in elasticity during unexpected problems. Such behaviour is considered to be an important trait for peer value co-creation behaviour as failure might occur during the value co-creation process.

Value co-creation behaviour antecedents and consequences

In this section, to understand the peer value co-creation behaviour better, different antecedents, peer perceived quality, peer identification, peer resources, peer

236 Alqayed, Foroudi, Dennis, Foroudi and Kooli

experience, peer value co-creation behaviour and consequences of peer value co-creation behaviour including peer satisfaction, peer motivation, relationship in the peer community, peer loyalty and peer active participation are discussed.

Perceived quality

As the marketing paradigm shifted from predominantly good-dominant to the service-dominant, the perceived quality has gained a considerable body of attention (Gummesson, 2008). Consequently, the interest in the perceived quality era has drawn attention from both practitioners and academics over the past few years (Martinez Garcia and Martinez Caro, 2010). Researchers have long realised that the perception of quality plays an important role in the success of any business relationship (Reichheld and Sasser, 1990; Carrillat et al., 2009). Scholars have also noted non-financial performance outcomes, such as satisfaction and loyalty (Silvestro and Cross, 2000; Newman, 2001). In this respect, Al-Hawari and Ward (2006) referred to perceived quality as a firm asset and the main contributor to both the financial and non-financial performance of the firm, which has a significant influence on the tangible and non-tangible probability for the firms.

In a broad view, there are two schools of thought associated with perceived quality: Nordic and American. In the Nordic school of thought, the most prevalent scholars include Grönroos (1984, 1990, 2001), and Lehtinen and Lehtinen (1982, 1991). In this school of thought, quality includes technical quality, functional quality and image quality. This school of thought proposes analysing what individuals receive from firms (technical) and how they received it (functional). The researchers in the Nordic school of thought argue that these qualities shape the business relationship. The Nordic school of thought predominantly concentrates on people-delivered services and results in favourable interaction during and after delivery. On the other hand, the American school of thought, mainly Brady and Cronin (2001), Cronin and Taylor (1992, 1994), Parasuraman et al. (1985, 1988, 1991a, 1994a, 1994b) and Teas (1993, 1994) focused on the notion of service encounters, maintaining that the services are intangible and that, ultimately, service shapes the perception of quality. However, the American school of thought on quality concentrates on delivery and tends to obscure outcome quality. The American school of thought on quality is more focused on the notion of service delivery as a measurement of service quality, whereas the Nordic school places more emphasis on the interaction of the service provider and the individuals as the main driver of service quality perception. Furthermore, the American school of thought focuses on the criticality of the service delivery outcomes, while the Nordic school focuses on the outcomes and the functionality of the service provision.

Mitra and Golder (2006) defined perceived quality as "the overall subjective judgment of quality relative to the expectation of quality. These expectations are based on one's own and others' experiences and various other resources, reputation, price and advertising" (p. 231). In a similar vein, Tsiotsou (2006) referred to perceived quality as the overall assessment of a product or service, where the objective quality shows the general product performance. Lewis and Booms (1983) referred to perceived quality as an individual's assessment of a product/service. Likewise, Zeithaml (1998) referred to the overall *evaluation of a specific consumption situation* as customer perceived quality. While Rao and Monroe (1989) suggested that price is the key determinant of quality perception, Dodds et al. (1991) suggested that the perception of value and external cues are the drivers of quality.

Parasuraman et al. (1988) defined perceived quality as a "global judgment, or attitude, relating to the superiority of the product/service" (p. 16), suggesting that perceived quality is not only different between the customer's expectation and actual service of brands but is also the customer's assessment of delivery. Similarly, Lehtinen and Lehtinen (1991), and Yoo and Park (2007) referred to perceived quality as a source of competitive advantage, which shows how well a firm/brand can accommodate a customer need.

Identification

While the term brand identification has received considerable attention from different scholars, the fact that customers identify with companies has earlier roots. According to the article of Bhattacharya and Sen (2003), customers can have their self-concept needs accommodated by brands. Later on, Ahearne et al. (2005) proposed the idea that identification can have an influence on both in-/ extra-role behaviour. In line with Bhattacharya and Sen (2003), firms can have meaningful self-concept with customers for identification, where identification is referred to as an active, selective act that accommodates individuals' self-definitional needs. In this vein, based on social identity theory, researchers (Ahearne et al., 2005; Bhattacharya and Sen, 2003) have suggested that customers who identify with firms are more likely to take part in activities that support brands (like positive word of mouth, or brand loyalty).

According to Bhattacharya and Sen (2003), during identification, customers perceive the firms as higher value in terms of social identity that aids customers to accommodate their self-concept needs. Based on the works of Belk (1988); Fournier (1998); and McCracken (1988), firms are a concrete actualisation of customers that represent the social categories that customers identify with through which the meaning between the self and brands is transferred. In this regard, Lam et al. (2012) proposed the idea that brands serve as a relationship partner to the private self. In other words, brands can help customers to define who they are and consider themselves to be part of a group by identifying with a brand. According to Lam et al. (2012), identification is the psychological state that shows the cognitive overlap between the self and the firms. Stokburger-Sauer et al. (2012) defined identification as the extent to which the supplier firm fits with an individual's self-concept through cognitive connection. Consequently, due to self-categorising, a cognitive connection can be formed between customers and the firm. The evaluative dimension shows how much customers value

238 Alqayed, Foroudi, Dennis, Foroudi and Kooli

their connection with a particular firm. This dimension describes customers' feeling about the firm and other assortments of the brand.

Researchers (e.g. Berger and Heath, 2007; Bhattacharya and Sen, 2003; Chernev et al., 2011) have tried to expand the knowledge about the antecedent of identification. Their results suggest that identification can be driven by a wide range of needs ranging from the need for self-improvement. Consequently, identification is likely to be associated with the person as a brand (i) having a similar personality to a customer, (ii) being considered prestigious by others and (iii) distinguishing himself/herself from the crowd. Additionally, these authors suggested factors, such as (i) when customers perceive their interaction with a brand helps them to have a higher social value, (ii) have memories during their consumption experience or (iii) assess a brand to be warm, in emotional terms instead of being cold. In this regard, Kunda (1999) suggested that individuals' needs for self-enhancement along with their self-continuity can encompass the affirmation and maintenance of a positive self-view, which can result in higher self-esteem. The results of different researchers (e.g. Escalas and Bettman, 2003; Thomson et al., 2005; Rindfleisch et al., 2009) suggested that such identity connected necessities can also be met via identification with respected brands. Brand prestige is also considered to be an antecedent of identification. Prestige is also considered to be an antecedent of customer identification. In this respect, Hughes and Ahearne (2010) defined identification as "the degree to which a person defines his or herself by the same attributes that he or she believes defines a brand" (p. 89).

Peer resources

As previously discussed with the shift of good-dominant logic towards service-dominant logic, the marketing literature has changed drastically (Pohlmann and Kaartemo, 2017). In the good-dominant logic, the firms are viewed as a value creator, and customers are referred to as value consumers. However, the service-dominant logic perspective challenged this point of view by suggesting that customers are not only the consumers of the value, but also, they are the main source of value for any firm. Furthermore, the service-dominant logic approach contends that value is evaluated by customers and is determined in a beneficiary context. In this context, the peer resources (both customers and provider) are considered to have a drastic influence on the value co-creation (Vargo, 2007; Vargo et al., 2008) on a peer platform.

In the service-dominant logic, resources are viewed as either intangible or tangible entities that are available to customers and firms for co-creating value (Barney, 1991). Although the term "resources" is common in marketing literature, the notion of resources has, predominantly, remained ambiguous (Seppänen and Mäkinen, 2010). As mentioned by Vargo and Lusch in their article in 2004, resource theory (R-A) was followed by resource advantage theory.

The resource-based theory (RBV) introduces the concept of intangible resources in the management and marketing literature. This perspective suggests that the application of valuable resources is the main driver of competitive advantage. RBV refers to resources as "all assets, capabilities, organisational processes, firm attributes, information, knowledge, etc., controlled by a firm that enable the firm to conceive of and implement strategies that improve its efficiency and effectiveness" (Barney, 1991, p. 101). Such a perspective can be regarded as the basis of resources on the peer platform or, more broadly, the sharing economy context as it sheds light on the importance of intangible resources (e.g. information and knowledge).

The resource-based theory resulted in the development of resource advantage theory (R-A) (Hunt and Morgan, 1995), which states that competitive advantage resources can result in sustainable competitive advantage for the firm (Hunt, 2000). In this theory, resources are intangible and tangible units that firms have access to and help firms to make an effective and efficient product/service for their customers (Hunt, 2000). The R-A theory provides a conceptual model for the studying of resources through the S-D logic lens by providing classification of resources (Madhavaram and Hunt, 2008).

Both resource-based theory and resource advantage theory resulted in the emergence of S-D logic. Despite the common thermotical foundation, the S-D logic has two major differences compared to its predecessor theories: (1) S-D logic focuses on the role of customer resource integration into value co-creation (Arnould and Thompson 2007) and (2) while R-A theory offers theoretical insight associated with the foundation of exploring the resources related to the different firms, the S-D logic investigates the resources beyond what firms possess by referring to the service ecosystem (Vargo and Lusch, 2008). In this regard, Vargo and Lusch (2016) classified resources in two distinctive categories:

Operant resources – a source that is "employed to act on operand resources (and other operant resources)" (Vargo and Lusch, 2004, p. 2). Operant resources are categorised as a higher-order resource and refer to the main source of sustainable competitive advantage for firms (FP4), (Vargo and Lusch, 2008). Customers have various types of resources (e.g. time and knowledge) that can be integrated with the firms' resources for co-creating value. Arnould and Thompson (2007) introduced the initial work on the customer resource classification required for service dominant logic (SDL). Drawn on resource-based theory, and customer culture theory, they argued that customer resources could be divided into three categories: cultural, social and physical resources.

Physical resources are the resources, which, in nature, are possessed and controlled by customers (e.g. strength and emotion). In this regard, customers have different mental and physical characteristics that can shape their lives. *Social resources* are fundamental in the SDL context and are the foundation of assessment of value in context. Social resources refer to relationships and networks (e.g. social class, ethnic groups). In this respect, the value co-creation can occur at two main levels (i) co-consumer experience, when individuals share their resources with other actors on a social and commercial

240 *Alqayed, Foroudi, Dennis, Foroudi and Kooli*

interchange platform to maximise their beneficiary value (Baron and Harris, 2008) and (ii) the consumer level, as individual value, incorporating the resources (Baron and Harris, 2008).

Peer experience

The concept of experience was initially introduced into the marketing literature by Holbrook and Hirschman in 1982. According to Hirsch and Levin (1999), customer experience can be referred to as an "umbrella construct; constructs that are a broad concept used to encompass and account for a diverse set of phenomena" (p. 199). However, to define customer experience, researchers take different approaches into account. One is the holistic experience approach, when a customer is opposed to a different form of interaction with a company (LaSalle and Britton, 2003); Another is based on extraordinary and memorable experience and, finally, there is the co-experience approach (Prahald and Ramaswamy, 2004).

A brief review of customer experience highlights the important characteristics of customer experience. Firstly, marketing highlights the importance of a memorable experience (Pine et al., 1999) with customers. Despite this, the literature review suggests that providing a memorable relationship and providing a memorable relationship with the company is more valuable than just selling a memorable experience to the customer. Secondly, the literature suggests that customer experience should be extraordinary and remain unique for each customer (LaSalle and Britton, 2003). Thirdly, the literature suggests that firms should be engaging customer senses at a personal level (Schmitt, 1999, 2003). Fourthly, the literature places emphasis on the importance of a uniquely designed experience for the customers (e.g. Homburg et al., 2017; McColl-Kennedy et al., 2019; Ponsignon et al., 2017; Zomerdijk and Voss, 2010). Finally, the researchers (e.g. Flavián et al., 2019; Gao et al., 2020; Meyer and Schwager, 2007) stated that the notion of customer experience is subjective in nature.

The theoretical foundation of the customer experience is that different touchpoints and cues can and will have influence on customer experience, which, in the marketing literature, is referred to as the overall customer experience (Homburg et al., 2015). Meyer and Schwager (2007) claimed that consumer experience is "the internal and subjective response that customers have to any direct or indirect contact with a company" (p. 18). On the other hand, in more recent years, Homburg et al. (2015) defined experience as "the evolvement of a person's sensorial, affective, cognitive, relational and behavioural responses to a brand by living through a journey of touch-points along with pre-purchase, purchase and post-purchase and continually judging this journey against response thresholds of co-occurring experiences" (p. 8). Consequently, researchers (e.g. Schembri, 2006; Verhoef et al., 2009) have suggested that experience can be regarded as a combination of affective and cognitive experience and can be treated as a holistic component.

Peer satisfaction

Satisfaction has been an increasingly researched and understudied construct since 1980 (Siebert et al., 2020). Researchers have conceptualised customer satisfaction as the post-consumption assessment of the firm offering, which is mainly dependent on customer expectation, customer perceived quality and customer perceived value. Similarly, Ageeva et al. (2018) referred to satisfaction as the degree to which a firm meets its customers' needs (Foroudi, 2020). Lim et al. (2020) referred to satisfaction as the post-consumption evaluation of customer expectation and the firm offering performance.

Satisfaction can result in repeated customer purchases and future recommendations (Hwang and Lee, 2019). Previous studies have confirmed that satisfied customers can make a significant contribution to company revenue (Song and Noone, 2017). Additionally, satisfaction can result in increasing market share (Anderson et al., 1994). Satisfaction causes customers to become less sensitive to the firm price and be more willing to pay premium prices. Furthermore, customer satisfaction indicates the improvement in the firm/brand offering compared to the competitors in the market (Peng et al., 2019), which results in firm promotion through word of mouth (Hwang and Lee, 2019; Matzler et al., 2019).

While some researchers (e.g. Peng et al., 2019; Leischnig et al., 2018) merely considered satisfaction as a multi-faceted construct that is preceded by behavioural intention, other lines of study separate this construct to capture more company-relevant outcome (Walsh and Bartikowski, 2013). In this respect, San Martín Gutiérrez (2006) suggested that the satisfaction construct has shifted from being a solely cognitive-based construct to a cognitive-emotional construct. Researchers widely use overall satisfaction for measuring customer satisfaction, which is based upon the total customer experience with a service/product market offering (Anderson et al., 1994).

Peer motivation

Motivation can be defined as a psychological force that drives goal-oriented behaviour. As such, motivation includes intention and activation (Ryan and Deci, 2000). Motivation can be defined as a mental state skilled in relation to targets or situations that have contributions for the entity's well-being or goals (Johnson and Stewart, 2005, p. 10), which influence the future of business relationships. Dellande et al. (2004) defined motivation as "customer's incentive to carry out their role" (p. 79).

Motivation possesses the vital energy for striving to the existing goals providing energy for setting up new goals. Furthermore, based on the nature of motivation, it can be categorised into two subcategories, including extrinsic or intrinsic. Self-determination theory (Ryan and Deci, 2000) suggests that intrinsic motivation is vital for continuing the activity for inherent satisfaction and can be driven by a motivation for competence or autonomy. Extrinsic motivation, on the other hand, is driven to attain a distinguishable outcome.

242   Alqayed, Foroudi, Dennis, Foroudi and Kooli

Intrinsic motivation refers to doing an action for the sake of the enjoyment and satisfaction of the activity (Ryan and Deci, 2000). The results of Hoffman and Novak (1996) and Füller (2006, 2010) indicate that intrinsically motivated individuals prefer doing experiential-oriented behaviours and search for enjoyable experience and activities. On the other hand, according to Ryan and Deci (2000) extrinsic motivation refers to when individuals are eager to do an activity to gain a separable outcome. West and Gallagher (2006) suggested that recognition by peers is one leading extrinsic motivation factor; other factors can be accommodating personal needs (West and Gallagher, 2006) or reciprocity (Füller, 2010).

Recent studies in social psychology suggest that motivation can be thought of as the antecedent of human behaviour prior to occurrence. Motivation can explain why people conduct a certain set of behaviours and the direction of their voluntary actions. Highly motivated customers result in better performance for firms (Becker, 2009). Consequently, firms focus on what motivates customers more than before (Schieffer and Leininger, 2008).

Peer loyalty

Loyalty is regarded as one of the oldest and most important constructs to marketing scholars (Toufaily et al., 2013); from a practitioner point of view, it is also one of the most competitive advantages a company can possess (Wolter et al., 2017). Establishing and keeping loyalty can aid businesses and develop long-term and, in most cases, mutual relationships (Pan et al., 2012) with their customers. Loyalty can be seen in commitment and attachment towards firms and stops individuals purchasing offerings from a firm's competitors (So et al., 2013) in the market. Additionally, loyalty can cause individuals to be willing to pay more (Diallo et al., 2015; Riquelme et al., 2019) and resist switching to a competitor (Hu et al., 2019).

The common definition of loyalty is an individual commitment to purchasing preferred products or services in a way that promotes its repeated purchase. Loyalty can cause individuals to repurchase from a service provider whenever they can and maintain a positive attitude towards them (Cheng et al., 2020). Based on the literature, there are two key types of loyalty – behavioural and attitudinal. On the one hand, from a behavioural perspective, loyalty can be expressed in customer behaviour towards a firm, the main indicator of which is repeated purchase (Maderer and Holtbrügge, 2019). On the other hand, attitudinal loyalty is regarded as a personal attitude that is made up of the different emotions an individual possesses towards a retailer or product. From the attitudinal perspective, individuals prefer a supplier to others and recommend its services to a third party. According to Cheng (2011), while behavioural loyalty is a substantial element, attitudinal loyalty is regarded as a psychological construct.

Peer relationship strength

Customer relationship is considered to be an effective and efficient marketing tactic as it can increase customer attachment with an e-retailer (Mandl and

Value co-creation behaviour   243

Hogreve, 2020). According to Arnott et al. (2007), the online community can not only aid customers to establish a close-knit relationship with other customers, but also motivate customers to keep their relationship with a firm. Individuals' participation in online customer communities can profoundly contribute to customer-company relations through commitment, satisfaction and trust (Wulf et al., 200). Oliver (2014) referred to satisfaction in a community as a positive evaluation of customers from their relationship in a community that is based upon a series of interactions in a community (De Valck et al., 2007).

Drawn on commitment-trust theory, both commitment and trust play a vital role in building and establishing a relationship in an online community. In this respect, business and interpersonal relationships are forged upon trust (Morgan and Hunt, 1994). Previous studies (e.g. Horppu et al., 2008; Porter and Donthu, 2008) signified the role of trust in an online community as a facilitator for customer eagerness in participating and establishing a relationship in an online community, which can result in increased social and economic transactions (Pavlou, 2003).

Anderson and Weitz (1992) defined commitment as the level of individual willingness in maintaining a stable relationship with other parties. Individuals' engagement in online communities can make individuals become committed to the community. Community engagement is the "emotional involvement with the virtual community, which is characterised by identification with, involvement in, and emotional attachment to the community" (Cheung and Lee, 2009, p. 283).

Active participation

In the past few years, global giant brands, such as Dell and Starbucks have demonstrated the importance of the concept of participation (Ramaswamy and Gouillart, 2010). Active participation refers to the level of customer involvement in goods and service production through contributing their resources (e.g. knowledge, time). Active participation can include different types of behaviour including decision-making, information provision, design, quality assurance (Kellogg et al., 1997; Yi and Gong, 2013) and a wide range of resources ranging from time to information (Arnould, 2008; Moreau and Herd, 2010), as through such contributions, customers can either positively or negatively influence the company process and its performance (Aarikka-Stenroos and Jaakkola, 2012). According to the literature, active participation plays a critical role in performance in terms of productivity and efficiency (Hsieh et al., 2004), accommodating customer needs (Dong and Sivakumar, 2017) and managing customer relationships (Chan et al., 2010).

Silpakit and Fisk (1985) referred to participation as the customer role in supplying activities instead of having contact with the employee during the service encounter. In a similar vein, Rodie and Kleine (2000) noted that the role of the customer possesses activities that include providing information that can contribute to raw material production and show a particular set of behaviours necessary for producing satisfactory results. Similarly, Uzkurt (2010) stated that participation is an expression of the physical, behavioural, emotional and informational

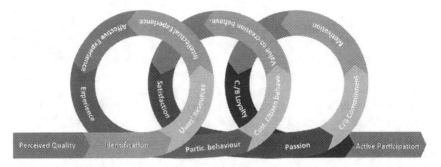

Figure 9.1 Value co-creation behaviour journey in online community.

contribution of customers to the service process and their ability and willingness to increase the service/product quality. In turn, Yi and Gong (2013) suggested that customer participation behaviour not only comprises responsible behaviour but also, to some extent, the personal interaction between the customer and the providers. Furthermore, Dong and Sivakumar (2017) suggested that customer participation can differ in respect to what resources individuals contribute (e.g. personal information), how customers participate (e.g. being passive, friendly) and to what extent they contribute (high, moderate or low) (figure 9.1).

Conclusion

Today because of the wide range of consequences of value co-creation, academics and practitioners have paid extensive attention to value co-creation behaviour. A great body of literature surrounding value co-creation exists. In this theoretical examination of the value co-creation, the literature explains the importance of value co-creation as an effective and important way of co-creating value by customers (Payne et al., 2008). This chapter reviewed the dominant schools of thought in marketing, including good-dominant logic and service-dominant logic. Then it briefly presented a historical review over the service-dominant logic, and how the good-dominant altered to service-dominant logic in the marketing literature. Then it discussed the difference between co-production and value co-creation. Afterwards, by applying the bibliometric analysis (multidimensional scaling), it systematically reviewed the value co-creation domain in the marketing literature. Additionally, based on the systematic review, the researcher proposed a future model. Then the value co-creation behaviour was explained. The key antecedents and outcomes of value co-creation behaviour were recognised.

Future research

This study is focused on the value co-creation behaviour, its antecedents and consequences from reviewing the related literature, which can provide a number

Value co-creation behaviour 245

of potentially fruitful future research avenues. Furthermore, further study should focus on investigating on the domain of the value co-creation behaviour on online platform (such as P2P) and add more antecedents and consequences. Future research can also discover whether the proposed associations in this study hold for other cultures or nations.

CASE STUDY

Airbnb is the world's biggest accommodation sharing platform which is a novel method of participating business-value, by co-creating among platform provider, host and users to create a novel authentic guests' experience in a networked environment. The company's name comes from "air mattress B&B". It covers 191 countries and 81,000 cities. The company takes between 6% and 12% commission from guests and 3% for every booking. Airbnb offers arrangement for lodging with diverse kinds of properties, such as moored yachts, entire houses, apartments, single rooms and more.

The rapid digitalisation procedure assists us to be more human-centric rather than firm-centric. It develops a concept of online value co-creation which is taking place inside the users who are managing their own value chain in peer-to-peer (P2) society. For example, users are able to do business wherever they are with whoever they wish. The rapid growth of Airbnb in the past decade where it has become the largest networked accommodation service has affected the traditional hospitality and tourism sector as they have lost their marketplace.

Case questions

To answer the below questions, please visit the Airbnb website.

Critically evaluate the Airbnb website and identify the strengths and weakness of the platform (e.g. navigation, information etc.) and provide suggestions for improvements.

By reviewing the platform and comments from the users, what key antecedents and consequences for peer value co-creation do you recognise?

Identify how the company could improve its active participations. Examples should be provided as appropriate.

Key terms and definitions

Peer perceived quality is a cognitive response and judgement about the overall excellence or superiority of a product or service, which is the primary driver of purchase intention and could measure thoroughly the three components

(i) perceived information quality, (ii) perceived system quality and (iii) perceived service quality.

Users' resources can be measured through four components: (i) knowledge, (ii) skills, (iii) creativity and (iv) connectedness.

Knowledge can be defined as "the extent to which the stakeholder is informed and experienced with a brand".

Skills: the extent to which the stakeholder is stimulated by the brand in terms of his/her capabilities.

Creativity: the extent to which the stakeholder is stimulated by the brand in terms of his/her use of imagination and development of original ideas.

Connectedness: the extent to which the stakeholder is associated, bonded or linked with others because of the brand.

Corporate brand identification is the degree to which the members and social group define themselves by the same attributes that they believes define the community meaning they identify themselves with, ie. the norms, traditions, customs and goals of the community.

Experience: Customer experience is multi-dimensional in nature and is a complex and dynamic term, which is a significant driver of a firm's success and competitive advantage surrounding customers'/users' reactions to all the interactions they have with a firm, other customers/users, intermediaries and wider network actors. Customer experience is "holistic in nature involving the customer's affective and intellectual responses to any indirect or direct contact with the brand, community, and other users across multiple touchpoints throughout the customer journey".

Affective experience: (moods and emotions) refers to the individual's emotional state after the introduction of stimuli, which affects each layer of an individual's behaviour and their decision-making process.

Intellectual experience: (cognitive, functional, educational, stimulation) refers to an individual's knowledge about the product and services.

Value co-creation behaviour is a desirable goal as it can assist firms in highlighting the customer's or consumer's point of view and in improving the front-end process of identifying customers' needs and wants. It occurs when a customer consumes, or uses, a product or service, rather than when the output is manufactured. It could be measured through subconstructs, participation behaviour and citizen behaviour.

Participation behaviour refers to role clarity, ability and motivation in participation in the community.

Information seeking: customers seek information about service status and service parameters to explain service requirements and satisfy other cognitive needs, how to perform their tasks as value co-creators as well as what they are expected to do and how they are expected to perform during a service encounter.

Information sharing is the key to the success of value co-creation. For successful value co-creation, customers should provide resources such as information for use in value co-creation processes.

Value co-creation behaviour 247

Responsible behaviour occurs when customers recognise their duties and responsibilities as partial employees. For successful value co-creation between themselves and employees, customers need to be cooperative, observing rules and policies and accepting directions from employees.

Responsible personal interaction refers to interpersonal relations between customers and employees, which are necessary for successful value co-creation.

Customer citizen behaviour as an extraordinary value to the firm refers to customers/users' procedural justice, distributive justice and interactional justice.

Feedback includes solicited and unsolicited information that customers provide to the employee, which helps employees and the firm to improve the service creation process in the long run.

Advocacy refers to recommending the business – whether the firm or the employee – to others such as friends or family. In the context of value co-creation, advocacy indicates allegiance to the firm and promotion of the firm's interests beyond the individual customer's interests.

Tolerance refers to customer willingness to be patient when the service delivery does not meet the customer's expectations of adequate service, as in the case of delays or equipment shortages.

Helping refers to customer behaviour aimed at assisting other customers. In a service co-creation process, customers usually direct helping behaviour at other customers rather than at employees because other customers in a service encounter may need help behaving in ways consistent with their expected roles.

Satisfaction is a post-customer service decision.

Motivation can be defined as mental states experienced in relation to situations or targets that have implications for the individual's goals or well-being, which influence the future of business relationships. People in business-to-business relationships appraise the situations they perform in, and the happenings that occur to them, and the resulting emotions and coping responses influence the course and outcomes of the relationship.

Trusting belief is a psychological state comprising the intention to accept vulnerability based on positive expectations of the intentions or behaviours of another which the stakeholder is confident about with regard to the brand.

Commitment arises from social exchanges and has been described as one's intention to continue a relationship for the brand and its success.

Passion: the extent to which the stakeholder has extremely positive feelings towards the brand.

Peer relationship strength is often a synonym for interpersonal loyalty and is an important concept in B2B/C services because of the personal contact between buyers and suppliers.

Peer loyalty is a collection of attitudes aligned with a series of purchase behaviours that systematically favour one entity over competing entities.

Attitude-based loyalty (cognitive-based loyalty or phantom loyalty) or pleasurable fulfilment that favours a particular entity derives from information about a company's offering, such as quality and price and is the weakest type of loyalty because it does not relate to the brand. This information indicates that the selected product or service is the best choice among its alternatives and thus preferable to others.

Behaviour-based loyalty entails repeated purchases that stem from conation or action orientation involving a readiness to act in the benefit of a particular entity.

Active participation is the key success factor for online communities. Active participation involves carrying out several activities on a regular basis (e.g. daily or weekly). These activities include logging on to the community website, keeping their profile up to date, complying with community rules and regulations, posting quality messages that engender discussions and replying to posted questions.

References

Aarikka-Stenroos, L. and Jaakkola, E. (2012). Value co-creation in knowledge intensive business services: a dyadic perspective on the joint problem solving process. *Industrial Marketing Management*, 41(1), 15–26.

Ageeva, E., Melewar, T. C., Foroudi, P., Dennis, C. and Jin, Z. (2018). Examining the influence of corporate website favorability on corporate image and corporate reputation: findings from fsQCA. *Journal of Business Research*, 89(Aug), 287–304.

Ahearne, M., Bhattacharya, C. B. and Gruen, T. (2005). Antecedents and consequences of customer-company identification: expanding the role of relationship marketing. *Journal of Applied Psychology*, 90(3), 574–585.

Akaka, M. A. and Vargo, S. L. (2015). Extending the context of service: from encounters to ecosystems. *Journal of Services Marketing*, 29(6/7), 453–462.

Al-Hawari, M. and Ward, T. (2006). The effect of automated service quality on Australian banks' financial performance and the mediating role of customer satisfaction. *Marketing Intelligence & Planning*, 24(2), 127–147.

Alves, H., Fernandes, C. and Raposo, M. (2016). Value co-creation: concept and contexts of application and study. *Journal of Business Research*, 69(5), 1626–1633.

Anderson, E. and Weitz, B. (1992). The use of pledges to build and sustain commitment in distribution channels. *Journal of Marketing Research*, 29(1), 18–34.

Anderson, E. W., Fornell, C. and Lehmann, D. R. (1994). Customer satisfaction, market share, and profitability: findings from Sweden. *Journal of Marketing*, 58(3), 53–66.

Antikainen, M. (2011). *Facilitating Customer Involvement in Collaborative Online Innovation Communities, VTT Publications 760.* Edita Prima Oy, Helsinki.

Arnott, D. C., Wilson, D., Kingshott, R. P. and Pecotich, A. (2007). The impact of psychological contracts on trust and commitment in supplier-distributor relationships. *European Journal of Marketing*, 41(9/10), 1053–1072.

Arnould, E. and Thompson, C. (2007). Consumer culture theory (and we really mean theoretics. In Belk, R. W. and Sherry, J. F. (Eds.), *Consumer Culture Theory (Research in Consumer Behavior, Vol. 11)* (pp. 3–22). Bingley: Emerald Group Publishing Limited.

Arnould, E. J. (2008). Service-dominant logic and resource theory. *Journal of the Academy of Marketing Science*, 36(1), 21–24.

Babin, B. J., James, K. W., Camp, K., Jones, R. P. and Parker, J. M. (2019). Pursuing personal constructs through quality, value, and satisfaction. *Journal of Retailing and Consumer Services*, 51(3), 33–41.

Ballantyne, D. and Varey, R. J. (2006). Creating value-in-use through marketing interaction: the exchange logic of relating, communicating and knowing. *Marketing Theory*, 6(3), 335–348.

Ballantyne, D. and Varey, R. J. (2008). The service-dominant logic and the future of marketing. *Journal of the Academy of Marketing Science*, 36(1), 11–14.

Barile, S. and Polese, F. (2010). Smart service systems and viable service systems: applying systems theory to service science. *Service Science*, 2(1–2), 21–40.

Barney, J. (1991). Special theory forum the resource-based model of the firm: origins, implications, and prospects. *Journal of Management*, 17(1), 97–98.

Baron, S. and Harris, K. (2008). Consumers as resource integrators. *Journal of Marketing Management*, 24(1–2), 113–130.

Becker, H. S. (2009). How to find out how to do qualitative research. *International Journal of Communication*, 3(4), 9–20.

Belk, R. W. (1988). Possessions and the extended self. *Journal of Consumer Research*, 15(2), 139–168.

Berger, J. and Heath, C. (2007). Where consumers diverge from others: identity signaling and product domains. *Journal of Consumer Research*, 34(2), 121–134.

Bettencourt, L. A. (1997). Customer voluntary performance: customers as partners in service delivery. *Journal of Retailing*, 73(3), 383.

Bhattacharya, C. B. and Sen, S. (2003). Consumer-company identification: a framework for understanding consumers' relationships with companies. *Journal of Marketing*, 67(2), 76–88.

Bonsu, S. K. and Darmody, A. (2008). Co-creating second life: market – consumer cooperation in contemporary economy. *Journal of Macromarketing*, 28(4), 355–368.

Bowman, C. and Ambrosini, V. (2000). Value creation versus value capture: towards a coherent definition of value in strategy. *British Journal of Management*, 11(1), 1–15.

Brady, M. K. and Cronin Jr, J. J. (2001). Some new thoughts on conceptualizing perceived service quality: a hierarchical approach. *Journal of Marketing*, 65(3), 34–49.

Carman, J. M. and Langeard, E. (1980). Growth strategies for service firms. *Strategic Management Journal*, 1(1), 7–22.

Carrillat, F. A., Jaramillo, F. and Mulki, J. P. (2009). Examining the impact of service quality: a meta-analysis of empirical evidence. *Journal of Marketing Theory and Practice*, 17(2), 95–110.

Chan, K. W., Yim, C. K. and Lam, S. S. (2010). Is customer participation in value creation a double-edged sword? Evidence from professional financial services across cultures. *Journal of Marketing*, 74(3), 48–64.

Chandler, J. D. and Vargo, S. L. (2011). Contextualization and value-in-context: how context frames exchange. *Marketing Theory*, 11(1), 35–49.

Chathoth, P., Altinay, L., Harrington, R. J., Okumus, F. and Chan, E. S. (2013). Co-production versus co-creation: a process based continuum in the hotel service context. *International Journal of Hospitality Management*, 32(March), 11–20.

Cheng, F. F., Wu, C. S. and Chen, Y. C. (2020). Creating customer loyalty in online brand communities. *Computers in Human Behavior*, 107(3), 105752.

Cheng, S. I. (2011). Comparisons of competing models between attitudinal loyalty and behavioral loyalty. *International Journal of Business and Social Science*, 2(10), 149–166.

Chernev, A., Hamilton, R. and Gal, D. (2011). Competing for consumer identity: limits to self-expression and the perils of lifestyle branding. *Journal of Marketing*, 75(3), 66–82.

250 Alqayed, Foroudi, Dennis, Foroudi and Kooli

Cheung, C. M. and Lee, M. K. (2009). Understanding the sustainability of a virtual community: model development and empirical test. *Journal of Information Science*, 35(3), 279–298.

Constantin, J. and Lusch, R. (1994). *Understanding resource management: how to deploy your people, products, and processes for maximum productivity*. Oxford, UK: Irwin Professional Publishing.

Converse, F. (1921). *Garments of Praise: A Miracle Cycle*. New York: EP Dutton.

Cossío-Silva, F. J., Revilla-Camacho, M. Á., Vega-Vázquez, M. and Palacios-Florencio, B. (2016). Value co-creation and customer loyalty. *Journal of Business Research*, 69(5), 1621–1625.

Cronin Jr, J. J. and Taylor, S. A. (1992). Measuring service quality: a reexamination and extension. *Journal of Marketing*, 56(3), 55–68.

Cronin Jr, J. J. and Taylor, S. A. (1994). SERVPERF versus SERVQUAL: reconciling performance-based and perceptions-minus-expectations measurement of service quality. *The Journal of Marketing*, 58(1), 125–131.

De Valck, K., Langerak, F., Verhoef, P. C. and Verlegh, P. W. (2007). Satisfaction with virtual communities of interest: effect on members' visit frequency. *British Journal of Management*, 18(3), 241–256.

Dellande, S., Gilly, M. C. and Graham, J. L. (2004). Gaining compliance and losing weight: the role of the service provider in health care services. *Journal of Marketing*, 68(3), 78–91.

Diallo, M. F., Coutelle-Brillet, P., Riviere, A. and Zielke, S. (2015). How do price perceptions of different brand types affect shopping value and store loyalty?. *Psychology & Marketing*, 32(12), 1133–1147.

Dodds, W. B., Monroe, K. B. and Grewal, D. (1991). Effects of price, brand, and store information on buyers' product evaluations. *Journal of Marketing Research*, 28(3), 307–319.

Dong, B. and Sivakumar, K. (2017). Customer participation in services: domain, scope, and boundaries. *Journal of the Academy of Marketing Science*, 45(6), 944–965.

Echeverri, P. and Skålén, P. (2011). Co-creation and co-destruction: a practice-theory based study of interactive value formation. *Marketing Theory*, 11(3), 351–373.

Edvardsson, B. (2005). Service quality: beyond cognitive assessment. *Managing Service Quality: An International Journal*, 15(2), 127–131.

Edvardsson, B., Tronvoll, B. and Gruber, T. (2011). Expanding understanding of service exchange and value co-creation: a social construction approach. *Journal of the Academy of Marketing Science*, 39(2), 327–339.

Elsharnouby, T. H. (2015). Student co-creation behavior in higher education: the role of satisfaction with the university experience. *Journal of Marketing for Higher Education*, 25(2), 238–262.

Ennew, C. T. and Binks, M. R. (1999). Impact of participative service relationships on quality, satisfaction and retention: an exploratory study. *Journal of Business Research*, 46(2), 121–132.

Escalas, J. E. and Bettman, J. R. (2003). You are what they eat: the influence of reference groups on consumers' connections to brands. *Journal of Consumer Psychology*, 13(3), 339–348.

Etgar, M. (2008). A descriptive model of the consumer co-production process. *Journal of the Academy of Marketing Science*, 36(1), 97–108.

Fagerstrøm, A. and Ghinea, G. (2013). Co-creation of value in higher education: using social network marketing in the recruitment of students. *Journal of Higher Education Policy and Management*, 35(1), 45–53.

Value co-creation behaviour   251

Firat, A. F. and Dholakia, N. (1998). *Consuming People: From Political Economy to Theaters of Consumption*. London: Psychology Press.

Flavián, C., Ibáñez-Sánchez, S. and Orús, C. (2019). The impact of virtual, augmented and mixed reality technologies on the customer experience. *Journal of Business Research*, 100(July), 547–560.

Fornell, C., Morgeson III, F. V. and Hult, G. T. M. (2016). Stock returns on customer satisfaction do beat the market: gauging the effect of a marketing intangible. *Journal of Marketing*, 80(5), 92–107.

Foroudi, P. (2020). Corporate brand strategy: drivers and outcomes of hotel industry's brand orientation. *International Journal of Hospitality Management*, 88(July), 1–14.

Foroudi, P., Yu, Q., Gupta, S. and Foroudi, M. M. (2019). Enhancing university brand image and reputation through customer value co-creation behaviour. *Technological Forecasting and Social Change*, 138(Jan), 218–227.

Fournier, S. (1998). Consumers and their brands: developing relationship theory in consumer research. *Journal of Consumer Research*, 24(4), 343–373.

Fuchs, V. R. (1965). The growing importance of the service industries. *The Journal of Business*, 38(4), 344–373.

Füller, J. (2006). *Why Consumers Engage in Virtual New Product Developments Initiated by Producers*. Minnesota: ACR North American Advances.

Füller, J. (2010). Refining virtual co-creation from a consumer perspective. *California Management Review*, 52(2), 98–122.

Füller, J., Mühlbacher, H., Matzler, K. and Jawecki, G. (2009). Consumer empowerment through internet-based co-creation. *Journal of Management Information Systems*, 26(3), 71–102.

Gale, B., Gale, B. T. and Wood, R. C. (1994). *Managing Customer Value: Creating Quality and Service That Customers Can See*. New York: Simon and Schuster.

Gallarza, M. G., Ruiz-Molina, M. E. and Gil-Saura, I. (2016). Stretching the value-satisfaction-loyalty chain by adding value dimensions and cognitive and affective satisfactions. *Management Decision*, 54(4), 981–1003.

Gao, L., Melero-Polo, I. and Sese, F. J. (2020). Customer equity drivers, customer experience quality, and customer profitability in banking services: the moderating role of social influence. *Journal of Service Research*, 23(2), 174–193.

Grönroos, C. (1984). A service quality model and its marketing implications. *European Journal of Marketing*, 18(4), 36–44.

Gronroos, C. (1990). Relationship approach to marketing in service contexts: the marketing and organizational behavior interface. *Journal of Business Research*, 20(1), 3–11.

Grönroos, C. (1997). Keynote paper from marketing mix to relationship marketing-towards a paradigm shift in marketing. *Management Decision*, 35(4), 322–339.

Grönroos, C. (2001). The perceived service quality concept – a mistake?, *Managing Service Quality*, 11(3), 150–152.

Grönroos, C. (2008). Service logic revisited: who creates value? And who co-creates? *European Business Review*, 20(4), 298–314.

Grönroos, C. (2011). A service perspective on business relationships: the value creation, interaction and marketing interface. *Industrial Marketing Management*, 40(2), 240–247.

Grönroos, C. and Gummerus, J. (2014). The service revolution and its marketing implications: service logic vs service-dominant logic. *Managing Service Quality*, 24(3), 206–229.

Grönroos, C. and Ravald, A. (2011). Service as business logic: implications for value creation and marketing. *Journal of Service Management*, 22(1), 5–22.

Grönroos, C. and Voima, P. (2013). Critical service logic: making sense of value creation and co-creation. *Journal of the Academy of Marketing Science*, 41(2), 133–150.

Groth, M. (2005). Customers as good soldiers: examining citizenship behaviors in internet service deliveries. *Journal of Management*, 31(1), 7–27.

Groth, M., Mertens, D. P. and Murphy, R. O. (2004). Customers as good soldiers: extending organizational citizenship behavior research to the customer domain. In D. L. Turnipseed (Ed.), *Handbook of Organizational Citizenship Behavior* (pp. 411–430). Hauppauge, NY: Nova Science Publishers.

Gummesson, E. (1994). Broadening and specifying relationshipmarketing. *Asia–Australia Marketing Journal*, 2(Aug), 31–43.

Gummesson, E. (2008). Quality, service dominant logic and many-to-many marketing. *The TQM Journal*, 20(2), 143–153.

Gummesson, E. and Mele, C. (2010). Marketing as value co-creation through network interaction and resource integration. *Journal of Business Market Management*, 4(4), 181–198.

Hamilton, M., Kaltcheva, V. D. and Rohm, A. J. (2016). Social media and value creation: the role of interaction satisfaction and interaction immersion. *Journal of Interactive Marketing*, 36(2), 121–133.

Han, H., Meng, B. and Kim, W. (2017). Bike-traveling as a growing phenomenon: role of attributes, value, satisfaction, desire, and gender in developing loyalty. *Tourism Management*, 59(3), 91–103.

Harmeling, C. M., Moffett, J. W., Arnold, M. J. and Carlson, B. D. (2017). Toward a theory of customer engagement marketing. *Journal of the Academy of Marketing Science*, 45(3), 312–335.

Harris, L., Russell-Bennett, R., Plé, L. and Cáceres, R. C. (2010). Not always co-creation: introducing interactional co-destruction of value in service-dominant logic. *Journal of Services Marketing*, 24(6), 430–437

Hatch, M. J. and Schultz, M. (2010). Toward a theory of brand co-creation with implications for brand governance. *Journal of Brand Management*, 17(8), 590–604.

Hennig-Thurau, T., Malthouse, E. C., Friege, C., Gensler, S., Lobschat, L., Rangaswamy, A. and Skiera, B. (2010). The impact of new media on customer relationships. *Journal of Service Research*, 13(3), 311–330.

Hietanen, J., Andéhn, M. and Bradshaw, A. (2018). Against the implicit politics of service-dominant logic. *Marketing Theory*, 18(1), 101–119.

Hirsch, P. M. and Levin, D. Z. (1999). Umbrella advocates versus validity police: a life-cycle model. *Organization Science*, 10(2), 199–212.

Hoffman, D. L. and Novak, T. P. (1996). Marketing in hypermedia computer-mediated environments: conceptual foundations. *Journal of Marketing*, 60(3), 50–68.

Homburg, C., Jozić, D. and Kuehnl, C. (2017). Customer experience management: toward implementing an evolving marketing concept. *Journal of the Academy of Marketing Science*, 45(3), 377–401.

Homburg, C., Schwemmle, M. and Kuehnl, C. (2015). New product design: concept, measurement, and consequences. *Journal of Marketing*, 79(3), 41–56.

Horppu, M., Kuivalainen, O., Tarkiainen, A. and Ellonen, H. K. (2008). Online satisfaction, trust and loyalty, and the impact of the offline parent brand. *Journal of Product & Brand Management*, 17(6), 403–413.

Hsieh, A. T., Yen, C. H. and Chin, K. C. (2004). Participative customers as partial employees and service provider workload. *International Journal of Service Industry Management*, 15(2), 25–45.

Hu, F., Teichert, T., Liu, Y., Li, H. and Gundyreva, E. (2019). Evolving customer expectations of hospitality services: differences in attribute effects on satisfaction and re-patronage. *Tourism Management*, 74(3), 345–357.

Hughes, D. E. and Ahearne, M. (2010). Energizing the reseller's sales force: the power of brand identification. *Journal of Marketing*, 74(4), 81–96.

Hunt, S. D. (2000). A general theory of competition: too eclectic or not eclectic enough? Too incremental or not incremental enough? Too neoclassical or not neoclassical enough?. *Journal of Macromarketing*, 20(1), 77–81.

Hunt, S. D. and Morgan, R. M. (1995). The comparative advantage theory of competition. *Journal of Marketing*, 59(2), 1–15.

Hwang, J. and Lee, J. (2019). Relationships among senior tourists' perceptions of tour guides' professional competencies, rapport, satisfaction with the guide service, tour satisfaction, and word of mouth. *Journal of Travel Research*, 58(8), 1331–1346.

Iansiti, M. and Levien, R. (2004). Creating value in your business ecosystem. *Harvard Business Review*, 3, 68–78.

Iglesias, O., Ind, N. and Alfaro, M. (2013). The organic view of the brand: a brand value co-creation model. *Journal of Brand Management*, 20(8), 670–688.

Iniesta-Bonillo, M. A., Sánchez-Fernández, R. and Jiménez-Castillo, D. (2016). Sustainability, value, and satisfaction: model testing and cross-validation in tourist destinations. *Journal of Business Research*, 69(11), 5002–5007.

Johnson, A. R. and Stewart, D. W. (2005). A reappraisal of the role of emotion in consumer behavior. In *Review of Marketing Research* (pp. 3–34). London: Emerald Group Publishing Limited.

Judd, R. C. (1964). The case for redefining services. *Journal of Marketing*, 28(1), 58–59.

Karjaluoto, H., Munnukka, J. and Kiuru, K. (2016). Brand love and positive word of mouth: the moderating effects of experience and price. *Journal of Product & Brand Management*, 25(6), 527–537.

Kelley, S. W., Donnelly Jr, J. H. and Skinner, S. J. (1990). Customer participation in service production and delivery. *Journal of Retailing*, 66(3), 315–345.

Kellogg, D. L., Youngdahl, W. E. and Bowen, D. E. (1997). On the relationship between customer participation and satisfaction: two frameworks. *International Journal of Service Industry Management*, 8(3), 206–219.

Khalifa, A. S. (2004). Customer value: a review of recent literature and an integrative configuration. *Management Decision*, 42(5), 645–666.

Kunda, Z. (1999). *Social Cognition: Making Sense of People*. Boston, MA: MIT press.

Kuzgun, E. and Asugman, G. (2015). Value in services–A service dominant logic perspective. *Procedia-Social and Behavioral Sciences*, 207(Oct), 242–251.

Lam, S. K., Ahearne, M. and Schillewaert, N. (2012). A multinational examination of the symbolic–instrumental framework of consumer–brand identification. *Journal of International Business Studies*, 43(3), 306–331.

Larson, K. and Watson, R. (2011). The value of social media: toward measuring social media strategies. *ICIS 2011 Proceedings*, 10. https://aisel.aisnet.org/icis2011/proceedings/onlinecommunity/10

LaSalle, D. and Britton, T. A. (2003). *Priceless. Turning Ordinary Products into Extraordinary Experience*. Boston, MA: Harvard Business School Press.

Lee, S. M., Olson, D. L. and Trimi, S. (2012). Co-innovation: convergenomics, collaboration, and co-creation for organizational values. *Management Decision*, 50(5), 817–831.

Lehtinen, U. and Lehtinen, J. R. (1982). *Service Quality: A Study of Quality Dimensions*. New York: Service Management Institute.

Lehtinen, U. and Lehtinen, J. R. (1991). Two approaches to service quality dimensions. *Service Industries Journal*, 11(3), 287–303.

Leischnig, A., Kasper-Brauer, K. and Thornton, S. C. (2018). Spotlight on customization: an analysis of necessity and sufficiency in services. *Journal of Business Research*, 89(Aug), 385–390.

Lehtinen, U. and Lehtinen, J. R. (1991). Two approaches to service quality dimensions. *Service Industries Journal*, 11(3), 287–303.

Leismann, K., Schmitt, M., Rohn, H. and Baedeker, C. (2013). Collaborative consumption: towards a resource-saving consumption culture. *Resources*, 2(3), 184–203.

Lengnick-Hall, C. A. (1996). Customer contributions to quality: a different view of the customer-oriented firm. *Academy of Management Review*, 21(3), 791–824.

Lengnick-Hall, C. A., Claycomb, V. C. and Inks, L. W. (2000). From recipient to contributor: examining customer roles and experienced outcomes. *European Journal of Marketing*, 34(3/4), 359–383.

Lewis, R. C. and Booms, B. H. (1983). The marketing aspects of service quality. *Emerging Perspectives on Services Marketing*, 65(4), 99–107.

Lim, W. M., Jee, T. W. and De Run, E. C. (2020). Strategic brand management for higher education institutions with graduate degree programs: empirical insights from the higher education marketing mix. *Journal of Strategic Marketing*, 28(3), 225–245.

Lusch, R. F. and Vargo, S. L. (2006). Service-dominant logic: reactions, reflections and refinements. *Marketing Theory*, 6(3), 281–288.

Lusch, R. F. and Vargo, S. L. (2014). *Service-dominant Logic: Premises, Perspectives, Possibilities*. Cambridge: Cambridge University Press.

Lusch, R. F., Vargo, S. L. and O'brien, M. (2007). Competing through service: insights from service-dominant logic. *Journal of Retailing*, 83(1), 5–18.

Macdonald, E. K., Wilson, H., Martinez, V. and Toossi, A. (2011). Assessing value-in-use: a conceptual framework and exploratory study. *Industrial Marketing Management*, 40(5), 671–682.

Maderer, D. and Holtbrügge, D. (2019). International activities of football clubs, fan attitudes, and brand loyalty. *Journal of Brand Management*, 26(4), 410–425.

Madhavaram, S. and Hunt, S. D. (2008). The service-dominant logic and a hierarchy of operant resources: developing masterful operant resources and implications for marketing strategy. *Journal of the Academy of Marketing Science*, 36(1), 67–82.

Maglio, P. P. and Spohrer, J. (2008). Fundamentals of service science. *Journal of the Academy of Marketing Science*, 36(1), 18–20.

Maglio, P. P. and Spohrer, J. (2013). A service science perspective on business model innovation. *Industrial Marketing Management*, 42(5), 665–670.

Mandl, L. and Hogreve, J. (2020). Buffering effects of brand community identification in service failures: the role of customer citizenship behaviors. *Journal of Business Research*, 107(Feb), 130–137.

Martín Gutiérrez, S. S. (2006). A model of consumer relationships with store brands, personnel and stores in Spain. *International Review of Retail, Distribution and Consumer Research*, 16(4), 453–469.

Martinez Garcia, J. A. and Martinez Caro, L. (2010). Rethinking perceived service quality: an alternative to hierarchical and multidimensional models. *Total Quality Management*, 21(1), 93–118.

Matzler, K., Teichmann, K., Strobl, A. and Partel, M. (2019). The effect of price on word of mouth: first time versus heavy repeat visitors. *Tourism Management*, 70(Feb), 453–459.

McColl-Kennedy, J. R., Zaki, M., Lemon, K. N., Urmetzer, F. and Neely, A. (2019). Gaining customer experience insights that matter. *Journal of Service Research*, 22(1), 8–26.

McCracken, G. (1988). *Culture and Consumption: New Approaches to the Symbolic Character if Consumer Goods and Activities*. Bloomington: Indiana University Press.

Merz, M. A., He, Y. and Vargo, S. L. (2009). The evolving brand logic: a service-dominant logic perspective. *Journal of the Academy of Marketing Science*, 37(3), 328–344.

Merz, M. A., Zarantonello, L. and Grappi, S. (2018). How valuable are your customers in the brand value co-creation process? The development of a Customer Co-Creation Value (CCCV) scale. *Journal of Business Research*, 82(Jan), 79–89.

Meyer, C. and Schwager, A. (2007). Understanding customer experience. *Harvard Business Review*, 85(2), 116.

Michaelidou, N., Siamagka, N. T. and Christodoulides, G. (2011). Usage, barriers and measurement of social media marketing: an exploratory investigation of small and medium B2B brands. *Industrial Marketing Management*, 40(7), 1153–1159.

Mitra, D. and Golder, P. N. (2006). How does objective quality affect perceived quality? Short-term effects, long-term effects, and asymmetries. *Marketing Science*, 25(3), 230–247.

Moreau, C. P. and Herd, K. B. (2010). To each his own? How comparisons with others influence consumers' evaluations of their self-designed products. *Journal of Consumer Research*, 36(5), 806–819.

Morgan, R. M. and Hunt, S. D. (1994). The commitment-trust theory of relationship marketing. *The Journal of Marketing*, 59(2), 20–38.

Morris, B. and Johnston, R. (1987). Dealing with inherent variability: the difference between manufacturing and service?. *International Journal of Operations & Production Management*, 7(4), 13–22

Newman, K. (2001). Interrogating SERVQUAL: a critical assessment of service quality measurement in a high street retail bank. *International Journal of Bank Marketing*, 19(3), 126–139.

Oh, H. and Kim, K. (2017). Customer satisfaction, service quality, and customer value: years 2000–2015. *International Journal of Contemporary Hospitality Management*, 29(1), 2–29

Oliver, R. L. (2014). *Satisfaction: A Behavioral Perspective on the Consumer: A Behavioral Perspective on the Consumer*. New York: Routledge.

Organ, D. W. (1990). The subtle significance of job satisfaction. *Clinical Laboratory Management Review*, 4(1), 94–98.

Osborne, P. (2013). *Anywhere or Not at All: Philosophy of Contemporary Art*. London: Verso Books.

Pan, Y., Sheng, S. and Xie, F. T. (2012). Antecedents of customer loyalty: an empirical synthesis and reexamination. *Journal of Retailing and Consumer Services*, 19(1), 150–158.

Parasuraman, A., Zeithaml, V. A. and Berry, L. L. (1985). A conceptual model of service quality and its implications for future research. *Journal of Marketing*, 49(4), 41–50.

256   *Alqayed, Foroudi, Dennis, Foroudi and Kooli*

Parasuraman, A., Zeithaml, V. A. and Berry, L. L. (1988). SERVQUAL: a multiple-item scale for measuring consumer perceptions of service quality. *Journal of Retailing*, 64(1), 12–40.

Parasuraman, A., Berry, L. L. and Zeithaml, V. A. (1991a). Refinement and reassessment of the SERVQUAL scale. *Journal of Retailing*, 67(4), 420.

Parasuraman, A., Berry, L. L. and Zeithaml, V. A. (1991b). Understanding customer expectations of service. *Sloan Management Review*, 32(3), 39–48.

Parasuraman, A., Zeithaml, V. A. and Berry, L. L. (1994a). Alternating scales for measuring service quality: a comparative assessment based on psychometric and diagnostic criteria. *Journal of Retailing*, 70(3), 201–230.

Parasuraman, A., Zeithaml, V. A. and Berry, L. L. (1994b). Reassessment of expectations as a comparison standard in measuring service quality: implications for further research. *Journal of Marketing*, 58(1), 111–124.

Pavlou, P. A. (2003). Consumer acceptance of electronic commerce: integrating trust and risk with the technology acceptance model. *International Journal of Electronic Commerce*, 7(3), 101–134.

Payne, A. F. and Frow, P. (2005). A strategic framework for customer relationship management. *Journal of Marketing*, 69(4), 167–176.

Payne, A. F., Storbacka, K. and Frow, P. (2008). Managing the co-creation of value. *Journal of the Academy of Marketing Science*, 36(1), 83–96.

Peng, L., Cui, G., Chung, Y. and Li, C. (2019). A multi-facet item response theory approach to improve customer satisfaction using online product ratings. *Journal of the Academy of Marketing Science*, 47(5), 960–976.

Pine, B. J., Pine, J. and Gilmore, J. H. (1999). *The Experience Economy: Work is Theatre & Every Business a Stage*. USA: Harvard Business Press.

Pitelis, C. (2012). Clusters, entrepreneurial ecosystem co-creation, and appropriability: a conceptual framework. *Industrial and Corporate Change*, 21(6), 1359–1388.

Podsakoff, P. M., MacKenzie, S. B., Paine, J. B. and Bachrach, D. G. (2000). Organizational citizenship behaviors: a critical review of the theoretical and empirical literature and suggestions for future research. *Journal of Management*, 26(3), 513–563.

Pohlmann, A. and Kaartemo, V. (2017). Research trajectories of service-dominant logic: emergent themes of a unifying paradigm in business and management. *Industrial Marketing Management*, 63(May), 53–68.

Ponsignon, F., Durrieu, F. and Bouzdine-Chameeva, T. (2017). Customer experience design: a case study in the cultural sector. *Journal of Service Management*, 28(4), 763–787.

Porter, C. E. and Donthu, N. (2008). Cultivating trust and harvesting value in virtual communities. *Management Science*, 54(1), 113–128.

Prahalad, C. K. and Ramaswamy, V. (2000). Co-opting customer competence. *Harvard Business Review*, 78(1), 79–90.

Prahalad, C. K. and Ramaswamy, V. (2003). The new frontier of experience innovation. *MIT Sloan Management Review*, 44(4), 12–19.

Prahalad, C. K. and Ramaswamy, V. (2004). Co-creation experiences: the next practice in value creation. *Journal of Interactive Marketing*, 18(3), 5–14.

Ramaswamy, V. and Gouillart, F. (2010). Building the co-creative enterprise. *Harvard Business Review*, 88(10), 100–109.

Ramaswamy, V. and Ozcan, K. (2016). Brand value co-creation in a digitalized world: an integrative framework and research implications. *International Journal of Research in Marketing*, 33(1), 93–106.

Ramirez, R. (1999). Value co-production: intellectual origins and implications for practice and research. *Strategic Management Journal*, 20(1), 49–65.

Ranjan, K. R. and Read, S. (2016). Value co-creation: concept and measurement. *Journal of the Academy of Marketing Science*, 44(3), 290–315.

Rao, A. R. and Monroe, K. B. (1989). The effect of price, brand name, and store name on buyers' perceptions of product quality: an integrative review. *Journal of Marketing Research*, 26(3), 351–357.

Reichheld, F. F. and Sasser, W. E. (1990). Zero defeofions: quoliiy comes to services. *Harvard Business Review*, 68(5), 105–111.

Rifkin, J. (2000). *The Age of Access: How the Shift from Ownership to Access is Transforming Modern Life* (p. 30). London: Penguin.

Rindfleisch, A., Burroughs, J. E. and Wong, N. (2009). The safety of objects: materialism, existential insecurity, and brand connection. *Journal of Consumer Research*, 36(1), 1–16.

Riquelme, I. P., Román, S., Cuestas, P. J. and Iacobucci, D. (2019). The dark side of good reputation and loyalty in online retailing: when trust leads to retaliation through price unfairness. *Journal of Interactive Marketing*, 47(3), 35–52.

Rodie, A. R. and Kleine, S. S. (2000). Customer participation in services production and delivery. *Handbook of Services Marketing and Management*, 4(2), 111–125.

Rosenbaum, M. S. and Massiah, C. (2011). An expanded servicescape perspective, *Journal of Service Management*, 22(4), 471–490.

Ryan, R. M. and Deci, E. L. (2000). Self-determination theory and the facilitation of intrinsic motivation, social development, and well-being. *American Psychologist*, 55(1), 68–78.

Saarijärvi, H., Kannan, P. K. and Kuuscla, H. (2013). Value co-creation: theoretical approaches and practical implications. *European Business Review*, 25(1), 6–19.

Schau, H. J., Muñiz Jr, A. M. and Arnould, E. J. (2009). How brand community practices create value. *Journal of Marketing*, 73(5), 30–51.

Schembri, S. (2006). Rationalizing service logic, or understanding services as experience?. *Marketing Theory*, 6(3), 381–392.

Schieffer, R. and Leininger, E. (2008). Customers at the core. *Marketing Management*, 17(1), 30–37.

Schmitt, B. H. (1999). *Experiential Marketing: How to Get Customers to Sense, Feel, Think, Act, Relate to Your Company and Brands*. New York: The Free Press.

Schmitt, B. H. (2003). *Customer Experience Management (CEM): A Revolutionary Approach to Connecting with Your Customer*. Hoboken, NJ: John Wiley and Sonc, Inc.

Schor, J. B. and Fitzmaurice, C. J. (2015). Collaborating and connecting: the emergence of the sharing economy. In *Handbook of Research on Sustainable Consumption*. Cheltenham: Edward Elgar Publishing.

Seppänen, M. and Mäkinen, S. (2010). Resources in academic discourse: an empirical investigation of management journals. *Journal of Industrial Engineering and Management*, 3(1), 116–137.

Shostack, G. L. (1977). Breaking free from product marketing. *Journal of Marketing*, 41(2), 73–80.

Siebert, J. U., Kunz, R. E. and Rolf, P. (2020). Effects of proactive decision making on life satisfaction. *European Journal of Operational Research*, 280(3), 1171–1187.

Silpakit, P. and Fisk, R. P. (1985). Services marketing in a changing environment. *In American Marketing Association*, 5(6), 117–121.

Silvestro, R. and Cross, S. (2000). Applying the service profit chain in a retail environment. *International Journal of Service Industry Management*, 11(3), 244–268.

Simula, H. and Ahola, T. (2014). A network perspective on idea and innovation crowdsourcing in industrial firms. *Industrial Marketing Management*, 43(3), 400–408.

Skålén, P. and Edvardsson, B. (2016). Transforming from the goods to the service-dominant logic. *Marketing Theory*, 16(1), 101–121.

So, K. K. F., King, C., Sparks, B. A. and Wang, Y. (2013). The influence of customer brand identification on hotel brand evaluation and loyalty development. *International Journal of Hospitality Management*, 34(3), 31–41.

Song, M. and Noone, B. M. (2017). The moderating effect of perceived spatial crowding on the relationship between perceived service encounter pace and customer satisfaction. *International Journal of Hospitality Management*, 65(Aug), 37–46.

Stephany, A. (2015). *The Business of Sharing: Making it in the New Sharing Economy*. New York: Springer.

Stokburger-Sauer, N., Ratneshwar, S. and Sen, S. (2012). Drivers of consumer–brand identification. *International Journal of Research in Marketing*, 29(4), 406–418.

Tapscott, D. and Williams, A. D. (2006). *Wikinomics: How Mass Collaboration Changes Everything*. New York: Portfolio.

Teas, R. K. (1993). Expectations, performance evaluation, and consumers' perceptions of quality. *Journal of Marketing*, 57(4), 18–34.

Teas, R. K. (1994). Expectations as a comparison standard in measuring service quality: an assessment of a reassessment. *Journal of Marketing*, 58(1), 132–139.

Thomson, M., MacInnis, D. J. and Whan Park, C. (2005). The ties that bind: measuring the strength of consumers' emotional attachments to brands. *Journal of Consumer Psychology*, 15(1), 77–91.

Tim, O. (2005). What is web 2.0? Design patterns and business models for the next generation of software. *International Journal of Digital Economics*, 65, 17–37.

Toufaily, E., Ricard, L. and Perrien, J. (2013). Customer loyalty to a commercial website: descriptive meta-analysis of the empirical literature and proposal of an integrative model. *Journal of Business Research*, 66(9), 1436–1447.

Tsiotsou, R. (2006). The role of perceived product quality and overall satisfaction on purchase intentions. *International Journal of Consumer Studies*, 30(2), 207–217.

Uusitalo, O. and Grønhaug, K. (2012). Service-dominant logic and licensing in international B2B markets. *Journal of Business Market Management*, 5(4), 265–284.

Uzkurt, C. (2010). Customer participation in the service process: a model and research propositions. *International Journal of Services and Operations Management*, 6(1), 17–37.

Vafeas, M., Hughes, T. and Hilton, T. (2016). Antecedents to value diminution: a dyadic perspective. *Marketing Theory*, 16(4), 469–491.

Vargo, S. L. (2007). Paradigms, pluralisms, and peripheries: on the assessment of the SD logic. *Australasian Marketing Journal (AMJ)*, 15(1), 105–108.

Vargo, S. L. and Akaka, M. A. (2009). Service-dominant logic as a foundation for service science: clarifications. *Service Science*, 1(1), 32–41.

Vargo, S. L. and Lusch, R. F. (2004). Evolving to a new dominant logic for marketing. *Journal of Marketing*, 68(1), 1–17.

Vargo, S. L. and Lusch, R. F. (2008). Service-dominant logic: continuing the evolution. *Journal of the Academy of Marketing Science*, 36(1), 1–10.

Vargo, S. L. and Lusch, R. F. (2011). It's all B2B... and beyond: toward a systems perspective of the market. *Industrial Marketing Management*, 40(2), 181–187.

Vargo, S. L. and Lusch, R. F. (2013). Service-dominant logic: prologue and prospects. *Die Betriebswirtschaft*, 73(2), 91–93.

Vargo, S. L. and Lusch, R. F. (2014). Inversions of service-dominant logic. *Marketing Theory*, 14(3), 239–248.

Vargo, S. L. and Lusch, R. F. (2016). Institutions and axioms: an extension and update of service-dominant logic. *Journal of the Academy of Marketing Science*, 44(1), 5–23.

Vargo, S. L., Maglio, P. P. and Akaka, M. A. (2008). On value and value co-creation: a service systems and service logic perspective. *European Management Journal*, 26(3), 145–152.

Verhoef, P. C., Lemon, K. N., Parasuraman, A., Roggeveen, A., Tsiros, M. and Schlesinger, L. A. (2009). Customer experience creation: determinants, dynamics and management strategies. *Journal of Retailing*, 85(1), 31–41.

Walsh, G. and Bartikowski, B. (2013). Exploring corporate ability and social responsibility associations as antecedents of customer satisfaction cross-culturally. *Journal of Business Research*, 66(8), 989–995.

West, J. and Gallagher, S. (2006). Challenges of open innovation: the paradox of firm investment in open-source software. *R&d Management*, 36(3), 319–331.

Wikström, S. (1996). Value creation by company-consumer interaction. *Journal of Marketing Management*, 12(5), 359–374.

Wilden, R., Akaka, M. A., Karpen, I. O. and Hohberger, J. (2017). The evolution and prospects of service-dominant logic: an investigation of past, present, and future research. *Journal of Service Research*, 20(4), 345–361.

Wilson, T. (2012). *A Review of Business–University Collaboration.*

Wirtz, J., den Ambtman, A., Bloemer, J., Horváth, C., Ramaseshan, B., van de Klundert, J., ... Kandampully, J. (2013). Managing brands and customer engagement in online brand communities. *Journal of Service Management*, 24(3), 223–244.

Wolter, J. S., Bock, D., Smith, J. S. and Cronin Jr, J. J. (2017). Creating ultimate customer loyalty through loyalty conviction and customer-company identification. *Journal of Retailing*, 93(4), 458–476.

Woodruff, R. B. and Flint, D. J. (2006). Marketing's service-dominant logic & customer value. In Robert F. Lusch and Stephen L. Vargo (Eds.), *The Service Dominant Logic of Marketing: Dialog, Debate & Directions*. New York: Sharpe.

Wyckham, R. G., Fitzroy, P. T. and Mandry, G. D. (1975). Marketing of services an evaluation of the theory. *European Journal of Marketing*, 9(1), 59–67.

Yi, Y. and Gong, T. (2008). If employees "go the extra mile," do customers reciprocate with similar behavior? *Psychology & Marketing*, 25(10), 961–986.

Yi, Y. and Gong, T. (2013). Customer value co-creation behavior: scale development and validation. *Journal of Business Research*, 66(9), 1279–1284.

Yi, Y., Nataraajan, R. and Gong, T. (2011). Customer participation and citizenship behavioral influences on employee performance, satisfaction, commitment, and turnover intention. *Journal of Business Research*, 64(1), 87–95.

Yoo, D. K. and Park, J. A. (2007). Perceived service quality. *International Journal of Quality & Reliability Management*, 24(9), 25–45.

Zeithaml, V. A. (1988). Consumer perceptions of price, quality, and value: a means-end model and synthesis of evidence. *Journal of Marketing*, 52(3), 2–22.

Zeithaml, V. A., Parasuraman, A. and Berry, L. L. (1985). Problems and strategies in services marketing. *Journal of Marketing*, 49(2), 33–46.

Zomerdijk, L. G. and Voss, C. A. (2010). Service design for experience-centric services. *Journal of Service Research*, 13(1), 67–82.

10 An assessment of customer experience concept

Looking back to move forward

Dongmei Zha, Reza Marvi, Pantea Foroudi, Charles Dennis, Akiko Ueno, Zhongqi Jin and T C Melewar

Introduction

The goals of this study are (1) to identify the main knowledge structure of customer experience and (2) to understand how the knowledge structure of customer experience has changed over time. The study is based on three bibliometric methods: i.e. multi-dimensional scaling, hierarchical cluster analysis and exploratory factor analysis. This chapter identifies insularity of service marketing contributions, ambiguities of experiential marketing contributions, as well as inadequacies of branding contributions as the three main issues to a fuller conceptualisation of customer experience.

Background to customer experience

It seems that customer experience (CX) has attracted considerable attention. Since the term first emerged in Carbone and Haeckel (1994) published in *Journal of marketing management* in an article on customer experience engineering, it has been a magnet of countless propositions and interpretations (Tynan and McKechnie, 2009). This growth of academic attention is most visibly demonstrated in the multiplicity of definitions in extant CX literature. In a CX review paper, Jain et al. (2017) combed through the labyrinth of CX literature and collected a total of 22 CX and CX-related (e.g., service experience, consumption experience) definitions. CX has been variously characterised as a journey (Rawson et al., 2013), a stage (Pine and Gilmore, 1999; Tynan and Mckechnie, 2009), an immersion (Grundey, 2008), or as a reaction to a series of touchpoints (Gentile et al., 2007; Homburg et al., 2017; Lemke et al., 2011; Lemon and Verhoef, 2016; Meyer and Schwager, 2007).

In a recent systematic review of CX literature, Kranzbuhler et al. (2018) made a call for "an integration and synthesis of the literature" (p. 436). Their review of CX literature (extending from 1982 to 2016) came to the conclusion that the CX construct suffers from what management literature called an *umbrella syndrome*. According to organisational behaviour theorists, Hirsch and Levin (1999) argued that popular umbrella constructs can become too all-encompassing for their own good; in other words, when something means *all things to all people*, it can end up meaning *less*. In a critical review of CX, Schmitt and Zarantonello

Assessment of customer experience concept   261

(2013) implored serious CX researchers to focus more on developing integrative framework based on existing constructs, rather than introducing *more and more constructs* and terminologies in an already crowded knowledge field. Lemon and Verhoef's (2016) extensive conceptual-historical narrative of the CX concept also noted with some dismay the multiple definitions in literature and the need for serious researchers to appropriate only widely accepted definitions.

If there is one thing the majority of reviewers agree on, it is that at this stage of concept development, theoretical consolidation must take precedence over enlargement. While most would agree with the prognosis, what remains highly problematic is still the prescription. What form and shape should the CX framework assume? How can we arrive at a structure that will sufficiently encapsulate the multifaceted nature of the CX concept? In their CX review, Homburg et al. (2017) suggest that to be successful in integration, the key is locating a novel, simple, parsimonious perspective, yet sufficiently generous in order to house the many strands of CX theories. Therefore, we assert that a rigorous examination of CX foundational intellectual structure is required.

Based on the overarching research purpose of this paper our two research objectives are (1) to identify the main knowledge structure of customer experience and (2) to understand how the knowledge structure of customer experience has changed over time. To achieve the research goal, our strategy is to use bibliometrics methods. The bibliometric analysis tracks customer experience literature over three intellectual eras (1996–2010, 2011–2016 and 2017–2019) providing researchers and readers with a longitudinal overview of the intellectual structure of CX. We noted that qualitative reviews offered valuable insight about CX concepts and all identified the underlying knowledge structure in CX literature. However, none has quantitatively investigated the knowledge structure of CX or identified the themes behind this construct through a quantitative literature review approach and bibliometrics methods.

This study makes two major contributions to the customer experience literature (CXL). First, it provides the first full-scale bibliometric analysis to date of the intellectual structure of CXL using co-citation metrics. Second, the deployment of bibliometrics is apt at this juncture because a number of CXL's difficulties arise from the complexities of its mixed and diverse literary traditions. An analysis of its intellectual structure allows us to ascertain with greater precision the sources and solutions to these persistent problems so that future CX research can be built on a stronger and sounder knowledge base and footing.

To begin with, we introduce the bibliometric approach with multi-dimensional analysis (MDS), the hierarchical cluster analysis (HCA) and the exploratory factor analysis (EFA) as the co-citation methods implemented, followed by the study findings. Finally, we conclude with a discussion of implications.

Method

Adhering to establishing a bibliometric protocol (Samiee and Chabowski, 2012; Chabowski et al., 2010, 2013, 2018), the identification of articles was initiated with a search for keywords. From an initial review of CX literature, 30 keywords were identified. To mitigate research bias, six independent reviewers with extensive background in CX research were invited to review this list. As a result, the following keywords were shortlisted: experience, customer experience, consumer experience, service experience, brand experience, service dominant logic, consumer research, services marketing and service design. Based on the final list of nine keywords, the search in the WOS database yielded 412 articles. Articles were selected based on a keyword being found in one of the following four fields in the WOS database: author keywords, abstract, reference-based article identifiers and title (McCain, 1990; Ramos-Rodríguez and Ruiz-Navarro, 2004; Schildt et al., 2006). In order to increase the validity of the results, all papers were reviewed. Furthermore, to reduce any bias, the exact selection criteria were defined beforehand, with three independent scholars having conducted the selection (Baumgartner and Pieters, 2003; Kunz and Hogreve, 2011; Zupic and C̆ater, 2015).

From the 412 articles, a total of 7,684 citations were retrieved. The data were classified under three periods: (1) 1996–2010 (hereafter P1); (2) 2011–2016 (hereafter P2); and (3) 2017–2019 (hereafter P3). In determining the span of the three eras, the development of key intellectual eras to CXL was applied as a guide. For example, citations in P1 (1996–2010) reflect early CXL writings dominated by service marketing literature. Citations in P2 (2011–2016), on the other hand, depict the "golden age" of experiential marketing literature with exemplars like Schmitt (1999), Pine and Gilmore (1999) and Gentile et al. (2007). Lastly, the citations in P3 (2017–2019) mirror the maturation of CXL as a whole with contributors taking a more integrative approach. Exemplars in this era are Schmitt and Zarantonello (2013), as well as Lemon and Verhoef (2016). A coding process was employed to ensure consistency. By using the frequency count in *bibexcel*, researchers were able to compile a list of highly cited articles from the sample.

Afterwards, the co-citation matrix was created where each value in the matrix demonstrates the number of times two papers were co-cited in a third document, since the most highly referenced CX articles can be perceived as the most influential in the CXL. Typically, to obtain a fair or good model for bibliometric analysis, the use of around 25 documents is considered optimal (Ramos-Rodríguez and Ruiz-Navarro, 2004). Adhering to this industry practice, the current study adopted for further analysis 26 publications for P1, 21 publications for P2 and 22 publications for P3.

To analyse the co-citation data, a multi-method was exerted: exploratory factor analysis, hierarchical cluster analysis and metri multidimensional scaling were used to investigate the intellectual structure of CXL; the advantages of using three methods allow for a comparison with bibliometric data, providing underexplored topics for future CX research (Samiee and Chabowski, 2012). MDS is the method used most in the research to identify influential works (McCain, 1990). Adhering to research-wide practices, stress values that are good (less than 0.10) or fair (between 0.10) are regarded as an acceptable standard (Ramos-Rodríguez and Ruiz-Navarro, 2004). In the current study, a good stress value of 0.058 was

Assessment of customer experience concept 263

obtained in the P1; 0.054 in P2; and 0.048 in the P3. A maximum standardised distance of 0.25 or less was then applied to determine which research groups were explicable and lucid. Research groups and cliques were then identified on the basis of this assumption. It should be noted that research groups are defined as groups consisting of at least two publications, while a research clique refers to three or more influential works grouped together. HCA, on the other hand, by using the bottom-up approach builds layers and layers of agglomerated data through the merging of clusters until they form a pyramidical hierarchy. In contrast, the EFA method, where the items can load on to more than one factor, can illustrate the span between multiple factors (Zupic and Cater, 2015).

Co-citation results

As indicated in our results, the intellectual structure of CX research is noticeable. In this section, the MDS, EFA and HCA findings are discussed, as they relate to the co-citation analysis for each time period (1996–2010, 2011–2016, 2017–2019) aiming to evaluate the longitudinal underpinnings of CX research.

Intellectual structure of customer experience

MDS Results

1996–2010 (P1)

An evaluation of Figure 10.1 demonstrates 11 research groups from the first period of our study. Three related groups in the general area of hedonic consumption experience (Groups 1, 6, 7) are centred on hedonic and service experiences (Hirshman and Holbrook, 1982; Shaw and Ivens, 2002). They also cover peripheral topics of extraordinary hedonic experience (Arnould and Price, 1993) and brand community (McAlexander et al., 2002). Together, these groups clearly demonstrate the experiential marketing literature in the early CX domain.

Group information is given in the following. Group 1 (v1 and v22): extraordinary hedonic experience; Group 2 (v2 and v19): experience economy and total customer experience; Group 3 (v3 and v4): servicescapes; Group 4 (v3 and v24): service dominant logic (SDL) and service encounters; Group 5 (v5 and v13): customer-brand relationship and brand community; Group 6 (v7 and v9): hedonic consumption and brand community; Group 7 (v7 and v22): hedonic and service experiences; Group 8 (v12 and v15): satisfaction and purchase, actual repurchase behaviors; Group 9 (v15 and v21): consumption emotions; **Group 10 (v17, v18 and v26): customer perception of service quality**; Group 11 (v20 and v23): experience design and loyalty behaviour.

Emphasising on service experience (Group 3 and Group 4), the concentration on servicescapes model (Bitner 1992), one aspect focuses on service dominant logic (Vargo and Lush, 2004) while another focuses on service encounters (Bitner, 1990). Relatedly, the research clique concentrating on customer perception of service quality (Group 10) provides a multi-item instrument for quantifying the

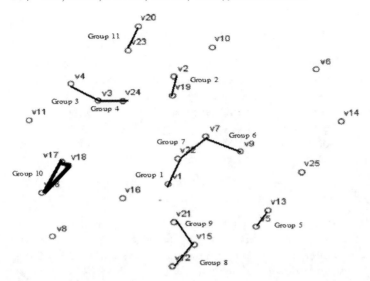

Figure 10.1 Customer experience literature intellectual structure pt 1 [1996–2010 (MDS)]. **Notes:** Stress value = 0.058; standardized Euclidean distance 0.25; bold faced text indicates research clique. v1 = Arnould and Price, 1993; v2 = Berry et al., 2002; v3 = Bitner, 1990; v4 = Bitner, 1992; v5 = Fournier, 1998; v6 = Hoffman and Novak, 1996; v7 = Holbrook and Hirshman, 1982; v8 = Lovelock, 1983; v9 = McAlexander et al., 2002; v10 = Mehrabian and Russell, 1974; v11 = Meuter et al., 2000; v12 = Mittal and Kamakura, 2001; v13 = Muniz and O'Guinn, 2001; v14 = Novak et al., 2000; v15 = Oliver, 1980; v16 = Oliver, 1997; v17 = Parasuraman et al., 1985; v18 = Parasuraman et al., 1988; v19 = Pine II and James, 1998; v20 = Pullman and Gross, 2004; v21 = Richins, 1997; v22 = Shaw and lvens, 2002; v23 = Shostack, 1984; v24 = Vargo and Lush, 2004; v25 = Zaichkowsky, 1985; v26 = Zeithaml et al., 1996.

service expectation perception (Parasuraman et al., 1985; Parasuraman et al., 1988) and the customer behavioural consequences of service quality (Zeithaml et al., 1996). This unveils the service marketing efforts in the CX domain.

Placing emphasis on consumer behaviour (Groups 8 and Group 9) is the basis for the research during this period. Rather than foregrounding the experience alone, the relevance of insights at a managerial level are indicated; this includes satisfaction and purchase, actual repurchase behaviours (Oliver, 1980; Mittal and Kamakura, 2001) and consumption-related emotions (Richins, 1997). In a related group (i.e. Group 11), the concentration on experience design and loyalty behaviour introduced an approach that includes emotional responses as mediating factors between the physical and relational elements and loyalty behaviours (Pullman and Gross, 2004; Shostack, 1984). This reveals the satisfaction and loyalty research efforts in the CX domain.

Research on customer-brand relationship and brand community (namely Group 5) provides the relationship premise at the level of consumers' lived experiences with their brands. By combining relationship and branding, sociological theories become associated with consumer behaviour (Fournier, 1998; Muniz and O'Guinn, 2001). In a related group, the concentration was on experience design and loyalty behaviour (Group 11).. In a related group, the concentration on total customer experience and economic experience (Group 2) is a unique topic. This theme shows that the holistic customer experience consists of both functional and emotional dimensions (Berry et al., 2002).

2011–2016 (P2)

We identified seven groups in this period (see Figure 10.2). A focus on service quality (Group 6 and Group 7) signals the continued significance of service marketing in the customer experience literature (CEL). Parasuraman et al. (1988) and Zeithaml et al. (1996) display the early effort of a service quality model in

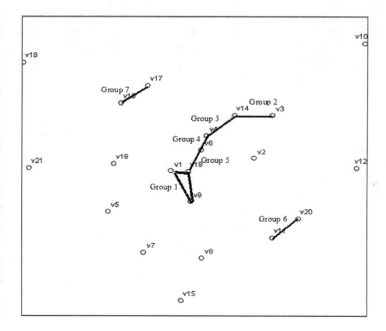

Figure 10.2 Customer experience literature intellectual structure pt 2 [2011–2016 (MDS)]. **Notes:** Stress value = 0.054; standardized Euclidean distance 0.25; bold faced text indicates research clique. v1 = Berry et al., 2002; v2 =. Bitner, 1992; v3 = Brakus et al., 2009; v4 = Gentile et al., 2007; v5 = Grewal and Kumar, 2009; v6 = Holbrook and Hirshman, 1982; v7 = Klaus et al., 2012; v8 = Lemke et al., 2001; v9 = Meyer and Schwager, 2007; v10 = Novak et al., 2000; v11 = Parasuraman et al., 1998; v12 = Parasuraman et al., 2005; v13 = Payne et al., 2008; v14 = Pine and Gilmore, 1998; v15 = Puccinelli et al., 2009; v16 = Pullman, 2004; v17 = Vargo and Lush, 2004; v18 = Vargo and Lush, 2008; v19 = Verhoef et al., 2009; v20 = Zeithaml et al., 1996; v21 = Zomerdijk, 2010.

CEL, while Vargo and Lush (2008) and Payne et al. (2008) focus on continuing the evaluation of new service dominant logic.

Group information is given in the following: **Group 1 (v1, v9 and v19): total customer experience**; Group 2 (v3 and v14): brand experience; Group 3 (v4 and v14): experience components and progression of economic value; Group 4 (v4 and v6): customer experience creation and holistic perspective of consumption; Group 5 (V6 and V19): customer experience and holistic perspective of consumption; Group 6 (v11 and v20): service quality; Group 7 (v13 and v17): co-creation value.

Four related groups emphasising brand experience (Groups 2–5) include four dimensions of brand experience on brand experience model and process (Brakus et al., 2009), as well as four components of CX (Pine and Gilmore, 1998). To complete this chain, one aspect is the focus on creating a hedonic experience for customers (Holbrook and Hirshman, 1982), while another emphasises customer experience creation at a managerial level (Gentile et al., 2007). As a set, this chain shows the multifaceted nature of experiential marketing and branding in the CX domain. A research clique emphasising total customer experience (Group 1) indicates the expansion of topics related to strategies for different stages of consumption experience in CXL.

2017–2019 (P3)

Figure 10.3 presents the four research groups in this period. An emphasis on brand experience and customer experience (Group 1) shows the comprehensive perspective in recent CX research. By incorporating topics related to branding process, research established a staged approach to CX during this time period (Brakus et al., 2009; Verhoef et al., 2009). The study of customer journey and brand experience (Group 2) reveals differentiated stages of purchase during the CX. This is important in the evaluation of CX (Brakus et al., 2009; Lemon and Verhoef, 2016). A research clique emphasising total customer experience was found in Group 3 (Gentile et al., 2007; Holbrook and Hirshman, 1982; Meyer and Schwager, 2007; Verhoef et al., 2009) and Group 4 (a conceptual model for customer experience quality and its impact on customer relationship outcomes).

Group information is given in the following: Group 1 (V4 and V20): brand experience; Group 2 (v4 and v10): customer journey; **Group 3 (v5, Vv8, v12 and v20): total customer experience;** Group 4 (v9 and v17): customer experience quality

HCA Results

1996–2010 (P1)

The HCA method identified four clusters in the P1 containing different intellectual structures which have had an influence on the knowledge structure of

Assessment of customer experience concept 267

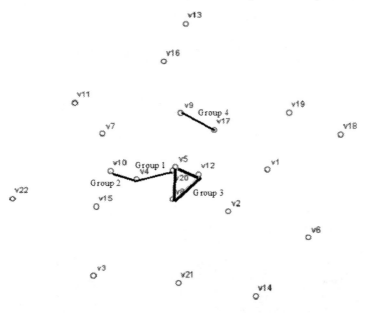

Figure 10.3 Customer experience literature intellectual structure pt 3 [2017–2019 (MDS)]. **Notes**: Stress value = 0.048; standardized Euclidean distance 0.25; bold faced text indicates research clique. v1 =. Bitner, 1992; v2 – Berry et al., 2002; v3 = Bitner, 1992; v4 = Brakus et al., 2009; v5 = Gentile et al., 2007; v6 = Pine and Gilmore, 1999; v7 = Grewal and Kumar, 2009; v8 = Holbrook and Hirshman, 1982; v9 = Lemke et al., 2001; v10 = Lemon and Verhoef, 2016; v11 = Mehrabian and Russell, 1974; v12 = Meyer and Schwager, 2007; v13 = Novak et al., 2000; v14 = Parasuraman et al., 1998; v15 = Pine and Gilmore, 1998; v16 = Rose et al., 2012; v17 = Schmitt ,1999; v18 = Vargo and Lush, 2004; v19 = Vargo and Lush, 2008; v20 = Verhoef et al., 2009; v21 = Zeithaml et al., 1996.

customer experience, as shown in Figure 10.4. The HCA findings for the P1 are similar to the MDS results; however, the differences in both methods show the precise nature of applying each method. Service quality (Cluster 1) reflects the scholarly attempts for developing scales for assessing service quality in retailing and service firms from a customer perspective. Service design (Cluster 2) investigates the influence of firm physical surroundings on customer experience. Similar to Cluster 2, branding (Cluster 4) represents the relationship among different aspects of service elements (both online and offline) associated with creating an enhanced customer experience as an important role in determining the success of a service/retailing firm. Finally, consumer research (Cluster 3) investigates the stimulus related to the symbolic, social and hedonic aspects of experience.

Cluster information is given in the following: Cluster 1 (v11, v17, v18, v26, v8): Service quality; Cluster 2 (v20, v23, v10, v2, v4, v3, v24, v19, v2): Service design; Cluster 3 (v15, v16, v1, v7): Consumer research, Cluster 4 (v6, v14, v9, v25, v13, v5, v21, v12): Branding

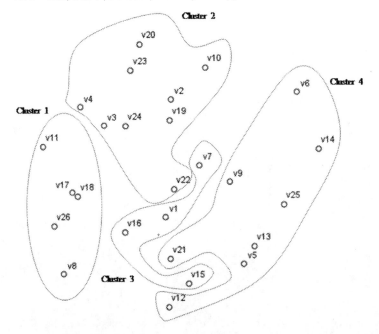

Figure 10.4 Customer experience literature intellectual structure pt 1 [1996–2010 (HCA)].
v1 = Arnould and Price, 1993; v2 = Berry et al., 2002; v3 = Bitner, 1990; v4 = Bitner, 1992; v5 = Fournier, 1998; v6 = Hoffman and Novak, 1996; v7 = Holbrook and Hirshman, 1982; v8 = Lovelock, 1983; v9 = McAlexander et al., 2002; v10 = Mehrabian and Russell, 1974; v11 = Meuter et al., 2000; v12 = Mittal and Kamakura, 2001; v13 = Muniz and O'Guinn, 2001; v14 = Novak et al., 2000; v15 = Oliver, 1980; v16 = Oliver, 1997; v17 = Parasuraman et al., 1985; v18 = Parasuraman et al., 1988; v19 = Pine II and James, 1998; v20 = Pullman and Gross, 2004; v21 = Richins, 1997; v22 = Shaw and Ivens, 2002; v23 = Shostack, 1984; v24 = Vargo and Lush, 2004; v25 = Zaichkowsky, 1985; v26 = Zeithaml et al., 1996.

2011–2016 (P2)

For P2, service dominant logics (Cluster 1) highlight that customer experience is not limited to a single form of a firm offering, while the entire service ecosystem impacts on customer experience in which it is intertwined with value. Drawing on overviewing of service and service quality literature, online marketing (Cluster 2) aims to provide a set of components of what makes an online experience compelling for customers. Additionally, this cluster aspires to identify the key outcomes of this compelling experience. In alignment with the two previous clusters, service marketing (Cluster 3) approaches customer experience as a strategic perspective by mainly focusing on how managers can create value in the form of experience for their customers (Figure. 10.5).

Cluster information is given in the following: Cluster 1 (v13, v17, v16, v9, v7, v8, v11): Service dominant logics, Cluster 2 (v10, v18, v20, v15): Online marketing; Cluster 3 (v2, V14, v3, v1, v19): Online marketing

Assessment of customer experience concept   269

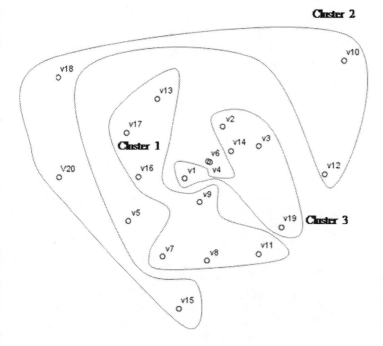

Figure 10.5 Customer experience literature intellectual structure pt 2 [2011–2016 (HCA)]. v1 = Berry et al., 2002; v2 =. Bitner, 1992; v3 = Brakus et al., 2009; v4 = Gentile et al., 2007; v5 = Grewal and Kumar, 2009; v6 = Holbrook and Hirshman, 1982; v7 = Klaus et al., 2012; v8 = Lemke et al., 2001; v9 = Meyer and Schwager, 2007; v10 = Novak et al., 2000; v11 = Parasuraman et al., 1998; v12 = Parasuraman et al., 2005; v13 = Payne et al., 2008; v14 = Pine and Gilmore, 1998; v15 = Puccinelli et al., 2009; v16 = Pullman, 2004; v17 = Vargo and Lush, 2004; v18 = Vargo and Lush, 2008; v19 = Verhoef et al., 2009; v20 = Zeithaml et al., 1996; v21 = Zomerdijk, 2010.

2017–2019 (P3)

For P3, service design (Cluster 1) depicts articles based on service-dominant logics, that are related to measuring customer experience in both online and offline environments. Closely linked to Cluster 1, (Experiential marketing) Cluster 2 offers a strategic framework for experimental marketing. It is noteworthy that the work of Lemon and Verhoef (2016) aims to empirically relate customer journey to customer experience. Finally, retailing (Cluster 3) focuses on the influence of macro factors on customer experience in a retailing setting (Figure. 10.6).

Cluster information is given in the following: Cluster 1(v6, v21, v14, v11, v19, v13, v22, v18, v1, v13): Service design, Cluster 2 (v7, v12, v15, v4, v2, v10, v9, v16, v17): Experiential marketing, Cluster 3 (v5, v8): Retailing.

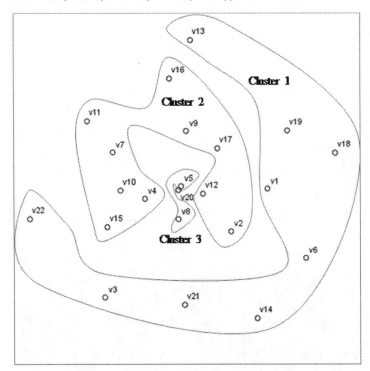

Figure 10.6 Customer experience literature intellectual structure pt 3 [2017–2019 (HCA)]. v1 =. Bitner, 1992; v2 = Berry et al., 2002; v3 = Bitner, 1992; v4 = Brakus et al., 2009; v5 = Gentile et al., 2007; v6 = Pine and Gilmore, 1999; v7 = Grewal and Kumar, 2009; v8 = Holbrook and Hirshman, 1982; v9 = Lemke et al., 2001; v10 = Lemon and Verhoef, 2016; v11 = Mehrabian and Russell, 1974; v12 = Meyer and Schwager, 2007; v13 = Novak et al., 2000; v14 = Parasuraman et al., 1998; v15 = Pine and Gilmore, 1998; v16 = Rose et al., 2012; v17 = Schmitt, 1999; v18 = Vargo and Lush, 2004; v19 = Vargo and Lush, 2008; v20 = Verhoef et al., 2009; v21 = Zeithaml et al., 1996;

EFA results

1996–2010 (P1)

For the first period of analysis four factors emerged from the EFA analysis. Service design (Factor 1) is concentrated on service design branding (Factor 2) shows how branding is related to customer experience. Service marketing (Factor 3) represents the relationship of service quality and customer satisfaction. Finally, online marketing (Factor 4) reveals how customers' experiences are related to online marketing (Figure. 10.7).

Factor information is given in the following: Factor 1 (v4, v11, v23, v18, v3, v25, v24, v17, v14, v10, v6, v20): Service design; Factor 2 (v21, v12, v1, v22, v5, v9, v13): Branding; Factor 3 (v26, v15, v16): Service marketing, Factor 4 (v23, v18, v10, v9, v8, v18, v19, v26): Online branding.

Assessment of customer experience concept 271

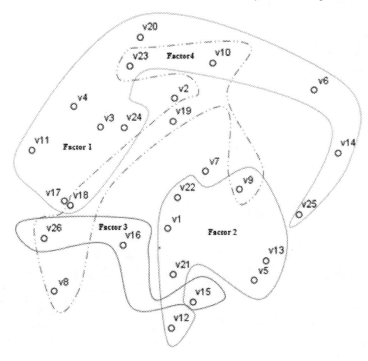

Figure 10.7 Customer experience literature intellectual structure pt 1 [1996–2010]. v1 = Arnould and Price, 1993; v2 = Berry et al., 2002; v3 = Bitner, 1990; v4 = Bitner, 1992; v5 = Fournier, 1998; v6 = Hoffman and Novak, 1996; v7 = Holbrook and Hirshman, 1982; v8 = Lovelock, 1983; v9 = McAlexander et al., 2002; v10 = Mehrabian and Russell, 1974; v11 = Meuter et al., 2000; v12 = Mittal and Kamakura, 2001; v13 = Muniz and O'Guinn, 2001; v14 = Novak et al., 2000; v15 = Oliver, 1980; v16 = Oliver, 1997; v17 = Parasuraman et al., 1985; v18 = Parasuraman et al., 1988; v19 = Pine II and James, 1998; v20 = Pullman and Gross, 2004; v21 = Richin,s 1997; v22 = Shaw and Ivens, 2002; v23 = Shostack, 1984; v24 = Vargo and Lush, 2004; v25 = Zaichkowsky, 1985; v26 = Zeithaml et al., 1996

2011–2016 (P2)

As for the second period, the results of EFA analysis also revealed four factors. Retailing (Factor 1) highlights how different elements have influence on customer experience in a retailing context. Service design (Factor 2), similar to Factor 1 in previous factors, stresses the importance of service design in delivering a satisfactory customer experience. Service dominant logics (Factor 3) aims to show how customer experience can positively result in value co-creation with the customers. Finally, along similar lines, service marketing (Factor 4) investigates how managers can co-create value with their customers in the form of customer experience (Figure. 10.8).

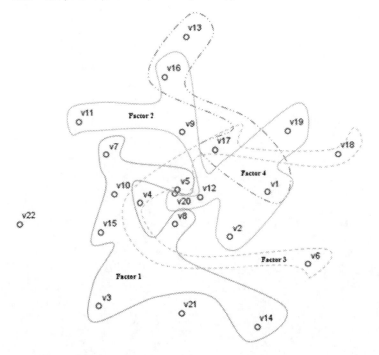

Figure 10.8 Customer experience literature intellectual structure pt 2 [2011–2016 (EFA)]. v1 = Berry et al., 2002; v2 =. Bitner, 1992; v3 = Brakus et al., 2009; v4 = Gentile et al., 2007; v5 = Grewal and Kumar, 2009; v6 = Holbrook and Hirshman, 1982; v7 = Klaus et al., 2012; v8 = Lemke et al., 2001; v9 = Meyer and Schwager, 2007; v10 = Novak et al., 2000; v11 = Parasuraman et al., 1998; v12 = Parasuraman et al., 2005; v13 = Payne et al., 2008; V14 = Pine and Gilmore, 1998; v15 = Puccinelli et al., 2009; v16 = Pullman, 2004; v17 = Vargo and Lush, 2004; v18 = Vargo and Lush, 2008; v19 = Verhoef et al., 2009; v20 = Zeithaml et al., 1996; v21 = Zomerdijk, 2010.

Factor information is given in the following: Factor 1 (v15, v10, v14, v3, v5, v8, v7): Retailing; Factor 2 (v9, v1, v16, v2, v19, V20, v12, v11): Service design; Factor 3 (v5, v4, v18, v6, v17): Service dominant logics; Factor 4 (v1, v16, v17, v13): Service marketing.

2017–2019 (P3)

As for the third period, Experiential marketing (Factor 1) reflects the experimental marketing. In addition, this factor aims to develop a framework for this approach to marketing. Retailing (Factor 2) highlights the importance of creating superior customer experience in a retailing context. Finally, sensory marketing (Factor 3) indicates the new trend in customer experience, also called sensory experience (Figure. 10.9)

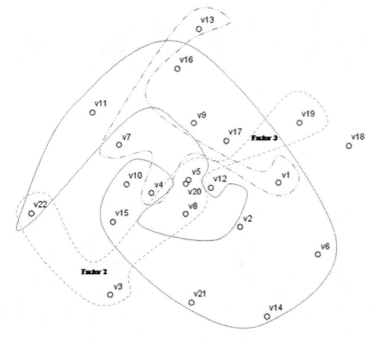

Figure 10.9 Customer experience literature intellectual structure pt 3 [2017–2019 (EFA)]. v1 = Bitner, 1992; v2 = Berry et al., 2002; v3 = Bitner, 1992; v4 = Brakus et al., 2009; v5 = Gentile et al., 2007; v6 = Pine and Gilmore, 1999; v7 = Grewal and Kumar, 2009; v8 = Holbrook and Hirshman, 1982; v9 = Lemke et al., 2001; v10 = Lemon and Verhoef, 2016; v11 = Mehrabian and Russell, 1974; v12 = Meyer and Schwager, 2007; v13 = Novak et al., 2000; v14 = Parasuraman et al., 1998; v15 = Pine and Gilmore, 1998; v16 = Rose et al., 2012; v17 = Schmitt, 1999; v18 = Vargo and Lush, 2004; v19 = Vargo and Lush, 2008; v20 = Verhoef et al., 2009; v21 = Zeithaml et al., 1996;

Factor information is given in the following: Factor 1 (v21, v11, v15, v2, v9, v14, v10, v4, v6, v17, v12, v22, v1, v16): Experiential marketing; Factor 2 (v22, v19, v3, v5, v20, v8): Retailing; Factor 3 (v7, v4, v1, v13): Sensory marketing

Discussion

Multi-method comparison

A bird's eye view of the MDS, HCA and EFA analysis shows the outlines of three major clusters that share an epistemological and ontological heritage of customer experience. Each period not only contains an intertwining of related research groups, clusters and factors agglomerated from the MDS, HCA and EFA analysis process, but also a constellation of independent events within its immediate proximity.

Although the data for all three applied methods have been identical, the outcomes of each method are different. However, all three applied techniques

274 *Zha, Marvi, Foroudi, Dennis, Ueno, Jin and Melewar*

established valuable tools for identifying the related subfields in the configuration of highly cited articles in each period. It is evident that each of the analysis yields different outcomes which could not have been attainable by a single method. In the following sections, these three main interrelated subgroups of customer experience are described.

Subgroup 1 – Service marketing

1996–2010 (P1)

In P1, the events representing service marketing literature congregate on Groups 1, 3, 4, 6, 7 in MDS analysis, Cluster 1 in HCA analysis and Factor 1 in EFA analysis as a single cluster on the left side of the map. Our papers originating from service marketing literature constitute the largest grouping in all three periods. The high citation metrics validate the received view among CX reviewers (Homburg et al., 2017), namely that early CX literature is heavily populated with contributions from service marketing literature. The confinement of service marketing literature within the bounds of a single cluster are closely interwoven with the focus of earlier citers exclusively on the service aspects of the CX, an observation also attested in Folstad and Vale's (2018) customer journey review.

This closely knitted cluster can be further decomposed into three service research theme groupings in the service marketing subgroups:

THEME 1: CUSTOMER EXPERIENCE DESIGN AND ANALYSIS

Research Group (11), Cluster (2) and Factor (1) mainly feature two papers on service design by Pullman and Gross (2004) and Shostack (1984), both pioneers of the concept of service marketing design. Folstad and Vale (2018) noted that service blueprinting, first developed by Shostack (1984) and later rehabilitated by Bitner et al. (2008), represents a precursor of the customer journey construct.

THEME 2: CUSTOMER EXPERIENCE MEASUREMENT

Research Group (10), Cluster (1) and Factor (4) comprise papers centred around the service quality measurement including the two papers featuring Parasuraman as the first author (1985, 1988) and Zeithaml et al. (1996).

THEME 3: EXTENSIONS OF CUSTOMER EXPERIENCE THEORY

The core is represented by the research Groups (3, 4), Cluster (2) and Factor (1) consisting of Bitner's (1992) paper on servicescape and Vargo and Lush's (2004) paper on service dominant logic. Service dominant logic brings an experiential dimension into CX literature through the concept of co-creation, while Bitner's servicescape opens the way for the integration of environmental factors into service marketing literature.

Three important observations should be made at this stage. First, in all streams of CX-related research, the context of the study is still service based. Second, while the emphasis of CX design and CX measurement is primarily processual, the high citation scores of Bitner (1992) as well as Vargo and Lush (2004) demonstrate a growing interest among contributors to integrate the more experiential aspects of CX experience into their analysis. Third, a firm-based or organisational perspective of CX is markedly absent. Questions like "How should organizations be structured in order to successfully manage the customer experience?" or "How do organisations need to adapt to the complexity of the customer journey?" are not addressed. According to Lemon and Verhoef (2016), so far, the customer journey and channel literature has made little progress in providing a meso level perspective of how firms can manage the entire customer journey and experience.

2011–2016 (P2)

In the second period, the service marketing mainly disintegrates into Group 7, Cluster 1 and Cluster 3, Factor 2, linked through service quality. Additionally, service marketing is anchored on Cluster 1 and Factor 4 through the value of co-creation. Such split alignment between these two concepts demonstrates a perspective shift among CX scholars. The movement away from a monotonic service-based context to a multi-varied context embraced inputs from other strands of CX writings in the experiential marketing. The carry-over of these two themes also indicates that co-creation and service quality remain important elements in the conception of CX among service marketing writers.

2017–2019 (P3)

In P3, the service marketing cluster underwent further changes. Relinquishing the intellectual structure of customer experience in three different periods, and Period 2, in Period 3, service marketing events are dispersed across the bibliometric results. First, six of the service marketing events (Bitner, 1992; Vargo and Lusch, 2008; Vargo and Lusch, 2004; Zomerdijk and Voss, 2010; Zeithaml et al., 1996; Parasuraman et al., 1988) are spread out on Cluster 1 in the plot. The only outlier in the radial is Pine and Gilmore (1999). Radial formations evolved because events that fail to achieve sufficient pooling to become a research group, find themselves entangled to core themes of experiential marketing literature. This thematic entanglement shows the inextricable links between the service marketing literature and the experiential marketing literature.

Secondly, service marketing events (Verhoef et al., 2009; Lemon and Verhoef, 2016; Lemke et al., 2011) have migrated to the core assimilating with other experiential marketing events, and they became integral components of the four major research groups in this Period 1 research Group (1, 2, 3, 4); Cluster (2, 3); Factor (1, 3). As an exemplar, Verhoef et al.'s (2009) paper, an agglomeration of the

276   Zha, Marvi, Foroudi, Dennis, Ueno, Jin and Melewar

factors that go into the creation of a customer experience model, transited from a distal position in P2 to emerge as the most highly cited paper in P3. Although the proposed model is built on service marketing theories, Verhoef et al. (2009) recognised a plurality of non-service factors: importance of past customer experiences, store environments, together with service interfaces including psychosocial factors such as store brands on future experiences.

Subgroup 2: Experiential marketing

1996–2010 (P1)

In P1, the seven events that make up the experiential marketing cluster congregate in the centre of the MDS plot. The cluster consists of an interlocking formation of four research Groups, (1, 2, 6, 7), Clusters (2, 3), and Factors (2, 4). Linking the research Groups 6 and 7 at the core, could represent Holbrook and Hirschman's (1982) paper on the experiential dimension of consumption. Holbrook (2018) has been very clear that the objective of their paper (Holbrook and Hirschman, 1982), was to bring attention to the lesser-known hedonic dimensions of consumer experience categorised as "fantasies, feelings and fun" in contrast to the more developed functional dimensions of consumption activities. Conserving the cognition-affect-behaviour-satisfaction (CABS) sequence of so-called information processing model, the authors associate a hedonistic character with the consumption experience (Hirschman and Holbrook, 1982). An experience is referred to as hedonic when its goal is the pursuit of pleasure (Hirschman and Holbrook, 1982).

Complementing the works of Holbrook and Hirschman, Mehrabian and Russell's (1974) paper on environmental psychology, represented by v10 on the MDS map, clarifies the interactions between the individual and the environment by identifying three basic emotional responses: pleasure, arousal and dominance. The work of Merhrabian and Russell (1974)'s Pleasure-Arousal-Dominance (PAD) Emotional State Model that are interwoven with experience in Holbrook and Hirschman's (1982) hedonic consumption model.

The interlocking of research Groups (1, 6, 7) represent a very interesting but telling alliance. An event (Holbrook and Hirschman, 1982) is centripetal, linking two papers with very different orientations. In research Group 6, it is linked to McAlexander et al. (2002) – an ethnographic study of Jeep owners as a brand community. In research Group 7, it is related to Shaw and Ivens 2002 work, a practitioner guide cataloguing the experiences of two senior executives from Dell Computers. This event is, in turn, linked to v1, Arnould and Price's (1993) interpretive study of the experience of river rafting. The conflation of papers of such divergent genres and categories exemplify the sense that the origins of the CX concept is as much rooted in the applied press (Tynan and Mckechnie, 2009) as it is in academia. This amalgamation would prove to be a conundrum for the development of theoretical development of experiential marketing literature.

Assessment of customer experience concept 277

2011–2016 (P2)

Period 2 can be described as the golden era of experiential marketing represented by a cluster of seven events organised as an interlocking network of five research Groups (1, 2, 3, 4, 5), Cluster (3); and Factor (1). In Period 2, the paper by Holbrook and Hirschman (1982), visualised in the MDS map, continues to maintain its pivotal position at the core. Linking research Group 4 and 5, it demonstrates once again that among citers, the paper continues to be perceived as the theoretical "dogma" of experiential marketing, also described as a "pillar of the so-called experience economy and experiential marketing" (Cova and Cova, 2012).

In the second paper, (Hirschman and Holbrook, 1982) exploring the propositions and premises of hedonic consumption, the authors defined hedonic experiences as "those facets of consumer behaviour that relate to the multisensory aspects of one's experience with products where multisensory means the receipt of experience in multiple sensory modalities including tastes, sounds, tactile impressions and visual images" (Hirschman and Holbrook, 1982, p. 92).

This conceptualisation is contingent on three a priori conditions: (1) embodied: embodiment in this context is the phenomenal state by which an individual feels located and active in an environment including a sense of location, bodily agency and ownership (Grabarczyk and Pokropski, 2016); (2) sensual: a representation of experience is multisensory in dimensions including auditory, visual, tactile, olfactory and taste; and(3) somatic: hedonic experience originates in a change in bodily state revolving around the two-stage afferent and efferent nature of a physio-psychological state (Hirschman and Holbrook, 1982). External changes displayed in the exteroceptive maps of vision or hearing may trigger an action programme that causes a change in body state, thus, arousing feelings or images of pleasure or displeasure.

In P2, the search for an experiential marketing model to *managerialize* the theoretical assumptions of hedonic consumption began in earnest. Pine and Gilmore's (1998) stated objective of the publication, namely "to supply the managerially inclined reader with the tools to begin staging compelling experiences" (Pine and Gilmore, 1998), is a typical piece of literature represented in this period. In spite of the misgivings with the many versions of experiential marketing in the popular press, Holbrook (2000) did find broad consent with the tenor of two prominent experiential marketing propositions. The conceptual heart of both Schmitt's and Pine and Gilmore's (1998) works, according to Holbrook (2000), is that memorable experiences involve different degrees of participation (embodied), engagement (sensual) and immersion, described as a state of deep engagement in a medium (somatic) and these features articulate in spirit the premises and propositions of hedonic consumption theory. Therefore, experiential marketing, at root, can be defined as the offering of experiential episodes with hedonic potential for (1) hedonic-oriented cognitions or fantasies; as (2) hedonic-related affects or feelings and (3) as hedonic lifestyle such as various play and leisure-oriented aspects of behaviour or simply, fun; that, in turn, results in the mental, emotional or physical experience of pleasure.

In P2, the most highly cited paper is Gentile et al.'s (2008) paper that provided the first theoretical outline of experiential marketing. Gentile et al. (2004) suggest that what contributes to the creation of experimental marketing value is not so much the selling of stand-alone experiential offerings, such as amusement parks, zoo or museum visits, movies or football matches but the embedment of hedonic potential in the transactional environment. In this perspective, companies do not sell or stage experiences, but they rather provide a palette of hedonic devices, artefacts, themes, multisensory settings, at different stages of the customer journey, conducive for the evocation of hedonic experiences.

Experiential marketing can include purposeful embedment of hedonic devises in the customer journey enabling the customer to live all the moments of the relationship with a company in a "delightful" way, even beyond expectations (LaSalle and Britton, 2003). Or, as Schmitt (1999) points out, a marketer can manipulate "the environment and setting for the desired customer experiences to emerge". Allowing customers to co-create their own hedonic experience with the company (Prahalad and Ramaswamy, 2004) transforms experiential marketing from an industry-specific concept into ubiquitous marketing logic. Hedonic episodes add spark, vitality and engagement to all stages of the consumption process (Hirschman and Holbrook, 1982). Pine and Gilmore (1998) rightly observed that the "concept of selling an entertainment experience is taking root in businesses far removed from theatres and amusement parks" (p. 99).

2017–2019 (P3)

In P3, with the exception of Verhoef et al. (2009), the highly cited works continue to be dominated by same staple papers from the experiential marketing cluster – Gentile et al., 2007; Holbrook and Hirschman, 1982; Pine and Gilmore, 1998; Brakus et al., 2009; Schmitt, 1999) and among them, they form the content of four research Groups (1, 2, 3, 4); Clusters (2, 3); and Factors (1, 2, 3) within the core of the experiential marketing cluster. Despite the increasing academic attention experiential marketing is garnering, much of the literature represented here remains descriptive and practitioner-oriented with no new inputs to advance the conceptualisation of the experiential marketing thought.

Subgroup 3: Branding meaning

1996–2010 (P1)

In P1, at the upper end of the axis, research Group 5, Cluster (4) and Factor (2) consist of two min articles: Fournier's (1998) seminal work which provides a framework for consumer-brand relationship, and Muniz and O'Guinn's (2001) article on brand community. At the lower end, the cluster is represented by research Group 8 and 9, pivoted around Oliver's two papers on satisfaction (1997, 1980). Oliver (1999) explores satisfaction as a staging ground for "loyalty

Assessment of customer experience concept   279

formation" since the satisfaction-retention dyad is the basis for developing long-term consumer-brand relationship.

Mittal and Kamakura (2001) argue for a more nuanced perspective of the construct beyond the disconfirmation structure. By arguing for context-dependent methodology, they advocate the inclusion of the nature/extent of response bias as a mediator of satisfaction rating. That is, satisfaction not only has a structure, but it also has a context and meanings as well. By overlooking meaning, prior research on satisfaction has produced only a faint resemblance to the culturally constituted and personally driven consumer experiences we observed (Fournier and Mick, 1999). It seems inarguable that expectations of consumption meanings arising from the individual, cultural and social context of the consumer are important factors in determining the meaning of satisfaction itself. Casting phenomenological and semiotic viewpoints, Fournier and Mick (1999) suggest that "meaningless satisfaction is no satisfaction at all".

This research oversight is not a problem confined to satisfaction studies. A consensus is now emerging that understanding brand personality and other brand relationship variables is contingent on the understanding of brand meanings (Batra, 2019). Researchers are beginning to realise the accrual of consumer-generated meanings (Arvidsson, 2005; Mick and Buhl, 1992) is the mechanism through which consumers can establish deep personal relationships with a brand (Elliott and Wattanasuwan, 1998; Fournier, 1998). Consumers modify brand meanings and use them for their own purposes. They may consume them personally, privately or join a "brand community" and become active co-creators of brand meanings (Muñiz and O'Guinn, 2001; Schau et al., 2009). Managing brands is, in essence, about managing brand meanings (Allen et al., 2008; McCracken, 2005).

2011–2016 (P2)

In P2, the events no longer exist as a cluster, represented in the MDS plot by a single event – i.e. that of Brakus et al., 2009. Since Brakus et al. (2009) is linked to Pine and Gilmore (1998) and onwards to the interlocking connection of the experiential marketing core, most citers effectively view Brakus et al. (2009) only as a "branding extension" of experiential marketing literature, rather than a separate literary representation. Although Brakus et al. (2009) provided a basis for conceptualising brand experience, as an experience by brand-related stimuli.

As a result, the intellectual inputs of branding meaning based on a branding paradigm were not further developed or exploited for CX consumption. For example, to date, few researchers in the CX field have acknowledged and integrated the semiotic doctrine that focuses on the morphology of signs and symbols. Semiotics positions meaning at the nucleus of consumer behaviour defining the meaning a brand as a system of signs and symbols that engages the consumer in an imaginary/symbolic process that contributes tangible value to a product offering (Oswald, 2007). As such, it provides a rich metalanguage for semiotic consumer research. Through its distinctive and wide-ranging literature, semiotics can advance theory development and substantiate expanded methodologies for symbolism research from acquisition and consumption to disposition behaviours.

2017–2019 (P3)

In P3, branding literature is still represented in the MDS space as a single event (Brakus et al., 2009). But in this MDS space, Brakus et al. (2009) is entrenched in the core of the experiential marketing cluster as a component of two important research Groups (1, 2); Cluster (2); and Factor (1).

The analysis of the service marketing cluster demonstrates that, while the research on the processual aspects of CX is vibrant and prolific, the content of CX remains captive to a service-oriented approach. To overcome the insularity, service marketing literature needs to deal with/address theoretical vulnerabilities in service marketing literature represented by the set of persistent problems that continues to hamper the intellectual development of the CX concept.

The analysis of the experiential marketing cluster shows that experiential marketing addresses a vital aspect of CX through the offering of hedonic experience. Different events of the customer journey evoke different types of customer experience(s) (Holbrook, 2000). Service-oriented events evoke service experience, brand-related stimuli evoke brand-based customer experience (Brakus et al., 2009) and hedonic-potentiated events evoke hedonic experiences.

The analysis of the brand meaning cluster shows that the existing contribution of branding knowledge to CX literature remains superficial and inadequate for the task of explicating the semiotic, symbolic and contextual dimensions of a customer journey. By ignoring the brand meaning context of a branding paradigm, many of the crucial socio-psychological aspects of CX remain unexplored. Different dimensions of customer experience require the application of different competences, different tools and devices based on a different marketing logic.

Based on the findings of MDS, EFA and HCA during the three periods (i.e. 1996–2011, 1993–2002, 2017–2019), we identified three general trends in the intellectual structure development of the CXL. As shown in Figure 10.10, this approach offers great detail about the CX domain changes over the time span of this study.

Conclusion

At the beginning of this chapter, we spelled out two research objectives as a roadmap to guide the development of the thesis. Objective 1 was to analyse the major intellectual components of the intellectual structure of CXL through a bibliometric analysis. The results from the bibliometric analysis of the three discreet literary periods enabled us to identify major clusters of writings, collages of influences and crucially, pinpoint the source of the persistent problems. Objective 2 was to

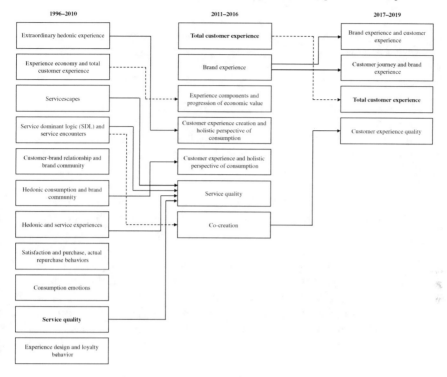

Figure 10.10 Longitudinal development of customer experience research.

understand how the knowledge structure of customer experience has changed over time. Based on these findings, we suggest a new schema to re-align the CX knowledge base rationalising and differentiating the contributions from service marketing literature, experiential marketing literature and branding literature.

CASE STUDY

Customer experience: ViewStream

ViewStream (not its real name) is one of the top three TV streaming services in Finland. ViewStream has hundreds of millions in revenue and tens of thousands of customers. The system provides on-demand broadcasts of TV channels and online content packages and also enables customers to watch live broadcasts on TV, computer, mobile phone or other mobile devices. There are four phases in the process of streaming TV services to customers: (1) impulse for purchasing; (2) purchasing; (3) implementation, use and maintenance; and (4) termination. Researchers from Lappeenranta University used interviews and focus groups to study the factors that affect customer experience and value-creating factors at different phases of the service process.

Customer-based factors

The most important customer-based factors during the impulse phase are consumption goals and personality traits. Consumption goals include price and "anytime and anywhere" availability. Personality traits concern the personalities of the image of the service provider as well as the customer. In the words of a Sales Manager:

> Some people just want an iPhone. When we ask them why, they claim that there is no rational reason, it just suits well with their personal traits.

The most important customer factors are resources and attitudes. If customers have resources such as finance, knowledge and skills, they are more likely to have positive experience in the purchasing and implementation phases, for example, by requesting customisation of the service. Attitudes are also important during the purchasing and implementation phases. The Marketing Director explained:

> Basically, we have two kinds of customers. The ones that know very well what they need and only want to purchase it. They want a fast and simple delivery process and nothing extra.

During the use and maintenance phase, the more skills or resources customers can use to take advantage of services, the more they are likely to have positive experiences with the service. Customers with open attitudes to new solutions are more likely to have positive experience with the service during this phase. In the words of the Marketing Director:

> Customers are continuously developing their digital skills and capabilities and hence they are more likely to have positive experience. That causes challenges for service providers to handle.

During the termination phase, the most important customer factors are attitudes related to the service. Decisions on whether a customer relationship is terminated or use of the service is stopped depend on the extent to which those factors were positive or negative. Customers who stop using the service for negative reasons or because of a negative experience are usually not willing to be engaged, while those who stop using the service but did not have negative experiences are more willing to engage. As the Customer Service Director explained:

We are following terminating customers and asking reasons. If the reasons behind leaving are negative customer experience, that has an effect to customer's willingness to be engaged to this phase of the process.

Summarising customer-based factors, implementation and use of services should be effortless. Solving customers' problems and turning them into positive experiences will help to build CEB. In the termination phase, it must be easy for the customer to stop the service because this enhances the customer's trust in the provider. However, it is also important to provide incentives for customers to extend their contract and that customers have a positive overall experience of the value of the streaming TV services. The main value-creating factors are broadcast quality, comprehensive content, the opportunity to watch on all types of devices, the opportunity to watch anytime and anywhere and the ease of purchasing and implementation. Customer experience is an important factor that affects CEB, especially in the use and maintenance phase.

Firm-based factors

The most important firm-based factors during the impulse phase are related to brand, rewards and incentives, which are especially important for special campaigns, such as those occurring during holidays. As the Customer Relationship Manager explained:

> Traditionally rewards and incentives are commonly used to enhance customer experience. Currently the brand makes customers want to have enhanced customer experience.

The social dimension together with processes and platforms are most important in the purchase and implementation phase. Platforms can be physical or digital, but customers want them to be social. As the Head of Customer Experience explains:

> Most digital services are still bought in traditional high street stores. The number of digitally purchased services is rising, but there still has to be a social dimension.

Alongside the social dimension, processes and platforms, rewards and other incentives are most important in the use and maintenance phase. Experience can be physical or digital. During the termination phase, the most important firm-based factors are reputation, brand, social factors, rewards and incentives that encourage customers to continue rather than terminate the service. Most importantly to firm-based factors, the company personally contacts customers in order to highlight the importance of customers, their own skills regarding the service and value co-creation in the form of identifying appropriate programme packages.

Context-based factors

Technological developments such as new platforms and social media are the most important context-based factors during the impulse and purchasing phases. Competitors' activities such as new services may also affect CEB during the termination phase. CEB particularly arises from value co-creation in the form of involving customers in channel package design. Summarising context-based factors, any content on any device, anytime and anywhere comprises a major influence on CEB. Summarising findings from the ViewStream case, for positive CEB, processes should be seamless and effortless. Firms need to listen to the customer voice and involve customers in co-creating service design.

Case questions

1. Assess the dimensions of customer experience with ViewStream.
2. Explore the ways to strengthen customer experience with ViewStream and discuss possible obstacles.
3. Consider potential contributions which customer experience would make to ViewStream.

Key terms and definitions

Customer experience: a multi-dimensional construct focusing on a customer's cognitive, emotional, behavioural, sensorial and social responses to a firm's offerings during the customer's entire purchase journey.

Servicescape: the physically built surroundings within consumption settings that influence the nature and quality of social interaction

Hedonic consumption experience: those facets of consumer behaviour that are related to the multisensory, fantasy and emotional aspects of one's experience with products.

Brand experience: a subjective, internal consumer responses (sensations, feeling, and cognitions) and behavioural responses evoked by brand-related stimuli that are part of a brand's design and identity, packaging, communications and environments.

References

Allen, Chris T., Susan Fournier and Felicia Miller (2008), "Brands and their meaning makers" in Curtis Haugtvedt, Paul Herr and Frank Kardes (Eds), *Handbook of Consumer Psychology*, 781–822, Taylor & Francis.

Assessment of customer experience concept   285

Arnould, E. J. and L. L. Price (1993), "River magic: extraordinary experience and the extended service encounter". *Journal of Consumer Research*, 20 (1), 24–45.

Arvidsson, A. (2005), "Brands: a critical perspective". *Journal of Consumer Culture*, 5 (2), 235–258.

Barnes, Donald C. and Alexandra Krallman (2019), "Customer delight: a review and Agenda for research". *Journal of Marketing Theory and Practice*, 27 (2), 174–195.

Batra, Rajeev (2019), "Creating brand meaning: a review and research agenda". *Journal of Consumer Psychology*, 29 (3), 535–546.

Baumgartner, H. and R. Pieters (2003), "The structural influence of marketing journals: a citation analysis of the discipline and its subareas over time." *Journal of Marketing*, 67 (2), 123–139.

Berry, Leonard L., Lewis P. Carbone, and Stephan H. Haeckel (2002), "Managing the total customer experience". *MIT Sloan Management Review*, 43 (3), 85–89.

Bitner, Mary Jo (1990), "Evaluating service encounters: the effects of physical surroundings and employee responses". *Journal of Marketing*, 54 (2), 69–82.

Bitner, Mary Jo (1992), "Servicescapes: the impact of physical surroundings on customers and employees". *Journal of Marketing*, 56 (2), 57–71.

Bitner, M. J., A. L. Ostrom and F. N. Morgan (2008), "Service blueprinting: a practical technique for service innovation". *California Management Review*, 50 (3), 66–94.

Brakus, J. Joško, Bernd H. Schmitt and Lia Zarantonello (2009), "Brand experience: what is it? How is it measured? Does it affect loyalty?". *Journal of Marketing*, 73 (3), 52–68.

Carbone, Lewis P. and Stephan H. Haeckel (1994), "Engineering customer experiences". *Marketing Management*, 3 (3), 8–19.

Chabowski, B. R., G. T. M. Hult, T. Kiyak and J. A. Mena (2010), "The structure of JIBS's social network and the relevance of intra-country variation: a typology for future research". *Journal of International Business Studies*, 41 (5), 925–934.

Chabowski, B. R., S. Samiee and G. T. M. Hult (2013), "A bibliometric analysis of the global branding literature and a research agenda." *Journal of International Business Studies*, 44 (6), 622–634.

Chabowski, B., P. Kekec, N. A. Morgan, G. T. M. Hult, T. Walkowiak and B. Runnalls (2018), "An assessment of the exporting literature: using theory and data to identify future research directions." *Journal of International Marketing*, 26 (1), 118–143.

Cova, B. and V. Cova (2012), "On the road to prosumption: marketing discourse and the development of consumer competencies". *Consumption Markets & Culture*, 15 (2), 149–168.

Elliott, R. and K. Wattanasuwan (1998), "Brands as symbolic resources for the construction of identity". *International Journal of Advertising*, 17 (2), 131–144.

Følstad, A. and K. Kvale (2018), "Customer journeys: a systematic literature review". *Journal of Service Theory and Practice*, 28 (2), 196–227.

Fournier, Susan (1998), "Consumers and their brands: developing relationship theory in consumer research". *Journal of Consumer Research*, 24 (4), 343–373.

Fournier, S. and D. G. Mick (1999), "Rediscovering satisfaction". *Journal of Marketing*, 63 (4), 5–23.

Gentile, Chiara, Nicola Spiller and Giuliano Noci (2007), "How to sustain the customer experience: an overview of experience components that co-create value with the customer". *European Management Journal*, 25 (5), 395–410.

Grabarczyk, Paweł and Marek Pokropski (2016), "Perception of affordances and experience of presence in virtual reality". *Avant. The Journal of the Philosophical-Interdisciplinary Vanguard*, 7, 2 .

Grewal, D., M. Levy and V. Kumar (2009), "Customer experience management in retailing: an organizing framework." *Journal of Retailing*, 85 (1), 1–14.

Grundey, D. (2008), "Experiential Marketing vs. Traditional Marketing: creating rational and emotional liaisons with consumers". *The Romanian Economic Journal*, 29 (3), 133–151.

Hirsch, Paul M. and Daniel Z. Levin (1999), "Umbrella advocates versus validity police: a life-cycle model". *Organization Science*, 10 (2), 199–212.

Hirschman, Elizabeth C. and Morris B. Holbrook (1982), "Hedonic consumption: emerging concepts, methods and propositions". *Journal of Marketing*, 46 (3), 92–101.

Hirshman, E. C. and M. B. Holbrook (1982), "The experimental aspects of consumption". *The Journal of Consumer Research*, 9 (2), 132–140.

Holbrook, Morris B. (2000), "The millennial consumer in the texts of our times: experience and entertainment". *Journal of Macromarketing*, 20 (2), 178–192.

Holbrook, Morris B. (2018), "Essay on the origins, development and future of the consumption experience as a concept in marketing and consumer research". *Qualitative Market Research: An International Journal*, 21, 421–444.

Holbrook, Morris B. and Elizabeth C. Hirschman (1982), "The experiential aspects of consumption: consumer fantasies, feelings, and fun". *Journal of Consumer Research*, 9 (2), 132–140.

Homburg, Christian, Danijel Jozić and Christina Kuehnl (2017), "Customer experience management: toward implementing an evolving marketing concept". *Journal of the Academy of Marketing Science*, 45 (3): 377–401.

Jain, Rajnish, Jayesh Aagja and Shilpa Bagdare (2017), "Customer experience–a review and research agenda". *Journal of Service Theory and Practice*, 27 (3), 642–662.

Klaus, P., B. Edvardsson and S. Maklan (2012, May), "Developing a typology of customer experience management practice–from preservers to vanguards". In *12th International Research Conference in Service Management*, La Londe les Maures, France.

Kranzbühler, Anne-Madeleine, Mirella H.P. Kleijnen, Robert E. Morgan and Marije Teerling (2018), "The multilevel nature of customer experience research: an integrative review and research agenda". *International Journal of Management Reviews*, 20 (2), 433–456.

Kunz, W. H. and J. Hogreve (2011), "Toward a deeper understanding of service marketing: the past, the present, and the future." *International Journal of Research in Marketing*, 28 (3), 231–247.

Lanier, C. D. Jr. and Hampton, R. D. (2009), "Experiential marketing: understanding the logic of memorable customer experiences", in Lindgreen, A., Vanhamme, J. and Beverland, M. B. (Eds), *Memorable Customer Experiences: A Research Anthology*, pp. 9–24, Gower Publishing Company, England.

LaSalle, D. and T. A. Britton (2003), *Priceless. Turning Ordinary Products Into Extraordinary Experience*. Boston, MA: Harvard Business School Press.

Lemke, Fred, Moira Clark and Hugh Wilson (2011), "Customer experience quality: an exploration in business and consumer contexts using reper- tory grid technique". *Journal of the Academy of Marketing Science*, 39 (6), 846–69

Lemon, Katherine N., and Peter C. Verhoef (2016), "Understanding customer experience throughout the customer journey". *Journal of Marketing*, 80 (6), 69–96.

Lovelock, C. H. (1983), "Classifying services to gain strategic marketing insights". *Journal of Marketing*, 47 (3), 9–20.

Lynn Shostack, G (1984), "Designing services that deliver". *Harvard Business Review*, 62 (1), 133–139.

McAlexander, James H., John W. Schouten and Harold F. Koenig (2002), "Building brand community". *Journal of Marketing*, 66 (1), 38–54.

McCain, K. W. (1990), "Mapping authors in intellectual space: a technical overview." *Journal of the American Society for Information Science (1986–1998)*, 41 (6), 433.

McCracken, G. D. (2005), *Culture and Consumption II: Markets, Meaning, and Brand Management (Vol. 2)*. Indiana University Press.

Mehrabian, A. and J. Russell (1974), *An Approach to Environmental Psychology*. Cambridge, MA: MIT Press.

Meuter, M. L., A. L. Ostrom, R. I. Roundtree and M. J. Bitner (2000), "Self-service technologies: understanding customer satisfaction with technology-based service encounters". *Journal of Marketing*, 64 (3), 50–64.

Meyer, Christopher and Andre Schwager (2007), "Understanding customer experience." *Harvard Business Review*, 85 (2), 116.

Mick, D. G. and C. Buhl (1992), "A meaning-based model of advertising experiences". *Journal of Consumer Research*, 19 (3), 317–338.

Mittal, Vikas and Wagner A. Kamakura (2001), "Satisfaction, repurchase intent, and repurchase behavior: investigating the moderating effect of customer characteristics". *Journal of Marketing Research*, 38 (1), 131–142.

Muniz, Albert M. and Thomas C. O'guinn (2001), "Brand community". *Journal of Consumer Research*, 27 (4), 412–432.

Novak, T. P., D. L. Hoffman and Y. F. Yung (2000), "Measuring the customer experience in online environments: a structural modeling approach." *Marketing Science*, 19 (1), 22–42.

Oliver, Richard L. (1980), "A cognitive model of the antecedents and consequences of satisfaction decisions". *Journal of Marketing Research*, 17 (4), 460 469.

Oliver, R. L. (1999), "Whence consumer loyalty?" *Journal of Marketing*, 63 (4_suppl1), 33–44.

Oswald, L. R. (2007), "Semiotics and strategic brand management". *Marketing Semiotics*, 10, 1–5.

Parasuraman, Anantharanthan, Valarie A. Zeithaml and Leonard L. Berry (1985), "A conceptual model of service quality and its implications for future research", *Journal of Marketing*, 49 (4), 41–50.

Parasuraman, Ananthanarayanan, Valarie A. Zeithaml and Leonard L. Berry (1988), "Servqual: a multiple-item scale for measuring consumer perc", *Journal of Retailing*, 64 (1), 12.

Parasuraman, A., V. A. Zeithaml and A. Malhotra (2005), "ES-QUAL: a multiple-item scale for assessing electronic service quality." *Journal of Service Research*, 7 (3), 213–233.

Payne, A. F., K. Storbacka and P. Frow (2008), "Managing the co-creation of value". *Journal of the Academy of Marketing Science*, 36 (1), 83–96.

Pine, Joseph B. and James H. Gilmore (1998), "Welcome to the experience economy". *Harvard Business Review*, 76, 97–105.

Pine, Joseph B. and James B. Gilmore (1999), *The Experience Economy*. Boston: Harvard Business School Press.

Prahalad, C. K. and V. Ramaswamy (2004), "Co-creation experiences: the next practice in value creation". *Journal of Interactive Marketing*, 18 (3), 5–14.

Puccinelli, N. M., R. C. Goodstein, D. Grewal, R. Price, P. Raghubir and D. Stewart (2009), "Customer experience management in retailing: understanding the buying process." *Journal of Retailing*, 85 (1), 15–30.

Pullman, Madeleine E. and Michael A. Gross (2004), "Ability of experience design elements to elicit emotions and loyalty behaviors", *Decision Sciences*, 35 (3), 551–578.

Ramos-Rodríguez, A. R. and J. Ruíz-Navarro (2004), "Changes in the intellectual structure of strategic management research: a bibliometric study of the strategic management journal, 1980–2000." *Strategic Management Journal*, 25 (10), 981–1004.

Rawson, Alex, Ewan Duncan and Conor Jones (2013), "The truth about customer experience". *Harvard Business Review*, 91 (9), 90–98.

Richins, Marsha L (1997), "Measuring emotions in the consumption experience". *Journal of Consumer Research*, 24 (2), 127–146.

Rose, S., M. Clark, P. Samouel and N. Hair (2012), "Online customer experience in e-retailing: an empirical model of antecedents and outcomes." *Journal of Retailing*, 88 (2), 308–322.

Samiee, S. and B. R. Chabowski (2012), "Knowledge structure in international marketing: a multi-method bibliometric analysis". *Journal of the Academy of Marketing Science*, 40 (2), 364–386.

Schau, H. J., A. M. Muñiz Jr and E. J. Arnould (2009), "How brand community practices create value". *Journal of Marketing*, 73 (5), 30–51.

Schildt, H. A., S. A. Zahra and A. Sillanpää (2006), "Scholarly communities in entrepreneurship research: a co–citation analysis." *Entrepreneurship Theory and Practice*, 30 (3), 399–415.

Schmitt, B. (1999), "Experiential marketing". *Journal of Marketing Management*, 15 (1–3), 53–67.

Schmitt, Bernd and Lia Zarantonello (2013), "Consumer experience and experiential marketing: a critical review". In *Review of Marketing Research*, 10(6),25–61.

Shaw, Colin and John Ivens (2002), *Building Great Customer Experiences*, 241. London: Palgrave.

Tynan, Caroline and Sally McKechnie (2009), "Experience marketing: a review and reassessment". *Journal of Marketing Management*, 25 (5–6), 501–517.

Vargo, S. L. and R. F. Lush (2004), "Evolving a services dominant logic". *Journal of Marketing*, 68 (1), 1–17.

Vargo, Stephen L. and Robert F. Lusch, (2008), "Service-dominant logic: continuing the evolution". *Journal of the Academy of Marketing Science*, 36 (1), 1–10.

Verhoef, Peter C., Katherine N. Lemon, A. Parasuraman, Anne Roggeveen, Michael Tsiros and Leonard A. Schlesinger (2009), "Customer experience creation: determinants, dynamics and management strategies". *Journal of Retailing*, 85 (1), 31–41.

Zaichkowsky, Judith Lynne (1985), "Measuring the involvement construct". *Journal of Consumer Research*, 12 (3), 341–352.

Zeithaml, Valarie A., Leonard L. Berry and Ananthanarayanan Parasuraman. "The behavioral consequences of service quality". *Journal of Marketing*, 60 (2), 31–34.

Zomerdijk, L. G. and C. A. Voss (2010), "Service design for experience-centric services". *Journal of Service Research*, 13 (1), 67–82.

Zupic, I. and T. Čater (2015), "Bibliometric methods in management and organization." *Organizational Research Methods*, 18 (3), 429–472.

11 Employee occupational identity

Maria J. Jerez-Jerez, T C Melewar and Pantea Foroudi

Introduction

This chapter aims in developing a better comprehension of the concept of employee occupational identity concept, its antecedents and consequences (employee turnover and work engagement); the importance of the stimuli and its influence on building corporate identity, image and reputation in the digital era explained by using salience as a moderator of this relationship.

Background

A considerable amount of research, in domains ranging from employees' turnover (Zopiatis et al., 2020), occupational identity (Hirschi, 2012) and stereotype (Hoyt et al., 2010) to, more recently, employer branding (Rathi et al., 2016) has attempted to comprehend and define how companies, or the individuals behind the brands (Kim and Lee, 2019), can construct deeper, more engaged relationships with employees which could be converted into success. As Gupta (2017) indicates, however, for most marketers, relationships such as these are unlikely to continue definably without a more accurate comprehension of why and when employees reply strongly and favourably to organisations' efforts at relationship-building, entering accordingly into the types of company-employee relations that alter them into keen devotees of the organisation and their products.

In their efforts to maintain success in the workplace, more and more organisations are managing a tactical framework that includes both human resources and marketing (Dabirian, 2020; Pride et al., 2015) so that an institution can appeal to maintain and incentivise those personnel. It seems that only a few organisations such as Marriot hotels, Google, Twitter and Pizza Hut have identified the benefits that a strong organisation-employee relationship can generate, not only in employee retention but also in promoting the organisation to others (Born and Kang, 2015). Therefore, this involves some knowledge of how the employment relationship may impact on a person's evaluation of her or his firm's employer branding and one part of the literature that focuses on this subject is the study of occupational identity in relation to organisational identification.

290 Jerez-Jerez, Melewar and Foroudi

Due to the relevant studies on occupational identities, and based on the evidence demonstrated above, this chapter provides a view of the latest knowledge on occupational identity, its antecedents and its influences on work engagement and turnover. Particularly, this chapter addresses (i) what are the specific antecedents and consequences of the construction of occupational identity; (ii) what is the relationship between occupational identity and its antecedents; (iii) what connects occupational identity, work engagement and turnover.

Several academic judgements depending on classic and contemporary research within social identity (Tajfel and Turner, 2004), dramaturgy (Goffman, 1959) and aesthetic (Warhurst et al., 2000) theories are central to this section to expand on the nature of occupational identity, which proposes the key occupational identity antecedents and consequences of such relationships in the place of work.

The concept of occupational identity has attracted attention from practitioners and researchers (Gabriel, 2000; Hirschhorn and Gilmore, 1989; Kahn et al., 2018) in previous studies, mainly because "work" as a life realm is mostly fundamental to identity construction. Indeed, most individuals spend the majority of their time working, especially when they are adults. As

> adults there is nothing that more preoccupies our lives. From the approximate ages of 21 to 70 we will spend our lives working. We will not sleep as much, spend time with our families as much, eat as much or recreate and rest as much as we work.
>
> (Gini, 1998, p. 707)

As evidence that work pervades every aspect of our lives – it is common to see people eating their lunch in front of the computer, people take their work home to carry on working, social conversations often centre on jobs and people often use their holidays to review their careers. Additionally, since researchers believe that identity is formed from relationships with others, everyday professional interactions are also central to the formation of individual work identities, and, similarly, these work identities will spread into everyday life (Dutton and Ragins, 2007; Leavitt and Sluss, 2015; Mahadevan and Mayer, 2017). To better understand the concept of occupational identity, the key identified theories are dramaturgy, social identity and aesthetic theory.

Dramaturgy theory: Goffman's (1959) model on the demonstration of identity is a figurative appraisal of the method by which people maintain and build a performance within a social setting. Its objective is not to understand how people see themselves, but to understand how people interact face to face; any social exchange can be interpreted using the theory (Conway, 2015; Goffman, 1959; Smutny et al., 2017); Tajfel and Turner's (1979, 2004) theory of social identity describes how an element of an individual's idea of self originates in groups of which that individual is a member (Stryker and Burke, 2000); Theory of aesthetic labour: "aesthetic labour" means the "recruitment, selection, development, and deployment of physical and presentational attributes geared towards

Employee occupational identity   291

looking good and sounding right" (Warhurst and Nickson, 2007, p. 104; Vijlbrief et al., 2020). Based on the above it is relevant to group occupational identity into two different themes, contractedness and value placed on work roles.

The contractedness of occupational identity

The contractedness of occupational identity is the first of these themes to which many academics have paid attention (Ashforth et al., 2020; Ibarra and Barbulescu, 2010). The creating of occupational identity consists of mending, developing, reinforcing, reviewing or preserving identities that already exist. Hence, instead of seeing the construction of identity as a simple process of adopting a work position, work identity is a problematic and interactive process (Gonzalez et al., 2018; Pettit and Crossan, 2020). Studies of occupational identity have concentrated on people's difficulties in forming work identities; for example, during a period of adjustment to occupational changes (Ibarra and Barbulescu, 2010), people may miss the comfort and security of their previous jobs. Although identities may develop out of stigmatised job roles (Ashforth et al., 2020), it is evident that certain jobs are more widely stigmatised while others have a great deal of social capital attached to them.

Identities are constantly at risk of being undermined because of unappealing jobs, or the integrity of occupational identities may be violated (Mannerstrom et al., 2017; Pettit and Crossan, 2020). Sometimes, employees attempt to retain what they believe to be a unique identity in opposition to the identities intended for them in their workplace. These individuals may have difficulty dealing with this situation, as will organisations and managers who face the challenge of trying to keep them under the same corporate umbrella (Radic et al., 2020; Praetorius et al., 2018). For example, on cruise ships where the employees are very multicultural – and where this issue is exaggerated as employees live and work together for up to six months at a time, employees have to adapt to a company standard identity and managers have the challenge of acknowledging the background identity of their employees while moving all of them in the same direction of the company purpose – a kind of cultural homogenisation.

However, Pettit and Crossan (2020) observe that, instead of developing aspects of identity into a proper occupational identity, practitioners are active in adapting their occupational identity to successfully gain a feeling of integrity. In Disney World, for example, employees seem to be happy and offer great customer service. Most of the employees work with feeling and successfully make customers believe that they are in a magical kingdom where their dreams become real (Disneyworld, 2018). Some of these employees may not naturally possess good interpersonal skills, but they have adapted to their role to create an adequate occupational identity. However, occupational identity is not just what one presents to the outside world: it also involves how we feel and how we react to difficult environments. While Disney employees may emit a magic "buzz", they may hate the falseness of their role. Another way of establishing an adequate occupational identity is to copy individuals in the public sphere

292   Jerez-Jerez, Melewar and Foroudi

whom one identifies with on a more private or fundamental level: this is a model advanced by Ibarra (1999; Selenko et al., 2018). For example, young trainees might copy their elders whom they believe to be authentic. They do not try to develop their own identity but imitate others whom they identify as more "real" (InterContinentalHotelsGroup, 2018).

Additionally, Ibarra (1999) states that people are capable of keeping an authentic identity during the course of adaptation and experimentation within the organisation that employs them. However, other academics (Sferrazzo, 2020) have shown that when a job inhibits the ability to create an intelligible sense of self in the workplace, there is the chance that it can be harmful to one's identity. Consequently, some employees who start their new job experience have a sense of not identifying with their work role. These people are caught between their existing identity and an occupational identity, which they regard to be unfamiliar (Corlett et al., 2017; Sferrazzo, 2020). This may happen to waiting employees in some cases: on starting jobs, instead of developing values on work roles, they may realise that it is not the right career for them; this could be another reason for the high turnover.

Value placed on work roles

The second theme centres on the value placed on work roles, a subject to which academics have also paid significant attention. According to Ashforth et al. (2020), occupational identity is "the set of central, distinctive components that are generated from one's history of occupational participation" (p. 417). Hirschi (2012) refers to it as "the clear perception of occupational interests, abilities, goals, and values, and the structure of the meaning that links these self-perceptions to career roles" (p. 4).

The problem arises when people do not have clarity regarding all these concepts, which is something that happens very often. It means that all of these domains (interest, abilities, goals and values) do not match with the job expectation. To cope with this issue, academics have developed several concepts that influence the formation of occupational identity, one being that people have a tendency to appraise themselves and are appraised by others, depending on the task they accomplish (Bauman, 2004; Williams et al., 2019; Mannerstrom et al., 2017). This involves a relationship between their work role and the formation of their occupational identity. Therefore, this can be a motivation for the individual to find the right job. Secondly, job titles influence the abilities of the employees and the way in which they are seen by sociologists (Williams et al., 2019). The individuals involved and others who they interact with of course define these roles and titles. If an individual has been given the chance to choose between increasing their salary or changing their job title, they may choose the second option, not only because of the perception of others but also to facilitate their career progression. For example, instead of being named Room Division Managers, some managers in hotels prefer to be called Assistant General Manager so, even if they have the same salary and responsibilities, it looks like they are not simply in charge of the accommodation sector (InterContinentalHotelGroup, 2018).

Personal identity

Thirdly, personal identity is influenced both by the customers (Fonagy, 2018; Mead, 1934) and by the occupational colleague group (Cooley, 1983). Employees' dignity, respectability and competence are always assessed in the place of work, misunderstood body language from the boss, an ambiguous comment from colleagues or lack of interest from customers, can destabilise the values of an employee with significant consequences. One can summarise this theme as Cameron and Spreitzer (2011) have argued, by saying that the three main stages of analysing occupational identity are the person, the work and the social level. Individual, because it is what an individual believes about their job, the workplace level is the context, and the societal level is the relation between the individual and the external (i.e. the customers) and the internal groups (i.e. work colleagues) (Cameron and Spreitzer, 2011).

Whereas the first theme looks at how identities are formed from external circumstances, the third theme looks at theories of a more active identity formation process. Snow and Anderson (1987) describe work identity as "the range of activities individuals engage in to create, present, and sustain personal identities that are congruent with and supportive of the self-concept" (p. 1348). This implies that individuals react to external influences in developing constructive identities, as well as being active agents in forming publicly validated occupational identities that present features that they believe to be most important to themselves. Occupational identity comprises a sequence of agentic strategies that people utilise to positively generate a sense of self in a given environment. Ibarra (1999) has argued that work identity is formed when individuals respond to divergences or threats to their identities. Waiting employees will need to respond to threats, such as stigma and stereotyping, homogenisation and globalisation, or the desire for social validity.

Nevertheless, individuals are restricted by the inflexible rules and policies imposed on them by the hospitality industry and, therefore, it is important to understand how these are also responsible for shaping identity (Lyubovnikova et al., 2017). Management in the industry in most situations have a tendency to omit the strategic integration of individual identities formed outside of the workplace. In its place, hoteliers prefer to develop a one-standard organism, completely overlooking the agency and creative potential of the individual (Cameron, 2001). To summarise, waiters' occupational identity is not narrowly defined by the work that they do, but rather extends to incorporate less tangible categories, namely, values, agency and the social and professional conditioning of identity.

Evolution of occupational identity

Based on dramaturgy theory, social identity and aesthetic theories, the content analysis of this study has recognised seven antecedents (employer branding, self-concept, work interaction, identity interference, authenticity, inter-groups and stereotype) of occupational identity that impact on the relationship to employee turnover and work engagement, and to explain the importance of the stimuli using salience as a moderator of this relationship. In line with the literature, this study highlighted the significance of sustaining and developing a favourable occupational identity, and stressed the importance of a constructive occupational identity, noting that it affects employees' perceptions of the role and organisation team, and emphasised its main influence in attracting and keeping employees in a competitive marketplace.

There are numerous aspects of the construction of occupational identity that symbolise the perception of waiters towards a workplace. This study reinforces the previous aspects developed from previous study results, commencing with the definition of occupational identity as "the clear perception of occupational interests, abilities, goals, and values, and the structure of the meaning that links these self-perceptions to career roles" (Hirschi, 2012, p. 4). This proposed definition reflects and captures the domain accurately.

Antecedents to occupational identity

The section below shows factors influencing employees' positive occupational identity:

Employer branding – employer branding has become as essential as services or goods in the marketplace. An employer branding symbolises a business's status as an employer (Rao and Patnaik, 2016). Achievements of every organisation mainly vary upon the talent and efficiency of its employees. Attracting and retaining talented people has become for organisations an enormous task in the current climate (Stysko-Kunkowska and Kwinta, 2020). Studies using different approaches continue to explore the association between occupational identity and employer branding, which has been studied from different approaches (Ashcraft, 2007; Highhouse et al., 2007; Wallace et al., 2014). With respect to the functional side of the whole occupational identity, the 'employer branding' as defined by Rao and Patnaik (2016) is an influencing aspect towards work engagement. The outcome is aligned with scholars (Ashcraft, 2007; Highhouse et al., 2007) who stressed that the employer branding in which employees' occupational identities are shaped, has an influence on potential personnel which implements an approach non-favourable/favourable to the company.

Self-concept – the outcomes of this study demonstrates that self-concept as a component of occupational identity is significant as a reflection of a person's feeling of self-worth and multifaceted cognitive structure, with characteristics of the "me" creating self-concept. (Loy, 2017; Sulphey, 2019; Tajfel and Turner, 1979). Career choice is an extension of self-concept, and that employees cultivate themselves and their understanding of work in their occupations (Holland, 1973; Super, 1951).

Employee occupational identity   295

Interaction – Isbell (2008) states that interaction in the workplace is the procedure that an individual applies, grows and establishes the responsibilities, activities and characteristics of exclusive to an occupation. This is important for the employees to obtain skills and crucial knowledge to extend an occupational role with professional and valued directions (Wolf, 2007). This occurs through professional education (Beck, 2009; Creary et al., 2015) and practice in the ambient work (Teskereci and Boz, 2019).

Interference – combining multiple identities can generate occasions for economic mobility, social interaction and the growth of abilities and skills; holding identities can, however, be complex (Settles, 2004). Identity interference can appear if two or more identities are noticed to be in conflict, (Dutton et al., 2010 Van Sell et al., 1981). The conflict of identity interference can be moderated by a management team by creating a sense of belonging and sense of career.

Authenticity – company standards and the management team often influence employee authenticity at work. On the basis of a previous study that has begun to analyse the impact of authenticity in the workplace, it was stated that the greater the employees' spirits of authenticity are, the greater their self-reported job satisfaction, performance and engagement (Van den Bosch and Taris, 2014). The main key is accomplishing a balance that can be true to individuals' selves with outcome success and prosperity within the company.

Stereotype – stereotype has already been discussed as an element that can generate an improvement in an employee's performance when it makes them be notable from those who have not been influenced by the stereotype (Dumas and Dunbar, 2014). Another way in which employees develop performance is when a stereotype threat is intentionally incited, and the stereotyped employees in the current environment are marginal (Hoyt et al., 2010; Kray et al., 2001). In these circumstances, people behave with "stereotype reactance", working harder to establish the opposite (Bargh et al., 1996).

Salience – salience can function as the degree to which clear stimuli are manifested to others in the workplace and structured as the origin of social salience connected to the situation where there is an occurrence of a stimulus (Taylor and Fiske, 2019). Stimuli are extremely important in the creation of occupational identity. Guido's salience dichotic theory (1995a, 1996; Shepherd and Williams, 2018) states that a stimulus is in-salient when it is incongruent in a precise setting, or it is re-salient when it is congruent in a precise situation; as a consequence, re-salience and in-salience are two contrasting features of the same concept.

Consequences of occupational identity

The literature indicates that occupational identity can lead to an outcome. A favourable occupational identity has to be established to lead to a positive result, such as a favourable work engagement and reduced employee turnover.

296 Jerez-Jerez, Melewar and Foroudi

Work engagement – Previous studies (e.g. Salanova et al., 2005) have verified that enhanced work engagement leads to developing work quality in terms of positive reactions, the capability to organise resources, improved self-efficacy and preventing workaholism. Shaufeli and Bakker's (2004) multi-sample analysis specifies that the relationship between employees' loyalty and available job resources is mediated by work engagement. Employee loyalty is known as sharing the same commitment and approach to the quality of work that directs to higher performance (Janta et al., 2011). The findings of this research indicated how a match between occupational identity and work engagement improved employee's perceptions of company belonging and pride. In turn, this pointed to extra progressive assessments of the employee's performance. Those results were consistent with former studies (Li et al., 2019; Simpson, 2009). Generally, work engagement is the external reflection of employee occupational identity; dedication, absorption and passion for work can affect how a business's employee perceives and can assist employees to construct an expectation framework concerning the business's nature of the work.

Turnover – turnover intention is related to poor service and disintegrated organisational success (Gustafson, 2002; Karatepe and Ngeche, 2012). Wang and Yin (2020) have presented that one of the signs of turnover is intent to leave an organisation. From the organisation's evaluation, employee turnover tends to render expenses arising from selection, recruitment and training (Morrell et al., 2004). Furthermore, it is possible that turnover might have an impact on the morale of employees (Morrell et al., 2004) as well as undermining the efficiency and productivity of the organisation (Purwayoga et al., 2019).

On the other side, employee engagement and retention and are linked to each other (Saad et al., 2018). Turnover continues to be an element of attention among management researchers. Empirical studies have established that an increased degree of work engagement leads to a reduction in employee turnover (Maslach et al., 2001; Schaufeli and Bakker, 2004). Additionally, Cole and Bruch (2006) have denoted that the observations of a robust organisational commitment and identification may impact on employees' turnover intent in specific situations, varying on the degree of responsibility in the workplace. Various studies have demonstrated that work engagement is definitively related to the determination to continue to work with one's firm (Soares et al., 2019; González-Gancedo et al., 2019). It is significant for companies to recruit people with assured attachment elements, which they can continue to develop in the workplace. It is imperative for the organisation to prize committed workers through promotion. The companies therefore should originate job programmes so that they uncover purpose in their work performance.

Moreover, this study will be the first research to recognise the construct of occupational identity and its relationship with work engagement and employee turnover; no theoretical validation was founded from earlier investigations. This

Employee occupational identity   297

research presents a wealth of data that stipulates the foundation to build and deliver greater comprehension of these research questions, namely: RQ1 – What factors affect occupational identity? RQ2 – What are the major influences of occupational identity on work engagement and employee turnover? The literature review results in the advance of the research conceptual framework. As a consequence, the framework detailed below is the result of the literature search and is reinforced by this research.

Issues for further discussion

The establishment of an interdisciplinary paradigm based on social sciences for occupational identity is the main presentation of this current chapter; the main achievement will be to build an interdisciplinary understanding of relationships, interpreted into results with operational significance to the research (Palmer and Bejou, 2006). Additional research needs to be undertaken in the following areas: further exploring and developing the effects of having multiple identities in institutions' performance; to analyse the cooperative behaviour of other employees to define whether occupational expectations of collaboration and altruism would succeed over the allegation of social identity theory; to investigate managerial and group-level policies to change the perspective so that stereotyping will be less prevalent in workplace environments; to present case studies of extreme organisations (businesses with a very favourable employer branding reputation and organisations with lower image); to clarify the correct nature of occupational identity in the setting of employer branding image; to measure individuals' salient identities and insights of the prospects offered by the company to accomplish in terms of those identities; to study the magnitude to which interpositions can generate a sense of duty that results in employees responding with greater degrees of commitment (Van der Zee et al., 2004; Walsh and Gordon, 2008).

Conclusion

This chapter concentrates on a comprehension of occupational identity, its antecedents and its effects on employee turnover and work engagement. Consequently, the literature review includes all these concepts and the antecedents that can have an influence on occupational identity within the workplace. The current scales linking to domains as well as items were obtained from various academic journals. On the foundation of the theoretic knowledge gained, the conceptual model was formed from the literature review (Figure 11.1).

The proposed conceptual framework model founded on the outcomes of the literature review has been confirmed, acknowledging seven antecedents of occupational identity that impact on the relationship to employee turnover and work engagement. In order to simplify the meaning of the stimuli, salience is used as a moderator of this relationship. Examples of antecedents that were disclosed are: employer branding, recognised by the scholars (Sullivan, 2004; Wallace et al., 2014); inter-groups and stereotype being part of the same discipline are

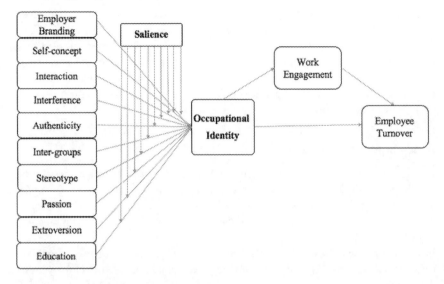

Figure 11.1 Conceptual framework.

distinguished (Van Rossem, 2019; Lyubomirova, 2013); self-concept (Hogg, 2003; Loy, 2017); and attitude in the workplace, such as social interaction, multiple identities, interference or authenticity. The last construct of this model is the consequences of occupational identity: work engagement and employee turnover.

CASE STUDY

Occupational identity – characterisation

Novel Solutions, a British consultancy firm, has been contracted by the American tour operator Suntours, to investigate employee occupational identity among European employers, and which factors can influence its development.

Three specific types of worker were studied by Novel:

- Workers who identified themselves primarily with an organisation, for example those working for the railway or postal service (German and Swedish case studies).
- Workers who identified themselves primarily with a profession, such as civil servants (Belgian, Hungarian, British case studies, core workers in Italian and Austrian case studies).
- Workers not specifically identifying with either an organisation or profession, such as call-centre employees (Austrian and Italian case studies).

The findings of this research have shown that the identity of these workers is not developed by specific education, and they do not consider themselves as part of a particular occupation but identify more with the organisation as opposed to a specific occupation. Likewise, for public organisation workers, the important reference for occupational identity is the institution they belong or belonged to, rather than the occupation itself.

This was particularly prevalent with large national institutions such as the railways. Here, workers were used to having a job for life, were in quite a closed, male-dominated, traditional industry, and therefore were able to identify very closely with a "railwayman" who exhibited close identity with colleagues, the enterprise and technical aspects of the institution. Furthermore, even the living arrangements were provided by the organisation as well. In this way, their entire lives were closely tied to the organisation.

Further, training in-house and a natural social network and good relationships with work colleagues reinforced organisational rather than occupational identity. In addition, occupational identity was also often related to customer service: "I am satisfied when I have succeeded in turning an angry customer into a satisfied one" (Swedish interviewee).

Occupational identity – changes related to restructuring

Privatisation, for example with German railways, resulted in many employers (with the creation of subsidiaries) rather than just a single employer, causing a move away from the traditional roles for railwaymen, towards service tasks being at the core of jobs, rather than just technical, compartmentalised job descriptions: in other words, a quality- rather than an administration-oriented model. No longer would a worker identify with a single organisation, and a single team, but more independent ways of working becomes increasingly the norm, with customer satisfaction at its core.

This is also evident with peripheral employees, such as at a call-centre, where customer satisfaction becomes personal satisfaction, which does not essentially relate to affinity with a business. Another trend, especially with call-centre workers as an example, is the lack of personal contact between sourced and outsourced organisations, with weak interactions between workers, resulting in, for example, low trade union affiliation.

Lastly, occupational identities are influenced by, for example, call-centre spatial location: being in physically separate locations for the central administrative core of a public organisation does not encourage communication. On the other hand, as in the British case, although spatial moving had happened with call-centre reorganisation, employees had been able to remain in contact with their old workplace, and from an administrative point of view, terms and conditions, pay scales and pension schemes remained unchanged, resulting in a more positive, collective atmosphere.

300   *Jerez-Jerez, Melewar and Foroudi*

> After the European senior management of Suntours had analysed the research report with all the information presented above, some queries still remained unanswered by Novel Solutions, specifically:

Case study questions

1. How has the contemporary workplace changed through changes to the organisations? Has this improved workers' sense of social cohesion with their colleagues?
2. What have been the main issues affecting occupational identity related to restructuring of these organisations and how have they changed workers' commitment to these organisations?
3. How has the definition of occupational identity been affected by the above issues and changes

Key terms and definitions

Occupational identity	Occupational identity is a set of perceptual components such as, goals, abilities, occupational interests and meanings connecting the individual's identity to their career perspectives as generated by previous experience.
Employer branding	The employer branding in which the employee's identity is created, constitutes the identity of the organisation as an employer. It is a long-term strategy that comprehends the company's values, behaviour system and policies towards the goals of holding the interest of, encouraging and maintaining the organisation's current and potential staff and correlated stakeholders with regard to an organisation.
Self-concept	Self-concept is what one perceives when one thinks of oneself. It is a person's feeling of self-worth, as well as a rich, multifaceted cognitive structure with characteristics of the "'me" creating self-concept and identities being part of self-concepts.
Interaction	Interaction refers to the procedure of exposure to multiple staff by which an untrained employee is accepted into an occupation and adopts the norms and values of the occupation in his/her self-concept and behaviour. It is also described as an outcome of the formation of self-esteem as an employee with the necessary responsibilities and knowledge.
Interference	Interference is the result of having multiple identities, which happens when the pressure of one identity hinders the performance of another identity and may create a number of physical and negative psychological outcomes.

Employee occupational identity 301

Authenticity   Individuals, in particular, look for an authentic identity – "being yourself" or "becoming yourself" – by the link between one's personal experiences and outer manifestations, and operating and communicating upon this personal experience in the workplace. On some occasions, authenticity can position itself as a rebellion against social order.

Inter-groups   Inter-groups occur when people from one group interrelate, individually or collectively, with another group or its components in relation to their group identification. As an example of inter-group conduct, group identification will bring about bonding, create well-being, companionship and personal security. Individuals often achieve a higher level of self-esteem by comparing their own group positively to others.

Stereotype   Stereotype provides the simplified essence of a group's overall perception of a person or group by downplaying individual differences and exaggerating commonalities as communicated between individuals and groups. Individuals tend to keep their stereotype of specific groups even after there is a significant indication that disconfirms the actual stereotype that they are using.

Salience   Salience theory is still an imprecise term. However, it has been defined as a property of a stimulus that permits it to be noticed and to stand out compared to others in their same context; therefore, and according to the dichotic theory of salience, this stimulus will be in-salient when it is incongruent with a specific environment and re-salient when it is congruent in a specific environment.

Work engagement   Work engagement is an optimistic occupational, emotional and incentivational state of mind that involves an honest disposition to make an effort in one's work and towards managerial achievement. It is typified by vigour, dedication, absorption and passion for work.

Turnover   Employee turnover is the movement, attrition, mobility, exits, migration or succession of employees between jobs, firms and occupations within the labour market, as well as the rotation between the states of unemployment and employment.

References

Ashcraft, K. L. (2007). Appreciating the "work" of discourse: occupational identity and difference as organising mechanisms in the case of commercial airline pilots. _Discourse and Communication_, 1(1), 9–36.

Ashforth, B. E., Schinoff, B. S. and Brickson, S. L. (2020). My company is friendly, "Mine's a Rebel": anthropomorphism and shifting organizational identity from "What" to "Who". _Academy of Management Review_, 45(1), 29–57.

Bargh, J. A., Chen, M. and Burrows, L. (1996). Automaticity of social behaviour: direct effects of trait construct and stereotype activation on action. _Journal of Personality and Social Psychology_, 71(2), 230–244.

302 Jerez-Jerez, Melewar and Foroudi

Bauman, Z. (2004). *Identity: conversations with Benedetto Vecchi*. Cambridge: Polity Press.

Beck, J. W. (2009). *Deconstructing student perceptions of incivility in the nursing education*. California: Louisiana State University.

Born, N. and Kang, S. K. (2015). *What are best practices in the space of employer branding that enable organizations attract and retain the best talent?* http://digitalcommons.ilr.cornell.e du/student/86 (Accessed: 26 January 2017).

Cameron, D. (2001). Chefs and occupational culture in a hotel chain: a grid-group analysis. *Tourism and Hospitality Research*, 3(2), 103–114.

Cameron, K. S. and Spreitzer, G. M. (2011). *The Oxford handbook of positive organizational scholarship*. New York: Oxford University Press.

Cole, M. S. and Bruch, H. (2006). Organizational identity strength, identification, and commitment and their relationships to turnover intention: does organizational hierarchy matter? *Journal of Organizational Behavior*, 27(5), 585–605.

Conway, J. A. (2015). *Relational leadership as meaningful co-action*. PhD thesis, University of Glasgow.

Cooley, C. H. (1983). *Human nature and the social order*. New Brunswick: Transaction Books.

Corlett, S., McInnes, P., Coupland, C. and Sheep, M. (2017). Exploring the registers of identity research. *International Journal of Management Reviews*, 19(3), 261–272.

Creary, S. J., Caza, B. B. and Roberts, L. M. (2015). Out of the box? How managing a subordinate's multiple identities affects the quality of a manager-subordinate relationship. *Academy of Management Review*, 40(4), 538–562.

Dabirian, A. (2020). *Unpacking employer branding in the information technology industry*. Doctoral dissertation, KTH Royal Institute of Technology.

Disneyworld (2018). *Magic kingdom*. https: //www.disneyworld.disney.go.com. (Accessed: 12 April 2018).

Dumas, D. and Dunbar K. N. (2014). Understanding fluency and originality: a latent variable perspective. *Thinking Skills and Creativity*, 14(1), 56–67.

Dutton, J. E. and Ragins, B. R. (2007). *Exploring positive relationships at work: building a theoretical and research foundation*. Mahwah: Lawrence Erlbaum Associates.

Dutton, J. E., Roberts, L. M. and Bednar, J. S. (2010). Pathways for positive identity construction at work: four types of positive identity and the building of social resources. *Academy of Management Review*, 35(1), 265–293.

Fonagy, P. (2018). *Affect regulation, mentalisation and the development of the self*. London: Routledge

Gabriel Y. (2000). *Storytelling in organizations*. Oxford: Oxford University Press.

Gini, A. (1998). Work, identity and self: how we are formed by the work we do. *Journal of Business Ethics*, 17(7), 707–714.

Goffman, E. (1959). *The presentation of self in everyday life*. New York: Anchor Books.

Gonzalez, J. A., Ragins, B. R., Ehrhardt, K. and Singh, R. (2018). Friends and family: the role of relationships in community and workplace attachment. *Journal of Business and Psychology*, 33(1), 89–104.

González-Gancedo, J., Fernández-Martínez, E. and Rodríguez-Borrego, M. A. (2019). Relationships among general health, job satisfaction, work engagement and job features in nurses working in a public hospital: a cross-sectional study. *Journal of Clinical Nursing*, 28(7–8), 1273–1288.

Guido, G. (1996). The theory of in-salience: effects on ad-message processing and memory. *Proceedings of the Third Golden Drum Forum*, 3(1), 36–43.

Gupta, M. (2017). Corporate social responsibility, employee–company identification, and organizational commitment: mediation by employee engagement. *Current Psychology*, 36(1), 101–109.

Gustafson, C. M. (2002). Employee turnover: a study of private clubs in the USA, *International Journal of Contemporary Hospitality Management*, 14(3), 106–113.

Highhouse, S., Thornbury E. and Little I. (2007). Social-identity functions of attraction to organizations. *Organisational Behavior and Human Decision Processes*, 103(1), 134–146.

Hirschhorn, L. and Gilmore, T. (1989). The psychodynamics of a cultural change: learning from a factory. *Human Resource Management*, 28(2), 211–233.

Hirschi, A. (2012). Callings and work engagement: moderated mediation model of work meaningfulness, occupational identity, and occupational self-efficacy. *Journal of Counseling Psychology*, 59(3), 479–855.

Hogg, M. A. (2003). *Social identity*. New York: Guilford Press.

Holland, J. L. (1973). *Making vocational choices: a theory of careers*. Englewood Cliffs, NJ: Prentice-Hall.

Hoyt, C. L., Johnson, S. K., Murphy, S. E. and Skinnell, K. H. (2010). The impact of blatant stereotype activation and group sex-composition on female leaders. *The Leadership Quarterly*, 21(5), 716–732.

Ibarra, H. (1999). Provisional selves: experimenting with image and identity in professional adaptation. *Administrative Science Quarterly*, 44(1), 764–791.

Ibarra, H. and Barbulescu R. (2010). Identity as narrative: prevalence, effectiveness, and consequences of narrative identity work in macro work role transitions. *Academy of Management Review*, 35(1),135–154.

InterContinentalHotelGroup (2018). *True hospitality for everyone*. https://www.ihgplc .com. (Accessed: 15 April 2018).

Isbell, D. S. (2008). Musicians and teachers: the socialisation and occupational identity of pre-service music teachers. *Journal of Research in Music Education*, 56(2), 162–178.

Janta, H., Ladkin, A., Brown, L. and Lugosi, P. (2011). Polish migrant workers in the UK hospitality industry: profiles, work experience and methods for accessing employment. *International Journal of Contemporary Hospitality Management*, 23(6), 803–819.

Kahn, W. A., Barton, M. A., Fisher, C. M., Heaphy, E. D., Reid, E. M. and Rouse, E. D. (2018). The geography of strain: organizational resilience as a function of inter-group relations. *Academy of Management Review*, 43(3), 509–529.

Karatepe, O. M. and Ngeche, R. N. (2012). Does job embeddedness mediate the effect of work engagement? A study of hotel employees in Cameroon. *Journal of Hospitality Marketing and Management*, 21(94), 440–461.

Kim, J. and Lee, K. H. (2019). Influence of integration on interactivity in social media luxury brand communities. *Journal of Business Research*, 99(1), 422–429.

Kray, L. J., Thompson, L. and Galinsky, A. (2001). Battle of the sexes: gender stereotype confirmation and reactance in negotiations. *Journal of Personality and Social Psychology*, 80(6), 942–958.

Leavitt, K. and Sluss, D. M. (2015). Lying for who we are: an identity-based model of workplace dishonesty. *Academy of Management Review*, 40(4), 587–610.

Li, Q., Chi, P., Hall, B. J., Wu, Q. and Du, H. (2019). Job stress and depressive symptoms among migrant workers in Macau: a moderated mediation model of self-esteem and perceived social support. *PsyCh Journal*, 8(3), 307–317.

304 Jerez-Jerez, Melewar and Foroudi

Loy, S. L. (2017). *Social identity theory and self-categorisation theory. The international encyclopedia of media effect.* New York: Wiley.

Lyubomirova N. (2013). Influence of intragroup dynamics and inter-group relations on authenticity in organizational and social contexts: a review of conceptual framework and research evidence. *Psychological Thought*, 2(6), 204–240.

Lyubovnikova, J., Legood, A., Turner, N. and Mamakouka, A. (2017). How authentic leadership influences team performance: the mediating role of team reflexivity. *Journal of Business Ethics*, 141(1), 59–70.

Mahadevan, J. and Mayer, C. H. (2017). *In Muslim minorities, workplace diversity and reflexive HRM.* London: Routledge.

Mannerstrom, R., Lonnqvist, J. E. and Leikas, S. (2017). Links between identity formation and political engagement in young adulthood. *Identity*, 17(4), 253–266.

Maslach, C., Schaufelli, W. B. and Leiter, M. P. (2001). Job burnout. *Annual Review of Psychology*, 52(1), 397–422.

Mead, G. H. (1934). *Mind, self, and society.* Chicago: University of Chicago Press.

Morrell, K., Loan-Clarke, J. and Wilkinson, A. (2004). The role of shocks in employee turnover. *British Journal of Management*, 15(1), 335–349.

Palmer, A. and Bejou, D. (2006). The future of relationship marketing. *Journal of Relationship Marketing*, 4(3/4), 1–10.

Pettit, K. L. and Crossan, M. M. (2020). Strategic renewal: beyond the functional resource role of occupational members. *Strategic Management Journal*, 41(6), 1112–1138.

Praetorius, G., Osterman, C. and Hult, C. (2018). Strategies and measures to improve the work environment of service crew on board Swedish passenger vessel. *International Journal on Marine Navigation and Safety of Sea Transportation*, 12(3), 587–595.

Pride, W., Ferrel, O. C., Lukas, B., Schembri, S. and Niininen, O. (2015). *Marketing principles.* South Melbourne: Cengage Learning Australia.

Purwayoga, P. V. S., Dharmanegara, I. B. A., Ngurah, P. and Yasa, S. (2019). Mediating role of work engagement and emotional exhaustion in the effect of work-family conflict on female workers' turnover intention. *International Journal of Academic Research in Business and Social Sciences*, 9(7), 176–190.

Radic, A., Ariza-Montes, A., Hernández-Perlines, F. and Giorgi, G. (2020). Connected at sea: the influence of the internet and online communication on the well-being and life satisfaction of cruise ship employees. *International Journal of Environmental Research and Public Health*, 17(8), 2840.

Rao, A. J. M. and Patnaik, K. G. K. (2016). Employer branding. The key HR success factor. *Open Journal of Advances in Business and Management*, 1(3), 93–103.

Rathi, S., Chopra, M., Chouduri, G., Sharma, P., Madan, K., Chhabra, M., Rai, R. R., Rubin, A. and Babbie, E. R. (2016). *Empowerment series: research methods for social work.* Boston: Cengage Learning.

Saad, Z. M., Sudin, S. and Shamsuddin, N. (2018). The influence of leadership style, personality attributes and employee communication on employee engagement. *Global Business and Management Research*, 10(3), 743.

Salanova, M., Agut, S. and Peiro, J. M. (2005). Linking organizational resources and work engagement to employee performance and customer loyalty: the mediation of service climate. *Journal of Applied Psychology*, 90(1), 1217–1227.

Schaufeli, W. B. and Bakker, A. B. (2004). Job demands, job resources and their relationship with burnout and engagement: a multisampling study. *Journal of Organizational Behavior*, 25(3), 293–315.

Selenko, E., Berkers, H., Carter, A., Woods, S. A., Otto, K., Urbach, T. and De Witte, H. (2018). On the dynamics of work identity in atypical employment: setting out a research agenda. *European Journal of Work and Organizational Psychology*, 27(3), 324–334.

Settles, I. H. (2004). When multiple identities interfere: the role of identity centrality. *Personality and Social Psychology Bulletin*, 30(1), 487–500.

Sferrazzo, R. (2020). The construction of workers' identity in liminal spaces. *PuntoOrg International Journal*, 5(1), 29–41.

Shepherd, D. A. and Williams, T. A. (2018). Hitting rock bottom after job loss: bouncing back to create a new positive work identity. *Academy of Management Review*, 43(1), 28–49.

Simpson M. R. (2009). Engagement at work: a review of the literature. *International Journal of Nursing Studies*, 46(7), 1012–1024.

Smutny, Z., Janoscik, V. and Cermak, R. (2017). Generation Y and internet privacy: implication for commercialization of social networking services. In: Benson, V., Saridakis, G. and Tuninga, R. (Eds.) *Analyzing the strategic role of social networking in firm growth and productivity* (95–119). Hershey: IGI Global.

Snow, D. and Anderson, L. (1987). Identity work among the homeless: the verbal construction and avowal of personal identities. *American Journal of Sociology*, 92(6), 1336–1371.

Soares, M. E. and Mosquera, P. (2019). Fostering work engagement: the role of the psychological contract. *Journal of Business Research*, 101, 469–476.

Stryker, S. and Burke, P. (2000). The past, present, and future of an identity theory. *Social Psychology Quarterly*, 63(1), 284–297.

Styśko-Kunkowska, M. A. and Kwinta, Z. (2020). Choice between salary and employer brand: the roles of materialism and inclination to develop an identity-motives-based relationship with an employer brand. *Frontiers in Psychology*, 11(1), 555.

Sullivan, J. (2004). *The 8 elements of a successful employment brand*. http://www.ere.net /2004/02/23/the-8-elements-of-a-successful-employment-brand. (Accessed: 1 May 2017).

Sulphey, M. M. (2019). The concept of workplace identity, its evolution, antecedents and development. *International Journal of Environment, Workplace and Employment*, 5(2), 151–168.

Super, D. E. (1951). Vocational adjustment: implementation of self-concept occupations. *Occupations*, 30(1), 88–92.

Tajfel, H. and Turner, J. C. (1979). *An integrative theory of inter-group conflict*. Monterey, CA: Brooks/Cole.

Tajfel, H. and Turner, J. C. (2004). *The social identity theory of inter-group behavior*. New York: Psychology Press.

Taylor, S. E. and Fiske, S. T. (2019). Interview with Shelley E. Taylor. *Annual Review of Psychology*, 70(1), 1–8.

Teskereci, G. and Boz, İ. (2019). "I try to act like a nurse": a phenomenological qualitative study. *Nurse Education in Practice*, 37(1), 39–44.

Van den Bosch, R. and Taris, T. W. (2014). Authenticity at work: development and validation of an individual authenticity measure at work. *Journal of Happiness Studies*, 15(1), 1–18.

Van der Zee, K. I., Atsma, N. and Brodbeck, F. C. (2004). The influence of social identity and personality on outcomes of cultural diversity in teams. *Journal of Cross-Cultural Psychology*, 35(1), 283–303.

306 Jerez-Jerez, Melewar and Foroudi

Van Rossem, A. H. (2019). Generations as social categories: an exploratory cognitive study of generational identity and generational stereotypes in a multigenerational workforce. *Journal of Organizational Behavior*, 40(4), 434–455.

Van Sell, M., Brief, A. P. and Schuler, R. S. (1981). Role conflict and role ambiguity: integration of the literature and directions for future research. *Human Relations*, 34(1), 43–71.

Vijlbrief, A., Saharso, S. and Ghorashi, H. (2020). Transcending the gender binary: gender non-binary young adults in Amsterdam. *Journal of LGBT Youth*,17(1), 89–106.

Wallace, M., Lings, I., Cameron, R. and Sheldon, N. (2014). *Attracting and retaining staff: the role of branding and industry image*. Singapore: Springer Science Business.

Walsh, K. and Gordon, J. (2008). Creating an individual work identity. *Human Resource Management Review*, 18(1), 46–61.

Wang, K. and Yin, J. (2020). Effects of work engagement on professional identity of young teachers in China's Ocean colleges – perspective of psychological capital. *Journal of Coastal Research*, 103(SI), 236–239.

Warhurst, C. and Nickson, D. (2007). Employee experience of aesthetic labour in retail and hospitality. *Work Employment and Society*, 21(1), 103–120.

Warhurst, C., Nickson, D., Witz, A. and Cullen, A. M. (2000). Aesthetic labour in interactive service work: some case study evidence from the "New" glasgow. *Service Industries Journal*, 20(3), 1–18.

Williams, R., Allen-Collinson, J., Middleton, G., Henderson, H., Crust, L. and Evans, A. (2019). "We have the time to listen": community health trainers, identity work and boundaries. *Qualitative Research in Sport, Exercise and Health*, 12(4), 597–611.

Wolf L. K. (2007). *A study of socialization of accelerated BSN Graduates*. Kent, OH: Kent State University College and Graduate School Education.

Zopiatis, A., Savva, C. S. and Lambertides, N. (2020). The non-inclusive nature of "all inclusive" economics: paradoxes and possibilities of the resort complex. *Tourism Management*, 78(1), 104054.

12 Behavioural intentions in the UK fashion industry

The impact of perceived fashion innovativeness on fashion brand image with the moderating role of social media marketing and lovemark

Helnaz Ahmadi Lari, Pantea Foroudi and Saheb Imani

Introduction

Given the importance of fashion innovativeness, this study aims to (i) explore the previous literature to evaluate the concept of fashion innovativeness, (ii) identify the aspects that have a significant influence on fashion innovativeness, (iii) develop and assess a conceptual framework concerning the relationships between fashion innovativeness, its antecedents and its consequences and (iv) investigates the impact of fashion innovativeness among British consumers.

Background to perceived fashion innovativeness on fashion brand image

Innovativeness has been mentioned as an area of interest in business, technology, sustainability and social science. Innovativeness within the context of business is represented in the marketing mantras of today that depict three categories: firm innovativeness, product innovativeness and consumer innovativeness which correspondingly reflect the ability of firms to introduce and develop new products and ideas, product innovation levels and the degree of consumer's intention towards purchasing innovative products more frequently than other consumers (Roehrich, 2004). In addition, innovativeness characterises a significant role in the diffusion of new practices, new thoughts and new products (Gatignon and Robertson, 1985). In a quest for generating behavioural intention towards innovativeness in a fashion marketplace, more and more brands and companies are struggling to stimulate the perceived level of innovativeness in the consumer's mind. Hence, brands such as Apple, Fitbit, Levi's and H&M seem to have consciously evoked the consumer expectation of innovativeness that in turn, leads to further behavioural intention.

What are the factors that influence the perceived fashion innovativeness favourably? Whether a fashion brand image has an effect on word of mouth and purchase intention? A large body of literature, in areas ranging from innovativeness (Rogers and Shoemaker, 1971; Midgley and Dowling, 1978; Hirschman, 1980; Foxall and Haskins, 1986; Goldsmith and Flynn, 1992), fashion innovativeness (Goldsmith and Reinecke Flynn, 1992; Goldsmith et al., 1999; Choo et al., 2014; Cho, 2018), fashion brand image (Roberts, 2005; Cho and Fiore, 2015) and behavioural intentions (Fishbien and Ajzen, 1975; Fishbein and Ajzen, 2010; Baker et al., 2016; Godey et al., 2016; Yusuf et al., 2018) to, more recently, lovemark (Hirschman and Holbrook, 1982; Schade et al., 2016; Brown, 2018) and social media marketing (Ashley and Tuten, 2015; Felix et al., 2017; Oberoi et al., 2017; Liu et al., 2021), has assessed the contribution of innovativeness for fashion marketers, fashion designers and firms through valuable insight about the role of innovativeness in the fashion market and fashion industry. However, for most marketers such relationships are likely to be indefinable without having a precise knowledge about consumer-brand relationships and without understanding of under what circumstances consumers respond more favourably to innovativeness.

This chapter contributes to the growing body of literature about fashion innovativeness by extending the notion of fashion innovativeness for fashion marketers, fashion designers and firms through valuable insight about the role of innovativeness in the fashion market and fashion industry tested in the British fashion market. Moreover, it draws on theory of diffusion of innovation (1983) by drawing a unique conceptual framework based on prior studies to postulate a comprehensible articulation between fashion innovativeness, its antecedents and its behavioural outcomes.

To date, innovativeness within the context of business has focused primarily on three categories: firm innovativeness, product innovativeness and consumer innovativeness which correspondingly reflect the ability of a firm to introduce and develop new products and ideas, product innovation levels and the degree of consumer's intention towards purchasing innovative products more frequent than other consumers (Roehrich, 2004). Central to the current chapter is the notion of innovativeness within a product field category (Danaeels and Kleinsvhmidt, 2001); product innovativeness, or "possession of newness" which is defined as the significant attribute of newness and uniqueness of a product (Roehrich, 2004). More specifically, we demonstrate the construct of fashion innovativeness as innovative fashion appearance-related products; fashion products with characteristics that differentiate those products with a focus on brand image dimensions that result in the amount of consumer effort expended in purchasing (Easey, 2009).

We draw on prior research (Louarn, 1997; Cho and Fiore, 2015; Cho, 2018) to conceptualise fashion innovativeness, its antecedents and its consequences. In doing so, we brought Le Louarn's innovativeness scale (1997) which is built upon prior innovativeness measurement (Midgley and Dowling, 1978; Hirschman, 1980). Le Louarn's scale (1997) exhibits a degree to which a decision-maker makes an innovative decision measured at product consumption level and brings insight to new product buying and consumption by containing three dimensions of innovativeness: attraction to newness, autonomy in innovative decision and the ability to take risks in trying newness that is correlated with innovative behaviour (Roehrich, 2004). In addition, we brought a unique fashion brand image scale (Roberts, 2005; Cho and Fiore, 2015) that incorporates brand awareness and three distinctive dimensions of brand associations (cognitive, sensory and affective), known as lovemark variables (mystery, sensuality and intimacy), proposed by Kevin Roberts (Roberts, 2005). Our study on conducted fashion brand image has incorporated more comprehensive understandings of mystery, the cognitive dimension of brand image; intimacy, the affective dimension and sensuality, the sensory dimension of brand image (Cho and Fiore, 2015). We also proposed the moderating impact of social media marketing and lovemark (brand respect, brand love) to enhance the relationship among the variables and the result.

In the following sections, we draw on current research to elaborate the nature of fashion innovativeness and articulate our proposed conceptual framework, which suggests schemes regarding the antecedents and consequences of fashion innovativeness. We subsequently develop possible approaches to test the hypothesis. We conclude with a discussion of the theoretical significance of fashion innovativeness and its possible implication for future study, contributions and limitations.

Fashion innovativeness

Our main statement, fashion innovativeness, is defined as the degree of interest in adopting a significant attribute of newness and uniqueness of fashion appearance-related products (Goldsmith and Reinecke Flynn, 1992; Goldsmith et al., 1999; Choo et al., 2014; Cho, 2018) which is a key concept to consumer's willingness to embrace new fashion-related products (Goldsmith et al., 1999).

Hirschman and Adcock were first to develop the fashion innovativeness paradigm by applying the Roger's innovativeness theory to textiles (Hirschman and Adcock, 1978). According to Goldsmith (1999), the nature of fashion innovativeness comprises better understanding of fashion innovators' behaviour and the process of fashion diffusion (Goldsmith et al., 1999).

The finding of previous recent research has examined the contribution of fashion innovativeness (FI) on perceived brand image dimensions by extending the Keller's Customer-Based Brand Equity (CBBE) theory to lovemarks (brand love and respect) and lovemarks' resulting effect on brand loyalty (Cho, 2018). This research has exhibited a positive correlation between FI and brand image dimensions which results in brand loyalty. Although results appear consistent with prior research; to achieve a more profound understanding of the end goal of brand loyalty, the notion of purchase intention towards brand image dimensions remains limited.

Support for this assertation comes from a piece of research that points out a more comprehensive inspection of FI associated with purchase tendency (Anić et al., 2017). This literature reviews the role of FI-related shopping reasons that had moderating effects which resulted in unplanned purchasing decisions for consumers. Existing research align FI to the context of fashion retail stores by providing adequate intermediary variables such as visual merchandising, retail setting, interior, atmosphere etc., during the purchase process, whereas scholars suggest that fashion innovativeness intermediary variables focused on opinion leadership have a smaller effect on fashion opinion leaders (Hirschman and Adcock, 1978; Goldsmith et al., 1991).

Moreover, further study has assessed the topic of fashion innovativeness in tandem with variables such as gender, channel choice and need for touch (Cho and Workman, 2011). The findings of this study discuss the decision-making process by indicating an equal relationship between the number of channels chosen to the degree of fashion innovativeness. Subject to other studies conceptualising the fashion innovativeness topic, few have greater emphasis on customer's level of innovativeness, shopping purchase behaviour of fashion innovators and their characteristics (Matthews and Rothenberg, 2017).

Building upon prior innovativeness measurement (Midgley and Dowling, 1978; Hirschman, 1980), Le Louarn's innovativeness scale (1997) exhibits a degree to which a decision-maker makes an innovative decision measured at product consumption level (Roehrich, 2004). Le Louarn's scale (1997) brings insight to new product buying and consumption by containing three dimensions of innovativeness: attraction to newness, autonomy in innovative decision and the ability to take risks in trying newness that is correlated with innovative behaviour (Roehrich, 2004).

Attraction to newness – Attraction towards newness is a tendency in search of novelty (Hirschman, 1980; Louarn, 1997; Roehrich, 2004). This conceptual development is further expanding the novelty seeking theory (Hirschman, 1980) by proposing that the need for stimulation leads individuals to seek out novel information to adopt product consumption in an effort to improve his/her performance (Hirschman, 1980). In this theory, consumers are considered to mediate by their "internal drive or motivating force" to seek out information (Hirschman, 1980). As an example, Apple watch, Fitbit or most of the famous branded smart watch companies are offering at least one valuable/added feature to every release to stimulate the novelty seeking behaviour in their consumers in order to acquire novel data.

Autonomy in innovative decision – Autonomy in innovative decision is defined as a degree to which an individual makes innovative decisions independently, based on individual experience (Midgley and Dowling, 1978; Louarn, 1997; Roehrich, 2004). This conceptualisation is underlying Midgely and Dowling's ideas in terms of defining innovation as a personality trait acquired by a lesser or a greater level within populations (Midgley and Dowling, 1978).

Ability to take risks in trying newness – Ability to take risks in trying newness is characterised as an observation of forming an attitude towards the innovation (Rogers, 1983; Louarn, 1997). This conceptualisation is closely linked to "relative time of adoption" methodology which is measured by the length of time required for members of a system to adopt an innovation (Rogers and Shoemaker, 1971).

Antecedents of fashion innovativeness

Mystery/cognitive association

Mystery, a cognitive association of a brand image mirrors an individual's internal consciousness, set of beliefs and evaluation towards products' attributes, service, performance and symbolic or psychological meaning of a brand (Venkatraman and Price, 1990; Keller, 1993; Roberts, 2005; Alwi and Kitchen, 2014; Cho et al., 2015; Cho and Fiore, 2015; Solomon, 2018). Cognitive associations are frequently used in educational brand image studies relating to product and service-oriented attributes (Alwi and Kitchen, 2014). Cognitive associations are empowered by direct and indirect interactions with the brand that result in functional benefit, symbolic benefit and non-product-related features (Cho and Fiore, 2015). Roberts relates cognitive association to the notion of combining past, present and future interaction within the brand including stories, dreams, icon and inspiration (Roberts, 2005).

As an example, great brands are inherently framed by stories stated by the firm or made by the consumers and visualised by the global icon (e.g. famous Japanese cat known as Hello Kitty, famous double Cs stands for Chanel, Nike's big swoosh) (Cho and Fiore, 2015). Moreover, the mystery/cognitive dimension accounts for dreamy and aspiration brands; for instance, Visionaire publishing is a wonderful example of fashion-related media that has incorporated creativity to the extent of reinventing a different theme for each issue (e.g. Louis Vuitton satchels, Tiffany & Co Visionaire love).

Sensuality/sensory association

Sensuality or sensory associations contribute in generating a scent for an identity of a brand or product by arousing the individual's five senses (including sound, sight, smell, touch and taste) (Roberts, 2005; Hultén, 2018). According to a majority of prior research studies; sensory associations are a set of experiential benefits reflected by consumer's direct interaction with product attributes, retail environment attributes as well as advertisements which consequently lead to creation of consumer value (Roberts, 2005; Krishna and Arbor, 2010; Hultén, 2018).

In the context of sensuality, experience is defined as indicators that consumers can relate to sensory elements of the product or the brand during consumption of that particular product or brand, using one or multiple of their senses (Krishna and Arbor, 2010). For instance, the famous and iconic Tiffany blue is now so solid and recognisable that any other product with the same colour tone is automatically allied with Tiffany blue. Another great example of sensory signature in fashion commodity is Christian Louboutin's red lacquer soles that have become a signature to this brand which evokes strong emotions towards the brand. As proposed by Roberts (2005), followed by scholars (Cho and Fiore, 2015), it has been proven that sensory drivers influence emotional enjoyment in the retail environment. Sensory elements can also be reliant on intangible retail traits such as the pleasant music, smell or even a vivid colour and unique appearance in the consumer's mind. According to Solomon, our sensory memory consists of our five senses working together to alert us; these sensations activate when we walk past a certain retail store or when we see a product and eventually, the perceived level of sensory association from that certain brand or retail store remains in the consumer's sensory memory (Solomon, 2018).

Additionally, sensory associations will persist in new demands on brand image conceptualisation since the growing impact of media and digital transformation increases the possibility of conveying the message and marketing a product or a brand (Krishna and Arbor, 2010). Similarly, a different perspective is derived from the theory of motivation (through the haptic system) that comparts sensory dimension based on consumer's perceptual preferences into hedonic and utilitarian, when shopping for fashion products (Wrokman, 2010).

To further clarify, for instance, ARIT, known as Augmented Reality Interactive Technologies, is recognisable as an immersive feature for consumers that considerably improves user's experience with the product or environment by transforming the digital transformation into real world experience (Huang and Liao, 2015). A recent example of using such a feature in the fashion industry is a Gap dressing room application where shoppers have the ability to try on garments in an augmented reality dressing room without having to step into a physical store.

Intimacy/affective association

Intimacy or affective associations, by definition, entitled to subjective feelings that conquer emotional goals towards a brand (Venkatraman and Price, 1990; Keller, 1993, 2001; Alwi and Kitchen, 2014; Cho and Fiore, 2015). Affective association captures consumer responses resulting from brand experience through an individual's direct and indirect interaction with the brand (Cho and Fiore, 2015).

A rich number of marketing literature examples have applied the triangular theory of love (Sternberg, 1986) to the "intimacy" by breaking down love in terms of three components; intimacy, passion and commitment by further defining intimacy as closeness, connectedness and bondedness in loving relationships (Sternberg, 1986; Shimp and Madden, 1987; Fournier, 1998). Although the intimacy theory of triangular love was originally implied over the course of relationship, empirical studies in consumer research have further transmitted the core element to brand love by relating intimacy to consumer-object emotional exchange (Shimp and Madden, 1987; Fournier, 1998). Coherently, Roberts conceptualised model supports a broad understanding of the originated triangular love theory and Keller's affective association together that formulated his

Behavioural intentions in UK fashion 313

intimacy dimension based on the level of love and respect. Lovemark theory posits intimacy as an affective and connective feeling perceived by consumers towards product-related and non-product-related attributes (Roberts, 2005). According to Roberts, intimacy captures three different subcomponents of empathy, commitment and passion that emerge from a brand's responding to its consumer's preferences, consumer's long-term commitment to a brand and gaining enjoyment from interacting with a brand (Roberts, 2005). Roberts further described intimacy association as a long-run customer-brand relationship that has a continuous effect on lovemark when compared to mystery and sensuality. As an example, Jordan as a part of the Nike brand is a great testament that has created a bonding with their consumers by creating a name relationship to affect their client's emotion. In support, a research study parallel to Roberts' theory has investigated a deeper understanding of the intimacy dimension relevant to fashion-related brands by confirming that intimacy is empowered by value creation (Cho and Fiore, 2015). For instance, brands use empathy by creating customer personas to reach their target audiences and to personalise their offering and services (e.g. birthday reminder, customisation).

Brand awareness

Brand awareness is the potential buyer's ability to recognise or recall a particular product category (Aaker, 1991; Cho and Fiore, 2015; Foroudi et al., 2018; Foroudi, 2019) which significantly empowers his/her consciousness and decision-making associated with a certain brand, product or services. Brand awareness affects the brand's presence in a consumer's mind set by conceptualising of brand recognition and brand recall that holds the ability of the consumer's mind to either identify the brand among various brands or provoke a brand name from memory (Keller, 1993; Foroudi et al., 2018; Foroudi, 2019). Furthermore, brand awareness has a vital effect on a consumer's decision-making by affecting the consumer's consideration set to classify between the brands that enter the consumer's mindset and the brands that are selected from the consumer's mindset (Macdonald and Sharp, 2000). Hence, brand awareness accentuates the brand associations in the consumer's mindset which results in the brand image building (Keller, 1993).

Consequences of fashion innovativeness

Purchase intention

In general terms, purchase intention defines the degree of anticipated consumer response behaviour that is transmitted to the level of consumer's future behaviour or likelihood towards buying behaviour (Fishbien and Ajzen, 1975). According to Fishbien and Ajzen, intention refers to a "person's location on subjective probability dimension involving a relation between himself and some action" (Fishbien and Ajzen, 1975). From a theory of planned behaviour perspective, purchase intention is determined by the relative contribution of attitude, perceived

314 H. A. Lari, P. Foroudi and S. Imani

norms and perceived behavioural control to further predict human social behaviour (Ajzen, 1991; Fishbein and Ajzen, 2010). Furthermore, Zeithaml pointed out that consumer purchase intention is forming under the basis of outstanding transaction, equivalently consumer purchase decision may alter by the effect of price, quality perception and value perception (Zeithaml, 1988; Zeithaml et al., 1996).

Word of mouth intention

Word of mouth is an interactive passing of information between a receiver and communicator (Arndt, 1967) about an evaluation of a product brand or services that is not commercially motivated (Lim and Chung, 2011; Baker et al., 2016; Godey et al., 2016; Yusuf et al., 2018). Word of mouth plays a vital role in transmitting information (Lim and Chung, 2011), forming consumer's behavioural intention (Baker et al., 2016), forming expectations (Krishnamurthy and Kumar, 2018) and perception (Buttle, 1998). Word of mouth as an actual or former user experience, accounts for a reliable and trustworthy informational cue (Lim and Chung, 2011; Yusuf et al., 2018) that has an impact on both negative and positive evaluations for consumers to rely on (Lim and Chung, 2011). Likewise, word of mouth is an effective marketing approach and a powerful marketing tool that can either be used by consumers or marketers, respectively known as organic WOM and fertilised WOM, for strategic purposes (Arndt, 1967).

Conceptual framework

This framework articulates the constructs in terms of the relationship between the variables (Figure 12.1). As it is shown, the first focus is on the link between perceived fashion innovativeness and fashion brand image. We suggest that in the fashion marketplace, as in other contexts, the consumer's evaluation of perceived level of innovativeness are determined based on a set of attributes associated with the brand. More importantly, we propose that consumers are likely to be interested in at least one of a fashion brand image associations. We also suggest that the link between fashion innovativeness and fashion brand image can be enhanced with the moderating role of social media marketing which impacts the cause-effect relationship between components. The second relationship focuses on the link between fashion brand image attributes and the constructs that build up the behavioural intentions. Although this link is likely to be enhanced by the moderating role of lovemark variables.

Fashion innovativeness and cognitive/mystery associations

Cognitive attributes are formed by the interaction between the learners and their environment and measure the individual's opinion and evaluation (Solomon, 2018). As previously mentioned, cognitive associations mainly capture an individual's memory according to a brand; therefore, how to create

Behavioural intentions in UK fashion 315

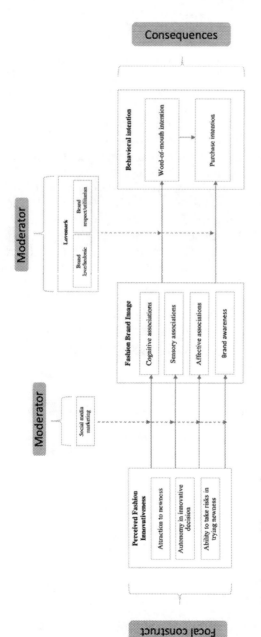

Figure 12.1 Conceptual framework.

the cognitive associations through fashion innovative products depends on consumers' learning processes (Cho et al., 2015). The ties between fashion innovativeness and cognitive attributes indicate the firm ability to develop a fashion-related product which is stored in everybody's memory. From a brand image perspective, Solomon relates cognitive associations to brand experiences that our brain encodes, stores and retrieves (Solomon, 2018). These saved cognitive attributes emphasize on creating inference from outcomes and they could be driven from several sources that consumers encode information from (Solomon, 2018). According to Venkatraman (1990), cognitive innovation is conceptualised as the desire to participate in new experiences that stimulate the mind. Furthermore, Pearson distinguished cognitive innovativeness into internal and external dimensions where internal cognitive innovation accounts for a tendency to like uncommon cognitive process that stimulates rational thinking whereas external cognitive innovativeness is a tendency to explore pragmatic facts and how things function (Pearson, 1970).

Advanced by prior scholars, fashion innovators with a high level of FI are correspondingly having a higher desire for searching information about the product, finding out how a product works and learning how to use it (Venkatraman and Price, 1990; Cho, 2018). Hence, consumers with the higher cognitive innovativeness will result in a higher tendency to purchase a product (Venkatraman and Price, 1990). Following the above argument, I hypothesised that consumers with higher innovativeness will have an impact on the perceived level of cognitive associations (mystery dimension) of brand image. Therefore, the first hypothesis of this research forms as follows:

H1. Perceived level of fashion innovativeness will have an impact on the cognitive/ mystery associations of fashion brand image.

Fashion innovativeness and sensory/sensuality associations

From a brand image perspective, sensory associations store a consumer's emotional responses gathered through any or all of the senses (Cho et al., 2015). In line with earlier discussion, research findings have suggested that sensory elements comprise the emotional and arousal desire towards a product-related attribute (Cho et al., 2015). By expanding the diffusion of innovation concept, sensory innovators and sensation seekers, are less likely to deliberate on the information; instead they tend to enjoy activities based on pleasurable principles (Venkatraman and Price, 1990). According to research (Park et al., 2010), customers who tend to have a higher sensory innovativeness are more likely to have a consciousness in their fashion shopping style and behaviour. Additionally, scholars (Venkatraman and Price, 1990; Cho et al., 2015; Cho, 2018), have revealed the relationship between sensory attributes and innovativeness. Sensory innovativeness tends towards engaging in and enjoying new experiences that arouse the senses internally and focuses on developments to improve the "touchy

Behavioural intentions in UK fashion   317

feely" characteristics of end products such as adventurous activities associated with the brand (Venkatraman and Price, 1990).

Furthermore, fashion consumers are considered to be multisensory when evaluating a fashion-related product. Therefore, sensory elements associated with brand image such as colour, material, retail environment and visual sensation would certainly affect the product performance judgement and further evaluation (Cho et al., 2015). Aligned with the importance of sensory attributes associated with brand image and by assuming innovativeness to be a personality trait that has an impact on consumer's behavioural decision, we expect the equivalent relationship between the perceived level of innovativeness and sensory associations of brand image. Thus, the second hypothesis forms as follows:

H2. Perceived level of fashion innovativeness will have an impact on the sensory/ sensuality associations of fashion brand image.

Fashion innovativeness and affective/ intimacy associations

Affective associations enhance consumers' propensity to obtain feeling about a product (Cho et al., 2015). From Robert's (2005) perspective; affective attribute depicts consumers with deep emotional connection and attachment to a brand. To explain under which conditions innovativeness can relate to affective associations, a research study (Gatignon and Robertson, 1985) has suggested that the speed of innovation diffusion will result higher among those consumers who already have related knowledge or experience of a product; therefore, we can assume that innovativeness would possibly have a consequent effect on affective associations. As a result, the knowledge of how to create affective associations through fashion innovative products is driven from a firm's ability to understand a consumer's opinion and preference. A firm's innovativeness creates pleasure and emotional attachment among consumers and consequently, consumers feel good about the product which further reinforces their hedonic value (Kunz et al., 2011). Because emotional connection with a brand is corelated with adaptation of the new product, we assume there is a relationship between fashion innovativeness and the affective dimension based on the above argument. Hence the third hypothesis of this study is as follows:

H3. Perceived level of fashion innovativeness will have an impact on the affective/ intimacy associations of fashion brand image.

Fashion innovativeness and brand awareness

Brand awareness as the fourth factor that contributes to the dimensions of fashion brand image, is defined as the ability of individuals to identify, recognise or recall a brand in a particular category (Aaker, 1991; Cho and Fiore, 2015; Foroudi et al., 2018; Foroudi, 2019). The enhancement of fashion innovativeness towards brand awareness has been discuses in the literature (Cho, 2018), confirming that consumers with

318   H. A. Lari, P. Foroudi and S. Imani

higher level of fashion innovativeness may cause a long-term brand success because they increase brand awareness. Furthermore, because of innovativeness, brands are more capable to fulfil their consumer's need which in turn leads to the likelihood that a brand or a product name comes up in a consumer's mind (Pappu and Quester, 2016). Keller (1993) claims that a minimum perceived level of brand awareness is adequate for product choice; therefore, we can eventually assume that adopting an innovative product can have a correlation with brand awareness. Accordingly, perceived level of fashion innovativeness will possibly have an impact on brand awareness and shape the fourth hypothesis of the study as provided below:

H4. Perceived level of fashion innovativeness will have an impact on the brand awareness.

Fashion brand image and purchase intention

Scholars Keller and Aaker suggest that behavioural intention can shape through strong brand association (Aaker and Keller, 1990). Therefore, it can be inferred that perceived level of brand image associations reflect a consumer`s behavioural formation. According to scholars (Hwang et al., 2019), a resultant behavioural intention can be formed over an individual`s belief, knowledge and information about that certain product; for this reason, brand image associations (cognitive, affective, sensory and brand awareness) partially account for product-related or non-product-related attributes that are holding a consumer's emotional experience, memories and commitment about the product that, in turn, these beliefs and information that the consumer has held in mind determines both the attitude towards the brand and further behavioural intention (Cho and Fiore, 2015).

Besides, brand awareness is regarded as a heuristic that simplifies decision-making (Macdonald and Sharp, 2000; Pappu and Quester, 2016) and further purchase intention (Keller, 1993). It has been shown that a higher level of brand awareness can possibly enhance the consumer's tendency to buy (Foroudi, 2019). Thus, brand awareness can further establish a former consideration in a consumer's mindset to purchase the products that they are already familiar with (Macdonald and Sharp, 2000; Foroudi, 2019). As a result, the fifth hypothesis of this study forms as below:

H5. Attributes towards fashion brand image which depend upon cognitive associations, affective associations, sensory associations and brand awareness will have an impact on purchase intention.

Fashion brand image and word of mouth

The studies on the relationship between brand image and word of mouth intention have been widely investigated (Krishnamurthy and Kumar, 2018). It has been proven that consumers develop their perspective of the brand image through electronic word of mouth (Krishnamurthy and Kumar, 2018). Further studies suggest the relationship among brand equity constructs (comprising brand image, brand awareness and

Behavioural intentions in UK fashion 319

brand associations) and electronic word of mouth (Pitta et al., 2016; Vahdati and Mousavi Nejad, 2016). Besides, word of mouth is considered to have a critical role in a consumer's preferences which implies that a consumer's stimulation to collect information about the brand is shaped in terms of their association with the brand (Pitta et al., 2016; Vahdati and Mousavi; Nejad, 2016). From the above arguments, the formation of fashion brand image will have an impact on word of mouth. Therefore, the sixth hypothesis of this study forms as:

H6. Attributes towards fashion brand image which depend upon cognitive associations, affective associations, sensory associations and brand awareness will have an impact on word of mouth.

Fashion brand image, lovemark and purchase intention

As previously mentioned, hedonic and utilitarian responses are the outcomes of consumer's evaluation from all the associations towards a given object, that form an attitude of the decision-maker (Schade et al., 2016). The impacts of the hedonic and utilitarian attitude of an individual is frequently a determinant factor towards purchase intention and willingness to pay and empirical evidence has long revealed the consequent effect of hedonic and utilitarian attitude towards purchase intention (Hirschman and Holbrook, 1982; Schade et al., 2016; Han et al., 2018). Consequently, consumer's purchase intention for hedonic and utilitarian reasons are derived from associations that are either cognitively or emotionally held in the consumer's mind about a product or a brand.

To better support the relationship between brand association and purchase intention with the moderating effect of hedonic and utilitarian attitude, an earlier example of Gap's virtual dressing room exemplifies how brands can harness their knowledge to tweak their messages in order to remark their brand as a fashion destination through cognitive associations, that in turn lead to transformative value in the consumer's mind. There exists a considerable body of literature on the subsequent effect of cognitive associations on attitude towards brand claiming that attitude can form by cognitive decisions by emphasising the customer's personal opinions and evaluations (Kim and Ko, 2012; Alwi and Kitchen, 2014). To intertwine the sensory association and attitude towards a global footwear brand, Melissa uses a scent feature to manufacture all their products with a signature bubble gum scent that influences the consumer's attitude because of this unique feature. To further support my hypothesis, scholars have reviled the impact of sensory associations on attitude (Haase and Wiedmann, 2018; Solomon, 2018). Lastly, literature (Kim and Ko, 2012; Alwi and Kitchen, 2014) has been developed on the hypothesis that attitude can form by affective associations. For instance, the famous brand Toms has created a slogan "one for one" meaning with every purchase you donate, a pair of shoes goes to someone in need. Coherently, the brand has created a bond with their consumers by evoking their client's emotion that in turn, leads to customer's emotional reaction and response. Based on the above explanations and because brand image associations correlate with attitude towards brand to develop further purchase intention, we assume the relationship between

320   H. A. Lari, P. Foroudi and S. Imani

fashion brand image associations, lovemark and purchase intention from the above argument. Therefore, the following hypothesis forms as:

> H7. Lovemark (which depends upon brand-love/ hedonic attributes and brand respect/utilitarian attributes) will have an impact on the relationships among fashion brand image (which depends upon cognitive associations, affective associations, sensory associations and brand awareness) and purchase intention.

Fashion brand image, lovemark and word of mouth

Following earlier discussion, hedonic/brand love and utilitarian/brand respect provide values for consumers through brand associations (Cho and Fiore, 2015; Hwang et al., 2019). While products presented by hedonic attributes focus on enhancing an emotional experience, utilitarian attributes transmit the functionality values. As a result, if customers are highly engaged with a brand or a product, they tend to show it by spreading it by word of mouth. Therefore, the stronger the impact of hedonic and utilitarian consumption, the stronger the consequent result on behavioural intention and further word of mouth intention. Empirical evidence has revealed the positive impact of hedonic and utilitarian values on word of mouth intention (Kudeshia et al., 2016).

In the context of fashion innovativeness, this relationship has practical implications for retailers and product developers in terms of emphasising apparel functionalities because when consumers perceive the innovativeness to be useful, it would directly influence their attitude as well as their behavioural intention. Among studies conducted on fashion innovativeness, plenty have pointed out innovativeness as a significant driver for decision-making (Cho and Workman, 2011; Anić et al., 2017; Matthews and Rothenberg, 2017).

Besides, Keller, (1993) has pointed out that brand image attributes can form through a direct or indirect depiction or source of information like word of mouth. From the above argument, hedonic and utilitarian attributes are expected to accelerate the relationship between perceived fashion brand image and word of mouth intention. According to the stated discussion and aligned with the body of previous research, the following hypothesis is proposed:

> H8. Lovemark (which depends upon brand love/hedonic attributes and brand respect/utilitarian attributes) will have an impact on the relationships among fashion brand image (which depends upon cognitive associations, affective associations, sensory associations and brand awareness) and word of mouth

Purchase intention and word of mouth

Based on empirical evidence, purchase intention is considered to be an outcome of the consumer's WOM (Arndt, 1967; Baker et al., 2016). The strength of word of mouth can alter the relative effect of purchase intentions in the consumer's mindset to flow from buyers to nonbuyers (Arndt, 1967) because consumers would prefer

Behavioural intentions in UK fashion 321

to reduce the perceived risk by acquiring reliable information. As a result, a positive word of mouth and a negative word of mouth is associated with the receiver's intention to make a purchase or other positive interactions, whereas negative WOM reduces the intentions and inhibits other brand behaviours (Baker et al., 2016).

In the context of fashion innovativeness, word of mouth can play a vital role in reflecting the consumer's mindset and making consumers more knowledgeable about their consumption; ultimately, related instances such as behavioural manifestation happen which triggers the consumer's purchase intention. Accordingly, a number of studies have investigated the positive relationship between eWOM and purchase intention (Erkan and Evans, 2016; Busalim, 2018), by inspecting whether consumers who are engaged in eWOM are more likely to develop a higher purchase intention. Thus, according to the discussion highlighting the significance impact of word of mouth on purchase intention, it is hypothesised that:

H9. Word of mouth will impact purchase intention.

Perceived fashion innovativeness, social media marketing and fashion brand image

Social media marketing activities are enhancing a brand's success by exchanging communication between brands and customers (Godey et al., 2016). Similarly, scholars disclose that social media marketing enhances brand equity creation (Kim and Ko, 2012; Godey et al., 2016). Based on a finding (Hollebeek et al., 2014), achieving strategic social media objectives are dependent on tactics and activities raising consumer affection and activation as opposed to cognitive processing.

For instance, providing consumers with testimonials through social media is a smart way for marketers to forward their messages and reach out to their potential buyers through related cognitive and affective brand associations. Moreover, sensory association through social media marketing can be used to trigger consumer perceptions of intellectual views about the product (e.g. quality, design). Furthermore, scholars have studied the link between social media marketing efforts and brand awareness by confirming that social media marketing reinforces brand awareness (Kim and Ko, 2012). Taken from above, fashion innovativeness can benefit the social media marketing by bringing the external and internal associations together. Accordingly, we declare that:

H. Social media marketing will impact the relationships among the perceived level of fashion innovativeness and (H10) cognitive/mystery associations, (H11) sensory/sensuality associations, (H12) affective/intimacy associations and (H13) brand awareness.

Research model and methods

The positivism (deductive) approach was followed to respond to the research questions and test the hypothesis in this research study. In a deductive approach, the study processes from the general to the certain conclusion by comprising

322   H. A. Lari, P. Foroudi and S. Imani

hypotheses to verify assumptions (Saunders et al., 2016). Accordingly, this research attempts to investigate perceived fashion innovativeness in the North London consumers with four objectives: (i) to explore prior literature to evaluate the importance of fashion innovativeness and to postulate a wider knowledge about the concept; (ii) to attempt to identify the essential dimensions that shape fashion innovativeness and are most likely to have influence on creation of fashion innovativeness; (iii) to attempt to develop and assess a conceptual model concerning the relationships between fashion innovativeness and its elements, fashion brand image and its behavioural intentions; and (iv) to evaluate the influence of fashion innovativeness on British consumers to determine their opinions about the concept. Consequently, two research questions have been formulated to achieve the research objectives: what are the factors that influence the perceived fashion innovativeness favourably? and whether fashion brand image has an effect on word-of-mouth and purchase intention?

According to fashion innovativeness literature, plenty have pointed out that innovativeness is a significant driver for decision-making (Anić et al., 2017; Cho and Workman, 2011; Matthews and Rothenberg, 2017) while not many studies have been directed to inspect and evaluate the fashion innovativeness on behavioural intentions. This research, as one of the first attempts, pursues to exhibit that perceived fashion innovativeness is built by attraction to newness, autonomy in innovative decision-making and ability to take risks in trying newness. Besides this, mystery/ cognitive association, sensuality/sensory, intimacy/affective association and brand awareness work together to generate fashion brand image. Further, this research attempts to prove that the fashion brand image, with moderating role of hedonic/ brand love and utilitarian/brand respect, is the outstanding cause of word of mouth intention and purchase intention which lead to fashion innovativeness.

Instrumental development and assessment

A Mono-method quantitative research design was selected as the preferred methodological choice for conducting the current study in order to understand and measure the extent of fashion innovativeness within British consumers. Mono-method quantitative design uses only one data collection method (i.e. questionnaire) and equivalent quantitative analytical procedure (Saunders et al., 2016). The quantitative research aim of researchers was to inspect and analyse the relationship between the variables which are measured statistically by using several statistical techniques (Saunders et al., 2016). Consequently, the designated quantitative method is most representable for this research. The research constructs were measured with a 7-point Likert scale ranging from 1 "strongly disagree" to 7 "strongly agree". Based on previous studies, Table 12.1 displays the scale of items for selected constructs after revising prior research.

Data collection and analysis methods

The relevant research method, deductive research approach, generally allied with survey method (Easterby-Smith et al., 2018) and is considered as one

Behavioural intentions in UK fashion 323

Table 12.1 Initial pool of items

Constructs	Items	Adapted from
Fashion inno-vativeness	In general, I am among the last in my circle of friends to buy a new fashion item when it appears. If I heard that a new fashion style was available in the store, I would be interested enough to buy it. Compared to my friends, I own few/new fashion items. In general, I am the last in my circle of friends to know the names of the latest fashions and styles. I know the names of new fashion designers before other people. I will buy a new fashion item, even if I have not heard of it yet.	(Cho, 2018)
Attraction to newness	I am the kind of person who tries every new product at least once. When I hear about a new product, I try to know more about it at the first occasion.	(Roehrich, 2004)
Autonomy in innovative decision	Before trying a new product, I try to learn what friends who possess this product think about it. I seek out the opinion of those who have tried new products or brands before I try them.	(Roehrich, 2004)
Ability to take risks in trying newness	I'd rather choose a brand that I usually buy rather than try something I am not confident in. I never buy something I don't know anything about with the risk of making a mistake.	(Roehrich, 2004)
Cognitive associations	This brand awakens good memories for me. This brand captures a sense of my life. This brand comes to mind immediately when I want to purchase a fashion product. This brand captures the times. This brand is a part of my life. This brand adds to the experience of my life.	(Cho et al., 2015)
Sensory associations	The design of this brand's ads is really well done. The well-ordered store environment appeals to me. The website design for this brand is really well done. The packaging of this brand is as pleasing as the product. This brand has incredible displays. The store environment of this brand appeals to me. This brand has a beautiful colour scheme.	(Cho et al., 2015)
Affective associations	I feel happy when I wear this brand. I have fun with this brand. I feel satisfied with this brand. I really enjoy wearing this brand. I have solid support for this brand. I like looking at the products of this brand. I can rely on this brand. I feel connected to this brand. I would stay with this brand.	(Cho et al., 2015)

(*Continued*)

324   H. A. Lari, P. Foroudi and S. Imani

Table 12.1 (Continued)

Constructs	Items	Adapted from
Brand awareness	I am interested in X. Compared to other people I know more about X. When I think of fashion items, X is one of the brands that come to mind. X is a brand of fashion I am very familiar with. I know what X looks like. I can quickly recognise the symbol or logo of X. Some characteristics of X come to my mind quickly.	(Foroudi et al., 2018)
Brand love / hedonic	Using smartwatch gives fun to me. Using smartwatch keeps me happy. Using smartwatch gives enjoyment to me. Using smartwatch stimulates my curiosity.	(0000000000)
Brand respect /utilitarian	(Effectiveness/ineffectiveness) (Functional/not functional) (Practical/impractical) (Useful/useless)	(Watchravesring-kan et al., 2010)
Word of mouth	How likely are you to spread positive WOM about (internet provider)'s online service? I would recommend (internet provider)'s online service to my friends. Given my experience with (internet provider), I would not recommend their service to my friends. If my friends were looking for an online service, I would tell them to try (internet provider).	(Maxham, 2001)
Purchase intention	If I have to choose among brands, X is definitely my choice. If I have to buy a fashion item, I plan to buy X even though there are other brands as good as X. If there is another brand as good as X, I prefer to buy X. I make my purchase selection of fashion items according to my favourite brand name, regardless of price.	(Foroudi et al., 2018)
Social media marketing	Websites Search engine optimisation Podcasts Blogs	(Melewar et al., 2017)

of the common strategies that provide efficiency in business and management studies (Saunders et al., 2016). The survey method is useful to acquire certain data from the respondents through a sample of the target population (Malhotra, 2010). Based on this approach, the current research was conducted in North London, as it represents be one of the biggest global hubs in the fashion industry and is a home to so many major brands with vibrant culture; this makes London an attractive destination to conduct a fashion-related topic research on. Therefore, it was decided to collect the data from consumers who live, work and study in North London and who had fashion shopping experience at least once, as it is believed that they represent the population. For conducting this research, a self-administrated online questionnaire with multiple open and closed questions was designed to collect data from a sample size of 300 respondents. Table 12.2 displays the statistical results of the respondents' demographic characteristics.

By completing the survey, the purchase history of the target population about their experience with fashion innovative products was also measured as they were requested to answer three questions. As it is illustrated in the below table, nearly 57% of the population which equals to 170 respondents had previous shopping experience with fashion innovative products. Depending on whether the respondents had the fashion innovative product or not, they were asked to specify the product and the price. The researcher summarised-categorised the products into five categorisations of *smart watch, clothing, accessories, sustainable apparel and footwear*. Survey respondents who claimed to have a smart watch comprised the majority of population among 170 respondents. The researcher also sorted the price range into eight categorisations as it is shown in Table 12.3. The majority claimed to invest an amount of up to 49 GBP.

To measure the different constructs stated in the framework, we used scaled items that previous studies had applied. Therefore, to study and observe the research hypothesis, all the data was analysed through SPSS 24.0 and structural equation modelling (SEM) with application Smart PLS 3.3.2 software.

Analysis and results

The present study's goal is to explore the role of fashion brand image in the nexus between perceived fashion innovativeness and behavioural intentions with the moderating role of social media marketing and lovemark. To evaluate the validity of these constructs, we used structural equation modelling with emphasis on the method of partial least squares (PLS) (Henseler et al., 2014). The constructs' reliability and validity were tested in order to examine the measurement model, and then the structural model was tested (Aparicio et al., 2017).

Model fit

Henseler et al. (2014) suggested the assessment of global model fit as the initial step of evaluating PLS model. Tenenhaus et al. (2004) proposed GoF index as a way of evaluating PLS-SEM path model. GoF index is assessed based on the mean geometric value for the mean communality score (average variance extracted – AVE values) and average R^2 value (Farooq et al., 2018) (for endogenous constructs). In this study, a GoF value of 0.565 was achieved, which reveals good model fit (see Table 12.4). Furthermore, we employed standardised root mean squared residual (SRMR) (Hu and Bentler, 1998) as a criterion for the approximate model fit, which indicates the significance of divergence between the empirical correlation matrix and the model.

326 *H. A. Lari, P. Foroudi and S. Imani*

Table 12.2 Demographic profile of the respondents (N=300)

	Frequency	Percent %
Gender		
Female	186	62.0
Male	105	35.0
LGBTI	9	3.0
Age		
19 and under	57	19.0
20 to 29	183	61.0
30 to 39	54	18.0
40 to 49	5	1.7
50 and above	1	0.3
Last qualification		
Associate degree (*e.g. AA, AS*)	19	6.3
Diploma	22	7.3
Doctorate (*e.g. PhD, EdD*)	2	0.7
High school degree	44	14.7
Postgraduate	56	18.7
Professional degree (*e.g. MD, DDS, DVM*)	5	1.7
Undergraduate	152	50.7
Ethnicity		
Asian/Asian Black (*Indian, Pakistani, Bangladeshi, Chinese, Other Asian background*)	62	20.7
Black/African/Caribbean/Black British	30	10.0
Hispanic, Latino or Spanish	21	7.0
Middle Eastern	44	14.7
Mixed/multiple ethnic group (*White and Black Caribbean, White and Black African, White and Asian, Other mixed/ multiple ethnic background*)	45	15.0
Mixed/ multiple ethnic group (*White and Black Caribbean, White and Black African, White and Asian, Other mixed/ multiple ethnic background*)	1	.3
White (*English, Welsh, Scottish, Northern Irish/British, Irish, Roma/Traveller, other White background*)	76	25.3
Other (*e.g Iranian, Greek, Turkish*)	21	7.0
Employment status		
Employed full time	36	12.0
Employed full time, Student	4	1.3
Employed part time	9	3.0
Employed part time, Student	89	29.7
Public service	1	0.3
Public service, Student	1	0.3
Self-employed	15	5.0
Self-employed, Student	7	2.3
Student	123	41.0
Student, Homemaker	1	0.3
Student, Unemployed/looking for work	8	2.7
Unemployed/looking for work	5	1.7
Unemployed/not looking for work	1	0.3
Material status		
Divorced	4	1.3
Living with partner	31	10.3
Married or domestic partnership	25	8.3
Single, never married	239	79.7
Widowed	1	0.3

Behavioural intentions in UK fashion 327

Table 12.3 Fashion innovative shopping experience (N=300)

Have you ever purchased a fashion innovative product? (keep in mind that your purchase doesn't necessarily have to be based on above examples and it can be any fashion innovative product)		
NO	130	43.3
YES	170	56.7
If yes, what fashion innovative product have you purchased?		
SMART WATCH (e.g. Apple watch, Fitbit, Garmin, Galaxy watch)	78	26.0
CLOTHING (e.g. reversible coat, tracker jacket, Arm strap jogger)	25	8.3
ACCESSORIES (e.g. touch screen gloves, bag with charger inside, mood ring)	34	11.3
SUSTAINABLE APPAREL (e.g. H&M conscious line)	14	4.7
FOOTWEAR (e.g. custom-made shoes, tracker trainees)	19	6.3
If yes, how much have you spent on your last purchase? (in **GBP**)		
1–49	38	12.7
50–99	25	8.3
100–199	35	11.7
200–399	37	12.3
400–599	19	6.3
600–799	11	3.7
800–999	3	1.0
1000 and above	2	0.7

Table 12.4 Summary of GoF indices for the global model

Fit indices	SRMR	Rms_Theta	GoF
Value in study	0.105	0.117	$\sqrt{R^2 \times \overline{AVE}} = \sqrt{0.4735 \times 0.6745} = 0.565$
Suggest value	<0.10	<0.12	$GoF_{small} = 0.1$; $GoF_{medium} = 0.25$; $GoF_{large} = 0.36$
References	(Shiri et al., 2017)	(Henseler et al., 2014)	(Wetzels et al., 2009)

Note: *SRMR*: standardised root mean squared residual; *Rms_Theta*: Root Mean Squared Residual Covariance Matrix.

Evaluation of the measurement model

According to the process developed by Anderson and Gerbing (1988), the conceptual research framework was tested by employing a two-stage approach. The first stage includes measuring the measurement model, structural model and total model. In the second stage, blindfolding procedures were used to determine and assess the accuracy of the tested hypotheses by using Smart PLS 3.3.2 and Q^2.

As a preliminary check of the measurement model, a confirmatory factor analysis (CFA) was used for testing this model with all measured constructs being modelled as correlated first-order factors. As seen in Table 12.5, reliability and

328 *H. A. Lari, P. Foroudi and S. Imani*

Table 12.5 Results of the measurement model

Construct/indicator	Loading	VIF	AVE	CR	Rho_A	C-α	DV?
Perceived fashion innovativeness			0.513	0.701	0.784	0.701	Yes
Attraction to newness			0.757	0.862			
ATN1	0.887	1.807					
ATN2	0.853	1.557					
Autonomy in innovative decision			0.818	0.900			
AID1	0.906	1.860					
AID2	0.904	1.839					
Ability to take risks in trying newness			0.741	0.851			
ATR1	0.861	1.391					
ATR2	0.860	1.415					
Fashion brand image			0.713	0.908	0.952	0.949	Yes
Cognitive associations			0.591	0.896			
CA1	0.700	1.640					
CA2	0.798	2.034					
CA3	0.773	1.838					
CA4	0.749	1.867					
CA5	0.771	1.989					
CA6	0.815	2.077					
Sensory associations			0.663	0.887			
SA1	0.771	1.483					
SA2	0.827	1.972					
SA3	0.854	2.189					
SA4	0.803	1.781					
Affective associations			0.640	0.934			
AA1	0.807	2.765					
AA2	0.822	2.676					
AA3	0.847	3.184					
AA4	0.762	1.970					
AA5	0.806	2.288					
AA6	0.753	2.129					
AA7	0.798	2.696					
AA8	0.800	2.519					
Brand awareness			0.701	0.921			
BA1	0.802	1.941					
BA2	0.797	1.951					
BA3	0.853	2.824					
BA4	0.865	3.102					
BA5	0.865	2.772					
Word of mouth intention			0.775	0.911	0.894	0.854	Yes
WoM1	0.930	3.279					
WoM2	0.931	3.287					
WoM3	0.770	1.583					

(*Continued*)

Behavioural intentions in UK fashion 329

Table 12.5 (Continued)

Construct/indicator	Loading	VIF	AVE	CR	Rho_A	C-α	DV?
Purchase intention			**0.697**	**0.902**	**0.873**	**0.856**	Yes
PI1	0.847	1.939					
PI2	0.883	2.422					
PI3	0.831	1.993					
PI4	0.774	1.808					
Lovemark			**0.727**	**0.955**	**0.947**	**0.946**	Yes
Brand love/hedonic			0.797	0.940			
BL1	0.914	3.474					
BL2	0.903	3.389					
BL3	0.915	3.913					
BL4	0.836	2.129					
Brand respect/ utilitarian			0.843	0.956			
BR1	0.905	3.333					
BR2	0.927	4.106					
BR3	0.906	3.490					
BR4	0.936	4.678					
Social media marketing			**0.823**	**0.831**	**0.813**	**0.738**	Yes
SM1	0.620	3.143					
SM2	0.822	2.417					
SM3	0.804	3.102					

Note: *VIF*: Variance inflation factor; *CR* = Composite reliability; *AVE* = Average variance extracted; *Rho_A*: Dijkstra-Henseler's indicator; *DV*: Discriminant validity.

convergent validity of the factors were estimated by Cronbach's alpha coefficients, composite reliability and average variance extracted. All alpha coefficients exceeded the 0.70 threshold suggested by Hair et al. (2011), and as well as this, composite reliabilities ranged from 0.701 to 0.955 thus satisfying the acceptance level (Bagozzi and Yi, 1988) for the reliability of study constructs (see Table 12.5). In addition, all the AVE values were above the suggested cut-off value of 0.50 (Hair et al., 2014). Indicator reliability was examined through the evaluation of factor loadings. Multidimensional data with lower than a 0.50 factor loading were eliminated because they were not considered to be within the acceptable range (Hair et al., 2010) and results indicating that all indicators were reliable. In the multi-collinearity test, which poses a threat to empirical model design, a criterion known as variance inflation factor (VIF) was used. According to Hair et al. (2011), values below 5 are considered appropriate for this criterion, and values close to 1 also indicate the acceptable limit of multi-collinearity. As for the composite reliabilities and Dijkstra-Henseler's indicator (Rho_A), they are well above the recommended 0.70 cut-off point (Bagozzi and Yi, 1988; Hair et al., 2010), indicating good internal consistency of all reflective constructs.

Finally, as shown in Table 12.6, measures were used to evaluate the discriminant validity of the measurement model including the HTMT ratio, which

330   H. A. Lari, P. Foroudi and S. Imani

Table 12.6 Discriminant validity

HTMT *ratio*

	1	2	3	4
1. Perceived fashion innovativeness	—			
2. Fashion brand image	0.505	—		
3. Word of mouth intention	0.390	0.742	—	
4. Purchase Intention	0.388	0.704	0.695	—

Note: Threshold of HTMT criterion: For conceptually similar constructs: HTMT <0.90; For conceptually different constructs: HTMT <0.85 (Hair et al., 2019).

Henseler et al. (2015) recommended as a modern means of analysing discriminant validity of constructs in the measurement models (Farooq et al., 2018). The HTMT is defined as the mean value of the item correlations across constructs relative to the (geometric) mean of the average correlations for the items measuring the same construct (Hair et al., 2019, p. 9). We concluded that all the constructs show evidence of acceptable discrimination.

Therefore, if the measurement model assessments meet all the acceptable criteria; then researchers went on to evaluate the structural model (Hair et al., 2017).

Testing the structural model

In this part, to test hypotheses about the exploration of the role of fashion brand image in the nexus between perceived fashion innovativeness and behavioural intentions with the moderating role of social media marketing and lovemark, we evaluated the structural model for general explanatory power of constructs using the R^2 value, predictive accuracy of the model by Q^2 value. But, before assessing the structural relationships, all constructs were tested for multicollinearity to make sure it does not bias the regression results. In this process the latent variable scores of the predictor constructs in a partial regression are used to calculate the VIF values (Hair et al., 2019). A maximum VIF value for each latent variable was computed resulting in a maximum VIF value of 1.872, which is below the cut-off point of 3, which is in accordance with Hair et al. (2019) who said that the VIF scores should be close to 3 and lower (see Table 12.7).

The bootstrap method with 1000 subsamples using the Smart PLS 3.2.8 software was applied to test the direction, strength and significance of the hypothesised path coefficients. To evaluate the quality of the model, the coefficient of determination (R^2), which represents the amount of explained variance of each endogenous latent variable was computed (Hair et al., 2017). Accordingly, the proportion of the total variance of each endogenous construct explained by the model is 79% for cognitive associations; 50% for sensory associations; 85.1% for affective associations; 74.8% for brand awareness; 46.6% for word of mouth intention; and 48.1% for purchase Intention. The R^2 ranges from 0 to 1, with higher values indicating a greater explanatory power. As a guideline, R^2 values of 0.75, 0.50 and 0.25 can be considered substantial, moderate and weak (Hair et

Behavioural intentions in UK fashion 331

Table 12.7 Full collinearity VIFs of constructs values for common method bias

Construct	VIFs					
	CA	SA	AA	BA	WOM	PI
Perceived fashion innovativeness	1.334	1.334	1.334	1.334		
Fashion brand image	1.334	1.334	1.334	1.334	1.000	1.872

Note: Threshold of VIFs: $\leq$ 3. CA: Cognitive associations; SA: Sensory associations; AA: Affective associations; BA: Brand awareness; WOM: Word of mouth intention; PI: Purchase intention.

al., 2019, p. 11). In addition, another means to measuring the model's predictive accuracy is Q^2 value (Geisser, 1974; Stone, 1974). As a result, Q^2 scores higher than 0.02, 0.15 and 0.35 demonstrate small, medium and large predictive relevance (Henseler et al., 2009). Hence, the predictive relevance of word of mouth intention and purchase intention in this study has been estimated at 0.339 and 0.308, respectively. Accordingly, it can be contended that the proposed model has an almost strong predictive relevance ($Q^2_{Large} = 0.339$; $Q^2_{Large} = 0.308$) for predicting variation in the endogenous constructs.

A graphical demonstration of the model results (path coefficient and t-value) is shown in Figure. 12.1. The impact of perceived fashion innovativeness on cognitive associations (H1: $\beta = 0.030$, t-value= 0.885, p>0.05) are not supported, which does not confirm the first hypothesis (H1), similarly the influence of perceived fashion innovativeness on sensory associations (H2: $\beta = -0.061$, t-value = 1.101, p>0.05), is not supported, followed by perceived fashion innovativeness to affective associations (H3: $\beta = -0.080$, t-value = 2.604, p < 0.05), and brand awareness (H4: $\beta = 0.133$, t-value = 2.967, p < 0.05) can be significantly explained by perceived fashion innovativeness. Therefore, H3 and H4 are confirmed. On the other hand, H5 and H6 were confirmed, indicating that fashion brand image could have a positive effect on purchase intention (H5: $\beta = 0.438$, t-value = 5.915, p < 0.001) and word of mouth intention (H6: $\beta = 0.683$, t-value = 19.882, p < 0.001) (see Table 12.8, and Figure 12.1). In direct effect, finally in H9, word of mouth intention has a positive effect on purchase intention (H9: $\beta = 0.346$, t-value = 4.271, p < 0.001).

Importance-performance map analysis (IPMA)

In the final phase, we explored the study of IPMA to better understand the most critical constructs affecting purchase intention in North London . IPMA is a very useful analytical tool in PLS-SEM, which graphically extends the standard path coefficient estimates in a more practical approach (Ringle and Sarstedt, 2016). More precisely, IPMA presents a contrast of *importance* (i.e., the total effect of predecessor constructs in predicting a target construct) and *performance* (i.e. average latent variable scores). The goal of IPMA is to identify predecessors which have a

332 H. A. Lari, P. Foroudi and S. Imani

Table 12.8 Results of hypotheses tests

Relationships	β-value	t-value	p-value	Remarks
Direct effects (overall model)				
H1: PFI → CA	0.030	0.885	0.376	Rejected
H2: PFI → SA	−0.061	1.101	0.271	Rejected
H3: PFI → AA	−0.080	2.604	0.009	Supported
H4: PFI → BA	0.133	2.967	0.003	Supported
H5: FBI → PI	0.438	5.915	0.000	Supported
H6: FBI → WOM	0.683	19.882	0.000	Supported
H9: WOM → PI	0.316	4.271	0.000	Supported
Moderating effects				
H7: LM → FBI → PI	−0.189	1.137	0.256	Rejected
H8: LM → FBI → WOM	−0.041	0.620	0.536	Rejected
H10: SMM → PFI → CA	−0.063	0.705	0.481	Rejected
H11: SMM → PFI → SA	−0.118	1.843	0.066*	Supported
H12: SMM → PFI → AA	−0.014	0.331	0.741	Rejected
H13: SMM → PFI → BA	−0.048	0.565	0.572	Rejected
Total effect				
FBI → WOM	0.683	19.882	0.000	—
FBI → PI	0.654	14.993	0.000	—

Note: Effect size: >0.350 large; >0.150 and ≤ 0.350 medium; >0.20 and ≤0.150 small (Chin, 1998).
$*p < 0.10$; $**p < 0.05$; $***p < 0.01$ (Hair et al., 2011; Henseler et al., 2009).

relatively low performance but high importance for the target constructs. A "one-unit point increase in the performance of predecessor construct will increase the performance of target construct, by the total effect size (i.e., importance) of the same predecessor construct" (Farooq et al., 2018, p. 176). As a result, conclusions can be drawn on two dimensions (i.e. both *importance* and *performance*), which is particularly important to prioritise managerial actions. Consequently, it is preferable to primarily focus on improving the performance of those constructs that exhibit high importance regarding their explanation of a specific target construct but, at the same time, have a relatively low performance (Hair et al., 2018).

According to the result in Figure 12.2 and Table 12.9, *fashion brand image* has the highest importance score (i.e. 0.712); if consumers in North London increases its fashion brand image performance by one-unit point; its overall intention to purchase will increase by 0.712. Moreover, our findings have revealed that there is the lowest performance in the North London consumers was with regard to fashion brand image (i.e. 58.160, that is lower than the average value = 60.054), which means that there is a great room for improvement in this area. Also, IPMA depicted that *Word-of-mouth intention* has the highest performance score, i.e. 61.949.

Future research directions

Of the several studies that can be followed within this particular area of study, the most insistent is the need to conduct this research within other living areas

Behavioural intentions in UK fashion 333

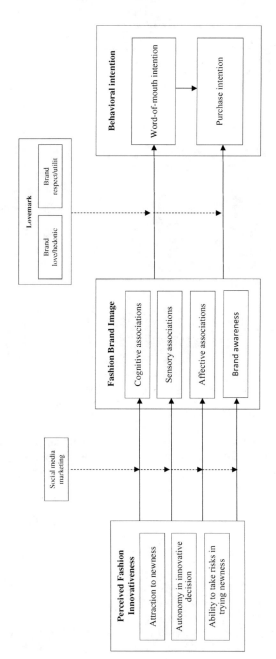

Figure 12.2 – Results.

Table 12.9 IPMA for purchase intention in North London consumers

Constructs	Importance	Performance
Fashion brand image	**0.712**	58.160
Word-of-mouth intention	0.271	**61.949**
Average value	0.491	60.054

Note: The bold values indicate the highest importance (total effect) and highest performance value.

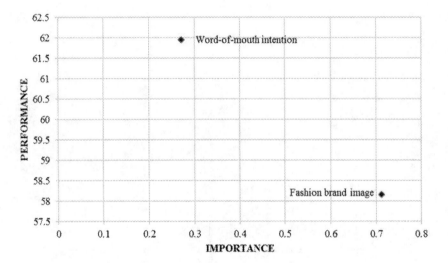

Figure 12.3 Importance-performance map analysis for purchase intention in NorthLondon consumers.

in London or other cities as the selected sample data to conduct this research was limited to consumers who live, work and study in North London; thus, the findings could have been distinctive. Accordingly, future research is recommended to conduct this study in different areas in London or other cities to be able to compare the result. The current study selected multiple examples of fashion innovative products, while the results might be different for a specific product/brand. Therefore, further study would be recommended to narrow down the research area and conduct this study for a specific product/brand. It is important to assess different research methodology as this research assessed using the quantitative research method to conduct this study; however, the result might differ with different approaches such as mixed research methodology and qualitative research.

This study focused on the convenience sampling method; however, the result might differ based upon the characteristics of the sample. Hence, it is recommended to conduct this study with different sample characteristics to achieve more reliable and precise data. Future studies have been recommended to expand on the research topic. Besides, the current literature proposed to provide value about the role of fashion innovativeness in the British fashion market. Therefore, this study would be taken as a starting point for future study about the same topic but in different cities to enhance the knowledge and understanding about this topic. Because of the limited time and resources, the examiner developed and conducted the research topic based on its prior dimensions. Thus, future study could replicate the conceptual framework to examine and validate the constructs of fashion innovativeness to prove their fundamentality for this concept. It also recommended studying fashion innovativeness based on its dimensions. Thus, future study is recommended to examine the construct validity and reliability of fashion innovativeness.

Conclusion

This research contributes to numerous other research studies by associating the knowledge about the relationships between fashion innovativeness, its antecedents and its behavioural outcomes. Specifically, we contend that fashion innovativeness as a key driver can generate a long-term consumer-brand relationship which will further generate positive behavioural intentions. Of course, consumers' relationships with a brand are also affected by other significant elements. However, a theoretical contribution of this research lies in the importance of fashion innovativeness accompanied with four fashion brand image dimensions which in turn contribute to purchase intention and word of mouth intention. In general, by advancing fashion innovativeness into product-related and non-product-related attributes, consumers can generate interactions with a selected brand. This study also adds to the extended notion of the theory of diffusion of innovation (1983) on the role of innovativeness in fashion marketplace.

More importantly, we suggest that our research aligns with prior studies (Matthews and Rothenberg, 2017) representing that the perceived level of innovativeness is influential towards behavioural intentions, brand loyalty (Cho, 2018) and hedonic and utilitarian shopping motives (Cho and Workman, 2011).

By equating the dynamics of consumer-brand relationship to innovativeness context, this study adds to the significant fashion innovation literature. Whereas fashion innovation literature has mainly developed the design and technology, our framework underlines the likelihood of adopting newness and uniqueness of fashion appearance-related products and pinpoints the role of consumer's motivation towards fashion innovativeness. The knowledge of these dynamics could be significant for marketing and branding studies within the fashion industry.

By expounding the degree of interest towards fashion innovativeness at product consumption level, our study adds a significant dimension to firms' understanding of the opportunities and boundaries of their customer relationship management. Specifically, our framework proposes that in adopting the fashion innovativeness at company–consumer contexts, managers are able to monitor how a consumer recognises their brand/company and how they get consumer's devotion to identify with their brand/company. In particular, if the perceived level of fashion innovativeness is believed to be desirable, brands/companies can articulate their characteristics through brand image attributes. A thoughtful communication method and positive impact of social media marketing efforts (such as websites, search engine optimisation, podcasts and blogs) is certainly essential towards developing the consumer's persuasive manner. Finally, we suggest that brands/companies must assign resources to hedonic and utilitarian shopping motives to advance the usefulness and uniqueness of the innovative product to evoke the user's consumption level.

Overall results suggest the moderating effect of social media marketing among perceived fashion innovativeness and sensory association scores as the most influential association among moderators. That is to say; positive impact of social media marketing efforts (such as websites, search engine optimisation, podcasts and blogs) will certainly generate a scent for f an innovative brand or product by arousing the individual's five senses (including sound, sight, smell, touch and taste). Therefore, fashion marketers and firms need to place emphasis on enhancing their brand awareness through social media marketing. Besides, the increasing power of social media marketing platforms allow fashion marketers, fashion designers and firms to reach out to their target audience, develop a relationship, communicate and promote their product innovativeness. Additionally, the trend of turning social media into e-commerce platforms allows the consumers to proceed with transactions in a more convenient way which certainly impacts consumer's behavioural intention towards innovativeness.

CASE STUDY

Established in 1971, Melissa, an iconic footwear company owned by Grendene Brazilian group, has developed as one of the largest jelly shoes inventors from São Paulo, Brazil.

Mellissa calls for innovation and their mission is to "transform plastic into extraordinary" and they have done this by turning plastic into fashion, art and design. The success of Melissa has been recognised by its threefold mission statement that focuses on the creation of *superior designs, sustainability growth* and *innovation* in footwear manufacturing. Melissa's brand strategy lies in interacting with their consumers beyond their visual level; aiming at reinforcing its brand awareness by being promoted as a playground for art and designers through its brand associations.

The rapid shift towards customer relationship marketing allows this global footwear brand to employ different brand elements in order to build its brand affinity. Applying product strategies, communication tools and further supporting elements allowed this unique Brazilian footwear brand to enhance their fashion brand image through multiple senses.

Through expanding their communication tools, this brand holds events and collaborative projects (hosting make up workshops, dance studio and

Behavioural intentions in UK fashion 337

Figure 12.4 Galleria Melissa – New York.

Figure 12.5 A collaboration with Pineapple dance studio held in London; based on Dance Machine Fall/Winter 2016 collection.

Figure 12.6 New York fashion week.

Art-Fashion Basel) to approach and introduce their products which enables the brand to use its incentives to increase the exposure and help with its overall marketing strategy while being fully engaged with the participants and having a return on investment. Using a complimentary discount exclusive to new consumers and offering a sample product to persuade potential buyers are other approaches used by Mellissa to build a relationship with their target audiences.

Bringing entertainment and experiential marketing together; Melissa use its Galleria spaces as an entertainer and networking area to bring many additional benefits associated with their business to develop its customer experience while boosting its customer engagement. Setting up online communities, supporting the potential of young creative minds by hosting a contest with the aim of creating a unique design to be launched, setting photo booth areas at their Gallerias and using specified #hashtag in the brand's favour to repost on their social pages are some major ways for Melissa to create a social tie with its consumers.

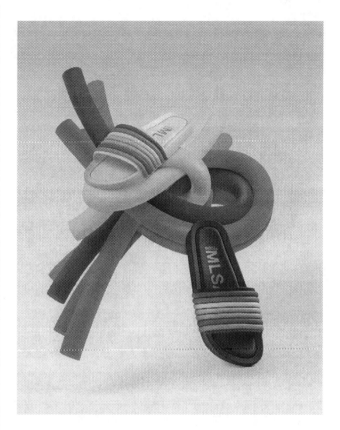

Figure 12.7 Melissa recyclable sandals.

Figure 12.8 The collaboration of Zaha Hadid (architecture) with Melissa extends the portfolio of Zaha Hadid in style.

Through expanding their **product strategies**, their colourful jelly products are distinguished from their signature "bubblegum" scent that indicates a touch point for Mellissa to strategically maintain its sensory associations. Having a different range of products and being famous for its collaboration with well-known designers like Jason Wu, Vivienne Westwood, Karl Lagerfeld and Viktor & Rolf brings out Mellissa's concept of giving luxury to all by reaching out to their consumers through cognitive associations. Concerning affective associations, Melissa embraces their sustainability element by incorporating innovative concepts with the use of mono-materials which are 100% recyclable, ideal for vegans, and advocating of animal rights. Another vessel for Melissa to preserve its brand characteristics by its products are through diversity of styles, graphic scheme and providing a platform for transmitting concepts on a different level by multiple sources.

Case questions

1. How does this brand manage to maximise its impact on potential buyers in order to have positive behavioural outcomes through enhancing its fashion brand image?
2. How does Melissa use its brand association to target the right market?
3. How would it be possible for Melissa to establish its product innovativeness through implementing its brand associations?

Key terms and definitions

Fashion innovativeness is defined as the degree of interest in adopting a significant attribute of newness and uniqueness of fashion appearance-related products (Goldsmith and Reinecke Flynn, 1992; Goldsmith et al., 1999; Choo et al., 2014; Cho, 2018) which is a key concept to consumer's willingness to embrace new fashion-related products (Goldsmith et al., 1999).

Attraction towards newness is a tendency in search of novelty (Hirschman, 1980; Louarn, 1997; Roehrich, 2004). This conceptual development is further expanding the novelty seeking theory (Hirschman, 1980) by proposing that the need for stimulation leads individual to seek out novel information to adopt product consumption in an effort to improve his/her performance (Hirschman, 1980).

Autonomy in innovative decision is defined as the degree to which an individual makes innovative decisions independently, based on individual experience (Midgley and Dowling, 1978; Louarn, 1997; Roehrich, 2004).

Ability to take risks in trying newness is characterised as an observation of forming an attitude towards the innovation (Rogers, 1983; Louarn, 1997).

Sensuality and sensory associations contribute in generating a scent for an identity of a brand or product by arousing the individual's five senses (including sound, sight, smell, touch and taste) (Roberts, 2005; Hultén, 2018).

Intimacy andaffective associations, by definition, entitled to subjective feelings that conquer emotional goals towards a brand (Venkatraman and Price, 1990; Keller, 1993, 2001; Alwi and Kitchen, 2014; Cho and Fiore, 2015). Affective association captures consumer responses resulting from brand experience through an individual's direct and indirect interaction with the brand (Cho and Fiore, 2015).

Brand awareness is the potential buyer's ability to recognise or recall a particular product category (Aaker, 1991; Cho and Fiore, 2015; Foroudi et al., 2018; Foroudi, 2019) which significantly empowers his/her consciousness and decision-making associated with a certain brand, product or services.

Purchase intention is defined as the degree to which anticipated consumers' response behaviour is transmitted to the level of consumer's future behaviour or likelihood towards buying behaviour (Fishbien and Ajzen, 1975; Kim et al., 2017).

Word of mouth is an interactive passing of information between a receiver and communicator (Arndt, 1967) about an evaluation of a product brand or services that is not commercially motivated (Lim and Chung, 2011; Baker et al., 2016; Godey et al., 2016; Yusuf et al., 2018).

Lovemark is a relationship hedonic and utilitarian experience and an object brand that a consumers enjoys by being in a relationship of respect and love with a brand, while the lovemark object will be explicitly termed lovemark brand (Hirschman & Holbrook, 1982; Schade, et al., 2016; Brown, 2018; Han, et al., 2018).

References

Aaker, D. A. and Keller, K. L. (1990). Consumer evaluations of brand extensions. *Journal of Marketing*, 54(1), 27–41.

Aaker, D. A. (1991). *Managing Brand Equity: Capitalizing on the Value of a Brand Name.* Free Press, New York.

Ajzen, I. (1991). The theory of planned behavior. *Organizational Behavior and Human Decision Processes*, 50(2), 179–211.

Alwi, S. F. S. and Kitchen, P. J. (2014). Projecting corporate brand image and behavioral response in business schools: cognitive or affective brand attributes? *Journal of Business Research*, 67(11), 2324–2336.

Anderson, J. C. and Gerbing, D. W. (1988). Structural equation modeling in practice: a review and recommended two-step approach. *Psychological Bulletin*, 103(3), 411–423.

Anić, I.-D., Mihić, M. and Milaković, I. K. (2017). Antecedents and outcomes of fashion innovativeness in retailing. *The Service Industries Journal*, 38(9–10), 1–18.

Aparicio, M., Bacao, F. and Oliveira, T. (2017). Grit in the path to e-learning success. *Computers in Human Behaviour*, 66, 388–399.

Arndt, J. (1967). Role of product-related conversations in the diffusion of a new product. *Journal of Marketing Research*, 4(3), 291–295.

Ashley, C. and Tuten, T. (2015). Creative strategies in social media marketing: an exploratory study of branded social content and consumer engagement. *Psychology & Marketing*, 32(1), 15–27.

Bagozzi, R.P. and Yi, Y. (1988). On the evaluation of structural equation models. *Journal of the Academy of Marketing Science*, 16(1), 74–94.

Baker, A. M., Donthu, N. and Kumar, V. (2016). Investigating how word-of-mouth conversations about brands influence purchase and retransmission intentions. *Journal of Marketing Research*, 53(2), 225–239.

Brown, J. R. (2018). The competitive structure of restaurant retailing: the impact of hedonic-utilitarian patronage motives. *Journal of Business Research*, 107, 233–244.

Busalim, A. (2018). Influence of e-WOM engagement on consumer purchase intention in social commerce. *The Journal of Services Marketing*, 32(4), 493–504.

Buttle, F. A. (1998). Word of mouth: understanding and managing referral marketing. *Journal of Strategic Marketing*, 6(3), 241–254.

Chin, W. W. (1998). The partial least squares approach to structural equation modeling. *Modern Methods for Business Research*, 295(2), 295–336.

Cho, E. and Fiore, A. M. (2015). Conceptualization of a holistic brand image measure fir fashion-related brands. *Journal of Consumer Marketing*, 32(4), 255–265.

Cho, E. (2018). Impact of fashion innovativeness on consumer-based brand equity. *The Journal of Consumer Marketing*, 35(3), 340–350.

Cho, E., Fiore, A. M. and Russell, D. W. (2015). Validation of a fashion brand image scale capturing cognitive, sensory, and affective associations: testing its role in an extended brand equity model. *Journal of Psychology and Marketing*, 32(1), 28–48.

Cho, S. and Workman, J. (2011). Gender, fashion innovativeness and opinion leadership, and need for touch. *Journal of Fashion Marketing and Management*, 15(3), 363–382.

Choo, H. J., Sim, S. Y., Lee, H. K. and Kim, H. B. (2014). The effect of consumers' involvement and innovativeness on the utilization of fashion wardrobe. *International Journal of Consumer Studies*, 38(2), 175–182.

Danaeels, E. and Kleinsvhmidt, E. J. (2001). Product innovativeness from the firm's prespective: it's dimensions and their relation with project selection and performance. *The Jurnal of Product Innovation Management*, 18(6), 357–373.

Easey, M. (2009). *Fashion Marketing*. 3rd ed. Wiley-Blackwell, Oxford.

Easterby-Smith, M., Thorpe, R., Jackson, P. R. and Jaspersen, L. J. (2018). *Management & Business Research*. 6th ed. SAGE, London.

Erkan, I. and Evans, C. (2016). The influence of eWOM in social media on consumers' purchase intentions: an extended approach to information adoption. *Computers in Human Behavior*, 61, 47–55.

Eun Park, J., Yu, J. and Xin Zhou, J. (2010). Consumer innovativeness and shopping styles. *Journal of Consumer Marketing*, 27(5), 437–446.

Farooq, M. S., Salam, M., Fayolle, A., Jaafar, N. and Ayupp, K. (2018). Impact of service quality on customer satisfaction in Malaysia airlines: a PLS-SEM approach. *Journal of Air Transport Management*, 67(March), 169–180.

Felix, R., Rauschnabel, P. and Hinsch, C. (2017). Elements of strategic social media marketing: a holistic framework. *Journal of Business Research*, 70, 118–126.

Fishbein, M. and Ajzen, I. (2010). *Predicting and Changing Behavior the Reasoned Action Approach*. Psychology Press, New York.

Fishbien, M. and Ajzen, I. (1975). *Belief, Attitude, Intention and Behavior: An Introduction to Theory and Research*. Addison Wesley, London.

Foroudi, P. et al. (2018). Perceptional components of brand equity: configuring the symmetrical and asymmetrical paths to brand loyalty and brand purchase intention. *Journal of Business Research*, 89, 462–474.

Foroudi, P. (2019). Influence of brand signature, brand awareness, brand attitude, brand reputation on hotel industry's brand performance. *International Journal of Hospitality Management*, 76, 271–285.

Fournier, S. (1998). Consumers and their brands: developing relationship theory in consumer research. *Journal of Consumer Research*, 24(4), 343–373.

Foxall, G. and Haskins, C. G. (1986). Cognitive style and consumer innovativeness: an empiricai test of Kirton's adaption-innovation theory in the context of food pnrchasing. *European Journal of Marketing*, 20(3), 63–80.

Gatignon, H. and Robertson, T. S. (1985). A propositional inventory for new diffusion research. *Journal of Consumer Research*, 11(4), 849–867.

Geisser, S. (1974). A predictive approach to the random effects model. *Biometrika*, 61(1), 101–107.

Godey, B. et al. (2016). Social media marketing efforts of luxury brands: influence on brand equity and consumer behavior. *Journal of Business Research*, 69(12), 5833–5841.

Goldsmith, R. and Flynn, L. (1992). Identifying innovators in consumer product markets. *European Journal of Marketing*, 26(12), 42–55.

Goldsmith, R., Hofacker, C. and Goldsmith, R. (1991). Measuring consumer innovativeness. *Journal of the Academy of Marketing Science*, 19(3), 209–221.

Goldsmith, R. E., Moore, M. A. and Bcaudoin, P. (1999). Fashion innovativeness and self-concept: a replication. *Journal of Product & Brand Management*, 8(1), 7–18.

Haase, J. and Wiedmann, K. (2018). The sensory perception item set (SPI): an exploratory effort to develop a holistic scale for sensory marketing. *Psychology & Marketing*, 35(10), 727–739.

Hair, J. F., Black, W. C., Babin, B. J. and Anderson, R. E. (2010). *Multivariate Data Analysis*. Prentice Hall, Upper Saddle River, NJ.

Hair, J. F., Ringle, C. M. and Sarstedt, M. (2011). PLS-SEM: indeed a silver bullet. *Journal of Marketing Theory & Practice*, 19(2), 139–152.

Hair, J. F., Black, W. C., Babin, B. J. and Anderson, R. E. (2014). *Multivariate Data Analysis*. Pearson New International Edition, Pearson, USA.

Hair, J. F., Hult, G. T. M., Ringle, C. M. and Sarstedt, M. (2017). *A Primer on Partial Least Squares Structural Equation Modeling PLS-SEM*. Second Edition, SAGE, Thousand Oaks, CA.

Hair, J. F., Sarstedt, M., Ringle, C. M. and Gudergan, S. P. (2018). *Advanced Issues in Partial Least Squares Structural Equation Modeling (PLS-SEM)*. SAGE, Thousand Oaks, CA.

Hair, J. F., Risher, J. J., Sarstedt, M. and Ringle, C. M. (2019). When to use and how to report the results of PLS-SEM. *European Business Review*, 31(1), 2–24.

Han, H., Lee, M. and Kim, W. (2018). Role of shopping quality, hedonic/utilitarian shopping experiences, trust, satisfaction and perceived barriers in triggering customer post-purchase intentions at airports. *International Journal of Contemporary Hospitality Management*, 30(10), 3059–3082.

Henseler, J., Ringle, C. M. and Sinkovics, R. R. (2009). The use of partial least squares path modeling in international marketing. In *New Challenges to International Marketing* (pp. 277–319). Emerald Group Publishing Limited.

Henseler, J., Dijkstra, T. K., Sarstedt, M., Ringle, C. M., Diamantopoulos, A., Straub, D.W., Ketchen, D. J., Hair, J. F., Hult, G. T. M. and Calantone, R. J. (2014). Common beliefs and reality about partial least squares: comments on Rönkkö & Evermann (2013). *Organizational Research Methods*, 17(2), 182–209.

Henseler, J., Ringle, C. M. and Sarstedt, M. (2015). A new criterion for assessing discriminant validity in variance-based structural equation modeling. *Journal of the Academy of Marketing Science*, 43(1), 115–135.

Hirschman, E. and Holbrook, M. (1982). Hedonic consumption: emerging concepts, methods and propositions. *Journal of Marketing*, 46(3), 92–101.

Hirschman, E. C. and Adcock, W. O. (1978). An examination of innovative communicators, opinion leaders and innovators for men's fashionapparel. *Advances in Consumer Research*, 5, 308–314.

Hirschman, E. C. (1980). Innovativeness, novelty seeking, and consumer creativity. *Journal of Consumer Research*, 7(3), 283–295.

Hollebeek, L. D., Glynn, M. S. and Brodie, R. J. (2014). Consumer brand engagement in social media: conceptualization, scale development and validation. *Journal of Interactive Marketing*, 28(2), 149–165.

Hu, L. T. and Bentler, P. M. (1998). Fit indices in covariance structure modeling: sensitivity to underparameterized model misspecification. *Psychological Methods*, 3(4), 424.

Huang, T.-L. and Liao, S. (2015). A model of acceptance of augmented-reality interactive. *Electronic Commerce Research*, 15(2), 269–295.

Hultén, B. (2018). *Sensory Marketing: Theoretical and Empirical Grounds*. Routledge, London.

Keller, K. L. (1993). Conceptualizing, measuring, and managing customer-based brand equity. *Journal of Marketing*, 57(1), 1–22.

Keller, K. L. (2001). Building customer-based brand equity. *Marketing Management*, 10(2), 14–19.

Kim, A. J. and Ko, E. (2012). Do social media marketing activities enhance customer equity? : an empirical study of luxury fashion brand. *Journal of Business Research*, 65(10), 1480–1486.

Kim, N., Chun, E. and Ko, E. (2017). Country of origin effects on brand image, brand evaluation, and purchase intention. *International Marketing Review*, 34(2), 254–271.

Krishna, A. and Arbor, A. (2010). *Sensory Marketing Research on the Sensuality of Products*. Routledge, London.

Krishnamurthy, A. and Kumar, S. (2018). Electronic word-of-mouth and the brand image: exploring the moderating role of involvement through a consumer expectations lens. *Journal of Retailing and Consumer Services*, 43, 149–156.

Kudeshia, C., Sikdar, P. and Mittal, A. (2016). Spreading love through fan page liking: a perspective on small scale entrepreneurs. *Computers in Human Behavior*, 54(C), 257–270.

Kunz, W., Schmitt, B. and Meyer, A. (2011). How does perceived firm innovativeness affect the consumer? *Journal of Business Research* , 64(8), 816–822.

Lim, B. C. and Chung, C. M. Y. (2011). The impact of word-of-mouth communication on attribute evaluation. *Journal of Business Research*, 64(1), 18–23.

Liu, X., Shin, H. and Burns, A. C. (2021). Examining the impact of luxury brand's social media marketing on customer engagement: using big data analytics and natural language processing. *Journal of Business Research*, 125, 815–826.

Louarn, P. L. (1997). La tendance à innover des consommateurs: analyse conceptuelle et proposition d'une échelle de mesure. *Recherche et Applications en Marketing*, 12(1), 3–19.

Macdonald, E. K. and Sharp, B. M. (2000). Brand awareness effects on consumer decision making for a common, repeat purchase product: a replication. *Journal of Business Research*, 48(1), 5–15.

Malhotra, N. K. (2010). *Marketing Research an Applied Orientation*. 6th ed. Pearson.

Matthews, D. and Rothenberg, L. (2017). An assessment of organic apparel, environmental beliefs and consumer preferences via fashion innovativeness. *International Journal of Consumer Studies*, 41(5), 526–533.

Maxham III, J. G. (2001). Service recovery's influence on consumer satisfaction, positive word-of-mouth, and purchase intentions. *Journal of Business Research*, 54(1), 11–24.

Melewar, T. C., Foroudi, P., Gupta, S., Kitchen, P. J. and Foroudi, M. M. (2017). Integrating identity, strategy and communications for trust, loyalty and commitment. *European Journal of Marketing*, 51(3), 572–604.

Midgley, D. F. and Dowling, G. R. (1978). Innovativeness: the concept and its measurement. *Journal of Consumer Research*, 4(4), 229–242.

Oberoi, P., Patel, C. and Haon, C. (2017). Technology sourcing for website personalization and social media marketing: a study of e-retailing industry. *Journal of Business Research*, 80, 10–23.

Pappu, R. and Quester, P. G. (2016). How does brand innovativeness affect brand loyalty? *European Journal of Marketing*, 50(1), 2–28.

Pearson, P. H. (1970). Relationships between global and specified measure of novelty seeking. *Journal of Consulting and Clinical Psychology*, 34(2), 199–204.

Pitta, D., Patino, A. and Maddox, L. (2016). Social media influences on building brand equity. *Journal of Marketing Development and Competitiveness*, 10(3), 17–25.

Ringle, C. M. and Sarstedt, M. (2016). Gain more insight from your PLS-SEM results: the importance-performance map analysis. *Industrial Management & Data Systems*, 116(9), 1865–1886.

Roberts, K. (2005). *Lovemarks: The Future beyond Brands*. Powerhouse Books, New York.

Roehrich, G. (2004). Consumer innovativeness: concepts and measurements. *Journal of Business Research*, 57(6), 671–677.

Rogers, E. M. and Shoemaker, F. F. (1971). *Communication of Innovation: A Cross-Cultural Approach*. 2nd ed. The Free Press, New York.

Rogers, E. (1983). *Diffusion of Innovations*. Free Press, New York.

Saunders, M., Lewis, P. and Thornhill, A. (2016). *Research Methods for Business*. 7th ed. Pearson.

Schade, M. et al. (2016). The impact of attitude functions on luxury brand consumption: an age-based group comparison. *Journal of Business Research*, 69(1), 314–322.

Shimp, T. A. and Madden, T. J. (1987). Consumer-object relations: a conceptual framework based analogously on Sternberg's triangular theory of love. *Advances in Consumer Research*, 15, 163–168.

Shiri, N., Shinnar, R. S., Mirakzadeh, A. A. and Zarafshani, K. (2017). Cultural values and entrepreneurial intentions among agriculture students in Iran. *International Entrepreneurship and Management Journal*, 13(4), 1157–1179.

Solomon, M. R. (2018). *Consumer Behavior: Buying, Having, and Being*. 12th ed. Pearson, London.

Sternberg, R. J. (1986). A triangular theory of love. *Psychological Review*, 93(2), 119–135.

Stone, M. (1974). Cross-validatory choice and assessment of statistical predictions. *Journal of the Royal Statistical Society*, 36(2), 111–147.

Tenenhaus, M., Amato, S. and Esposito Vinzi, V. (2004). A global goodness-of-fit index for PLS structural equation modelling. *Proceedings of the XLII SIS Scientific Meeting*, 1, 739–742.

Vahdati, H. and Mousavi Nejad, S. H. (2016). Brand personality toward customer purchase intention the intermediate role of electronic word-of-mouth and brand equity. *Asian Academy of Management Journal*, 21(2), 1–26.

Venkatraman, M. P. and Price, L. L. (1990). Differentiating between cognitive and sensory innovativeness concepts, measurement, and implications. *Journal of Business Research*, 20(4), 293–315.

Watchravesringkan, K., Hodges, N. N. and Kim, Y. H. (2010). Exploring consumers' adoption of highly technological fashion products. *Journal of Fashion Marketing and Management: An International Journal*, 14(2), 263–281.

Wetzels, M., Odekerken-Schröder, G. and van Oppen, C. (2009). Using PLS path modeling for assessing hierarchical construct models: guidelines and empirical illustration. *MIS Quarterly*, 33(1), 177–195.

Wrokman, J. E. (2010). Fashion consumer groups, gender, and need for touch. *Clothing and Textiles Research Journal*, 28(2), 126–139.

Yusuf, A., Hussin, A. and Busalim, A. (2018). Influence of e-WOM engagement on consumer purchase intention in social commerce. *Journal of Services Marketing*, 32(4), 493–504.

Zeithaml, V. A. (1988). Consumer perceptions of price, quality and value: a means-end model and synthesis of evidence. *Journal of Marketing*, 52(3), 2–22.

Zeithaml, V. A., Berry, L. L. and Parasuraman, A. (1996). The behavioral consequences of service quality. *Journal of Marketing*, 60(2), 31–46.

13 Corporate brand image

Technology and innovation in e-tailing

Virginia Vannucci and Eleonora Pantano

Introduction

Chapter 13 discusses the role of technology (i.e. virtual and augmented reality, social media, etc.) and innovation in improving corporate branding in the context of electronic retailing (e-tailing), with emphasis on the consumers online interactions with retailers, and on the massive amount of data emerging from these interactions. It finally proposes a theoretical framework synthetising how retailers would generate competitive advantage in the new settings enriched with advanced technology. The chapter concludes with the case study of the Gucci app, which merges several innovative features like augmented reality for users' virtual try-on.

Key points

Innovation management, technology management, e-tailing, retailing, omnichannel retail, data-driven strategy, consumer-computer-interaction and luxury branding are discussed.

Background

Technology and innovation management strategies for retailers

The phenomenon of digitalisation is largely transforming the retail sector (Hagberg et al., 2016; Pantano et al., 2018; Willems et al., 2017). This phenomenon has become even more dramatic for retailers because of the effect of the COVID19 pandemic in 2020, which pushed retailers to move online to survive. In other words, retailers have been pushed to develop digital capabilities and reinforce their infrastructure to satisfy consumers' online demand (Pantano et al., 2020). Indeed, retailers are forced to constantly monitor the technological and environmental changes in order to maintain business competitiveness and profitability (Vannucci and Pantano, 2019). Accordingly, new business opportunities, retail models and forms of commerce and consumption experiences emerge.

The recent literature about the integration of interactive and innovative technologies in retail and e-tailing (online retailing) settings mainly focused on

348   Vannucci and Pantano

(i) consumer acceptance of digital technologies through the extension of the Technology Acceptance Model (TAM) (Davis, 1989) and Innovation Diffusion Theory (IDT) (Rogers, 1962 revised in Rogers, 2017); (ii) new management strategies for technology integration; and (iii) number of patents in the retail domain. In particular, TAM is based on perceived ease of use, usefulness and attitude as drivers of the consumer's behavioural intention to use a certain technology, such as virtual mirrors and augmented reality apps for virtual try-on, smart retail technologies (SRT) as voice controller for, personal shopping assistance, near-field communications (NFC) systems, etc. (Roy et al., 2018; Pantano et al., 2017b). Also, new constructs have extended the TAM such as social influence, personality traits, product features, etc. (Bailey et al., 2017; Chi, 2018; Kaushik and Rahaman, 2015; Perry, 2016). Similarly, IDT evaluates the actual adoption of the technology in a certain market, providing a clear and updated overview of the number of adopters in the market, while defining the characteristics of each adopter based on specific categories: innovators, early adopters, early majority, late majority and laggards (Rogers, 2017). In other words, the theory explains when potential users decide to adopt an innovation considering their beliefs and opinion about the innovation. The new management strategies might include the extension of offering, new price strategies, the collaboration of human and digital technologies and the successful integration of different technologies to shift traditional retail management to a smart scenario (Hagberg et al., 2016; Pantano et al., 2018; Poncin et al., 2017; Roy et al., 2017; Vrontis et al., 2017; Willems et al., 2017). The number of patents provides an overview of the technological trends in retail, by synthetising the evolution of the sector in terms of innovative technology (Pantano and Pizzi, 2020), which can be used to predict the future availability of new systems to enhance retail management (Pantano et al., 2018). To this end, the Knowledge Push Curve (KPC) (Pantano et al., 2018) predicts the future developments of technologies for retailing by stating that the number of patents tripled every five years until 2005 and doubled every two years after.

Main focus of the chapter

Corporate brand image in e-tailing

The brand image might be conceived as a mental representation and a subjective perception that customers feel about a specific brand (Keller, 2003). Therefore, the more a firm can create a positive brand image in customers' memory, the higher its positioning and competitive advantage (Parker, 2009). To this end, literature has recognised the importance of building a strong corporate brand image as the measure of intangible brand assets, which are difficult to imitate, and which may help to achieve sustained superior financial performance (Roberts and Dowling, 2002; Martenson, 2007). The corporate brand image provides credibility to other brands, and it is a vehicle to clarify and synthetise the organisational culture and values inside the organisation (Aaker, 1996;

Martenson, 2007). Thus, the corporate brand image is based on what people associate the company with, while summarising all the information (such as perceptions, values and beliefs) about the company that people hold (Martenson, 2007). Branding literature also argued that a positive brand image has a positive impact on consumers' attitude towards the brand, such as their purchase decision of buying at premium prices, more loyalty and more positive word-of-mouth (Martenson, 2007).

From a retailing perspective, the favourable store image (including the online store image) increases consumers' satisfaction, which in turn increases store loyalty (Osman, 1993; Bloemer and de Ruyter, 1998; Martenson, 2007). Specifically, the store (either physical or online) image can be defined as the way that consumers view the store, such as their impression or perception of the store (Hartman and Spiro, 2005). This element plays a critical role especially in luxury retailing, which is characterised by the communication of the essence of luxury through any element composing the store image (Dion and Arnould, 2011). Indeed, luxury retailing aims to strengthen the consumers' perception of the luxury brand image through product that consumers consider (i) of high quality; (ii) capable of offering authentic value and benefits, whether functional or emotional; (iii) built on qualities such as artisanship, craftsmanship or service quality; (iv) worthy of commanding a premium price; and (v) capable of inspiring a deep connection with the consumer (Ko et al., 2019).

In order to reinforce the connection with the customer and influence positively their brand image, luxury retailers are also largely investing in social media channels (Kim and Ko, 2012; Godey et al., 2016; Passavanti et al., in press). Accordingly, scholars are emphasising the importance for retailers of constantly monitoring what their consumers say about them through social media, in order to build a positive brand image and, consequently, increase store brand loyalty and stimulate positive future purchase behaviour (Keller and Lehmann, 2006; Kim and Ko, 2012; Godey et al., 2016; Giglio et al., 2020). In particular, literature has shown that brand-related user generated content (UGC) posted online has a substantial impact on behavioural outcomes, highlighting the importance of monitoring what consumers are saying, not only about a brand (Kim and Johnson, 2016). For instance, Walasek, Bhatia and Brown (2017) collected tweets to evaluate how much consumers talk online of luxury brands compared with other brands. Johnen and Schnittka (2019) collected 90,260 consumers comments (including initial comments and replies) to 227 specific brand posts, which were categorised through a sentiment analysis to understand how to optimise the response to consumers' online complaints. Peng et al. (2019) evaluated consumers' hotel rating on TripAdvisor and beer rating on BeerAdvocate to understand consumers' evaluation of hotels and beers, respectively. Finally, Giglio et al. (2020) investigated consumers' perceptions of luxury hotel brands through evaluating of consumers' visual data as uploaded pictures on TripAdvisor. However, research on how to extract knowledge from the data consumers produce online to evaluate retailers' brand image is still in progress.

Data-driven e-tailing

Any time that a consumer interacts with a technology (i.e. self-service check-out, searching the virtual catalogue, etc.), s/he produces data that can be of a certain value for retailers. However, the interactions can be different, including both technologies in the physical stores and online (i.e. website navigation, social media presence, online purchases, etc.), by resulting in a rapid and massive amount of data from multiple sources (big data). Thus, the opportunities emerging from the use of big data in the retail, with emphasis on e-tailing, are enormous. To this end, big data analytics allow retailers to follow their customers without geographical and time constraints (Newell and Marabelli, 2015; Wieland et al., 2016). Despite the massive availability of data, much data has never been used to extract knowledge (consumers' insights) or value to firms (Wahyudi et al., 2018). Therefore, companies still might fail to extract value from big data due to the lack of knowledge and skills useful to analyse data generated by consumers (Sivarajah et al., 2017).

Literature suggests that successful big data analytics consist of the "collection, analysis, visualization, use and interpretation of data for various functional division with a view to gaining actionable insights, creating business value and establishing competitive advantage" (Motamarri et al., 2017, p. 625). However, these actions go beyond the traditional business intelligence and decision support systems (Wang et al., 2018). Indeed, this massive amount of data generated by consumers results in new challenges for e-retailers in storing, efficiently managing and analysing huge data sets due to the lack of scalability, flexibility and performance essential in this context (Sivarajah et al., 2017). To this end, advanced techniques for performing more complex and effective analysis are required to achieve more precise and effective results from big data to build and reinforce strong image (Sheng et al., 2018; Wamba et al., 2017).

Accordingly, Verhoef and colleagues (2016) proposed a model of big data value creation highlighting the strategies and solutions to create value. In particular, the model is based on four main components: (i) big data assets, (ii) big data capabilities, (iii) big data analytics and (iv) big data value. (i) Big data assets are the resources stored by companies, which are tangible (e.g. buildings) and intangible (e.g. customers, products). Actually, the variety of data generated and collected by retailers arises from different sources simultaneously. This change induces retailers to realise that data have become valuable assets to be used for commercial steering. By investing in the right data, it is possible to develop successful processes and sustainable relationships with consumers either online or offline (Erevelles et al., 2016). To exploit data is necessary to highlight the relevant elements through which retailers are able to coordinate their activities and their assets. (ii) Big data capabilities ensure better assets management while allowing their more rewarding deployment (Day, 1994). The big data capabilities are based on (Verhoef et al., 2016) people, systems, processes and organisation. People are the key to a successful analytical performance, while identifying the right analytical people is the main step to developing a big data strategy. With

Corporate brand image   351

regard to the systems, retailers should internally train employees to strengthen their analytical skills in order to have sufficient knowledge from big data (Verhoef and Lemon, 2013). The selection of the right system for the analysis is the key element to guaranteeing high-quality results, in which new big data solutions and traditional business analytics coexist. This solution would lead to an integrated data ecosystem that allows the analysis of data from different sources without having a single system for everything (Verhoef et al., 2016). The processes are the procedures that define guideline for data access, data management and communication within companies (Verhoef and Leeflang, 2009). Organisations concern the organisational structure and the embeddedness of analytical function within the companies. (iii) Big data analytics (the analysis and interpretation of findings) allows retailers to improve retail plans and retail business models (Gandomi and Haider, 2015). Big data analytics is further based on two forms of analytics: (1) analytics to gain insights and (2) analytics to develop models (Verhoef et al., 2016). The achievement of insights and the development of models can generate value for firms with regard to marketing decisions (Humby et al., 2008), actions and campaign improvement (Feld et al., 2013; Marr, 2015) and development of big-data-based solutions for customers (Thaler and Tucker, 2013). Finally, (iv) big data value consists of value creation from big data through analytics. Indeed, the exploitation of big data analytics leads to the generation of value while converting data into knowledge: knowledge in business value and in products or services (Kunz et al., 2017; Wamba et al., 2017). In particular, consumers' value creation allows understanding customer needs in order to propose them products or services considering the competitive advantage over competitors (Cossío-Silva et al., 2016). A firm's value creation allows examining any difficulty inside the firm's operations in order to optimise business process models (Verhoef et al., 2016).

Omnichannel integration

The availability of digital technologies has allowed retailers to create new channels to show and sell products and services. For a long time, there was only one main sales channel in traditional retailing, the physical one. With the progresses in technologies, many retailers have launched the online channel, shifting the offer and competition to more than one channel (the brick-and-mortar and the online one). Subsequently, the diffusion of smartphones allowed the development of mobile commerce (mobile channel), and the affirmation of social media enabled further sales channels (social media channels).

Thus, the concepts of multichannel, cross-channel and omnichannel, underlining their differences emerged in the new retail settings (Beck and Rygl, 2015; Piotrowicz and Cuthbertson, 2014; Verhoef et al., 2015). Specifically, multichannel retailing is the set of activities concerning the sale of products or services on multiple channels, including the traditional brick-and-mortar (physical channel), the online channel and the catalogue, where these channels coexist without the possibility for the consumer to trigger an interaction among them, and

352 *Vannucci and Pantano*

without the retailers' ability to provide the same experience through them (Beck and Rygl, 2015) adequately. Therefore, the multichannel strategy allows a retailer to reach different customer segments through different channels and to increase the overall value offer (Neslin et al., 2006; Verhoef et al., 2010). An evolution of multichannel retailing is the cross-channel retailing. Cross-channel is defined as the set of activities that involve the sale of goods or services across multiple channels, where the customer can activate partial interactions between those channels, and the retailer controls the partial integration of them (Beck and Rygl, 2015). Despite this partial integration among channels, only omnichannel management provides the total integration among channels. Indeed, omnichannel retailing is an interconnected system of all sales channels. The strategies adopted in each channel are consistent through each other. There is a complete transfer of data, so that consumers can interact with the retailer and live the same shopping experience on all channels without any interruption between them. For instance, the customer can start a shopping experience on one channel (such as searching for pre-purchase information online) and continue it on another (such as the effective purchase through the brand/retailer mobile app). As a consequence, the boundaries between different channels have blurred, allowing consumers to move freely from the online channel to mobile devices and physical stores, within a single transaction process. The channels are therefore used interchangeably, offering continuity during the search and purchase process. There is complete homogenisation of business processes that aim to meet consumer demand regardless of location or time and create a seamless shopping experience (Jocevski et al., 2019). Specifically with regard to the omnichannel, the retailers can interact in a synchronised manner with customers at every point of contact: the result is a consistent, continuous and personalised experience across multiple devices using consistent data from customers.

Summarising, omnichannel retailing (i) involves different channels in an interrelated manner; (ii) eliminates the boundaries between channels; and (iii) allows a unique and consistent customer experience with the brand/retailer (Jocevski et al., 2019). Furthermore, in this omnichannel perspective, also new shopping behaviours emerge based on the different usage of the available channels: showrooming and webrooming. The first consists of the practice of researching products in a brick-and-mortar store to physically evaluate the good and then making the purchase online; while the second is based on assessing the product online and making the purchase in the brick-and-mortar store (Bell et al., 2018; Rapp et al., 2015; Verohef et al., 2015). Indeed, showrooming and webrooming behaviours combine online, mobile and brick-and-mortar retail opportunities (Kang, 2018). The customer can easily change channels without losing information: he/she can search products online and then buy them on social media or through the mobile channel, and then he/she can request home delivery.

On the one hand, the implementation of an omnichannel strategy requires substantial investments both in financial and management terms, considerably increasing the organisational complexity. On the other one, omnichannel management increases customer loyalty and satisfaction (Grewal et al., 2017).

Solutions and recommendations

The chapter described the disruptive forces actually affecting retailing, with emphasis on e-tailing from the brand management perspective. To this end, our research employed a review of technologies and innovation strategies to extract the brand image formation from consumers' interaction with the technology, with emphasis on the online channel (e-tailing).

Indeed, the deeper understanding of the consumers' interactions would allow measuring brands' images more accurately via measurement instruments that are better focused on specific areas of consumers' interest. Subsequently, brand managers can shape the image in ways that resonate well with retail and marketing strategy and consumers' priorities when visiting a particular online store, as successful retail and brand strategies depend on the creation of strong pairings between the brand and each element of the online store (including products display, virtual atmospherics and so on). To this end, managers might adopt specific strategies to emphasise the high quality of the product, the service quality, authenticity, values and benefits of the brand, and inspire deep connections with the brand.

The combination of technologies, software applications and communications media would offer a really extraordinary manifestation of a superior brand image (either in the online or offline context).

Therefore, in the new scenario characterised by the increasing of both consumers' interaction with the technologies and availability of consumers' data, retailers are required to (i) adopt new technologies, (ii) develop efficient innovation management strategies, (iii) exploit new and advanced techniques and metrics, (iv) extract knowledge on consumers from the new analytics and (v) evaluate the brand image to generate the new competitive advantage (Figure 13.1).

Future research directions

First, the online identification of particular words and themes extracted by consumers' spontaneous (online) communications would allow the deeper

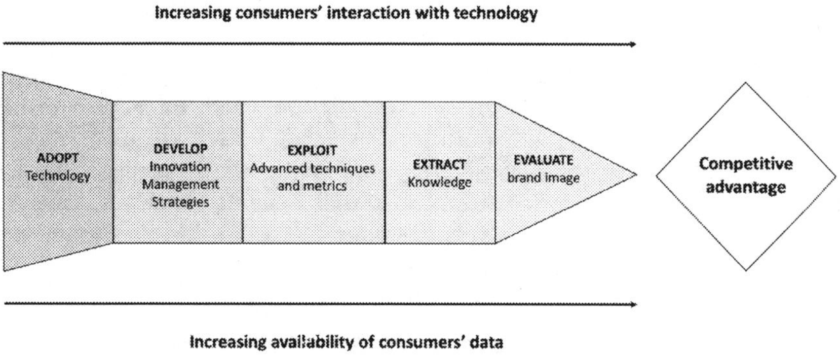

Increasing consumers' interaction with technology

ADOPT Technology — DEVELOP Innovation Management Strategies — EXPLOIT Advanced techniques and metrics — EXTRACT Knowledge — EVALUATE brand image — Competitive advantage

Increasing availability of consumers' data

Figure 13.1 Retailers' competitive advantage creation in the technology-enriched scenario. Source: the authors.

354 Vannucci and Pantano

understanding of the process to develop the brand image online, by achieving a general idea of "what consumers say" about the brand. If the data collection is to be limited to the presence of specific words (in addition to the name of the brand), additional analyses could provide more detailed information on consumers' perceptions of particular services, initiatives, products, strategies, etc. Since usual computing performances limit the analyses to a certain number of texts in a very specific period of time (i.e. one specific month), high performing computers are recommended for those kinds of analyses, requiring an additional monetary investment in hardware, while data collection and analysis reiterated constantly would increase the data volume and the related consumer insights.

Secondly, current algorithms (i.e. IBM Watson, Microsoft Azure, etc.) are able to conduct sentiment analysis of consumers' spontaneous communications, by assigning the label of "positive" or "negative", with a certain error. Future developments in cognitive software should allow clearer identification of the positive and negative sentiment involved in any consumers' communication with a reduced error, to provide a more precise overview of the proportions of satisfied and dissatisfied consumers with the brand image, and easily distinguish consumers who love the brand (brand love) and consumers who hate the brand (brand hate).

Third, consumers with different backgrounds might behave differently when online. Current advances in technology offer several analytical techniques that brand managers might successfully employ and that could become fundamental to future marketing research to better identify and target consumers. Thus, we recommend future studies to analyse this new domain and propose an inclusive taxonomy of new techniques and metrics for research in branding and retailing, developed both by academic research and by results obtained in the real world. The emerging taxonomic framework and research perspective will lay a foundation for the future development of big data analytics theory and practice for retail and brand management.

Conclusion

The new technologies contribute to the formation of brand image, with emphasis on e-tailing, which is largely characterised by consumers' interactions with the technology and online spontaneous communications. Our chapter may help scholars and practitioners to deeply understand the effect of new technologies on the brand image, which can be measured more accurately via new metrics and analytics.

From a managerial viewpoint, especially the analyses of unsolicited consumers' communications on social media like Twitter and Instagram can be an additional tool for management that they can integrate into strategies. Accordingly, retailers should integrate and extend current practices to collect and analyse insights into consumers through low-cost tools, to make big data such as those generated in social media scalable and manageable. Thus, such an approach can be used

Corporate brand image   355

systematically (almost instantly) and is feasible for many companies with varying financial resources.

Drawing upon the consumers' interactions with the technology and consumers' unsolicited online communications, managers can better develop the brand images as these are perceived by consumers. Subsequently, managers can shape these images in ways that resonate well with retail and marketing strategy and consumers' priorities when experiencing a particular brand/store online and offline, as successful retail and brand strategies depend on creating strong pairings between the luxury brand and each element of the store (including products, atmospherics and so on).

The combination of technologies, software applications, communications media, structures and hardware would offer a really extraordinary manifestation of superior brands.

CASE STUDY: GUCCI APP

In 2011, the luxury fashion brand Gucci launched its app with basic functions. In 2019, after huge improvements, the brand added several additional functionalities such as augmented reality (AR) technology and innovative features. To date, this app is a very entertaining and engaging app where customers can not only see and browse Gucci products, but also interact with the brand through a playful and exciting experience.

The main functionalities for the user to explore are the home page, the try-on page, the runway page, the arcade page and, finally, the podcast page. However, this app is quite unique, since the goal is not selling products, while it is sharing the brand's values, creating engagement between the brand and the user and reinforcing the brand attachment.

On the home page, there are the primary campaigns of the moment; the user can see it all scrolling the page or click each campaign to see what it is about and the related products. All the products shown can be bought on the app or through the link at the end of the page giving access to Gucci's website landing page. The home page shows Gucci's brand personality with campaigns like "The MX project", a curated selection of items across categories and collections that live beyond gender, underling that Gucci is a for-all gender brand. The "Equilibrium" campaign shows Gucci's commitment to generate positive change for people and the planet. In this section, the brand explains how Gucci is working for a sustainable world, with eco-friendly initiatives and actions to fight gender-based violence and discrimination. Through the very content-rich home page, the user can also access art galleries, like the Gucci Garden, a Florence (Italy) based museum about the Gucci brand and its iconic products that also offers a polished restaurant in the core of the historical city centre. The home page further shows the new products, such as new perfumes, watches (with 3D images), nail polishes, sneakers, sunglasses, mascaras and new collections. The home page also offers a "Do it yourself" (DIY) tool where knitwear styles and Gucci wallets can be personalised with letters in diverse colours. Two initials can be selected in a mix of leathers and fabrics that are appliquéd on either side of the Ophidia tote bag.

There is also a specific page about donation: through the app, the user can donate money in Italy or globally to fight the Covid-19 pandemic, in support of the World Health Organisation.

Another engaging feature available on the home page is the possibility to use the photo booth to "guccify yourself", which allows adding stickers or frames with the Gucci logo, or downloading wallpaper from the Gucci gallery, to any picture or selfie.

A very innovative tool is the integration of AR technology for browsing the iconic bags. Indeed, the app allows visualising the Gucci's iconic bags in the space, how they would look like if bought. Through this function, the user can decide where to put the bag in the real space (through the smartphone camera) to see the bag's actual dimensions and features. The user can also switch colour, material and model. Similarly, the app offers its users the "try-on" tool. Thanks to the AR technology, the user can virtually try on sneakers, lipsticks, eyewear, hats and some masks to share funny pictures. By framing the face with the phone's camera, consumers can try different models of glasses, lipsticks, or hats, choosing from those highlighted by the app. Likewise, by framing the feet with the camera, consumers can wear virtually different models of sneakers (Figure 13.2). For each product, it is also possible to choose different colours or themes. The "try-on" section also allows users to virtually decorate spaces, through furniture and pieces featuring the brand motifs and patterns. Once the objects are virtually tried on, the user can buy them through the app. The images look real, and this is an excellent support in mobile shopping, where usually it is not possible to physically try products before buying them. This option would help reduce the phenomenon of webrooming, and the customer can use a single channel to complete the purchase. Furthermore, the Gucci app allows users to virtually participate in runways, which are interactive and artistic shows usually difficult to join in person (the invitation is very restrictive). In the same app section, it is possible also to see past runways again through videos and pictures of the previous collections.

Another innovative tool in the app is the arcade section, where users can play with some vintage games, revisited with Gucci brand. For instance, in a "mascara hunt" game, the player needs to hunt Gucci mascaras throwing a bowling ball to collect points. The more the user receives scores in the arcade section, the more s/he can collect badges to discover the story behind each game. Finally, the last section of the Gucci app offers a podcast with several feeds. The saved podcasts are about different topics, from a

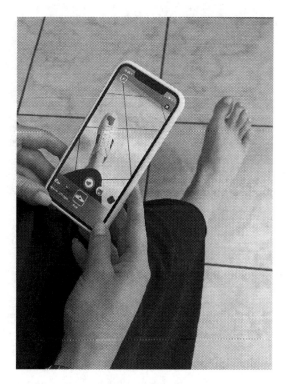

Figure 13.2 A consumer playing with the Gucci app to virtual try-on a certain pair of Gucci sneakers. Source: the authors.

food podcast to a technology podcast and to a beauty podcast. Several podcasts are about fashion inspiration and suggestions to wear Gucci products.

The Gucci app presents itself as a high-tech tool that allows the user to enjoy an engaging and innovative shopping experience, while interacting with the brand. The Gucci app is an example of how luxury brands might open up to technological innovations to get closer to consumers and communicate directly the brand's values and personality. Although users are not expected to always finalise the purchase when using the app, the app generates positive attitudes towards the brand. It still provides updates on Gucci's new collections and campaigns, creating a relationship with the brand and developing a sense of attachment.

Case questions (three questions)

1. How does the Gucci app contribute to the building and maintaining of the brand image?

358 *Vannucci and Pantano*

2. Which kind of new functionalities can Gucci add to the app to catch new consumers?
3. What are the backfire effects of the excessive usage of the Gucci app for brick-and-mortar stores?

Key terms and definitions

Big data analytics: the process of examining big data to uncover information (such as hidden patterns, correlations, market trends and customer preferences) that can help companies make more informed business decisions.

Big data value: The creation of value for companies from the collection of a huge amount of data from multiple sources.

Brand awareness: the degree of consumer recognition of a product by its name.

Brand image: the current view of the customers about a brand.

Innovation diffusion theory: the process by which a new technology/innovation is adopted over time among the users in a certain social system.

Omnichannel retailing: a fully integrated approach to commerce, providing shoppers a unified experience across all channels or touchpoints.

Showrooming: the practice of researching products in a brick-and-mortar store to physically evaluate the good first, and to make the purchase online secondly.

Technology acceptance model: consumer's behavioural intention to use a certain technology, based on the constructs of perceived ease of use, usefulness and attitude.

Webrooming: the practice of evaluating the product online first, and making the purchase in the brick-and-mortar store secondly.

References

Aaker, D. (1996). *Building Strong Brands*. Free Press, New York.

Bailey, A. A., Pentina, I., Mishra, A. S. and Ben Mimoun, M. S. (2017). Mobile payments adoption by US consumers: An extended TAM. *International Journal of Retail and Distribution Management, 45*(6), 626–640.

Beck, N. and Rygl, D. (2015). Categorization of multiple channel retailing in multi-, cross-, and omni-channel retailing for retailers and retailing. *Journal of Retailing and Consumer Services, 27*, 170–178.

Bell, D. R., Gallino, S. and Moreno, A. (2018). Offline showrooms in omnichannel retail: Demand and operational benefits. *Management Science, 64*(4), 1629–1651.

Bloemer, J. and de Ruyter, K. (1998). On the relationship between store image, store satisfaction and store loyalty. *European Journal of Marketing, 32*(5/6), 499–513.

Chi, T. (2018). Understanding Chinese consumer adoption of apparel mobile commerce: An extended TAM approach. *Journal of Retailing and Consumer Services, 44*, 274–284.

Cossío-Silva, F. J., Revilla-Camacho, M. Á., Vega-Vázquez, M. and Palacios-Florencio, B. (2016). Value co-creation and customer loyalty. *Journal of Business Research, 69*(5), 1621–1625.

Davis, F. D. (1989). Perceived usefulness, perceived ease of use, and user acceptance of information technology. *MIS Quarterly, 13*(3), 319–340.

Day, G. S. (1994). The capabilities of market-driven organizations. *Journal of Marketing*, 58(4), 37–52.

Dion, D. and Arnould, E. (2011). Retail luxury strategy: Assembling charisma through art and magic. *Journal of Retailing*, 87(4), 502–520.

Erevelles, S., Fukawa, N. and Swayne, L. (2016). Big data consumer analytics and the transformation of marketing. *Journal of Business Research*, 69(2), 897–904.

Feld, S., Frenzen, H., Krafft, M., Peters, K. and Verhoef, P. C. (2013). The effects of mailing design characteristics on direct mail campaign performance. *International Journal of Research in Marketing*, 30(2), 143–159.

Gandomi, A. and Haider, M. (2015). Beyond the hype: Big data concepts, methods, and analytics. *International Journal of Information Management*, 35(2), 137–144.

Giglio, S., Pantano, E., Bilotta, E. and Melewar, T. C. (2020). Branding luxury hotels: evidence from the analysis of consumers' "big" visual data on TripAdvisor. Journal of Business Research. doi: 10.1016/j.jbusres.2019.10.053.

Godey, B., Manthiou, A., Pederzoli, D., Rokka, J., Aiello, G., Donvito, R. and Singh, R. (2016). Social media marketing efforts of luxury brands: Influence on brand equity and consumer behavior. *Journal of Business Research*, 69(12), 5833–5841.

Grewal, D., Roggeveen, A. L., Runyan, R., Nordfaldt, J. and Lira, M. E. V. (2017). Retailing in today's world: Multiple channels and other strategic decisions affecting firm performance. *Journal of Retailing and Consumer Services*, 34(1), 261–263.

Hagberg, J., Sundstrom, M. and Egels-Zandén, N. (2016). The digitalization of retailing: An exploratory framework. *International Journal of Retail & Distribution Management*, 44(7), 694–712.

Hartman, K. B. and Spiro, R. L. (2005). Recapturing store image in customer-based store equity: A construct conceptualization. *Journal of Business Research*, 58(8), 1112–1120.

Humby, C., Hunt, T. and Phillips, T. (2008). *Scoring Points: How Tesco Is Winning Customer Loyalty*. Kogan Page Publishers, London.

Jocevski, M., Arvidsson, N., Miragliotta, G., Ghezzi, A. and Mangiaracina, R. (2019). Transitions towards omni-channel retailing strategies: A business model perspective. *International Journal of Retail & Distribution Management*, 47(2), 78–93.

Johnen, M. and Schnittka, O. (2019). When pushing back is good: The effectiveness of brand responses to social media complaints. *Journal of the Academy of Marketing Science*, 47, 858–878.

Kang, J. Y. M. (2018). Showrooming, webrooming, and user-generated content creation in the omnichannel era. *Journal of Internet Commerce*, 17(2), 145–169.

Kaushik, A. K. and Rahaman, Z. (2015). An alternative model of self-service retail technology adoption. *Journal of Services Marketing*, 29(5), 406–420.

Keller, K. L. (2003). Brand synthesis: The multidimensionality of brand knowledge. *Journal of Consumer Research*, 29(4), 595–600.

Keller, K. L. and Lehmann, D. R. (2006). Brands and branding: Research findings and future priorities. *Marketing Science*, 25(6), 740–759.

Kim, A. J. and Ko, E. (2012). Do social media marketing activities enhance customer equity? An empirical study of luxury fashion brand. *Journal of Business Research*, 65(10), 1480–1486.

Kim, A. J. and Johnson, K. K. (2016). Power of consumers using social media: Examining the influences of brand-related user-generated content on facebook. *Computers in Human Behavior*, 58, 98–108.

Ko, E., Costello, J. P. and Taylor, C. R. (2019). What is a luxury brand? A new definition and review of the literature. *Journal of Business Research*, 99, 405–413.

Kunz, W., Aksoy, L., Bart, Y., Heinonen, K., Kabadayi, S., Ordenes, F. V. and Theodoulidis, B. (2017). Customer engagement in a big data world. *Journal of Services Marketing*, 31(2), 161–171.

Marr, B. (2015). *Big Data: Using SMART Big Data, Analytics and Metrics to Make Better Decisions and Improve Performance*. John Wiley & Sons, Chichester, UK.

Martenson, R. (2007). Corporate brand image, satisfaction and store loyalty. *International Journal of Retail & Distribution Management*, 35(7), 544–555.

Motamarri, S., Akter, S. and Yanamandram, V. (2017). Does big data analytics influence frontline employees in services marketing? *Business Process Management Journal*, 23(3), 623–644.

Neslin, S. A., Grewal, D., Leghorn, R., Shankar, V., Teerling, M. L., Thomas, J. S. and Verhoef, P. C. (2006). Challenges and opportunities in multichannel customer management. *Journal of Service Research*, 9(2), 95–112.

Newell, S. and Marabelli, M. (2015). Strategic opportunities (and challenges) of algorithmic decision-making: A call for action on the long-term societal effects of "datification". *The Journal of Strategic Information Systems*, 24(1), 3–14.

Osman, M. Z. (1993). A conceptual model of retail image influences on loyalty patronage behavior. *International Review of Retailing, Distribution & Consumer Research*, 3(2), 133–148.

Pantano, E., Priporas, C. V. and Stylos, N. (2017a). "You will like it!"using open data to predict tourists' response to a tourist attraction. *Tourism Management*, 60, 430–438.

Pantano, E., Rese, A. and Baier, D. (2017b). Enhancing the online decision-making process by using augmented reality: A two country comparison of youth markets. *Journal of Retailing and Consumer Services*, 38, 81–95.

Pantano, E., Priporas, C. V. and Dennis, C. (2018). Retailer innovation push behaviour in the new service economy: A smart retailing model. *International Journal of Retail and Distribution Management*, 46(3), 264–282.

Pantano, E., Pizzi, G., Scarpi, D. and Dennis C. (2020). Competing during a pandemic? Retailers' ups and downs during the COVID-19 outbreak. *Journal of Business Research*, 116, 209–213.

Pantano, E. and Pizzi, G. (2020). Forecasting artificial intelligence on online customer assistance: Evidence from chatbot patents analysis. *Journal of Retailing and Consumer Services*, 55, art. 102096.

Parker, B. T. (2009). A comparison of brand personality and brand user-imagery congruence. *Journal of Consumer Marketing*, 26(3), 175–184.

Passavanti, R., Pantano, E., Priporas, C.-V. and Verteramo, S. (2020). The use of new technologies for corporate marketing communication in luxury retailing: Preliminary findings. *Qualitative Market Research: An International Journal*, 23(3), 503–521.

Peng, L., Cui, G., Chung, Y. and Li, C. (2019). A multi-facet item response theory approach to improve customer satisfaction using online product ratings. *Journal of the Academy of Marketing Science*, 47, 960–976.

Perry, A. (2016). Consumers' acceptance of smart virtual closets. *Journal of Retailing and Consumer Services*, 33, 171–177.

Piotrowicz, W. and Cuthbertson, R. (2014). Introduction to the special issue information technology in retail: Toward omnichannel retailing. *International Journal of Electronic Commerce*, 18(4), 5–16.

Corporate brand image   361

Poncin, I., Garnier, M., Mimoun, M. S. B. and Leclercq, T. (2017). Smart technologies and shopping experience: Are gamification interfaces effective? The case of the smartstore. *Technological Forecasting and Social Change*, *124*, 320–331.

Rapp, A., Baker, T. L., Bachrach, D. G., Ogilvie, J. and Beitelspacher, L. S. (2015). Perceived customer showrooming behavior and the effect on retail salesperson self-efficacy and performance. *Journal of Retailing*, *91*(2), 358–369.

Roberts, P. W. and Dowling, G. R. (2002). Corporate reputation and sustained superior financial performance. *Strategic Management Journal*, *23*, 1077–1093.

Rogers, E. M. (2017). *Diffusion of Innovations*, 4th Edition. Free Press, New York.

Roy, S. K., Balaji, M. S., Sadeque, S., Nguyen, B. and Melewar, T. C. (2017). Constituents and consequences of smart customer experience in retailing. *Technological Forecasting and Social Change*, *124*, 257–270.

Roy, S. K., Halaji, M. S., Quazi, A. and Quaddus, M. (2018). Predictors of customer acceptance of and resistance to smart technologies in the retail sector. *Journal of Retailing and Consumer Services*, *41*, 147–160.

Sheng, J., Amankwah-Amoah, J. and Wang, X. (2020). Technology in the 21st century: New challenges and opportunities. *Technological Forecasting and Social Change*, *143*, 321–335.

Sivarajah, U., Kamal, M. M., Irani, Z. and Weerakkody, V. (2017). Critical analysis of big data challenges and analytical methods. *Journal of Business Research*, *70*, 263–286.

Thaler, R. H. and Tucker, W. (2013). Smarter information, smarter consumers. *Harvard Business Review*, *91*(1), 45–54.

Vannucci, V. and Pantano E. (2019). Digital or human touchpoints? Insights from consumer-facing in-store services. *Information Technology and People*, *33*(1), 296–310.

Verhoef, P. C. and Leeflang, P. S. (2009). Understanding the marketing department's influence within the firm. *Journal of Marketing*, *73*(2), 14–37.

Verhoef, P. C. and Lemon, K. N. (2013). Successful customer value management: Key lessons and emerging trends. *European Management Journal*, *31*(1), 1–15.

Verhoef, P. C., Venkatesan, R., McAlister, L., Malthouse, E. C., Krafft, M. and Ganesan, S. (2010). CRM in data-rich multichannel retailing environments: A review and future research directions. *Journal of Interactive Marketing*, *24*(2), 121–137.

Verhoef, P. C., Kannan, P. K. and Inman, J. J. (2015). From multi-channel retailing to omni-channel retailing: Introduction to the special issue on multi-channel retailing. *Journal of Retailing*, *91*(2), 174–181.

Verhoef, P. C., Kooge, E. and Walk, N. (2016). *Creating Value with Big Data Analytics: Making Smarter Marketing Decisions*. Routledge, Oxon, UK.

Vrontis, D., Thrassou, A. and Amirkhanpour, M. (2017). B2C smart retailing: A consumer-docused value-based analysis of interactions and synergies. *Technological Forecasting and Social Change*, *124*, 271–282.

Wahyudi, A., Kuk, G. and Janssen, M. (2018). A process pattern model for tackling and improving big data quality. *Information Systems Frontiers*, *20*(3), 457–469.

Walasek, L., Bhatia, S. and Brown, G. D. A. (2017). Positional goods and the social rank hypothesis: Income inequality affects online chatter about high- and low-status brands on twitter. *Journal of Consumer Psychology*, *28*(1), 138–148.

Wamba, S. F., Gunasekaran, A., Akter, S., Ren, S. J. F., Dubey, R. and Childe, S. J. (2017). Big data analytics and firm performance: Effects of dynamic capabilities. *Journal of Business Research*, *70*, 356–365.

Wang, Y., Kung, L. and Byrd, T. A. (2018). Big data analytics: Understanding its capabilities and potential benefits for healthcare organizations. *Technological Forecasting and Social Change*, *126*, 3–13.

Wieland, A., Handfield, R. B. and Durach, C. F. (2016). Mapping the landscape of future research themes in supply chain management. *Journal of Business Logistics*, *37*(3), 205–212.

Willems, K., Brengman, M. and van de Sanden, S. (2017). In-store proximity marketing: Experimenting with digital point-of-sales communication. *International Journal of Retail & Distribution Management*, *45*(7/8), 910–927.

Part IV

Building a corporate brand reputation

14 Take a new turn

Relationships between corporate identity management and corporate reputation in a hospitality context

Pantea Foroudi, Reza Marvi, Javad Izadi, Mohammad M. Foroudi and Pouya Pirzadeh

Introduction

What are the main factors influencing corporate identity management? and what are the key factors that influence corporate reputation favourably? Results from our study show that philosophy, vision, mission and top management driving force positively influence corporate identity management.

Background

The role of corporate identity management on corporate reputation

Corporate identity management and corporate reputation are today's buzz words of marketing (Ageeva et al., 2019). In its search for continuous achievement in a marketplace, corporate identity management is characterised by philosophy (Ghodeswar, 2008), vision (Harris and De Chernatony, 2001), mission (Urde, 2003), corporate history (Konecnik and Go, 2008),, and top management driving force (Yin Wong and Merrilees, 2005)). Also, innovation adoption is related to corporate identity management and corporate reputation. With so-called ties, an increasing number of corporations seek to establish profound, purposeful and long connections with their customers (Akarsu et al. 2020).

What is the relationship between philosophy, vision and mission, corporate history, country-of-origin and top management driving force with corporate identity management? What is the connection between corporate identity management and corporate reputation? What is the connection between corporate identity management and innovation adoption? What is the relationship between innovation adoption and corporate reputation? A vast body of research, ranging from corporate identity management (Abdullah et al., 2013), philosophy (e.g. De Chernatony, 1999), vision (e.g. Harris and Chernatony, 2001), mission (e.g. Dermol and Širca, 2018), corporate history (e.g. Blombäck and Brunninge, 2013), country-of-origin (e.g. Barbarossa et al., 2018; Che-Ha et al. 2016), top management driving force (Melewar et al. 2018) and brand reputation (e.g. Foroudi, 2018), has attempted to recognise and describe how organisations, or the "individuals behind the corporate brands" (McAlexander et al., 2002, p. 50), can make deeper, more faithful associations. Though this chapter has introduced brand new relationships: the moderation effect of diversity between corporate history and corporate identity management, and the moderation effect of diversity between country-of-origin and corporate identity management. These relationships have not been examined before and it is the first time that they are pointed out in this article (Melewar et al., 2018).

This chapter contributes to the growing study on employee–company associations by suggesting the opinion of gender diversity and equality as the essential managerial foundation for the kind of profound, promised and purposeful associations which marketers are progressively seeking to establish with their customers.

In the next sections, corporate identity and reputation are portrayed in extant research to develop the employee–company personalities and articulate the research model, which provides hypotheses concerning the main consideration and outcomes of reputation in the market. We then offer approaches to test these hypotheses. Finally, the chapter ends with a discussion of the theoretical significance of employee–company reputation and its implications for companies seeking diverse employees.

Theoretical background

Brand identity plays an important role for companies to distinguish themselves from their opponents in the market (Black and Veloutsou, 2017). A brand identity aids firms in building an image with their internal and external stakeholders, resulting in adding value to the firm's reputation. Brand identity can be the first impression of a customer of a brand (Törmälä and Gyrd-Jones, 2017; Foroudi, 2019). Corporate identity has significant influence on customer purchase decisions (Godey et al., 2012).

Corporate identity is rooted in social identity theory. Social identity theory suggests customers seek their self-concept from being members of different social groups. According to Tajfel (1981), social identity is way in which the more an individual identifies the sameness with a specific group or product, the more it moves towards the sense of oneself with that group membership.

Corporate identity management

Leuthesser et al (2015) describes corporate identity as the manner by which corporate philosophy and strategy is shown to internal and external stakeholders (Foroudi, 2020) is via correspondence, behaviour and symbolism. Also, brand identity management refers to the qualities, features, attributes or traits of an organisation that are recognised to be key, long-lasting and specific through a company's guidelines, nature and positioning (Balmer, 2001; He and Balmer, 2005, 2009; Van Riel and Balmer, 1997). Foroudi et al. (2017) describe corporate identity management as the collection of explanations by which people on the outside know a company and through those explanations people can explain, recall and connect to that company. Fisher et al. (2016) stated that with a corporation's growing strategy, corporation identity will wane. Companies struggle for a differentiating identity to grab the attention of stakeholders to show they can do things that their competitors could not. Corporate identity and its aspects are formed by values and beliefs of all personnel of an organisation from top to bottom (King, 2017). In other words, corporate identity management is established fundamentally through inside connections, including staff at different levels (Koporcic and Halinen, 2018).

In order to become successful in the market, companies need to manage corporate identity (Melewar et al., 2017). Identity gives power to employees to connect with a corporation and they can find out their roles in connection with the corporation (; Fisher et al., 2016). Furthermore, another corporate identity definition is "organizational attributes that are central, enduring and distinct" (Skilton and Purdy, 2017, p. 13). Corporate identity management includes different features of a corporation, such as business strategy, corporate culture, behaviour and corporate design, all of which collaborate together and its consequence is distinguishing one company from another (Foroudi et al., 2017; Melewar et al., 2017). It is evident that corporate identity management is completely different from changing a company's name (Fetscherin and Usunier, 2012). Balmer et al. (1999) suggested that people might have various understandings of the identity of a company according to their sentiments, feelings and beliefs (Foroudi et al., 2018; Karaosmanoğlu et al., 2011). Hence, as corporate identity is seen by several people inside (Gioia et al., 2000; Rode and Vallaster, 2005; Simões et al., 2005) and outside (Shymko and Roulet, 2017; Sun et al., 2016) of a company, corporate identity management would be inevitable for each of those individuals (Karaosmanoğlu et al., 2010).

Corporation identity is formed by the founder's experiences and outlook on the world (Koporcic and Halinen, 2018). Corporate identity management was the origin of graphic design (Chajet and Schatman, 1993; Schmidt, 1995) where it was connected to elements affecting organisational graphics and imagery that are utilised to encompass and depict a company's characteristics to the outside world (Balmer, 1994; Pérez and Del Bosque, 2014).

Conceptual framework

Philosophy, vision, mission→corporate identity management

Philosophy is not only a strategic intention (Dermol and Širca, 2018); it can have a strong effect on employee motivation (Taylor et al., 2010). Corporate philosophy can impact on corporate identity (Tuna et al., 2016) and corporate branding (balmer et al., 2017). As a result, we can observe all corporate branding and corporate identity management activities through the corporate philosophy framework (Balmer, 2017). Also, philosophy is the basic, distinguishing and persevering idea, belief and feeling directing a business, which in turn is essential in preparing and writing a mission (Analoui and Karami, 2002; Wang, 2011). In other words, different execution and implementation outcomes rooted in philosophy and mission which finally benefit the company (Davis et al., 2007; Palmer and Short, 2008; Pearce and David, 1987, Wang, 2011). One of the usages of mission statements is informing and connecting stakeholders (Lin et al., 2018; Kemp and Dwyer, 2003). In addition, organisations obtain their meaning from the mission statement (Suvatjis et al., 2012). Besides, the mission statement has a critical role in attracting customers by emphasising company qualities and values (David, 2012)

The ultimate purpose of corporate philosophy is to express the essential values of a company, which are demonstrated in the vision and mission statement (Dessupoio et al., 2018). Corporate identity management is responsible for solidifying corporate philosophy (Abdullah et al., 2013). Thus, understanding corporate identity means realising the impact of cultural influence because values and vision are affected by cultural elements (Abdullah et al., 2013; Dessupoio et al, 2018). It is the duty of the vision statement to prepare and empower the present and potential employees (Ramus and Steger, 2000), customers (Cova and Pace, 2016) and stakeholders (Li et al., 2018) of the company. In the tourism industry, vision is not only the identity of every hotel, but also the implementing of unique management activities and service standards across the hotels (Edghiem and Mouzughi, 2018). Bart et al. (2001) stated employees enable putting into effect and carrying out the mission with deep interest. Essential messages are intended to connect a corporation with the external environment containing values and mission of the organisation (e.g. through websites, yearly reports) (Moriuchi and Takahashi, 2018).

Van Riel (1995) suggested that leading corporate communications should be directed by the basic philosophy of "directing the company's communications policies from within the corporate strategy-corporate identity-corporate image triangle" (p. 19). Vision statement is the main guidance of all company's exercises (Kohles et al., 2012; Locke et al., 1991). Also, if shared values and prescriptive mental models illustrate in a formal manner, it can be named vision statements that reveal a perfect future state (House, 1977; Kohles et al., 2012; Shipman et al., 2010; Strange and Mumford, 2002, 2005). Furthermore, vision statement is associated with the company's corporate identity management (Maitlis and Sonenshein, 2010). Vision and mission are referred to as the organisation's identity (Kohles et al., 2012) by all top managers. Corporate identity, at a strategic level, establishes the organisation's quality and uniqueness mirrored in its philosophy, mission and values (He et al., 2013; Simões et al., 2017). However, there is a sufficient body of evidence that only writing a mission statement is inadequate (Kemp and Dwyer, 2003). Desmidt and Prinzie (2009) highlighted the significance of a written mission statement as a tool inside an organisation. Company mission and organisational values are a crucial factor of giving strength to inner awareness of corporate identity management and its external broadcast (Chong, 2007; Dermol and Širca, 2018). As discussed above, we propose the following hypothesis:

H1: Philosophy, mission and vision positively influence corporate identity management.

Take a new turn 369

Moderation effect of diversity on philosophy, mission and vision→corporate identity management

Diversity has been a controversial subject for management scholars and managers at all levels (Tasheva and Hillman, 2018, Gehman and Grimes, 2017). In terms of demography, although diversity has wide outcomes both for staff and organisations, managing that diversity is not easily attainable (Chung et al., 2015). Companies take different strategic decisions towards better managing their increasingly diverse workforce (Gröschl, 2011). Researchers have concentrated on how to conduct teams and organisations that are diverse in terms of gender (Hogg et al., 2012). To differ between diversity management positions and the HR function, and to shape corporate identity that develops from top-level management to all operational and managerial levels is of great importance (Gröschl, 2011). All factors of corporation life such as the company's culture, philosophy, vision and mission form corporate identity (Martins and Parsons, 2007). Combining elements like diversity in philosophy, vision and mission statement give the minority members of the organisation better feeling (Cole and Salimath, 2013). So, as discussed above we propose the following hypothesis:

> H1a: Gender diversity as a moderator has an effect on philosophy, mission, vision and corporate identity management.

Corporate history→corporate identity management

When employees together create a company's history, corporate identity would be shaped and maintained (Anteby and Molnar, 2012). Organisational memory is rooted in corporate history (Levitt et al., 1988; Mena et al., 2016; Rowlinson et al., 2014; Schrempf-Stirling et al., 2016). For instance, for universities the establisher is the one who has influence on the university's identity (Melewar, 2003, 2016). History can be a competitive advantage that a company is able to use and refer to (Schrempf-Stirling et al., 2016). Realising the relation between corporate identity and corporate history is of paramount importance (Blombäck and Brunninge, 2013). Researchers (e.g., Mena et al., 2016; Rowlinson et al., 2014) believe that all founded corporation have a history (Urde et al., 2015). On the other hand, some companies' history is a prominent part of their identity and they employ it as a constituent of defined corporate heritage (Urde et al., 2015). In this regard, communicating company history appears to grow in popularity.

Ravasi et al. (2018) studied how corporate history legitimises the day-to-day work of a company, such as corporate identity. History is one aspect that can have influence on identity in the marketing academic literature, and it seems to repeatedly contributes to corporate identity and branding (Blombäck and Brunninge, 2009, 2013; Melewar, 2003; Moingeon and Ramanantsoa, 1997). Simultaneously, various scholars have discussed that corporate identity management is excessively internalised in organisation history and culture can be used as

370   *Foroudi, Marvi, Izadi, Foroudi and Pirzadeh*

a tool (Blombäck and Brunninge, 2009). Identity has several aspects that one of them is history (Micelotta and Raynard, 2011).

The story of corporation can be conveyed in a way that preserves corporate history and corporate identity forever (Essamri et al., 2018). Natural uniqueness and imitation are two reasons for applying a corporation's history to describe identity (Barney, 1991). Scholars uncovered how building blocks of history are being used to establish corporate identity and the way that corporate identity can be conveyed to stakeholders outside of the company (Blombäck and Brunninge, 2013; Lundström, 2006; Urde et al., 2007). Furthermore, company founders become a constitutional part of corporate identity management (Fan et al., 2018). Thus, corporation identity could connect powerfully and sensitively with generations to come, and also this generation can clearly join in a company's history (Hall, 2004).

H2: Corporate history positively influences corporate identity management.

Moderation effect of diversity between corporate history→corporate identity management

For a long time, diversity and equality have been a controversial subject that made different governments pass laws in favour of diversity in the workplace, and persuading organisations in the public sector to show impartiality and clarity both in the industry and recruitment processes (Senyucel and Phillpott, 2011). By these laws, different people should have access equally to public services and fairly have the chance to be employed and go up the organisation ladder apart from any bias. This ethical discussion is especially identified with public service, whereby the company as a privately based business responsible for enhancing the quality of life, looking for supporting working force (Senyucel and Phillpott, 2011).

Establishing equality policies that provide sufficient foundation to make sure legal compliance in companies is provided, so numerous organisations begin to offer an explanation to this moral discussion (Cornelius et al., 2001; Senyucel et al., 2011). A Company might improve its attraction to hire talented people from labour market by this beneficence (Cox and Blake, 1991; Senyucel and Phillpott, 2011). Thus, lower absence rates (Diestel et al., 2014), higher retention (Kulik et al., 2016), expanded levels of morale (Fast et al., 2014) and effective responsibility (Kraimer et al., 2012) might be seen in the corporation. As discussed above we propose the following hypothesis:

H2a: Gender Diversity as a moderator has an effect between corporate history and corporate identity management.

Country-of-origin→corporate identity management

Country-of-origin is explained as the country to which a customer relates a specific product or brand as its source (Roth and Diamantopoulos, 2009; Kimet al.,

Take a new turn 371

2013). In other resources, the COO is defined as "a set of strengths and weaknesses related to the country-of-origin that incorporates or subtracts the value supplied by a brand or service to the manufacturer and/or its clients" (García-Gallego and Chamorro Mera, p. 17). Also, we can define COO as "the overall perception consumers form of products from a particular country, based on their prior perceptions of the country's production and marketing strengths and weaknesses" (Roth and Romeo, 1992, p. 480). The country-of-origin is used as an external signal by consumers to verify quality and features of a product (Maruyama and Wu, 2014). COO's aspects can affect quality of products and service, which are assessed by consumers. This influence can change purchase intention (Kim et al., 2017; Pharr, 2005).

Consumers' assessment of a product and their perceptions will be satisfied by COO as an external informational key (Kim et al., 2017). The fact is that numerous companies are failing to keep all or a portion of their local corporate identity because of constant changes and mergers. García-Gallego and Chamorro Mera (2017) suggested that with any economic and financial decision to incorporate with former rivals, there is an important thing called marketing decision which must be made: to keep the origins of brands or to let them be lost. An extensive factor in corporate identity management is the country-of-origin which impacts different aspects of a product such as consumer perceptions, quality perceptions, reliability differences and performance (Melewar, 2003; Veloutsou and Taylor, 2012). A COO is a powerful symbol and can considerably help the corporate identity management and also in the minds of consumers, the product's image (Aiello et al., 2008; Foroudi et al., 2016a). In the world of tourism, there is a need for countries to promote their position to attract more customers and several are modifying the brands of places in the minds of main stakeholders to develop special and different identities (Foroudi et al., 2016; Middleton and Clarke, 2012; Kumar, 2014).

H3: Country-of-origin positively influences corporate identity management.

Moderation effect of diversity on the country-of-origin→corporate identity management

In the preceding years, corporations have realised the importance of their employees' diversity. For instance, problem-solving (Nishii, 2013), innovation (King et al., 2011) and creativity (Godart et al., 2015) are some benefits of diversity for each firm. A diverse team can convey different and varied practices, opinions and implicit knowledge to the corporation (Bowen et al., 2003; Senyucel and Phillpott, 2011). Besides, diversity assures stakeholders that the management board is performing their duty appropriately (Wahid, 2018). Also, diversity has an impact on the products' features as well due to cultural differences (Wyer Jr., 2011). Immigrants with racial diversity have appeared in different countries (Kalargyrou and Costen, 2017). As diversity is not essentially noticeable, it can be difficult to appreciate. Manoharan and Singal (2017) stated that diversity is

372 Foroudi, Marvi, Izadi, Foroudi and Pirzadeh

the perception about being different from peers. Bowen and Blackmon (2003) stated that diversity is a hidden attribute as it is not easily understandable. Senyucel (2011) suggested that sexual diversity is significant for an organisation due to its effect on effectiveness. When members of a team rival for promotion, generosity and amiability have to be characters in gender-diverse groups because philanthropy, and assistance are the human qualities that these groups very much needed (Apesteguia et al., 2012; Barclay, 2010; Farrelly, 2011; Lee et al., 2018; Ortmann and Tichy, 1999; Williams and Polman, 2014). Furthermore, during working in mixed groups in terms of gender, members of a team prevent others from saying or doing things that may seem offensive and aggressive (e.g., Hirschfeld et al., 2005; Myaskovsky et al., 2005). Results show that people in groups which are gender-diverse do not greatly like to experience social stress and hostility among members in the workplace developing from disputes (Lee et al., 2018). As discussed above, we propose the following hypothesis:

> H3a: Gender diversity as a moderator has an effect on country-of-origin and corporate identity management.

Top management driving force→corporate identity management

The main responsibility of senior managers is communicating inside and outside of a company (Madera et al., 2014). On the basis of their organisational power and having knowledge to work, they know how to change the company in the right way, and according to research results, the role of top management in forming corporate identity is undeniable (He, 2012). Expressing the corporation's main idea to the stakeholders (internal and external) is the approach of senior management that builds foundation of top management driving force (Hatch and Schultz, 1997; Melewar et al., 2003; 2018). For instance, a university's main strategy is conveyed from top executives to its stakeholders and top executives are highly associated with the environment and take each opportunity to emphasise the university's main values publicly (Melewar et al., 2018). On the other hand, investors draw more attention to companies whose board of directors consist of women. Moreover, it gives a good signal to society and stakeholders that they are perfect leaders and know how to deal with different groups in an organisation (Cumming et al., 2015). In relation to top management, hotel managers use corporate identity to identify their rivals who want to present a threat against them (Mohammed et al., 2014).

The top management has a critical role in setting attitudes, values, and ideas, which are expressed in administrative policies impacting corporate identity management (Suvatjis et al., 2012). The constant management of senior executives could guarantee that front staff perceive corporate identity management, acknowledge corporate values, create a high level of belief and certainty within the corporation, and subsequently improve positive thinking (Terglav et al., 2016; Vallaster and de Chernatony, 2006). Aaker and Joachimsthaler (2000) suggested that organisational role models are the leading technique to communicate corporate identity management. Studies on internal branding demonstrate that if the process is backed by top executives' comments and deeds, staff have motivation and try their best. Hence corporate internal changes must begin at the top with the CEO and top managers and transfer to the lower organisational level (Burmann and Zeplin, 2005; Terglav et al., 2016). Executives have to highlight part of the corporate identity management that cannot be realised easily, such as a corporation's core values (Terglav et al., 2016). As discussed above we propose the following hypothesis:

H4: Top management driving force positively influences corporate identity management.

Moderation effect of Diversity between Top Management Driving Force→Corporate Identity Management

corporations should provide an organisation that value different cultures and ensure people can work there with ease (Madera et al., 2013). Besides, companies seem to assign women to the board of directors or CEO when they encounter a ratio of women outsmarting men (Bugeja et al., 2012). Konrad et al. (1995) revealed that diversity and well-behaved individuals in different manners for the purpose of behaving correctly as identity-conscious structures. In the hospitality industry, employment should be based on identity-conscious practices by which a hotel effectively employs from various nations and/or provides English language classes for chosen employees. Konrad and Linnehan (1995) argued identity-conscious actions are normally backed by Asians as they believe that such acts support them to conquer negative racial stereotypes (being uncommunicative and passive) which prevent them from promotion. Black employees support identity conscious to identity blind when appraising their future managers (Highhouse et al., 1999).

There has been great progress in the hotel industry which offers considerable opportunity to women to be in higher positions (Marco, 2012). By diversity, not only the board of directors can be easily controlled but also the interests of shareholders will be preserved (Cumming et al., 2015). In reference to effectiveness, identity conscious diversity programmes like affirmative action plans (Leslie et al., 2014), diversity committees and workforces (Baum et al., 2016), diversity managers (Kong et al., 2018), diversity training (Reynolds et al., 2014), diversity evaluations for managers (Tatli, 2011), networking programmes (Madera et al., 2013), and mentoring programmes (Kim et al., 2015) are effective in increasing management diversity. Some diversity management methods, which try to be identity-conscious, are connected to more powerful managers' opposition (Linnehan and Konrad, 1999). Working in an atmosphere with "different cultures has been a very significant aspect of diversity in countries which welcome immigrants" (Shen et al., 2009, p. 235). Because of that, identity-conscious actions could contribute to corporations to a great degree drawing attention, expand and retain diverse employees (Manoharan et al., 2014). As discussed above we propose the following hypothesis:

374 *Foroudi, Marvi, Izadi, Foroudi and Pirzadeh*

H4a: Gender diversity as a moderator has an effect between top management driving force and corporate identity management.

Corporate identity management→corporate reputation

Corporation reputation is an instant image of a brand relying on the collective different pictures held by both its internal and external stakeholders over the long term (Foroudi et al., 2018; Fombrun, 1995). Corporate reputation is explained as a perception of an organisation in the minds of present and future stakeholders (Koporcic and Halinen, 2018). Past and present deeds of a company have an effect on corporate reputation (Akdeniz et al., 2013). It may be a product signal that buyers repeatedly utilise to deal with ambiguity when they want to make a decision (Akdeniz et al., 2013; Baek et al., 2010; Dodds et al., 1991; Gammoh et al., 2006; Washburn et al., 2004).

Understanding the relationship between the chief executive officer and corporate reputation is important. While reputation is not a tangible asset for the company, it can result in tangible benefits (Love et al., 2017, Zavyalova et al., 2016). Researchers (Li et al., 2015; Su et al., 2015; Weigelt and Shittu, 2016) have found that customers prefer to buy a product/service from a particular corporation when the corporation reputation is perceived to be high (Sun, 2014). As individuals choose products/services that suit them, corporate reputation has an impact on the brand image (Cretu and Brodie, 2003) transferred by brand signature (Foroudi et al., 2017, 2018). Additionally, employee recruitment and retention depend on corporate reputation (Kuo and Kalargyrou, 2014). Corporation reputation results in employee self-esteem (Akgunduz, 2015), employee job satisfaction (Song et al., 2015) and employee emotional commitment (Tanford, 2013). Individuals consciously measure the corporate reputation when assessing an organisation; though, they try to base their assessments on the emotional appeal that a corporation holds for them (Karaosmanoğlu et al., 2011).

Corporate identity management is a crucial means to impact corporate reputation (Balmer, 2008; Flint et al., 2018). However, there is a similarly strong understanding that corporate identity and corporate reputation are interconnected (Aaker, 2004; Fombrun and Van Riel, 2004; Kapferer, 2012; Roper and Fill, 2012; Urde et al., 2016). Despite these relationships, corporate reputation and identity are distinctive (Balmer, 2010). While corporate reputation refers to the external stakeholder perception (Xie et al., 2015), corporate identity is based on the employee (Urde et al., 2016). An organisation employs its reputation to modify its identity for the purpose of legitimising its existence (Podnar and Golob, 2017). This process is called adaptation and flows from identity to reputation (Podnar and Golob, 2017). Accepting feedback on reputation is necessary for corporate identity management (Podnar and Golob, 2017). When it is lacking, corporate top management are "flying blind" (Gray and Balmer, 1998, p. 700). Reputation provides information that leads to the company's identity, process, activities and communications. As discussed above, reputation is characterised through retention and adaption (Podnar et al., 2017). As discussed above, we propose the following hypothesis:

H5: Corporate identity management positively influences corporate reputation.

Corporate identity management→innovation adoption→corporate reputation

Innovation plays an important role in many developed and developing countries. Innovation is conceptualised as an approach to making a proper, flexible business model, and plain, which can assist the benefits of consumers or managers in a competitive marketplace (Foroudi et al., 2016), makes firms distinguishable (Gupta and Malhotra, 2013) and produces better products/services (Foroudi et al., 2016). The results of Adner and Kapoor's (2010) research revealed that positive innovations are highly context-specific and should be strategic to enable the smooth functioning of actors contributing to the brand. Adopting these new innovations not only can result in high uncertainty for top managers (De Massis et al., 2015) but is also a difficult process (Holt and Daspit, 2015). Innovation adoption is implementation of new products/services in an organisation (De Massis et al., 2015). Through innovation adoption, consumers assess new products based on their relative advantages, compatibility and complexity (Rogers, 1962, 2003; Sääksjärvi and Samiee, 2011; Sarmah et al., 2017). Innovation enables firms to be distinguishable from their opponents in a market (Gupta and Malhotra, 2013).

Having a proper innovation strategy in a company can result in corporate identity enhancement (Beverland et al., 2010). The results of Micheli et al. (2018) revealed that long-term thinking is more effective than short-term thinking styles for supporting innovation strategy. Additionally, his results showed that innovation implementation should be in the shade of corporate identity. Findings of Amable et al. (2016) suggested that each innovation has a value, and this value will change with corporate identity management.

Different studies show that reputation score is dependent on some factors such as innovation adoption (Abratt and Kleyn, 2012; Himme and Fischer, 2014). Gaining such invaluable reputation is a very daunting task for firms (Brexendorf and Keller, 2017). Consumers are able to convey the attempt to build reputation for innovation to a new product/service (Brexendorf et al., 2015). Bearden and Shimp (1982) suggested that manufacturer reputation and quality improvement help to decrease the risk. As discussed, we propose the following hypothesis:

H6a: Corporate identity management positively influences innovation adoption.

H6b: Innovation adoption positively influences corporate reputation.

Methodology

Sampling and survey administration

This study used offline surveys in Tehran, Iran from small- and medium-sized hotels as there is no large hotel in Iran. Iran is a country which presents cultural glory and a varied, seductive scenery; though, Iran is a destination with low number of tourists and is an under-researched country in the context of place branding. Iran has an affluent cultural and historical background with a diverse climate and environment, which does not participate in the global market (Foroudi et al., 2016); thus, Iran offers tremendous possibilities for observation of the growth of the country's tourism industry from the perspective of place branding. Investigating place branding activities in Iran therefore emphasises the challenges untouched by indigenous managers and policy makers. The hospitality industry is growing its operations in the global market (Kim et al., 2017) and according to Foroudi et al. (2016), Iran desires to advance branding policies that allow them to answer diverse marketplace segments.

For data collection, we employed two research assistants. We had eight researchers in a similar field examine the item measurements for reliability. The items were initially in the English language. We have translated the questionnaire into Persian. To inspect the phraseology and terms, Ageeva et al. (2019) and Harpaz et al. (2002) suggested translation of the items and translation of the transcriptions in a non-mechanical way and we discussed "each question and the alternatives in a small group of persons fluent in both languages…until an agreement was reached" (p. 236). As a result, there were some alterations to improve the survey respondents' understanding. We also examined the dimensionality, acceptance level, validity and reliability of the measurement among postgraduate hospitality management programmes in Iran (89) to avoid employing hotels which might take part in this research (Table 14.1). After the validation process, 332 valid questionnaires were conducted offline over five months in 2017 from medium-sized hotels (56.9%) and small-sized hotels (43.1%). Of the 332 participants, 192 were female with an average age of 45 to 54 years (34.6%), and 35 to 44 years old (32.5%) and 51.8% were postgraduate and 36.4% were undergraduate. Table 14.1 illustrates 43.4% were working as middle managers and senior management (33.1%).

The survey measures

The survey was divided into two sections. The first section contained measures based on previous research. There were two main constructs (i) corporate identity management which was measured via six items (Cole and Bruch, 2006; Gioia and Thomas, 1996) and (ii) corporate reputation with seven item measurements (Foroudi, 2019; Foroudi et al., 2014, 2016). Based on the contexts, four antecedents for corporate identity management were recognised for this study as (i) philosophy, vision and mission (Sinkula et al., 1997; Baker and Sinkula, 1999; Simoes et al., 2005) (ii) corporate history (Melewar et al., 2003, 2018),

Table 14.1 The main scale dimensions, item sources and reliability measures for each construct

Construct and item	Factor loading	Mean	Std.D	Cronbach's alpha
Corporate identity @ .913	Cole and Bruch (2006); Gioia and Thomas (1996)			
The top management team has a strong sense of the hotel's history.	0.843	5.2801	1.29716	Removed – The top management team members do not have a well-defined set of goals or objectives for the hotel. (R)
All employees have sense of pride in the Hotel's goals and missions.	0.844	5.2169	1.35127	
All employees feel that the hotel has carved out a significant place in the community.	0.816	5.4759	1.23495	All employees are knowledgeable about the hotel's history and traditions.
All employees identify themselves strongly with the hotel.	0.842	5.1596	1.39327	
Philosophy, mission and value @ .865	Sinkula et al. (1997); Baker and Sinkula (1999); Simoes et al. (2005)			
All employees are committed to achieving the company's goals in this hotel.	0.684	5.4910	1.16465	Removed – Employees view themselves as partners in charting the direction of the hotel unit.
This Hotel has a clear concept of who we are and where we are going.	0.776	5.7500	1.17662	We do not have a well-defined mission. (R)
The company's values and mission are regularly communicated to employees.	0.771	5.6235	1.18135	Managers periodically discuss corporate mission and values.
Senior management shares the corporate mission with employees.	0.776	5.9578	1.14164	All employees are aware of the relevant values (norms about what is important, how to behave and appropriate attitudes).
Corporate history @ .909	Melewar et al. (2003, 2018)			
The hotel's core values are established by its history.	0.865	5.4458	1.35756	Removed – The character of the founder(s) has formed the building blocks of the core values.
I like the hotel's corporate history.	0.947	5.7319	1.22307	
The hotel's corporate history is aligned with the hotel's corporate identity.	0.926	5.6898	1.26186	
Country-of-Origin @ .895	Melewar et al. (2003, 2018)			
The values of the hotel's home country are one of the determinants of what the hotel stands for.	0.886	5.6235	1.30989	

(Continued)

378 Foroudi, Marvi, Izadi, Foroudi and Pirzadeh

Table 14.1 (Continued)

Construct and item	Factor loading	Mean	Std.D	Cronbach's alpha
The hotel's country-of-origin imagery is the picture, reputation and the stereotype that consumers attach to its products and services.	0.918	5.6867	1.28367	
The hotel's country-of-origin has positive influence on the hotel's brand.	0.910	5.3705	1.39640	
Top management driving force @ .859	Balmer and Stotvig (1997); Melewar (2003); Melewar and Saunders (1998); Olins (1990)			
The top manager of our hotel is not pushing the corporate identity topic in our Hotel at all. (R)	0.799	5.9157	1.06813	Removed – The top manager of our hotel regularly gives out new tasks saying the use of our identity guidelines have to be considered as one element of corporate identity management.
The top manager of our hotel is very passionate when it comes to identity of our company.	0.858	5.8163	1.13152	
Our hotel top managers consider brand identity to be important for hotel communication activities.	0.815	5.5934	1.26073	
Corporate reputation @ .960	Foroudi et al. (2014, 2016, 2019)			
I have a good feeling about the hotel.	0.834	5.7410	1.22625	Removed – The hotel offers products and services that are good value for money. The hotel has excellent leadership. The hotel is an environmentally responsible hotel.
I admire and respect the hotel.	0.924	5.9608	1.23701	
I trust the hotel.	0.923	5.9759	1.23372	
The hotel is well managed.	0.904	5.9518	1.23302	
Diversity @ .917	Carters and Jennings (2004); Sawyerr et al. (2005)			
I feel everyone is treated fairly, regardless of gender.	0.883	5.3163	1.35061	Removed – The hotel is committed to creating an environment where diversity is celebrated. I feel everyone is treated fairly, regardless of religion or belief. I feel everyone is treated fairly, regardless of sexual orientation. I feel everyone is treated fairly, regardless of marital status. I feel everyone is treated fairly, regardless of nationality.
I feel everyone is treated fairly, regardless of disability.	0.776	5.4789	1.27117	
I feel everyone is treated fairly, regardless of ethnic origin.	0.903	5.4608	1.16662	
I feel everyone is treated fairly, regardless of age.	0.919	5.4307	1.24785	

(Continued)

Take a new turn 379

Table 14.1 (Continued)

Construct and item	Factor loading	Mean	Std.D	Cronbach's alpha
Innovation adoption @ .912	Avlonitis et al. (1994); Jaworski and Kohli (1993); Pallister and Foxall (1998); Tang (1999); Wang and Ahmed (2004)			
If our competitor adopts an important innovation, our hotel reacts immediately by adopting the innovation too.	0.872	4.9910	1.33619	Removed – We are usually one of the last hotels in our industry sector to accept something new.
We are suspicious of new inventions and new ways of thinking.	0.769	5.1928	1.39882	
We are reluctant about adopting new ways of doing things until we see them working for hotels around us.	0.903	4.9880	1.40129	
We do consider new innovations even before other hotels are using them.	0.895	5.0090	1.34071	

country-of-origin (Melewar et al., 2003, 2018) and top management driving force (Balmer and Stotvig, 1997; Melewar, 2003; Melewar and Saunders, 1998; Olins, 1990). Diversity was measured as a moderator with nine items based on a study by Melewar et al. (2018). Also, this study identifies innovation adoption as an outcome of corporate identity management and antecedents of corporate reputation. Innovation adoption was examined based on previous studies (Avlonitis

Table 14.2 Demographic characteristics

Characteristics	Relative frequency (%)	Frequency			
Size of the company			Education		
Small	143	43_1	PhD	24	7.2
Medium	189	56_9	Postgraduate	172	51_8
Gender			Undergraduate	121	36_4
Male	140	42_2	Pre university	15	4_5
Female	192	57_8	Position		
Age			Chief Executive	24	7_2
Under 25	1	_3	Senior Management	110	33_1
25–34	45	13_6	Middle Management	144	43_4
35–44	108	32_5	Junior Management	54	16_3
45–54	115	34_6			
55–64	57	17_2			
65 and over	6	1_8			

380 *Foroudi, Marvi, Izadi, Foroudi and Pirzadeh*

et al., 1994; Jaworski and Kohli, 1993; Pallister and Foxall, 1998; Tang, 1999; Wang and Ahmed, 2004). The second section was comprised of questions on the demographics of the sample (e.g., education, age, gender etc.). We used a 7-point Likert-type scale to measure the model's constructs.

Data analysis

We employed Anderson and Gerbing (1988) and Hair et al.'s (2006) two-stage approach using structural-equation-modelling based on their suggestions. In the first stage, we examined the measurement-model by employing AMOS24 which is used to categorise the causal-relationships between the observed variables and the unobserved variables to evaluate Cronbach's α, composite reliability and convergent and discriminant validity of the model. The outcome displays a high degree of reliability (0.859 > 0.70) (De Vaus, 2002; Hair et al., 2006). The composite reliability was recommended to be greater than 0.7 (Hair et al., 2006). We also used discriminant and convergent validity. Table 14.3 demonstrates that the outcome of average variance extracted (0.619 to 0.859 > 0.5) is greater than the squared correlation estimates, which supports discriminant validity (Fornell and Larcker, 1981; Hair et al., 2006). The results illustrate the good rule of thumb and adequate convergent validity. The correlation matrix for the constructs is illustrated in Table 14.3.

According to researchers (Lambert and Harrington, 1990; Malhotra et al., 2006), we used non-response-bias by measuring the difference through the Mann-Whitney U-test among 50 early and 50 late participants. The results presented that significance value in any variable is equal to or not less than a 0.5 probability value that is insignificant. So, there was no statistically major difference among early and late participants. So, there was non-response bias in this research.

The current research used the common method-variances which refer to "possibility arises from the method variance to inflate the observed correlations between the variables artifactually, are the frequently mentioned concern of researchers in empirical study" (Zhang and Chen, 2008, p. 245). We used Harman's one-factor examination to inspect the common-latent-factor and common-method-bias and chi-square difference among the primary and fully constrained model by the suggestions of previous studies (Harman, 1976; Lindell and Whitney, 2001; Malhotra et al., 2006). The results suggested that two models are statistically different and share a variance. Additionally, we used four categorisation sources of common method variances CMVs. Hereafter, the extent of common-method-variance in this research was mostly involving measurement context effects.

In the second stage, we assessed the structural model (Tabachnick et al., 2007) which estimates the expected covariance and causal linear relationship between the independent and dependent latent variables. The structural model fit was examined throughout goodness-of-fit to measure how well the model fits with its data. The comparative fit index (CFI) (0.942 > 0.90 designates good fit) and the root-mean-squared-approximation-of-error (RMSEA) (0.066 < 0.08

Table 14.3 Corporate reputation

	CR	AVE	MSV	ASV	Coiporatc reputation	Coiporatc identity	Philosophy, mission and values	Coiporatc history	Top management driving force	Country-of-Origin	Innovation adoption
Corporate reputation	0.960	0.859	0.277	0.102	0.927						
Corporate identity	0.914	0.728	0.288	0.136	0.387	0.854					
Philosophy, mission and values	0.866	0.619	0.293	0.168	0.526	0.537	0.787				
Corporate history	0.917	0.787	0.035	0.022	0.093	0.183	0.171	0.887			
Top management driving force	0.865	0.681	0.293	0.120	0.302	0.421	0.541	0.188	0.825		
Country-of-Origin	0.897	0.745	0.018	0.011	0.098	0.134	0.056	0.135	0.112	0.863	
Innovation adoption	0.917	0.738	0.147	0.079	0.280	0.384	0.347	0.085	0.337	0.064	0.859

382 Foroudi, Marvi, Izadi, Foroudi and Pirzadeh

indicates acceptable fit) are an incremental-index that assesses the fit of a model with the null baseline model. The incremental fit index (IFI), Tucker-Lewis-index (TLI) and the normed-fit-index (NFI) were 0.943, 0.935 and 0.907, respectively. The results were greater than the recommended threshold of 0.90; thus, the results identified the unidimensionality of the item measuremnts (Anderson and Gerbing, 1988; Hair et al., 2006).

The finding demonstrated that the t-values and structural-path-coefficients for each constructs' association and with squared-multiple-correlations (R2) for each endogenous construct. H1 proposed the direct effect of philosophy, vision and mission on corporate identity management (H1: $\beta = 0.579$, t = 6.359) was statistically supported. With regard to research Hypothesis 2 (corporate history -> corporate identity management) and Hypothesis 3 (country-of-origin -> corporate identity management), the unexpected results show the relationship between the constructs ($\beta = 0.064$, t = 1.267, p = 0.205; $\beta = 0.089$, t = 1.622, p = 0.105, respectively) were non-significant. H4 addresses the impact of top management driving force on corporate identity management (H3: $\beta = 0.239$, t = 2.579) and a significant relationship was confirmed. The findings signify that the relationship between corporate identity management and corporate reputation (H5) and innovation adoption (H6) were significant ($\beta = 0.311$, t = 5.761; $\beta = 0.417$, t = 6.927, respectively). The result of H7 shows the relationship between innovation adoption and corporate reputation ($\beta = 0.120$, t = 2.466) was significant.

To examine the moderation impact of diversity between philosophy, vision and mission (H1a), corporate history (H2a), country-of-origin (H3a) and top management driving force (H4a), we use interaction moderations (Figure 14.1). The results show that diversity strengthens the positive relationship between philosophy, vision, mission and corporate identity management (H1a). Diversity dampens the positive relationship between corporate history (H2a), country-of-origin (H3a) and corporate identity management. In addition, the results illustrated that diversity dampens the negative relationship between top management driving force and corporate identity management (H4a).

Discussion

This chapter introduces the concept of corporate identity management, defined as the qualities, features, attributes or traits of an organisation that are recognised to be key, long-lasting and specific through a company's guidelines, nature and positioning (Balmer, 2001; He and Balmer, 2005; 2009; ; Van Riel and Balmer, 1997). Irrespective of the industry which a company is involved in or what type of companies they are competing with, it is crucial that top management determine corporate identity management to show staff, customers and stakeholders what the corporation's nature is. Based on the research gap which has been identified by academic writers (Anteby and Molnar, 2012; Garrett et al., 2017; Kohles et al., 2012, Suvatjis et al., 2012), this chapter has initiated a study on corporate identity management and elements which have an effect on it.

Take a new turn 383

Diversity strengthens the positive relationship between Philosophy, Vision, Mission and Corporate Identity Management.

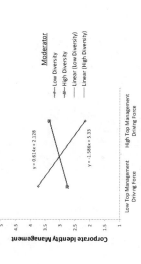

Diversity dampens the positive relationship between Corporate History and Corporate Identity Management.

Diversity dampens the positive relationship between Country-of-Origin and Corporate Identity Management.

Diversity dampens the negative relationship between Top Management Driving Force and Corporate Identity Management.

Figure 14.1 The research conceptual model.

Table 14.4 Results of hypothesis testing

Hypothesis				Estimate	S.E.	C.R.	P	Results
H1	Philosophy, vision and values	->	Corporate identity management	0.579	0.091	6.359	***	Accepted
H2	Corporate history			0.064	0.050	1.267	0.205	Rejected
H3	Country -of-origin			0.089	0.055	1.622	0.105	Rejected
H4	Top management driving force			0.239	0.093	2.579	0.010	Accepted
H5	Corporate identity management	->	Corporate reputation	0.311	0.054	5.761	***	Accepted
H6	Corporate identity management	->	Innovation adoption	0.417	0.060	6.527	***	Accepted
H7	Innovation adoption	->	Corporate reputation	0.120	0.049	2..466	0.014	Accepted

*** $p < 0.001$. *Notes*: Path = Influence of independent variable on dependent variable; β = Standardised regression coefficient; S.E. = Standard error; p = Level of significance.

The results of the research demonstrate that corporate identity management based on the research model consists of two factors, philosophy, vision and mission and top management driving force. Philosophy, vision and mission show the direction of the corporation, where it comes from, what it is doing and where it is going. Top management driving force reveals the power of top management in communication with internal and external stakeholders. This issue builds the basis of top management (Hatch et al., 1997; Melewar et al., 2003, 2018). This study showed that successful corporate identity management is in the hands of top managers and their decisions; as they decide what philosophy, vision and mission there should be, how to communicate with staff, and how to build relationship with outsiders.

Unfortunately, in this study the hypothesis about the relationship of corporate history and corporate identity management is not accepted. Also, the chapter does not support the idea of there being a relationship between country-of-origin and corporate identity management.

Moreover, there is a mediating factor, gender diversity, in this research. As can be seen in the charts, diversity strengthens the positive relationship between philosophy, vision and mission and corporate identity management. It means that in a diversified corporation, staff serve more efficiently and effectively in the direction of future goals. In addition, diversity weakens the positive relationship between corporate history and corporate identity management. It can be seen in the relationship between country-of-origin and corporate identity management. Diversity weakens the negative relationship between top management driving force and corporate identity management.

Corporate identity management on the other side of the model has a relationship with innovation adoption. Additionally, it is related to corporate reputation as proved in previous research (Flint et al., 2018; Foroudi and Marvi, 2020; Foroudi et al., 2014; Ingenhoff and Fuhrer, 2010; Urde et al., 2016).

Solutions and recommendations

This research suggests that, in order to improve corporate reputation, corporations should have a vivid understanding of favourable corporate identity management, which is influenced by two important factors, mainly, philosophy, vision and mission and top management driving force. The results revealed that top management driving forces have slightly more influence compared to philosophy, vision and mission. Tourism managers should note that the philosophy, vision and mission are the backbone of corporate identity management and shape what identity is (Foroudi et al. 2020a). Besides, top management driving forces should pay close attention to the way they influence corporate identity.

Additionally, diversity was found to weaken the relationship between top management driving forces. On the other hand, diversity strengthens the relationship between philosophy, vision and mission and corporate identity management. The more diverse the individuals participating in forming the philosophy, vision and mission, the better corporate identity management is possible for the corporations. However, having more diversity can lessen the relationship between top management driving forces and corporate identity management. This result suggests that a corporation can benefit from having more top management driving force due to diverse perspectives. Also, with mixing gender diversity in a corporation, top managers should improve or amend key documents according to new situations. They have to identify new shifts to be made by discussing gender diversity to know this topic well. They have to know different cultures, traditions, behaviours and generally seek new people. What is more, top managers and policy makers should know that having different staff, especially in the hospitality industry, is a normal phenomenon and even an advantage. Being ready for this phenomenon in developing countries is vital. Developing new strategies both for female and male employees can make it simple to face new challenges and in competition with rivals.

The results showed that there is no meaningful relationship between corporate history, and country-of-origin with corporate identity management. What is more, the results revealed that diversity weakens the relationship between corporate history, country-of-origin and corporate identity management. It falls to managers to familiarise all employees with history of the corporation and show them what their achievements are and what their failures are, how they can make these achievements in the future and beyond that, encourage them to innovate (Foruid et al. 2020b).

The results also shown that there is a positive relationship between corporate identity management and corporate reputation, suggesting that the way a company presents its identity to its customers has a positive influence on its reputation. In this respect, a corporation should closely monitor corporate identity management as it shapes their corporate reputation. Also, the results indicated that corporate identity management positively impacts on innovation adoption. Because identity is what a corporation is in terms of its attributes (Foroudi et al., 2019), innovativeness and innovation adoption can be influenced by corporate identity management. Tourism managers should consistently concentrate on corporate identity management as it shapes the innovativeness of their corporation.

Finally, innovation adoption was found to have a positive influence on corporate reputation. In this respect, a corporation can have a reputation for adopting innovative ways to accommodate its customers' needs. In this regard, managers should place emphasis on innovation adoption as it makes their corporation become well known for being innovative. Encouraging innovative culture or imitating one is the top managers' authority. Thus, it is the responsibility of managers to encourage and motivate employees to think and present innovative product or maintain this morale to adopt innovation from outside and decrease resistance. Top management teams and executives have a critical role not only in corporate identity management, but also in corporate reputation.

Future research directions

Like all research, the current research has a number of limitations. To the authors' knowledge, this is the first research investigating the antecedents of corporate identity management, including philosophy, vision and mission, corporate history, country-of-origin, top management driving force and corporation reputation. The first implication of this study is the context of the research. The focus of this study is Tehran (Iran); however, the results could be different in other places like the United States due to different cultures. To overcome this problem, future studies can investigate the moderating role of culture as well. Besides, future studies can also analyse and investigate the model in bigger and more diverse countries. Also, future researchers can investigate the proposed model in other industries and compare the results with the following results. In conclusion, the model examines the antecedents of corporation identity management.

Conclusion

Corporate identity has gained considerable attention and has been under investigation for a long time. However, there is limited understanding of corporate identity management in the tourism industry. The main theoretical implication of this research is of concern to corporate identity management. Previous researchers have analysed the antecedents of corporate identity management, mainly job involvement and organisational citizenship behaviour (Wang, 2011), job satisfaction and decision-making (Kohles et al., 2012), corporate sustainability (Simões et al., 2017), managerial perceptions (He, 2012), brand loyalty (Pratihari et al., 2018) and culture (Dessupoio et al., 2018). However, no researchers have investigated the influence of philosophy vision and mission, corporate history, country-of-origin, and top management driving force on corporate identity management.

CASE STUDY

The University of West London (UWL): corporate identity management and corporate reputation in a higher education context

All organisations have responsibilities to both their clients and other stakeholders. Corporate identity management and corporate reputation are crucial factors for organisations that help organisations to reach more profit. The case study examines how the University of West London – UWL (uwl.ac.uk/about-us/how-university-works/history, 2020) has a constructive approach towards corporate identity management and corporate reputation in a hospitality context. Also, this case study puts a light on that positive working strategy and responsible actions which are focused on corporate identity management.

The UWL is one of the UK public universities that has two campuses in London, one at Berkshire and one at Reading. The UWL draws on 150 years of heritage, history and experience in professional education. The UWL has origins back to the 19th century when the first school was originated in 1860 and named as Lady Byron; some years after, its name was changed to Ealing College. The Ealing College became a university in 1992 and after 18 years, its name was changed to the UWL.

In January 1912, a secondary school under the name of the Slough campus was founded. This campus becomes Slough College by the 1960s. After that, in the 1980s, the Slough College was nominated as Thames Valley College for Higher Education but it was shut down in 2011.

In 1990, all colleges including Queen Charlotte's, Thames Valley, Music and Ealing Colleges were merged together under the name of Polytechnic of West London (PWL). In line with *the Further and Higher Education Act 1992*, the PWL improved to the Thames Valley University (TVU). The Reading College and Arts and Design School was joined with the Thames Valley University. The Paragon is one of the campuses of the UWL that is located in Brentford and was formerly TVU Branding. Finally, the university name was changed to the University of West London. Following a massive growth from 1860 to 2009, the UWL corporate identity management was improved sharply.

Now, there are eight schools in the UWL which include Computing and Engineering, Nursing, Business School, Midwifery and Healthcare, the London Geller College of Hospitality and Tourism, the School of Music and Law and Criminology, London College of Music, the School of Human and Social Sciences, Media and Design, and the London School of Film. Also, UWL offers PhD programmers and Professional Doctorates. In 2018, The UWL was ranked in *The Sunday Times* as Good University in 56th place nationally in 2017 and in 52nd place in 2020. The UWL has jumped 31 places in "The Times and The Sunday Times Good University Guide 2020" which is the biggest rise in the UK. Also, 98% of the UWL alumni are employed or started further study within six months after graduation. "The Complete University Guide in 2020" ranked the UWL as 7th in the UK for facility spending. The following are descriptions of the recognitions corporate identity management and corporate reputation in the UWL received:

- The UWL was recognised with a Silver award for a high standard of teaching in the Teaching Excellence Framework (TEF).
- The UWL ranked top for teaching quality and student experience in London by "The Times and Sunday Times Good University Guide 2018".
- The University's Vice-Chancellor, Professor Peter John, was made a Commander of the Order of the British Empire (CBE) in the Queen's 2020 New Year honours list for his outstanding work and service to higher education.
- The UWL won the Outstanding Financial Performance Award at *The Times* Higher Education Awards 2019.
- The UWL Leadership was recognised as an "Outstanding Leadership and Management Team" at THE Leadership and Management Awards 2017.

The University of West London has recorded the best results of any university in Greater London in the annual National Student Survey (NSS) in 2016.

Case questions

1. What does the UWL do while putting into practice its approach to continuing progress?
2. What are the main features of the UWL approach to improving corporate reputation, including all of its benefits? Analyses what this strategy has to offer to communities, the society and to the student market as well.
3. What approach (and model) to corporate identity management is followed by UWL?

Key terms and definitions

Corporate identity management is the collection of explanations by which people on the outside know a company and through those explanations people can explain, recall and connect to that company.

Corporate reputation is explained as a perception of an organisation in the minds of present and future stakeholders.

Philosophy is the basic, distinguishing and persevering idea, belief and feeling directing a business, which in turn is essential in preparing and writing a mission statement.

Vision is a forward-looking statement which tries to identify a societally benefitial purpose for an organization.

Mission is a tool inside an organisation and refers to the organisation's identity as decided by all top managers. It is a crucial factor of giving strength to inner awareness of corporate identity management and its external broadcast.

Corporate history is history of the company and the company's ownership.

Country-of-origin is explained as the country to which a customer relates a specific product or brand as its source.

Top management driving force is expressing the corporation's main idea to the stakeholders (internal and external) and is the approach of senior management that builds foundation.

Diversity is perception about being different from peers.

Innovation adoption is the implementation of new products/services in an organisation.

References

Aaker, D. A. (2004). Leveraging the corporate brand. *California Management Review*, 46(3), 6–18.

Aaker, D. A. and Joachimsthaler, E. (2000). *Brand Leadership*. Free Press, New York.

Abdullah, Z., Shahrina, Nordin, M. and Abdul Aziz, Y. (2013). Building a unique online corporate identity. *Marketing Intelligence & Planning*, 31(5), 451–471.

Adner, R. and Kapoor, R. (2010). Value creation in innovation ecosystems: How the structure of technological interdependence affects firm performance in new technology generations. *Strategic Management Journal*, 31(3), 306–333.

Abratt, R. and Kleyn, N. (2012). Corporate identity, corporate branding and corporate reputations: Reconciliation and integration. *European Journal of Marketing*, 46(7/8), 1048–1063.

Ageeva, E., Melewar, T. C., Foroudi, P. and Dennis, C. (2019). Cues adopted by consumers in examining corporate website favorability: An empirical study of financial institutions in the UK and Russia. *Journal of Business Research*, 98, 15–32.

Akarsu, T. N., Foroudi, P. and Melewar, T. C. (2020). What makes Airbnb likeable? Exploring the nexus between service attractiveness, country image, perceived authenticity and experience from a social exchange theory perspective within an emerging economy context. *International Journal of Hospitality Management*, 91, (Just published).

Akdeniz, B., Calantone, R. J. and Voorhees, C. M. (2013). Effectiveness of marketing cues on consumer perceptions of quality: The moderating roles of brand reputation and third-party information. *Psychology & Marketing*, 30(1), 76–89.

Akgunduz, Y. (2015). The influence of self-esteem and role stress on job performance in hotel businesses. *International Journal of Contemporary Hospitality Management*, 27(6), 1082–1099.

Amable, B., Ledezma, I. and Robin, S. (2016). Product market regulation, innovation, and productivity. *Research Policy*, 45(10), 2087–2104.

Analoui, F. and Karami, A. (2002). CEOs and development of the meaningful mission statement. *Corporate Governance: International Journal of Business and Society*, 2(3), 13–20.

Anteby, M. and Molnar, V. (2012). Collective memory meets organizational identity: Remembering to forget in a firm's rhetorical history. *Academy of Management Journal*, 55(3), 515–540.

Apesteguia, J., Azmat, G. and Iriberri, N. (2012). The impact of gender composition on team performance and decision making: Evidence from the field. *Management Science*, 58(1), 78–93.

Avlonitis, G. J., Kouremenos, A. and Tzokas, N. (1994). Assessing the innovativeness of organizations and its antecedents: Project innovstrat. *European Journal of Marketing*, 28(11), 5–28.

Baek, T. H., Kim, J. and Yu, J. H. (2010). The differential roles of brand credibility and brand prestige in consumer brand choice. *Psychology & Marketing*, 27(7), 662–678.

Baker, W. E. and Sinkula, J. M. (1999). The synergistic effect of market orientation and learning orientation on organizational performance. *Journal of the Academy of Marketing Science*, 27(4), 411–427.

Balmer, J. M. T. (1994). The BBC's corporate identity: Myth, paradox and reality. *Journal of General Management*, 19(3), 33–49.

Balmer, J. M. T. (2001). Corporate identity, corporate branding and corporate marketing-Seeing through the fog. *European Journal of Marketing*, 35(3/4), 248–291.

Balmer, J. M. T. (2008). Identity based views of the corporation: Insights from corporate identity, organisational identity, social identity, visual identity, corporate brand identity and corporate image. *European Journal of Marketing*, 42(9/10), 879–906.

Balmer, J. M. T. (2010). Explicating corporate brands and their management: Reflections and directions from 1995. *Journal of Brand Management*, 18(3), 180–196.

Balmer, J. M. T. (2017). Advances in corporate brand, corporate heritage, corporate identity and corporate marketing scholarship. *European Journal of Marketing*, 51(9/10), 1462–1471.

Balmer, J. M. T. and Stotvig, S. (1997). Corporate identity and private banking: A review and case study. *International Journal of Bank Marketing*, 15(5), 169–184.

Barbarossa, C., De Pelsmacker, P. and Moons, I. (2018). Effects of country-of-origin stereotypes on consumer responses to product-harm crises. *International Marketing Review*, 35(3), 362–389.

Barclay, P. (2010). Altruism as a courtship display: Some effects of third-party generosity on audience perceptions. *British Journal of Psychology*, 101(1), 123–135.

Baum, M., Sterzing, A. and Alaca, N. (2016). Reactions towards diversity recruitment and the moderating influence of the recruiting firms' country-of-origin. *Journal of Business Research*, 69(10), 4140–4149.

Bearden, W. O. and Shimp, T. A. (1982). The use of extrinsic cues to facilitate product adoption. *Journal of Marketing Research*, 19(2), 229–239.

Beverland, M. B., Napoli, J. and Farrelly, F. (2010). Can all brands innovate in the same way? A typology of brand position and innovation effort. *Journal of Product Innovation Management*, 27(1), 33–48.

Black, I. and Veloutsou, C. (2017). Working consumers: Co-creation of brand identity, consumer identity and brand community identity. *Journal of Business Research*, 70, 416–429.

Blombäck, A. and Brunninge, O. (2009). Corporate identity manifested through historical references. *Corporate Communications: An International Journal*, 14(4), 404–419.

Blombäck, A. and Brunninge, O. (2013). The dual opening to brand heritage in family businesses. *Corporate Communications: An International Journal*, 18(3), 327–346.

Bowen, F. and Blackmon, K. (2003). Spirals of silence: The dynamic effects of diversity on organizational voice. *Journal of Management Studies*, 40(6), 1393–1417.

Brexendorf, T. O. and Keller, K. L. (2017). Leveraging the corporate brand: The importance of corporate brand innovativeness and brand architecture. *European Journal of Marketing*, 51(9/10), 1530–1551.

Bugeja, M., Matolcsy, Z. P. and Spiropoulos, H. (2012). Is there a gender gap in CEO compensation? *Journal of Corporate Finance*, 18(4), 849–859.

Burmann, C. and Zeplin, S. (2005). Building brand commitment: A behavioural approach to internal brand management. *Journal of Brand Management*, 12(4), 279–300.

Carter, C. R. and Jennings, M. M. (2004). The role of purchasing in corporate social responsibility: A structural equation analysis. *Journal of Business Logistics*, 25(1), 145–186.

Chajet, C. and Schatman, T. (1993). *Image by Design*. Addison-Wesley, Reading, MA.

Che-Ha, N., Nguyen, B., Yahya, W. K., Melewar, T. C. and Chen, Y. P. (2016). Country branding emerging from citizens' emotions and the perceptions of competitive advantage: The case of Malaysia. *Journal of Vacation Marketing*, 22(1), 13–28.

Chong, M. (2007). The role of internal communication and training in infusing corporate values and delivering brand promise: Singapore Airlines' experience. *Corporate Reputation Review*, 10(3), 201–212.

Chung, Y., Liao, H., Jackson, S. E., Subramony, M., Colakoglu, S. and Jiang, Y. (2015). Cracking but not breaking: Joint effects of faultline strength and diversity climate on loyal behavior. *Academy of Management Journal*, 58(5), 1495–1515.

Cole, B. M. and Salimath, M. S. (2013). Diversity identity management: An organizational perspective. *Journal of Business Ethics*, 116(1), 151–161.

Cole, M. S. and Bruch, H. (2006). Organizational identity strength, identification, and commitment and their relationships to turnover intention: Does organizational hierarchy matter? *Journal of Organizational Behavior: The International Journal of Industrial, Occupational and Organizational Psychology and Behavior*, 27(5), 585–605.

Cornelius, N., Gooch, L. and Todd, S. (2001). Managing difference fairly: An integrated 'partnership' approach. In D. Collinson (Ed.), *Equality, Diversity and Disadvantage in Employment* (pp. 32–50). Palgrave Macmillan, London.

Cox, T. H. and Blake, S. (1991). Managing cultural diversity: Implications for organizational competitiveness. *Academy of Management Perspectives*, 5(3), 45–56.

Cumming, D., Leung, T. Y. and Rui, O. (2015). Gender diversity and securities fraud. *Academy of Management Journal*, 58(5), 1572–1593.

Davis, J. H., Ruhe, J. A., Lee, M. and Rajadhyaksha, U. (2007). Mission possible: Do school mission statements work? *Journal of Business Ethics*, 70(1), 99–110.

De Chernatony, L. (1999). Brand management through narrowing the gap between brand identity and brand reputation. *Journal of Marketing Management*, 15(1–3), 157–179.

De Massis, A., Di Minin, A. and Frattini, F. (2015). Family-driven innovation: Resolving the paradox in family firms. *California Management Review*, 58(1), 5–19.

Dermol, V. and Širca, N. T. (2018). Communication, company mission, organizational values, and company performance. *Procedia: Social and Behavioral Sciences*, 238, 542–551.

Desmidt, S. and Prinzie, A. A. (2009, August). The effectiveness of mission statements: An explorative analysis from a communication perspective. In Guclu Atinc (Ed.),

Academy of Management Proceedings (Vol. 2009, No. 1, pp. 1–6). Academy of Management, Briarcliff Manor.

Dessupoio, N., da Costa Vieira, P. R. and Troccoli, I. R. (2018). Impact of the relevant dimensions in the corporate identity of a public higher education. *International Journal of Business Management and Economic Research*, 9(3), 1258–1269.

Diestel, S., Wegge, J. and Schmidt, K. H. (2014). The impact of social context on the relationship between individual job satisfaction and absenteeism: The roles of different foci of job satisfaction and work-unit absenteeism. *Academy of Management Journal*, 57(2), 353–382.

Dodds, W. B., Monroe, K. B. and Grewal, D. (1991). Effects of price, brand, and store information on buyers' product evaluations. *Journal of Marketing Research*, 28(8), 307–319.

Edghiem, F. and Mouzughi, Y. (2018). Knowledge-advanced innovative behaviour: A hospitality service perspective. *International Journal of Contemporary Hospitality Management*, 30(1), 197–216.

Essamri, A., McKechnie, S. and Winklhofer, H. (2018). Co-creating corporate brand identity with online brand communities: A managerial perspective. *Journal of Business Research*, 96(7), 366–375.

Fan, D., Lo, C. K., Yeung, A. C. and Cheng, T. C. E. (2018). The impact of corporate label change on long-term labor productivity. *Journal of Business Research*, 86, 96–108.

Farrelly, D. (2011). Cooperation as a signal of genetic or phenotypic quality in female mate choice? Evidence from preferences across the menstrual cycle. *British Journal of Psychology*, 102(3), 406–430.

Fast, N. J., Burris, E. R. and Bartel, C. A. (2014). Managing to stay in the dark: Managerial self-efficacy, ego defensiveness, and the aversion to employee voice. *Academy of Management Journal*, 57(4), 1013–1034.

Fetscherin, M. and Usunier, J. C. (2012). Corporate branding: An interdisciplinary literature review. *European Journal of Marketing*, 46(5), 733–753.

Fisher, G., Kotha, S. and Lahiri, A. (2016). Changing with the times: An integrated view of identity, legitimacy, and new venture life cycles. *Academy of Management Review*, 41(3), 383–409.

Flint, D. J., Signori, P. and Golicic, S. L. (2018). Corporate identity congruence: A meanings-based analysis. *Journal of Business Research*, 86(May), 68–82.

Fombrun, C. J. (1995). *Reputation: Realizing Value from the Corporate Image*. Boston, MA: Harvard Business School Press.

Fombrun, C. J. and Van Riel, C. B. M. (2004). *Fame and Fortune: How Successful Companies Build Winning Reputations*. Pearson Education, Upper Saddle River, NJ.

Fornell, C. and Larcker, D. F. (1981). Structural equation models with unobservable variables and measurement error: Algebra and statistics, 18(2), 382–388.

Foroudi, P. (2019). Influence of brand signature, brand awareness, brand attitude, brand reputation on hotel industry's brand performance. *International Journal of Hospitality Management*, 76, 271–285.

Foroudi, P. (2020). Corporate brand strategy: drivers and outcomes of hotel industry's brand orientation. *International Journal of Hospitality Management*, 88(8), 1–14.

Foroudi, P. and Marvi, R. (2020). Some like it hot: the role of identity, website, co-creation behavior on identification and love. *European Journal of International Management*, (Just published).

Foroudi, P., Melewar, T. C. and Gupta, S. (2014). Linking corporate logo, corporate image, and reputation: An examination of consumer perceptions in the financial setting. *Journal of Business Research*, 67(11), 2269–2281.

Foroudi, P., Gupta, S., Kitchen, P., Foroudi, M. M. and Nguyen, B. (2016a). A framework of place branding, place image, and place reputation: Antecedents and moderators. *Qualitative Market Research: An International Journal*, 19(2), 241–264.

Foroudi, P., Jin, Z., Gupta, S., Melewar, T. C. and Foroudi, M. M. (2016b). Influence of innovation capability and customer experience on reputation and loyalty. Journal of Business Research, 69(11), 4882–4889.

Foroudi, P., Jin, Z., Gupta, S., Foroudi, M. M. and Kitchen, P. J. (2018). Perceptional components of brand equity: configuring the symmetrical and asymmetrical paths to brand loyalty and brand purchase intention. *Journal of Business Research*, 89, 462–474.

Foroudi, P., Gupta, S., Nazarian, A. and Duda, M. (2017). Digital technology and marketing management capability: Achieving growth in SMEs. *Qualitative Market Research: An International Journal*, 20(2), 230–246.

Foroudi, P., Yu, Q., Gupta, S. and Foroudi, M. M. (2019). Enhancing university brand image and reputation through customer value co-creation behaviour. *Technological Forecasting and Social Change*, 138, 218–227.

Foroudi, P., Cuomo, M. T., Foroudi, M. M., Katsikeas, C. S. and Gupta, S. (2020a). Linking identity and heritage with image and a reputation for competition. *Journal of Business Research*, 113(2), 317–325.

Fouroudi, P., Kitchen, P. J., Marvi, R., Akarsu, T. N. and Uddin, H. (2020b). A bibliometric investigation of service failure literature and a research agenda. *European Journal of Marketing* (Just accepted).

Gammoh, B. S., Voss, K. E. and Chakraborty, G. (2006). Consumer evaluation of brand alliance signals. *Psychology & Marketing*, 23(6), 465–486.

García-Gallego, J. M. and Chamorro Mera, A. (2017). COO vs ROO: Importance of the origin in customer preferences towards financial entities. *International Marketing Review*, 34(2), 206–223.

Garrett, T. C., Lee, S. and Chu, K. (2017). A store brand's country-of-origin or store image: What matters to consumers? *International Marketing Review*, 34(2), 272–292.

Gehman, J. and Grimes, M. (2017). Hidden badge of honor: How contextual distinctiveness affects category promotion among certified B corporations. *Academy of Management Journal*, 60(6), 2294–2320.

Gerbing, D. W. and Anderson, J. C. (1988). An updated paradigm for scale development incorporating unidimensionality and its assessment. *Journal of Marketing Research*, 25(2), 186–192.

Gioia, D. A. and Thomas, J. B. (1996). Identity, image, and issue interpretation: Sensemaking during strategic change in academia. *Administrative Science Quarterly*, 41(13), 370–403.

Ghodeswar, B. M. (2008). Building brand identity in competitive markets: a conceptual model. *Journal of Product & Brand Management*, 17, 4–12.

Gioia, D. A., Schultz, M. and Corley, K. G. (2000). Organizational identity, image, and adaptive instability. *Academy of Management Review*, 25(1), 63–81.

Godey, B., Pederzoli, D., Aiello, G., Donvito, R., Chan, P., Oh, H., … Weitz, B. (2012). Brand and country-of-origin effect on consumers' decision to purchase luxury products. *Journal of Business Research*, 65(10), 1461–1470.

Gray, E. R. and Balmer, J. M. T. (1998). Managing corporate image and corporate reputation. *Long Range Planning*, 31(5), 695–702.

Gröschl, S. (2011). Diversity management strategies of global hotel groups: a corporate web site based exploration. *International Journal of Contemporary Hospitality Management*, 23, 224–240.

Gupta, S. and Malhotra, N. (2013). Marketing innovation: A resource-based view of international and local firms. *Marketing Intelligence & Planning*, 31(2), 111–126.

Gupta, S., Malhotra, N. K., Czinkota, M. and Foroudi, P. (2016). Marketing innovation: A consequence of competitiveness. *Journal of Business Research*, 69(12), 5671–5681.

Hair, J. F., Tatham, R. L., Anderson, R. E. and Black, W. (2006). *Multivariate Data Analysis*. Pearson Prentice Hall, Upper Saddle River, NJ.

Harris, F. and De Chernatony, L. (2001). Corporate branding and corporate brand performance. *European Journal of Marketing*, 35, 441–456.

Harman, H. H. (1976). *Modern Factor Analysis*. Chicago, USA: University of Chicago Press.

Harpaz, I., Honig, B. and Coetsier, P. (2002). A cross-cultural longitudinal analysis of the meaning of work and the socialization process of career starters. *Journal of World Business*, 37(4), 230–244.

Hatch, M. J. and Schultz, M. (1997). Relations between organizational culture, identity and image. *European Journal of Marketing*, 31, 356–365.

He, H. W. (2012). Corporate identity anchors: A managerial cognition perspective. *European Journal of Marketing*, 46(5), 609–625.

He, H. W. and Balmer, J. M. (2005). The saliency and significance of generic identity: An explanatory study of UK building societies. *International Journal of Bank Marketing*, 23(4), 334–348.

He, H. W. and Mukherjee, A. (2009). Corporate identity and consumer marketing: A process model and research agenda. *Journal of Marketing Communications*, 15(1), 1–16.

Highhouse, S., Stierwalt, S. L., Bachiochi, P., Elder, A. E. and Fisher, G. (1999). Effects of advertised human resource management practices on attraction of African American applicants. *Personnel Psychology*, 52(2), 425–442.

Hillestad, T., Xie, C. and Haugland, S. A. (2010). Innovative corporate social responsibility: The founder's role in creating a trustworthy corporate brand through "green innovation". *Journal of Product & Brand Management*, 19(6), 440–451.

Himme, A. and Fischer, M. (2014). Drivers of the cost of capital: The joint role of non-financial metrics. *International Journal of Research in Marketing*, 31(2), 224–238.

Hirschfeld, R. R., Jordan, M. H., Feild, H. S., Giles, W. F. and Armenakis, A. A. (2005). Teams' female representation and perceived potency as inputs to team outcomes in a predominantly male field setting. *Personnel Psychology*, 58, 893–924.

Hogg, M. A., Van Knippenberg, D. and Rast III, D. E. (2012). Intergroup leadership in organizations: Leading across group and organizational boundaries. *Academy of Management Review*, 37(2), 232–255.

Holt, D. T. and Daspit, J. J. (2015). Diagnosing innovation readiness in family firms. *California Management Review*, 58(1), 82–96.

House, R. J. (1977). A 1976 theory of charismatic leadership. In J. G. Hunt and L. L. Larson (Eds.), *Leadership: The Cutting Edge* (pp. 189–207). Carbondale: Southern Illinois University Press.

Ingenhoff, D. and Fuhrer, T. (2010). Positioning and differentiation by using brand personality attributes: Do mission and vision statements contribute to building a unique corporate identity? *Corporate Communications: An International Journal*, 15(1), 83–101.

Jaworski, B. J. and Kohli, A. K. (1993). Market orientation: Antecedents and consequences. *Journal of Marketing*, 57(3), 53–70.

Jo Hatch, M. and Schultz, M. (1997). Relations between organizational culture, identity and image. *European Journal of Marketing*, 31(5/6), 356–365.

Kalargyrou, V. and Costen, W. (2017). Diversity management research in hospitality and tourism: Past, present and future. *International Journal of Contemporary Hospitality Management*, 29(1), 68–114.

Kemp, S. and Dwyer, L. (2003). Mission statements of international airlines: a content analysis. *Tourism Management*, 24(6), 635–653.

Kapferer, J. N. (2012). *The New Strategic Brand Management: Advanced Insights and Strategic Thinking*. London, UK: Kogan Page Publishers.

Karaosmanoğlu, E., Baş, A. B. E. and Zhang, J. (2011). The role of other customer effect in corporate marketing: Its impact on corporate image and consumer-company identification. *European Journal of Marketing*, 45(9/10), 1416–1445

Kim, M. Y., Choi, L., Knutson, B. J. and Borchgrevink, C. P. (2017). Hotel employees' organizational behaviors from cross-national perspectives. *International Journal of Contemporary Hospitality Management*, 29(12), 3082–3100.

Kim, S. S., Im, J. and Hwang, J. (2015). The effects of mentoring on role stress, job attitude, and turnover intention in the hotel industry. *International Journal of Hospitality Management*, 48, 68–82.

King, E. B., Dawson, J. F., West, M. A., Gilrane, V. L., Peddie, C. I. and Bastin, L. (2011). Why organizational and community diversity matter: Representativeness and the emergence of incivility and organizational performance. *Academy of Management Journal*, 54(6), 1103–1118.

Kohles, J. C., Bligh, M. C. and Carsten, M. K. (2012). A follower-centric approach to the vision integration process. *The Leadership Quarterly*, 23(3), 476–487.

Kong, H., Jiang, X., Chan, W. and Zhou, X. (2018). Job satisfaction research in the field of hospitality and tourism. *International Journal of Contemporary Hospitality Management*, (just accepted).

Konecnik, M. and Go, F. (2008). Tourism destination brand identity: the case of Slovenia. *Journal of Brand Management*, 15(3), 177–189.

Konrad, A. M. and Linnehan, F. (1995). Formalized HRM structures: Coordinating equal employment opportunity or concealing organizational practices? *Academy of Management Journal*, 38(3), 787–820.

Koporcic, N. and Halinen, A. (2018). Interactive network branding: Creating corporate identity and reputation through interpersonal interaction. *IMP Journal*, 12(2), 392–408.

Kraimer, M. L., Shaffer, M. A., Harrison, D. A. and Ren, H. (2012). No place like home? An identity strain perspective on repatriate turnover. *Academy of Management Journal*, 55(2), 399–420.

Kulik, C. T., Perera, S. and Cregan, C. (2016). Engage me: The mature-age worker and stereotype threat. *Academy of Management Journal*, 59(6), 2132–2156.

Kumar, A. (2014). Place branding: A way to correct the negative image of sex tourism. *International Journal of Business Research and Development*, 3(1), 1–7.

Kuo, P. J. and Kalargyrou, V. (2014). Consumers' perspectives on service staff with disabilities in the hospitality industry. *International Journal of Contemporary Hospitality Management*, 26(2), 164–182.

Lambert, D. M. and Harrington, T. C. (1990). Measuring nonresponse bias in customer service mail surveys. *Journal of Business Logistics*, 11(2), 5.

Lee, H. W., Choi, J. N. and Kim, S. (2018). Does gender diversity help teams constructively manage status conflict? An evolutionary perspective of status conflict,

396 *Foroudi, Marvi, Izadi, Foroudi and Pirzadeh*

team psychological safety, and team creativity. *Organizational Behavior and Human Decision Processes*, 144(Sep.), 187–199.

Leslie, L. M., Mayer, D. M. and Kravitz, D. A. (2014). The stigma of affirmative action: A stereotyping-based theory and meta-analytic test of the consequences for performance. *Academy of Management Journal*, 57(4), 964–989.

Leuthesser, L. and Kohli, C. (2015). Mission statements and corporate identity. In *Proceedings of the 1996 Academy of Marketing Science (AMS) Annual Conference* (pp. 145–148). Springer, Cham.

Li, J., Xia, J. and Zajac, E. J. (2018). On the duality of political and economic stakeholder influence on firm innovation performance: Theory and evidence from Chinese firms. *Strategic Management Journal*, 39(1), 193–216.

Lin, Y. H., Ryan, C., Wise, N. and Low, L. W. (2018). A content analysis of airline mission statements: Changing trends and contemporary components. *Tourism Management Perspectives*, 28, 156–165.

Lindell, M. K. and Whitney, D. J. (2001). Accounting for common method variance in cross-sectional research designs. *Journal of Applied Psychology*, 86(1), 114.

Linnehan, F. and Konrad, A. M. (1999). Diluting diversity: Implications for intergroup inequality in organizations. *Journal of Management Inquiry*, 8(4), 399–414.

Locke, E. A., Kirkpatrick, S. A., Wheeler, J., Schneider, J., Niles, K., Goldstein, H., et al. (1991). *The Essence of Leadership*. Lexington Books, New York.

Love, E. G., Lim, J. and Bednar, M. K. (2017). The face of the firm: The influence of CEOs on corporate reputation. *Academy of Management Journal*, 60(4), 1462–1481.

Lundström, B. (2006). *Grundat 1876. Historia och Företagsidentitet Inom Ericsson*, doctoral dissertation. Royal Institute of Technology. Stockholm.

Madera, J. M., Dawson, M. and Neal, J. A. (2013). Hotel managers' perceived diversity climate and job satisfaction: The mediating effects of role ambiguity and conflict. *International Journal of Hospitality Management*, 35, 28–34.

Madera, J. M., Dawson, M. and Neal, J. A. (2014). Managing language barriers in the workplace: The roles of job demands and resources on turnover intentions. *International Journal of Hospitality Management*, 42, 117–125.

Mael, F. and Ashforth, B. E. (1992). Alumni and their alma mater: A partial test of the reformulated model of organizational identification. *Journal of Organizational Behavior*, 13(2), 103–123

Maitlis, S. and Sonenshein, S. (2010). Sensemaking in crisis and change: Inspiration and insights from Weick (1988). *Journal of Management Studies*, 47(3), 551–580.

Malhotra, N., Hall, J., Shaw, M. and Oppenheim, P. (2006). *Marketing Research: An Applied Orientation*. Pearson Education, Australia.

Manoharan, A. and Singal, M. (2017). A systematic literature review of research on diversity and diversity management in the hospitality literature. *International Journal of Hospitality Management*, 66, 77–91.

Manoharan, A., Gross, M. J. and Sardeshmukh, S. R. (2014). Identity-conscious vs identity-blind: Hotel managers' use of formal and informal diversity management practices. *International Journal of Hospitality Management*, 41 (Aug.), 1–9.

Marco, R. (2012). Gender and economic performance: Evidence from the Spanish hotel industry. *International Journal of Hospitality Management*, 31(3), 981–989.

Martins, L. L. and Parsons, C. K. (2007). Effects of gender diversity management on perceptions of organizational attractiveness: The role of individual differences in attitudes and beliefs. *Journal of Applied Psychology*, 92(3), 865–875.

Maruyama, M. and Wu, L. (2014). The relevance of retailer country-of-origin to consumer store choice: Evidence from China. *International Marketing Review*, 31(5), 462–476.

McAlexander, J. H., Schouten, J. W. and Koenig, H. F. (2002). Building brand community. *Journal of Marketing*, 66(1), 38–54.

Melewar, T. C. (2003). Determinants of the corporate identity construct: A review of the literature. *Journal of Marketing Communications*, 9(4), 195–220.

Melewar, T. C., Foroudi, P., Dinnie, K. and Nguyen, B. (2018). The role of corporate identity management in the higher education sector: an exploratory case study. *Journal of Marketing Communications*, 24(4), 337–359.

Melewar, T. C. and Saunders, J. (1998). Global corporate visual identity systems: Standardization, control and benefits. *International Marketing Review*, 15(4), 291–308.

Melewar, T. C. and Walker, C. (2003). Global corporate brand building: guidelines and case studies. *Journal of Brand Management*, 11(2), 157–170.

Melewar, T. C., Foroudi, P., Gupta, S., Kitchen, P. J. and Foroudi, M. M. (2017). Integrating identity, strategy and communications for trust, loyalty and commitment. *European Journal of Marketing*, 51(3), 572–604.

Melewar, T. C., Foroudi, P., Dinnie, K. and Nguyen, B. (2018). The role of corporate identity management in the higher education sector: An exploratory case study. *Journal of Marketing Communications*, 24(4), 337–359.

Mena, S., Rintamäki, J., Fleming, P. and Spicer, A. (2016). On the forgetting of corporate irresponsibility. *Academy of Management Review*, 41(4), 720–738.

Micelotta, E. R. and Raynard, M. (2011). Concealing or revealing the family? Corporate brand identity strategies in family firms. *Family Business Review*, 24(3), 197–216.

Micheli, P., Perks, H. and Beverland, M. B. (2018). Elevating design in the organization. *Journal of Product Innovation Management*, 35(4), 629–651.

Middleton, V. T. and Clarke, J. R. (2012). *Marketing in Travel and Tourism*. Oxfordshire, UK: Routledge.

Mohammed, I., Guillet, B. D. and Law, R. (2014). Competitor set identification in the hotel industry: A case study of a full-service hotel in Hong Kong. *International Journal of Hospitality Management*, 39(May), 29–40.

Moingeon, B. and Ramanantsoa, B. (1997). Understanding corporate identity: The French school of thought. *European Journal of Marketing*, 31(5/6), 383–395.

Moriuchi, E. and Takahashi, I. (2018). An empirical investigation of the factors motivating Japanese repeat consumers to review their shopping experiences. *Journal of Business Research*, 82(Jan), 381–390.

Myaskovsky, L., Unikel, E. and Dew, M. A. (2005). Effects of gender diversity on performance and interpersonal behaviour in small work groups. *Sex Roles*, 52(9–10), 645–657.

Nishii, L. H. (2013). The benefits of climate for inclusion for gender-diverse groups. *Academy of Management Journal*, 56(6), 1754–1774.

Olins, W. (1990). *Corporate Identity: Making Business Strategy Visible Through Design*. Boston, USA: Harvard Business School Press.

Ortmann, A. and Tichy, L. K. (1999). Gender differences in the laboratory: Evidence from prisoner's dilemma games. *Journal of Economic Behavior & Organization*, 39(3), 327–339.

Pallister, J. G. and Foxall, G. R. (1998). Psychometric properties of the Hurt–Joseph–Cook scales for the measurement of innovativeness. *Technovation*, 18(11), 663–675.

Palmer, T. B. and Short, J. C. (2008). Mission statements in US colleges of business: An empirical examination of their content with linkages to configurations and performance. *Academy of Management Learning & Education*, 7(4), 454–470.

Pearce, J. A. and David, F. (1987). Corporate mission statements: The bottom line. *Academy of Management Perspectives*, 1(2), 109–115.

Pérez, A. and Del Bosque, I. R. (2014). Organizational and corporate identity revisited: Toward a comprehensive understanding of identity in business. *Corporate Reputation Review*, 17(1), 3–27.

Pharr, J. M. (2005). Synthesizing country-of-origin research from the last decade: Is the concept still salient in an era of global brands?. *Journal of Marketing Theory and Practice*, 13(4), 34–45.

Podnar, K. and Golob, U. (2017). The quest for the corporate reputation definition: Lessons from the interconnection model of identity, image, and reputation. *Corporate Reputation Review*, 20(3–4), 186–192.

Ravasi, D., Rindova, V. and Stigliani, I. (2018). History, material memory and the temporality of identity construction. *Academy of Management*, 62(5), 1523–1555.

Reynolds, D., Rahman, I. and Bradetich, S. (2014). Hotel managers' perceptions of the value of diversity training: An empirical investigation. *International Journal of Contemporary Hospitality Management*, 26(3), 426–446.

Rode, V. and Vallaster, C. (2005). Corporate branding for start-ups: the crucial role of entrepreneurs. *Corporate Reputation Review*, 8(2), 121–135.

Romenti, S. (2010). Reputation and stakeholder engagement: An Italian case study. *Journal of Communication Management*, 14(4), 306–318.

Roper, S. and Fill, C. (2012). *Corporate Reputation: Brand and Communication*. Pearson, Harlow.

Roth, K. P. and Diamantopoulos, A. (2009). Advancing the country image construct. *Journal of Business Research*, 62(7), 726–740.

Roth, M. S. and Romeo, J. B. (1992). Matching product category and country image perceptions: A framework for managing country-of-origin effects. *Journal of International Business Studies*, 23(3), 477–497.

Rowlinson, M., Hassard, J. and Decker, S. (2014). Research strategies for organizational history: A dialogue between historical theory and organization theory. *Academy of Management Review*, 39(3), 250–274.

Sääksjärvi, M. and Samiee, S. (2011). Assessing multifunctional innovation adoption via an integrative model. *Journal of the Academy of Marketing Science*, 39(5), 717–735.

Sarmah, B., Kamboj, S. and Rahman, Z. (2017). Co-creation in hotel service innovation using smart phone apps: An empirical study. *International Journal of Contemporary Hospitality Management*, 29(10), 2647–2667.

Sawyerr, O. O., Strauss, J. and Yan, J. (2005). Individual value structure and diversity attitudes. *Journal of Managerial Psychology*, 20(6), 498–521.

Schmidt, K. (1995). *The Quest for Identity*. Cassell, London.

Schrempf-Stirling, J., Palazzo, G. and Phillips, R. A. (2016). Historic corporate social responsibility. *Academy of Management Review*, 41(4), 700–719.

Senyucel, Z. and Phillpott, S. (2011). Sexual equality and diversity in UK local councils. *Equality, Diversity and Inclusion: An International Journal*, 30(8), 702–718.

Shen, J., Chanda, A., D'netto, B. and Monga, M. (2009). Managing diversity through human resource management: An international perspective and conceptual framework. *The International Journal of Human Resource Management*, 20(2), 235–251.

Shipman, A. S., Byrne, C. L. and Mumford, M. D. (2010). Leader vision formation and forecasting: The effects of forecasting extent, resources, and timeframe. *The Leadership Quarterly*, 21(3), 439–456.

Shymko, Y. and Roulet, T. J. (2017). When does Medici hurt da Vinci? Mitigating the signaling effect of extraneous stakeholder relationships in the field of cultural production. *Academy of Management Journal*, 60(4), 1307–1338.

Simões, C., Dibb, S. and Fisk, R. P. (2005). Managing corporate identity: An internal perspective. *Journal of the Academy of Marketing Science*, 33(2), 153–168.

Skilton, P. F. and Purdy, J. M. (2017). Authenticity, power, and pluralism: A framework for understanding stakeholder evaluations of corporate social responsibility activities. *Business Ethics Quarterly*, 27(1), 99–123.

Song, Z., Chon, K., Ding, G. and Gu, C. (2015). Impact of organizational socialization tactics on newcomer job satisfaction and engagement: Core self-evaluations as moderators. *International Journal of Hospitality Management*, 46, 180–189.

Strange, J. M. and Mumford, M. D. (2002). The origins of vision: Charismatic versus ideological leadership. *The Leadership Quarterly*, 13(4), 343–377.

Strange, J. M. and Mumford, M. D. (2005). The origins of vision: Effects of reflection, models, and analysis. *The Leadership Quarterly*, 16(1), 121–148.

Su, L., Swanson, S. R. and Chen, X. (2015). Social responsibility and reputation influences on the intentions of Chinese Huitang Village tourists: Mediating effects of satisfaction with lodging providers. *International Journal of Contemporary Hospitality Management*, 27(8), 1750–1771.

Sun, J. (2014). How risky are services? An empirical investigation on the antecedents and consequences of perceived risk for hotel service. *International Journal of Hospitality Management*, 37, 171–179.

Sun, P., Hu, H. W. and Hillman, A. J. (2016). The dark side of board political capital: Enabling blockholder rent appropriation. *Academy of Management Journal*, 59(5), 1801–1822.

Suvatjis, J., De Chernatony, L. and Halikias, J. (2012). Assessing the six-station corporate identity model: A polymorphic model. *Journal of Product & Brand Management*, 21(3), 153–166.

Tabachnick, B. G., Fidell, L. S. and Ullman, J. B. (2007). *Using Multivariate Statistics* (Vol. 5, pp. 481–498). Pearson, Boston, MA.

Tasheva, S. N. and Hillman, A. (2018). Integrating diversity at different levels: Multi-level human capital, social capital, and demographic diversity and their implications for team effectiveness. *Academy of Management Review*, 44(4), 746–765.

Tatli, A. (2011). A multi-layered exploration of the diversity management field: Diversity discourses, practices and practitioners in the UK. *British Journal of Management*, 22(2), 238–253.

Taylor, G. S., Templeton, G. F. and Baker, L. T. (2010). Factors influencing the success of organizational learning implementation: A policy facet perspective. *International Journal of Management Reviews*, 12(4), 353–364.

Terglav, K., Ruzzier, M. K. and Kaše, R. (2016). Internal branding process: Exploring the role of mediators in top management's leadership–commitment relationship. *International Journal of Hospitality Management*, 54(Apr.), 1–11.

Törmälä, M. and Gyrd-Jones, R. I. (2017). Development of new B2B venture corporate brand identity: A narrative performance approach. *Industrial Marketing Management*, 65(Aug), 76–85.

Tuna, M., Ghazzawi, I., Yesiltas, M., Tuna, A. A. and Arslan, S. (2016). The effects of the perceived external prestige of the organization on employee deviant workplace behavior: The mediating role of job satisfaction. *International Journal of Contemporary Hospitality Management*, 28(2), 366–396.

Urde, M. (2003). Core value-based corporate brand building. *European Journal of Marketing*, 37, 1017–1040.

Urde, M. and Greyser, S. A. (2015). The Nobel Prize: the identity of a corporate heritage brand. *Journal of Product & Brand Management*, 24, 318–332.

Urde, M., Greyser, S. A. and Balmer, J. M. (2007). Corporate brands with a heritage. *Journal of Brand Management*, 15(1), 4–19.

Vallaster, C. and de Chernatony, L. (2006). Internal brand building and structuration: The role of leadership. *European Journal of Marketing*, 40(7/8), 761–784.

Van Riel, C. B. and Balmer, J. M. (1997). Corporate identity: The concept, its measurement and management. *European Journal of Marketing*, 31(5/6), 340–355.

Vaus, D. (2002). *Analyzing Social Science Data: 50 Key Problems in Data Analysis*. New York, USA: SAGE.

Veloutsou, C. and Taylor, C. S. (2012). The role of the brand as a person in business to business brands. *Industrial Marketing Management*, 41(6), 898–907.

Wahid, A. S. (2018). The effects and the mechanisms of board gender diversity: Evidence from financial manipulation. *Journal of Business Ethics*, 147(Jan.), 1–21.

Wang, C. L. and Ahmed, P. K. (2004). The development and validation of the organisational innovativeness construct using confirmatory factor analysis. *European Journal of Innovation Management*, 7(4), 303–313.

Wang, Y. (2011). Mission-driven organizations in Japan: Management philosophy and individual outcomes. *Journal of Business Ethics*, 101(1), 111–126.

Washburn, J. H., Till, B. D. and Priluck, R. (2004). Brand alliance and customer-based brand-equity effects. *Psychology & Marketing*, 21(7), 487–508.

Weigelt, C. and Shittu, E. (2016). Competition, regulatory policy, and firms' resource investments: The case of renewable energy technologies. *Academy of Management Journal*, 59(2), 678–704.

Williams, M. and Polman, E. (2014). Is it me or her? How gender composition evokes interpersonally sensitive behaviour on collaborative cross-boundary projects. *Organization Science*, 26(2), 334–355.

Wong, H. Y. and Merrilees, B. (2005). A brand orientation typology for SMEs: a case research approach. *Journal of Product & Brand Management*, 14, 155–162.

Wyer Jr, R. S. (2011). Procedural influences on judgments and behavioral decisions. *Journal of Consumer Psychology*, 21(4), 424–438.

Xie, C., Bagozzi, R. P. and Meland, K. V. (2015). The impact of reputation and identity congruence on employer brand attractiveness. *Marketing Intelligence & Planning*, 33(2), 124–146.

Zavyalova, A., Pfarrer, M. D., Reger, R. K. and Hubbard, T. D. (2016). Reputation as a benefit and a burden? How stakeholders' organizational identification affects the role of reputation following a negative event. *Academy of Management Journal*, 59(1), 253–276.

Zhang, X. and Chen, R. (2008). Examining the mechanism of the value co-creation with customers. *International Journal of Production Economics*, 116(2), 242.

15 Islamic brand love

Waleed Yousef and Najwa Yousef

Introduction

Islamic brand love introduces the concept of corporate religious branding and how beliefs and brand love influence on brand loyalty, word-of-mouth and purchase intention. This chapter examines religious beliefs as a new antecedent to brand love, and proposes a new construct, that of Islamic brand love. In addition, this chapter investigates some phycological antecedents to brand love such as cultural identity, religiosity or strongly held values. This chapter aims to address the following objectives: (i) to explore the relationship between religious beliefs and brand love; (ii) to offer a better understanding of Muslim consumer behaviour towards branding; (iii) to explore how *Sharia* sources affect Muslim consumers regarding brand love; (iv) to propose Islamic brand love as a new construct; (v) to offer a new scale for brand love based on religious beliefs.

Background

Islamic brand love

Islamic brand love is defined as the degree of passionate emotional attachment and positive evaluation (Albert and Merunka, 2013; Batra et al., 2012; Nguyen et al., 2013) that a satisfied Muslim consumer has for a particular trade name that matches his/her beliefs (Abdin, 2004; Alserhan, 2010). In addition, Fournier (1998) stated that consumers could develop a relationship with a brand in different categories such as love and passion. Similarly, Caroll and Ahuvia (2006) categorised the consumer/brand relationships as passion for brand, brand attachment or declaration of love towards the brand.

The theory of interpersonal love has been used in the marketing context (e.g. Shimp and Madden, 1988); however, Batra et al. (2012) stated that the theories of interpersonal love were not suitable for brand love research. They supported their argument by highlighting the differences between the different types of interpersonal love, such as parental love and romantic love; they argued that theories of interpersonal love could not therefore be applied to brand love. On the contrary, it is argued that brand love can be measured using interpersonal love theories only if an exploratory study is included beforehand (Albert et al., 2008).

Muslim consumer

The Muslim population is growing at a rate of 1.8% annually, while the total global Muslim population is 1.56 billion (Kearney, 2006, p. 7) and increased to 1.8 billion (Khan et al., 2017). Asia and the Middle East have the largest Muslim populations, with 870 million and 190 million, respectively (Soon and Wallace, 2017). While other consumer segments are reaching saturation point, Muslims are a potential segment on which to build a base for future growth. The market in products and services which comply with *Sharia* is worth $2 trillion and is growing annually (Khan et al., 2017). Kearney (2006, p. 5) defines Muslim consumers "as the market dominated by Muslims following Islamic cultures and beliefs". There is a misconception that Muslims are found only in the United Arab Emirates and the Middle East; they also exist in the developing world economy. Although Muslim consumers' lives are characterised by the lifestyle, dietary and financial laws of the Islamic faith, they are not homogeneous. For instance, Muslims across the globe wear different attire, speak various languages and consume different foods (Soon and Wallace, 2017). This indicates that, although Muslims share a similar faith, their behaviours are different. It is important to understand the growth of the Muslim population in order to make decisions to target them.

Levels of consumption in the Quran

Economic conditions differ from one age to another and from one society to another. Moreover, incomes within each society differ greatly. The reason for these differences is that God is the one who allocates livelihoods. God says, "Is it they who allocate the mercy of your Lord? It is We who have allocated their livelihood in this life" (43:32). Variation is a requisite to straighten things on Earth. If all people had the same capabilities and talents, there would be so many jobs that no one would do. God Almighty, the Creator of the universe, made people with variations in capabilities so that life could go smoothly and people could carry out the order of populating the Earth (Atwan, 1997). God says, "God has favoured some of you over others in livelihood. Those who are favoured would not give their properties to their servants" (16:71). Since people vary in their incomes, they also vary in their consumption. Not all people consume at the same level. Therefore, it is possible to classify consumption into three levels as set out in the following paragraphs.

Subsistence (basic necessities) – the subsistence level refers to the existence of basic necessities in a Muslim society, which are necessary and without which life would not be possible, to the extent that if these necessities were to disappear, life would disappear too. The Muslim, therefore, is called on to endeavour tirelessly to secure these necessities so that society does not stagnate and lag behind. A society that does not secure basic necessities cannot carry out the order of populating the Earth which has been entrusted to it. Therefore, Muslims have to go beyond this threshold of basic consumption, since any shortfall in this basic level threatens people's lives, and as a result the security and stability of society as a whole. Consequently, crime and theft become rampant, and other negative

Islamic brand love 403

phenomena associated with a poor level of consumption that is lower than the basic minimum are also seen in Al-Elyani, 2006). Overall, a basic subsistence level is one that provides for the basic necessities of life such as food, drink, clothing and shelter.

In the second level of sufficiency/adequacy (of needs), the term "sufficiency" refers to the first step towards wealth, where all basic legitimate needs have been satisfied (Al-Abbadi, 1985). The level of sufficiency is that in which a reasonable standard of living is attained for members of the community. Needs come in second place to necessities, and here, variations between people occur according to their social status, their capabilities, conditions and family obligations (Al-Elyani, 2006). God says, "The wealthy shall spend according to his means; and he whose resources are meagre shall spend according to what God has given him. God never burdens a soul beyond what He has given it. God will bring ease after hardship" (65:7).

This level of "sufficiency" consumption is considered as the first step towards being wealthy since it falls in a median position between the level of subsistence and that of luxury. And as such, it should be controlled by the restrictions of the Islamic *Sharia*, so that it does not fall into either indulgence or stinginess. Verses in the Holy Quran have indicated observance of this level of consumption when God says, "God desires ease for you, and does not desire hardship for you" (1:185). The righteous Islamic *Sharia*, which has been given to the Messenger (SAAWS) is based on ease and facility, not on hardship and difficulty.

The third level, that of luxury, refers to abundance, tenderness and ease of living (Al-Khayyat, 1982, p. 5). Luxury means exploiting and enjoying the good things in life. However, this should be enjoyed within the good things permitted by God (Al-Elyani, 2006). Luxury items include all that relates to ornamentation and decoration in clothes, food, drinks, housing, perfumes, permissible jewellery, means of transport, entertainment and others that are part of luxury life and easy or "soft" living for the individual and society (Afar, 1979). Luxury things add beauty and pleasure to human life without excess or indulgence. And they are part of the permissible good things and subventions that God has bestowed on His servants to enjoy and praise Him for. Consumption of such luxuries should be circumscribed and commensurate with people's income without excess or miserliness, and without impacting negatively on the production of basic necessities necessary for society (Afar, 1979, p. 163). God says, "Who forbade God's finery which He produced for His servants, and the delights of livelihood"; "They are for those who believe, in this present world, but exclusively theirs on the Day of Resurrection" and "We thus detail the revelations for people who know" (7: 32).

Muslim consumer and love

Muslims believe that Islam governs all aspects of their lives, and that all the Islamic laws can be derived from the Holy Quran, and that Almighty God motivates true

404 Waleed Yousef and Najwa Yousef

followers by love in different verses. For instance, the following verse includes advice for followers to judge equitably if they are ever asked to judge:

> Listeners to falsehoods, eaters of illicit earnings. If they come to you, judge between them, or turn away from them. If you turn away from them, they will not harm you in the least. But if you judge, judge between them equitably. Allah loves the equitable.
>
> (5:42)

Therefore, Muslims are expected to follow what comes in the Holy Quran if they want to be loved by God. The next section includes an explanation of Muslim consumer behaviour from a marketing perspective. True believers are mentioned in the Holy Quran as those who have the greatest love "But those who believe have greater love for Allah" (2:165). On the other hand, Almighty God describes himself in the Holy Quran in the following way: "Allah does not love the aggressors" (2:190).

Another example referring to love in the Holy Quran includes the following reference: "and spend in the cause of Allah, and do not throw yourselves with your own hands into ruin, and be charitable. Allah loves the charitable" (2:195). In this verse, Almighty God advises Muslims to spend their money for the sake of God, and states that those who spend will be rewarded by being loved by God. Love in the Holy Quran comes as a reward from God for those who are truly following him; for instance: "Allah loves the repentant, and He loves those who keep clean" (2:222). Another example is where Almighty God uses love as a reward for those who are seeking for the good things in this life, as in the following reference: "So Allah gave them the reward of this world, and the excellent reward of the Hereafter. Allah loves the doers of good" (3:148).

Main focus of the chapter

Religious beliefs and Islamic brand love

A few previous studies investigated the influence of religious beliefs on branding. However, Alserhan (2010) defined Islamic branding as those brands which are *Sharia*-compliant. Similarly, Temporal (2011a) stated that Islamic brands had to consider the five pillars of Islam (*Shahada, Salat, Sawm, Zaka* and *Hajj*) in order to attract Muslim consumers. On the other hand, the brand love concept has been discussed in the literature considering various antecedents and consequences (Batra et al., 2012; Carroll and Ahuvia, 2006; Rageh and Spinelli, 2012; Christodoulides et al., 2009; Rossiter, 2012) Figure 15.1 illustrates the main factors that influence brand love and the key outcomes of brand love.

Therefore, this chapter builds on the work of Batra et al. (2012), who stated that beliefs and strongly held values were influential factors in brand love. In addition, some researchers (Alserhan, 2010; Alserhan and Alserhan 2012; Temporal, 2011a) have stated that further studies are needed to link Muslim consumers with branding. Therefore, this

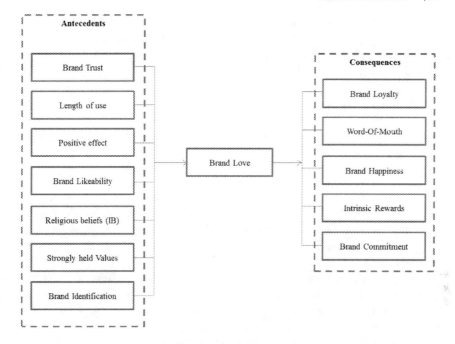

Figure 15.1 The major antecedents and consequences of brand love. Source: Albert and Merunka (2013); Batra et al. (2012); Nguyen et al. (2013).

chapter seeks to bridge the gap in the literature by proposing Islamic brand love as a new construct, and by examining the influence of religious beliefs on brand love.

Religious beliefs are known as an individual's positive or negative evaluation of a particular behaviour based on the beliefs held (Ajzen, 1991). For Muslims, *Sharia* sources are the main source of their belief, as they encompass all aspects of life (Addis and Holbrook, 2001). Therefore, Muslim religious beliefs can be considered as Muslim behavioural beliefs. In this regard, Abdin (2004) states that religious beliefs in Islam are the state in which the heart accepts the truth and lives by it. In addition, Alserhan (2010) states that brands cannot be separated from faith, and Muslim consumers love, hate and consume in line with their religious beliefs. Similarly, Batra et al. (2012) found that religiosity and deeply held values were positively correlated with brand love. Overall, Muslims are expected to be controlled by Islamic rules which are taken from the Holy Quran (Bakar et al., 2013). Love is specifically mentioned in the Holy Quran 83 times, in two forms, the first describing Almighty God and the second describing true believers (Abdin, 2004). Thus, love in the Islamic context is a controlled love, rather than an emotional love.

Culture and Islamic brand love

Culture is a unique concept which is defined differently in various contexts. Melewar et al. (2005, p. 60) define culture as shared practices, traditions, beliefs

406   Waleed Yousef and Najwa Yousef

and norms within a particular group of people. Furthermore, culture is defined as a set of beliefs, practices, values, traditions, norms and religious values shared by a group of people in a particular region. Culture is shared and learnt, and influences individuals in their daily lives. Hofstede (1983), in his theory of cultural dimensions, states that culture is unique to a country, and different countries may have different cultures. From the religious perspective, beliefs, practices, values and norms determine the cultural connotations of followers of a particular religion. For instance, some types of behaviour by Muslims are not common among Christians or Hindus because of religious differences.

Culture influences consumer behaviour in different ways, and it is important for marketers to understand the culture of their target markets to avoid cultural conflicts in their marketing endeavours or business operations. Elliott and Jankel-Elliot (2003, p. 215) have argued that culture influences consumer perceptions towards goods and services and brands in the market. Therefore, the religious beliefs of Muslims may influence their brand perception. Muslims are controlled by *Sharia* teachings, which explain the practices they have to follow in their lives, including their consumption patterns. For example, *Sharia* clearly prohibits the consumption of some products. For some products, *Sharia* may have certain rules of consumption: for example, banking products should be free from *Riba* (interest). *Sharia* comes from four sources, which are explained in Table 15.1.

Muslims believe that *Sharia* sources encompass all aspects of life (Bakare et al., 2013). The Quran is the main source of the Islamic belief system, considered as the book of God by Muslims. Fisher (1997, p. 338) defines the Quran

Table 15.1 The four sources of *Sharia*

Source	Definition
The Quran (primary)	The main contents and structure of *Sharia* law come from the Quran, which serves as the final arbiter on discussions of law. Muslims believe that the Quran is a compilation of the words of Allah (the Arabic word for God), a revelation from Allah that was sent down to the Prophet Muhammad through the Angel Gabriel. Despite differences in ideology among Muslim groups, it is the most fundamental belief of all Muslims that the Quran is the word of Allah.
The Sunnah (secondary)	In Islamic law, the primary role of the Sunnah is to clarify the Quran. The Quran describes the Sunnah as the essential guide for Muslims.
Ijma (tertiary)	Ijma is a consensus among ulama that results in a fatwa. The ijma is used to rule on an issue that is not explicitly discussed in the Quran and Sunnah. Usually, it is used to settle dubious issues and to revise a previous fatwa in light of superior arguments regarding the issue.
Ijtihad (tertiary)	Similar to ijma, the key players in ijtihad are the ulama. But instead of representing the consensus of several ulama, ijtihad refers to a sole alim's judgements (for example, opinion, analogy) on new issues that are not found explicitly in the Quran, Sunnah and ijma.

Source: Muhamad and Mizerski (2010).

as a set of revelations to the Prophet Mohammed from God, which were made over a period of 23 years. According to Islamic beliefs, these revelations were made in two stages. In the first stage, the messages focused on describing God and insisting that humans should worship only God. In the second stage, the messages focused on the social life of Muslims, including details of relationships with friends, relatives, neighbours and partners. Islam insists that Muslims should follow the guidelines from God in all aspects of their lives, and that even their emotions should be regulated by the teachings of Islam. Therefore, their love and hate should not be driven by mere human desires, but they should always seek guidance from the book to express their emotions (Alserhan, 2010).

According to Ajzen (1991), the social factor indicators of consumers' behaviour are known as the subjective norms, and it is defined as the social pressure on individuals to behave in accordance with the teachings or values followed by their reference groups (e.g. religious groups) or community (Ajzen, 1991). Herrero et al. (2008) state that subjective norms represent how a consumer is influenced by the perception of referents important to him or her. George (2004, p. 7) concludes,

An individual's normative structure, i.e. his or her beliefs about what important others think about the behaviour in question, should directly influence his or her subjective norms, or perceptions of the social pressure to comply with expectations about engaging in the behaviour. Subjective norms should in turn influence the individual's proclivity to engage in the behaviour. If social expectations are that people should engage in the behaviour in question, then the individual should be more likely to do so'.

Alam and Sayuti (2011) suggest that social pressure (e.g. from family, friends or religious people) is expected to influence religious individuals' behaviour. In addition, social pressure can influence religious people to a level where their intention to perform the behaviour leads them to prefer products/brands which match their religious beliefs (Hansen, 2008; Nur Haslizatual Liza, 2011). In addition, customers' subjective norms are considered as among the factors that impact on their attitudes (Ajzen and Fishbein, 1980). Overall, subjective norms and society's beliefs are two important factors in relation to consumer behaviour (Fame et al., 2004).

According to Batra et al. (2012), a brand can be loved as a result of different factors which include cultural identity. Additionally, Souiden and Rani (2015) state that Islam encourages its followers to pray, live and eat together, and therefore Muslims tend to belong to a collectivist culture, where the influence of social pressure is significant (Al-Gahtani et al., 2007). Additionally, Muslims believe that true love is part of God's love, and His love is the ultimate love; therefore, for Muslims, following Islamic teachings is one of the ways that makes them loved by God (Abdin, 2004). In addition to the influence of culture, Muslims' self-judgements of brands/products that consider Islamic teachings are expected to be positive, because as a result of following Islamic teachings, Muslims will be loved by God (Alserhan, 2010). Batra et al. (2012) state that strongly held

408 *Waleed Yousef and Najwa Yousef*

values influence an individual's judgement towards brand love. And for Muslims, Islam is a religion that covers all aspects of life (Alserhan, 2010; Souiden and Rani, 2015). However, it is suggested that Muslims behave differently when it comes to consumption, as the level of ease or difficulty varies depending on their perception of the behaviour and the level of religiosity they have (Muhamad and Mizerski, 2013). However, Muslims are more conservative when it comes to consumption, as they tend to develop love for brands that consider their beliefs, since they love and hate in line with Islamic teachings (Alserhan, 2010).

Outcomes of Islamic brand love

Fournier and Mick (1999) asserted that love and satisfaction were strongly correlated constructs, and they considered love as the highest level of satisfaction a consumer could have. More recently, Roy et al. (2013) suggested that brand love mediated the satisfaction/brand loyalty correlation, considering satisfaction as an antecedent to brand love, and finding that satisfaction and brand love were positively correlated. Their study was based on work by Caroll and Ahuvia (2006), who stated that satisfaction was one of the reasons behind brand love; however, they found that satisfied customers were not necessarily in love with the brand.

Affection has been linked with brand love and is considered as one of the brand love core elements (Feher, 2006; Richins, 1997, in Batra et al., 2012). In addition, Batra et al. (2012) found that affection was one of the positive effects a consumer could have when he/she loved a brand. Affection and love are similar constructs. However, affection has been used as one of the items to measure brand love, as brand love is a broader concept (Albert and Valette-Florence, 2010).

Brand loyalty is defined as the degree to which a consumer is committed to repurchase the brand. It is also viewed as a special case of relationship marketing, where the consumer has a significant psychological attachment to the brand entity consumed (Punniyamoorthy and Raj, 2007). In addition, Oliver (1999) defines brand loyalty as a deeply held commitment to rebuy a preferred product/ service consistently in the future.

Brand loyalty includes purchase intention and positive word of mouth (Cengiz and Yayla, 2007), which are also considered to be consequences of brand love (Caroll and Ahuvia, 2006). Therefore, consumers who love a brand will be loyal to it by repurchasing it and recommending it to other customers (Albert and Merunka, 2013; Rageh et al., 2012). In addition, brand love can lead to brand loyalty, positive word of mouth, brand commitment and intrinsic rewards. Albert and Merunka (2013) state that once consumers trust a brand, they are willing to love it, and a high level of brand love can be gained through brand identification as well. Consumers can also come to love a brand through having a long history with it (Batra et al., 2012). It is suggested that strongly held values such as religiosity, cultural identities and intrinsic rewards can lead to brand love (Batra et al., 2012). Overall, three important outcomes are considered as the main Islamic brand love outcomes which are brand loyalty, word of mouth and purchase intention.

Future research directions

This study offers Islamic brand love as a new construct, with religious beliefs, subjective norms and perceived behavioural control as key factors. Future researchers would be able to build on the current study of Islamic brand love from different dimensions. Some examples are given below.

1. The brand love construct should be investigated considering different determinants.
2. Islamic brand love found to be a vital construct leads to word of mouth, purchase intention and brand loyalty. More potential consequences of brand love can be examined in the future research.
3. This chapter examines brand love in the context of Islam; future research can consider brand love from different religious contexts.
4. A comparison research between collectivistic and individualistic cultures is recommended to examine the influence of culture on brand love.

Conclusion

This chapter contributes to the existing literature by offering a new construct, that of Islamic brand love. The Islamic brand love construct was developed by investigating the correlation between religious beliefs and brand love within the Islamic context. In addition, a new definition for Islamic brand love was provided, as a result of the relationship between religious beliefs and brand love. It can be concluded that Islamic brand love is a vital construct that is worth being considered by managers who seek to target Muslim consumers.

CASE STUDY

The AlBaik brand is a brand that is represented in a chain of restaurants based in Saudi Arabia, which is known by most Muslims who have performed *Hajj*. It is well known as a brand that communicates with its customers through considering their religious beliefs (AL-Sabban et al., 2014). Moreover, AlBaik as a brand promises its stakeholders that it will perform in line with God's teachings; it strives to position itself in society as a brand that considers Muslims' religious beliefs (AlBaik, 2017). As the company is based mainly in Jeddah and Makkah, where Muslims from all over the world gather to perform the *Hajj*, which is one of the pillars of Islam, the AlBaik brand is also linked with the Islamic holy places, which has helped it become a popular brand among Muslims.

In addition, AlBaik is a highly trusted company among its stakeholders. In 1998 the company was invited by the government of the Kingdom of Saudi Arabia, to serve food for the pilgrims during the *Hajj* time, the company served all pilgrims as a non-profit base service, with high food quality (Khan, 2014). Finally, in 2005, the company launched several corporate social responsibility programmes, such as the "clean up the world" campaign. The campaign was launched in line with the United Nations support programme (UNSP) (Khan, 2014).

Case questions

1. Based on the definition of Islamic brand love, do you think AlBaik brand can be loved by Muslims? Why?
2. Are there any other actions that can be taken by AlBaik in order to become a loved brand among Muslims?
3. Would you spread positive word of mouth about a brand that pays a lot of attention to cultural factors, such as religious beliefs, customs or language?

Key terms and definitions

Islamic brand love: The degree of passionate emotional attachment and positive evaluation (Albert and Merunka, 2013; Batra et al., 2012; Nguyen et al., 2013) that a satisfied Muslim consumer has for a particular trade name that matches his/her beliefs (Abdin, 2004; Alserhan, 2010).

Religious beliefs: the degree to which a follower is living according to the guidelines of his/her religious beliefs with a significant influence on their behaviour (Shachar et al., 2011), as their hearts accept the truth and live by it, out of free will and with love (Abdin, 2004).

Subjective norms: the perceived social pressure (Ajzen, 1991) from people important to an individual, who think he/she should/not perform certain actions.

Perceived behavioural control: the beliefs in personal ease or difficulty in performing the behaviour of interest (Ajzen, 1991).

Word of mouth: informal communications transferred from one individual to another about the usage or ownership of a particular brand, good or service (Brown et al., 2005; Lam et al., 2009).

Brand loyalty: a strong commitment to rebuy a product/service consistently in the future (Oliver, 1999), where the consumer has a significant psychological attachment to the brand entity consumed (Punniyamoorthy and Raj, 2007).

Purchase intention: consumer's judgement about buying a particular product or brand (Hellier et al., 2003; Porral et al., 2015).

Bibliography

Abdin, A. S. (2004). Love in Islam. *European Judaism*, 92–102.

Addis, M. and Holbrook, M. (2001). On the conceptual link between mass customization and experiential consumption: an explosion of subjectivity. *Journal of Consumer Behaviour*, 1(1), 50–66.

Ahmad Alserhan, B. and Ahmad Alserhan, Z. (2012). Researching Muslim consumers: do they represent the fourth-billion consumer segment? *Journal of Islamic Marketing*, 3(2), 121–138.

Ahuvia, A. C. (2005). Beyond the extended self: loved objects and consumers' identity narratives. *Journal of Consumer Research*, 32(1), 171–184.

Ajzen, I. (1991). The theory of planned behavior. *Organizational Behavior and Human Decision Processes*, 50(2), 179–211.

Ajzen, I. and Fishbein, M. (1977). Attitude-behavior relations: a theoretical analysis and review of empirical research. *Psychological Bulletin*, 84(5), 888.

Ajzen, I. and Fishbein, M. (1980). *Understanding Attitudes and Predicting Social Behavior*. New Jersey: Prentice-Hall.

Al-Abbadi, A.-S. (1985). *The Islamic Conception of Basic Needs and Its Relationships to Contemporary Conditions: A Paper as Part of a Symposium Entitled "Contemporary Social and Economic Conditions and Shapes of Change in in the Islamic World"*. Oman: Royal Council of Islamic Civilization.

Alam, S. S. and Sayuti, N. M. (2011). Applying the theory of planned behavior (TPB) in Halal food purchasing. *International Journal of Commerce and Management*, 21(1), 8–20.

Albaik (2017). http://www.albaik.com/en/article/corporate/the-albaik-promise.html [Accessed on January 2016].

Albert, N. and Merunka, D. (2013). The role of brand love in consumer-brand relationships. *Journal of Consumer Marketing*, 30(3), 258–266.

Albert, N. and Valette-Florence, P. (2010). Measuring the love feeling for a brand using interpersonal love items. *Journal of Marketing Development and Competitiveness*, 5(1), 57.

Albert, N., Merunke, D. and Pierre Valette-Florence, P. (2008). When consumers love their brands: exploring the concept and its dimensions. *Journal of Business Research*, 61(10), 1062–1075.

Al-Elyani, S. (2006). *Economic Education in the Holy Quran and Application in the Family and the School: An.* Unpublished MA Dissertation, Umm AL-Qura University.

Al-Gahtani, S. S., Hubona, G. S. and Wang, J. (2007). Information technology (IT) in Saudi Arabia: culture and the acceptance and use of IT. *Information Management*, 44(8), 681–691.

Al-Khayyat, A. A. (1982). *"Development and Luxury from an Islamic Perspective"*: A *Research Paper Presented at a Symposium Entitled "Islamic Economics"*. Oman: University of Jordan.

Al-Sabban, N., Al-Sabban, Y. and Rahatullah, M. K. (2014). Exploring corporate social responsibility policies in family owned businesses of Saudi Arabia. *International Journal of Research Studies in Management*, 3(2), 51–58.

Alserhan, B. A. (2010). On Islamic branding: brands as good deeds. *Journal of Islamic Marketing*, 1(2), 101–106.

Alserhan, B. A. and Alserhan, Z. A. (2012). Researching Muslim consumers: Do they represent the fourth-billion consumer segment? *Journal of Islamic Marketing*, 3(2), 121–138.

412 Waleed Yousef and Najwa Yousef

Armitage, C. J. and Conner, M. (2001). Efficacy of the theory of planned behaviour: a meta-analytic review. *British Journal of Social Psychology*, 40(4), 471–499.

Atwan, R. A. M. (1997). *The Role of Islamic Education in Rationalizing Spending: An.* Unpublished MA Dissertation, Yarmuk University, Faculty of Sharia and Islamic Studies.

Bakar, A., Lee, R. and Noor, H. (2013). Parsing religiosity, guilt and materialism on consumer ethics. *Journal of Islamic Marketing*, 4(3), 232–244.

Batra, R., Ahuvia, A. and Bagozzi, R. (2012). Brand love. *Journal of Marketing*, 76(2), 1–16.

Beckerleg, S. (1995). "Brown sugar" or Friday prayers: youth choices and community building in coastal Kenya. *African Affairs*, 94(374), 23–38.

Berry, L., Carbone, L. and Haeckel, S. (2002). Managing the total customer experience. *MIT Sloan Management Review*, 43(3), 85–89.

Brown, T. J., Barry, T. E., Dacin, P. A. and Gunst, R. F. (2005). Spreading the word: Investigating antecedents of consumers' positive word-of-mouth intentions and behaviors in a retailing context. *Journal of the Academy of Marketing Science*, 33(2), 123–138.

Carroll, B. A. and Ahuvia, A. C. (2006). Some antecedents and outcomes of brand love. *Marketing Letters*, 17(2), 79–89.

Cengiz, E. and Erdoøan Yayla, H. (2007). The effect of marketing mix on positive word-of-mouth communication: evidence from accounting offices in Turkey. *Innovative Marketing*, 3(4), 73–86.

Chaudhuri, A. and Holbrook, M. B. (2001). The chain of effects from brand trust and brand affect to brand performance: the role of brand loyalty. *Journal of Marketing*, 65(2), 81–93.

Christodoulides, G. (2009). Branding in the post-internet era. *Marketing Theory*, 9(1), 141–144.

Christodoulides, G., Michaelidou, N. and Li, C. H. (2009). Measuring perceived brand luxury: an evaluation of the BLI scale. *Journal of Brand Management*, 16(5–6), 395–405.

Elliott, R. and Jankel-Elliott, N. (2003). Using ethnography in strategic consumer research. *Qualitative Market Research An International Journal*, 6(4), 215–223.

Essoo, N. and Dibb, S. (2004). Religious influences on shopping behaviour: an exploratory study. *Journal of Marketing Management*, 20, 683–712.

Fam, K. S., Waller, D. S. and Erdogan, B. Z. (2004). The influence of religion on attitudes towards the advertising of controversial products. *European Journal of Marketing*, 38(5/6), 537–555.

Fehr, B. (1988). Prototype analysis of the concepts of love and commitment. *Journal of Personality and Social Psychology*, 55(4), 557.

Fehr, B. (2006). A prototype approach to studying love. *The New Psychology of Love*, 225–246.

Foroudi, P., Akarsu, T. N., Ageeva, E., Foroudi, M. M., Dennis, C. and Melewar, T. C. (2018). Promising the dream: changing destination image of London through the effect of website place. *Journal of Business Research*, 83, 97–110.

Fournier, S. (1998). Consumers and their brands: Developing relationship theory in consumer research. *Journal of Consumer Research*, 24(4), 343–373.

Fournier, S. and Mick, D. G. (1999). Rediscovering satisfaction. *Journal of Marketing*, 63(4), 5–23.

George, J. F. (2004). *The Theory of Planned Behavior and Internet Purchasing*. Internet.

Hansen, T. (2008). Consumer values, the theory of planned behaviour and online grocery shopping. *International Journal of Consumer Studies*, 32(2), 128–137.

Hazan, C. and Shaver, P. (1987). Romantic love conceptualized as an attachment process. *Journal of Personality and Social Psychology*, 52(3), 511.

Hellier, P. K., Geursen, G. M., Carr, R. A. and Rickard, J. A. (2003). Customer repurchase intention: a general structural equation model. *European Journal of Marketing*, 37(11/12), 1762–1800.

Herrero Crespo, Á. and Rodríguez del Bosque, I. (2008). The effect of innovativeness on the adoption of B2C e-commerce: a model based on the theory of planned behaviour. *Computers in Human Behavior*, 24(6, 2830–2847.

Hofstede, G. (1983). The cultural relativity of organizational practices and theories. *Journal of International Business Studies*, 14(2), 75–89.

Hofstede, G. (1984). The cultural relativity of the quality of life concept. *Academy of Management Review*, 9, 389–398.

Izberk-Bilgin, E. (2012). Infidel brands: unveiling alternative meanings of global brands at the nexus of globalization, consumer culture, and Islamism. *Journal of Consumer Research*, 39(4), 663–687.

Jafari, A. and Süerdem, A. (2012). An analysis of material consumption culture in the Muslim world. *Marketing Theory*, 12(1), 61–79.

Kearney, A. T. (2006). Addressing the Muslim market. *Reuters*, 1–26.

Khan, M. N., Islam, M. M., Islam, M. R. and Rahman, M. M. (2017). Household air pollution from cooking and risk of adverse health and birth outcomes in Bangladesh: A nationwide population-based study. *Environmental Health*, 16(1), 57.

King, J. and Crowther, R. (2004). The measurement of religiosity and spirituality: examples and issues from psychology. *Journal of Organizational Change Management*, 17, 83–101.

Kirkpatrick, L. A. (1992). An attachment-theory approach psychology of religion. *International Journal for the Psychology of Religion*, 2(1), 3–28.

Kirkpatrick, L. A. (1997). A longitudinal study of changes in religious belief and behavior as a function of individual differences in adult attachment style. *Journal for the Scientific Study of Religion*, 36(2), 207–217.

Kirkpatrick, L. A. (1998). God as a substitute attachment figure: a longitudinal study of adult attachment style and religious change in college students. *Personality and Social Psychology Bulletin*, 24(9), 961–973.

Lam, D., Lee, A. and Mizerski, R. (2009). The effects of cultural values in word-of-mouth communication. *Journal of International Marketing*, 17(3), 55–70.

Lasswell, T. E. and Lasswell, M. E. (1976). I love you but I'm not in love with you*. *Journal of Marital and Family Therapy*, 2(3), 211–224.

Liao, C., Chen, J.-L. and Yen, D. C. (2007). Theory of planning behavior (TPB) and customer satisfaction in the continued use of e-service: an integrated model. *Computers in Human Behavior*, 23(6), 2804–2822.

Ma, F. (2014). The concept of love in Shakespeare's Sonnets. *Journal of Language Teaching and Research*, 5(4), 918–923.

Melewar, T. C., Karaosmanoglu, E. and Paterson, D. (2005). Corporate identity: concept, components and contribution. *Journal of General Management*, 31(1), 59–81.

Mende, M. and Bolton, R. N. (2011). Why attachment security matters how customers' attachment styles influence their relationships with service firms and service employees. *Journal of Service Research*, 14(3), 285–301.

414   Waleed Yousef and Najwa Yousef

Mokhlis, S. (2009). Relevancy and measurement of religiosity in consumer behavior research. *International Business Research*, 2(3), 75.

Muhamad, N. and Mizerski, D. (2010). The constructs mediating religions' influence on buyers and consumers. *Journal of Islamic Marketing*, 1(2), 124–135.

Muhamad, N. and Mizerski, D. (2013). The effects of following Islam in decisions about taboo products. *Psychology and Marketing*, 30(4), 357–371.

Mukhtar, A. and Mohsin Butt, M. (2012). Intention to choose Halal products: the role of religiosity. *Journal of Islamic Marketing*, 3(2), 108–120.

Nguyen, B., Melewar, T. C. and Chen, J. (2013). The brand likeability effect: can firms make themselves more likeable? *Journal of General Management*, 38(3), 25–36.

Oliver, R. L. (1999). Whence consumer loyalty? *Journal of Marketing*, 63(4), 33–44.

Porral, C. C., Valentín Alejandro, M. F., Boga, O. J. and Mangín, J. L. (2015). Measuring the influence of customer-based store brand equity in the purchase intention. *Cuadernos De Gestión*, 15(1), 93–118.

Punniyamoorthy, M. and Raj, M. P. M. (2007). An empirical model for brand loyalty measurement. *Journal of Targeting, Measurement and Analysis for Marketing*, 15(4), 222–233.

Rageh Ismail, A. and Spinelli, G. (2012). Effects of brand love, personality and image on word-of-mouth: the case of fashion brands among young consumers. *Journal of Fashion Marketing and Management: An International Journal*, 16(4), 386–398.

Rauschnabel, P. A. and Ahuvia, A. C. (2014). You're so lovable: anthropomorphism and brand love. *Journal of Brand Management*, 21(5), 372–395.

Richins, M. L. (1997). Measuring emotions in the consumption experience. *Journal of Consumer Research*, 24(2), 127–146.

Rippin, A. (2015). *Muslims: Their Religious Beliefs and Practices*. London: Routledge.

Rossiter, J. R. (2012). A new C-OAR-SE-based content-valid and predictively valid measure that distinguishes brand love from brand liking. *Marketing Letters*, 23(3), 905–916.

Roy, S. K., Eshghi, A. and Sarkar, A. (2013). Antecedents and consequences of brand love. *Journal of Brand Management*, 20(4), 325–332.

Schifter, D. E. and Ajzen, I. (1985). Intention, perceived control, and weight loss: an application of the theory of planned behavior. *Journal of Personality and Social Psychology*, 49(3), 843.

Shabbir, M. S. (2010). The relationship between religiosity and new product adoption. *Journal of Islamic Marketing*, 1(1), 63–69.

Shachar, R., Erdem, T., Cutright, K. M. and Fitzsimons, G. J. (2011). Brands: The opiate of the nonreligious masses? *Marketing Science*, 30(1), 92–110.

Shimp, T. A. and. Madden, T. J. (1988). Consumer-object relations: a conceptual framework based analogously on Sternberg's triangular theory of love. *NA – Advances in Consumer Research*, 15.

Soon, J. M. and Wallace, C. (2017). Application of theory of planned behaviour in purchasing intention and consumption of Halal food. *Nutrition & Food Science*, 47(5), 635–647.

Souiden, N. and Rani, M. (2015). Consumer attitudes and purchase intentions toward Islamic banks: the influence of religiosity. *International Journal of Bank Marketing*, 33(2), 143–161.

Sternberg, R. J. (1986). A triangular theory of love. *Psychological Review*, 93(2), 119.

Temporal, P. (2011a). 23 the future of Islamic branding and marketing: a managerial perspective. *Handbook of Islamic Marketing*, 465.

Temporal, P. (2011b). *Islamic Branding and Marketing: Creating a Global Islamic Business*. John Wiley and Sons.

16 Societal corporate branding and political discourse

where brand ethics meets with consumers' clicktivism

*Rossella Gambetti, Silvia Biraghi,
T C Melewar and Angela Beccanulli*

Introduction: societal corporate branding

The role corporations should play in society, in terms of their social engagement and ethical responsibilities, has been increasingly questioned in recent times (Aßländer and Curbach, 2014; Buchholtz and Carroll, 2009; Leisinger, 2009). Governments, activists, communities and stakeholders expect companies to account for the social consequences of their activities (Porter and Kramer, 2006). These expectations are reconfiguring the rationale and the dynamics of business-society relations (Logsdon and Wood, 2002; Matten and Crane, 2005) since corporations are recognising that it is their duty to fulfil obligations to society (Stokes, 2002). This imbues firms with an ethical ethos that leads to corporation social responsiveness (Balmer and Gray, 2003). That emphasises honest and respectful dialogue informed by the ongoing exchange between business and society jointly shaping purposes, rights, duties and priorities (Bhattacharya, Korschun and Sen, 2009).

Corporations are claimed to act as if they were metaphorically citizens in that their commitments to society resemble those of citizens (Moon, Crane and Matten, 2005). As corporate citizens, companies participate in society in various forms ranging from indirect participation as pressure groups to direct participation in order to resolve communitarian problems (Moon, Crane and Matten, 2005). In acting as quasi-governmental entities, corporations become part of the political community and are inspired by the will to contribute to society getting involved in public discourse, civil endeavours and political rule-making (Aßländer and Curbach, 2014).

In that sense, the corporate brand, meant as the embodiment of the bilateral engagements between a company and society (Balmer and Greyser, 2002; Balmer and Gray, 2003) that encapsulates the covenant of their ongoing reciprocal commitments (Hatch and Schultz, 2009, 2010; Järventie-Thesleff, Moisander and Laine, 2011; Cornelissen, Christensen and Kinuthia, 2012; Melewar, Gotsi and Andriopoulos, 2012), represents an asset that in the essence of its promise embeds and harmoniously expresses the citizenship status of the corporation in

416   *Gambetti, Biraghi, Melewar and Beccanulli*

society. We name this approach to corporate brand management *societal corporate branding* and it is referred to as

> the humanistic tension of a company to use the corporate brand as an enabler of social discourses and actions through which the company carries out quasi-governmental interventions in favor of society. Doing so, corporations take on a role as sociopolitical citizens thanks to their societal CB actions to get engaged in the community and to actively contribute to the common good (Aßländer and Curbach, 2014), embedding it in their value proposition.
>
> (Biraghi, Gambetti and Schultz, 2017, 208)

In this chapter, we explore the current humanistic tension of companies to use the corporate brand as an enabler of political discourses and actions that are felt as cogent in the society. In particular we illustrate and discuss cases of corporate branding practices conducted by companies as a reaction to Donald Trump's political and social discourse and how these have been received by consumers. The aim is to contribute to, identify and understand the blurred contours of contemporary marketing ethics as related to corporate brand management and reflect on how brand and consumer political discourse currently get interlaced to reinforce brand symbols, meanings and actions.

Societal corporate branding, a criticism between Trump's humanism and pragmatism

The word "humanism" refers to a system of thought in which human values, interests and dignity are considered relevant (Law, 2011). It is an abstract concept that affirms people universally possess subjective identity and dignity that is an absolute inner value all human beings possess (Misztal, 2012).

If humanism regards all the abstract concepts that are referred to the "inner person", another concept exists that is always related to the person: the pragmatism. It specifically refers to the evident demonstrations of the "inner self", to the practical actions clearly recognisable and addable.

Therefore, humanism fundamentally treats abstract and ethical concepts while pragmatism sustains practical activities.

In the last years of the 20th and beginning of the 21st centuries, the adhesion to these two notions has profoundly involved companies in the economic system, deeply affecting their corporate branding campaigns.

Corporate branding is nowadays used to treat relevant moral and practical discourses and some companies decide to show their commitment by addressing abstract concepts such as dignity and morality, so the humanistic aspects behind an issue, or directly referring to practical actions and events, so the pragmatic parts of an issue.

A clear topic on which to study different corporate branding actions addressing a humanistic tension or a practical one is the cultural, social and political

Societal corporate branding and politics   417

diatribe related to the election of the new president of the United States, Donald Trump. Specifically, because some firms criticised directly the identity, morality and values of Donald Trump, while others addressed his conservative decisions and actions, pointing that distinction between humanistic and pragmatic principles.

In the next section, we illustrate some recent compelling case studies of companies that have shown their humanistic tension by criticising some aspects of Trump's personality and morality.

A critique of Donald Trump's humanism

In the context of societal corporate branding, many brands have embraced the humanistic tension, expressing in their citizenship campaigns judgements on the *morality and identity* of Donald Trump, especially on his image as a man of power, characterized by non-transparent behaviours and personal life and on his values and dignity.

Historically, political campaigns have been fought using slanders and infamies directed to the candidates' personal image and morality to erode popularity and reputation (Latin *dignitas*). By every possible means, politicians strived to defend and exalt their own image and fame and attack the ones of the adversaries (Laurence, 1994, 62–74). The major part of these leaks was orally entrusted and, occasionally, handwritten in satirical pamphlets or graffiti (Gascou, 1984, 676–706), equally as occurs today by satirical cartoons, memes and eventually billboards. Everything that belongs to the private and personal sphere had been used by adversaries to point out the leading political leader in order to demolish his personal qualities and so his political choices (Gascou, 1984, 719–735). In history, one of the first politicians to be persecuted for unethical private behaviours and scandalous love affairs was Julius Caesar. Recently, examples of politicians such as Jack Profumo, Silvio Berlusconi, and Donald Trump have been strongly criticized by both adversaries and public opinion for similar reasons.

Nowadays, as we live in the defined "image society", "in which the image plays an essential role in both processes of constitution of a new imagery and mass information" (Goodman, 1968, 103–142), the cultural model focuses on exteriority and how appearance is more important than ideas and content and this has legitimised more humanistic attacks on personal qualities and identities.

These attacks have been visible during the election campaign and political mandate of Donald Trump. Indeed, the president was inundated throughout his mandate by fierce public critiques on his interpersonal behaviors that were variously held sexist, arrogant, bossy, and culturally disrespectful. So, after his election the (electoral) world split into two: those who loved the president and those who hated him and the haters saw the new president as brutal, cruel, cynical and inhumane.

The hatred shown comes from the fact that Donald Trump is somehow breaking the continuity between republicans and democrats of the previous years, seeming to be the "not welcome outsider". The treatment that the media and

418   *Gambetti, Biraghi, Melewar and Beccanulli*

companies reserve for Donald Trump nowadays seems to transcend the normal criticism and strays into a demonisation, involving comparisons of the million-aire with dictators such as Mussolini or Hitler.

A predominant role is played by his manifestation of rough and coarse expressiveness in contrast with the identification of polite behaviours as principles of education and civilisation.

Another element of reprobation is the verbal prose used by the President, consisting of a simple, direct and pragmatic terminology, strongly incisive on people with a less sophisticated life and language, instead of what is rather expressed by personalities with a more intellectual and probably cultured *habitus*.

Much of the media, but also companies, continuously compare the tycoon figure with fascist and Nazist dictators; this recourse is due to the fact that these regimes were established after strong political and economic crises, similar to our current condition, but even more so because, culturally, in the collective imagination there is no better terminology to define"bad". [1]

As for the brands that have based their corporate citizenship campaigns on humanism and so on the criticism of the person, ethics, expressive inadequacy and morality of Trump, two interesting corporate cases are *The Simpsons* and Cucapà. In both these business cases, the criticism addresses indirectly both the personality and physicality of the president in a way that describes him as inadequate to fill his presidential role.

The Simpsons case: a critique of Donald Trump's personality and look

The Simpsons, the animated television series by 21st Century Fox (21CF), launched a succession of episodes with indirect political propaganda in which, repeatedly, Donald Trump was depicted as an unpresidential, narcisistic and unreliable person with a dictator soul comparable to Hitler's personality. Specifically, his inappropriateness is conveyed by depicting the president always lying in bed, refusing to read norms or answer emergency calls but just busy in increasing his Twitter followers. Then, his narcisism is underlined by all his personal photos hanged all over the cartoon house while his untrustworthiness is prompted by clear references to the Russiagate scandal. Moreover, his dictator soul is emphasized by the show of a book of Hitler speeches on his presidential bed. Finally, there are critiques on his personal aspect, especially on his height and hair that are depicted as a dog-top toupee.

21st Century Fox is an American multinational mass media corporation involved in the film and television industries that distinguished itself over time for an established commitment in engaging viewers on the current most pressing issues with an irreverent sense of humour.

Politics is a common theme in the series and the action against Trump is in line with the core values of the company. Indeed, since the beginning, 21CF

1   https://medium.com/@ItPutrino/perché-odiano-donald-trump-97bf2096cb02

Societal corporate branding and politics 419

and the tv series producer, Matt Groening, were arrayed on the front line in sustaining diversity and integration. Due to this reason, the mass media company expressed its corporate citizenship by taking its distance from Trump, showing their authentic commitment to their core values of diversity and inclusivity.

The Cucapà corporate citizenship project: a critique of Donald Trump's personality

A further example of a critical communication campaign against the humanism of Donald Trump was produced by **Cucapà**. This brand is a Mexican brewery company which carried out an original guerrilla campaign selling t-shirts to Trump supporters, stating "I support Donald", in the streets of Los Angeles. Unfortunately, this statement was a "catch" because as the temperature raised the supporting words on the t-shirt transformed into: "Donald el que lo lea" (which is a Spanish expression meaning "whoever reads this is a stupid") showing Donald Trump's face with a clown's nose.

This critical campaign against Donald Trump was actually part of a broader corporate citizenship project.

Specifically, the funds collected with the sale of the garments, went towards the financing of a huge party, by which Cucapà lived up to their statement: "Donald Trump (or his supporters) is going to pay for our beers, even though he doesn't know it yet"[2] following the rhetoric of Trump's declaration "Mexico will pay for the wall, they just don't know yet" referring to the intended construction on the Mexican border, that will be better explained in the next section.

The implicit critique that Cucapà directs to Donald Trump refers both to his person and his decisions.

Focusing on the personal structure, in the "con calor" t-shirt, Trump appears as a clown, so as a clumsy and puerile person whom people laugh at. The clown figure is not casual because usually that character is a synonym of unpredictability and untrustworthiness and moreover, culturally, is referred to as an obscene figure; all characteristics that the brand uses implicitly to refer to Trump.

Moreover, evidently, Cucapà changed an offensive Spanish colloquial phrase using the name of Trump referring to him as a laughable person.

Cucapà showed its corporate citizenship to its fellow citizens. As a Mexican brand, Cucapà felt the duty to refer to a huge issue for its own country showing its reluctance against Trump. The brand took a position in defence of Mexican citizens reclaiming its Mexicans roots.

These two corporate branding campaigns are clear cases of corporate citizenship combined with the notion of humanism. Companies critique the personality of Trump in order to remain loyal to their corporate values and to take a stand for employees and stakeholders. See Figure 16.1.

---

2 https://www.theguardian.com/us-news/2016/oct/18/mexico-brands-advertising-donald-trump

Figure 16.1 Cucapa's t-shirts in comparison: with calor and sin calor. https://www.entrepreneur.com/article/283573

CASES' HIGHLIGHTS

In sum, these two citizenship campaigns against the figure of Donald Trump, have identified, and therefore criticised, specific dimensions of Trump's humanism.

Respectively, *The Simpson's* judgement revolves around showing the inadequacy of the president's personality. The unsuitability is demonstrated by the repeated narcissistic references and the refusal to comply with political demands and duties.

Cucapà, in its criticism, addresses the presumed unreliability of the president in various ways. First, it is highlighted by comparing Trump to a clown, a character who, by definition, makes unexpected jokes and therefore cannot be trusted. Second, Cucapà refers to the decision to build a wall on the border with Mexico. Building a wall on the border means turning a back to part of the American population and therefore being a president people can't trust. Third, since Cucapà had already used Trump's rhetoric in the campaign, the brand does so also in his criticism of the president. Indeed, Cucapà sells shirts that change with the heat; this means that the original message of the shirts is not reliable. Since the shirts are sold to Trump's supporters, Cucapà wants to relay the message that they serve the supporters with the same unreliability as the president they vote for.

The next paragraph will instead provide examples of criticism against Trump's pragmatism, that is, on his decisions and political actions. In particular, the cases that will be examined criticise his immigration policies and his decisions on global warming.

Societal corporate branding and politics   421

A critique of Donald Trump's pragmatism

Despite going beyond a criticism of the person and addressing instead the practical activities, there are all those companies that have used the corporate branding combined with the notion of "pragmatism".

In particular, Trump has been criticised by companies for some decisions taken in stark contrast to those of the previous American neocons.

Specifically, the president has been attacked for the actions perpetuated in the sphere of foreign policy, such as the "Ban immigration" (which prohibited citizens of the five largest Muslim nations from entering America) and the already mentioned building of the wall on the Mexican border and for his convictions on global warming.

Countries all over the world have had growing interest in the effect of global warming and in December 2015, the United Nations Framework Convention on Climate Change (UNFCC) signed a Paris Climate Agreement in an attempt to mitigate global warming.3

Nevertheless, Donald Trump during his presidential campaign declared his intention to exit from the "Paris Agreement", communicating his view in different ways, especially on social media platforms.[4]

Donald Trump wrote on his Twitter feed: "Global Warming is nothing else, but an overpriced and artificially raised issue, which is targeted to make US economy less compatible".[5]

Trump also stated that the United States would actually benefit, rather than lose from global warming, even if it is an issue.

In the screenshots below, there are some comments published by Trump on his Twitter account: See Figure 16.2.[6]

There are relevant cases of corporate branding campaigns addressing the pragmatism of Donald Trump, in particular criticising the above-mentioned decisions. Notable of mention are the Airbnb, Nike and Moma branding campaigns.

The Airbnb case: a critique of "The Ban Immigration" to support values of diversity and acceptance

The first campaign is the one realised by Airbnb, the community marketplace used to list, discover and book accommodation around the world, that produced a campaign video against racial politics, to celebrate equality among people, during the Super Bowl of 2017. The video campaign, named #weaccept is a 30-second video showing a multi-ethnic group of people of different ages and genders that share a common message: "We believe no matter who you are, where you are

---

3   https://unfccc.int/process-and-meetings/the-paris-agreement/what-is-the-paris-agreement
4   https://www.theguardian.com/us-news/2018/may/31/paris-climate-deal-trump-exit-resistance
5   Donald J. Trump @realDonaldTrump official Twitter profile.
6   Donald J. Trump @realDonaldTrump official Twitter profile.

Figure 16.2 President Donald Trump's tweet on global warming. Donald J. Trump @ realDonaldTrump official Twitter profile.

from, who you love or who you worship, we all belong. The world is more beautiful the more you accept. #weaccept".

To support this message, the company also published on its website, in the section "Diversity and Belonging",[7] a press release explaining that the meaning behind the video was the promotion of acceptance of all human beings.

The brand showed its corporate citizenship embracing the concept of "pragmatism", in particular indirectly opposing Trump's policies against immigrants.

This campaign is consistent with the cultural policy of the company based on values as "the acceptance of diversity" and "the importance of having a place to belong and to call "home". Along with the campaign, the company expresses its corporate citizenship also with practical actions such as providing short-term housing for 100,000 refugees and disaster survivors[8] and money to organisations that help refugees (Figure 16.3).

Nike's corporate branding campaigns against Trump's declarations on diversity and global warming. A project to support equality and sustainability

A second case is **Nike**, that in February 2017, published an advertising campaign named "Equality", in reaction to Trump's Travel/Immigration Ban and his speech on people other than the White community and heterosexuals.

In this campaign, Nike shows different sport celebrities, such as LeBron James and Serena Williams, coming together against discrimination, communicating how equality should be in the world. The video states that if everybody can be equal in sports, equality can be everywhere.

---

7   https://www.airbnb.it/weaccept
8   https://www.theverge.com/2017/2/5/14517708/airbnb-super-bowl-ad-donation-aid

Societal corporate branding and politics 423

Figure 16.3 "We Accept" manifesto on Airbnb corporate website.

The power of the video derives not only from the message but also from the use of the images.[9] By making everything black and white, it reflects on what Nike is trying to communicate; there should be no colour and/or difference in the society.

In addition, the CEO of Nike, Mark Parker, made a declaration on Trump's travel and immigration ban.

"Nike believes in a world where everyone celebrates the power of diversity. Regardless of whether or how you worship, where you come from or who you love, everyone's individual experience is what makes us stronger as a whole".[10]

When it comes to equality, Nike is very passionate. The company expresses its corporate citizenship communicating clearly its beliefs and reasons to believe, not only in the United States but also in the rest of the world using social media and celebrities' endorsements.

Moreover, it is necessary to say that Nike is so committed in terms of equality also because a lot of its employees are immigrants and the brand strongly believes that people should celebrate diversity and not diminish it.

9   http://griotmag.com/it/equality-spot-della-nike-parla-veramente-uguaglianza/
10 https://www.refinery29.com/en-us/2017/01/138751/nike-trump-immigration-ban-mo-farah-letter

424   *Gambetti, Biraghi, Melewar and Beccanulli*

Nike also took a stand against Trump's decision to exit from the Paris Agreement.

Indeed, Mark Parker, the CEO, declared:

> Nike believes that climate change poses a serious global threat and that the world will have a more sustainable future and the industrial systems and economies in order to allow an economy of low-carbon growth.[11]

The brand decided to take part in the "We are still in" movement[12] that groups all those companies that would like to remain in the Paris Agreement to fight global warming. Practically, Nike also launched two sustainable actions: **FlyKnit** and **Nike Grind**. The Flyknit technology avoids the production of tonnes of waste and, in addition, gives life to lighter, stronger and more easily adaptable shoes. The aim is to significantly reduce waste and prevent tonnes of waste.

Nike Grind, on the other hand, regenerates existing products and materials into a range of materials par excellence. These materials will go far beyond single use and will continue to live from one product to another.

Nike Grind technology has led to many eco-sustainable initiatives, including "Recycle a shoe".[13] See Figures 16.4 and 16.5.

The MoMa case: a critique against the Travel and Immigration Ban

The last case in this section regards a protest generated by an artistic institution, accompanied by the relative non-profit organisations: **MoMa** and **MoMa PS1**.

The **MoMa** (Museum of Modern Art of New York), is the foremost museum of modern art in the world that, in the actual American context, in alignment with its mission and values, has immediately positioned itself against the politics of the new American President Donald Trump. Specifically, through exhibitions and programmes the museum has expressed its acceptance, promotion and welcoming of diversity. The most famous strong action of the museum has been the response to Trump's "Travel and Immigration ban" by introducing seven works made by artists from nations whose citizens were denied to entry into the United States by Trump, to the 5th floor permanent-collection galleries.[14]

Moreover, in accordance with respect and promotion of diversity, the museum concentrated on three other initiatives. Firstly, the displaying of 176 original emojis (until March 2017) across its collection beside the Picasso and Matisse masterpieces. These giant emojis became part of the exhibition because the museum considered them as a user meta-language that reaches humanity, a way

---

11 https://www.businessoffashion.com/articles/news-analysis/trump-climate-reversal-means-fashion-industry
12 https://www.businessinsider.com/we-are-still-in-group-represents-62-trillion-of-the-us-economy-plans-to-stay-in-paris-agreement-2017-6?IR=T
13 https://www.green-talk.com/nike-turns-sneaker-love-into-playground-hubs/
14 https://www.noisiamofuturo.it/2017/05/18/moma-anche-larte-protesta-trump/

Societal corporate branding and politics 425

Figure 16.4 "Equality" advertising campaign.

Figure 16.5 Gina Rodriguez and Serena Williams for Nike Equality campaign. Official Instagram profiles.

of bridging communication gaps between different communities, the integration of mixed-race families, different skin tones and same-sex couples that push the reaction activists for different social causes.

Secondly, MoMa specifically stood up in support of lesbian, gay, bisexual and transgender (LGBT) community launching the programme "Open Art

426 *Gambetti, Biraghi, Melewar and Beccanulli*

Space" to take care of the growth process of teenagers that are discovering their sexual identity, supporting them in a daily life where discrimination is still common.

Finally, the MoMa's "Modern Jazz Social" a settled live music performance, encouraged public awareness of African American artists, supporting them and encouraging their participation at MoMa's initiatives; this action was in line with MoMa's mission of respect and promotion of diversity.

Contextually, MoMa PS1, in April 2017, took a clear position against Trump's decision to build a wall on the Mexican border, thanks to an exhibition about the concept of "wall", both real and metaphorical, evoking and denouncing the birth of new nationalistic and xenophobic movements. See Figure 16.6.

Cases' highlights

These three cases have been examples of corporate citizenship campaigns against Trump's pragmatism. All the brands protested against the most compelling practical decisions and actions taken by the president. Their choice to criticise the racial and global warming policies depend on the fact that they were the most debated topics among the citizens. Thanks to these campaigns, brands stayed faithful to their core values, rousing a positive social impact on employees, consumers and communities with which they are in relation with.

In regard to creating a social impact, in the next section some cases of anti-Trump corporate citizenship campaigns will be examined, which not only dealt with social issues but also created a social impact on consumers. The effects will be analysed in an ascendant climax, from one that created the smallest social impact to the one that enlarged an existing social movement.

Figure 16.6 Emoji installation at MoMa. https://www.moma.org/calendar/exhibitions/3639

Corporate citizenship campaigns with a social impact: from counter-narrative to consumers' boycott to social movements' enlargement

Today, more than ever, consumers are putting their faith in brands to stand for something to help solve societal and political problems. People are weighing a brand's principles as much as its products. The 2018 Edelman Earned Brand study reveals that nearly two-thirds (64%) of consumers around the world now buy on belief. "These Belief-Driven Buyers will *support, boycott or follow* a brand based on where it stands on the political or social issues they care about".15 Regarding this new way of choosing, some companies are reacting proactively by creating corporate citizenship campaigns in which they openly or indirectly communicate their political or social ideology. In realising these campaigns, most of the companies are inspired by contemporary issues spread by media or directly by politicians but some of them, emphasising the importance they give to their consumers, are inspired by the inputs they collect directly from the communication flows already in the centre of public interest.

Along with these premises, it is important to analyse the social impact that these campaigns have on consumers, meaning to investigate how consumers perceive the role of companies and how they react to their communication policies.

The type and flow of reactions, that businesses can elicit depends on the positive or negative emotions brands create with their actions. Consumers, usually, express positive emotions for those companies whose they share values and from which they feel represented, protected and supported. This kind of positive emotions creates reactions such as "brand loyalty" and "brand love" (Roberts, 2006) that boost consumers likelihood to support the brand. When the support is particularly strong, consumers tend to aggregate in "movements behind the brand" (Roberts, 2006).

On the other hand, some brand's actions may not be shared by consumers and thus arouse negative emotions from which adverse reactions such as "brand dislike" or "brand hate" can derive. These negative emotions, at their maximum manifestation, could also cause consumers to boycott the brand (Dalli, Romani and Grappi, 2012). "Brands, however, always elicit the action or the resistance of the consumer" (Arvidsson, 2006, 36).

It is evident that these two orders of emotions can be manifested also if a brand decides to take sides in a communication flow already at the centre of public interest.

In the following, corporate branding cases against Donald Trump policies that had a strong social impact will be analysed.

The cases will be analysed according to an ascendant climax scheme, from the one that created the smallest impact on consumers to the one with the greatest social return.

15 https://www.edelman.com/earned-brand

428   Gambetti, Biraghi, Melewar and Beccanulli

The first and last cases regard brands engaged with a topic of conversation already widespread among media and consumers.

In the first example, Dove, using a counter-narrative technique, causes such positive reactions to create an online affiliate movement in which consumers, using the campaign rhetoric, broaden the message of the campaign on social media.

To continue in the ascendant climax scheme, the second case, Starbucks, regards a corporate citizenship campaign able to create both positive and negative reactions in consumers. Negative reactions promulgated by Trump's supporters created a boycotting movement against the firm on social networks. This "boycotting movement" not only created conversations on social media and cast doubt on Trump's word as the previous movement but undermined the company's image and sales. This movement reached a size such as to generate a countermovement in support of the brand, whose famous figures have become spokesmen.

Finally, we discuss Nike, with its corporate citizenship campaign that entered a particularly delicate subject area in America: racism. The topic had already found its wide diffusion among consumers, media and famous people when the analysed brand decided to leverage on the wave of communication to express its commitment on the issue. Its citizenship campaign while becoming part of an existing social movement, managed to have a wide diffusion.

In the next section, we illustrate a corporate branding case which leveraged on an already spread theme of conversation among customers. The brand, using a counter-narrative technique, generated, as social impact, an online movement in which consumers used the same rhetoric as the corporate branding campaign.

The Dove case: a counter-narrative citizenship campaign against Donald Trump

In the context of social citizenship campaign, many companies use the counter-narrative technique. Since brands are asked to take a side on political and social issues, the technique of counter-narrative serves to dismantle or demystify and directly discredit political messages by resorting to irony or revealing hypocrisies, lies or false information. In addition, it serves to promote the "critical spirit", that is consumers' ability to reflect on the authenticity of a message pronounced by a political or public figure. Currently, the most used technique of counter narrative is the "hashtag hijacking" (Romero, Meeder and Kleinberg, 2011), a form of media dissent, in which a hashtag is created with the same message shared by the person to contradict but with a different purpose than the one originally intended.[16] Usually the hashtag hijacking is used to frame an issue and to spread it because it is assumed by the company that consumers could use it on social networks and so broaden the message of the advertising and create virtual debate (Davolio and Lenzo, 2017).

---

16   https://smallbiztrends.com/2013/08/what-is-hashtag-hijacking-2.html

Societal corporate branding and politics   429

An interesting case of counter-narrative is the corporate branding campaign created by **Dove**, the personal care brand owned by Unilever. The brand took a stand against Donald Trump with an advertising campaign based entirely on the "alternative facts"[17] wording inspired by Trump's counsellor's phrase which referred to the inaccurate inauguration attendance number. The coined phrase "alternative facts" was already a small topic of discussion on social media when the brand decided to leverage on it creating the hashtag hijacking #AlternativeFacts. The brand uses corporate citizenship engagement in matters regarding Trump's administration that creates stronger relationship with the stakeholders. Indeed, nowadays the company's activities involve the social responsibility of their business to increase a positive social impact. Dove stood out of the competitors and became more visible because it wanted to make people talk about them and about #AlternativeFacts. Originally the ad was only released in the UK, and immediately after it was published in *The Guardian*, its social impact was massive because it became very popular among society, within social conversations on Twitter, Facebook and dozens of publications on web pages. As soon as the print ads were published in *The Guardian* and *The Times of London*, there was already a craze about #AlternativeFacts going on social media which continued with Dove.

Their communication strategy in terms of political engagement was a brilliant move since they received positive feedback on social media both from their permanent and new customers, engaging them in creation of shared value. Moreover, their approach which combines comments on social issues with simple tag lines proved to be successful in maintaining existing conversations and creating new ones around the topic that assured the brand a positive impact in creating new relationships with customers on a personal level.

Following the ascendant climax, in the next section, we illustrate a corporate branding case that created, as social impact, a boycotting movement and a counterresponse within consumers. See Figures 16.7 and 16.8.

Boycotting phenomena of corporate branding campaigns against Donald Trump: the Starbucks case

Nowadays, as already mentioned, firms using corporate branding campaigns, have stepped in to fill the void left by nonresponsive political parties and government agencies, taking a side on problems, that in the past, governments handled. But this has created new tensions and new social impacts (Bryant, 2011). "As brands have become more political, they have become at the same time, more vulnerable to political attacks" (Bryant, 2011). Indeed, as contemporary consumers are attempting to shape policy and be heard in the corridors of states of power, they have increasingly started to express their political ideas against companies with different ideological commitment by either not buying their products or boycotting them using the easy and inexpensive connections of social networking and

---

17   http://www.adnews.com.au/news/dove-trolls-trump-with-alternative-facts-ad

430 *Gambetti, Biraghi, Melewar and Beccanulli*

Figure 16.7 Dove Print Campaign #AlternativeFacts.

social media. "This is one of the most dynamic form of political expression today" (Bryant, 2011). So, corporate branding campaigns can become really courageous actions because communicating directly or indirectly political messages to the "wrong target" (opposite party) might make a company a target of an angry audience and ruin their reputation. An interesting example of consumers' expression of political resentment against a brand is the #BoycottStarbucks phenomenon and the counterresponse #DrinkStarbucks. **Starbucks**, the giant coffee chain, after the declaration of President Donald Trump on refugee policy, tried to promote a message of unity serving, a week before Election Day, its seasonal holiday drinks in new green cups with an illustration by Shogo Ota that showed the faces of more than one hundred people drawn with a single continuous line.18 See Figure 16.9.

18 https://www.news.com.au/finance/business/retail/starbucks-unity-cups-outrage-trump-fans/news-story/03d612d9e68070edc9cf9e9c9ab45d69

New Dove antiperspirant helps you remember distant relatives' names at family gatherings.

New Dove antiperspirant is a really good listener.

New Dove antiperspirant makes the lift arrive when you feverishly press the button.

New Dove antiperspirant knows a guy who can get you on the guest list.

#AlternativeFacts

Figure 16.8 Positive comments on Dove's campaign via Twitter.

This selling had a huge social impact because on social media Trump supporters started different boycotting actions against the brand that caused and were followed also by counter protests supporting the brand. The fact that Starbucks got rid of Christmas colour (red), replacing it with Islamic colour (green), all in the name of tolerance, actually stirred the thought that the Starbucks's CEO had them produced in support of Hillary Clinton, as he was known to be a supporter of the democratic party. Thus, the green cups became a trend topic of discussion on the major social media, creating viral content about progressive causes, including ethical sourcing and racial equality. People started to ask why the holiday spirit had become a political agenda defining the company a "Killary"[19] supporter against America. Moreover, some Christians saw this as an attack against Christmas, a forced political action. In reaction, many Trump supporters with the operation "#TrumpCup", continued to take to Twitter, proudly sharing photos of the drinks they've purchased at the chain they claimed to hate. Protesters used the hashtag #TrumpCups to instruct followers to place their Starbucks orders using the name "Trump", thereby forcing the coffee waiter to write the name on a coffee cup and once the order was ready sharing it online.

Then people decided to boycott Starbucks again in response to the CEO's declaration that Starbucks would hire 10.000 refugees worldwide over the next five years. Many Trump supporters denounced Starbucks's CEO and explained the real desire to boycott the brand, claiming that the company was giving away

19 https://www.businessinsider.com.au/starbucks-green-cups-spark-anger-2016-11

Figure 16.9 Green cups featuring an illustration by Shogo Ota showing the faces of more than a hundred people.

jobs that could be filled by Americans or American veterans. It raised a common online belief with which customers said that they had put Trump in the White House so they could also put Starbucks out of business using the hashtag #BoycottStarbucks. The movement to boycott Starbucks had already inspired a counter-protest #BuyStarbucks and #DrinkStarbucks with supporters including actress Jessica Chastain[20] that created a common sense of reinforced beliefs that the company fought against the uncertainty of Trump's actions without silence and without fear.

Finally, to conclude the climax of corporate branding campaigns, the next section will illustrate how brands can leverage on already popular conversation topics and enlarge social discourses and movements. See Figure 16.10.

The Nike case: expanding anti-Trump social movements

If Donald Trump can be seen as a movement leader who mobilised a mass following his charismatic appeals, the so-called "resistance", that opposes him, operates as a countermovement. A countermovement is defined as a movement

---

20 https://twitter.com/jes_chastain/status/826106536611168256

Societal corporate branding and politics   433

Figure 16.10 Examples of positive and negative reactions on Twitter.

that makes contrary claims simultaneously to those of the original movement (Tarrow and Meyer, 2018). Resistance is the set of sudden and strong emergent countermovements that overtly resist to the presidency of Donald Trump (Tarrow and Meyer, 2018). With the perils emerging after the start of the Trump era, public outrage began to coalesce into powerful social movements capable of creating large-scale progressive change. This process began at the very start of the Trump administration, when millions of people around the world took to the streets during the Women's March to protest against injustice. It continued with the #Takeaknee movement against the administration's travel ban, and, more recently, in the #MeToo movement and the March for Our Lives against gun violence. Even before Trump's elections, women, environmentalists, immigrants and ethnic and racial minorities began to organise to oppose the assault on rights and regulations they expected to be coming. As the enormities of the Trump presidency became clear, pre-existing groups, like Black Lives Matter and the LGBT movement, began to merge with the new groups that emerged from the elections. (Tarrow and Meyer, 2018). The emerging Resistance had two main organisational conduits: new groups, like Indivisible, that were formed out of ad hoc initiatives (Brooker, 2018) and older ones, like the already mentioned ones, that has been working for progressive causes. Social movements often arise in response to unpredictable discontinuous triggers, which catalyse action. All we have seen over the past two years suggests that the election of President Trump has been such a trigger (Tarrow and Meyer, 2018). His actions seem to have stimulated a shift towards progressive thinking in the United States, opening the door to transformative, generational change. This social movements also called "collective effervescence" (Durkheim, 1995) has been fertile soil for companies to explicate their effort in corporate citizenship.

The interesting cases selected have seen a brand leveraging on already existing social movements against specific decisions and actions of the Trump's presidency and inserting their corporate citizenship campaign on these existent dialogues siding with citizens and broadening and legitimising the phenomenon more.

The existent dialogue regards racial discrimination that in the United States is a latent state that permeates all aspects of daily life and extends to all minority communities. The incidents that triggered a strong public reaction in Trump's

434   *Gambetti, Biraghi, Melewar and Beccanulli*

mandate and brought the issue of discrimination back to the centre of the debate, prompting companies and public actors to deal with such a delicate and heartfelt issue from a large part of their stakeholders, have been the "Muslim Ban" and the construction of the wall on the Mexican border. Immediately, civil rights activists condemned the measures launched by the President and hundreds of American citizens took to the streets to protest. The culmination of the protest was when videos shooting violent scenes in which African American citizens were beaten during their arrest were shot on social networks. From this event, even public figures have expressed their protest.

In the summer of 2016, Colin Kaepernick, star of the National Football League, decided, before a game, to remain seated during the national anthem to denounce violence against African Americans. He publicly declared:

> I am not going to stand up to show pride in a flag for a country that oppresses black people and people of colour. To me this is bigger than football and it would be selfish on my part to look the other way. There are bodies in the street and people getting paid leave and getting away with murder.[21]

A few days later, before another game, Kaepernick continued the protest kneeling during the national hymn: the gesture was severely criticised so as to induce the team leaders to decide to dismiss him.

However, the protest took on a huge media significance following the words spoken by President Trump during an official speech in Alabama on September 22nd:

> "Wouldn't you love to see one of these NFL owners when somebody disrespects our flag to say get off the field right now, out, he's fired, he's fired".[22]

Among the first to stand up to the President's words was the basketball star Stephen Curry who, speaking to the press, said he wanted to refuse the invitation to the White House reserved for his team.

The protest also spread to the world of basketball and baseball and even to the world of European sport. From there, even some music stars started to kneel, names like Stevie Wonder, John Legend and Pharell Williams.

The gesture of kneeling has become the symbol of a protest that has rapidly spread from the world of sport to the world of music and cinema as well as on social networks where many stars support the #takeaknee campaign.

Nike, one of the most influential companies in the sportswear sector, decided as part of its citizenship commitment to leverage on the #takeaknee social movement. On September 1, 2018, the brand released a new commercial

---

21   https://www.theguardian.com/sport/2018/sep/04/nike-controversial-colin-kaepernick-campaign -divisive

22   https://www.sutori.com/story/taking-a-knee--YKbvv6M5SiDvASs2JpQ4iWZ1

starring the football player Colin Kaepernick. Nike's vice-president said that Kaepernick is one of the most inspirational athletes of this generation, who has leveraged the power of sport to help move the world forward. That's why they wanted to energise its meaning and introduce "Just Do It" to a new generation of athletes.

Nike's ad was published on Monday 1st and in just one day it arose an enormous level of attention. Between midday Monday and midday Tuesday, there were 2.7 million mentions of Nike. According to social media analysis firm Talkwalker, this massive social media movement means, for Nike's image, an increase of 1400% views over the prior day. In 24 hours, the reactions were booming. Then, the social buzz still increased thanks to many outstanding American characters who took a social part in the controversy. By 72 hours after the ad launch, Nike's mentions on their account were more than 5,2 million. As soon as Nike published its decision to hire Kaepernick for its commercial, the NFL player himself tweeted the ad. Right after his publication, in just a few days, the tweet had amassed 912,327 likes and 358,975 retweets.

Nike has chosen to undertake a branding strategy that includes brand positioning within social issues. The decision to include Colin Kaepernick – the image of an outstanding "Black Lives Matter" exponent – is a clear political and social declaration even if the commercial has not explicitly mentioned the protests, police shootings or anything controversial. The message is clear, hard and bold: Nike is taking a precise position against brutality, police shootings and violence towards Black people. Nike has always supported the Afro-American population both by employing a notably diverse staff and speaking out against racism many times so this citizenship commercial is consistent with its culture and value. By choosing and taking on Kaepernick as the protagonist of the ad, Nike has decided to amplify and make the message, that he has already spread, even more known around the country. The brand with this decision makes America aware of the fact that a powerful force, Nike, was listening and willing to support the cause. See Figures 16.11 and 16.12.

Conclusion

Our study extends the literature on societal corporate branding by providing empirical analysis of how brands took a stand on sociopolitical issues, joining the sustained social conversations already in the centre of public interest.

By examining several brand campaigns, realised between summer 2015 and February 2017, we underscored a number of key points.

First, brands are filling the void left by nonresponsive political parties and government agencies to the point that they comprehend in their purpose something bigger than just the economic objective. Brands act according to their "brand purpose" that reveals their essence: why the brand has been launched, why it is relevant and necessary for the consumers and how it should improve society for the better (Biraghi, Gambetti and Quigley, 2019). Doing so, corporations take on a role as sociopolitical citizens thanks to their efforts to get engaged in the community and to actively

Figure 16.11 Nike's first release of advertisement starring Colin Kaepernick.

Figure 16.12 Nike's advertisement "Dream crazy" published on YouTube.

contribute to the common good (Aßländer and Curbach, 2014), becoming the spokesman of their customers and employees' protests.

In this chapter, we focused on brands which covered the role of "macro-citizens" supporting a specific patriotic issue, the presidential election, as bait to show their commitment. The cited campaigns were not only useful to show companies' political or social ideology but also to manifest their understanding and closeness to employees and customers.

Societal corporate branding and politics   437

Second, brands acting like a quasi-governmental entity, find their raison d'etre in a strong community participating in the most cogent discourses generated in the social arena (Biraghi and Gambetti, 2017). This involvement allows brands to understand the issues, the concerns and the expectations of consumers, implementing actions to support society well-being and advancement. These actions when perceived as incongruent with the brand DNA may also become issues for brands, since consumers use their purchasing power as a political act to take positions that unmask untruthful communicative messages that are not compatible with the brand culture. Indeed, the new task for brands is to push through relevance, in particular to ensure that the social causes they support are in line with their mission, culture and values. The above-mentioned brand strategies show how different companies have lined up with those conversation topics in conflict both with the citizens' values and with brand culture and mission. In expressing themselves, corporations bear duties to accomplish virtuous social activities such as remaining faithful to their origins and value propositions. As consumers recognise the consistency between the messages and the corporate values, they perceive the real commitment of firms and their support. Consistency not only creates a positive impact on the communities, but also boosts consumers' trust and loyalty, thus increasing the reputation and profitability of corporations.

Finally, all these campaigns were powerful in terms of the social impact they created or amplified. Most of the consent/dissent on Donald Trump was expressed through social media, as these platforms have turned the traditional one-way communication approach of companies towards consumers into a two-way channel that leverages on consumer engagement (Ismail, Nguyen and Melewar, 2018). The click-reactions propagated the campaigns and their cultural values through the loops of social conversations (Kozinets, Patterson and Asham, 2017) giving awareness and authority to the firms' actions, and elevating consumers' conversations to a new sort of techno-mediated social activism. This form of activism has been named "clicktivism" (Halupka, 2014). It gets people to pay attention to cogent topics and, in some cases, to produce real activist actions as in the case of the "Take a knee movement" or the Starbucks protest and counter-protest.

Future research directions

Future works could better examine the influences on consumers of societal corporate branding campaigns especially in the techno-mediated context. It could be examined how corporate citizenship strategies are co-opted through brand activism and how massive citizens' activation such as "clicktivism" can be used by brands to encourage consumer engagement.

Key terms and definitions

Cultural branding: the cultural branding perspective acknowledges brands' representational and rhetorical power both as cultural artefacts and as engaging

438 *Gambetti, Biraghi, Melewar and Beccanulli*

and deceptive bearers of cultural and ideological codes. Within this framework, brands themselves have become ideological referents that shape cultural rituals, economic activities and social and political norms.

Corporate citizenship: by corporate citizenship, we refer to the fact that corporations are claimed to act as if they were metaphorically sociopolitical citizens, becoming part of the political community and being inspired by the will to contribute to society and getting involved in public discourse. Thanks to this new role, the brand is evolving from being a self-referential corporate asset embodying a company-centred attitude, towards being an asset that is socially inspired.

Societal corporate branding: by societal corporate branding, we refer to the humanistic tension of a company to use the corporate brand as an enabler of social discourses and actions through which the company carries out quasi-governmental interventions in favour of society. Doing so, corporations take on a role as sociopolitical citizens thanks to their societal corporate branding actions to get engaged in the community and to actively contribute to the common good, embedding it in their value proposition.

Clicktivism: traditionally considered as a form of lazy activism and as a non-committal act, clicktivism has been currently revisited as a form of civic engagement and quick activism expressed by likes, comments and content sharing that could eventually lead to more committed forms of social-political activation. Due to its ease of replication and non-specialised boundaries of use, clicktivism typifies the engagement norms of post-modernity and the most popular forms of political participation.

Brand DNA: is the sum of values that form the brand's core and defines its personality, creating a clear identity essential both for external and internal stakeholders. The brand DNA, therefore, defines the credibility limits of a brand. Indeed, consumers perceive the real commitment of a company's action when it is coherent with its DNA.

Case questions

1. Which are the advantages and the criticalities for a brand participating in social conversations assuming a citizen role?
2. What is the role played by techno-mediated platforms in societal corporate branding?
3. After reading this chapter, can you explain what it means for a brand to be a cultural resource that is co-constructed by the company and the society?
4. Do you think that *The Simpson's* appraisal was in line with its corporate DNA? Why?
5. Referring to Dove's campaign "Alternative Facts", what is the pragmatic action of Trump that is criticised? Do you recognise a critique of his humanism in this campaign?
6. Which were Nike's reasons for choosing Colin Kaepernick for the campaign?

Bibliography

Aßländer, M. S. and Curbach, J. (2014). The corporation as citoyen? Towards a new understanding of corporate citizenship. *Journal of Business Ethics*, 120(4), 541–554.

Arvidsson, A., (2006). *La marca nell'economia dell'informazione*. Milano: Franco Angeli, 36–36.

Balmer, J. M. T. and Gray, E. R. (2003). Corporate brands: what are they? What of them? *European Journal of Marketing*, 37(7–8), 972–997.

Balmer, J. M. T. and Greyser, S. A. (2002). Managing the multiple identities of the corporation. *California Management Review*, 44(3), 72–86.

Bhattacharya, C. B., Korschun, D. and Sen, S. (2009). Strengthening stakeholder–company relationships through mutually beneficial corporate social responsibility initiatives. *Journal of Business Ethics*, 85(2), 257–272.

Biraghi, S. and Gambetti, R. C. (2017). Is brand value co-creation actionable? A facilitation perspective. *Management Decision*, 55(7), 1475–1488.

Biraghi, S., Gambetti, R. C. and Schultz, D. E. (2017). Advancing a citizenship approach to corporate branding: a societal view. *International Studies of Management & Organization*, 47(2), 206–215.

Biraghi, S., Gambetti, R. C. and Quigley, S. (2019). Brand purpose as a cultural entity between business and society. In J. Marques and S. Dhimar (Eds.). *Social Entrepreneurship and Corporate Social Responsibility* (pp. 401–422). Cham: Springer.

Brooker, M. E. (2018). Invigorating and redirecting the grassroots. In D. S. Meyer and S. Tarrow (Eds.), *The Resistance. The Dawn of the Anti-Trump Opposition Movement* (pp. 162–184). New York: Oxford University Press.

Bryant, S. (2011). Not going to starbucks: boycotts and the out-sourcing of politics in the branded world. *Journal of Consumer Culture*, 11(2), 145–167.

Buchholtz, A. K. and Carroll, A. B. (2009). *Business and Society*. Mason, OH: South-Western Cengage Learning.

Cornelissen, J. P., Christensen, L. T. and Kinuthia, K. (2012). Corporate brands and identity: developing stronger theory and the call for shifting debate. *European Journal of Marketing*, 46(7–8), 1093–1102.

Dalli, D., Romani, S. and Grappi, S. (2012). Emotions that drive the consumers away from brands: measuring negative emotions toward brands and their behavioral effect. *International Journal of Research in Marketing*, 29(1), 55–67.

Durkheim, E. (1995). *Elementary Forms of the Religious Life*. Oxford: Oxford University Press.

Gascou, J. (1984). *Suètone Historien*. Roma: Ecole Rome.

Goodman, N. (1968). *Languages of Art: An Approach to a Theory of Symbols*. New York: Bobbs-Merril Company, INC.

Halupka, M. (2014). Clicktivism: a systematic heuristic. *Policy & Internet*, 6(2), 115–132.

Hatch, M. J. and Schultz, M., (2009). Of bricks and brands: from corporate to enterprise branding. *Organizational Dynamics*, 38(2), 117–130.

Hatch, M. J. and Schultz, M. (2010). Toward a theory of brand co-creation with implications for brand governance. *Journal of Brand Management*, 17(8), 590–604.

Ismail, A. R., Nguyen, B. and Melewar, T. C. (2018). Impact of perceived social media marketing activities on brand and value consciousness: roles of usage, materialism and conspicuous consumption. *International Journal of Internet Marketing and Advertising*, 12(3), 233–254.

440 Gambetti, Biraghi, Melewar and Beccanulli

Jarventie-Thesleff, R., Moisander, J. and Laine, P. M. (2011). Organizational dynamics and complexities of corporate brand building – a practice perspective. *Scandinavian Journal of Management, 27*(2), 196–204.

Kozinets, R., Patterson, A. and Ashman, R. (2017). Networks of desire: How technology increases our passion to consume. *Journal of Consumer Research, 43*(5), 659–682.

Laurence, R. (1994). Rumour and communication in Roman politics. *Greece & Rome, 41*(1), 62–74.

Law, S. (2011). *Humanism: A Very Short Introduction.* Oxford: Oxford University Press.

Leisinger, K. M., (2009). On corporate responsibility for human rights. In H. Spitzeck, M. Pirson, W., Amann, S. Khan and E. von Kimakowitz (Eds.), *Humanism in Business* (pp. 175–203). Cambridge: Cambridge University Press.

Logsdon, J. M. and Wood, D. J. (2002). Business citizenship. *Business Ethics Quarterly, 12*(2), 155–187.

Matten, D. and Crane, A. (2005). Corporate citizenship: toward an extended theoretical conceptualization. *Academy of Management Review, 30*(1), 166–179.

Melewar, T. C., Gotsi, M. and Andriopoulos, C. (2012). Shaping the research Agenda for corporate branding. *European Journal of Marketing, 46*(5), 600–608.

Misztal, B. A. (2012). The idea of dignity: its more significance. *European Journal of Social Theory, 16*(1), 101–121.

Moon, J., Crane, A. and Matten, D. (2005). Can corporations be citizens? Corporate citizenship as a metaphor for business participation in society. *Business Ethics Quarterly, 15*(3), 429–453.

Porter, M. E. and Kramer, M. R. (2006). Strategy & society: the link between competitive advantage and corporate social responsibility. *Harvard Business Review, 84*, 78–85.

Roberts, K., (2006). *Lovemarks: The Future Beyond Brands.* New York: Powerhouse Books.

Romero, D. M., Meeder, B. and Kleinberg, J. (2011). Differences in the mechanics of information diffusion across topics: idioms, political, hashtags and complex contagion on twitter. In *WW1 Proceedings of the 20th International Conference on World Wide Web* (pp. 695–704).

Stokes, G., (2002). Democracy and citizenship. In A. Carter & G. Stokes (Eds.), *Democratic Theory Today* (pp. 23–52). Cambridge: Polity Press.

Tarrow, S. and Meyer, S. D. (2018). Challenges of the Anti-Trump movement. *Partecipazione e Conflitto, 11*, 614–645.

Sitography

Agostini, S. D. (2017). *Il MoMa capofila nelle proteste contro il "muslim ban" di Trump.* Retrieved at IlSole24Ore.com, https://www.ilsole24ore.com/art/arteconomy/2017-02 -04/il-moma-capofila-proteste-contro-muslim-ban-trump-185637.shtml?uuid=AEd V9QO&refresh_ce=1

Airbnb Official Website (2017). https://www.airbnb.it/weaccept

Baker, R. (2017). *Dove Trolls with "Alternative Facts" Ad.* Retrieved at Adnews.com, http://www.adnews.com.au/news/dove-trolls-trump-with-alternative-facts-ad

Black Lives Matter Official Web Page. (2013). Retrieved at https://blacklivesmatter.com /about/herstory/

BWW News Desk (2017). *MoMa Modern Jazz Social to Transform Museum into Jazz Club.* Retrieved at Broadwayworld.com, https://www.broadwayworld.com/bwwclassical/article/ MoMA-Modern-Jazz-Social-To-Transform-Museum-Into-Jazz-Club-427-20170402

Societal corporate branding and politics 441

Byford, S. (2017). *Airbnb's Super Bowl Ad Says "We Accept" Everyone*. Retrieved at Theverge.com, https://www.theverge.com/2017/2/5/14517708/airbnb-super-bowl-ad-donation-aid

Campbell, A. (2013). *What Is Hashtag Hijacking?* Retrieved at Smallbiztrends.com, https://smallbiztrends.com/2013/08/what-is-hashtag-hijacking-2.html

Cau, E. (2018). *La falsa emergenza della carovana di migranti*. Retrieved at IlFoglio.it, https://www.ilfoglio.it/esteri/2018/10/25/news/la-falsa-emergenza-della-carovana-di-migranti-220904/

CultureGrrl. (2017). *Solves for Trump Bumps: Getty's Direct Salvo vs MoMa's Discreet Indirection*. Retrieved at Artsjournal.com, http://www.artsjournal.com/culturegrrl/2017/02/salves-for-trump-bumps-gettys-direct-salvo-vs-momas-discreet-indirection.html

Danziger, P. N. (2018). *Starbucks Needs a Reputation Boost: Will Closing for Racial-Bias Education Do It?* Retrieved at Forbes.com, https://www.forbes.com/sites/pamdanziger/2018/04/25/starbucks-needs-a-reputation-boost-will-closing-for-racial-bias-education-do-it/#6cd5c0ad397e

Davolio, M. E. and Lenzo, D. (2017). *Contro-narrative e narrative alternative: una ricerca di approfondimento, Giovani e Media*. Retrieved at Giovaniemedia.ch, https://www.giovaniemedia.ch/fileadmin/user_upload/2_Chancen_und_Gefahren/Radikalisierung_Extremismus/Rapporto_contro-narrative_Eser_Lenzo_2017.pdf

Delano, J. W. (2016). *This Is What the US-Mexico Border Wall Actually Looks Like*. Retrieved at NationalGeographic.com, https://news.nationalgeographic.com/2016/03/160304-us-mexico-border-fence-wall-photos-immigration/

Edelman's Official Website. (2018). *Earned Brand 2018*. Retrieved at https://www.edelman.com/earned-brand

Editorial Board. (2017). *Strategie di persuasione a confronto: Trump vs Corona*. Retrieved at http://www.performancestrategies.it/blog/vendite-e-negoziazione/trump-vs-corona/

Egan, M. (2017). *Corona Has a Trump-Mexico Problem*. Retrieved at Money.com, https://money.cnn.com/2017/01/17/investing/corona-trump-constellation-brands/index.html

Elbaor, C. (2017). *MoMa Creates "Safe Space" for LGBTQ Teens and Allies*. Retrieved at Artnet.com, https://news.artnet.com/art-world/moma-safe-art-space-lgbtq-teens-833342

Fernandez, C. (2017). *What Trump's Climate Reversal Means for the Fashion Industry*. Retrieved at Businessfashion.com, https://www.businessoffashion.com/articles/news-analysis/trump-climate-reversal-means-fashion-industry

Huffington Post's Editorial Board. (2007). *Il Moma espone le opere di sette artisti colpiti dal bando anti immigrazione di Trump*. Retrieved at Huffingtonpost.it https://www.huffingtonpost.it/2017/02/05/moma-contro-trump_n_14629078.html

Joseph, A. (2017). *Steph Curry Spoke Out and Burned Donald Trump*. Retrieved at Cnbc.com, https://www.cnbc.com/2017/02/08/steph-curry-spoke-out-and-burned-donald-trump.html

Kaplan, J. (2017). *Coca-Cola Opposes Trump Travel Ban, Assesses Employes Impact*. Retrieved at Bloomber.com, https://www.bloomberg.com/news/articles/2017-01-30/coca-cola-opposes-trump-travel-ban-will-assess-employee-impact

Kaufman, A. C. (2016). *Nike Is Now Making Most of its Shoes From its Own Garbage*. Retrieved at Huffingtonpost.com, https://www.huffpost.com/entry/nike-recycled-shoes_n_5733436fe4b0bc9cb048b398

442 Gambetti, Biraghi, Melewar and Beccanulli

Kelner, M. (2018). *Nike's Controversial Colin Kaepernick Ad Campaign its Most Divisive Yet.* Retrieved at TheGuardian.com, https://www.theguardian.com/sport/2018/sep/04/nike -controversial-colin-kaepernick-campaign-divisive

Kennedy, R. (2017). *At MoMa PS1, Tomas Rfa Explores Walls Real and Metaphorical.* Retrieved at NyTimes.com, https://www.nytimes.com/2017/04/05/arts/design/tomas -rafa-explores-walls-in-new-nationalisms-moma-ps1.html

Kirshner, A. (2017). *Airbnb Sends Strong Message for Refugees with "We Accept" Super Bowl Ad.* Retrieved at Sbnation.com, https://www.sbnation.com/nfl/2017/2/5/14517376/air bnb-super-bowl-ad-we-accept-trump

Larbi, M. (2017). *Dove Is Brilliantly Trolling Trump with Their Alternative Facts Advert.* Retrieved at Metro.co., https://http://metro.co.uk/2017/02/02/dove-is-brilliantly-tr olling-trump-with-their-alternative-facts-advert-6422563/

Ledbetter, C. (2017). *Dove Deodorant's #AlternativeFacts Campaign Trolls the Trump Administration.* Retrieved at Huffingtonpost.com, https://www.huffpost.com/entry/ doves-alternativefacts-campaign-perfect-trolls-the-trump-administration_n_5891f effe4b02772c4ea67db

Leininger, A. (2018). *Trump Supporters Launch #TrumpCup as a Protest Against Starbucks.* Retrieved at Edition.cnn, https://edition.cnn.com/2016/11/18/living/trump-cup-starb ucks/index.html

Lubitz, R. (2017). *In the Face of the Trump Presidency, Nike Just Released a Star-Studded Campaign Celebrating Equality.* Retrieved at Mic.com, https://www.mic.com/articles /168453/in-the-face-of-the-trump-presidency-nike-just-released-a-star-studded-camp aign-celebrating-equality

Maheshwari, S. (2017). *Super Bowl Commercials Feature Political Undertones and Celebrity Cameos.* Retrieved at NyTimes.com, https://www.nytimes.com/2017/02/05/business/m edia/commercials-super-bowl-51.html?_r=

Mastrolilli, P. (2019). *Il Messico rafforza il controllo dei confini e scongiura i dazi Usa.* Retrieved at LaStampa.it, https://www.lastampa.it/2019/06/09/esteri/il-messico-rafforza-il-contr ollo-dei-confini-e-scongiura-i-dazi-usa-bLEm6BSxPHZzEnVqb80dWK/pagina.html

Milman, O. (2018). *Paris Deal: A Year after Trump Announced US Exit, a Coalition Fights to Fill the Gap.* Retrieved at TheGuardian.com, https://www.theguardian.com/us-news /2018/may/31/paris-climate-deal-trump-exit-resistance

Mittal, P. (2016). *World's First Emojis on Display at New York's MoMa.* Retrieved at Aljazeera.com, https://www.aljazeera.com/blogs/americas/2016/12/world-emojis-dis play-york-moma-161226184836568.html

MoMa Official Website, *Open Art Space: A Free Drop-In Program for LGBTQ Teens and Their Allies.* Retrieved at https://www.moma.org/calendar/events/3679

Nichols, J. M. (2017). *MOMA Is Creating Safe Spaces for LGBTQ Teens Who Love Art.* Retrieved at Huffingtonpost.com, https://www.huffpost.com/entry/moma-lgbtq-teens -safe-space_n_5888f6bce4b0024605fd49e6

Palazzo, C. (2017). *Airbnb Says #Weaccept as Super Bowl LI Ads Get Political.* Retrieved at Telegraph.co.uk, https://www.telegraph.co.uk/technology/2017/02/06/airbnb-says-wea ccept-super-bowl-li-ad/

Passera, V. (2016). *Il MoMa di New York sfida Donald Trump.* Retrieved at Mame.it https:/ /www.mam-e.it/arte/moma-ne-work-trump-donald/

Perkins, M. S. (2017). *A Group Representing $6.2 Trillion of the US Economy Says They're "Still in" the Paris Climate Agreement.* Retrieved at Businessinsider.com https://www.bus inessinsider.com/we-are-still-in-group-represents-62-trillion-of-the-us-economy-plans -to-stay-in-paris-agreement-2017-6?IR=T

Societal corporate branding and politics   443

Peterson, H. (2017). *Dove Blasts Trump Administration in New Ad.* Retrieved at Businessinsider.com, https://www.businessinsider.com/dove-blasts-trump-administration-in-new-ad-2017-2?IR=T

Reid, E. (2017). *Eric Reid: Why Colin Kaepernick and I Decided to Take a Knee.* Retrieved at NyTimes.com, https://www.nytimes.com/2017/09/25/opinion/colin-kaepernick-football-protests.html

Reints, R. (2018). *Colin Kaepernick Pushes Nike's Market Value Up $6 Billion, to an All-Time High.* Retrieved at Fortune.com, http://fortune.com/2018/09/23/nike-market-value-colin-kaepernick-ad/

Rodionova, Z. (2017). *Donald Trump's Supporters Call for Starbucks Boycott after CEO Announces Plan to Hire 10,000 Refugees.* Retrieved at Independent.co.uk, https://www.independent.co.uk/news/business/news/starbucks-boycott-donald-trump-muslim-ban-supporters-ceo-howard-shultz-plan-hire-10000-refugees-a7554686.html

Sahoo, S. (2016). *Unilever Boss Says Look at What Trump Does, Not What He Says.* Retrieved at Thenational.ae, https://www.thenational.ae/business/unilever-boss-says-look-at-what-trump-does-not-what-he-says-1.195446

Spotti, V. (2018). *Nike e Colin Kaepernick: cosa succede quando un brand fa una campagna controversa.* Retrieved at Techeconomy.it https://www.techeconomy.it/2018/09/10/nike-colin-kaepernick/

Stack, L. (2017). *Starbucks Is Criticized for its Holiday Cups, Yes, Again.* Retrieved at NyTimes.com, https://www.nytimes.com/2017/11/20/style/starbucks-gay-agenda.html

Taylor, K. (2017). *Starbucks Has Become a Target of Trump Loving Conservatives- And That's Great News for the Brand.* Retrieved at Businessinsider.com, https://www.businessinsider.com/why-trump-supporters-boycott-starbucks-2017-2?IR=T

Twitter Page #Alternativefacts. (2017). Retrieved at https://twitter.com/search?q=%23alternativefacts%20%40dove&src=typd

United Nations Climate Change Official Website. (2015). Retrieved at https://unfccc.int/process-and-meetings/the-paris-agreement/what-is-the-paris-agreement

Wyche, S. (2016). *Colin Kaepernick Explains Why He Sat During National Anthem.* Retrieved at Nfl.com, http://www.nfl.com/news/story/0ap3000000691077/article/colin-kaepernick-explains-why-he-sat-during-national-

Zogbi, E. (2018). *Celebrities Who Supper Colin Kaepernick's Nike Ad.* Retrieved at Newsweek.com, https://www.newsweek.com/celebrities-show-their-support-colin-kaepernicks-nike-ad-1104236

Zuccheri, R. (2019). *Trump Ferma I Boeing: "Ordine con effetto immediato".* Retrieved at IlGiornale.it, http://www.ilgiornale.it/news/mondo/trump-ferma-i-boeing-ordine-e-ffetto-immediato-1662063.html

17 Brand knowledge, brand community and brand engagement

Suraksha Gupta, Dongmei Cao and Aisha Abuelmaatti

Introduction

The ways of brand management have changed. Brand communities have become one of the popular branding tools for marketers to engage consumers and build up brand image and brand knowledge with. This chapter aims to understand the interactive impact of brand knowledge and brand community engagement on purchase intention with an examination of the Honda car communities in the city of Jakarta.

Background

The development of a brand implies communicating a specific brand image in such a way that the company's target group links a brand and its products with a set of associations (Keller, 1993, 2013). According to the World Intellectual Property Report (2013), the image of a brand has the tendency to impact consumers' intention to purchase and brand sustainability in the long run.

It is worth noting that ten of the top 30 growing global brands are from the automotive industry, according to Interbrand (2017). This industry has been estimated to grow by 4.4% by 2030 (McKinsey and Company, 2016). Consumers adopt cars as conscious expressions of their identities, and the cars they select are often a symbolic representation of their personality and lifestyles. A vehicle, as a product, is usually purchased following careful consideration and often demands high capital value (Jiang et al., 2013). In this competitive market, cluttered with different products, consumer brand choice has been made more difficult. As such, consumers are presented with an array of brands to meet their needs. As a result, a lot of caution often predates the decision-making process. It can be deduced as such, given the preceding content, that focusing merely on product development does not suffice to fulfil consumers' needs. In fact, as consumers have to make buying decisions, they develop specific rules of thumb used in decision-making (Scammon, 1977). Brands are the most common rule of thumb in the contemporary marketplace. They facilitate many purchase decisions and offer reassurance as they connect current and future decisions to experiences, satisfactions and knowledge (Keller, 2003; Kapferer, 2008). Hence, brands play an important role

Brand knowledge, community and engagement 445

in consumer decision-making in the automotive industry and guide consumers in the process of making a purchase decision (Zarantonello and Schmitt, 2010).

It is interesting to note that, in Indonesia, the Association of Automotive Industries (2015) recorded a substantial 57% increase in growth of car sales compared to the previous year, reaching 1,208,028 units. The total number of passenger cars on the streets until 2016 amounted to 14,580,666 units according to the Badan Pusat Statistik (2016). This is reflected in the vast number of brand choices of cars and brand communities to compare and evaluate, ranging from Japanese, European, American, to Korean, before making a purchase decision. Marketers are interested in how these communities can create value for the company, influence consumer perceptions and evaluations through brand knowledge and attract consumers to become members of the community, to influence their purchasing intentions. To this end, understanding how consumer's buying intentions are influenced by brand knowledge and brand community engagement is of utmost importance.

Theoretical grounding

A brand is defined as a name, term, sign, symbol, design or a combination of these that identifies the maker or seller of a product or services (Kotler and Keller, 2009). Brands serve as strategic business assets essential for firms to develop a competitive advantage (Bertilsson, 2009) or build brand identity in competitive markets (Ghodeswar, 2008).

Branding is the process for a brand to be known by consumers, and various marketing programmes conducted by the producer of goods or services are also included in branding (Kotler and Keller, 2009). This branding process will then make consumers have the experience in knowing, using, even to liking a good or service with a particular brand. It will be easier for consumers to determine their choice if they already know and have the information about a brand. Moreover, consumers attach meanings, feelings, beliefs or opinions to their favourite brands (Mumby, 2013). Keller (2003, 2013) mentioned that consumers' knowledge, feelings and perceptions of the brand, as the outcome of their experience, are the foundations of a strong brand.

Concepts of brand knowledge and brand community engagement

Brand knowledge

Brand knowledge is defined as the existence of information about a brand in the memory of consumers, along with brand associations (Keller, 1993). Keller (1993) proposes that consumers' brand awareness and brand image are the two primary dimensions of brand knowledge. Brand awareness can be quantified from the consumer's capacity to recognise brands under contrasting circumstances (Keller, 2013). Chen and He (2003) mentioned that brand awareness leads to a significant role in consumer's decision-making because consumers must remember a specific brand when they buy related products. Kotler and Keller (2009)

446 *Gupta, Cao and Abuelmaatti*

described a brand image as the perceptions and beliefs held by consumers about the brand. Brand image, based on Keller's exposition (1993), is defined as the thought of a brand that reflects brand associations processed in the consumer's memory. The more associations are involved and related in the brand, the stronger the brand image of the brand's product. Information is an essential and critical part of forming a brand image and hence brand knowledge. The various items of provided information will reach consumers and be stored in their minds. In this regard, the multiple associations that connect the minds of consumers to a brand can be regarded as brand knowledge. Moreover, brand image is formed of the consumer's experiences, perceived quality, and self-image congruence with the brand image (Aaker, 1997; Sasmita and Suki, 2014). It is important to note that brand image exists in each consumer's mind and can differ, depending on the associations held by the consumer.

Brand community engagement

Brand identity is central to the brand's strategic vision since it embodies the essential characteristics that will sustain it over time (Aaker, 1996). It can be argued that a brand's identity is the sum of unique associations that consumers have when confronted with the brand (Keller, 2003). It is of utmost importance to consider the strength of the consumer's relationship with the brand community, which can be characterised through brand community identification whereby the person construes themselves to be a member belonging to the brand community. In contrast to other identities, which may render a person unique and separate, this is a shared or collective identity (Tajfel and Turner, 1985). Community engagement results from the overlaps that members perceive between their unique self-identity and their group-based identity.

A brand community is an important marketing tool and a strategy building up consumer attachment to a brand identity (Kotler and Keller, 2009). Liaw's (2011) study suggests that consumers' participation in a brand community influences purchase intention. Frank and Shah (2003) investigated how communities support innovative activities, maximising opportunities to bind and collaborate with loyal customers. In today's marketing environment, where the situation tends to be less structured, many marketers believe that channelling marketing funds to the brand community has a positive and effective impact. Indeed, marketers are interested in organising and facilitating the community of a brand (McAlexander et al., 2002).

Community members of a brand community are characterised by three primary elements, in which three points of characteristic features for the formation are summarised, namely mutual or shared consciousness, legitimacy and oppositional brand loyalty (Liaw, 2011). Shared awareness is when every member of the community feels that stronger brand relationships are essential. Still, more importantly, they think that relations between community members are stronger with one another. The most critical element of a community is public awareness of a product. Some important aspects are not verbal expressions that differentiate

Brand knowledge, community and engagement 447

their members from others and make them similar to each other. Such demarcation usually includes brand references for different or specific users compared to other brand users. This becomes clear in the behaviour when they have a way and a unique name to greet their members. The awareness of this kind that is found in the brand community is not limited to a geographic area. The brand community is not only recognised, but it is also celebrated. The brand community's members will be influenced by the brand and will be tied to each other. The fact that members perceive a stronger bond to the awareness and ownership on a common level is essential. The members of the brand community are also conscious of the different characteristics of other members. What the brand community differentiates between members and non-members of the community is legitimacy. A brand community is an open institution which does not reject its potential members and is also able to form its personalised system of hierarchy in the community. There are two elements of this characteristic, namely legitimacy and oppositional brand loyalty.

Legitimacy is the process by which members of the society categorise between community members and non-members of the community or the ones who have different rights. The brand community, in general, opens a social organisation that does not reject any members, but they have a hierarchical status. Anyone loyal to a particular brand may become a member of a community without ownership on the condition of having a right and genuine reason. What distinguishes members of the community who have a belief in the brand and those who just happen to have the brand's product is their concern for the brand. But legitimacy does not always exist in a brand community. On the other hand, through opposition in brand competition, brand community members get essential experiences in their communities, as well as a vital component of the brand's meaning. This serves as an illustration of what the brand is not and who is not a member of the brand community.

Brand community engagement of members can draw great benefits from a fruitful exchange with other customers, namely brand-related interactions, or personally developing and deriving social benefits by identifying with other members of a peer-group (Kuo and Feng, 2013). According to Nitzan and Libai (2011), these benefits can influence customers' decision-making as customers are more likely to trust other customers whose preferences they share and will ultimately lead to increased relations and loyalty towards that brand.

Examples of brand community engagement cited from published research include Harley Owners Group (HOG) from the Harley-Davidson brand (Fornier et al., 2001). This community is actively supported and governed by the company. Generally, the company persuades the customers to join local HOG branches, take part in its diverse events and show up in the meetings, when customers buy Harley-Davidson motorcycles. The local dealer usually arranges this HOG branch, and often the location of the meeting is at the dealer itself. Harley-Davidson usually funds HOG. Some agencies provide useful support such as caring and riding information, plus social and intellectual support, provided through learning experiences, social activities and friendships, to this

448   Gupta, Cao and Abuelmaatti

community's members. Increase in members' interest, commitment and reliance on the Harley-Davidson brand have been shown to result from taking part in the HOG (Fornier et al., 2001).

A similar thing happened within the Toyota car community in Indonesia (Liputan6.com, 2015). Toyota Owner Club (TOC) also invited representatives of Toyota car users community across Indonesia from all dealers in a regional event gathering held on 19 August 2015. This first local gathering aimed to invite all members of the Toyota community in Indonesia to provide information on the development of Toyota products and services. The purpose was to build an inter-community network that can provide mutual benefits in the long run.

This has also taken place within the Honda community engagement. *Honda Day 2016*, the first and biggest Honda car communities gathering in Indonesia, was held as a form of appreciation to consumers and all Honda lovers in Indonesia.[1] Various activities were designed at the event, not only to show the character and advantages of Honda's cars but also to strengthen the excellent relationship between Honda and the community as well as all consumers. The Honda Day is intended to be held routinely every year emphasising that the existence of the community is considered positive as people in this community are active consumers. They share various items of knowledge and inputs about Honda products.

Hypothesis development

Brand knowledge and brand community engagement

A community is a group of individuals who are united along with a set of purposes and common interest and intentions in a certain area. The community members knowledge about specific issues is built through communicating with others within the community. The community members have an insight of dedication and responsibility to deliver back the benefit to the community by passing on information and sharing their skill; this is the traditional viewpoint of a community (Cegarra-Navarro et al., 2009).

Communities both co-consume and co-produce knowledge; they co-consume it through information direction amidst people of the community. The attitudes and behaviours of community members in a group objective are affected by the ongoing flow of information. The power of the group in influencing brand desire in consumers and non-consumers is demonstrated in some studies that are conducted within brand communities. For example, the conclusive responsibility of brand communities in encouraging brand engagement and brand commitment was confirmed by the field study conducted by Kim et al. (2008). In addition, the changes in attitude and behaviour mediated by knowledge diffusion have been indicated in the study conducted by Wu and Sukoco (2010). Concurrently,

---

1   Source: Merdeka.com. Available online at https://www.merdeka.com/otomotif/honda-day-2016-kumpulkan-20-komunitas-mobil-honda.html.

Brand knowledge, community and engagement 449

giving information and feedback to the industry and producers co-produces knowledge. Cooperation with brand communities in the expansion of their marketing schemes is emphasised by many organisations such as Apple, Volkswagen and Nike, to name a few. Generating knowledge through active interactions with members of the community may be encouraged by the companies. It can be argued that the original source of concept for production and innovation might derive from long-term entrenched communities with stable activity between its members (Ewing, 2008).

Based on the sensitivity, ideas and faiths of the community members, the knowledge exchange in a community may be subjective, as much as objective, through giving actual information (Kim et al., 2008; Wu and Sukoco, 2010). For example, customers might share their fondness or disapproval of certain products, with advice to buy or not buy or notify each other accurately or mistakenly on elements, trademarks, store locations etc. Attitudes and behaviours are affected by both subjective and objective knowledge (Kim et al., 2008). Yet, the accuracy, dependability and objectivity of the shared information may grow as the community acquires expertise (Ewing, 2008).

The influence of customers' brand knowledge and the size of the brand community were examined in a study based on a sample of members of a European car club conducted by Wilimzig (2011). Accordingly, the effect of brand community on its members is abated by both the brand knowledge of the consumer and the size of the brand community. Besides, knowledgeable customers, about a brand, experience higher levels of identification, engagement and pressure than novices. Therefore, it is more important for the company to recruit competent consumers, rather than novices into brand communities if they aim to have an impact on customers. The results of research conducted by Wilimzig (2011) states the positive effect of brand knowledge variables on brand community. As such, the following hypotheses can be deduced in view of the preceding content:

H1: Brand knowledge has a positive and significant effect on brand community.

Brand knowledge and purchase intention

Purchase intention has been defined as the likelihood that the consumer will plan to purchase a brand's product, consider purchasing or prefer purchasing it (Grewal et al.,1998). Positive purchase intention does not necessarily mean the consumer will buy the brand, but it is much more likely.

Consumer purchase intention is affected by many factors. According to Dodds et al. (1991), purchase intentions rest on price and quality of the product, which means that before buying the product, customers' primary attention is on the affordability and the quality offering. Consumers' purchase intention is not only confined to price and quality but moves beyond to cultural, psychological and social aspects (Kotler, 2011). Moreover, user experience, social network and word of mouth are all associated with purchase intention. For instance, if the

450 *Gupta, Cao and Abuelmaatti*

experience of using the car was good, then consumers recommend it to family and friends. The vast array of studies shows that brand community engagement and communication shape and influence consumers' attitudes towards brands and brand equity and thus significantly influence the intent to purchase (Wang and Hazen, 2016).

Brand knowledge is an underexplored influential factor. Brand knowledge could be gained through consumers' experience with the brand (Huang, 2017). Moreover, every company competes to create a good brand image through brand knowledge in the views of consumers, whether it is about products, companies or users. With a good brand image and brand knowledge in the minds of consumers, it is easier for companies to market their products and also be well received by consumers.

Consumers need to find, collect and understand some information about products in making decisions about them. Brand knowledge can have a significant impact on the customers' image and perception of the respective brand (Chevalier and Mayzlin, 2006). Positive brand image increases customers' likelihood to buy a certain brand, whereas negative brand image can be damaging. Positive brand image produces higher brand loyalty and creates barriers against competitors' actions (Keller, 1993). A decision to purchase will not be taken if a consumer does not have any knowledge about both the product and the desired brand. Consumers will tend to buy products with well-known brands compared to products whose brands are still foreign to their ears. Buying interest is also based on consumer knowledge they get from the media about the product brand's information. Esch et al. (2006) state that the higher the level of one's brand knowledge, the more the consumer's buying interest in the product with the brand increases because the brand is the first thing that they remember.

Similarly, the research conducted by Lawu (2015) uses dimensions of brand knowledge as independent variables and purchase intention as the dependent variable. The study's results show that the dimensions of brand knowledge significantly influence the purchase intention variable. It also shows that the dimensions of brand knowledge have a significant effect on purchase intention. In the automobile industry, customers' brand knowledge of different automobile brands forms distinctive brand images of the corresponding brands, which influence the consumer purchase intention of certain brands of cars. As such, the following hypotheses can be deduced in view of the preceding content:

H2: Brand knowledge has a positive and significant effect on purchase intention.

Brand community engagement and purchase intention

The notion that the markets are active and target-oriented, and not only quiet receivers of information, is the basis of the uses and gratifications theory. Gratification can be explained as a positive sensibility reaction to having one's ambitions or objectives fulfilled. It is feasible to determine how members' utilisation of societies can affect their interest to purchase by applying gratification as the standard of favourable outcome while examining brand communities. Gratification can be hard to measure because it is an emotion, in which each consumer will go through at distinct levels.

A theoretical model of how the relationship of customers with brand community affects their intentions and behaviours is developed by Algesheimer et al. (2005). Beneficial effects, such as engagement of larger society, and unfavourable effects, such as the pressure of normative society and eventually reactance, are generated by the brand community.

Businesses that take advantage of arranging virtual communities will be splendidly remunerated with both unequalled customer loyalty and great economic returns, as stated by Hagel and Armstrong (1997). Furthermore, the Yankee Group Report is referred to by Holland and Baker (2001), in which a review of organisations implementing a community action demonstrated growth in brand loyalty. Moreover, across an array of websites, online consumers, who are the brand community members, purchase at a much higher rate than non-members, as indicated by the survey.

According to a study conducted by Wilimzig (2011), there is a strong indication that brand community members have a higher probability of purchasing. This outcome can be a demonstration for brands that their community members are and will be more approachable to marketing and advertising efforts. Brand communities give a positive impact on consumer's purchase intention, as stated by the results of research conducted by Wilimzig (2011). As such, the following hypotheses can be deduced in view of the preceding content:

> H3: Brand community has a positive and significant effect on purchase intention.

Research model

The above hypotheses are depicted in Figure 17.1, which is our research model. The research model is underpinned by the social influence theory, which is proposed by Kelman (1958). According to Kelman (1958), social influence appears when an individual's attitudes, beliefs and subsequent actions are influenced by referent others through three processes: compliance, identification and internalisation. This

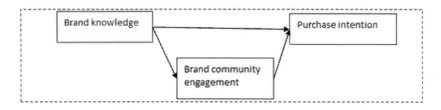

Figure 17.1 Research model.

452   Gupta, Cao and Abuelmaatti

would be especially relevant to brand identity, brand community identity (Black and Veloutsou, 2017), brand community and brand engagement behaviours (Cao et al., 2020). Social influence theory is particularly relevant to consumer behaviours in collectivism cultures like Indonesia and India (Gupta and Shukla, 2019). The customers in a collectivist society like Indonesia are influenced by the social norms (Thøgersen et al., 2015). As the Honda car brand is well established, purchasing this product has become a norm for society. Given the preceding content, this research will analyse consumers' purchase intention by two parameters, namely brand knowledge and brand community engagement as can be seen in Figure 17.1.

The impact of brand knowledge and brand community engagement on the individual's action and brand consumption represents social influence on purchase intention (Vigneron and Johnson, 2004; Tsai, 2005; Wiedmann et al., 2009; Wang, 2014; Varshneya et al., 2017). Social influence occurs when individuals change their thoughts, feelings or behaviours in response to their society or surroundings (Turner, 1991; Liu et al.,2020). It can be argued that people manipulate or modify their thoughts and actions to conform to the other groups or society (Chen-Yu and Seock, 2002). It can be attributed to the concept of homophily which can be considered as the social dynamics in which individuals try to affiliate with others by displaying similar behaviour (Ryan, 2001). It may be regarded as a salient factor because people seek social proof before trying a product category (Thøgersen et al., 2015). In other words, the consumers who are socially adapted are motivated to gain brands to display their status and achievements to their aimed social groups (Tsai, 2005).

Research methods

Measurement

Measurement of constructs is all adapted from validated literature. Brand knowledge is measured by four items which are adapted from Osei-Frimpong et al. (2019). Four measurement items of brand community engagement are adapted from Algesheimer et al. (2018). Purchase intention is measured by three items, which are adapted from Prentice et al. (2019). Respondents are required to use a 5-point Likert scale to assess the questionnaire items.

Sampling and data

The questionnaire survey was designed for data collection. It was uploaded to Jisc Online-Surveys, an online survey tool designed for academic research. After the survey was launched, a web link was generated for accessing the survey.

A convenient sampling method was used. We contacted 12 popular Honda car brand communities in Jakarta (Table 17.1). The questionnaire's web link was sent to those Honda car brand community members via Line and Whatsapp messenger as well as email. After a few times of sending reminder emails to contacts, a sample of 209 valid replies was collected.

Brand knowledge, community and engagement   453

Table 17.1 Respondent profile (n=209)

Indicator	Category	Frequency (%)
Gender	Male	125 (60%)
	Female	84 (40%)
Age	18–29 years	123 (59%)
	30–39 years	58 (28%)
	≥ 40 years	28 (13%))
Occupation	Student	50 (24%)
	Non-government employees	118 (56%)
	Entrepreneur	29 (14%)
	Government employees	12 (6%)
Personal monthly expense budget	<USD100	23 (11%)
	USD101–170	35 (17%)
	USD171–240	43 (20%)
	USD241–310	33 (16%)
	≥ USD311	75 (36%)
Membership* of Honda Brand communities in Jakarta	Jazz Fit Club Indonesia	130 (62%)*
	Brio Project Indonesia	85 (41%)
	Mobilio Indonesia Community	68 (33%)
	C-RV Nation Indonesia	60 (29%)
	FD Squad Jakarta	27 (13%)
	Accord CM 5 Indonesia	21 (10%)
	Run GK5	9 (4%)
	Other (Civic Jakarta, Basis Bintaro, HRV devotee, HOFOS Honda Freed Owners, ICC)	10 (5%)

Note: *Most of the respondents are members of more than one Honda brand community in Jakarta. Therefore, the sum of the frequency is more than the sample size, 209.

Table 17.1 reports the profile of the survey respondents, including gender, age, occupation and monthly expense budget. Our sample represents younger generations of the Indonesian population. Among the three age groups, the majority (59%) of them are between 18 and 29 years old; only 13% of them are 40 years old and over. The rest are between 30 and 39 years old. The male group accounts for 60% and females account for 40% of respondents. With regard to the occupation profile, the majority (62%) half are professionals (including government and non-government employees), and there were some students (24%) and entrepreneurs (14%) in the sample.

According to the World Bank statistics, Indonesia is an upper-middle-income economy with gross national income (GNI) per capita of USD4050 in 2019.[2] The middle class accounted for 20% of the population in 2019.[3] The growing

2   Source: World Bank. Available online at https://data.worldbank.org/indicator/NY.GNP.PCAP.C D?locations=ID.
3   Source: World Bank. Available online at https://www.worldbank.org/en/news/press-release/2020 /01/30/expanding-middle-class-key-for-indonesia-future#:~:text=Over%20the%20past%2015 %20years,currently%20belonging%20to%20this%20group.

454   *Gupta, Cao and Abuelmaatti*

middle class accounts for 43% of total household consumption and constitutes a main purchasing power in the automotive market.[4] Table 17.1 indicates that 62% of correspondents were from the ever-increasing middle class (i.e. with personal monthly expense budget within the range of USD171–310) and 36% from the wealthy class (i.e. with monthly expense budget of more than USD311). The middle class and the wealthy class together constitute the biggest proportion of car consumers across the Indonesian population.

Our sample indicates some of the most popular Honda brand communities in Jakarta, such as Jazz Fit Club Indonesia (its memberships representing 62% of the sample), Brio Project Indonesia (41%) and Mobilio Indonesia Community (33%).

Results and analysis

Measurement validation

Table 17.2 displays constructs and measurement items and reports the test results of construct reliability and validity. All loadings are higher than the threshold value 0.7; values of Cronbach's alpha and composite reliability (CR) are all higher than the suggested threshold value 0.7 (Hair et al., 2014). Both suggest good convergence of the measurement. Scores of average variance extracted (AVE) range from 0.765 to 0.819, indicating excellent reliability of the three constructs (Hair et al., 2014).

Table 17.3 displays the construct discriminant validity using the HTMT (heterotrait-monotrait ratio) criterion. The results of HTMT range from 0.546 to 0.806, which are lower than the threshold value 0.85, suggesting sufficient discriminant measurement of each construct (Ringle et al., 2015).

Structural model test

Structural relationships were tested, and the results are reported in Table 17.4. Our results suggest that brand knowledge (β = 0.561, t = 8.883) is a crucial determinant of purchase intention of Honda cars. Meanwhile, brand community engagement (β = 0.321, t = 4.681) also significantly influences the purchase intention of Honda cars. Brand knowledge significantly contributes to brand community engagement (β = 0.502, t = 9.668) and hence brand knowledge indirectly impacts purchase intention via the mediator brand community engagement. The brand community model and the interactive effects of brand knowledge and brand community engagement explain 60% of purchase intention of Honda cars in Jakarta.

---

4   Source: The Association of Indonesia Automotive Industries. Available online at https://www.gaikindo.or.id/en/growing-middle-class-encourages-automotive-market/.

Brand knowledge, community and engagement   455

Table 17.2 Constructs reliability and validity

Construct (**reference**)	Measurement		Loading
Brand knowledge (*Osei-Frimpong et al.*, *2019*) Cronbach's α (0.898) CR (0.929) AVE (0.765)	BK1	I know pretty much about the Honda brand.	0.881
	BK2	I know the unique advantages of the Honda brand.	0.885
	BK3	Compared to most other people, I know quite much about the Honda brand.	0.869
	BK4	I consider myself to be an expert in the Honda brand.	0.864
Brand community engagement (*Algesheimer et al.*, *2018*) Cronbach's α (0.926) CR (0.948) AVE (0.819)	BCE1	I benefit from following the brand community's rules.	0.926
	BCE2	I am motivated to participate in the brand community's activities because I feel better afterwards.	0.918
	BCE3	I am motivated to participate in the brand community's activities because I can support other members.	0.895
	BCE4	I am motivated to participate in the brand community's activities because I can reach personal goals.	0.879
Purchase intention (*Prentice et al.*, *2019*) Cronbach's α (0.887) CR (0.930) AVE (0.817)	PI1	I would buy a Honda brand car through this community.	0.937
	PI2	Honda would be my first choice to buy a car.	0.921
	PI3	I would gather more information for buying a Honda car.	0.850

Table 17.3 Discriminant validity: HTMT criterion

Construct	BCE	BK	PI
Brand community engagement (BCE)	*		
Brand knowledge (BK)	0.546	*	
Purchase Intention (PI)	0.665	0.806	*

Table 17.4 Structural parameter estimates with standardised coefficients

Path (hypothesis)	Coefficients	T value	Support
BK→BCE	0.502***	9.669	Yes
BK→PI	0.561***	8.883	Yes
BCE→PI	0.321***	4.681	Yes
Model Fit Summary: SRMR = 0.053; NFI = 0.883; Chi-Square = 224.0636. PI (R^2 = 0.600); BCE (R2 = 0.252).			

***$p<0.001$ (two-tailed test)

Multigroup analysis

To understand the behavioural difference within the sample, we generated five data groups based on two profile indicators, i.e. age and gender: G1 (aged 18 to 29), G2 (aged 30 to 39), G3 (aged 40 to 41), G4 (Female) and G5 (Male). Then we performed algorithm and bootstrapping testing with the data groups. Results of path coefficients of the group samples and the complete sample are displayed in Figure 17.2.

We found that the three hypotheses are all statistically significant across the five group's data, which is the same as that of the complete sample. The multiple group analysis (MGA) results show that the behavioural pattern between the two gender groups is different slightly. However, the results indicate that each age group sample has a distinctive feature. For instance, R square of purchase intention (PI) (0.754) is the highest score in G3, suggesting purchase intention of the eldest age group (G3) is most likely to be explained by their brand knowledge and

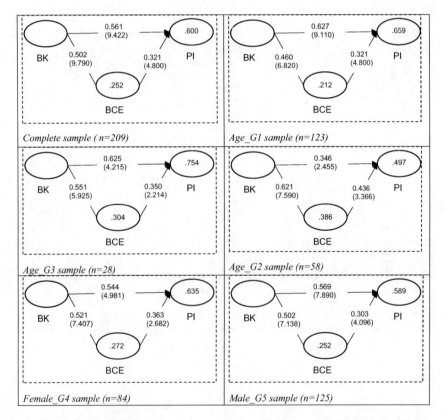

Figure 17.2 Multigroup comparison: path coefficients, T values and R squares. Note: T values are in brackets; R square values are inside circles; BK = brand knowledge; PI = purchase intention; BCE = brand community engagement.

Brand knowledge, community and engagement   457

brand community engagement. On the contrary, R square of purchase intention (0.497) has the lowest score in AgeG2, suggesting purchase intention of the middle age group (G2) is least likely to be explained by their brand knowledge and brand community engagement.

It shows that the behavioural pattern in AgeG2 is opposite to that of AgeG1. For instance, among the five groups, brand knowledge (BK) is the strongest determinant of purchase intention (BK→PI: 0.627) in Age G1, while brand knowledge has the smallest effect size on purchase intention (BK→PI: 0.346). Brand community engagement (BCE) has the lowest effect on purchase intention (BCE→PI: 0.302) in AgeG1, while brand community engagement has the most potent impact on purchase intention (BCE→PI:0.436) in AgeG2.

To further check if the behavioural differences among the five group samples are significant, we ran multiple group analysis. The results of path coefficients differences between five groups and their significance was obtained using both PLS-MGA and Welch-Satterthwait Test. Table 17.5 displays the MGA results. The MGA results show that none of the path-differences are statistically significant based on t-values in brackets. The results indicate that the biggest path coefficients-differences are associated with the effect of brand knowledge on purchase intention, e.g. the path coefficients-difference between AgeG1 and AgeG2 (0.281), between AgeG2 and AgeG3 (0.279) and between AgeG2 and MaleG2 (0.223).

Conclusion

This chapter set out to investigate the impact of brand community engagement and brand knowledge on purchase intention in the Honda car brand communities in Jakarta, Indonesia, one of the Asian emerging automotive markets. Our results suggest that brand knowledge has a strong effect on purchase intention. That is, the higher the Honda consumer's knowledge of the Honda brand, the higher the engagement of consumers in Honda communities, and vice versa. The finding behind this result reflects consumers' reasonable assessment of product information for the purchase decision to make. This finding is in line with relevant studies (e.g. Wilimzig, 2011).

Also, our empirical results suggest that brand community engagement is positively and significantly related to purchase intention. Moreover, we found that the interaction effect of brand knowledge and brand community engagement on purchase intention is positive and statistically significant. Our findings are consistent with some of the relevant studies on brand management and brand community (e.g. Zheng et al., 2015; Prentice et al., 2019). Zheng et al. (2015) suggest that user engagement in online brand communities on social networking sites help build brand loyalty. Tiruwa et al. (2016) found that brand community engagement influences the customer's intention to purchase. Although brand loyalty and purchase intention are the different effects of brand community engagement, they share one common theoretical implication. That is, the influence of social identity (ID) drives engaging consumers and motivating purchase

Table 17.5 Multiple group analysis (MGA): PLS-MGA and Welch-Satterthwait Test (WST)

Path	Test	Path coefficients-diff									
		AgeG1-AgeG2	AgeG1-AgeG3	Age G1-FemaleG1	AgeG1-MaleG2	AgeG2-G3	Age G2-FemaleG1	Age G2-MaleG2	Age G3-FemaleG1	Age G3-Male G2	FemaleG1-Male G2
BCE → PI	PLS-MGA	0.134	0.048	0.062	0.001	0.087	0.073	0.133	0.014	0.047	0.061
		(0.898)	(0.274)	(0.382)	(0.009)	(0.452)	(0.408)	(0.944)	(0.068)	(0.279)	(0.394)
	WST	0.134	0.048	0.062	0.001	0.087	0.073	0.133	0.014	0.047	0.061
		(0.898)	(0.268)	(0.386)	(0.010)	(0.437)	(0.404)	(0.948)	(0.067)	(0.273)	(0.401)
BK → BCE	PLS-MGA	0.161	0.091	0.061	0.041	0.069	0.100	0.119	0.030	0.050	0.020
		(1.466)	(0.805)	(0.596)	(0.401)	(0.594)	(0.943)	(1.120)	(0.277)	(0.452)	(0.198)
	WST	0.161	0.091	0.061	0.041	0.069	0.100	0.119	0.030	0.050	0.020
		(1.536)	(0.800)	(0.626)	(0.424)	(0.571)	(0.941)	(1.125)	(0.264)	(0.433)	(0.198)
BK → PI	PLS-MGA	0.281	0.002	0.083	0.058	0.279	0.198	0.223	0.081	0.056	0.025
		(1.855)	(0.012)	(0.631)	(0.568)	(1.446)	(1.142)	(1.460)	(0.456)	(0.357)	(0.187)
	WST	0.281	0.002	0.083	0.058	0.279	0.198	0.223	0.081	0.056	0.025
		(1.868)	(0.011)	(0.633)	(0.587)	(1.399)	(1.142)	(1.477)	(0.437)	(0.342)	(0.189)

Brand knowledge, community and engagement   459

intention and is underpinned by the social influence theory in social marketing and brand community management (Algesheimer et al., 2005).

Implications and recommendations

The results provide practical implications for brand markets to develop branding strategy, e.g. to enhance consumers' brand image through providing product information and product knowledge; to strengthen the brand-consumer relationship through engaging brand community members with the brand identity.

The MGA results provide practical implications for brand markets to make strategies of market segmentation. From the MGA, we found that the behavioural patterns between the two gender groups share more similarity than difference. This result suggests that there is no need to segment into male or female groups with different brand community engagement strategies.

However, we found that the effect size of brand knowledge on purchase intention differs substantially between the three age-group samples. Our results suggest that the model best explained the purchase intention behaviour of the group aged 30–39 among the three age groups. Therefore, Honda needs to form a more engaging community environment and events to invite and engage this particular group. Also, we found that brand knowledge is the highest effect size predicting purchase intention among the group aged 18–29. Therefore, Honda could notice this particular group and make a specific effort to provide brand and product knowledge in the community.

Future research directions

This research contains some limitations. One of the limitations is related to the sample; our sample is more representative of younger generations in Jakarta, Indonesia. Therefore, care should be taken for generalisation of the findings to other age groups of the population or different social and cultural countries.

In recent years, studies on brand community have changed with a focus more on the online social media brand community context. Digital and virtual engagement is a different context and meet a distinct need for some groups of people but not all. Also, evidence shows that people are conscious of the social distancing rule, and at the same time, desire to be socialised and included in virtual and real communities. With the social distancing measures due to the COVID-19 pandemic, study on brand management and brand marketing needs to pay more attention to the different needs of social and cultural groups and both virtual and real brand communities' engagement. The other limitation of the study is that we focused on the link between brand and consumer. The interaction of the self with the other members and social influencers also affect brand consumers' engagement with a brand and their purchase decisions (Hughes et al., 2019). This limitation in our study opens other future research directions.

CASE STUDY5

"F*ck off Google": protest against Google Campus Berlin (Fritze et al., 2019)

Introduction

In November 2016, Google announced plans to rent a building in the trendy, multicultural Kreuzberg district of Berlin to open a Google Campus – a business incubator for tech start-ups, offering support, workshops and networking opportunities for entrepreneurs. But soon after the announcement, disaffected local communities organised several protests, asserting that "It's extremely violent and arrogant of this mega-corporation, whose business model is based on mass surveillance and which speculates like crazy, to set up shop here", according to a protest leader known by his alias, Larry Pageblank. Berlin's local government supported Google's plan, yet Kreuzberg inhabitants' fierce protests to combat gentrification and Google's commercial exploitation of the neighbourhood sought to reject its potentially huge impact on their privacy and lifestyle. In the face of this challenge, was it still possible for Google to continue its plans in Berlin?

Berlin: a rising star in the start-up scene

In 2016, Berlin was a popular site for German start-ups, accounting for 17% of all German start-ups. A new tech start-up was being founded every 17 hours in the city, with about 500 of them launching every year. The city offered various incubators, accelerators and co-working spaces, as well as good access to capital and financial support. In addition, Berlin provided a safe city with high living standards, parks, low rental prices, a rich cultural and art scene and people from diverse international backgrounds. Moreover, Berlin's renowned universities contributed to the knowledge-intensive environment, and Germany maintained a stable legal and political system. Together, these features made Berlin highly attractive for creative, international entrepreneurs to set up shop, while also providing pull factors for recruiting employees. Berlin's start-ups thus took pride in their ecosystem and famously adopted an inclusive attitude, known as the "Berlin Spirit". All of these elements were pertinent to Google's 2016 plan to open a campus in Berlin.

Google campus: a breeding ground for entrepreneurs

The "Google for Entrepreneurs" project was designed particularly to promote technology start-ups. It revolved around Google Campuses, which feature connecting spaces that seek to bring together like-minded problem solvers and provide facilitative conditions for entrepreneurs.

---

5   The case study material is edited from Fritze et al. (2019). Relevant references, tables and figures are removed from the original source.

When Google chose the city for a new campus, Berlin's politicians were optimistic. The city's mayor Michael Müller viewed the plans as an opportunity, calling it "an important day for Berlin". Local politicians also expressed their hope that Google, as a successful company, would invest in growing neighbourhoods, spur digitalisation of the city and help link the city's scientific institutions and businesses. As it moved forward with the plan, Google chose the vibrant Kreuzberg neighbourhood, known for its creative, diverse culture and unconventional scene, filled with entrepreneurs and artists. In 2016, Google started renting a building in the heart of Kreuzberg and preparing for the campus opening, initially scheduled for 2017. The project would hire six to ten Google employees, with room for around 20 start-ups. The pieces thus were in place for a fruitful cooperation between Google and Berlin, but there was one thing nobody had reckoned with: the residents of Kreuzberg!

Kreuzberg: a special neighbourhood?

Berlin's Kreuzberg district has long been renowned for its art scene, student spirit, environmentalism, underground nightlife and radical political activism. In addition, the neighbourhood's strong sense of community has prompted highly invested efforts to protect the local ecosystem. Inhabitants were proud to call themselves "Kreuzbergers". The area is only 10.38 km^2 in size, yet its increasing popularity has led to greater population density and soaring rents, such that "The problem of rising rents and lack of living space is one of the most important issues for Berlin", according to Petra Rohland, a spokesperson for the city's Department of Urban Development and Housing. The Kreuzbergers, known for their liberal, left-minded political attitudes, have responded to these developments by forming activist groups and coalitions that work to address issues surrounding gentrification, displacement and the privatisation of public space.

Google: caught in the battle against gentrification and displacement

When Google decided to open its campus in Kreuzberg, it added fuel to the fiery debate about gentrification, rents and displacement of small shops and inventive businesses, which has long been integral to Kreuzberg's culture. Protestors argued that Google Campus would spur these negative developments, possibly leading to a situation like that in San Francisco, where extreme poverty and technology wealth live side by side. Protestors perceived that the multinational corporation would kill off their very identity, threatening the loss of their individualistic lifestyle and start-up scene through a profit-oriented restructuring of the neighbourhood. They also noted that Google's business model conflicts with the liberal, progressive and creative spirit of Kreuzberg. People were particularly suspicious of the company's collection and monetisation of personal data, reflecting previous critiques of Google's data protection policies. Finally, protestors highlighted news reports of Google's tax evasion and mass surveillance practices.

462   *Gupta, Cao and Abuelmaatti*

> This distrust in the company and its ethics, combined with the ongoing fight against gentrification, led to fierce protests targeting the Google Campus. The multiple campaigns included animated Twitter activity and the creation of online platforms such as "fuckoffgoogle.com". In 2018, protestors even occupied the area where the campus was planned to be, prompting their arrest by local authorities. Confronted with such opposition, Google had no choice but to postpone the opening of its campus.

Case questions

What are the fundamental reasons behind the conflict between the Google Campus initiative and the inhabitants of Kreuzberg?

Do you think that the conflict has somehow ruined Google's image in the long term?

What should Google have done to communicate with the protestors and handle the issue?

How would Google avoid such similar things happening in the future?

Key terms and definitions

Brand community is a community formed by a group of non-geographically bound members and is associated with a brand. Community members are socially connected with each other and the brand as well.

Brand community engagement refers to the process of forming emotional or behavioural interactions of community members and member with the brand. It is a brand management tool for enhancing brand connection and brand attachment.

Brand knowledge refers to a consumer's understanding of a brand and its products. Brand knowledge is typically concerned with the consumer's ability to remember, say or associate a brand.

Acknowledgement

We thank Nadira Femitri Asri for her assistance in data collection.

References

Aaker, D. A. (1996). *Building Strong Brands*. New York: Free Press.

Aaker, J. (1997). Dimensions of brand personality. *Journal of Marketing Research*, 34, 347–356.

Algesheimer, R., Dholakia, U. M. and Herrmann, A. (2005). The social influence of brand community: evidence from European car clubs. *Journal of Marketing*, 69, 19–34.

Brand knowledge, community and engagement 463

Algesheimer, René, Dholakia, Utpal M. and Herrmann, Andreas. (2018). The social influence of brand community: Evidence from European car clubs. *Journal of Marketing*, 69(3), 19–34.

Badan Pusat Statistik (2016). *Pengendara Mobil*. Available from: https://bps.go.id/linkTableDinamis/view/id/1133 [18 May 2018].

Bertilsson, J. (2009). *The Way Brands Work; Consumers' Understanding of the Creation and Usage of Brands*. Lund: Lund Business Press.

Black, I. and Veloutsou, C. (2017). Working consumers: co-creation of brand identity, consumer identity and brand community identity. *Journal of Business Research*, 70, 416–429.

Cao, D., Meadows, M., Wong, D. and Xia, S. (2020). Understanding consumers' social media engagement behaviour: an examination of the moderation effect of social media context. *Journal of Business Research*. Available from: https://doi.org/10.1016/j.jbusres.2020.06.025

Cegarra-Navarro, J. G., Cordoba-Pachon, J.-R. and Fernandez de Bobadilla, G. W. (2009). Creating environmental knowledge through green communities in the Spanish pharmaceuticals industry. *The Service Industries Journal*, 29(12), 1745–1761.

Chen, R. and He, F. (2003). Examination of brand knowledge, perceived risk and consumers intention to adopt an online retailer. *TQM & Business Excellence*, 14(6), 677–693.

Chen-Yu, J. H. and Seock, Y. K. (2002). Adolescents' clothing purchase motivations, information sources, and store selection criteria: a comparison of male/female and impulse/nonimpulse shoppers. *Family and Consumer Sciences Research Journal*, 31(1), 50–77.

Chevalier, J. A. and Mayzlin, D. (2006). The effect of word of mouth on sales: online book reviews. *Journal of Marketing Research*, 43(3), 345–354.

Dodds, B. K., Monroe, K. B. and Grewal, D. (1991). Effect of price, brands and store information on buyers' product evaluation. *Journal of Marketing Research*, 28(3), 307–319.

Esch, F.-R., Langner, T., Schmitt, B. H. and Geus, P. (2006). Are brands forever? How brand knowledge and relationships affect current and future purchases. *Journal of Product & Brand Management*, 15(2), 98–105.

Ewing, T. (2008). Participation cycles and emergent cultures in an online community. *International Journal of Market Research*, 50(5), 575–590.

Fornier, S., Sensiper, S., McAlexander, J. and Schouten, J. (2001). *Building Brand Community on the Harley- Davidson Posse Ride (Multimedia Case)*. Harvard: Harvard Business Publishing.

Frank, N. and Shah, S. K. (2003). How communities support innovative activities: an exploration of assistance and sharing among end-users. *Research Policy*, 32, 157–178.

Fritze, M. P., Ganser-Stickler, G. M., Turk, S. and Zhao, Y. (2019). "F*ck off Google": protest against Google Campus Berlin. *The Case Journal*, 15(6), 669–688.

Ghodeswar, B. M. (2008). Building brand identity in competitive markets: a conceptual model. *Journal of Product & Brand Management*, 17(1), 4–12.

Grewal, D., Monroe, K. B. and Krishnan, R.(1998). The effects of price-comparison advertising on buyers' perceptions of acquisition value, transaction value, and behavioral intentions. *Journal of Marketing*, 62(2), 46–59.

Gupta, A. K. and Shukla, A. V. (2019). Online retail format choice behavior of Indian customers for reasoned purchase: a cultural perspective. *Journal of International Consumer Marketing*, 31(5), 469–491.

Hagel, J. and Armstrong, A. G. (1997). *Net Gain: Expanding Markets Through Virtual Communities*. Cambridge, MA: Harvard Business School Press.

Hair, J. F., Black, W. C., Babin, B. J. and Anderson, R. E. (2014). *Multivariate Data Analysis* (7th ed.). Essex: Pearson Education Limited.

Holland, J. and Baker, S. M. (2001). Customer participation in creating site brand loyalty. *Journal of Interactive Marketing*, 15, 34–45.

Huang, C.-C. (2017). The impacts of brand experiences on brand loyalty: mediators of brand love and trust. *Management Decision*, 55(5), 915–934.

Hughes, C., Swaminathan, V. and Brooks, G. (2019). Driving brand engagement through online social influencers: an empirical investigation of sponsored blogging campaigns. *Journal of Marketing*, 83(5), 002224291985437-96.

Interbrand (2017). *Top Growing Brands*. Available from: http://interbrand.com/best-bra nds/best-global-brands/2016/.

Jiang, L., Yang, Z. and Jun, M. (2013). Measuring consumer perceptions of online shopping convenience. *Journal of Service Management*, 24(2), 191–214.

Kapferer, J.-N. (2008). *The New Strategic Brand Management*. London: Kogan Page.

Keller, K. L. (1993). Conceptualizing, measuring, and managing customer-based brand equity. *Journal of Marketing*, 57, 1–22.

Keller, K. L. (2003). Brand synthesis: the multidimensionality of brand knowledge. *Journal of Consumer Research*, 29(4), 595–600.

Keller, K. L. (2013). *Strategic Brand Management* (4th ed.). USA: Pearson Education.

Kelman, H. C. (1958). Compliance, identification, and internalization: three processes of attitude change. *Journal of Conflict Resolution*, 2 (1), 51–60.

Kim, J. W., Choi, J., Qualls, W. and Han, K. (2008). It takes a marketplace community to raise brand commitment: the role of online communities. *Journal of Marketing Management*, 24(3–4), 409–431.

Kotler, P. (2011). Reinventing marketing to manage the environmental imperative. *Journal of Marketing*, 75(4), 132–135.

Kotler, P. and Keller, K. L. (2009). *Marketing Management* (13th ed.). Upper Saddle River, NJ: Pearson Education.

Lawu, B. J. (2015). Pengaruh Elemen brand knowledge dan Brand Equity Terhadap 78 repurchase intention. *Journal of Management*, 14, 197–221.

Liaw, G. F. (2011). A study on the influence of consumers' participation in a brand community on purchase intention. *Journal of International Management Studies*, 6(1). Available from: http://www.jimsjournal.org/pi.html [10 July 2020].

Liputan6 (2015). *Komunitas dan Dealer Bersinergi Sukseskan Jambore Toyota*. Available from: http://otomotif.liputan6.com/read/2377208/komunitas-dan-dealer-bersinergi-s ukseskan-jambore-toyota [18 May 2020].

Liu, X., Min, Q. and Han, S. (2020). Understanding users' continuous content contribution behaviours on microblogs: an integrated perspective of uses and gratification theory and social influence theory. *Behaviour & Information Technology*, 39(5), 525–543.

McAlexander, J. H., Schouten, J. W. and Koenig, H. F. (2002). Building brand community. *Journal of Marketing*, 66(1), 38e54.

McKinsey & Company (2016). *Automotive Revolution – Perspective Towards 2030*. Available from: https://www.mckinsey.de/files/automotive_revolution_perspective_t owards_20 30.pdf

Mumby, D. K. (2013). *Organizational Commitment: A Critical Approach*. Thousand Oaks, CA: SAGE, p. 411.

Nitzan, I. and Libai, B. (2011). Social effects on customer retention. *Journal of Marketing*, 75(6), 24e38.

Osei-Frimpong, K., McLean, G. and Famiyeh, S. (2019). Social media brand engagement practices. *Information Technology & People*, 33(4), 1235–1254.

Prentice, C., Han, X. Y., Hua, L.-L. and Hu, L. (2019). The influence of identity-driven customer engagement on purchase intention. *Journal of Retailing and Consumer Services*, 47, 339–347.

Ringle, C. M., Wende, S. and Becker, J.-M. 2015. SmartPLS 3. *Boenningstedt: SmartPLS GmbH*. Available from: http://www.smartpls.com

Ryan, A. M. (2001). The peer group as a context for the development of young adolescent motivation and achievement. *Child Development*, 72(4), 1135–1150.

Sasmita, J. and Suki, N. M. (2014). Young consumers' insights on brand equity: effects of brand association, brand loyalty, brand awareness, and brand image. *International Journal of Retail & Distribution Management*, 43(4), 276–292.

Scammon, D. L. (1977). Information load and consumers. *Journal of Consumer Research*, 4(3), 148–155.

Tajfel, H. and Turner, J. C. (1985). The social identity theory of intergroup behavior. In *Psychology of Intergroup Relations*, S. Worchel and W. G. Austin, (Eds.) Chicago: Nelson-Hall, 6–24.

Thøgersen, J., Dutra de Barcellos, M., Gattermann Perin, M. and Zhou, Y. (2015). Consumer buying motives and attitudes towards organic food in two emerging markets. *International Marketing Review*, 32(3/4), 389–413.

Tiruwa, A., Yadav, R. and Suri, P. K. (2016). An exploration of online brand community (OBC) engagement and customer's intention to purchase. *Journal of Indian Business Research*, 8(4), 295–314.

Tsai, S-P. (2005). Impact of personal orientation on luxury brand purchase value, *International Journal of Market Research*, 47(4), 429–454.

Turner, J. C. (1991). *Social Influence*. Bristol: Thomson Brooks/Cole Publishing Co.

Varshneya, G., Pandey, S. and Das, G. (2017). Impact of social influence and Green consumption values on purchase intention of organic clothing: a study on collectivist developing economy. *Global Business Review*, 18(2), 478–492.

Vigneron, F. and Johnson, L. W. (2004). Measuring perceptions of brand luxury. *Journal of Brand Management*, 11(6), 484–506.

Wang, S. (2014). Consumer's characteristics and social influence factors on green purchasing intentions. *Journal of Life and Social Sciences*, 32(7), 738–753.

Wang, Y. and Hazen, B. T., (2016). Consumer product knowledge and intention to purchase remanufactured products. *International Journal of Production Economics*, 181(Part B), 460–469.

Wiedmann, K-P., Hennigs, N. and Siebels, A. (2009). Value-based segmentation of luxury consumption behaviour. *Psychology and Marketing*, 26(7), 625–651.

Wilimzig, B. J. (2011). *Online Communities: Influence on Members Brand Loyalty and Purchase Intent*. Available from: https://pdfs.semanticscholar.org/b700/d0a6d97a18f5 53eb4a11e8a91fd8c212e0b0.pdf

World Intellectual Property Report (2013). *Brands – Reputation and Image in the Global Marketplace*. Available from: https://www.wipo.int/edocs/pubdocs/en/intproperty/944/wipo_pub_944_2013.pdf

Wu, W.-Y. and Sukoco, B. M. (2010). Why should I share? Examining consumers' motives and trust on knowledge sharing. *Journal of Computer Information Systems*, 50(4), 11–19.

Zarantonello, L. and Schmitt, B. H. (2010). Using the brand experience scale to profile consumers and predict consumer behaviour. *Journal of Brand Management*, 17(7), 532–540.

Zheng, X., Cheung, C. M. K., Lee, M. K. O. and Liang, L. (2015). Building brand loyalty through user engagement in online brand communities in social networking sites. *Information Technology & People*, 28(1), 90–106.

18 Building and sustaining personal brand

Examining the effectiveness of personal branding in the context of education

Marwa Tourky, Pantea Foroudi and Fatma Haji Al-Zadjali

Introduction

Personal branding offers huge potential benefits for job-hunting and career development. This chapter advances theoretical and practical understanding of its strategic use. It presents a unique framework – drawing on social and cultural capital and impression management theories – that shows students, graduates and young professionals how to develop their personal brand.

Background

Personal branding is built on a set of unique characteristics that an individual possesses, such as values, attributes, beliefs, personality, opinions and life goals (Rampersad, 2009a), and which affect the way others perceive them. It is a marketing strategy in which a person uses these individual characteristics to differentiate themselves from others, by realising who they are, what they do and how they present their views (Dolak, 2008). Personal branding helps people to understand their own identity (Kornberger, 2010) and to discover themselves. It can then be used as a promotional vehicle to attract a target market, by matching a person's own needs to market needs while also influencing and controlling other people's perceptions of themselves and seeing themselves as a brand (Peter and Gomez, 2019).

The growing significance of personal branding in today's world is driven by its ability to empower individuals to represent themselves and to deliver their message in a way that can influence the perceptions of their audience (Bastos and Levy, 2012). Students and graduates are therefore potential beneficiaries: they can use personal branding to understand themselves, and to position themselves well with their target audiences (current or potential employers, colleagues, peers and friends). Its benefits continue within the workplace. Employees can use it to gain competitive advantage over colleagues and to enhance their professional presence, culminating in creating positive impressions on organisational leaders (Morgan, 2011), and competing for a better professional standing (Rampersad, 2009b). Entrepreneurs and freelancers can harness its power to help them stand

468   M. Tourky, P. Foroudi and F. H. Al-Zadjali

out in the crowd: with the right communication tools and messages, they can use personal branding to articulate their values and differentiate themselves from others in the field, communicating how they are better than their rivals, and providing other individuals and companies with reasons why they should be chosen over hundreds of similar providers. Employers, meanwhile, are using personal branding to foster differentiation between workers in a highly competitive marketplace (Sills, 2008). By understanding where employees excel, organisations can ensure that their talents are put to use in the best way possible (Clark, 2014).

It is an essential concept, which enhances students' ability to succeed in a dynamic labour market and should be part of ongoing career planning – throughout all the stages of one's career – given the current challenging employment environment. In every field, the people at the top are those who have been proactive in managing their careers.

It is also important to note that the responsibility for managing one's career is now in the hands of the individual rather than resting with employers (Corkindale, 2008). This adds to the importance of students and graduates understanding how to brand themselves, initially by expressing their attributes in the course of responding to interview questions. This is not a straightforward task. For example, while previous studies have identified a number of generic attributes that employers seek when hiring graduates, such as knowing their own skills and strengths, awareness of their career objectives, independence, the ability to learn new things, and knowledge of the firm (Ryan, 2016), not all these attributes will match a specific employer's requirements. Students therefore need to understand the criteria or attributes which a particular employer may value, depending on the field or the post. Based on this, students can choose a specialism that will help them succeed after graduating (Strimbu et al., 2018).

This chapter therefore not only explains the concept of personal branding (its meaning, dimensions, building process and outcomes), but also sheds light on a distinctive set of factors that help to build an individual personal brand and sustain it over time.

Personal branding: an overview

The concept of individual branding was instituted in 1980 by Al Ries and Jack Trout in their book *Positioning the Battle of Your Mind*, but the term "personal branding" was made more popular by Tom Peters in his 1997 article "The Brand Called You". Since then, the concept has attracted the interest of both academics and practitioners, and while it has become increasingly popular, mainly among practitioners, the literature on the topic remains under-developed (Keller, 2008). As a result, there are very few views about the meaning, process or dimensions of the concept, and no clear definition exists (Slaughter, 2015). Personal branding has been examined in relation to celebrities, athletes and political leaders, and has been extended to human brands competing in the job market (Khedher, 2015).

Building and sustaining personal brand 469

From a practitioner perspective, a personal brand can be defined as "the combination of personal attributes, values, drivers, strengths, and passions you draw from that differentiates your unique promise of value from your peers, and helps those assessing you to determine if they should hire you or do business with you" (Guiseppi, 2017). Put more simply, "a personal brand identifies, clarifies, and communicates who you are to the world around you, whether it is a business environment, an academic field, or an entrepreneurial setting" (Arruda, 2009). From an academic perspective, a personal brand can be defined as "a strategic process of creating, positioning, and maintaining a positive impression of oneself, based on a unique combination of individual characteristics, which signal a certain promise to the target audience through a differentiated narrative and imagery" (Suddaby, 2010). A common theme among the existing definitions of personal branding is perception: it relates to how others perceive you, which is different from, but related to, self-perception and self-esteem (Rampersad, 2008). Implicit in the meaning of personal branding is the value that you can contribute to whichever organisation hires you.

Any person wishing to present themselves in a unique way and to differentiate themselves from others needs to follow a systematic approach. This entails assessing, identifying, positioning and communicating their individual abilities, attributes, interests and motivation, thereby supporting their success (Khedher, 2015; Manai and Holmlund, 2014). The process of building a personal brand (see Figure 18.1) involves four steps, which are described in the following paragraphs.

Feedback and continuous self-assessment

Step 1 in building a personal brand entails carrying out a self-assessment: an introspective, self-analytical exercise in which people seek to understand their personal values, motivation and passion, and to gain clarity about their personal and professional goals, mission, and vision in both the short and long term (Ilies, 2018). This step involves self-knowledge, self-esteem and social perceptions through people understanding their own competences and the distinctive elements that may position them differently in social groups (such as their level of personal development, emotional maturity and personality type). This careful observation and examination of feelings, actions and aspirations can be carried out using the SWOT (strengths, weaknesses,

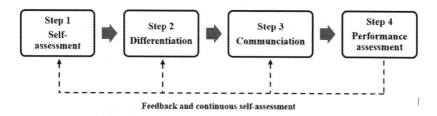

Figure 18.1 Building and sustaining personal building.

470   M. *Tourky, P. Foroudi and F. H. Al-Zadjali*

opportunities and threats) technique (Peter and Gomez, 2019). This self-analysis process involves a person listing their personal attributes, achievements, strengths, values and distinguishing their valuable personal assets, before evaluating their weaknesses and giving themselves honest feedback. The goal is to capitalise on the opportunities that arise from their informational, educational and social background, to eliminate or change what they realise is not useful, and to understand what is required for specific career paths (Evans, 2017). This also might lead to people adjusting their short- and long-term personal and professional goals.

Step 2 in building a personal brand involves a person positioning themselves with their target audience by emphasising what is unique and distinguishable about them and desirable to the target audience. This might involve identifying emotional and functional appeals: in other words *how* a person makes others feel about them and *what* service they can offer that makes them stand out from the crowd. A good technique is for a person to ask trusted family members, friends and colleagues to describe their personality in a few words. It is important to adjust any gaps between what the audience thinks and feels about the person and what the person wants them to think and feel (Bence, 2008). This means that personal branding is not self-centred but is also about the audiences (Evans, 2017). Professionally, it is suggested that people design a simple, eye-catching statement that summarises who they are, what they stand for and what is unique about them, which can be used in any communications.

Step 3 involves communicating the personal brand, which includes people deciding which channels they will use to share their message (Evans, 2017). The use of social media is popular given its high reach and low cost. It is also an interactive medium that allows prompt feedback, enabling messaging to be adjusted and favourable performance to be speedily measured, among other advantages. However, there are a number of major challenges associated with the use of social media, including lack of information control. For example, the high accessibility of information by different people (friends and the general public) gives audiences the power to evaluate a person's brand, which can result in branding failures if people find mismatches between the person's stated goals and their own assessment of them (Labrecque et al., 2011). Gioia et al. (2014) noted that "careers have become personal brands that need to be managed in a virtual age". Employees and graduates therefore need to be armed with sufficient technical and communication skills to create ongoing consistent communication with their target audiences. Moreover, norms for posting information and interacting on the internet are changing, causing conflict across users' different roles (Kang, 2010).

Step 4 involves evaluating personal brand performance by assessing the effectiveness of the activities undertaken in the previous steps – for example measuring the extent to which the person has attracted the attention of the right audience, has created a favourable personal brand image among them and has achieved the intended personal and professional goals, such

Building and sustaining personal brand   471

as getting the desired job. This final step also involves sustaining a personal brand over time; in other words, continuously updating it. Individual brand performance can be improved by using reflexivity to control image (Khedher, 2015, 2019; Ilies, 2018) and other personal brand performance outcomes. This involves people reassessing their capabilities, knowledge and social capital, updating their personal goals, adjusting their communication message and refreshing their personal look, while re-evaluating their performance against the goals they set themselves. This continuous process is affected by external factors such as labour market and employability trends, which affect the skills and capability that employers are seeking (Khedher, 2015, 2019). Reflexivity is essential for continuous development and improvement of personal branding, as it leads people to emphasise or de-emphasise certain things, responding to further feedback in a dynamic, recursive process (Khedher, 2015), resulting in a sustainable personal brand.

Dimensions of personal branding

Personal branding is a multi-dimensional concept comprising different components that should be taken into consideration during the creation process. For example, a personal brand includes an individual vision and mission, which identify a person's current situation and where they want to be in the future (Ilies, 2018). It is also shaped by ambition, as this affects people's ability to identify their objectives, networks and career. Other important components that should be given considerable attention include personal values, differentiation, authenticity and visual appearance. Since personal branding relates to a set of values and qualities that assist in self-differentiation and reflect accurate self-identification by clarifying strengths and weaknesses (Khedher, 2019; Ilies, 2018; Thompson-Whiteside et al., 2018; Amoako and Adjaison, 2012), the process of building a personal brand entails identifying values and characteristics that define what a person stands for, and then fitting them to the target audience to create the intended impression (Gorbatov et al., 2018; Hood et al., 2014; Parmentier et al., 2013; Rampersad, 2008). Reflecting an authentic self-identity is also important for professional success (Peter and Gomez, 2019; Rampersad, 2008). Each person has their own set of talents, passions, knowledge and skills that can be discovered through self-examination. If these truths are positioned in the right way, they will be immensely useful to the right target market (e.g. employer), and will deliver financial benefits and happiness for the person behind the brand (Khedher, 2019). Physical appearance is an integral component of personal branding. Looking polished and professional enhances a person's brand through the presentation of self-image, which influences professional image in the workplace (Khedher, 2019).

Overall, there are four key dimensions of a personal brand: differentiation, authenticity, visual appearance and self-presentation (as shown in Figure 18.2), which are set out in more detail in the following paragraphs.

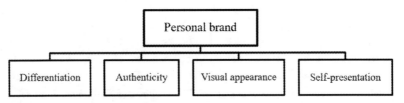

Figure 18.2 Key dimensions of a personal brand.

Differentiation

Differentiation, a vital element of personal branding, refers to unique characteristics in a person which the target audience views as desirable (Gorbatov et al., 2018). As Arruda and Dixson (2007) put it: "What makes you unique, makes you successful". Differentiation helps in reflecting strategic communication by constructing a mission and describing a person, predicated on values, personality, interests and strengths (Hood et al., 2014; Poeppelman and Blacksmith, 2014; Rampersad, 2008; Lair et al., 2005; Peters, 1999). Differentiation acts as a parity point, similar to product branding (Parmentier et al., 2013). An individual has to choose their most potent characteristics to send a clear brand message that fits their desired audience, as this helps create a positive brand image and will gain better career opportunities (Gorbatov et al., 2018; Parmentier et al., 2013).

Differentiation is based on both tangible and intangible credentials. The former are objective, easily measured accomplishments (Evans, 2017), such as education, number of years of experience, positions held, responsibilities, membership of professional bodies etc. The latter are subjective and sometimes more difficult to convey, for example the reputation of current and past employers, team leadership skills, level of motivation, contribution to the success of an employer etc. Investing in both forms is viewed as a form of cultural capital which will determine the success and effectiveness of personal branding (Khedher, 2019).

Authenticity

Authenticity refers to a person's real character (Peter and Gomez, 2019) and the quality of being true to oneself and others (Khedher, 2019). It is based on a person's valid values, strengths, uniqueness and intelligence (Rampersad, 2008). It entails maintaining a constant, relevant and meaningful brand statement which reflects individual actions and behaviour that support a positive image and favourable impression on others (Peter and Gomez, 2019; Rampersad, 2008; Gorbatov et al., 2018). Aligning one's words and actions is key to authenticity (Hagenbuch, 2015), and promotes personal brand sustainability (Ilies, 2018). This is considered to be one of the core elements of building personal branding; however, though a challenging practice for individuals as they develop their self-brand to satisfy the market (Thompson-Whiteside et al., 2018; Ilies, 2018). Individuals who are transparent in terms of how they present themselves to others are seen as having more credibility by stakeholders and have more professional opportunities, in addition to being seen as trustworthy and more likely to convince others (Khedher, 2019).

Visual appearance

Visual appearance refers to the look that contributes to the formation of a first impression and is considered an integral component of a personal brand (Khedher, 2019). It includes self-care, personal look, wardrobe and grooming (Arruda and Dixson, 2007; Montoya et al., 2002). In the work environment, appearance forms part of the construction of a person's professional image. People use their body shape and appearance as a means of expressing their individual identity, developing them into social symbols that give messages about their self-image to others (Motion, 1999).

Simons (2012) argues that people who are encountered in the course of professional life (potential employers, colleagues and others) notice what an individual wears and how they present themselves overall. The management of physical appearance is therefore becoming a standard of managerial judgement, which requires conscious thought and ongoing self-control by individuals following an implicit model, and which might differ from one profession to another. For example, an athlete's attractiveness could be defined by physical qualities and characteristics that viewers find aesthetically pleasing, a pleasing personal style and the fitness of their body for their sport (Arai et al., 2013); while fashion professionals follow the prevailing understanding of beauty in their daily choices of clothing, makeup and hairstyle, which are all critical to success (Parmentier et al., 2013). With the growing popularity of selfies, a form of self-expression as an image, appearance is becoming a narrative performance in the creation of personal branding (Eagar and Dann, 2016).

Self-presentation

Self-presentation refers to the use of verbal and non-verbal cues to present oneself and to increase the likelihood of creating favourable perceptions among a target audience. This can be done using both direct and indirect impression management strategies (Roberts, 2005). Khedher (2019) argues that personal branding is a form of self-presentation in which people, through impression management in their everyday lives, use their words and actions to give a particular impression (Goffman, 1959). According to Hearn (2008), personal branding needs communicative capabilities and persuasive linguistic discourse to strategically conceal personal information and create the desired impression.

Theoretical underpinning for personal branding

Different theories have been used to explain the development and management of personal branding. In this study we rely on cultural capital, social capital and impression management theories to explain the dynamics of personal brand building, and to provide a theoretical underpinning for the proposed dimensions of personal branding.

The first of these three theoretical planks, cultural capital, has been described as "a form of knowledge, skills, education, and advantages that individuals have, which give them a higher status in society" (Khedher, 2019, p. 100). This includes a broad range of elements such as formal and informal knowledge, general culture, diplomas, linguistic competence, specific attitudes and personal style (Bourdieu, 1983). Social capital, meanwhile, is defined as "the sum of the resources, actual or virtual, that accrue to an individual or a group by virtue of possessing a durable network of more or less institutionalised relationships of mutual acquaintance and recognition" (Bourdieu, 1983). This consists of networks, connections, group memberships, affiliations etc. (Khedher, 2015).

The notions of both cultural and social capital, underpinned by Bourdieu's theory (1983, 1984), provide a theoretical foundation which explains the process of personal branding in an organisational context. Drawing on Bourdieu, personal brand development happens through processes that help to portray a person as having field-specific social and cultural capital that allows them to "stand out", while acquiring the habitus that allows them to comply with field and occupation-specific expectations in order to "fit in" (Parmentier et al., 2013). Furthermore, an issue of Bourdieu's theory suggests that bridging the divide between those who have a strong personal branding and those who do not depends on successfully investing in and acquiring the relevant social and cultural capital.

The third theoretical plank of personal branding, impression management theory, relates to how the early stages of brand building – self-awareness, assessment and the identification of personal strengths (tangible and intangible credentials) – are then used to differentiate a person from others and to send a message about the added value they bring. Impression management is defined as "the process by which individuals attempt to control the impressions others form of them" (Leary and Kowalski, 1990, p. 34), and has also been described as the "vehicle by which professional image construction occurs" (Roberts, 2005). People often use impression management to display valued aspects of themselves to the public at appropriate times (Roberts, 2005). It involves generating an awareness of and monitoring how one is perceived in a given situation. Khedher (2019) and Nolan (2015) argue that personal positioning can be managed by applying impression management, which assists in boosting the value of both individuals and their corporations.

People can deploy self-presentation tactics, including both assertive and defensive strategies, to present information about their own traits, abilities and accomplishments (Cialdini and Richardson, 1980). Assertive strategies are those that are used to create images promoting desirable qualities, e.g. self-promotion that draws attention to personal accomplishments so as to appear competent, and ingratiation that involves doing favours for other people in order to appear likeable (Jones and Pittman, 1982). Defensive strategies, on the other hand, are aimed at maintaining a particular image, minimising

Building and sustaining personal brand   475

deficiencies or avoiding looking bad after a predicament or "event that cast aspirations on one's lineage, character, conduct or skills" (Schlenker, 1980, p. 125). They include apologies, excuses and justifications, all of which are used to repair a "spoiled" or negative identity (Tedeschi and Melburg, 1984). Both assertive and defensive strategies are important for constructing viable professional images, since they are a means of signalling that people possess a high degree of competence and character (Luaura, 2005). These direct tactics are usually used by people to respond to social identity devaluation and legitimacy threats to their professional image. In the face of such threats, individuals may also use indirect tactics to help shape perceptions of their personal identities, such as "managing information about the people and things with which one is simply associated" (Cialdini, 1989: 46).

Theoretical framework

This study presents a conceptual framework that explains the process of building a personal brand emphasising (i) the antecedents of personal branding; (ii) the mediating effects of personal branding; (iii) the moderating effect of communication on the process of personal branding; and (iv) the consequences of personal brand performance, stressing the influences of personal branding on personal and organisational gains. These are set out in detail in the following paragraphs.

Antecedents of personal branding

Self-knowledge → personal branding

Self-knowledge refers to "the careful, intentional, conscious and permanent observation of [one's] own feelings, emotions, actions and results of the actions taken" (Ilies, 2018, p. 47). It entails self-assessment of body image (physical self), personal beliefs (cognitive self), personal feelings and emotions (emotional self), social relationships (social self) and existential values, aspirations and skills (spiritual self) (Ilies, 2018). This leads people to a better understanding of themselves in terms of both intrinsic cues (how they perceive themselves) and extrinsic cues (how they are perceived by others), which is considered the first step in building a personal brand (Kucharska and Mikołajczak, 2018).

It is argued that self-knowledge improves both self-confidence and knowledge about social perceptions, which in turn help the person to design achievable personal development goals. People who recognise and acknowledge their achievements have higher self-esteem than those who do not. Engaging in personal branding can therefore be relatively easy or difficult, depending on a person's existing level of self-esteem (Zinko and Rubin, 2015). This means that individuals with spectacular outcomes are likely to express and distinguish themselves better than others (Wioleta and Mikołajczak, 2018), therefore culminating in an effective personal branding process (Khedher, 2015).

476   M. Tourky, P. Foroudi and F. H. Al-Zadjali

Social capital → personal branding

Social capital refers to the process of forming and consolidating good relationships over time (Khedher, 2019), which requires a continuous effort for establishment, genuine collaboration and a positive attitude (Arruda and Dixson, 2007; Parmentier and Fischer, 2012). This involves practising networking in order to nurture personal and professional links, which in turn generate resources such as references, support and useful information.

Social capital enables graduates to access a wider range of opportunities in the labour market. Peter and Gomez (2019) argue that the more people one connects with, the more one's personal brand is recognised. For Parmentier et al. (2013), cultivating and demonstrating upward affiliations (in the modelling industry) facilitates access to desirable contacts and provides graduates with symbolic capital by association. In this respect, networks serve as a signalling mechanism for human brands and can be actively used to shape job market outcomes (Khedher, 2019).

Mediating effects of personal branding

Personal branding → personal brand positioning

Personal branding is a planned process in which people make efforts to market themselves (Khedher, 2014) on the basis of tangible and intangible credentials (Evans, 2017). There is a strong relationship between personal branding and personal brand positioning (Parmentier et al., 2013; Khedher, 2014, 2015; Gorbatov et al., 2018). Brand positioning is considered as the second phase of personal branding (Khedher, 2014), since the identification of personal uniqueness can favourably position a personal brand in professional life and in social groups. Studies have highlighted that people looking for work in the late 1990s used personal brand positioning to be competitive – a similar strategy to that used in the marketplace to differentiate between products (Khedher, 2014; Parmentier et al., 2013). The individual's brand needs to be positioned in other people's minds by highlighting their unique characteristics and the point of parity (Gorbatov et al., 2018; Khedher, 2014; Parmentier et al., 2013).

Moderating effect of communication

Communiction → personal brand

Individuals need to promote and present themselves in a way that differentiates them from others (Khedher, 2014), and creates favourable perceptions in the mind of their target audience. These perceptions are conveyed through different online and offline channels (Ward and Yates, 2013; Khedher, 2014; Ilies, 2018; Gorbatov et al., 2018). Studies indicate that personal brand positioning can be accomplished using a combination of online and offline communication strategies (Gorbatov et al., 2018; Ward and Yates, 2013). Ward and Yates (2013) point out that communication techniques in personal branding result in a better professional life, by increasing the person's visibility, accessibility and engagement with the target audience (Peter and Gomez, 2019; Ilies, 2018; Khedher, 2015; Amoako and Adjaison, 2012). Thus, the moderating role of communication in the process of building a personal brand needs to be acknowledged.

Consequences

Personal brand positioning → personal brand performance

Brand performance refers to how successful a brand is in the market (Wong and Merrilees, 2008). In commercial contexts, brand awareness, reputation and loyalty have been suggested as important elements of brand performance (Chaudhuri, 2002; Wong and Merrilees, 2008). Likewise, personal branding can have an effect on an individual's performance.

Effective personal branding and positioning can also lead to personal gains represented in greater self-awareness and evaluation (Gorbatov et al., 2018) which in turn lead to reflexivity as a person attempts to position their self-identity in the social environment. Other results include greater motivation, credibility and influence (Ward and Yates, 2013), self-realisation and the acquisition of self-promotion skills (Garbatov et al., 2018). Effective personal branding also enhances personal visibility (Lee and Cavanaugh, 2016) and prestige, furthering people's careers and creating a type of social capital. Its other personal outcomes include differentiation, which can enable a connection with the target audience (Brems et al., 2016), and the use of that connection to receive preferential treatment over those competing for the same resources (Parmentier et al., 2013). In addition, there is clear evidence that it has monetary outcomes (Gorbatov et al., 2018).

Alongside these personal gains, organisational performance can also benefit from employee branding (Gorbatov et al., 2018). Personal branding is positively correlated to a company's competitive advantage. Organisational benefits can take the form of (i) predicting individuals' behaviours; (ii) basking in their reflected glory; and (iii) organisational signalling (Zinko and Rubin, 2015).

Personal brand positioning → personal brand image

Personal brand image can be described as how one is viewed and perceived by others. It results from building a point of parity and then differentiating oneself from others (Peter and Gomez, 2019; Gorbatov et al., 2018; Khedher, 2015). It is seen as an outcome of personal brand performance, which generally happens after the process of self-knowledge, assessment and differentiation. Positioning a brand in the marketplace on the basis of brand distinctiveness can project an image to customers, who see the unique values offered to them (Kucharska and Mikołajczak, 2018; Wong and Merrilees, 2008): personal brands can also be used in this way to create a favourable impression on others (Gorbatov et al., 2018;

478   M. Tourky, P. Foroudi and F. H. Al-Zadjali

Khedher, 2015). As a consequence, assets can be advanced and personal brand value strengthened (Khedher, 2019; Karaduman, 2013).

Personal brand image → personal and organisational gains

Studies have shown that there is a strong relationship between personal brand image and personal brand performance (Peter and Gomez, 2019; Wioleta and Mikołajczak, 2018; Khedher, 2015). Rampersad (2008) asserts that a clear process for personal branding may improve brand performance by building an authentic image and reputation in the market. Furthermore, having a distinctive personal brand image can increase the level of recognition among audiences, which can be used as an indicator of how successful the brand is in the market, which in turn reflects brand performance. Creating a personal brand image is therefore considered one of the brand management activities that impacts on personal brand performance (Wioleta and Mikołajczak, 2018; Khedher, 2015).

From an organisational perspective, studies have shown that employees who relate the organisation's branding to their own branding through different communication channels can enhance corporate reputation among different stakeholders (Khedher, 2019; Nolan, 2015; Karaduman, 2013).

In personal branding, it is important to clearly identify the intended outcomes, since evaluating personal brand performance can be used as a tool for personal improvement and development purposes (Amoako and Adjaison, 2012).

Discussion and conclusion

Personal branding is seen as a new and evolving topic (Khedher, 2015) with no clear view or thoughts around it (Slaughter, 2015). However, its relevance for individuals is already clear: personal brand management can lead to personal and professional success (Morgan, 2011; Bastos and Levy, 2012; Wioleta and Mikołajczak, 2018; Amoako and Adjaison, 2012). It requires people to discover themselves in the initial stages and then to match their personal needs to market requirements to gain competitiveness (Morgan, 2011). The use of personal branding by students results in explicit self-identification, which enhances their quality as graduates and leads to better opportunities after graduation.

The framework provided by the authors (shown in Figure 18.3) for building a personal brand is underpinned by Bourdieu's social and culture capital theories and by impression management theory, which explain the antecedents and consequences of the process. This unique model updates previous frameworks by integrating different theories and models used in past studies. In the framework, the authors highlight the three core elements of building a personal brand: differentiation, authenticity, visual appearance and self-presentation. The process also requires clear self-knowledge – which involves intrinsic and extrinsic self-perceptions – and investment in social capital and interpersonal relationships. The authors have also shown the importance of communication in terms of presenting the brand to the intended audience and have discussed the meaning and

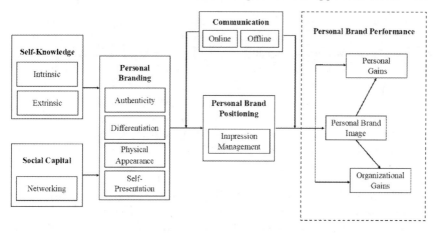

Figure 18.3 Personal branding theoretical framework.

dimensions of all the relevant concepts. Overall, building an effective personal brand through positioning has been shown to have a positive impact on personal image and other brand performance measures, culminating in a better personal and professional life.

This chapter also provides a full understanding of the relationship between personal branding and employability – and sheds particular light on the relevance of the concept to students in higher education. Personal branding enables graduates to promote themselves to enterprises that fit their identity in the desired industry (Khedher, 2019). This is valuable for both students and academics, expanding the available body of literature on the subject by applying branding theories (Thompson-Whiteside et al., 2018) and also helping decision-makers in institutions of higher learning to set their programme objectives in a way that appeals to both quality and employability.

The authors strongly believe that the university experience should include providing students with the tools they need for effective personal brand management. This should begin early in their studies and continue throughout their time at university – and indeed beyond it. There is no doubt that students should turn their attention to the need for personal branding as they approach graduation or immediately afterwards. Any delays may disadvantage them in their search for meaningful, satisfying employment, because personal branding is a long-term strategy that should ideally be started long before graduation, and whose benefits can be expected to last throughout their careers.

Future research

In the current highly competitive jobs market, personal branding is a strategic tool for self-promotion, and is essential for maximising personal and professional success (Morgan, 2011; Rampersad, 2009). As a result, there has been noticeable attention in the literature to the need to develop a useful model for building an individual personal brand, building on brand identity and communications as key components while using several theories (Khedher, 2015, 2019; Ilies, 2018). However, this study is conceptually based, proposing a conceptual framework based on previous studies. The implications of personal branding in higher education institutions, along with the relationships between different factors, need to be tested with cross-sectional data investigating how students approach personal branding management in a variety of higher education institutions, regions and cultures. It would also be useful to study these relationships among students over time, and to conduct experiments with different university programmes that assist students in these endeavours. We believe this is important and worthwhile because, when students effectively present an authentic brand, they attain greater levels of self-actualisation. This has implications for their career progression.

The authors also recommend further study on the power of using social media for creating brand communities, applying social identity theory in building the personal brand and measuring its impact on corporate branding and brand performance. The use of social media strengthens both self-identity and social identity, which aligns individuals with a specific brand community (Helal et al., 2018; Fujita et al., 2018). Helal et al. (2018) and Fujita et al. (2018) point out the importance of applying social identity theory, which supports creating a brand image with a brand community, where people can express themselves and share similar characteristics with the group they follow (Helal et al., 2018; Fujita et al., 2018; Turner et al., 1994). Employing a sharp brand image within a specific community supports a person in building their brand and leads on to better brand performance (Tanha, 2018; Helal et al., 2018; Fujita et al., 2018; Paschen et al., 2017).

CASE STUDY

Ahmed Abou Hashima is a well-known Egyptian entrepreneur who has been working in the steel industry since the late 1990s. In 2011 he established his own steel company, which has become one of the largest and best-known firms in the Middle East. Five years later, he invested in the media field and following that, he set up a construction company in 2017 (*Arabian Business*, 2020). He aims to provide high-quality products and services using the most creative and innovative techniques and technologies available (*Arabian Business*, 2020). The rapid expansion of his business empire suggests that he had unlimited ambitions, with a strategic plan to fulfil his dreams within a short period of time.

Ahmed is a powerful example of the application of personal branding resulting in business success. He identified himself as a hard-working risk-taker with a clear vision to overcome difficulties in order to achieve his desired goals (Esquireme.com, 2018). As a result, his audience's opinions of him are based on these attributes. These characteristics could

Building and sustaining personal brand 481

be seen in 2011, when he launched his steel company during Egypt's political and economic crisis despite it being a very difficult period to survive in the market (Thomas, 2020). However, he had a clear vision and dream to succeed, which he shares with his entire organisation (Thomas, 2020).

In terms of investing in cultural and social capital, Ahmed is considered a successful role model for younger generations. In addition to becoming one of the most significant young players in the steel industry within a short period of time, he enjoys enormous public popularity. He focuses heavily on corporate social responsibility (Thomas, 2020), earning his reputation not only by empowering and supporting the youth population, but also by promoting the welfare of underprivileged and marginalised communities (*Arabian Business*, 2020; Esquireme.com, 2018).

In terms of communication, Ahmed uses both online and offline tools to create favourable perceptions among his target audience. For example, he has addressed university students to share his success story (Ahmedabouhashima.com, 2018), he participates in conferences and other media events and he uses online tools to present entrepreneurial competitions that have millions of young viewers. He strategically employs critical branding tools that have catapulted him to great personal and professional success and have created positive perceptions in the minds of his audience. He represents the successful creation of a personal brand in the market (Ahmedabouhashima.com, 2018).

Ahmed is a clear example of successful personal branding. He has effectively promoted himself and now holds a very strong market position.

Case questions

1. What new strategies are worth implementing for effective personal branding?
2. To what extent do you think Ahmed's self-branding serves his commercial branding?
3. Which kind of capital (social or cultural) delivers greater competitive advantage when building an individual brand?
4. Do you think the personal branding strategy used by Ahmed can be implemented by others to achieve their dreams in different fields?

Key terms and definitions

Personal brand is a set of characteristics of an individual, reflecting their attributes, values, beliefs etc., which is rendered into a differentiated narrative and imagery with the intent of establishing a competitive advantage in the minds of a target audience (Gorbatov et al., 2018). It is the individual name of a real person, connected with a set of notions intended to identify them and to differentiate them from others (Kucharska and Mikołajczak, 2018).

Personal branding (also known as self-branding and self-promotion) is a strategic process of creating, positioning and maintaining a positive impression of oneself, based on a unique combination of individual characteristics, which signal a certain promise to a target audience through a differentiated narrative and imagery (Amoako and Adjaison, 2012). It involves capturing and promoting an individual's strengths and uniqueness to the target audience (Labrecque et al., 2011; Khedher, 2019). This entails an introspective process by which a person defines themselves professionally and can serve as a pathway to career success. The result is a clear, powerful and positive ideology that comes to the target audience's mind every time they think of the person; it constitutes their abilities, values and actions, as well as informing the audience of who they are, what they do and what makes them different (Wee and Brooks, 2010).

Personal brand positioning refers to active marketing efforts by an individual that are designed to communicate their personal brand identity to a specific target market by highlighting positive attributes that are of value to the target audience and differentiating themselves from other individuals in the marketplace (Khedher, 2014). It is a person-centric activity that focuses on managing how others view the individual (Gorbatov et al., 2018) and highlights the unique characteristics that distinguish them from the competition (Parmentier et al., 2013).

Personal brand image refers to how an individual is viewed and perceived by others (Peter and Gomez, 2019). It involves the desired and perceived components of the personal brand that are based on perceptions of the person's competence and character (Gorbatov et al., 2018). It is also the way the individual wants to be perceived, experienced and appreciated by others (Khedher, 2015).

References

Amoako, G. K. and Adjaison, G. K. (2012). Non-empirical analysis of the relationship between personal branding and individual performance. *Journal of Marketing and Operations Management Research*, 2(3), 117.

Arabian Business (2020). *World's Most Powerful Arabs 2019: Ahmed Abou Hashima*. Retrieved from https://www.arabianbusiness.com/423073-worlds-most-powerful-arabs -2019-2nd-abou-hashima [accessed 6 May 2020].

Arai, A., Ko, Y. J. and Kaplanidou, K. (2013). Athlete brand image: Scale development and model test. *European Sport Management Quarterly*, 13(4), 383–403.

Arruda, W. (2009). Brand communication: The three Cs. *Thunderbird International Business Review*, 51(5), 409–416.

Arruda, W. and Dixson, K. (2007). *Career Distinction, Stand Out by Building Your Brand*. Hoboken: Wiley.

Bastos, W. and Levy, S. J. (2012). A history of the concept of branding: Practice and theory. *Journal of Historical Research in Marketing, 4*, 347–368.

Bence, Brenda. (2008). Personal branding quiz: How are you doing? *American Salesman, 53*(8), 26–29.

Bourdieu, P. (1983). The forms of capital. In E. J. Richardson (Ed.), *Handbook of Theory and Research for the Sociology of Education* (pp. 241–258). New York: Greenwood Publishing Group.

Bourdieu, P. (1984). *Distinction: A Social Critique of the Judgment of Taste*. Cambridge, MA: Harvard University Press.

Brems, C., Temmerman, M., Graham, T. and Broersma, M. (2016). Personal branding on twitter. *Digital Journal, 5*, 443–459.

Cialdini, R. B. (1989). Indirect tactics of image management: Beyond basking. *Impression Management in the Organization, 45*(1), 45–56.

Cialdini, R. B. and Richardson, K. D. (1980). Two indirect tactics of image management: Basking and blasting. *Journal of Personality and Social Psychology, 39*, 406–415.

Chaudhuri, A. (2002). How brand reputation affects the advertising-brand equity link. *Journal of Advertising Research, 42*(3), 33–43.

Clark, D. (2014). How to promote yourself without looking like a jerk. *Harvard Business Review Press*. Retrieved from https://hbr.org/2014/12/how-to-promote-yourself-without-looking-like-a-jerk [accessed 27 June 2020].

Corkindale, G. (2008). The return of the personal brand. *Harvard Business Review*. Retrieved from https://hbr.org/2008/02/the-return-of-the-personal-bra [accessed 27 June 2020].

Dolak, D. (2008). *Building a Strong Brand and Branding Basics*. Retrieved from https://www.google.al/url?sa=t&rct=j&q=&esrc=s&source=web&cd=1&ved=0ahUKEwi

Eagar, T. and Dann, S. (2016). Classifying the narrated selfie: Genre typing human-branding activity. *European Journal of Marketing, 50*(9/10): 1835–1857.

Evans, J. (2017). *Branding in Perspective: Self-branding for Professional Success*. Hempstead: Hofstra University.

Fujita, M., Harrigan, P. and Soutar, G. N. (2018). Capturing and co-creating student experiences in social media: A social identity theory perspective. *Journal of Marketing Theory and Practice, 26*(1–2), 55–71.

Gioia, D. A., Hamilton, A. L. and Patvardhan, S. D. (2014). Image is everything: Reflections on the dominance of image in modern organizational life. *Research in Organizational Behavior, 34*, 129–154.

Goffman, E. (1959). *The Presentation of Self in Everyday Life*. New York: Anchor Books.

Gorbatov, S., Khapova, S. N. and Lysova, E. I. (2018). Personal branding: Interdisciplinary systematic review and research agenda. *Frontiers in Psychology, 9*, 2238.

Guiseppi, M. (2017. The 10-step personal branding worksheet. *Career Cast*. Retrieved from https://www.careercast.com/career-news/10-step-personal-branding-worksheet [accessed 27 June 2020].

Hagenbuch, D (2015). *Infallible Principles for Personal Branding from Pope Francis*. Retrieved from https://www.entrepreneur.com/article/251326 [accessed 29 June 2020].

Hearn, A. (2008). Meat, mask, burden: Probing the contours of the branded self. *Journal of Consumer Culture, 8*(2), 197–217.

Helal, G., Ozuem, W. and Lancaster, G. (2018). Social media brand perceptions of millennials. *International Journal of Retail & Distribution Management, 46*(10), 977–998.

Hood, K. M., Robles, M. and Hopkins, C. D. (2014). Personal branding and social media for students in today's competitive job market. *Journal of Research in Business Education*, 56(2), 33–47.

Ilies, V. (2018). Strategic personal branding for students and young professionals. *Cross-Cultural Management Journal*, 20(1), 43–51.

Jones, E. E. and Pittman, T. S. (1982). Toward a general theory of strategic self-presentation. In J. Suls (Ed.), *Psychological Perspectives on the Self* (Vol. 1, pp. 231–262). Hillsdale, NJ: Erlbaum.

Kang, C. (2010). Is internet privacy dead? No, just more complicated: Researchers. *The Washington Post*. Retrieved from http://voices.washingtonpost.com/posttech/2010/03/is_internet_privacy_dead_no_ju.html [accessed 27 June 2020].

Karaduman, İ. (2013). The effect of social media on personal branding efforts of top level executives. *Procedia – Social and Behavioral Sciences*, 99(C), 465–473.

Keller, K. (2008). *Strategic Brand Management*. 3rd ed. Upper Saddle River, NJ: Pearson/Prentice Hall.

Khedher, M. (2014). Personal branding phenomenon. *International Journal of Information, Business and Management*, 6(2), 29–40.

Khedher, M. (2015). A brand for everyone: Guidelines for personal brand managing. *Global Business Issues*, 9(1), 19–27.

Khedher, M. (2019). Conceptualizing and researching personal branding effects on the employability. *Journal of Brand Management*, 26(2), 99–109.

Kornberger, M. (2010). *Brand Society: How Brands Transform Management and Lifestyle*. Cambridge: Cambridge University Press.

Kucharska, W. and Mikołajczak, P. (2018). Personal branding of artists and art-designers: Necessity or desire? *Journal of Product & Brand Management*, 27(3), 249–261.

Labrecque, L. I., Markos, E. and Milne, G. R. (2011). Online personal branding: Processes, challenges, and implications. *Journal of Interactive Marketing*, 25, 37–50.

Lair, D. J., Sullivan, K. and Cheney, G. (2005). Marketization and the professionalization of self. *Management Communication Quarterly*, 18, 307–343.

Leary, M. R. and Kowalski, R. M. (1990). Impression management: A literature review and two-component model. *Psychological Bulletin*, 107(1), 34–47.

Lee, J. W. and Cavanaugh, T. (2016). Building your brand: The integration of infographic resume as student self-analysis tools and self-branding resources. *Journal of Hospitality, Leisure, Sport & Tourism Education*, 18, 61–68.

Manai, A. and Holmlund, M. (2014). Self-marketing brand skills for business students. *Marketing Intelligence & Planning*, 33(5), 749–762.

Montoya, P., Vandehey, T. and Viti, P. (2002). *The Personal Branding Phenomenon: Realize Greater Influence, Explosive Income Growth and Rapid Career Advancement by Applying the Branding Techniques of Oprah*. Personal Branding Press, USA.

Morgan, M. (2011, August). *Personal Branding: Create Your Value Proposition*. Retrieved from http://www.imanet.org/docs/default-source/career/your-valueproposition

Motion, J., (1999). Personal public relations: Identity as a public relations commodity. *Public Relations Review*, 25(4), 465–479.

Nolan, L. (2015). The impact of executive personal branding on non-profit perception and communications. *Public Relations Review*, 41(2), 288–292.

Parmentier, M. A. and Fischer, E. (2012). How athletes build their brands. *International Journal of Sport Management and Marketing*, 11(1–2), 106–124.

Parmentier, M. A., Fischer, E. and Reuber, A. (2013). Positioning person brands in established organizational fields. *Journal of the Academy of Marketing Science*, 41(3), 373–387.

Building and sustaining personal brand 485

Paschen, J., Pitt, L., Kietzmann, J., Dabirian, A. and Farshid, M. (2017). The brand personalities of brand communities: An analysis of online communication. *Online Information Review*, *41*(7), 1064–1075.

Peter, A. J. and Gomez, S. J. (2019). Building your personal brand: A tool for employability. *IUP Journal of Soft Skills*, *13*(2), 7–20.

Peters, T. (1999). The brand called you. *Fast Company*, *10*, 83–90.

Poeppelman, T. and Blacksmith, N. (2014). Personal branding via social media: Increasing SIOP visibility one member at a time. *TIP: The Industrial-Organizational Psychologist*, *51*(3), 112–119.

Rampersad, H. K. (2008). A new blueprint for powerful and authentic personal branding. *Perform. Improv*, *47*, 34–37.

Rampersad, H. K. (2009a). *Be the CEO of Your Life*. New Delhi: Global Vision Publishing House.

Rampersad, H. K. (2009b). *Authentic Personal Branding: A New Blueprint for Building and Aligning a Powerful Leadership Brand*. Charlotte, NC: Information Age Publishing, Inc.

Roberts, L. M. (2005). Changing faces: Professional image construction in diverse organizational settings. *Academy of Management Review*, *30*(4), 685–711.

Ryan, L. (2016). 12 qualities employers look for when they're hiring. Retrieved from https ://www.forbes.com/sites/lizryan/2016/03/02/12-qualities-employers-look-for-when-theyre-hiring/ [accessed 27 June 2020].

Schlenker, B. R. (1980). *Impression Management: The Self-concept, Social Identity, and Interpersonal Relations*. California: Brooks/Cole.

Sills, J. (2008). Becoming your own brand. *Psychology Today*. Retrieved from https://www .psychologytoday.com/us/articles/200801/becoming-your-own-brand [accessed 27 June 2020].

Simons, A. (2012). Branding you! *Texas Library Journal*, *88*(1), 10–12.

Slaughter, J. (2015). *Identifying the Characteristics of a Personal Brand: A Qualitative Study*. Doctoral dissertation, Colorado Technical University.

Strimbu, J., Muller, D., Lockhort, P., Pinar, M. and Trapp, P. (2018). Examining the factors relevant for creating a strong student brand: Perceptions of importance and evaluation. *Marketing Management Association Annual Conference Proceedings*, 53–60.

Suddaby, R. (2010). Editor's comments: Construct clarity in theories of management and organization. *Academy of Management Review*, *35*, 346–357.

Tanha, M. (2018). An introduction to brand building via social media. *International Journal of Management Research & Review*, *8*(6), 1–12.

Tedeschi, J. T. and Melburg, V. (1984). Impression management and influence in the organization. *Research in the Sociology of Organizations*, *3*, 31–58.

Thomas, A. (2020). Follow the leader: Ahmed Abou Hashima, Chairman & CEO, Egyptian steel. *Entrepreneur*. Retrieved from https://www.entrepreneur.com/article/279 236. [accessed 6 July 2020].

Thompson-Whiteside, H., Turnbull, S. and Howe-Walsh, L. (2018). Developing an authentic personal brand using impression management behaviours. *Qualitative Market Research*, *21*(2), 166–181.

Turner, J., Oakes, P., Haslam, S. and McGarty, C. (1994). Self and collective: Cognition and social context. *Personality and Social Psychology Bulletin*, *20*(5), 454.

Ward, C. and Yates, D. (2013). Personal branding and e-professionalism. *Journal of Service Science*, *6*(1), 101.

Wee, L. and Brooks, A. (2010). Personal branding and the commodification of reflexivity. *Cultural Sociology*, *4*(1), 45–62.

Wioleta, K. and Mikołajczak, P. (2018). Personal branding of artists and art-designers: Necessity or desire? *Journal of Product and Brand Management*, *27*(3), 249–261.

Wong, H. Y. and Merrilees, B. (2008). The performance benefits of being brand-orientated. *Journal of Product & Brand Management*, *17*(6), 372–383.

Zinko, R. and Rubin, M. (2015). Personal reputation and the organization. *Journal of Management & Organization*, *21*, 217–236.

19 How the digital environment and its user experience effects the customer's perception of luxury brands and co-creation of brand value

Nastaran Norouzi Richards-Carpenter and Thimo Grantz

Introduction

The chapter focuses on digital sensory branding in luxury marketing. Online engagement has become a primary branding tool, especially in the context of a continuously growing customer audience and its engagement in luxury industry. This study explores sensory aspects which interact with users to identify the digital relationship, as well as the effects a virtual environment has on brands perception.

Key points include luxury fashion marketing; digital branding; sensory marketing; webmosphere; multi-sensory brand-experience; multi-sensory integration; and interactive technologies.

Background to multi-sensory integration and interactive technologies

The importance of the concept of digital environment is continuously increasing in the world of marketing as it is a continuous touchpoint between brand and customer. The digital environment, in its customer perception, is founded on a sensory relationship between brand and customer aiming to touch on many different areas: from physical tools to interact with the digital world, to the actual digital environment itself. The digital interactive technologies help to enable a sensory-based relationship with the users which helps create a "webmosphere" (i.e. the conscious designing of web environments to create positive effects) (Petit et al., 2019).

The concept of "sensory marketing" defined by authors (Krishna et al., 2016; Rodas-Areiza and Montoya-Restrepo, 2018; Petit et al., 2019) as a "comprehensive system" that communicates the most important aspects about the brand while not just taking into account the traditional channels of interaction with the consumer, but also the participation of new channels and methods that impact the five senses of the human being or customers. In addition, in the discipline of marketing, sensory marketing engages the consumers' senses with the goal of affecting their perception, judgement and behaviour. "In a digital world, sensory marketing focuses on the integration and use of digital technologies especially in an online context" (Petit et al., 2019). As a relatively new field of marketing in the online world, it has become more evident that in many cases, this area is a missed opportunity for many brands, as the online world has become a primary interaction tool (Petit et al., 2019).

Although there are various studies (Hultén, 2011; Bradford and Desrochers, 2009) which examine sensory marketing in relation to brands, the impact of sensory marketing in brand co-creation is understudied. Hultén (2011) examined how different people react when a company interacts and supports their purchase and consumption processes through the involvement of the five human senses, in respect to enhancing customer value, experiences and the overall brand as an image. However, current literature lacks theories in relation to digital sensory marketing and customer value co-creation and brand equity. At the core of co-created brand value sits the concept and desire to create a seamless experience across channels as well as taking advantage of the synergies that are created between different channels to further enhance the customer experience as well as brand value (Lemon and Verhoef., 2016).

Iglesias et al. (2017) highlighted that the interaction between channels talking about relationships ultimately creates "brand knowledge". The value creation which is the result of a good branding strategy results in customer relationship and which leads to creation of value-in-context (Edvardsson et al., 2011) and then brand o-creation. Co-created brand value in its essential benefit for the brand deals with brand equity. However, the importance of digital sensory marketing is such that co-creation has been overlooked.

How does the user perception change in respect to the digital environment? How does the brand and its management react and adapt to certain user and customer input in the digital environment? Is the digital brand experience founded from a customer-centric approach or a business and professional centric foundation? How does an enhanced digital/virtual environment help customer satisfaction in a co-created brand value?

The online participation of some brands in the luxury sector has encouraged and directed new consumption habits, which had an impact on the marketing and communication strategies on a managerial level, especially with regard to digital communication (Rios, 2016). The importance in respect to the new digital luxury environment can not be underestimated as it could help companies to structure their experience-based approaches from either a customer or business centric approach. The following sections will then go further and explore the effects of a digital enhanced luxury environment in terms of brand value created.

While sensory marketing is focused on the communication in respect to the senses, the multi-sensory brand experience incorporates a different level of the company when it comes to the customer perception. The multi-sensory brand-experience primary objective is to support "individual value creation", while referring to the reactions of the customers in respect to the purchase and consumption

Customer's perception of luxury brands   489

behaviour (Hultén, 2011; Pine and Gilmore, 1998; Richards and Jones, 2008). Previous scholars (Hultén, 2011; Rodas-Areiza and Montoya-Restrepo, 2018) further note the importance of the involvement of the five human senses, resulting in the customer value, experience and perception of a brand as an image. In this customer-centric approach, it is important to note the willingness of the consumers to process these sensory impressions such as ambient scent consciously (Bradford and Desrochers, 2009).

Methodology

A qualitative approach was used to investigate the digital environment and how user experience affects the customer's perception of luxury brands and co-creation of brand value. Qualitative research design is a useful strategy for studying as it can uncover patterns, themes and categories in order to make judgements about "what is really significant and meaningful in the data" (Patton, 1990, p. 406). Seven in-depth interviews were conducted over two months: two in the digital sector, three in the customer sector and two from the designer and brand perspective. The purpose was to sample a broad and rich cross-section of views and triangulation in relation to the sensory marketing to gather in-depth and authoritative knowledge on the research topic. The initial plan for interviews was to have in-depth face-to-face interviews with key organisational managers and designers who were selected because of their status as knowledgeable respondents and drawn from organisations engaged in sensory marketing in the luxury fashion sector. However, considering the global pandemic as a result of Covid-19, interviews were conducted online using various social platforms such as Zoom, Skype etc.

The interviews encouraged interviewees to elaborate their own interpretations, beliefs, attitudes and feelings (Aaker et al., 2001) about sensory marketing and its constructs. The interviewees decided the timing of interviews Interviews on average lasted an hour, and interviews were recorded and transcribed to ensure reliability (Andriopoulos and Lewis, 2009). All key industry insiders requested to remain anonymous and they mentioned they did not want the name of their firm to be known.

In accordance with Arnould and Wallendorf (1994), the aim was to create a "conversation-like dialogue rather than asking questions that impose categorical frameworks on informants' understanding and experiences" (p. 492). The use of open-ended questions enhanced and increased the validity of the responses, as is appropriate for studies of an exploratory nature. To produce a refined and complete synthesis and interpretation of the material collected from the qualitative data, QSR NVivo software Version 8 was used which is appropriate for data administration and analysis. The researchers found NVivo to be useful for mapping out the themes of the interviews diagrammatically and assisted researchers in viewing the whole text, enabling inter-relationships of the codes to be seen at a glance and was thus also made more appropriate for data storage and retrieval. The use of NVivo as computer-assisted qualitative data analysis software made the data analysis more reliable, easier, more accurate and more transparent as well as making manipulation and analysis of the data easier. The researchers first manually coded the data and then imported the data in NVivo. Combining NVivo and manual coding increases the trustworthiness of data. This analysis process meets criteria of trustworthiness for qualitative study by employing multiple methods to check internal validity and credibility, providing detailed description of the research setting (external validity and transferability), protecting cases' and informants' confidentiality, using rigorous, multiple stages of coding (reliability and dependability) and word-by-word interview transcription (objectivity and confirmability).

The primary data was divided into three categories based on the expertise of the interviewees and after the data analysis, the presence (or absence) of the seven constructs which were originally identified in the literature were organised under these three categories. Each category offers a slightly different approach to understanding the influence of a digital environment in respect to brand perception. The first category set the foundation for luxury customers. The second category of the designers or brands elaborated on their perception on the digital influence. The last category of the programmers/IT-companies explained how they actively adapted and created digital environments for brands. With each category, a new level of understanding is unveiled and when combined, presents a complete picture of the different influences as well as reactions.

Findings and discussion

As discussed earlier, to answer the research question, seven main constructs were identified as follow: (i) customer relationship; (ii) digital sensory impression; (iii) digital environment opens; (iv) engagement with digital environment; (v) brand implemented adoption (reaction); (vi) customer experience and finally, (vii) co-creation of brand value. The NVivo data analysis identified the existence of each of the constructs (or otherwise) in relation to the three categories of interviewees. The findings have been presented below:

(i) Customer relationship

At the core of any successful brand stands a solid "customer relationship". This is best implemented in a company through customer relationship management (CRM). At the core of customer relationship management sits the effective applications of customer knowledge, to enhance the performance of an organisation. Lemon and Verhoef (2016) understand customer relationship management as "the foundation for a customer experience response orientation". While both approaches define CRM as the "management of mutually beneficial relationship(s) from the seller's perspective" (Richards and Jones, 2008), it is the future applications of customer relationship management in a digital environment that are particularly interesting. Here it has become clear that CRM has entered into an evolution in which information technology and organisational

Customer's perception of luxury brands   491

changes are of greatest importance to the customer-centric processes. Such a definition connects us with the definition of sensory marketing which communicates the most important aspects about the brand while not just taking into account the traditional channels of interaction with the consumer but through engaging the five senses of the human being or customers.

Within this section, it is important to highlight the two different aspects: "multi-sensory integration" and "interactive technologies"' Multi-sensory integration is defined as "the statistical difference between the number of impulses received within a cross-modal combination of stimuli and the evoked number of the most effective stimuli" (Stein and Stanford, 2008). As Stein and Stanford (2008) further note, it is the benefits of the integration that provide a better insight into the neural mechanisms and their integration and reaction of the sensory information. Interactive technologies further enable a new form of integration of the senses. Being in an interactive system facilitates a higher level of feedback to report the service quality.

From a customer-centric approach, it is further important to define the supplied feedback customers supply in respect to the service quality. Service quality can be defined as "the operating system's ability to meet customers' needs consistently" (Voss et al., 2004). Customer experience is defined in rather simple terms. It is defined as "all the offerings a company presents and manages" (Pine and Gilmore, 1998). While consumers are widely led by product recommendations, it is important to note that the trustworthiness is higher on more independent websites (Senecal and Nantel, 2004).

In the context of the digital environment, the term e-service quality should be defined. The definition of e-service quality identifies "the service quality of the internet as the extent on which a website facilitates efficient and effective shopping, purchasing, and delivery of products and services" (Zeithaml et al., 2000).

Category 1: *Consumers/Customers* – The interviewed customers have outlined that they perceive their relationship as "the accumulation of experiences and interactions a company has had with the customer. This can include pre/during/post purchase and a positive relationship which can lead to acquisition and retention" (Customer 1). Others in simpler terms have highlighted the "emotional connection they associate with a brand" (Customer 2). They further outlined that if a brand takes all these factors into account, they result in a very positive brand relationship. A further interviewee outlined that they perceive customer relationship as a "bond which is created between a customer and the service that is required" (Customer 3). Of significant importance is the "bond". To have a cohesive relationship, customers have stated that a flawless experience between the physical store to online environment is vital. In both the analogue as well as digital environment, customers have found sensory interactions extremely important noting that videos are more important than pictures. In respect to the customer relationship, it could therefore be outlined that in order to have a successful customer relationship, the brand needs to have a clear branding strategy that translates well between the physical as well as online environment resulting in positive interactions that set the foundation of a cohesive experience for the customer.

Category 2: *Digital Professional* – The interviewed digital professionals or programmers have outlined that they perceive customer relationship as "having the same expectations of the brand across all its touchpoints. No matter if it's the online store or customer support it needs to be the same everywhere" (Professional 1). They further pointed out that they understand customer relationship as the effective way in which a "business finds clients, serves them and keeps them" (Professional 2). As part of the common issues that are part of the luxury fashion industry, they outline that "Video overview, detailed images and 3D would solve the problem quite well" in terms of convincing the customer to purchase. To secure a smooth shopping experience, they say that "good filtering system, light and fast UI with all commonly used features" help create a smooth customer perception. In respect to the customer relationship, it could therefore be outlined that following a more technical approach, the customer relationship is based on a cohesive offline/online relationship that fulfils expectations on all touchpoints.

Category 3: *Brand Designer* – The interviewed brands or designers have outlined that for them their customer relationship is the most important part of their brand as they would not exist without it. "A brand doesn't exist without its customers, so relationship with them means everything" (Brand 1). Being set in the lifestyle business, they further noted that "repetitive engagement is a must. Our brand creates feelings through sensory environment" (Brand 2). As part of the customer relationship, they note the information basis: "We add an extra content to create more informative digital environment as well. Such content as how designs were made, some inspirations for collections, pictures and videos of creative process" (Brand 2). In respect to the customer relationship, it could therefore be outlined that from a brands point of view, the customer relationship sets the foundation of their existence while using repetitive tactics to engage the customers in gaining more information about its identity.

(ii) Digital sensory impression

The primary sensory interactions of interest in this specific digital context are the haptic, audio and visual senses. Lesser known but of great importance are the sense of perception as well as the perception of space. Both play an important role in the digital/virtual environment. In a digital/virtual context, the traditional senses that are engaged have mostly been of a visual as well as an auditory nature (Petit et al., 2019). Virtual augmented solutions that are made available to people, meaning to their computers – human interactions, such as touch screens and augmented reality will lead to an enhanced emotional sense. Such interactions through touch screens will help to enhance the consumer's sense of psychological

Customer's perception of luxury brands 493

ownership (Krishna and Schwarz, 2014). The sensory interaction can be categorised as follows:

Haptic – The sense of touch (or haptic sense) has been defined as the hierarchically highest of the sensations (Krishna, 2012). It is the only sense that covers and engages the entire body, giving it an advantage in terms of easy engagement (Rodrigues et al., 2017). As a result, the "need for touch" or "NFT" which defines the consumers' need to identify products through their haptic sense (Rodrigues et al., 2017). According to Peck and Childers (2006), touch has been identified in increasing the customers' impulse in purchasing.

Audio – The auditory sense in its most basic definition uses soundwaves in its interaction (Girard et al., 2019). In a more branded orientation, the term "audio branding" is defined as the interaction strategy with the consumer (Malenkaya and Andreyeva, 2016). This interaction strategy is, of course, closely linked to the overall auditory communication. Krishna (2012) has defined the auditory communication in a much wider sense. According to Krishna (2012), the auditory sense is linked to the read word. Language as a phonetic loop lets consumers encode their words in their mind while maintaining a close connection to the brand (Krishna, 2012).

Visual – In simple terms, this is defined as the reliance of the visual system on light waves (Girard et al., 2019). In a brand context, the visual stimuli are closely connected to the memory code or mental visual imagery, while in its response it does not necessarily have to be a conscious experience (Kim and Lennon, 2008). It has, however, become evident that visuals (pictures and videos) are an essential part of the consumer's approach in making judgements, also defined as perceptually based expectancies (Raghubir and Krishna, 1999).

Perception of movement –The perception of movement, while an older construct, has yet to be defined in a digital context. Here, the perception of movement is generally defined as correlative events. Mack (1970) has defined the perception of movement as the "perception of an object motion that correlates between the visual retinal image and other sensory information".

Virtual perception of space – The virtual perception of space is (in its digital application) a continuously developing field. The "space" should be defined as "virtual adaptive environment which engages human interactions with computer-based technologies" (Loomis and Knapp, 2003).

Sensory digital communication is interdependent on digital/virtual environment. Digital/virtual environment has been defined as a "computer-based environment" through which "users" or consumers can interact via avatars (Littlefield, Evil Twin Studios Inc, 2006). In this context, the online environment should be considered as an embodiment of interactions through a digital interface (Petit, Velasco and Spence, 2019). The environment supports a multitude of social activities around objects, while generating the opportunity to

494   N. N. Richards-Carpenter and T. Grantz

engage in chat and, ideally, have the system provide topics for chat (Brown and Bell, 2004).

In both the analogue, as well as digital environment, a brand in its essential function has to be clear about its identity and differentiation (Zha et al., 2020; Davies and Chun, 2003). Zha further suggests that the foundation of a brand is to make sure that the communicated experience results in a returning customer that wants to reengage in the experience. A vital component of the customer experience is ultimately measurable and can be defined as a transaction process in the marketplace. Within digital/virtual environments, technology has greatly influenced not only the growth of the market and its sectors (such as the luxury industry), but online participation has encouraged a new consumption habit that has greatly influenced the communication strategies (Rios, 2016). The next section looks into digital environment and investigates its construction.

Category 1: *Consumers/Customers* – One of the key elements that have been outlined by the customers is the importance of video content. Customers have further highlighted the importance of audio content. "(Music) has the power to create a positive emotional relationship with a clothing piece" (Customer 3). While these are the actively perceived interactions, there is also a subconscious level. Described as the "sense of movement", customers have agreed that they "perceive the quality and texture of the dress or product (through its movement)" (Customer 2). Further interactions such as a 360-degree view on items has been noted as specifically important and useful (Customer 1). Linked to the sensory interaction is the "sense of space". On this, customers have said that the "presentation is something that is very important to me, as it helps me distinguish quality straight away in an item" (Customer 1). They further agreed on the definition of the "sense of space" being the "the capability of representing a particular clothing piece with other pieces which help to support the effect of this piece".

In respect to the virtual/digital sensory interaction, it could therefore be outlined that at the core of a virtual/digital sensory interaction sits the interaction of a consumer visually or through other senses such as the "sense of movement" or "sense of space" that allows them to judge and determine the quality of a product. The "sense of movement" here constitutes the visual perception which helps consumers to intuitively judge the quality of a product.

Category 2: *Digital Professional* – The virtual/digital sensory interactions for the digital professionals depend very much on the tool you are using. They therefore stated that "Mobile is different to web. On your mobile you might not be able to have sounds as you are in a public environment. In online we are missing of course texture. Here we definitely need to step it up to have a better textualised sense through movement for example" (Professional 1). While most feedback has encouraged video display, it also holds a certain danger. "video might destroy an 'illusion' of some chosen items" (Professional 2). This does however help the brand in the long run. In respect to the virtual/digital sensory interaction it could therefore be outlined that the digital virtual sensory interaction is based upon the different tools that are available to the customer with the goal to convey as much sensory information in order to create a good brand and product experience.

Category 3: *Brand/Designer* – The brands have similarly to the customers highlighted that the visual stimulation especially through video content has become most important. They further note that "Multisensory posts make a rich digital environment" (Brand 2). The visual content is essential for the customer to understand the product "(The softness of a product) is shown through videos and HD photos" (Brand 1). To build a flawless sensory interaction process from analogue to digital, the brand further explained

in order to increase the suspense because it takes 7 seconds to open (a box) during that time you increase the desire to see what there is inside, we repeat that we were born as e-commerce, so until you do not receive your purchase, you do not know how is it because you could not touch it in advance. We use the perfume which floods the person who opens the box.

(Brand 1)

To integrate the "sense of movement" brands are beginning to understand its importance in terms of perceiving quality through movement in the digital world. "The sense of movement and other similar sensory impressions let them to form a less false view about specific items" (Brand 2). The brands similarly understand the "sense of space" as an overall connection that binds together a cohesive experience for the customer. "Sense of space is something that can destroy everything or make an overall view much better" (Brand 2). In respect to the virtual/digital sensory interaction, it could therefore be outlined that the virtual/digital environment needs to engage as many senses as possible in order to create a useful customer relationship through which the brand interacts and conveys as much of its information about its identity as well as product information.

(iii) Digital environment opens

The digital/virtual environment has been defined as a "computer-based environment" through which "users" or consumers can interact via avatars (Littlefield et al., 2006). In this context, the online environment should be considered as an embodiment of interactions through a digital interface (Petit et al., 2019). The environment supports a multitude of social activities around objects, while generating the opportunity to engage in chat and, ideally, have the system provide topics for chat (Brown and Bell, 2004).

In both the analogue, as well as digital environment, a brand in its essential function has to be clear about its identity and differentiation (Zha et al., 2020). Zha et al. (2020) further suggest that the foundation of a brand is to make sure that the communicated experience results in a returning customer that wants to reengage in the experience. A vital component of the customer experience is ultimately measurable and can be defined as a transaction process in the marketplace. The following section looks into customer engagement in the digital environment.

Category 1: Consumers/Customers

Utilising the help of search engines, all interviewed customers have noted that it is easy for them to find their searched for brands. Through the initial engagement they have further noted that they are searching through multiple pages at the same time before settling for a product: "if one clothing site doesn't have anything that I'd like, I search on different websites. I tend to have a very directed search behaviour, but not associated with brands" (Customer 1). Other customers have noted that they prefer to search for the desired product on the original webpage and only use other pages if they can't find what they are looking for "if I buy a clothing product. I usually visit my favourite brands directly" (Customer 3). The digital environment also plays an important role in terms of inspiration: "you can see what the item would look like on a variety of different styles, body shapes and matching items" (Customer 1). While this is also the case in the analogue environment, the digital platform has the option to showcase many more variations.

In respect to the customer engagement digital (online) environment, it could therefore be outlined that brands need to understand that the search behaviour of customers in the online environment is quick and multi-paged. The most inspiring content made available to the customer is an effective tool to help increase the engagement of the customer with the digital environment.

Category 2: Digital Professional

The digital professionals when interviewed stated the importance of the digital environment as "Every brand should have their own space to present themselves" (Professional 1). They further noted that this space holds the main benefit in terms of communicating the brand's benefits to the customer. They further highlight that "brand identity in my digital environment are some settings on filter or additional word in my search request" (Professional 2). The biggest benefit they highlight is the fact that a brand has a better chance at representing themselves world-wide (Professional 2).

In respect to the digital (virtual/online) environment, it could therefore be outlined that ideally, the digital environment is a space through which the brand can present itself following its own rules while communicating the benefits in a globalised market.

Category 3: Brand/Designer

From the brands perspective, the digital virtual environment "is a driving factor, an atmosphere by which your brand is surrounded by and being placed in a digital world, it enhances the communication with your consumers" (Brand 2). The brand further stated that reactive technologies are of great importance to the digital environment: "implemented adaptation tools used in digital environment help to increase your customer circle" (Brand 2). As part of their communication the brand further stated,

> Our brand was born to fight against an illness, so we absolutely do not show unhealthy body. We prefer to use our friends as models and not the "perfect Angels". We have our community called Caramì team where all the women who purchase a product, take a selfie or a photo.
>
> (Brand 1)

In respect to the digital (virtual/online) environment, it could therefore be outlined that the communication is the main part of the digital environment for the brands. Not just as part of their values but also as part of the senses they aim to engage in their customers.

(iv) Engagement with digital environment

In order to understand customer engagement in the context of the digital (online) environment, it is important to first define customer engagement in general. Customer engagement is defined as the "incorporation of all brand interactions with the readiness of a customer to actively participate with the brand" (Islam and Rahman, 2017; Doorn et al., 2010). Cheung et al. (2015) on a more customer centric approach, identify customer engagement as the "psychological process which manifests in the customers behaviour and motivational psychological state". All approaches, however, ultimately lead to and touch on the customer journey. Here, the customer journey within the environment has multiple touchpoints which affecting each other, with the end result of a focus on the sales and conversion effects (Lemon and Verhoef., 2016). Customer engagement is therefore a multi-dimensional concept, which reflects on a psychological state occurring by the virtue of the interactive customer experience (Marbach et al., 2016).

Search engine optimization (SEO)-led – One of the most important fields of study in respect to a successful brand, customer engagement in the digital (online) environment is directed though SEO. Search engine optimisation can be defined as all the work that is necessary to enhance a high volume of referral hits from a search engine with the goal to make the brands webpage as popular as possible. To make a webpage successful, it is necessary to fully understand how search engines work and stay up to date on the latest developments. Bahuguna further defines SEO as the "theoretical technique employed by a search engine to rank webpages in response to the search

498   N. N. Richards-Carpenter and T. Grantz

query". At the core of search engine optimisation resides the organisation of keywords. Through search engine optimisation, the search engine tries to effectively rank the given keywords in respect to the most useful web page or domain (Evans, 2007).

Search intent – While SEO is a direct technical response from the search engine in response to users' search query, it is important to identify the customer's approach within the process. As such, it is vital to define the terminology of search intent. Search behaviour is closely connected to past and previous searches from a user, which are founded on the intent of a user's past searches (Gross et al., 2006). Determining the intent as part of a successful search is incredibly important, as it will result in a more relevant and informed search (Manolescu et al., 2009). As part of a filtered and intent-led successful search query, Manolescu et al. (2009) further identify inputs such as "the user's current or ambient context, calendar, social network, rules or policies, user profiles, and so forth" as utilities that can help refine a more efficient search. Search intent is therefore based on type of content which is specified and operationalised in their specific classifications (Jansen et al., 2007). To support the search engines on the other side, intent tags have been put in place. These intent tags however do not always define the content of a document but rather how the document is to be used (Steele et al., 2007).

Inspiration – Leading from the search intent of a customer the importance of the inspiration aspect of a customer's search in respect to finding the best possible product naturally follows. Kraft et al. (2005) introduced a widget through which search context can provide simplistic access to the point of inspiration. The importance of inspiration is that the user's work or search flow is not interrupted and leads to augmented search queries that ultimately improve the relevant search query.

Perception – The perception stage binds the previous sections together. The perception stage can be defined as the "element through which the processing of the senses takes place". Perception therefore equals awareness and the understanding of sensory information (Krishna, 2012). Within the online or digital environment, this perception stage has a significant impact on the purchasing behaviour of customers in respect to the online store environment such as colour and layout (Kim et al., 2007). They further remark that the perception affects the enjoyment, shopping involvement and "desire to stay" in the online store.

Category 1: Consumers/Customers

Utilizing the help of search engines all interviewed customers have noted that it is easy for them to find their searched for brands. Through the initial engagement they have further noted that they are searching through multiple pages at the same time before settling for a product "if one clothing site doesn't have anything that I'd like, I search on different websites. I tend to have a very directed search

Customer's perception of luxury brands   499

behaviour, but not associated with brands." (customer 1). Other customers have noted that they prefer to search for the desired

product on the original webpage and only use other pages if they can't find what they are looking for "if I buy a clothing product. I usually visit my favourite brands directly." (customer 3). The digital environment also plays an important role in terms of inspiration "you can see what the item would look like on a variety of different styles, body shapes and matching items" (customer 1). While this is also the case in the analogue environment, the digital platform has the option to showcase many more variations.

In respect to the Customer Engagement Digital (Online) Environment it could therefore be outlined that Brands need to understand that the search behaviour of customers in the online environment is quick and multi-paged. The best inspiring content made available to the customer is an effective tool to help increase the engagement of the customer with the digital environment.

Category 2: Digital Professional

One of the main tools in engagement is SEO. On this, professionals highlighted the importance of:

> good product and content descriptions. There are structuring tools that can help display the data in the search result. This is text only. The more you describe and define the better the search engine can obtain the data and display it.
>
> (Professional 1)

To be specifically successful in the online world, a brand has to be displayed in the "top 5, have descriptions that fulfil the users needs" (Professional 2). The search intent as an important part of the shopping experience as they understand as "actively directed and encouraged through the system. Example is 'Related searches about...' section at the bottom of the Google Search Results page" (Professional 2).

In respect to the customer engagement digital (online) environment, it could therefore be outlined that in order to have good online engagement, the brands need to be as descriptive as possible in order to achieve a high ranking position in search engines. The search intent can hereby be directed through relevant searches.

Category 3: Brand/Designer

a key factor for brands is the usage of SEO technology. They utilise small but regular tricks to gain a high ranking: "Keywords, hashtags in the case of Instagram, optimised mobile versions of websites" (Brand 2) can help to have a high ranking. They further note the importance of price-directed search queries "The intent of the customer is 'To find the best product at the best price'. In Italian we say 'fare l'affare'" (Brand 1).

In respect to the customer engagement digital (online) environment, it could therefore be outlined that for brands, their customer engagement in the digital world is mainly directed through search engines as well as price-optimised searches that fit the customer's need.

Brand implemented adoptions (reaction) – when it comes to including new technologies such as artificial intelligence (AI), brands have stated, "AI helps to optimise a lot of categories. It's definitely a next step towards revolutionary future of fashion" (Brand 2). Brands have further highlighted the importance of reacting quickly to online statements as the digital world is quick and can leave permanent damage in terms of reputation (Brand 2).

In respect to the brand implemented adaptations (reaction), it could therefore be outlined that new technologies are becoming an essential part of brand identities that if utilised correctly, can result in a positive customer relationship.

(v) Brand implemented adoption (reaction)

The stage of "brand implemented adaptations" deals with the direct response from the brand in regard to the customer's experience and journey. This, of course, needs to be defined to fully understand its effects. Here, the implemented adaptations go through specific touch points which generate the experience of the different stages (Lemon and Verhoef., 2016 of brand "experience" which directly reflects on the "brands image as the accrual of a variety of experiences" (Zha et al., 2020). There are of course many different approaches in the academic literature when it comes to defining the term "brand", therefore, it remains somewhat elusive in its nature (Tynan et al., 2010). The brand in its reaction will ultimately have to react to the consumer's responses, which are based on sensation, feelings and cognition that founded on behavioural stimuli are a direct response to the brand's identity (Kent et al., 2015).

The following categories will further investigate the existing literature and help define the different approaches when it comes to brand implemented adaptations.

Artificial Intelligence-Supported – AI-supported systems are a somewhat elusive area of study and require careful defining in order to be of benefit to both customers and a company. A general definition of AI or artificial intelligence is the development of a computer system to be able to engage in a human-like thought process (Kok et al., 2009). They further identify the ability of the system to interact, think and act rationally as the core components of artificial intelligence. A vital component of a successful AI system is the element of trust. It is not just the human component that needs to develop trust with the system but also the system's ability through its behaviour to enhance the trust of the human into the system (Rai, 2020). One way to achieve this behavioural trust is through generated AI fairness (Rai, 2020). On a more technical level, AI technology is further defined as a computer-generated display that allows the user to have

Customer's perception of luxury brands   501

a feeling of actively engaging while being present in a different environment (Schroeder, 2002). The active integration of all these components will prove of upmost importance for a brand in its representation and interaction with customers.

User (Customer) Experience Adaptations –Following the AI support is the user or customer experience adaptations. It is by following and further developing the scope of these antecedents that sets the basis to develop the understanding of the factors that will enhance the future way of interactive shopping (Childers et al., 2001). While there is much to say about the experience, the academic literature has a limited perception of the empirical work that is directly related to customer experience (Lemon and Verhoef., 2016). One of the biggest difficulties in the adaptations is the fact that customer experiences in their nature are social and result in a state where firms have less control over the journey and experience (Lemon and Verhoef., 2016).

Category 1: Consumers/Customers

Once a customer engages with a brand through a digital platform, it is important that the brand reacts appropriately to enhance the customer experience. One tool can be AI. While some customers have noted they don't believe that they have interacted with AI (Customer 3), other customers have noticed that they understand it as "if I was to view a black dress, my phone would show me more black dresses in the future, or Instagram (etc.) would advertise me similar clothing stores, for the style that I tend to shop for" (Customer 1). Customers have further outlined certain trust issues they have when it comes to sharing personal data with an AI. "I believe they would share my data based on my search and their accuracy isn't spot on" (Customer 2).

In respect to the brand implemented adaptations (reaction), it could therefore be outlined that it is of vital importance for brands to react to customers' preferences by using tools such as AI to create an improved digital experience. They further have to establish secure ways that strengthen the customers' trust in their data security in relationship to the brand.

Category 2: Digital Professional

If a brand uses the latest technology, it will be able to react quickly: "In simple ways through offering a tailored experience through the gathered data" (Professional 1). A good system that interacts with the brand will have an interactive element. This is elaborated in the following: "Most of systems tend to customize their feed using information about previous activities (preferences) of the current user, all users of the system, some groups of users. Also advertised content sometimes breaks the organic feed" (Professional 2).

In respect to the brand implemented adaptations (reaction), it could therefore be outlined that the brand ideally reacts through a customised approach where the system is able to have a customised feed and suggestions for every customer.

502   N. N. Richards-Carpenter and T. Grantz

(vi) Customer experience

The customer experience management, however, is a much more direct business section. An effective customer experience management captures and deals with an immediate response that happens between a customer and the business, going so far as to manage what the customer thinks in their immediate response about a company (Meyer and Schwager, 2007). In its basic definition, customer experience, and therefore its management, deals with the brand's physical performance as well as all sense-stimulated emotions that the brand evokes with the customer at all moments of contact (Andajani, 2015). It is further important to note that the interaction between customer and brand is strictly personal in this portrayal and the involvement is therefore based on the rational, emotional, sensorial, physical and spiritual involvement (Verhoef et al., 2009).

Smart assistant – A key aspect of new technologies within the customer environment is that it enables new forms of interactions between brands and customers, leading to a transformation of the marketplace through technology (Yadav and Pavlou, 2020). One new technological aspect which has been under significant development is a virtual or digital smart assistant. The main element of a smart assistant in the online environment is composed of a system that helps to communicate between a customer's personal memory store, as well as point of sale terminals in a retail environment (Suzuki Fujitsu Ltd, 2000). A SSA or Smart Shopping Assistant is therefore a form of digital interaction, for example a mobile device with the goal to enhance the customer experience in the shopping process (Nguyen et al., 2012).

Customer experience satisfaction – Following the customer experience, it is ultimately important to measure and determine the output through the level of satisfaction. It is, by definition, the customer satisfaction that holds the leading criteria for determining the quality, such as service quality, product quality etc. which defines the overall satisfaction of a customer (Pizam and Ellis, 1999). Customer satisfaction is further measurable as positive feedback holds a significant impact on the financial performance of a company (Chi and Gursoy, 2009). Not only does it hold a financial improvement, but it is also the main determinant of a successful customer retention strategy (Hennig-Thurau and Klee, 1997). The literature further identifies customer satisfaction as the perception of the value received in the brand–customer relationship by the customer (Hallowell, 1996). Customer experience satisfaction can be divided into two categories: satisfaction and effective response:

As part of the effective service and quality response of a customer, the organisation should shift its main focus to the customer's spontaneous responses and reactions linked to their offer-related stimuli (Becker and Jaakkola, 2020). Within the management side, quality and its customer response are defined within two sections, talking about the reliability as well as the product being free from deficiencies (Wang et al., 2004). The luxury industry service is closely linked to the overall perceived quality and is therefore defined as a global judgement or attitude

Customer's perception of luxury brands   503

which relates to the superiority of a service, product or offering (Yang et al., 2004). In the end it all of course comes back to a customer centric approach. It is therefore defined as customer-perceived preferences for an evaluation of the different product attributes such as performance and the way it achieves expected goals.

Category 1: Consumers/Customers

Customer experience satisfaction is an important aspect in terms of brands to evaluate past experiences and create a positive customer–brand relationship (Pizam and Ellis, 1999). Customers have noted that it is important to them that they receive a response on their feedback. "If I do (give feedback) I expect some sort of acknowledgement" (Customer 2). They further noted that incentives can be a useful tool to receive more feedback. All interviewed customers have stated that they believe that brands are listening to feedback as it "helps make a brand more trustworthy – then ultimately creating a larger following, and a community of people that trust that brand" (Customer 1).

In respect to the customer experience satisfaction, it could therefore be outlined that the customer satisfaction is a direct channel which needs careful maintaining from the brand's side in order to create a larger following base resulting in a continued cycle of brand trust and eventually "customer loyalty" (Srinivasan et al., 2002).

Category 2: Digital Professional

Customer experience, as outlined by the professionals, can be analysed through the tools of click time and purchase. This, however, is not enough. "We need more input from direct content that reflects on the direct communication" (Professional 1). Ideally, the system will sort the products by relevance: "Usually products which are rarely clicked and bought goes to the bottom of the 'most popular' products. But if user chose 'sort by price' or 'sort buy date' order, customers feedback will be ignored" (Professional 2). Further tools such as "offering coupons, email reminders, announcements and support" (Professional 2) can help to sustain customer experience.

In respect to the customer experience satisfaction, it could therefore be outlined that from a digital platforms point of view, the customer satisfaction is closely linked to the interaction process of the system itself. Tools such as customisation and ease of use through good search options and sorting will help maintain high customer satisfaction.

Category 3: Brand/Designer

As part of customer satisfaction, the brand stated that "loyalty and satisfaction are core features for retention" (Brand 2). They further understand it as their "evaluation of how strong your branding is in general" (Brand 2). Another

504   N. N. Richards-Carpenter and T. Grantz

important part of the satisfaction is presented through feedback. "We accept all types of feedback. We were born only four years ago, so we are at the beginning but ready to listen to the feedback of our customers and to improve our experience" (Brand 1).

In respect to the customer experience satisfaction, it could therefore be outlined that in order to have a high level of customer satisfaction, the brands must value customer feedback the highest with the goal of building upon customer loyalty.

(vii) Co-creation of brand value

At the core of co-created brand value sits the concept and desire to create a seamless experience across channels as well as taking advantage of the synergies that are created between different channels to further enhance the customer experience as well as brand value (Lemon and Verhoef., 2016). There are of course many more factors that play into co-created brand value. While it primarily focuses on diagnosing and developing an improved customer relationship through its value creation, it also actively involves customers through which the interaction further co-creates brand value (Iglesias et al., 2017). They also highlight that this form of interaction between channels talking about relationships ultimately creates "brand knowledge". The value which is the result of a good usage of a functioning brand leads to customer relationship and then results in value-in-context (Edvardsson et al., 2011). Co-created brand value in its essential benefit for the brand deals with brand equity. Brand equity is defined as brand knowledge resulting from awareness and association in respect to the customer response (Del Rio et al., 2001). Co-creation brand value can be categorised as the three following constructs:

Benefits of virtual environment for brand –The virtual environment, as previously defined, is ideally a reflection of the features that are presented in the overall design as well as shopping media (Childers et al., 2001). Ideally, the online or virtual environment as a shopping platform has several benefits for the customer which include saving time, as well as maximising convenience instead of having to visit the physical store (Sarkar, 2011). Another great benefit is the enhancement of the consumer's trust resulting out of perceived benefits from the virtual environment (Loureiro, 2013). On an essential level brand trust in defined as the customer's secure belief that a company/brand will perform as expected upon the promised consumption (Kang, 2011).

Enhanced emotional response from consumers – In order to understand the possibilities of enhancing the emotional responses from consumers, it is important to first define the emotional responses that consumers frequently engage in. These emotional types can be defined as anger, disgust or contempt in a negative setting with further dissatisfaction originating from shame/shyness or guilt which is usually connected to unplanned or excessive purchases (Machleit and Eroglu, 2000). There are, however, certain difficulties in defining adequate measures in regard to consumers' behaviour and the effective responses, which build a key component to enhance the responses (Kuehnl et al., 2019). To gain a favourable status of enhanced emotional responses from consumers, brands and retailers are manipulating the available ambient factors to tip the emotional responses of their consumers into a positive state while also minimising any negative responses (Machleit and Eroglu, 2000).

Loyalty – An essential aspect of co-created brand values is loyalty and does therefore need to be defined. Customer loyalty can be defined as a "deeply held commitment to rebuy or repatronize a preferred product or service with consistent engagement in the future" (Hsu., 2008). Bloemer et al. (1995) have defined true brand loyalty within six stages. These stages are

> (1) the biased customer, (2) the behavioural response from a customer, (3) the ability of the consumer to express loyalty over time, (4) by decision magnitude, (5) with the ability to choose out of multiple brands which (6) they define as a functionality of the psychological decision making process in respect to brand commitment.

In the digital world, the definition of loyalty is more difficult. Here, the definition of loyalty in the online world is defined as "the favourable attitude of consumers towards a product, website or brand resulting in repeated purchasing behaviour" (Islam et al., 2017). Another important aspect of brand loyalty can be found in personalisation which has been proven to enhance the consumer's loyalty towards a brand as it becomes a closer part of their own identity (Srinivasan et al., 2002).

Category 1: Consumers/Customers

Co-created brand value combines the different tools and channels that are part of an enhanced customer–brand relationship. Customers have noted that the digital environment for them has a positive effect on a "Easier shopping experience, a more aesthetically pleasing experience to the eye and the benefit of creating a community of loyal customers" (Customer 1). Customers further understand the value as "the chance of saving time and effort and have an even better experience. Furthermore, it allows us to search more specifically for a product" (Customer 3).

In respect to the co-creation of brand value, it could therefore be outlined that co-created brand value is created through the synergies of the different tools and channels that help to create a better brand experience for the customer. The digital environment as one of the primary touchpoints does hereby hold the power to immediately strengthen and build on that relationship.

Category 2: Digital Professional

From the digital professional perspective, the co-created brand value is part of the enhanced sensory interaction with the customer through the digital environment (Professional 1). If utilised correctly, they further state that "remembering

506   N. N. Richards-Carpenter and T. Grantz

this (interaction level) will make you come back and create loyalty". They further highlight that "If you are not in the digital environment, you do not exist" (Professional 2).

In respect to the co-creation of brand value, it could therefore be outlined that the different digital tools help to encourage an ease of use with a high customer satisfaction. The main important factor and benefit being that without the digital environment a brand hardly exists. Only through the professional display and communicated identity does a brand generate true brand value.

Category 3: Brand/Designer

Co-created brand value (Brand 1) "supports the 'win–win' strategy: creating collaborations where both the brands have positive results". With a focus on the digital/online industry they state that the "Digital environment creates Loyalty only when the customer is satisfied: 'they' receive 'their' products fast (and) find what (they) were looking for". Brand 2 stated that online environment is accessible any time creating huge value to the brand "(the online shop) is there at anytime, anywhere in the world, prepared to interact with your audience".

In respect to the co-creation of brand value, it could therefore be outlined that fro a brand perspective, the core of co-created brand value is set in having an ongoing never-ending customer interaction process through which they can enhance customer loyalty.

Conclusion

The conclusion can generally be separated into two sections. One being managerial centric and the other one being customer/consumer based. While both continuously affect and interact with each other, it is important to have a distinction in the two as both have different initial approaches to the topic.

Managerial conclusive benefits

From a managerial point of view, it is important to highlight the importance of an interactive and well-presented digital representation of the brand. Without it the danger of seeming not trustworthy is greatly encouraged. The digital environment as a branding tool further helps to engage customers further into a daily brand experience. The digital environment does hereby allow the brand to have a continuous exchange and interaction with its customers which will ultimately encourage their loyalty. The digital professionals and brand managers should therefore be encouraged to interact with each other even more. A digital display of the brand and its overall brand management go hand in hand. Understanding every point of the designed construct can help to further streamline the importance of every touch point between brand and customer. A streamlined design can help to create a continuously encouraged and forward-thinking branding approach.

Customer-based conclusive benefits

From a customer-based point of view, it can be highlighted that their interactions with and feedback towards the digital environment can be one of the most important touch points for a brand in order to correct or enhance its identity. The digital environment does provide an extremely important continuous environment through which customers can continuously interact. In return, the customer will be able to have a more comprehensive relationship with the brand. The communicated benefits such as identity but also sales, promotions or special events are direct benefits that are even more accessible through the digital environment.

Future research

This research can be conducted via a bigger sample via survey to add to the validity of the findings. Also, if this research is conducted in other countries and across various cultures, a comparative study can be conducted which would provide more rich, multi-dimensional and reliable findings. Of course, such a research is interdependent on technological advances and customer familiarity with social and digital platforms as many of these multi-sensory marketing efforts are channelised via social media. Therefore, future research should include the validation of the findings of this study, especially in other cultural and technological settings. A replication study is recommended to demonstrate greater generalisability and validity of the relationships. Furthermore, the developed model could be investigated in future research using other research approaches and especially, confirmatory statistical techniques.

Additionally, this research can be integrated into a neuromarketing field of study for a measurement of physiological and neural signals to gain insight into customers' reactions to the multi-sensory marketing activities.

Finally, a future study can look into the findings of this research and compare it with the results of a different luxury or even non-luxury sector such as the luxury car sector or the travel and tourism industry to see if there are any differences in findings across various sectors and industries.

CASE STUDY

I guess you have been to a Nike store by now; if not, you might want to pay a visit to see how Nike are using multi-sensory marketing to encourage the potential customers to immediately go for the most expensive shoes in the store. Do you know why?

Nike found that when scents were added to stores, purchase intent among customers increased by up to 80%. Four hundred shoppers at a selected Nike store rated the store and products better and were more likely to come back to shop again when a pleasant smell was present in the store.

Essentially, Nike stores use a mixed flower scent to direct you towards the more expensive shoe designs inside. Studies show that you are willing to spend up to 10€ more on their shoes if they are diffusing flowery scents in the store. Alan Hirsch, in 1993, conducted an interesting study to explore the use of ambient scent on Nike shoes; identical pairs of Nike running shoes where presented in two different rooms; one room was diffused with a floral scent and the other room was without scent. Interestingly, the shoes presented in the room with the floral scent were estimated to be 10$ more expensive, and the participants were 84% more willing to purchase the pair in the scented room. This study clearly demonstrates the power of ambient scents as a marketing tool. It is a well-known and proven fact that your memory and smells are tied closely together – a scent can really bring back memories and invoke emotions.

Also, the shops are light and often have white walls with black decorations or images in neutral colours, which makes you relaxed enough to make you pay for their shoes.

Nowadays, companies know this all too well and make use of scents and sounds to jolt your brain into liking or enjoying their product.

Brands using sensory branding know that if they want to build lasting connections with their audience, they need to strategically manage their sensory messaging as much as their visual or verbal appeal. This means thinking beyond the impact that logo or website design will have on the audience and considering how brands can create new touch points through other senses.

Case questions

1. What other senses in addition to sense of smell can be employed in a Nike store? How?
2. How can sensory marketing methods be applied to the Nike website to encourage the visitor to purchase the products?
3. What do you understand by "sense of movement"? How can "sense of movement" as a sensory marketing tool be employed in a Nike shop as a stimulus to encourage visitors to purchase the products?
4. What digital sensory interactions are most important to you when you consider purchasing activewear and why? (Videos, pictures, touch etc.)

Key terms and definitions

Customer relationship: customer relationship marketing (CRM) is a technique based on client relationships and customer loyalty. Using customer data and feedback, companies utilising this marketing strategy develop long-term relationships with customers and develop laser-focused brand awareness.

Digital sensory marketing: integrating new technologies into multi-sensory online experience.

Webmosphere: the conscious designing of web environments to create positive effects.

Digital/virtual environment: the definition of a digital environment is one that touches on many different areas from physical tools to interact with the digital world to the actual digital environment itself.

Artificial Intelligence (AI): the theory and development of computer systems able to perform tasks normally requiring human intelligence, such as visual perception, speech recognition, decision-making and translation between languages.

Customer experience management (CEM) is the practice of designing and reacting to customer interactions to meet or exceed their expectations, leading to greater customer satisfaction, loyalty and advocacy.

Co-creation of brand value: collaborative development of new value (concepts, solutions, products and services) together with experts and/or stakeholders (such as customers, suppliers etc.). Less specifically, the term is also used for any way in which a business allows consumers to submit ideas, designs or content.

Bibliography

Aaker, D. A. and Joachimsthaler, E. (2000). The brand relationship spectrum: The key to the brand architecture challenge. *California Management Review*, 42, pp. 8–23.

Aaker, J. L., Benet-Martínez, V. and Garolera, J. (2001). Consumption symbols as carriers of culture: A study of Japanese and Spanish brand personality constucts. *Journal of Personality and Social Psychology*, 81(3), pp. 492–508. doi:10.1037/0022-3514.81.3.492

Akarsu, T. N., Melewar, T. C. and Foroudi, P. (2019). Sensory branding. *Contemporary Issues in Branding*, 1, pp. 210–223.

Akarsu, T. N, Marvi, R. and Foroudi, P. (2020). Forty-nine years of sensory research: A bibliometric analysis for the intellectual structure, trends and research agenda. *European Journal of Marketing*, (Just published).

Andajani, E. (2015). Understanding customer experience management in retailing. *Procedia: Social and Behavioral Sciences*, 211, pp. 629–633.

Andriopoulos, Constantine and Lewis, Marianne. (2009). Exploitation-exploration tensions and organizational ambidexterity: Managing paradoxes of innovation. *Organization Science*, 20, pp. 696–717. 10.1287/orsc.1080.0406.

Arnould, Eric and Wallendorf, Melanie. (1994). Market-oriented ethnography: Interpretation building and marketing strategy formulation. *Journal of Marketing Research*, 31, pp. 484–504. 10.2307/3151878.

Becker, L. and Jaakkola, E. (2020). Customer experience: Fundamental premises and implications for research. *Journal of the Academy of Marketing Science*, 48(4), pp. 1–19.

Berry, L. L., Carbone, L. P. and Haeckel, S. H. (2002). Managing the total customer experience. *MIT Sloan Management Review*, 43, pp. 85–89.

Bloemer, J. M. and Kasper, H. D. (1995). The complex relationship between consumer satisfaction and brand loyalty. *Journal of Economic Psychology*, 16(2), pp. 311–329.

Bitner, M. J. (1995). Building service relationships: It's all about promises. *Journal of the Academy of Marketing Science*, 23(4), 246–251.

Bloch, P. H. (1995). Seeking the ideal form: Product design and consumer response. *Journal of Marketing*, 59(3), 16–29.

Bloch, P. H. and Richins, M. L. (1983). A theoretical model for the study of product importance perceptions. *Journal of Marketing*, 47(3), 69–81.

Bolton, R., Gustafsson, A., McColl-Kennedy, J., Sirianni, N. and Tse, D. (2014). Small details that make big differences: A radical approach to consumption experience as a firm's differentiating strategy. *Journal of Service Management*, 25, pp. 253–274.

Bradford, K. D. and Desrochers, D. M. (2009). The use of scents to influence consumers: The sense of using scents to make cents. *Journal of Business Ethics*, 90(S2), 141–153.

Brakus, J. J., Schmitt, B. H. and Zarantello, L (2009). Brand experience: What is it? How is it measured? Does it affect loyalty? *Journal of Marketing*, 73(3), 52–68.

Brodie, R. J., Ilic, A., Juric, B. and Hollebeek, L. (2013). Consumer engagement in a virtual brand community: An exploratory analysis. *Journal of Business Research*, 66, pp. 105–114.

Broniarczyk, S. M. and Alba, J. W. (1994). The importance of the brand in brand extension. *Journal of Marketing Research*, 31(2), 214–228.

Brown, B. and Bell, M. (2004), November. CSCW at play: "there"as a collaborative virtual environment. In *Proceedings of the 2004 ACM Conference on Computer Supported Cooperative Work* (pp. 350–359).

Burrell, Q. L. (2003). Predicting future citation behavior. *Journal of the American Society for Information Science & Technology*, 54, pp. 372–378.

Business Wire. (2017). *See, Hera and Feel the Evolution of Visa Through Sensory Branding.* Available at: https://www. businesswire.com. [Accessed: 7 December 2017].

Calder, B. J., Malthouse, E. C. and Schaedel, U. (2009). An experimental study of the relationship between online engagement and advertising effectiveness. *Journal of Interactive Marketing*, 23(4), pp. 321–331.

Caru, A. and Cova, B. (2003). Revisiting consumption experience: A more humble but complete view of the concept. *Marketing Theory*, 3, pp. 267–286.

Chen, I. J. and Popovich, K. (2003). Understanding customer relationship management (CRM). *Business Process Management Journal*, 9(5), pp. 672–688.

Cheung, C. M., Shen, X. L., Lee, Z. W. and Chan, T. K. (2015). Promoting sales of online games through customer engagement. *Electronic Commerce Research and Applications*, 14(4), pp. 241–250.

Chi, C. G. and Gursoy, D. (2009). Employee satisfaction, customer satisfaction, and financial performance: An empirical examination. *International Journal of Hospitality Management*, 28(2), pp. 245–253.

Childers, T.L., Carr, C. L., Peck, J. and Carson, S. (2001). Hedonic and utilitarian motivations for online retail shopping behavior. *Journal of Retailing*, 77(4), pp. 511–535.

Collier, J. E. and Bienstock, C. C. (2006). Measuring service quality in e-retailing. *Journal of Service Research*, 8(3), pp. 260–275.

Datta, S. K. and Coughlin, T. (2016), September. An IoT architecture enabling digital senses. In *2016 IEEE 6th International Conference on Consumer Electronics-Berlin (ICCE-Berlin)* (pp. 67–68). IEEE.

Davies, G. and Chun, R. (2003). The use of metaphor in the exploration of the brand concept. *Journal of Marketing Management*, 19, pp. 45–71.

Customer's perception of luxury brands   511

Del Rio, A. B., Vazquez, R. and Iglesias, V. (2001). The effects of brand associations on consumer response. *Journal of Consumer Marketing*, 6(11), pp. 4048–4056, 21 March, 2012.

Doorn, V., Lemon, N., Mittal, V., Nass, S., Pick, D., Pirner, P., Verhoef, P. C.(2010). Customer engagement behaviour: Theoretical foundations and research Dubois, B. and Duquesne, P. 1993. *The Market for Luxury Goods: Income Versus Culture. European Journal of Marketing.*

Edvardsson, B., Tronvoll, B. and Gruber, T. (2011). Expanding understanding of service exchange and value cocreation: A social construction approach. *Journal of the Academy of Marketing Science*, 39(2), pp. 327–339.

Evans, M. P. (2007). Analysing Google rankings through search engine optimization data. *Internet Research*, 17(1), pp. 21–37.

Gardner, B. B. and Levy, S. J. (1955). The product and the brand. *Harvard Business Review*, 33(2), pp. 33–39.

Girard, A., Lichters, M., Sarstedt, M. and Biswas, D. (2019). Short-and long-term effects of nonconsciously processed ambient scents in a servicescape: Findings from two field experiments. *Journal of Service Research*, 22(4), pp. 440–455.

Gross, W., McGovern, T. and Sturtevant, R., Perfect Market Technologies Inc. 2006. *Search Engine Using User Intent.* U.S. Patent Application 11/234,769.

Hallowell, R. (1996). The relationships of customer satisfaction, customer loyalty, and profitability: An empirical study. *International Journal of Service Industry Management*, 7(4), pp. 27–42.

Hennig-Thurau, T. and Klee, A. (1997). The impact of customer satisfaction and relationship quality on customer retention: A critical reassessment and model development. *Psychology & Marketing*, 14(8), pp. 737–764.

Homburg, C., Jozić, D. and Kuehnl, C. (2017). Customer experience management: Toward implementing an evolving marketing concept. *Journal of the Academy of Marketing Science*, 45(3), pp. 377–401

Hsu, S. H. (2008). Developing an index for online customer satisfaction: Adaptation of American customer satisfaction index. *Expert Systems with Applications*, 34(4), pp. 3033–3042.

Hultén, B. (2011). Sensory marketing: The multi-sensory brand-experience concept. *European Business Review*, 23(3), pp. 256–273

Iglesias, O., Ind, N. and Alfaro, M. 2017. The organic view of the brand: A brand value co-creation model. In *Advances in Corporate Branding* (pp. 148–174). Palgrave Macmillan, London.

Iglesias, O., Markovic, S. and Rialp, J. (2019.) How does sensory brand experience influence brand equity? Considering the roles of customer satisfaction, customer affective commitment, and employee empathy. *Journal of Business Research*, 96, pp. 343–354.

Islam, J. U. and Rahman, Z. (2017). The impact of online brand community characteristics on customer engagement: An application of stimulus-organism-response paradigm. *Telematics and Informatics*, 34(4), pp. 96–109.

Jansen, B. J., Booth, D. L. and Spink, A. (2007, May). Determining the user intent of web search engine queries. In *Proceedings of the 16th International Conference on World Wide Web* (pp. 1149–1150).

Kang, J. (2011). *Social Media Marketing in the Hospitality Industry: The Role of Benefits in Increasing Brand Community Participation and the Impact of Participation on Consumer Trust and Commitment Toward Hotel and Restaurant Brands.*

512 N. N. Richards-Carpenter and T. Grantz

Kent, A., Dennis, C., Cano, M. B., Schwarz, E., Brakus, J. J. and Alamanos, E. (2015) *Branding, Marketing and Design: Experiential Experiential In-Store Digital Environments Environments.*

Kim, J., Fiore, A. M. and Lee, H. H. (2007). Influences of online store perception, shopping enjoyment, and shopping involvement on consumer patronage behavior towards an online retailer. *Journal of Retailing and Consumer Services*, 14(2), pp. 95–107.

Kim, M. and Lennon, S. (2008). The effects of visual and verbal information on attitudes and purchase intentions in internet shopping. *Psychology & Marketing*, 25(2), pp. 146–178.

Kok, J. N., Boers, E. J., Kosters, W. A., Van der Putten, P. and Poel, M. (2009). Artificial intelligence: Definition, trends, techniques, and cases. *Artificial Intelligence*, 1, pp. 1–20.

Kraft, R., Maghoul, F. and Chang, C. C. (2005), October. Y! q: Contextual search at the point of inspiration. In *Proceedings of the 14th ACM International Conference on Information and Knowledge Management* (p. 816823).

Krishna, A. (2012). An integrative review of sensory marketing: Engaging the senses to affect perception, judgment and behavior. *Journal of Consumer Psychology*, 22(3), pp. 332–351

Krishna, A. and Schwarz, N. (2014.) Sensory marketing, embodiment, and grounded cognition: A review and introduction. *Journal of Consumer Psychology*, 24(2), pp. 159–168.

Krishna, A., Cian, L. and Sokolova, T. (2016). The power of sensory marketing in advertising. *Current Opinion in Psychology*, 10, pp. 142–147.

Kuehnl, C., Jozic, D. and Homburg, C. (2019). Effective customer journey design: Consumers' conception, measurement, and consequences. *Journal of the Academy of Marketing Science*, 47(3), pp. 551–568

Lemon, K. N. and Verhoef, P. C. (2016). Understanding customer experience throughout the customer journey. *Journal of Marketing*, 80(6), pp. 69–96.

Littlefield, A., Evil Twin Studios Inc 2006. *System and Method for Organizing Online Communities and Virtual Dwellings Within a Virtual Environment.* U.S. Patent Application 11/292,702.

Loomis, J. M. and Knapp, J. M. (2003). Visual perception of egocentric distance in real and virtual environments. *Virtual and Adaptive Environments*, 11, pp. 21–46.

Loureiro, S. M. C. (2013). The effect of perceived benefits, trust, quality, brand awareness/associations and brand loyalty on internet banking brand equity. *International Journal of Electronic Commerce Studies*, 2, p. 139158.

Machleit, K. A. and Eroglu, S. A. (2000). Describing and measuring emotional response to shopping experience. *Journal of Business Research*, 49(2), pp. 101–111.

Mack, A. (1970). An investigation of the relationship between eye and retinal image movement in the perception of movement. *Perception & Psychophysics*, 8(5), pp. 291–298.

Malenkaya, Y. and Andreyeva, A. (2016). Fashion and audio branding: The analysis and interpretation of luxury fashion marketing concepts. *Journal of Global Fashion Marketing*, 7(4), pp. 291–304.

Manolescu, D. A., Meijer, H. J. M. and Kern, L. J., Microsoft Corp (2009). *Intent-aware Search.* U.S. Patent Application 12/044,362.

Marbach, J., Lages, C. R. and Nunan, D. (2016). Who are you and what do you value? Investigating the role of personality traits and customer-perceived value in online customer engagement. *Journal of Marketing Management*, 32(5–6), pp. 502–525.

Meyer, C. and Schwager, A. (2007). Understanding customer experience. *Harvard Business Review*, 85(2), p. 116.

Nguyen, V. T., Le, T. N., Bui, Q. M., Tran, M. T. and Duong, A. D. (2012), July. Smart shopping assistant: A multimedia and social media augmented system with mobile devices to enhance customers' experience and interaction. In *PACIS* (p. 95).

Patton, M. Q. (1990). *Qualitative Evaluation and Research Methods* (2nd ed.). Sage Publications, Inc.

Peck, J. and Childers, T. L. (2006). If I touch it I have to have it: Individual and environmental influences on impulse purchasing. *Journal of Business Research*, 59(6), pp. 765–769.

Petit, O., Velasco, C. and Spence, C. (2019). Digital sensory marketing: Integrating new technologies into multisensory online experience. *Journal of Interactive Marketing*, 45, pp. 42–61.

Pine, B. J. and Gilmore, J. H. (1998). Welcome to the experience economy. *Harvard Business Review*, 76, p. 97105.

Pizam, A., Shapoval, V. and Ellis, T. (2016). Customer satisfaction and its measurement in hospitality enterprises: A revisit and update. *International Journal of Contemporary Hospitality Management*, 28(1), pp. 2–35.

Raghubir, P. and Krishna, A. (1999). Vital dimensions in volume perception: Can the eye fool the stomach?. *Journal of Marketing Research*, 36(3), pp. 313–326.

Rai, A. (2020). Explainable AI: From black box to glass box. *Journal of the Academy of Marketing Science*, 48(1), pp. 137–141.

Richards, K. A. and Jones, E. (2008). Customer relationship management: Finding value drivers. *Industrial Marketing Management*, 37(2), pp. 120–130.

Rios, A. E. (2016). The impact of the digital revolution in the development of market and communication strategies for the luxury sector (fashion luxury). *Central European Business Review*, 5(2), pp. 17–36.

Rodas-Areiza, J. A. and Montoya-Restrepo, L. A. (2018). Methodological proposal for the analysis and measurement of sensory marketing integrated to the consumer experience. *Dyna*, 85(207), pp. 54–59.

Rodrigues, T., Silva, S. C. and Duarte, P. (2017). The value of textual haptic information in online clothing shopping. *Journal of Fashion Marketing and Management: An International Journal*, 23(2), pp. 257–276.

Sarkar, A. (2011). Impact of utilitarian and hedonic shopping values on individual's perceived benefits and risks in online shopping. *International Management Review*, 7(1), pp. 58–65.

Schroeder, R. (2002). Social interaction in virtual environments: Key issues, common themes, and a framework for research. In *The Social Life of Avatars* (pp. 1–18). Springer, London.

Senecal, S. and Nantel, J. (2004). The influence of online product recommendations on consumers' online choices. *Journal of Retailing*, 80(2), pp. 159–169.

Srinivasan, S. S., Anderson, R. and Ponnavolu, K. (2002). Customer loyalty in e-commerce: An exploration of its antecedents and consequences. *Journal of Retailing*, 78(1), pp. 41–50

Steele, M. and Aziz, I., Microsoft Corp 2007. *Intent Based Search*. U.S. Patent Application 11/448,646.

Stein, B. E. and Stanford, T. R. (2008). Multisensory integration: Current issues from the perspective of the single neuron. *Nature Reviews. Neuroscience*, 9(4), pp. 255–266.

Stern, B. B. (2006). What does brand mean? Historical-analysis method and construct definition. *Journal of the Academy of Marketing Science*, 34(2), pp. 216–223

514 N. N. Richards-Carpenter and T. Grantz

Suzuki, H., Fujitsu Ltd (2000). *System and Method for Updating Shopping Transaction History Using Electronic Personal Digital Shopping Assistant.* U.S. Patent 6,129,274.

Tafesse, W. (2016). Conceptualization of brand experience in an event marketing context. *Journal of Promotion Management*, 22, pp. 34–48.

Thaler, R. (1985). Mental accounting and consumer choice. *Marketing Science*, 4, pp. 199–214.

Thaler, R. H. (1999). Mental accounting matters. *Journal of Behavioral Decision Making*, 12, pp. 183–206.

Tynan, C., McKechnie, S. and Chhuon, C. (2010). Co-creating value for luxury brands. *Journal of Business Research*, 63(11), pp. 1156–1163

Verhoef, P. C., Lemon, K. N., Parasuraman, A., Roggeveen, A., Tsiros, M. and Schlesinger, L. A. (2009). Customer experience creation: Determinants, dynamics and management strategies. *Journal of Retailing*, 85(1), pp. 31–41.

Voss, C. A., Roth, A. V., Rosenzweig, E. D., Blackmon, K. and Chase, R. B. (2004). A tale of two countries' conservatism, service quality, and feedback on customer satisfaction. *Journal of Service Research*, 6(3), pp. 212230.

Wang, Y., Lo, H. P. and Yang, Y. (2004). An integrated framework for service quality, customer value, satisfaction: Evidence from China's telecommunication industry. *Information Systems Frontiers*, 6(4), p. 325340.

Yadav, M. S. and Pavlou, P. A. (2020). Technology-enabled interactions in digital environments: A conceptual foundation for current and future research. *Journal of the Academy of Marketing Science*, 48(1), pp. 132–136

Yang, Z., Jun, M. and Peterson, R. T. (2004). Measuring customer perceived online service quality. *International Journal of Operations & Production Management*, 24(11), pp. 1149–1174.

Zeithaml, V. A., Parasuraman, A. and Malhotra, A. (2000). *E-service Quality: Definition, Dimensions and Conceptual Model.* Working Paper. Marketing Science Institute, Cambridge, MA.

Zha, D., Melewar, T. C., Foroudi, P. and Jin, Z. (2020). An assessment of brand experience knowledge literature: Using bibliometric data to identify future research direction. *International Journal of Management Reviews*, 20(3), pp. 287–317. ISSN 1460-8545 [Article] (doi:10.1111/ijmr.12226)

20 Celebrity endorsement, theories, models, existing literature and corporate identity, image and reputation

Shahzeb Hussain

Introduction

This chapter starts with a brief introduction on celebrity endorsement. Next, it covers outstanding models on the topic, followed by commonly used theories, studies done on celebrity negative publicity, effects of demographics on celebrity endorsement, use of celebrity endorsement in social media, effects of celebrity endorsement on corporate identity, image and reputation and finally, gives some detail on potential future contributions.

Background

A celebrity endorser is an individual, who enjoys public recognition and uses the recognition on behalf of a consumer's good by appearing with it in an advertisement (McCracken, 1989). Celebrity endorsers are suggested to be an effective marketing communication tool. They appear in various modes of advertising and influence reference groups with th3eir charm, beauty, expertise and credibility. Consumers value their symbolic meanings and use these meanings to enhance their own selves. They connect with the endorsed products and brands through the symbolism attached with the celebrity endorser and transfer these meanings to themselves by consuming the brands, which have meanings relevant to them or sufficient to build their own self-concepts (Escalas and Bettman, 2009). These meanings are critical in enhancing consumers' own self-identity, which as a result provide a business to marketers and advertisers to hire celebrities.

The history of celebrity endorsement goes all the way back to Queen Victoria, who was once associated with Cadbury's chocolate. Between 1875 and 1900, trade cards used pictures of popular celebrities to create brand awareness. In the same period, tobacco firms like Goodwin and Co. and Kodas Cigarettes signed various similar contracts with famous personalities and used them on their cigar packs. This legacy continued throughout the early 20th century, where various showbusiness personalities associated themselves with industries like tobacco, beauty, fashion, electronic equipment and alcoholic and non-alcoholic beverages. A new level of sophistication emerged, whereby instead of just co-branding an existing product with a celebrity, companies started making new products

516   *Shahzeb Hussain*

for celebrities (Francis and Yazdanifard, 2013). In recent decades, the use of celebrity endorsers has become standard practice. A rough estimate suggests that approximately 25% of all advertisements in the United Stated and the United Kingdom consist of celebrity endorsers (Carroll, 2008). These numbers are a bit higher in some of the other countries' contexts, such as in countries like India and Japan, where 75% of advertising endorsements are made by celebrity endorsers (Carroll, 2008). Various successful individuals from fields ranging from cuisines, entertainment, business, politics and sports are affiliated today with brand endorsements. They don't only enjoy high profiles and live luxurious style of lives, but also possess glamourous images in the eyes of the public (Choi et al., 2005).

Employing an appropriate celebrity endorser for a product or brand is a critical and expensive task. At the time of celebrity endorsers' hiring, firms and their advertising agencies take various factors into account, such as image, familiarity, likeability, expertise, trustworthiness, attractiveness, fit between the celebrity and brand etc. – most of which are discussed in later sections of this chapter. Along with other highly ranked tasks, costs of securing a celebrity endorser is another debatable and controversial matter. Celebrity endorsements are an expensive strategy for the firms. Estimates suggest that as much as 10% of a firm's annual budget is spent on celebrity endorsements (Bergkvist and Zhou, 2016). Depending on the status and experience of celebrities, firms pay them in millions and billions of dollars. Sports star Tiger Woods earned an estimated $60 million a year, David Beckham earned $75 million in 2014, Beyonce made $115 million from her various endorsements in 2014, Rihanna earned $220 million from her endorsements in 2016, Catherine Zeta-Jones earned $20 million for endorsing T-Mobile, Nike spent $110 million on advertisements with Michael Jordan, while American Express and CoverGirl spent $75 million on advertisements featuring Ellen DeGeneres.

In return, these celebrities have a positive impact on firms' overall profits. According to a rough estimation, the impact of celebrity endorsers' announcements on stock returns is found to be marginally positive with a +0.44% only on the day of the announcement (Ding et al., 2011). They also bring other benefits, such as they capture consumers' attention, increase advertisement and brand recall rates, influence on advertising effectiveness, improve communication, transfer their qualities and credibility to products and brands, and rise purchase behaviour (Erdogan, 1999; Spry et al., 2011).

Although, the benefits of celebrity endorsers are some of the important prerequisite, but these benefits are impossible without various attributes, which a celebrity endorser should complement to the products, brands or advertisings – these attributes are discussed below. If the endorser does not possess these attributes, then the campaign surrounded on celebrity can be unsuccessful (Glover, 2009). Selection of the right celebrity endorser with sufficient attributes plays a major role in the effectiveness of celebrity endorsement. These attributes have also been termed as models within the literature of celebrity endorsement. Some of these models are illustrated below.

Models on celebrity endorsement

There are various models based on the topic of celebrity endorsement; however, only three most frequently used models are discussed below:

Celebrity credibility

The concept of celebrity credibility has been and will continue to be of interest to scholars and practitioners in marketing and advertising. It is defined as celebrity's positive characteristics that affect the receiver's acceptance of a messages (Ohanian, 1990). It refers to whether the celebrity is considered as having expertise relevant to the communication topic, can be trusted to give an opinion on the topic and possesses physical characteristics and attributes which are attractive (Ohanian, 1990; Suki, 2014). The concept of celebrity credibility has been originated from Hovland and his colleagues' work in 1953 on source credibility. Ohanian (1990) adopted a source credibility scale and developed measures of celebrity credibility using two exploratory and two confirmatory American samples. His scale consisted of dimensions, such as trustworthiness, expertise and attractiveness. Trustworthiness refers to the degree to which the audience perceives that celebrity endorser can convey a sense of believability, honesty and integrity through the medium to the brand (Kim et al., 2014). Expertise is defined as the extent to which a celebrity endorser is suggested as skilled, experienced and knowledgeable (Magnini et al., 2008). Attractiveness refers to celebrity endorsers' physical appearance, features, beauty, sexual appeal and etiquettes (Amos et al., 2008). Evidence suggests that high celebrity credibility dimensions are suggested to be important and influential constructs in persuading consumers' attitudes, beliefs, brand recall, brand credibility, brand equity, brand image, corporate image, corporate credibility, corporate reputation and self-brand connection (Lafferty et al., 2002; Spry et al., 2011; Singh and Banerjee, 2018; Yoo et al., 2018).

Meaning transfer theory

McCracken (1989) proposed the concept of meaning transfer theory and suggested that meaning is transferred in the society through marketing processes, such as communication, arts and sometimes, also through famous and renowned individuals, namely celebrities. Celebrities bring meanings, which are adopted by individuals in the society. Marketers use these celebrities and attach them with brands and send their meanings to the public. This model has been called as meaning transfer theory in the literature.

Meaning transfer theory was developed due to the inadequacies which celebrity credibility brings (McCracken, 1989; Jain and Roy, 2016). According to a few researchers (McCracken, 1989; Roy, 2018), celebrity credibility has failed to explain the reasons why one celebrity is effective to endorse one brand but does not show any effectiveness to endorse the other. Celebrities stand for different meanings to the consumers and their personality or lifestyle traits in some cases

518   *Shahzeb Hussain*

are unable to be right for the brand. The purpose of meaning transfer theory is to communicate or transfer the symbolic or cultural meanings from celebrity endorsers to the products and brands. These meanings are transferred from celebrity endorsers to the brand and give them new representations in the market.

In 1989, McCracken, based on the importance of meaning transfer theory, proposed a three-stage meaning transfer process. In the first stage, meanings are developed from a celebrity endorser's roles, traits, accomplishments etc. In the second stage, meanings are transferred to the product or brand by virtue of the endorsement. In the last stage, meanings are transferred from the product or brand to the consumers through purchase and consumptions.

Studies done on this topic are fewer compared to the number of studies done on the celebrity credibility model. Earlier studies (Langmeyer and Walker, 1991; Byrne et al., 2003; Batra and Homer, 2004; Peetz et al., 2004; Jain and Roy, 2016) on this topic examined the transference of celebrity endorsers' meanings (i.e. quality, image, credibility, personality, physical appearance, feelings, performance, values and power) to the product or brand meanings. Results suggested that different celebrities' meanings have significant effects on products or brands. Few (Till, 2001) also examined the transference of negative meaning from celebrity endorsers to the brands. Results suggested that negative meanings have higher impact on the endorsed products or brands. Later, researchers (Charbonneau and Garland, 2006) have explored the reverse meaning transfer from the product/brand to celebrity endorser.

Match-up hypothesis

The next model, which has taken significant importance in the literature, is the match-up hypothesis. It has also been termed as congruence, relevancy and similarity in the literature (Parmar et al., 2020). This model suggests that highly relevant characteristics of celebrity endorsers should have congruency with the highly relevant attributes of brands (Choi and Rifon, 2012). To emphasise the importance of this model, previous researchers (Watkins, 1989; Erdogan, 1999) have suggested that there should be an appropriate tie between the firms' products and celebrity endorsers' personas and images. Absence of connection between celebrity endorsers and products endorsed can make consumers believe that celebrity endorsers have been bought and are highly paid to endorse the products and brands (Erdogan, 1999).

Previous research on this topic is not very extensive. Friedman and Friedman (1983) gave their perspective and suggested that celebrity endorsers with high products match were important, when purchases of products involved high social and psychological risks. Kahle and Hosmer (1985) and Kamins (1990) suggested that attractiveness was one of the core dimensions in enhancing the effectiveness of products and increasing purchase intentions. Till and Busler (2000) and Mishra and Beatty (1990) examined the similar relationship based on expertise and image, respectively. Their findings revealed that a good match-up could increase brand attitude and purchase intention. These findings were not evident

Celebrity endorsement, theories and, models 519

by Mishra et al. (2015) on attitude towards brand and purchase intention based on personality congruency, but they found a positive effect on celebrity endorser suitability, celebrity endorser credibility, ad believability and attitude towards ad. It is also evident in the literature that celebrity endorsers compared to non-celebrity endorsers can have higher effects on more congruent products than less congruent products (Kamins and Gupta, 1994; Na, 2007). A higher level of congruency can result in higher persuasion and attitudes, attitudes and recall, while a low level of congruency can badly damage consumers' attitudes and intentions (Misra and Beatty, 1990; Ilicic and Webster, 2011; Mishra, 2015; Albert et al., 2017). Recently, a few researchers also found that congruency does not matter for all types of celebrity endorsers, rather it only matters for some (Parmar et al., 2020). There is also some weak evidence which suggests that incongruency or mismatch between celebrity endorser and brand generates longer ad viewing times, higher brand attitudes, brand interest, purchase intention and positive word-of-mouth communication (Torn, 2012).

Theories used with the context of celebrity endorsement

There are various theories in the literature; however, some of the most frequently used theories are described below:

Social influence theory

The effectiveness of celebrity endorsers has been linked by some researchers to the process of social influence theory (Friedman and Friedman, 1979; Choi and Rifon, 2012). Social influence theory takes into account how individuals are influenced by others to display certain behaviours (Osei-Frimpong et al., 2019, p. 105). It is noted as accepting certain pressurised behaviour to recognise oneself in any environment. There are two forms of social influence theory, so-called informational social influence theory and normative social influence theory. The first theory explains that individuals when influenced accept information obtained from others as evidence about the reality, while the second theory explains that individuals conform to the influence of other people that leads them to conformity in order to be accepted by others (Kelman, 1961; Casey et al., 2003). These theories are related to Kelman's (1961) process of social influence theory. Kelman (1961) suggested that there are three processes, which when pursued, facilitate the potential that an individual will accept an influence from others (Kamins, 1989, p. 5). These processes are called identification, internalisation and compliance. Identification occurs when individuals adopt behaviour of others because they have preferences to be like others. It is related to Deutsch and Gerard's earlier mentioned normative influence theory (Choi and Rifon, 2012; Um, 2013). Internalisation occurs when individuals conform to the attitudes or behaviours of others because these actions are thought to be credible and are highly congruent with individuals' own values and thoughts. Compliance occurs when individuals accept influence from others because they hope to receive a

520   *Shahzeb Hussain*

likeable response from them (McCormick, 2016). Out of these three processes, identification and internalisation influence individuals' attitudes and beliefs towards celebrity endorsers. Identification process is based on a desire to be like the favourite celebrity endorsers, i.e. by copying their behaviours including using their favourite celebrity endorsers' products and brands. Internalisation is when consumers internalise a message, i.e. when they are persuaded by the behaviours of celebrity endorsers. Both identification and internalisation theories have been used in the literature to illustrate the importance of celebrity endorsement context (Choi and Rifon, 2012; McCormick, 2016).

Social learning theory

Social learning theory is another theory heavily used in the celebrity endorsement context. Studies on social learning theory within the context of celebrity endorsement context has its origins in studies by Bandura et al. (1961). This theory suggests that individuals learn from their family members, peers, surrounding culture and other media entities including celebrity endorsers (Chan and Zhang, 2007). People learn by observing the behaviour of others (Brace-Govan, 2013, p. 114). The reason to learn or act alike others is to receive rewards, such as receiving a similar status, name, designation etc., within the society. This process is also called observational learning. It is a cognitive process and therefore, also called social cognitive theory. It consists of four processes, so-called attentional processes, retention processes, motor reproduction processes and motivational processes. Attentional processes define to what extent celebrity behaviours and characteristics are perceived by the individuals; retention processes relate tot how far celebrity behaviours and characteristics are retained or remembered; motor reproduction processes regards whether celebrity's behaviours and characteristics are decisive and whether individuals are able to transfer these characteristics into actions; and finally, motivational processes look at whether correct observational learning is performed in reality after observing a celebrity endorser (Schafer and Quiring, 2015). Further, Basil (2012) suggested that individuals are more likely to perform behaviours of celebrities, when they see or think of themselves as identical to others. These perceptions of similarity can be influenced by celebrities' age, gender, physical attractiveness or status and make them want to acquire their characteristics and associate themselves with their endorsed brand (Hung, 2014; Phua et al., 2018).

Elaboration likelihood model

The elaboration likelihood model (ELM) is based on the assumption that individuals' response to a celebrity endorser depends on various situational factors and thus, their replies can be distinguished between high and low (Karasiewicz and Kowalczuk, 2014). In the first case, i.e. high involvement, individuals will have a permanent change in their attitudes as individuals pay attention to the arguments contained in the message. They will elaborate more strongly towards the content of the message and are involved cognitively (Freeman and Chen, 2015; Von Sikorski et al., 2018). This path is also called central route because individuals will have stronger mental activities involved (Lammers, 2000; Wheeler, 2009). While in the second case, i.e. low involvement, the reception of the message will be peripheral and heuristic, and will have a weaker effect on individuals' attitudes (Karasiewicz and Kowalczuk, 2014). Individuals will be less likely to consider the implications of the arguments in the message, less likely to process complex information and less motivated to process the communication (Sanbonmatsu and Kardes, 1988; Freeman and Chen, 2015). They will have high focus towards the peripheral, ancillary cues associated with the communication, such as the attractiveness, trustworthiness, expertise or level of fame of the celebrity endorser. Low involvement usually involves products such as shoes, beauty products, soft drinks and other beverages. These are well-established products and there is less need to process the information. They are very often endorsed by the celebrity endorsers to make the product and its message memorable. Previous studies on the elaboration likelihood model within the context of celebrity endorsement have confirmed that under conditions of high involvement, arguments influence attitude, while, in the case of low involvement, celebrities influence attitudes (Petty et al., 1983; Byrne et al., 2003; Anghel, 2009; Jain et al., 2011).

Associative network theory

The next theory, which is heavily used in the celebrity endorsement context is of associative network theory. According to associative network theory, human memory is made of interconnected nodes, where each node holds information and is connected with other nodes, based on an associative link (Cuomo et al., 2019). When individuals think of something, s/he also activates information on other associated nodes (Lord and Putrevu, 2009; Spry et al., 2011). Celebrity and brand are an example of a similar node, where celebrity is linked with the brand through the endorsement process (Um, 2018). When the individuals think about the brand, they also activate the associated link on the celebrity, and when they think about the celebrity, they also activate the associated link on the brand (Spry et al., 2011). It means that feelings and attitudes towards the celebrity endorser are transferred to the brand and vice versa (Phua et al., 2018). If the stored information based on celebrity endorser or brand is strong and positive, then it also generates positive information on the other connected source (Um, 2018; Yang, 2018). Similarly, when the information on celebrity endorser or brand is negative, it equally generates the negative information on the other connected source (Till and Shimp, 1998; Um and Kim, 2016; Um, 2018). Prior research on the celebrity endorsement context confirms the importance of associative network and suggests that it does enhance the importance of other connected source (Magnini et al., 2008; Spry et al., 2011; Um, 2018; Cuomo et al., 2019).

522 Shahzeb Hussain

Literature on other widely used topics in the context of celebrity endorsement

This section covers some of the literature on other contexts of celebrity endorsement contexts, such as celebrity endorsement and negative publicity, celebrity endorsement and demographic factors and celebrity endorsement presence on social media

Celebrity endorsement and negative publicity

Despite the beneficial aspects, celebrity endorsers also come with risks and at times, are also found involved in negative publicities (Akturan, 2011). Negative publicities of celebrity endorsers are evaluated more negatively than positive or moderate evaluated information is (Money et al., 2006). Negative publicities attract more negative attention, increase bad press, help in easily memorising and recalling the adverse events, affect brand/corporate image and reputation, and most importantly decrease firms' sales (Thwaites et al., 2012). When these events occur, most firms distance themselves from the celebrity endorsers, while others cease the endorsement for a short period, to avoid the transfer of negative publicities' effects from celebrity endorsers to the endorsed products and brands, and also to show disapproval of celebrity endorsers' behaviours (Akturan, 2011; Prameswara and Sjabadhyni, 2018). Incidents such as O. J. Simpson's involvement in murder charges, Mike Tyson's sexual abuse of women, Michael Jackson's accusation of child abuse, Michael Vick's involvement in dog fighting, Madonna's release of offensive videos, Tiger Wood's extra =marital infidelities, Justin Bieber's racist jokes and John Terry's verbal racist remarks are all evident in the literature (Akturan, 2011; Wang and Kim, 2020).

Similar to benefits of celebrity endorsers, researchers have also examined the topic based on celebrity negative publicity. Literature on this topic is divided into two parts. In the first part, researchers have examined the negative effects of celebrity negative publicity on attitude towards brand, purchase intentions, stick prices and similar brands of competitors (Till and Shimp, 1998; Louie et al., 2001; Carrillat et al., 2014). They have found that negative information about a celebrity endorser negatively affects consumers' evaluation of the endorsed brand, company's stock value and also lowers the evaluation of the celebrity endorser's sponsor and competitor's similar brands (Till and Shimp, 1998; Money et al., 2006). Current researchers (Um, 2013; Um and Kim, 2016; Yoon and Shin, 2017) on the study have examined the effects on topics such as identification, commitment, attribution and transgressions. They have found that consumers with high levels of identification, attribution and commitment towards the brand are less likely to be influenced by celebrity scandals (Um, 2013; Um and Kim, 2016). Celebrity transgression that are high inseverity would elicit negative consumer responses towards the celebrity, brand and purchase intention (Wang and Kim, 2020). The stronger the associative link present between the brand and the celebrity endorser, leads to higher brand evaluation as well as purchase intention (Um and Kim, 2016).

Celebrity endorsement, theories and, models   523

Celebrity endorsement and parasocial relationships

In 1956, Horton and Wohl developed the concept of parasocial relationship, which is defined as a one-sided, pseudo-intimate relationship with famous and well-known personalities, such as show characters, news anchors, talk show hosts and importantly, celebrities (Claessens and Van den Buck, 2015). These are long-term connections developed through mediated repeated encounters, where one party feels a deep and abiding connection to the other and the other does not reciprocate (Hwang and Zhang, 2018). These relationships are formed based on empathy, emotional connections and involve a sense of intimacy and comprehension (Hwang and Zhang, 2018). They are considered an important part of the social world and help individuals to grow or approach their own ideal selves (Lee et al., 2020). Mostly, these relationships are formed based on media consumptions, such as television, radio and other showbiz tools, but out of all these, social media provides a perfect platform for the growth of parasocial relationships (Lueck, 2012; Rasmusses, 2018; Lim et al., 2020).

Literature on parasocial relationships within the context of celebrity endorsement is very limited. However, it has been overtly suggested that parasocial relationships help individuals to form relationships with the celebrities (Gong and Li, 2017). These relationships are usually formed through vicarious interactions, most importantly, through repeated media exposures, which lead individuals to create a sense of intimacy, liking and friendship with celebrities (Chung and Cho, 2017). It is suggested that parasocial relationships with celebrities create a positive bond between two, bring a positive attitude towards advertising, endorsed products and brands and purchase intentions (Gong and Li, 2017; Kurtin et al., 2018). Further, studies also suggest that parasocial relationships change perceptions and lead to values of customer equity, credibility, satisfaction and loyalty (Lim and Kim, 2011; Young et al., 2012; Labrecque, 2014; Kim et al., 2015; Yuan et al., 2019).

Celebrity endorsement and social media

Social media is defined as an application for users to generate content, share materials and take part in social networking (Ahmad et al., 2019). It is a group of internet-based applications that permits creation and exchange of information among internet users (Danniswara et al., 2017). Various media such as Facebook, Twitter, YouTube and Instagram are some of the most frequently used social media platforms. According to recent consensus, there are over 2.7 billion users on Facebook, over 2 billion on YouTube, 330 million on Twitter and over 1 billion on Instagram (Statista, 2020). It is evident from various sources that social media anticipation has increased from 10% in 2008 to a whopping 77% in 2018 (Phua et al., 2018). Along with this growing importance, individuals today spend 46 minutes each day on these sites, 70% of these users login daily, while 43% of them login multiple times in a day (Clarke et al., 2016). These importance make it a significant tool to be used by businesses to promote and advertise themselves. By using social media, firms can keep their followers up to date on

524   *Shahzeb Hussain*

recent developments, make their presence more obvious, build two-way real-time effective communications, enhance their images and create successful relationships (Clarke et al., 2016; Danniswara et al., 2017).

Trends suggest that celebrities play an important role on social media in increasing the influence of products and brands (Phua et al., 2018). They have a huge number of followers and have an ability to turn the traffic. They use social media to keep their fans updated on their upcoming projects including their endorsed brands (Chung and Cho, 2017). Exclusive communication on products and brands encourages fans to relate themselves with celebrities and buy their endorsed products and brands. Interactions with favourite celebrities make the spectators create parasocial relationships (explained earlier), create interactions with them and buy their endorsed brands (Kim and Kim, 2020). Research on this topic suggests that celebrity endorsement presence on social media can help firms to increase brand satisfaction, brand credibility, attitudes, purchase intention, word of mouth and commitment, but as suggested in the earlier theories, there needs to be a similarity and self-congruency between the celebrity endorsers and individuals (Um, 2016; Chung and Cho, 2017; Danniswara et al., 2017; Kim and Kim, 2020).

Celebrity endorsement and demographics

There appear to be other factors, i.e. consumers' demographics, which also have a significant effect on the topic of celebrity endorsement. Although, findings on the topic are very mixed up. People have different types of decision-making styles based on their ages, genders, income levels and ethnicities. Usually, younger, low-income, female and ethnic individuals have been found to be highly persuaded by celebrity endorsers compared to older, high-income, male and majority-ethnicity individuals (Djafarova and Rushworth, 2017, Hussain et al., 2020). Young individuals try to disengage with their parents or guardians in order to construct and define their own identities and lifestyles in their own ways (Djafarova and Rushworth, 2017). Celebrities play a role in order to influence and communicate the traits that are required and looked at by the young consumers and thus make them have a positive effect towards celebrity endorsers (Isaksen and Roper, 2008). Similarly, men and women are effected differently by celebrity endorsers (Meyers-Levy and Strenthal, 1991; Bhutada and Rollins, 2015). Men use salient cues to process information, while women use relevant information and are easily persuaded and have a higher willingness to accept claims compared to men (Bhutada and Rollins, 2015). Furthermore, specific cultures and ethnicities prefer their own ethnic celebrities due to their similarities with them (Kim and Cheong, 2012; Hussain et al., 2020). Most of these assumptions are confirmed in the literature (Bhutada and Rollins, 2015; Djafarova and Rushworth, 2017). But, as mentioned earlier, there are a few studies that have confirmed that genders, ages and ethnicities are effected similarly by celebrity endorsers and there is no significant difference found among these demographics (Bush et al., 2004; Sierra et al., 2009; Hussain et al., 2020).

Celebrity endorsement and corporate identity, image and reputation

Along with the effects of celebrity endorsers on advertising and brand, celebrity endorsers have positive effects on consumers' views on the firm's identity, image and reputation (Hussain et al., 2020). Celebrity endorsers that promote trustworthiness, possess expertise in the field, bring attractiveness and meanings, have a match-up with brands and products and contribute towards a firm's approach to produce corporate social responsibility are thought to be highly beneficial for the success of the firm (Kim et al., 2014; Ghotbivayghan et al., 2015). Consumers are usually fond of celebrities, their way of life, how they dress, glamour etc. They adore, choose their way of lives and buy the products and brands, which their favourite celebrities endorse. When similar individuals also find that their favourite celebrities are credible and thoughtful about the surroundings, they get much closer and a faith in them is created (Zakari et al., 2019). Information from a highly reputable celebrity endorser can heavily help to influence the attitudes, beliefs and opinions not only towards the products and brands, but also towards other connected sources, such the firm (Van Norel et al., 2014). A firm's identity, image and reputation are heavily based on the signals relayed by a credible and reputable celebrity endorser. Although, there is not a lot of research available on the effects of celebrity endorsers on a firm's identity, image and reputation, but limited research on this topic supports the idea that celebrity endorsers play a significant role in the establishment of the positive identity, image and reputation of a firm (Kim et al., 2014; Zakari et al., 2019; Hussain et al., 2020; Lee et al., 2020).

Future direction

Based on the importance of the topics covered by this book, we have a few suggestions for future researchers to investigate. As one can notice, from the last topic of celebrity endorsers' effects on corporate identity, image and reputation, we suggest future researchers explore this topic in more detail as there is a limited amount evidence on the topic, especially on the effect of celebrity endorsers on corporate identity. Further, we also suggest future researchers explore the topic based on different type of firms including their types, sizes, locations etc. Next, our suggestion is to explore the topic based on consumers' demographics, advertising types and brand types etc. Finally, future researchers should examine the importance of this topic within the context of cutting-edge marketing.

Conclusion

Celebrity endorsement is not a new phenomenon. It is in debate from last few decades especially since the study of Ohanian (1990) on celebrity credibility. The first few studies on the topic are based on examining the effects of celebrity endorsers on attitudinal and behavioural constructs (Goldsmith et al., 2000), while the most current studies are based on examining the effects of celebrity

526   *Shahzeb Hussain*

endorser on self-brand connection, brand equity, brand image, brand credibility, brand loyalty, advertising credibility, corporate image, corporate credibility, corporate loyalty, corporate social responsibility, etc. (Spry et al., 2011; Dwivedi et al., 2016; Hussain et al., 2020; Lee et al., 2020). There is still room for future researchers to examine this topic based on other constructs including the ones, which are suggested in the future directions.

CASE STUDY

Eldrick "Tiger Woods" is a professional American golfer and CEO to TGR Design, The TGR Foundation, TGR Live and The Woods Jupiter. He was born on December 30, 1975, to a retired African American Lieutenant Colonel Earl Woods and his Asian American wife Kultida Tida Woods. He was named Tiger after a Vietnamese soldier who was also a friend of his father. Woods grew up in Orange County, California. He started taking interest in golf at the age of 6 months and started playing the game at the age of 5 and played his very first professional tournament in 1992 at the age of 16. In 1996, Woods made an unprecedented record. In 2000, Woods became the youngest British Open Champion at St. Andrews. His second Masters victory in 2001 made him the first golfer to hold all four professional majors at one time. His major victories include the five Masters Tournaments, three U.S. Open Championships, four PGA Championships and three British Open Championships. He also has been declared PGA player of the year 11 times, player of the year ten times, leading money winner seven times, Vardon Trophy winner 12 times, Bryson Nelson Award winner nine times, FedEx Cup Champion nearly twice and won the Presidential Medal of Freedom in 2019.

In late 2009, Tiger Woods' extramarital scandals came on the surface. Numerous women came forward and confirmed their affairs with the champion Woods. His marriage ended, but his main sponsor Nike stood by his side. Phil Knight, the then chairman and co-founder of Nike, gave his backing to Woods especially when other sponsors were distancing themselves from the world-renowned golfer. Knight added that when his career would be over, his wrongdoings would be seen as slight glitches. Other sponsors, such as Proctor & Gamble and Gillette limited their sponsorship and a few others also dropped Woods from their sponsorships. The Tiger-Nike relationship proved one of the most iconic deals in the overall history of endorsements. Nike, which already had a signed contract with Woods in 1996 (reportedly for $40 million), an estimated $100-million contract in 2001 and $20–40-million contract in 2006, extended their contract in 2013 for an undisclosed sum.

Although, this relationship has created few enduring memories at the time and brought millions of dollars in business for both sides, some

Celebrity endorsement, theories and, models 527

stakeholders associated with Nike criticised their association after the scandals came out. Of course, the main criticism was of Wood's scandals and his treatment by Nike, which rather than dissolve their partnership, their relationship with Woods became stronger and fruitful "year in and year out".

Case questions

1. What do you think Nike should have done with Tiger Woods's sponsorship, after his scandal came out?
2. Critically discuss the negative effects that Woods's scandal might have brought towards Nike's image and reputation?
3. What kind of corporate identity has Phil Knight created based on Woods's scandal?

Key terms and definitions

Celebrity endorser: a celebrity endorser is an individual, who enjoys public recognition and uses the recognition on behalf of a consumer's good by appearing with it in an advertisement (McCracken, 1989).

Celebrity credibility refers to whether the celebrity is considered as having expertise relevant to the communication topic, can be trusted to give an opinion on the topic and possesses physical characteristics and attributes which are attractive (Ohanian, 1990; Suki, 2014).

Meaning transfer theory: McCracken (1989) proposed the concept of meaning transfer theory and suggested that meaning is transferred in the society through marketing processes, such as communication, arts and sometimes, also through famous and renowned individuals, namely celebrities.

Meaning transfer theory: this model suggests that there should be higher congruency between the celebrity endorser and the relevant attributes of brand (Choi and Rifon, 2012).

Social influence theory: this theory refers to the way in which individuals change their behaviour to meet the demands of a social environment.

Social learning theory: this theory suggests that individuals learn from their family members, peers, surrounding culture and other media entities including celebrity endorsers (Osei-Frimpong et al., 2019, p. 105).

Elaboration likelihood model: this theory is based on the assumption that individuals' response to a celebrity endorser depends on various situational factors and thus, their replies can be distinguished between high and low (Karasiewicz and Kowalczuk, 2014).

Associative network theory: this theory explains that human memory is made of interconnected nodes, where each node holds information and is connected

528 *Shahzeb Hussain*

with other nodes, based on an associative link (Spry et al., 2011; Cuomo et al., 2019).

Parasocial relationships are defined as one-sided, pseudo-intimate relationships with famous and well-known personalities, such as show characters, news anchors, talk show hosts and importantly, celebrities (Claessens and Van den Buck, 2015).

References

Ahmed, Y. A., Ahmad, M. N., Ahmad, N. and Zakaria, N. H. (2019). Social media for knowledge-sharing: A systematic literature review. *Telematics and Informatics, 37*, 72–112.

Akturan, U. (2011). Celebrity advertising in the case of negative associations: Discourse analysis of weblogs. *Management Research Review.*

Albert, N., Ambroise, L. and Valette-Florence, P. (2017). Consumer, brand, celebrity: Which congruency produces effective celebrity endorsements?. *Journal of Business Research, 81*, 96–106.

Amos, C., Holmes, G. and Strutton, D. (2008). Exploring the relationship between celebrity endorser effects and advertising effectiveness: A quantitative synthesis of effect size. *International Journal of Advertising, 27*(2), 209–234.

Anghel, C. (2009). The effect of celebrity endorsements on gift-giving purchases: An application of the elaboration likelihood model.

Bandura, A., Ross, D. and Ross, S. A. (1961). Transmission of aggression through imitation of aggressive models. *Journal of Abnormal & Social Psychology, 63*(3), 575–582

Basil, M. (2012). Admiration: An important determinant of celebrity effectiveness. *Marketing Theory and Applications, 229.*

Batra, R. and Homer, P. M. (2004). The situational impact of brand image beliefs. *Journal of Consumer Psychology, 14*(3), 318–330.

Bergkvist, L. and Zhou, K. Q. (2016). Celebrity endorsements: A literature review and research agenda. *International Journal of Advertising, 35*(4), 642–663.

Bhutada, N. S. and Rollins, B. L. (2015). Disease-specific direct-to-consumer advertising of pharmaceuticals: An examination of endorser type and gender effects on consumers' attitudes and behaviors. *Research in Social and Administrative Pharmacy, 11*(6), 891–900.

Brace-Govan, J. (2013). More diversity than celebrity: A typology of role model interaction. *Journal of Social Marketing.*

Bush, J., Martin, A. and Bush, D. (2004). Sports celebrity influence on the behavioural intentions of Generation-Y. *Journal of Advertisement Research, 44*(1), 108–118.

Byrne, A., Whitehead, M. and Breen, S. (2003). The naked truth of celebrity endorsement. *British Food Journal.*

Carrillat, F. A., d'Astous, A. and Christianis, H. (2014). Guilty by association: The perils of celebrity endorsement for endorsed brands and their direct competitors. *Psychology & Marketing, 31*(11), 1024–1039.

Carroll, A. (2009). Brand communications in fashion categories using celebrity endorsement. *Journal of Brand Management, 17*(2), 146–158.

Casey, M. K., Allen, M., Emmers-Sommer, T., Sahlstein, E. R. I. N., Degooyer, D. A. N., Winters, A. M. and Dun, T. I. M. (2003). When a celebrity contracts a disease: The example of Earvin "Magic" Johnson's announcement that he was HIV positive. *Journal of Health Communication, 8*(3), 249–265.

Chan, K. and Zhang, C. (2007). Living in a celebrity-mediated social world: The Chinese experience. *Young Consumers.*

Celebrity endorsement, theories and, models 529

Charbonneau, J. and Garland, R. (2006). The use of celebrity athletes as endorsers: Views of the New Zealand general public. *International Journal of Sports Marketing and Sponsorship*.

Choi, S. M. and Rifon, N. J. (2012). It is a match: The impact of congruence between celebrity image and consumer ideal self on endorsement effectiveness. *Psychology & Marketing*, 29(9), 639–650.

Choi, S. M., Lee, W. N. and Kim, H. J. (2005). Lessons from the rich and famous: A cross-cultural comparison of celebrity endorsement in advertising. *Journal of Advertising*, 34(2), 85–98.

Chung, S. and Cho, H. (2017). Fostering parasocial relationships with celebrities on social media: Implications for celebrity endorsement. *Psychology & Marketing*, 34(4), 481–495.

Claessens, N. and Van den Bulck, H. (2015). Parasocial relationships with audiences' favorite celebrities: The role of audience and celebrity characteristics in a representative Flemish sample. *Communications*, 40(1), 43–65.

Clarke, T. B., Murphy, J. and Adler, J. (2016). Celebrity chef adoption and implementation of social media, particularly pinterest: A diffusion of innovations approach. *International Journal of Hospitality Management*, 57, 84–92.

Cuomo, M. T., Foroudi, P., Tortora, D., Hussain, S. and Melewar, T. C. (2019). Celebrity endorsement and the attitude towards luxury brands for sustainable consumption. *Sustainability*, 11(23), 6791.

Danniswara, R., Sandhyaduhita, P. and Munajat, Q. (2017). The impact of ewom referral, celebrity endorsement, and information quality on purchase decision: A case study of Instagram. *Engineering Computer Science*, 30(2), 23–44.

Ding, H., Molchanov, A. E. and Stork, P. A. (2011). The value of celebrity endorsements: A stock market perspective. *Marketing Letters*, 22(2), 147–163.

Djafarova, E. and Rushworth, C. (2017). Exploring the credibility of online celebrities' Instagram profiles in influencing the purchase decisions of young female users. *Computers in Human Behavior*, 68, 1–7.

Dwivedi, A., Johnson, L. W. and McDonald, R. (2016). Celebrity endorsements, self-brand connection and relationship quality. *International Journal of Advertising*, 35(3), 486–503.

Erdogan, B. Z. (1999). Celebrity endorsement: A literature review. *Journal of Marketing Management*, 15(4), 291–314.

Escalas, J. E. and Bettman, J. R. (2009). Self-brand connections: The role of reference groups and celebrity endorsers in the creation of brand meaning.

Francis, D. and Yazdanifard, R. (2013). The impact of celebrity endorsement and its influence through different scopes on the retailing business across United States and Asia. *International Journal of Commerce, Business and Management*, 2(1), 35–40.

Freeman, K. S. and Chen, C. C. (2015). Wither the impact of celebrity endorsement. In *International Conference on Communication, Media, Technology and Design*, 661–676.

Friedman, H. H. and Friedman, L. (1978). Does the celebrity endorser's image spill over the product. *Journal of the Academy of Marketing Science*, 6(4), 291–299.

Friedman, H. H. and Friedman, L. (1979). Endorser effectiveness by product type. *Journal of Advertising Research*, 63–71.

Ghotbivayghan, B., Hoseinzadehshahri, M. and Ebrahimi, M. (2015). Effect of celebrity endorsement on consumer's perception of corporate image, corporate credibility and corporate loyalty. *Case Studies in Business and Management*, 2(1), 51–67.

Glover, P., 2009. Celebrity endorsement in tourism advertising: Effects on destination image. *Journal of Hospitality and Tourism Management*, 16(1), 16–23.

530 *Shahzeb Hussain*

Goldsmith, R. E., Lafferty, B. A. and Newell, S. J. (2000). The influence of corporate credibility on consumer attitudes and purchase intent. *Corporate Reputation Review*, 3(4), 304–318.

Gong, W. and Li, X. (2017). Engaging fans on microblog: The synthetic influence of parasocial interaction and source characteristics on celebrity endorsement. *Psychology & Marketing*, 34(7), 720–732.

Horton, D. W. R. and Wohl, R. (1956). Mass communication and parasocial interaction: Observation on intimacy at a distance. *Psychiatry*, 19(3), 215–229.

Hovland, C. I., Janis, I. L. and Kelley, H. H. (1953). Communication and persuasion, Yale university, USA.

Hung, K. (2014). Why celebrity sells: A dual entertainment path model of brand endorsement. *Journal of Advertising*, 43(2), 155–166.

Hussain, S., Melewar, T. C., Priporas, C. V., Foroudi, P. and Dennis, C. (2020). Examining the effects of celebrity trust on advertising credibility, brand credibility and corporate credibility. *Journal of Business Research*, 109, 472–488.

Hwang, K. and Zhang, Q. (2018). Influence of parasocial relationship between digital celebrities and their followers on followers' purchase and electronic word-of-mouth intentions, and persuasion knowledge. *Computers in Human Behavior*, 87, 155–173.

Ilicic, J. and Webster, C. M. (2011). Effects of multiple endorsements and consumer–celebrity attachment on attitude and purchase intention. *Australasian Marketing Journal (AMJ)*, 19(4), 230–237.

Isaksen, K. J. and Roper, S. (2008). The impact of branding on low-income adolescents: A vicious cycle?. *Psychology & Marketing*, 25(11), 1063–1087.

Jain, V. (2011). Celebrity endorsement and its impact on sales: A research analysis carried out in India. *Global Journal of Management and Business Research*, 11(4).

Jain, V. and Roy, S. (2016). Understanding meaning transfer in celebrity endorsements: A qualitative exploration. *Qualitative Market Research: An International Journal*.

Kahle, L. R. and Homer, P. M (1985). Physical attractiveness of celebrity endorser: A social adaptation perspective. *Journal of Consumer Research*, 11(1), 954–961.

Kamins, M. A. and Gupta, K. (1994). Congruence between spokesperson and product type: A matchup hypothesis perspective. *Psychology and Marketing*, 11(6), 569–586.

Kamins, M. A. (1989). Celebrity and noncelebrity advertising in a two-sided context. *Journal of Advertising Research*, 29, 34.

Kamins, M. A. (1990). An investigation into the "match-up" hypothesis in celebrity advertising: When beauty may be only skin deep. *Journal of Advertising*, 19(1), 4–13.

Karasiewicz, G. and Kowalczuk, M. (2014). Effect of celebrity endorsement in advertising activities by product type. *International Journal of Management and Economics*, 44(1), 74–91.

Kelman, Herbert C. (1961). Process of opinion change. *Public Opinion Quarterly*, 25(4), 57–78.

Kim, H., Ko, E. and Kim, J. (2015). SNS users' para-social relationships with celebrities: Social media effects on purchase intentions. *Journal of Global Scholars of Marketing Science*, 25(3), 279–294.

Kim, K. and Cheong, Y. (2012). The effects of athlete-endorsed advertising: The moderating role of the athlete-audience ethnicity match. *Journal of Sport Management*, 25(2), 143–155.

Kim, M. and Kim, J. (2020). How does a celebrity make fans happy? Interaction between celebrities and fans in the social media context. *Computers in Human Behavior*, 106419.

Kim, S. S., Lee, J. and Prideaux, B. (2014). Effect of celebrity endorsement on tourists' perception of corporate image, corporate credibility and corporate loyalty. *International Journal of Hospitality Management*, 37, 131–145.

Celebrity endorsement, theories and, models 531

Kurtin, K. S., O'Brien, N., Roy, D. and Dam, L. (2018). The development of parasocial interaction relationships on YouTube. *The Journal of Social Media in Society, 7*(1), 233–252.

Labrecque, L. I. (2014). Fostering consumer–brand relationships in social media environments: The role of parasocial interaction. *Journal of Interactive Marketing, 28*(2), 134–148.

Lafferty, B. A., Goldsmith, R. E. and Newell, S. J. (2002). The dual credibility model: The influence of corporate and endorser credibility on attitudes and purchase intentions. *Journal of Marketing Theory and Practice, 10*(3), 1–11.

Lammers, H. B. (2000). Effects of deceptive packaging and product involvement on purchase intention: An elaboration likelihood model perspective. *Psychological Reports, 86*(2), 546–550.

Langmeyer, L. and Walker, M. (1991). A first step to identify the meaning in celebrity endorsers. *ACR North American Advances.*

Lee, G., Cho, S. Y., Arthurs, J. and Lee, E. K. (2020). Celebrity CEO, identity threat, and impression management: Impact of celebrity status on corporate social responsibility. *Journal of Business Research, 111*, 69–84.

Lim, C. M. and Kim, Y. K. (2011). Older consumers' TV home shopping: Loneliness, parasocial interaction, and perceived convenience. *Psychology & Marketing, 28*(8), 763–780.

Lim, J. S., Choe, M. J., Zhang, J. and Noh, G. Y. (2020). The role of wishful identification, emotional engagement, and parasocial relationships in repeated viewing of live-streaming games: A social cognitive theory perspective. *Computers in Human Behavior, 106327.*

Louie, T. A., Kulik, R. L. and Jacobson, R. (2001). When bad things happen to the endorsers of good products. *Marketing Letters, 12*(1), 13–23.

Lord, K. R. and Putrevu, S. (2009). Informational and transformational responses to celebrity endorsements. *Journal of Current Issues & Research in Advertising, 31*(1), 1–13.

Lueck, J. (2012). Friend-zone with benefits: The parasocial advertising of Kim Kardashian. *Journal of Marketing Communications, 21*(2), 91–109.

Magnini, V. P., Honeycutt, E. D. and Cross, A. M. (2008). Understanding the use of celebrity endorsers for hospitality firms. *Journal of Vacation Marketing, 14*(1), 57–69.

McCormick, K. (2016). Celebrity endorsements: Influence of a product-endorser match on millennials attitudes and purchase intentions. *Journal of Retailing and Consumer Services, 32*, 39–45.

McCracken, G. (1989). Who is the celebrity endorser? Cultural foundations of the endorsement process. *Journal of Consumer Research, 16*(3), 310–321.

Meyers-Levy, J. and Sternthal, B. (1991). Gender differences in the use of message cues and judgments. *Journal of Marketing Research, 28*(1), 84–96.

Mishra, A. S. (2015). Brand-celebrity match and its impact on advertising effectiveness. *DLSU Business & Economics Review, 25*(1), 16–27.

Mishra, A. S., Roy, S. and Bailey, A. A. (2015). Exploring brand personality–celebrity endorser personality congruence in celebrity endorsements in the Indian context. *Psychology & Marketing, 32*(12), 1158–1174.

Misra, S. and Beatty, S. E. (1990). Celebrity spokesperson and brand congruence: An assessment of recall and affect. *Journal of Business Research, 21*(2), 159–173.

Money R. B., Shimp T. A. and Sakano T. (2006). Celebrity endorsements in Japan and the United States: Is negative information all that harmful? *Journal of Advertising Research, 46*(1):113–123.

532   Shahzeb Hussain

Na, Y. J. K. J. H. (2007). Effects of celebrity athlete endorsement on attitude towards the product: The role of credibility, attractiveness and the concept of congruence. *International Journal of Sports Marketing & Sponsorship*.

Ohanian, R. (1990). Construction and validation of a scale to measure celebrity endorsers' perceived expertise, trustworthiness, and attractiveness. *Journal of Advertising*, 19(3), 39–52.

Osei-Frimpong, K., Donkor, G. and Owusu-Frimpong, N. (2019). The impact of celebrity endorsement on consumer purchase intention: An emerging market perspective. *Journal of Marketing Theory and Practice*, 27(1), 103–121.

Parmar, Y., Mann, B. J. S. and Ghuman, M. K. (2020). Impact of celebrity endorser as in-store stimuli on impulse buying. *International Review of Retail, Distribution and Consumer Research*, 30(5), 576–595.

Peetz, T. B., Parks, J. B. and Spencer, N. E. (2004). Sport heroes as sport product endorsers: The role of gender in the transfer of meaning process for selected undergraduate students. *Sport Marketing Quarterly*, 13(3).

Petty, R. E., Cacioppo, J. T. and Schuman, D. (1983). Central and peripheral routes to advertising effectiveness: The moderating role of involvement. *Journal of Consumer Research*, 10(4), 135–146.

Phua, J., Lin, J. S. E. and Lim, D. J. (2018). Understanding consumer engagement with celebrity-endorsed e-cigarette advertising on Instagram. *Computers in Human Behavior*, 84, 93–102.

Prameswara, D. H. and Sjabadhyni, B. (2018). The effect of negative celebrity publicity and celebrity identification towards purchase intention. In *Universitas Indonesia International Psychology Symposium for Undergraduate Research (UIPSUR 2017)*. Atlantis Press.

Rasmussen, L. (2018). Parasocial interaction in the digital age: An examination of relationship building and the effectiveness of YouTube celebrities. *The Journal of Social Media in Society*, 7(1), 280–294.

Roy, S. (2018). Meaning transfer in celebrity endorsements: An explanation using metaphors. *Journal of Marketing Communications*, 24(8), 843–862.

Sanbonmatsu, D. M. and Kardes, F. R. (1988). The effects of physiological arousal on information processing and persuasion. *Journal of Consumer Research*, 15(3), 379–385.

Schäfer, M. and Quiring, O. (2015). The press coverage of celebrity suicide and the development of suicide frequencies in Germany. *Health Communication*, 30(11), 1149–1158.

Sierra, J., Hyman, M. R. and Torres, I. M. (2009). Using a model's apparent ethnicity to influence viewer responses to print ads: A social identity theory perspective. *Journal of Current Issues and Research in Advertising*, 31(2), 41–68.

Singh, R. P. and Banerjee, N. (2018). Exploring the influence of celebrity credibility on brand attitude, advertisement attitude and purchase intention. *Global Business Review*, 19(6), 1622–1639.

Spry, A., Pappu, R. and Cornwell, T. B. (2011). Celebrity endorsement, brand credibility and brand equity. *European Journal of Marketing*.

Statista (2020). Twitter account the most followers worldwide as of May 2020. Retrieved August 20, 2020, from https://www.statista.com/statistics/273172/twitter-accounts-with-the-most-followers-worldwide/.

Suki, N. M. (2014). Does celebrity credibility influence Muslim and non-Muslim consumers' attitudes toward brands and purchase intention?. *Journal of Islamic Marketing*.

Till, B. D. and Busler, M. (1998). Matching products with endorsers: Attractiveness versus expertise. *Journal of Consumer Marketing*, 15(6), 576–586.

Till, B. D. and Busler, M. (2000). The match-up hypothesis: Physical attractiveness, expertise, and the role of fit on brand attitude, purchase intent and brand beliefs. *Journal of Advertising*, 29(3), 1–13.

Till, B. D. and Shimp, T. A. (1998). Endorsers in advertising: The case of negative celebrity information. *Journal of Advertising*, 27(1), 67–82.

Thwaites, D., Lowe, B., Monkhouse, L. L. and Barnes, B. R. (2012). The impact of negative publicity on celebrity ad endorsements. *Psychology & Marketing*, 29(9), 663–673.

Torn, F. (2012). Revisiting the match-up hypothesis: Effects of brand-incongruent celebrity endorsements. *Journal of Current Issues & Research in Advertising*, 33(1), 20–36.

Um, N. H. (2013). Celebrity scandal fallout: How attribution style can protect the sponsor. *Psychology & Marketing*, 30(6), 529–541.

Um, N. H. (2018). What affects the effectiveness of celebrity endorsement? Impact of interplay among congruence, identification, and attribution. *Journal of Marketing Communications*, 24(7), 746–759.

Um, N. H. and Kim, S. (2016). Determinants for effects of celebrity negative information: When to terminate a relationship with a celebrity endorser in trouble? *Psychology & Marketing*, 33(10), 864–874.

Van Norel, N. D., Kommers, P. A., Van Hoof, J. J. and Verhoeven, J. W. (2014). Damaged corporate reputation: Can celebrity Tweets repair it?. *Computers in Human Behavior*, 36, 308–315.

Von Sikorski, C., Knoll, J. and Matthes, J. (2018). A new look at celebrity endorsements in politics: Investigating the impact of scandalous celebrity endorsers and politicians' best responses. *Media Psychology*, 21(3), 403–436.

Watkins, A. (1989). Simply irresistible? Pepsi learns there is a down-side to signing up rock stars. *Beverage Industry*, 1–41.

Wang, S. and Kim, K. J. (2020). Consumer response to negative celebrity publicity: The effects of moral reasoning strategies and fan identification. *Journal of Product & Brand Management*, 29(1), 114–123.

Wheeler, R. T. (2009). Nonprofit advertising: Impact of celebrity connection, involvement and gender on source credibility and intention to volunteer time or donate money. *Journal of Non-profit & Public Sector Marketing*, 21(1), 80–107.

Yang, W. (2018). Star power: The evolution of celebrity endorsement research. *International Journal of Contemporary Hospitality Management*, 30(1), 389–415.

Yoo, J. W., Lee, H. S. and Jin, Y. J. (2018). Effects of celebrity credibility on country's reputation: A comparison of an Olympic star and a political leader. *Corporate Reputation Review*, 21(3), 127–136.

Yoon, S. W. and Shin, S. (2017). The role of negative publicity in consumer evaluations of sports stars and their sponsors. *Journal of Consumer Behaviour*, 16(4), 332–342.

Young, A. F., Gabriel, S. and Sechrist, G. B. (2012). The skinny on celebrities: Parasocial relationships moderate the effects of thin media figures on women's body image. *Social Psychological and Personality Science*, 3(6), 659–666.

Yuan, C. L., Moon, H., Kim, K. H. and Wang, S. (2019). The influence of parasocial relationship in fashion web on customer equity. *Journal of Business Research*.

Zakari, M., Dogbe, C. S. K. and Asante, C. (2019). Effect of celebrity endorsement on telecommunication companies' reputation. *Management Research Review*.

Index

Note: Page numbers in *italics* indicate figures and **bold** indicate tables

Aaker, D. A. 22, 318, 372
Aaker, J. L. 154
Abdin, A. S. 405
ability: of customers/buyers/consumers 229, 244, 313, 428; decision-making and 322; employees 85; of human asset 80; marketers 151; multisensory stimulation 147; of organisations/firms 28, 86, 93–94, 96, 171, 210, 307–308, 317; retailers 352; risk taking 309–310; students 468; to take risks in trying newness 310–311, **323**
Abratt, R. 21, 31, 37, **44, 47, 52–53**, 87
acceptance 25, 329, 421–422, 424, 517
Ackerman, L. D. **53–54**
active participation in value co-creation 243–244
actual, conceived, communicated, ideal, and desired (ACID) test 28
actual identity 28–29; *see also* identity
Adcock, W. O. 309
Adner, R. 375
advocacy 233, 235
aesthetic(s) 5; and atmospherics 182, 184–185; and cultural artefacts 183–184; in cyberspace 191; labour 290; London Heathrow Terminal 5 132; marketing 184; of products 146; and servicescape 185; symbolic artefacts 85, 115
aesthetic heritage and corporate branding 181–194; and atmospherics 184–185; background 181; case study 192–194; corporate brand heritage 186–188; and cultural artefacts 183–184; in digital age 188–189; future research 190; issues, controversies, problems 188–189; service-dominant (S-D) logic 185–186;

and servicescape 185; solutions and recommendations 189–190; visual brand identity 182–183; *see also* societal corporate branding
affective associations 312, 317–320, 322, **323**, 330–331, 340
affective brand meaning 141; *see also* brand meaning
affective experience 140–141, 148, 154–155, 183, 191, 240, 312–313, 317, 322
Ageeva, E. 241, 376
Ahearne, M. 238
Ahmad, M. A. 95
Ahuvia, A. C. 401, 408
AI *see* artificial intelligence
Airbnb 220, 245, 421–422, *423*
Ajzen, I. 313, 407
Akaka, M. A. 224
Alam, S. S. 407
Alba, J. W. 146, 154
AlBaik 409–410
Albert, A. 14, 16
Albert, N. 408
Albert, S. **53**
Alessandri, S. W. **44, 53**
Algesheimer, R. 451–452
Al-Hawari, M. 236
Allee, V. 81
Alpen Swiss Style Muesli *159*, 159–160
Alserhan, B. A. 404–405
alternative facts 429
Amable, B. 375
ambidexterity 187
ambient conditions/physical stimuli 76, 84, 115–117, 130, 185
American Express 516

536 Index

Anderson, E. 243
Anderson, J. C. 126, 327, 380
Anderson, L. 293
Ani-Mumuney, F. 213
Ansoff, H. I. 77
ANT *see* associative network theory
anthropomorphisation 178
Apple 174–178, *176–177*, 307, 310, 449
architectural design 83, 113, 116
architecture 26; aesthetic aspects 55;
 companys/firms 18, 55, 130, 182;
 components of 115, 118; corporate
 visual identity 37, 95; covenanted or
 corporate brand identity 29; customer
 behaviour 26; layout and 12; ontological
 153; in retail setting 113–114; role in
 brand awareness 36; Zaha Hadid 339
Argenti, P. A. 212
ARIT *see* Augmented Reality Interactive
 Technologies
Armstrong, A. G. 451
Arnott, D. C. 243
Arnould, E. J. 239, 276, 489
Arruda, W. 472
artefacts *see* cultural artefacts
artificial intelligence (AI) 500–501;
 see also augmented reality
Ashforth, B. E. 23, 25–26, 292
Askegaard, S. **44**
assets *see* cultural assets
Association of Automotive Industries 445
associative network theory (ANT)
 154, 521
atmospherics: aesthetics and 182,
 184–185; brand 191; consumer
 environment studies 148; literature 152;
 sensory brand experiences (SBE) 140;
 stores **144**, 149, 151–152, 155; *see also*
 specific types
attitude(s): behaviour and 25, 34,
 448–449; beliefs and 38, 520; of
 companies towards online consumers
 170; customers/consumers 185, 282,
 318–319, 348–349, 450; hedonic
 and utilitarian 319; physical stimuli
 influencing employees 84; positive
 242, 357, 476, 523; reflecting brand
 reliability/durability 82; towards
 advertisements 3; trust as subjective 81;
 values and 25
attraction: atmospheric environment
 of heritage 184; to newness 309–310,
 322, **323**

attribution theory 114, 131
auditory atmospherics 149; *see also*
 atmospherics
auditory sense 493
auditory stimuli 142, 145, 147, 149,
 159–160, 184, 189, 277, 492–493
augmented reality (AR) 181, 312, 347–
 348, 355–356, 492; *see also* artificial
 intelligence
Augmented Reality Interactive
 Technologies (ARIT) 312
authenticity 13, 295; brand heritage
 187; consumers ability to reflect 428;
 personal branding 472–473; of touristic
 heritage sites 188; transparency and 209
automatic behaviour 155–156; *see also*
 behaviour
autonomy in innovative decision 309–310,
 322, **323**
average variance extracted (AVE) 121,
 325, 329, 380, 454
avoidance behaviour 184; *see also*
 behaviour
Ayranci, E. 82

Badan Pusat Statistik 445
Baker, M. J. 20, **48**, **50**, 148
Baker, S. M. 451
Bakker, A. B. 296
Ballantyne, D. 189, 228, 232
Balmer, J. M. T. 13–14, 16–23, 26, 28–33,
 39–44, **46–48**, **50**, **52–55**, 87–88, 171,
 182, 187, 367
Bandura, A. 520
Ban Immigration policy 421–422
Barnett, M. L. L. **41**
Bart, Y. 368
Bartlett's test of sphericity (BTS) 121
Basil, M. 520
Batra, R. 401, 404–405, 407–408
BCE *see* brand community engagement
Bearden, W. O. 375
Beatty, S. E. 518
Beckham, D. 516
BeerAdvocate 349
behaviour: attitudes and 25, 34, 448–449;
 automatic 155–156; avoidance 184;
 customers/consumers 15, 26, 34, 36, 38,
 85, 115, 142, 145–147, 154, 169, 182,
 264–265, 277, 279, 313, 406–407, 498;
 design and loyalty 264–265; employee
 15, 25, 36, 38, 84, 297; institutional
 and/or individual 16; organisational 15,

17, 19, 23, 29, 84, 87, 116, 172; value co-creation 218–245
behavioural intentions *see* UK fashion industry
behavioural school 19
Belk, R. W. 237
Bentler, P. M. 117
Berman, B. 149
Bernstein, D. 21, **52–53**
Berry, L. L. 22
Bettencourt, L. A. 234–235
Beyonce 516
Bhatia, S. 349
Bhattacharya, C. B. 30, 237
bibexcel 262
Bick, G. 21
Bieber, J. 522
big data: analytics 350–351, 354; capabilities 350; value creation 350–351
Binks, M. R. 234
Birkigt, K. **54**
Bitner, M. J. 26, 36, 149, 185, 274
Black Lives Matter 433, 435
Blackmon, K. 372
Bloemer, J. M. 505
Böhme, G. 184
Bonn, M. A. 184
Booms, B. H. 237
Bourdieu, P. 474, 478
Bowen, F. 372
boycotting movement 428–429
Bradley, A. J. 94
Brady, M. K. 236
Brakus, J. J. 141–142, 145, 151, 156–157, 279–280
brand atmospherics 191; *see also* atmospherics
brand awareness 313, **324**; and consumers decision-making 445; fashion brand image scale 309; fashion innovativeness and 317–318; as heuristics 318; link of social media marketing and 321; staff appearance, colour and architecture 36, 83
brand community engagement (BCE) 446–448, 457; hypothesis development 448–451; and purchase intention 450–451
brand core 35
brand culture 183, 437
brand designer 492, 495, 497, 499–500, 503–504, 506
brand DNA 437

brand experience *see* sensory brand experience
brand image: brand identity and 184; cognitive association 311; competitive advantage and 182; defined 446; innovativeness on fashion 307–309, 314, 316, 321, 335; media and digital transformation 312; patents 93; personal 477–478; and purchase intention 318–320; through electronic word of mouth 318; visibility of 142; *see also* corporate brand image; corporate brand identity; corporate image; corporate reputation
brand implemented adaptations 500–501
branding meaning 278–280
brand knowledge (BK) 445–446, 448–450, 457; case study 460–462; future research 459; hypothesis development 448–451; implications and recommendations 459; measurement 452, 454; multigroup analysis 456, 456–457; and purchase intention 449–450; research model 451–454; sampling and data 452–454; structural model test 454; *see also* knowledge
brand love/hedonic 320, **324**, 405, 427; *see also* Islamic brand love
brand loyalty 155, 218, 220, 309, 349, 386, 401, 408, 427, 446–447, 450–451, 505
brand management 33, 183, 211, 353–354, 416, 457, 459, 478–479
brand meaning 145–146, 151, 518; affective 141; analysis of 280; characterisation of 141, 153, 155; co-creation in consumer's mind 156; consumers modifying 279; natural occurrence or happenstance 157; and value 183
brand personality 154, 157, 182, 279, 355
brand-related antecedents 151
brand respect/utilitarian 309, 320, 322, **324**
British Airways Airline Ltd. 132
Brown, G. D. A. 349
Brown, T. J. 22, 35, **43**
Bruch, H. 296
Brunel Business School (BBS) 55–59, 57
Brunel University 56
Burghausen, M. 187
business identity 17; *see also* corporate identity
business strategies 75, 91, 226, 367
business-to-customer/business-to-business (B2C/B) 218
Busler, M. 518

538 *Index*

Callahan, A. L. 25
Cameron, K. S. 293
Carbone, L. P. 260
Cardador, M. T. 14
Carroll, B. A. 401, 408
case study(ies): aesthetic heritage and
  corporate branding 192–194; Airbnb
  245; AlBaik 409–410; Alpen Swiss
  Style Muesli *159*, 159–160; Apple
  174–178, *176–177*; brand knowledge
  460–462; celebrity endorsement
  526–527; corporate brand identity/
  image 174–178, 355–357; corporate
  identity management 387–388;
  corporate multi-channel branding
  213–214; corporate reputation 132;
  Cucapà corporate citizenship project
  419–420, *420*; customer experience
  281–284; customers perception of
  luxury brands 507–508; Dove 428–429;
  employee occupational identity
  298–300; FirstBank 213–214; Gucci app
  355–357, *357*; Hermès International
  S.A. 192–194; Islamic brand love
  409–410; London Heathrow Terminal
  5 132; marketing competencies 100;
  Melissa (footwear company) 336–340,
  337–339; MoMa 421, 424–426, *426*;
  Next Plc 100; Nike 421, 422–424,
  428, 432–435, *436*, 507–508; Novel
  Solutions 298–300; personal branding
  480–481; positioning and branding of
  London-based business school 55–59;
  sensory brand experiences (SBE) 159–
  160; *Simpsons, The* 418–420; Starbucks
  429–432; University of West London
  (UWL) 387–388; value co-creation
  245; ViewStream 281–284; Woods, T.
  526–527
CBIM *see* Corporate Brand Identity
  Matrix
celebrity credibility 517–518
celebrity endorsement 208–209,
  515–527; associative network theory
  521; background 515–516; case study
  526–527; celebrity credibility 517;
  corporate identity, image and reputation
  525; demographics and 524; elaboration
  likelihood model (ELM) 520–521;
  future direction 525; literature 522–
  525; match-up hypothesis 518–519;
  meaning transfer theory 517–518;
  models 517–519; negative publicity and

  522; parasocial relationship and 523;
  social influence theory 519–520; social
  learning theory 520; social media and
  523–524; theories 519–521
celebrity endorser: attractiveness 517,
  521; behaviours 522; characteristics of
  518; consumers positive effect towards
  524; defined 515; effectiveness of
  519; hiring of 516; mismatch between
  brand and 519; transference of 518;
  trustworthiness 517, 521, 525; use in
  advertisements 516
21st Century Fox (21CF) 418–419
CFA *see* confirmatory factor analysis
Chamorro Mera, A. 371
Chandler, J. D. 232
Chathoth, P. 231
Chen, C. F. 188
Chen, F. S. 188
Chen, R. 445
Chen, W. 188
Cheng, S. I. 242
Cheung, C. M. 497
Childers, T. L. 146, 493
Chou, C. P. 117
Christensen, L. T. **44**
Churchill, G. A. Jr. 97
citizenship behaviour 233, 235–236, 386
clicktivism 437
Clinton, H. 431
co-creation of brand value 489, 504–506;
  see also customers perception of luxury
  brands
co-creativity 155–156
cognition-affect-behaviour-satisfaction
  (CABS) 276; *see also* implicit cognition
cognitive/mystery associations 314–316
cognitive revolution 23
cognitive schema 17
cognitive structure 23, 294
Cohen, L. M. 75
Çolakoğlu, N. 82
Cole, M. S. 296
collective learning 91
commitment: advocacy 235; brand
  attachment and 188; brand engagement
  and 448; citizenship 434; employee
  emotional 374; human capital 82;
  organisational 296; personal 165; of
  stakeholders in organisation 28, 34;
  trust and 75, 82, 243; word of mouth
  and 524
commitment-trust theory 243

Index   539

communicated identity 28, 506
communication 34–35; capabilities 93–95; cost-minimising 212; defined 35; digital 181, 488; effective 15, 20; employees role in communication with external stakeholders 18; integrated approach 20–21; interpersonal relations 81; moderating effect of 476–477; non-controlled 28; online 208–211; personal branding 476–477; strategies 19, 176; tertiary 20; unsuccessful 22
company-employee relations 289
comparative fit index (CFI) 126, 380
competence: brand 93; defined 94, 96; development 91; marketing 92–93, 95–97, 100; measurement 96; technological advances 76; theory 91; *see also* core competence; marketing competencies
competitive advantage 11, 80, 89–90, 99, 174, 178, 182, 353, 477
competitive market 58, 75, 114, 294, 375, 444–445, 468
composite reliability (CR) 454
conceived identity 28–29
concept of service 221–224, 274
conceptual framework: corporate identity management 367–375; employee occupational identity 298; fashion innovativeness 314, 315; research 78, 79
conceptual model 97, 115–117, 126, 128, 239, 297, 322, 383
confirmatory factor analysis (CFA) 114, 121, **122–124**, 327
connectedness/connected 23, 96, 190, 238, 312, 352, 367, 373–374, 498, 521, 525
constructs reliability **455**
construct validity 120–126, 335, **455**
consumers/customers 491–492, 494, 496, 498–499, 501, 503, 505; behaviour 15, 26, 34, 36, 38, 85, 115, 142, 145–147, 154, 169, 182, 264–265, 277, 279, 313, 406–407, 498; boycott 427–435; demographic profile of **118**; emotional response from 504–505; environment studies **144**, 148–149; experiences 142, 502; identity 33; loyalty 4, 26, 90, 115, 141, 156, 176, 182, 446, 505; perceptions 82, 114, 229, 349; relationship 94, 336, 490–492; satisfaction 90, 115, 141, 156, 224, 270; value co-creation 221, 233

consumption experience 145–146
consumption in the Quran 402–403
consumption studies **143**, 145–146
content/face validity 119; *see also* construct validity
continuous self-assessment 469–471
contract-based intangible assets 90
contractedness of occupational identity 291–292
controlled communications 28; *see also* communication
convergent validity 121, 329, 380
co-production 231–232
core competence 75–77, 96–97; competitive advantage 100; defined 96; marketing capabilities and 76, 97, 100; tangible and intangible assets 75; technological advances 76; *see also* competence
Cornelissen, J. P. 38, **41, 45**
corporate awareness 36
corporate behaviour 20, 27, 172, 174
corporate beliefs 31
corporate brand heritage 186–188
corporate brand identity 29, 169–178; background 169–170; case study 174–178; future research 174; image and reputation 170–172, 173; management 89, 93; solutions and recommendations 173–174; virtual space 170
Corporate Brand Identity Matrix (CBIM) 173, 173–174
corporate brand image 347–357; case study 355–357; competitive advantage 353; data-driven e-tailing 350–351; in e-tailing 348–349; future research 353–354; innovation management 347–348; omnichannel integration 351–352; solutions and recommendations 353; technology management 347–348
corporate branding *see* aesthetic heritage and corporate branding; societal corporate branding
corporate citizenship: campaigns 418, 427–435; Cucapà project 419, 420; engagement 429; pragmatism 422
corporate core values 32–33
corporate culture 18, 20, 27, 31–32, 34–36, 95, 212, 367
corporate design *see* corporate visual identity
corporate guidelines/leadership 87
corporate heritage brand 187, 190, 192

540 *Index*

corporate heritage identity stewardship (CHIS) 187, 191
corporate history: corporate identity management 369–370; cultural assets 87
corporate identity: background of 11–14; celebrity endorsement 525; communication 34–35; defined 14, 37–55, **39–55**; intrinsic nature of 14–17; management 26, 28, 30; perspectives 18–30; philosophy, mission and value 30–34; quindrivium 18; schools of thought 19; study 17–18; visual identity 36–37
corporate identity management 365–388; case study 387–388; conceptual framework 367–375; corporate history 369–370; corporate reputation 374–375, **381**; country-of-origin 370–372; data analysis 380–382; defined 366–367; future research 386; innovation adoption 375; methodology 376–382; philosophy, vision, mission 367–369; research conceptual model 383; results of hypothesis testing **384**; role in corporate reputation 365–366; sampling and survey administration 376; solutions and recommendations 385–386; survey measures 376–380, **377–379**; theoretical background 366; top management driving force 372–374
corporate image 19, 170–172; acquisition of 26, 32; celebrity endorsement 525; composed of 12; corporate identity and 26; defined 14; management of 13; need for 206–207; organisational culture and 33; *see also* corporate reputation
corporate mission 31–32, 34, 87
corporate multi-channel branding 205–214; background 205–206; case study 213–214; celebrity endorsement 208–209; corporate reputation 207–208; future research 212; need for corporate image 206–207; online corporate communication 210–211; online stakeholder (customer) engagement 209–210; social media 208; solutions and recommendations 211–212
corporate performance 82, 171
corporate personality 12–13, 38
corporate philosophy 27, 31, 34, 38, 87
corporate principles 27, 31–32, 87
corporate reputation 4, 29, 113–132, 170–172, *173*, 207–208, **381**;

ambiguity about 14; architecture in retail setting 113–114; case study 132; celebrity endorsement 525; corporate identity management 374–375, **381**; data analysis 119–120; in digital era 207–208; implications 128–130; intellectual and emotional assets 78–80; management 13; model 115–117; research 115–119, 130–131; results 120–128; *see also* corporate image
corporate sensory identity 3
corporate strategy 19–20, 27, 32–33, 58, 87, 207, 210, 212, 368
corporate values 27, 33–34, 36, 38, 87, 211, 372; *see also* value; value co-creation (VCC)
corporate vision 19, 32–33, 87; *see also* vision
corporate visual identity (CVI) 3, 17–19, 34, 36–37, 55, 95, 182; defined 37; physical (tangible assets) 83
corporate visual identity systems (CVIS) 182
country-of-origin (COO) 88–89, 152, 365–366, 370–372, 384–385
CoverGirl 516
COVID-19 pandemic 206, 210–212, 347, 356, 459
creativity 175, 191, 193–194, 218, 311, 371; *see also* co-creativity
Cronbach's alpha 121, 329, 380, 554
Cronin, J. J. Jr. 236
Crossan, M. M. 291
cross-channel 181, 351–352
Cucapà corporate citizenship project 419–420, *420*
cultural artefacts 183–184, 194, 437
cultural assets 78, 86–91, 100
cultural/intangible assets 76, 78, 90–91, 97–98; *see also* intangible assets
cultural values 34, 90–91, 188, 437
culture: brand 183; capital theories 478; conceptualised as collective programming 76; corporate/ organisational 18–20, 22–23, 27, 31–36, 88, 90, 95, 348; defined 406; of honesty and integrity 87; Islamic brand love 405–408; outcomes of 408; perceptions of 83, 85
Cummings, E. M. 32
customer-based brand equity (CBBE) theory 309
customer-based conclusive benefits 507

Index   541

customer-based factors 282–283
customer-brand relationship focus 186
customer citizenship behaviour 233;
    see also citizenship behaviour
customer engagement digital (online)
    environment 499–500
customer experience (CX) 152, 260–268,
    502–504; background 260–261;
    branding meaning 278–280; case study
    281–284; co-citation results 263–273;
    design and analysis 274; experiential
    marketing 276–278; extensions
    of theory 274–276; longitudinal
    development of 281; measurement
    274; method 261–263; multi-method
    comparison 273–274; service marketing
    274–276
customer experience literature (CXL)
    261–262, 264, 267, 269–273
customer-perceived quality 82
customer-related intangible assets 90
customer relationship management
    (CRM) 89, 93–94, 490
customers perception of luxury brands
    487–508; brand implemented
    adaptations 500–501; case study
    507–508; co-creation of brand value
    504–506; customer-based conclusive
    benefits 507; customer experience 502–
    504; customer relationship 490–492;
    digital sensory impression 492–495;
    digital/virtual environment 495–497;
    engagement with digital environment
    497–500; findings 490–506; future
    research 507; interactive technologies
    487–489; managerial conclusive benefits
    506; methodology 489–490; multi-
    sensory integration 487–489
CX see customer experience
cyberspace 189, 191–192

Dacin, P. A. 35, **43**, 156
data analysis: corporate identity
    management 380–382; corporate
    reputation 119–120, **120**; fashion
    innovativeness 322–325
data collection: corporate reputation 117–
    118; fashion innovativeness 322–325
data-driven e-tailing 350–351
Davies, P. T. 32
Davis, T. R. V. 116
de Barnier, V. 187–188
de Chernatony, L. **43**

Deci, E. L. 242
decision-making 172, 322; active
    participation 243; aggressive reactions
    in 171; brand awareness 318;
    consumers/customers 185, 313, 445,
    447; fashion innovativeness 310, 322;
    in-store environment 146; role of
    performance management to support
    managerial 96; styles 524
de Dreux, A. 194
Deighton, J. 154
Dell 243
Dell Computers 276
demographics **326**; celebrity endorsement
    and 524; characteristics 325, **379**; of
    consumers **118**
design-as-fashion school 19
desired identity 22, 26, 28–29
Desmidt, S. 368
Dewett, T. 86
Dickson, K. 56
differentiation: consumer behaviour
    and 182; identity and 145; personal
    branding usage in 468, 471–472, 477;
    and positioning 87; of status between
    employees 85; visual branding favouring
    product 182
digital professional 492, 494–496, 499,
    501, 503, 505–506
digital sensory impression 492–495
digital sensory marketing 488
digital technology 76, 85–86, 99
digital/virtual environment 488, 492–500
Dijkstra-Henseler's indicator 329
discriminant validity 121, 329–330,
    380, **455**
Disney World 291
diversity 141, 176, 421–422; acceptance
    422; atmospherics 140; gender and
    equality 366, 369, 385; and global
    warming 422–424; immigrants with
    racial 371; moderation effect between
    corporate history 370; moderation effect
    between top management driving force
    373–374; moderation effect on country-
    of-origin 371–372; moderation effect
    on philosophy, mission and vision 369;
    negative relationship 384; workforce 15
Dixson, K. 472
Dodds, B. K. 449
Dodds, W. B. 237
"Do it yourself" (DIY) tool 356
Dong, B. 244

542 *Index*

Donovan, R. 148
Dooley, R. 176
Doran, R. 31
Dove 428–429, *430–431*
Dowling, G. R. **45, 52, 54**
Downey, S. M. **52**
dramaturgy theory 290, 293
Dukerich, J. M. 16, 23
Duncan, T. 20, 35
Dutton, J. E. 16, 23–24

Ealing College 387
Eatwith 220
economic and social actors 228–229
Edelman Earned Brand 427
education *see* higher education; personal brand/branding
Edvardsson, B. 226
Edward (Prince of Wales) 193
elaboration likelihood model (ELM) 520–521
Elizabeth II (queen) 132
Elliott, R. 406
ELM *see* elaboration likelihood model
Elsbach, K. D. 40, 85, 115
emotional assets *see* intellectual and emotional assets
emotional intelligence 82
emotional response from consumers 504–505
employee behaviour 15, 25, 36, 38, 84, 297; *see also* behaviour
employee-company: associations 366; personalities 366; relationships 77; reputation 366
employee occupational identity 289–300; antecedents to 294–295; background 289–291; case study 298–300; characterisation 298–299; conceptual framework 298; consequences of 295–297; contractedness of 291–292; evolution of 293–294; personal identity 293; restructuring 299–300; value placed on work roles 292–293
employer branding 289, 293–294, 297
Ennew, C. T. 234
environmental antecedents 151
equality: advertising campaign *425*; gender diversity and 366; policies 370; and sustainability 422–424
"Equilibrium" campaign 355
Erdem, O. 154
Erikson, E. 12

Esch, F.-R. 450
e-tailing 348–349, 350–351
ethical values 34
Evans, J. R. 149
Everett, S. 20
experiential marketing 4, 140, 142, **143**, 145, 157–158, 271; customer experience 276–278; entertainment and 338; hedonic devises 278; literature 262–263, 275, 279
explicit objective knowledge 81
exploratory factor analysis (EFA) 121, **122–124**, 263, 270–273, *271–273*
extrinsic motivation 228, 241–242

Facebook 208, 429, 523
face-to-face questionnaires 117
Fahy, J. 91
fashion brand image: conceptual framework 314; lovemark 319–320; perceived fashion innovativeness 307–309, 321; and purchase intention 318–320; and word of mouth 318–320
fashion industry *see* UK fashion industry
fashion innovativeness (FI) 307–321, **323**; ability to take risks in trying newness 310–311; affective/intimacy associations 312–313, 317; antecedents of 311–313; attraction to newness 310; autonomy in innovative decision 310; brand awareness 313, 317–318; cognitive/mystery associations 314–316; conceptual framework 314; consequences of 313–321; data analysis 322–325; data collection 322–325; evaluation of measurement model 327–330; fashion brand image 318–321; importance-performance map analysis (IPMA) 331–332; instrumental development and assessment 322; lovemark 319–320; model fit 325–327; mystery/cognitive association 311; purchase intention 313–314, 318–321; sensory/sensuality associations 311–312, 316–317; shopping experience **327**; social media marketing 321; testing structural model 330–331; word of mouth 314, 318–321
feedback 208, 235; communication strategy 429; and continuous self-assessment 469–471; in corporate identity management 374; customer satisfaction 502, 504; defined 235; online communication 210

Index 543

feeling states 152–154, 156
FI *see* fashion innovativeness
Fill, C. 14, **49**, **51**, **54**, 208
firm-based factors 283–284
FirstBank 213–214
Fishbien, M. 313
Fisher, G. 367
Fisk, R. P. 243
Fitbit 307, 310
FlyKnit 424
Fombrun, C. J. 34, **45**, 80, 210
Foreman, J. 212
Foroudi, M. M. 26, 118, 182, 219, 366, 376
Fournier, S. 237, 278, 401, 408
Frank, N. 446
Frow, P. 228
Fruhling, A. L. 86
Fujita, M. 480
Füller, J. 242
fuzzy set qualitative comparative analysis (fsQCA) 97, 114; corporate reputation 119–120; findings from 126–128

Gagliardi, P. 183
Gallagher, S. 242
Gammoh, B. S. 93
García-Gallego, J. M. 371
generative capacity 15
Gentile, C. 262, 278
George, J. F. 407
Gerbing, D. W. 126, 327, 380
Gestalt theory 182
Giglio, S. 349
Gilmore, J. H. 145, 262, 275, 277–278
Gioia, D. A. 23, **45**, 470
global warming 421–424, 422, 426
Goffman, E. 290
Golder, P. N. 236
Goldsmith, R. 309
Gomez, S. J. 476
Gong, T. 233–234, 244
good dominant logic (G-D logic) 222–225, **223**, 236, 238, 244
goodness-of-fit index 126
Goodwin and Co. 515
Google 289
Google Campus 460–462
Google for Entrepreneurs project 460
Gouillart, F. 226
Goulding, C. 188
graphic design *see* visual identity
gratification 450–451

Gray, E. R. 32, **43–45**, **47**, **53–54**
Gregory, J. R. **46**
Greyser, S. A. 16
Groening, M. 419
Grönroos, C. 220–221, 226, 228, 230, 236
Gross, M. A. 274
Groth, M. 235
Guardian, The 429
Gucci app 355–357, 357
Gucci Garden 355
Guido, G. 295
Gulbrandsen, I. T. 209
Gummesson, E. 225
Gupta, S. 289

Ha, Y. W. 146
Haeckel, S. H. 260
Hafeez, K. 78, 92, 94
Hagel, J. 451
Hair, J. F. 121, 329–330, 380
Hajj 409
Hall, R. 80
Hamel, G. 77
haptic sense 142, 147, 157, 312, 492–493
Harley-Davidson 447–448
Harley Owners Group (HOG) 447–448
Harman's one-factor examination 380
Harpaz, I. 376
Harrington, T. C. 119
Harris, P. 38
Hashima, A. A. 480–481
Haslam, S. A. 182
Hatch, M. J. 17, 33, **45**, **48–49**
Hawke, R. 92
He, F. 445
He, H. 15, 17, 22–23, 30, **39**, **41–43**, **54**
Hearn, A. 473
hedonic consumption 140, 142, 146, 153, 263, 276–277
hedonic experiences 146, 153, 155, 157, 263, 266, 277–278, 280
hedonico-sensory stimuli 153
hedonic profiles 153
Helal, G. 480
helping 169, 175, 235, 479
Henseler, J. 325, 330
Hermès, A 193
Hermès, C.-E. 192–193
Hermès, E.-M. 193–194
Hermès, T. 192
Hermès International 192–194
heterotrait-monotrait ratio (HTMT) 329–330, **330**, 454, **455**

544 *Index*

hierarchical cluster analysis (HCA)
261–263, 266–269, *270*
higher education 55–56, 387–388,
479–480
Higher Education Funding Council 58
Hirsch, P. M. 240
Hirschman, E. C. 146, 153, 240,
276–277, 309
H&M 307
Hoch, S. J. 146, 154
Hoegg, J. 146
Hoffman, D. L. 242
Hofstede, G. 76, 406
Holbrook, M. B. 145–146, 153, 155, 240,
276–277
Holland, J. 451
Homburg, C. 240
Homer, P. M 518
Honda 448, 452, 454, 457, 459
Hooley, G. J. 90
Horton, D. 523
Hovland, C. 517
Hughes, D. E. 238
Hultén, B. 142, 152, 488
human capital 81–82, 86, 89, 92
humanism 416–427
Hutchinson, J. W. 154
hypothesis development in brand
knowledge 448–451
hypothesis testing in corporate identity
management **384**

Ibarra, H. 292–293
ideal identity 28–29
identification 237–238; characteristics 18;
core competence 100; corporate identity
and 16; online 353; organisational 16–
17, 23, 25, 289, 296; research identity
and 15; social 24–25; stakeholder/s 18,
22, 30
identity: change 32–33; characteristics
18; conceived 28–29; corporate
sensory 3; defined 12; desired 22, 26,
28–29; differentiation and 145; ideal
28–29; perspectives 18; powers 14–15;
research 15; *see also* corporate identity;
organisational identification
IDT *see* innovation diffusion theory
IFI *see* incremental fit index
Iglesias, O. 142, 220, 488
Ikonen, M. 81
IMC *see* integrated marketing
communications

immigration ban 424–426
IMP *see* industrial marketing and
purchasing
implicit cognition 155
importance-performance map analysis
(IPMA) 331–332, **334**, *334*
incremental fit index (IFI) 126, 382
Ind, N. 21
India 452, 516
individual identity 12
individual value creation 488
Indonesia 445, 448, 452–453
industrial marketing and purchasing
(IMP) 224
information processing **143**, 146–147,
154–155
information quality 85–86
information seeking 233–234
information sharing 233–234
innovation adoption 365, 375, 379, **379**,
382, 385–386
innovation diffusion theory (IDT) 348
innovation management 95, 347–348
innovative decision *see* autonomy in
innovative decision
innovativeness *see* fashion innovativeness
Instagram 208, 354, 499, 523
intangible assets: capability 89; contract-
based 90; customer-related 90; digital
technology 85–86; intellectual and
emotional 75; marketing capability
90–91; organisational 76–77
intangible capital 81
intangible resources 80–81, 89, 238–239
integrated capabilities 94
integrated communication approach 20–21
integrated corporate communication 19
integrated marketing communications
(IMC) 35; *see also* communication
integrative capacity 15
intellectual and emotional assets 78–82;
and marketing capability 89
intellectual assets 75, 80, 82
intellectual capital 80–82, 89
intellectual property 89
intellectual structure of customer
experience 263–273; *see also* customer
experience (CX)
interaction in the workplace 295
interactive technologies 487–489, 491
Interbrand 444
interdisciplinary/multi-disciplinary
approach 27–30

interference in the workplace 295
internalisation 25, 451, 519–520
interpersonal interactions 81
intimacy/affective association 312–313
intrinsic motivation 241–242
intrinsic nature of corporate identity
14–17; *see also* corporate identity
IPMA *see* importance-performance map
analysis
Iran 376
Irani, Z. 56
Isbell, D. S. 295
Islamic brand love 401–410; case study
409–410; consumption in the Quran
402–403; culture and 405–408; defined
401; future research 409; love 403–404;
Muslim consumer 402–404; religious
beliefs and 404–405; *see also* brand love/
hedonic

Jackson, M. 522
Jain, V. 260
Jakarta 452, **453**, 454
James, L. 422
Jankel-Elliott, N. 406
Japan 516
Jazz Fit Club Indonesia 454
Jenkins, E. **44, 54**
Jisc Online-Surveys 452
Joachimsthaler, E. 22, 372
Jobs, S. 175–176, 178
Johnen, M. 349
joint value creation sphere 221
Jordan, M. 209, 516
Just, S. N. 209

Kaepernick, C. 434–435, 436
Kahle, L. R. 518
Kaiser-Meyer-Olkin (KMO) 121
Kamakura, W. A. 279
Kamins, M. A. 518
Kapoor, R. 375
Karaosmanoglu, E. 14, 34, **41**
Kashyap, V. 82
Kavida, V. 80–81
Keller, K. L. 154, 156, 169, 318, 320,
445–446
Kellogg, D. L. 234
Kelman, H. C. 451, 519
Kennedy, S. H. 18, 20, 206
Khalifa, A. S. 232
Khedher, M. 473–474
Kim, J. W. 448

Kiriakidou, O. **45**
Kissler, G. D. 32
Kleine, S. S. 243
Knight, C. 182
Knight, P. 526
knowledge: brand 445–446, 448–450;
capital 89; collective 91; competencies
96; defined 80; economy 75; firm
capability to learn and acquire 86;
intellectual and emotional assets 80–81;
sensory brand experiences (SBE) 142,
143–144
Knowledge Push Curve (KPC) 348
Kodas Cigarettes 515
Kohli, C. **50**
Konrad, A. M. 373
Kotler, P. 148, 184, 445–446
Kottasz, R. **40**
Kraft, R. 498
Kranzbühler, A.-M. 260
Kress, G. R. 183
Krishna, A. 147, 153, 493
Kunda, Z. 238
Kunene, S. 208

Lam, S. S. 237
Lambert, A. **53**
Lambert, D. M. 119
Lappeenranta University 281
Larson, K. 208
Lawu, B. J. 450
Ledford, J. 31, 33
legitimacy 446–447, 475
Lehtinen, J. R. 236–237
Lehtinen, U. 236–237
Le Louarn's innovativeness scale 308, 310
Lemon, K. N. 261–262, 269, 275, 490
lesbian, gay, bisexual and transgender
(LGBT) 425, 433
Leuthesser, L. **50**, 366
Levin, D. Z. 240
Levin, M. L. 27, 32
Levi's 307
Lewis, R. C. 237
Liao, M. N. **41**
Liaw, G. F. 446
Libai, B. 447
Likert scales 97, 119, 126, 322
Lim, W. M. 241
Linnehan, F. 373
Ljungquist, U. 92
London-based business school 55–59
Louboutin, C. 311

546 *Index*

lovemark and purchase intention 319–320

loyalty *see* brand loyalty; consumers/ customers

Lusch, R. F. 219–226, **227**, 228, 231–232, 238–239, 266, 274–275

luxury 403; brands 181, 349, 489; industry 502; items 403; retailing 349; valorisation of aesthetic heritage 192–194

Lynn Shostack, G. 274

Mack, A. 493

Maclaren, P. 188

macro-citizens 436

Madonna 522

Mael, F. A. 23, 25–26

Magee, K. C. 95

Maglio, P. P. 222–223

management construct 30

managerial antecedents 151, 157–158

managerial cognition 17, 23

managerial conclusive benefits 506

managerial contribution 129–130

managerial implications of SBE 157–158; *see also* sensory brand experiences (SBE)

Mann-Whitney U-test 119, 380

Manoharan, A. 371–372

Manolescu, D. A. 498

March for Our Lives 433

Margulies, W. P. 18, **53–54**

marketing approach 21–23

marketing capability 75–78, 91–92; combination with technology 86; core competence and 76, 97, 100; defined 76; intangible assets 90–91; and intellectual and emotional assets 89; physical/ tangible assets 89–90

marketing communications 4, 19–20, 22, 35–36, 181, 208

marketing competencies 75–100; background 77–78; case study 100; communication key capability 94–95; competencies 91–92, 96–97; core competencies 96–97; corporate brand identity management 93; cultural assets 86–91; customer relationship management 93–94; design management 95; emotional assets 78–82; innovation management 95; intellectual assets 78–82; marketing capability 75–78, 91–92; market-sensing capability 92–93; model testing

97; performance management 95–96; physical assets 83–86; propositions development 77–78; research 99; social media 94–95; *see also* competence

marketing strategies 176, 338, 353, 355, 467

marketing theory 20, 100

market orientation 90

market-sensing capability 92–93

Markwick, N. 14, **48**, **51**, **54**

Marriot hotels 289

Martineau, P. 12

Martín Gutiérrez, S. S. 241

Massiah, C. 235

match-up hypothesis, celebrity endorsement 518–519

McAlexander, J. H. 276

McCabe, D. B. 146

McColl-Kennedy, J. R. 149

McCracken, G. 237, 517–518

McDonald, M. P. 94

McGrath, M. A. 148

meaning transfer theory, celebrity endorsement 517–518

measurement of brand knowledge 452, 454

Mehrabian, A. 155, 276

Melewar, T. C. 34, **41**, **44–46**, **54**, 87, 95, 379, 405

Melissa (footwear company) 336–340, 337–339

mergers/acquisitions 16, 371

Merunka, D. 408

Merz, M. A. 186, 219

#MeToo movement 433

Meyer, C. 240

Micheli, P. 375

Mick, D. G. 408

Middle East 402, 480

Milliman, R. 148–149, 152

Millward, L. J. **45**

minimalism 175–178

Mishra, A. S. 519

Misra, S. 518

mission: corporate 26–27, 31–32, 34; corporate identity management 367–369; cultural 87; philosophy and value 30–34; statements 27, 31, 336

Mitra, D. 236

Mittal, V. 279

model(s): on celebrity endorsement 517–519; CHIS 187; conceptual 115–117, 239, 322; consumer learning 154; of corporate reputation 115–117; customer experience 149; economy experience 145; fit 325–327; measurement 327–330; multimodality 142; research *451*, 451–452; servicescapes 263; structural model test 454; testing 97

Modern Jazz Social 426

Moingeon, B. **52**, 88

MoMa 421, 424–426, *426*

mono-method quantitative research 322

Monroe, K. B. 237

Morgan, N. A. 91

Moriarty, S. E. 35

Moussa, A. 187

Moustaghfir, K. 80

Mujeeb, E. M. 95

Mukherjee, A. 15, **39**, **54**

Müller, M. 461

multi-dimensional analysis (MDS) 261, 263–266, *264–265*, 267

multi-disciplinary approach 20, 23, 27–30

multiple group analysis (MGA) *456*, 456–457, **458**

multiple sensory modalities 146

multisensory atmospherics 149; *see also* atmospherics

multi-sensory brand experience 183

multi-sensory integration 487–489, 491

Muniz, A. M., Jr. 278

Murray, J. H. 94

Muslim consumer 402–404

mystery/cognitive association 311

National Student Survey (NSS) 59

near-field communications (NFC) 348

need for touch (NFT) 146, 493

negative publicity and celebrity endorsement 522

New York fashion week *338*

Next Plc 100

NFC *see* near-field communications

NFI *see* normed-fit-index (NFI)

NFT *see* need for touch

Nguyen, N. 22

Nike 421, 422–424, 428, 432–435, *436*, 449, 507–508, 516, 526–527

Nike Grind 424

Nilsson, E. 189

Nitzan, I. 447

Nolan, L. 474

non-controlled communications 28

non-response bias 380

normed-fit-index (NFI) 126, 382

North London 322, 325, 332, 334, **334**, *334*

Novak, T. P. 242

Novel Solutions 298–300

Nowlis, S. M. 146

NSS *see* National Student Survey

occupational identity *see* employee occupational identity

O'Gorman, C. 31

O'Guinn, T. C. 278

Ohanian, R. 517, 525

Oksiutycz, A. 208

olfactory atmospherics 149; *see also* atmospherics

olfactory stimuli 142, 145, 147, 149, 159, 184, 189, 191, 277

Olins, W. 19–20, **44**, **47**, **52**, **54–55**

Oliveira, P. 95

Oliver, R. L. 243, 278, 408

Olson, J. 141

omnichannel integration 351–352

omnichannel retailing 352

Onasanya, B. 213

online corporate communication 210–211; *see also* communication

online identification 353; *see also* identification

online stakeholder (customer) engagement 209–210

operant resources **223**, 239

organisational approach 23–27

organisational behaviour 15, 17, 19, 23, 29, 84, 87, 116, 172; *see also* behaviour

organisational change 15–17

organisational cognition 17, 23

organisational culture 18–19, 33, 95

organisational gains 478

organisational history 34

organisational identification 15–17, 23, 25, 289, 296; *see also* identification

organisational identity 13–15, 24; defined 17; mutual recognition between corporate identity and 17; studies 25; subdivision 18

organisational image 24–25

organisational mission 26–27, 31–32, 34, 38

organisational performance 14, 78, 477

organisational philosophy 32, 34

organisational psychology 17

organisational reputation 24; *see also* corporate reputation

organisational structure 28, 116, 351

organisational values 33–34, 38

548 *Index*

organisation beliefs 32, 187
organisation core values 33
organisation resource 78
organisation strategy 33
organisation values 32–34, 38, 368
organisation vision 27
Osborne, P. 223
Osei-Frimpong, K. 452
Otnes, C. 188

Pan, Y. **52**
parasocial relationship and celebrity
 endorsement 523
Parasuraman, A. 236–237, 265, 274
Paris Agreement 424
Paris Climate Agreement 421
Park, J. A. 237
Parker, M. 423–424
Parmentier, M. A. 476
partial least squares (PLS) 325
participation behaviour 233–234, 244
passion 7, 205, 212, 296, 312–313,
 469, 471
Patnaik, K. G. K. 294
Payne, A. F. 226, 228–229, 266
Pearson, P. H. 316
Peck, J. 146, 493
Pecot, F. 187–188
peer experience 240
peer loyalty 242
peer motivation 241–242
peer perceived quality 235; *see also*
 perceived quality
peer relationship strength 242–243
peer resources 238–240
peer satisfaction 241
peer-to-peer (P2P) 218, 220, 245
Peng, L. 349
perceived behavioural control 314, 409
perceived brand value 20, 35
perceived quality 82, 236–237
perception 498; customers/consumers
 82, 114, 149, 349, 354, 371, 406;
 employees 294; mastication and
 orosensory 147; of movement
 493; organisational members 23;
 purchasing organisation 91; sensory
 brand experiences (SBE) 152–154;
 stakeholders 22, 33–35, 130, 210
performance management 78, 92, 95–96
personal brand/branding 467–481;
 antecedents of 475–476; authenticity
 472–473; background 467–468; case

study 480–481; communiction 476–477;
continuous self-assessment 469–471;
differentiation 472; dimensions of
471, 472; feedback 469–471; future
research 479–480; image 470, 477–478;
mediating effects of 476; overview
468–469; performance 470–471, 475,
477–478; personal brand positioning
476; self-knowledge 475; self-
presentation 473; social capital 476;
theoretical framework 475–478, 479;
theories 473–475; visual appearance 473
personal brand positioning: personal brand
 image 477–478; personal branding 476;
 personal brand performance 477
personal gains 477
personal identity 25, 85, 115, 129,
 176, 293
personal interaction 233–234
Peter, A. J. 476
Peter, J. P 141
Peters, T. 468
Pettit, K. L. 291
physical assets 75, 83–86
physical resources 239–240
physical stimuli/ambient conditions *see*
 ambient conditions/physical stimuli
physical structure/spatial layout and
 functionality 76, 83–84
physical/tangible assets: marketing
 capability 89–90
Pilditch, J. **53**
Pine, J. B. 145, 262, 275, 277–278
Pizza Hut 289
Pleasure-Arousal-Dominance (PAD)
 Emotional State Model 276
Plummer, J. T. 12
political discourse *see* societal corporate
 branding
Pondar, K. **42**
positioning: and branding 55–59; and
 competitive advantage 348; corporation
 29; differentiation and 87; personal 474;
 strategic 207
Positioning the Battle of Your Mind
 (Ries and Trout) 468
positive attitudes 242, 357, 476, 523;
 see also attitude(s)
positivism (deductive) approach 321
Powell, S. M. **39–40**
pragmatism 416–427
Prahalad, C. K. 77
Pratt, M. G. 14

predictive validity 131
Prentice, C. 452
Price, L. L. 276
primitive brand variables 155–156
Prinzie, A. A. 368
product strategies 336, 340
Project Management Institute 96
propositions: corporate reputation 115–117; development 77–78; experiential marketing 277; model testing 97; value 437; value co-creation 228
provider value creation sphere 221
psychoanalysis 12
Public Health England 211
Pullman, M. E. 274
purchase intention 313–314, 318–320, **324**; brand community engagement and 450–451; brand knowledge and 449–450; lovemark and 319–320; word of mouth and 320–321
Puth, G. **51**

QSR NVivo software Version 8 489–490
qualitative research design 489

Ramanantsoa, B. **52**, 88
Ramaswamy, V. 226
Rampersad, H. K. 478
Rani, M. 407
Ranjan, K. R. 231
Rao, A. J. M. 294
Rao, A. R. 237
Ravald, A. 226
Ravasi, D. 369
Read, S. 231
relative fit index (RFI) 126
religious beliefs and Islamic brand love 404–405
Research Assessment Exercise (RAE) 58
research conceptual framework 78, 79
resource advantage theory (R-A) 78, 80, 239
resource-based theory (RBV) 75–78, 100, 238–239
resource-based view 77–78, 80, 91, 99
resources 229–230; intangible 80–81, 89, 238–239; operant **223**, 239; organisational 78; peer 238–240; physical 239–240; value co-creation (VCC) 229–230
responsible behaviour 233–234, 244
responsible personal interaction 244
Richard Wohl, R. 523

Ries, A. 468
Rifkin, J. 229
Rindell, A. 206
Rindova, V. P. 34
Roberts, K. 309, 312–313, 317
Rodie, A. R. 243
Rodriguez, G. 425
Rogers, P. S. 31
role theory 12
root-mean-squared-approximation-of-error (RMSEA) 126, 380
Roschk, H. 155
Rose, G. M. 188
Rosenbaum, M. S. 235
Rossen, P. E. T. 90
Rossiter, J. 148
Roth, A. V. 95
Roy, S. K. 408
Russell, J. A. 155, 276
Russiagate scandal 418
Ryan, R. M. 242

salience 17, 24, 294–295, 297
salience dichotic theory 295
sampling and data, brand knowledge 452–454
sampling and survey administration, corporate identity management 376
Santos, F. P. 188
Saunders, J. **46**
Sayuti, N. M. 407
Schaufeli, W. B. 296
Schmitt, B. H. **51–52**, 145, 184, 260–262, 277–278
Schnittka, O. 349
schools of thought in marketing **222**
Schultz, M. 17, 33, **48–49**
Schwager, A. 240
search engine optimization (SEO)-led 497–498
search intent 498
Selame, E. **53**
Selame, J. **53**
self-concept 23, 237, 293–294, 515
self-determination theory 241
self-knowledge 469, 475, 477–478
self-presentation 13, 20, 38, 90, 471, 473–473, 478
Sen, S. 30, 237
sensation: auditory 147; brand-related 145; gustative 160; haptic 493; and perception 147, 153; sensory brand experiences (SBE) 152–154

550 *Index*

sense of movement 494–495
sense of touch 146–147, 493
sensory brand experiences (SBE) 140–160, **143**; antecedents of 151–152; automatic behaviour 155–156; background 140–141; brand experience 142–145; brand personality and engagement 157; case study 159–160; co-creativity 155–156; consumer environment studies 148–149; consumption experience 145–146; defined 141; experiential marketing 145; feeling states 152–154; future research 149–151; information processing 146–147, 154–155; integrative framework of 150; knowledge fields 142, **143–144**; managerial implications 157–158; nature of 152–154; outcomes of 155–156; perception 152–154; primitive brand variables 155–156; sensation 152–154; sensory marketing 147–148; service marketing 149
sensory marketing (SM) 4, 142, **144**; defined 487–488; sensory brand experiences (SBE) 147–148
sensory/sensuality associations 311–312, 316–317, 319, 321, **323**, 331
Senyucel, Z. 372
service design 218, 262, 267, 269, 270–272, 274, 284
service-dominant logic (S-D logic) 185–186, 196, **223**, 224–226, **227**, 239, 263, 271
service-driven antecedents 151
service marketing **144**; customer experience 274–276; sensory brand experiences (SBE) 149
service quality 82, 270; customer behavioural consequences 264; defined 491; measurement 236; in retailing 267; service functions and 185
servicescapes 149, 152, 185, 190–191, 263
set-theoretic approach 119
Shah, S. K. 446
Shanley, M. **45**
Sharia 402–406, **406**
sharing economy business model 220
Shen, H. 155
Sherry, J. F. Jr. 148
Shih, C. M. 91
Shimp, T. A. 375
Shostack, G. L. 222

showrooming 352
Shultz, M. **45**
Siau, K. 86
Silpakit, P. 243
Simoes, C. **41**, **54**
Simons, A. 473
Simonson, A. **51**, 184
simplicity 175–177, *177*
Simpson, O. J. 522
Simpsons, The 418–420
Singal, M. 371–372
Sivakoumar, N. 80–81
Sivakumar, K. 244
skills: analytical 351; communication 470; digital 282; intellectual and emotional assets 80–81; interpersonal 291; marketing 94; self-promotion 477; of staff 89
small and medium-sized enterprises (SMEs) 77, 80–82, 89, 91
smart assistant 502
smart retail technologies (SRT) 348
Smith, D. C. 156
Snow, D. 293
social capital 81, 476
social identification 16, 24–25; *see also* identification
social identity 19, 25, 131, 290
social identity theory 15, 24–25, 30, 114, 366, 480
social influence theory 519–520
social learning theory 520
social media 4, 93–95, 169, 177–178, 208; celebrity endorsement and 523–524; marketing 321, **324**
social movements 427–435
social networks 208
social strategy 178
societal corporate branding 415–437; consumers' boycott 427–435; corporate citizenship campaigns 427–435; future research 437; humanism 416–427; pragmatism 416–427; social movements 427–435; Trump, D. 416–427
Soenen, G. B. 33, **46**, **54**
Souiden, N. 407
Spector, A. J. 13
Spence, C. 149, 152
spin-offs 16
Spohrer, J. 222–223
Spreitzer, G. M. 293
Stadler, M. M. **54**
stakeholder-focus brand era 186

standardised root mean squared residual (SRMR) 325
Stanford, T. R. 491
Starbucks 243, 429–432
Steenkamp, N. 82
Stein, B. E. 491
Steiner, L. **43**
stereotype 88, 289, 293–295, 297
Stevens, J. 117
Stimulant-Organism-Response (S-OR) model 148, 154–156
Stokburger-Sauer, N. 237
store atmospherics **144**, 149, 151–152, 155; *see also* atmospherics
store image 12, 349
Stotvig, S. **48**
Strati, A. 183
structural equation modelling (SEM) 97, 114, 325
structural model test 454
Stuart, H. **43**, **50**
subculture 88–89
subjective norms 407, 409
subsistence (basic necessities) 402
Suciu, M. C. 81
sufficiency consumption 403
Sukoco, B. M. 448
Sumita, T. 82
Suntours 298–300
superior designs 336
survey instrument, corporate reputation 118–119
survey measures, corporate identity management 376–380, **377–379**
sustainability: challenges 206; corporate 386; and equality 422–424; growth 336; personal brand 472; and social science 307
Sutton, R. I. 25
Suvatjis, J. Y. **43**
Swales, J. M. 31
symbolic artefacts/decor and artefacts 76, 84–85
symbolism 13, 18–19, 26–27, 30, 37–38, 151, 160, 280, 366, 515

tactile atmospherics 149; *see also* atmospherics
tactile stimuli 145–149, 159, 184, 189, 277
Tajfel, H. 290
tangible assets 75–78, 83–86
Tapscott, D. 229

taste atmospherics 149; *see also* atmospherics
taste stimuli 142, 145, 147, 149, 151–152, 157, 183, 191, 277, 311, 336
Taylor, S. A. 236
Teas, R. K. 236
technology acceptance model (TAM) 348
technology-based intangible assets 90
technology management 347–348
Teece, D. J. 92
Tehran (Iran) 376, 386
Tenenhaus, M. 325
Terry, J. 522
testing structural model 330–331
themed experiences 145
theoretical contribution 128–129
theoretical framework, personal branding 475–478, 479
theory of complexity 114
theory of social identity 290
Thompson, C. 239
three spheres of value co-creation 221
Till, B. D. 518
Times of London, The 429
Tiruwa, A. 457
tolerance 233, 235, 431
Tombs, A. 149
Topalian, A. 18, **43**
top management driving force 372–374
total corporate communication 20–21, 28, 206
Toyota Owner Club (TOC) 448
transformational leadership 95
travel ban 424–426
triangular theory of love 312
TripAdvisor 349
Trout, J. 468
Trump, D. 416–435, *422*
trust 4; and commitment 75, 243; credibility and corporate image 171; customers/consumers 22, 504; intellectual and emotional assets 81–82; stakeholders 210; of target audiences 25; time and 94
Tsai, M. T. 91
Tsiotsou, R. 236–237
Tucker-Lewis-index (TLI) 126, 382
Turley, L. 148–149, 152
Turner, J. C. 290
turnover 289–290, 294–298
Twitter 208, 289, 354, 429, 433, 523
Tyson, M. 522

552 *Index*

Uber 220
UGC *see* user generated content
UK fashion industry 307–340; analysis and results 325–332, 333–334; fashion brand image 307–309; fashion innovativeness 307–321; future research 332–335; research model and methods 321–325
umbrella syndrome 260
Unilever 429; *see also* Dove
United Arab Emirates 402
United Kingdom 132, 516
United Nations Framework Convention on Climate Change (UNFCC) 421
United Nations support programme (UNSP) 410
United States 386, 421, 423–424, 433, 516
University of West London (UWL) 387–388
Urde, M. 33, **45**, 173
user (customer) experience adaptations 501
user generated content (UGC) 349
U.S. Show Jumping Team 193
Uzkurt, C. 243

Vafeas, M. 233
value 30–34; and beliefs 367; citizens 437; companies 22–23, 33–34, 87, 211; mutual cultural 90; placed on work roles 292–293; proposition 185, 230
value co-creation (VCC) 218–245; active participation 243–244; antecedents and consequences 235–236; case study 245; citizenship behaviour 235–236; concept of service 221–224; co-production and 231–232; customer value co-creation behaviour 233; and development 218–225; economic and social actors 228–229; future research 244–245; identification 237–238; importance of 219–220; mechanisms 230–233; in online community 244; participation behaviour 233–234; peer experience 240; peer loyalty 242; peer motivation 241–242; peer relationship strength 242–243; peer resources 238–240; peer satisfaction 241; perceived quality 236–237; resources 229–230; service-dominant logic 224–226, **227**; three spheres of 221
value-in-use approach *see* consumers/ customers
Van den Bosch, A. L. M. 40

Van Heerden, C. H. **46**, **51**
Van Leeuwen, T. 183
Van Maanen, J. 88
Van Rekom, J. 31, **44**, **50**, **54**
Van Riel, C. B. M. 20, 29, **44**, **47–48**, **50–51**, **54–55**, 87, 210, 368
Varey, R. J. 228, 232
Vargo, S. L. 155, 219–226, **227**, 228, 231–232, 238–239, 266, 274–275
variance inflation factor (VIF) 329–330
Varlander, S. 116
VCC *see* value co-creation
Venkatraman, M. P. 316
Verhoef, P. C. 149, 152, 261–262, 269, 275–276, 278, 350, 490
Vick, M. 522
Victoria (queen) 515
ViewStream 281–284
VIF *see* variance inflation factor
virtual environment for brand 504
virtual perception of space 493
virtual space 170
visible system approach (VSA) 224
vision: corporate 32–33, 87; corporate identity management 367–369; cultural assets 87; mission and 27, 32; organisation 27
visual appearance, personal branding 473
visual atmospherics 149; *see also* atmospherics
visual behavioural school 19
visual brand identity 182–183
visual identity/identification 17–20, 22, 26, 36–37, 76; *see also* corporate visual identity
visual sense 493
visual stimuli 493
Voima, P. 220–221
Volkswagen 449
Vorhies, D. W. 91
VSA *see* visible system approach

Wakefield, K. 148
Walasek, L. 349
Wallendorf, M. 489
Wang, K. 296
Wang, M. C. 75
Ward, C. 476
Ward, T. 236
Watson, R. 208
webmosphere 487
webrooming 352, 356
Weitz, B. 243

Welch-Satterthwait Test (WST) 457, **458**
West, J. 242
Whetten, D. A. **53**
Wilimzig 449, 451
Williams, A. D. 229
Williams, S. 422, 425
Wilson, A. 34, **44**, **48**, **54**
Wilson, T. 233
Wirtz, J. 156
Woods, A. 56
Woods, E. 526
Woods, T. 209, 516, 522, 526–527
Wooldridge, A. **45**
word of mouth (WOM) 154–155, 237, 314, 318–321, **324**, 408, 519
work engagement 290, 294–298
World Bank 453
World Health Organisation 356
World Intellectual Property Report 444

Wu, P. L. 126
Wu, W.-Y. 448
Wyckham, R. G. 221

Yankee Group Report 451
Yates, D. 476
Yi, Y. 233–235, 244
Yin, J. 296
Yoo, D. K. 237
YouTube 523

Zaha Hadid (architecture) 339
Zarantonello, L. 260–262
Zeithaml, V. A. 225, 232, 237, 265, 274, 314
Zeta-Jones, C. 516
Zha, D. 494, 496
Zheng, X. 457
Zinkhan, G. M. **45**

Printed in the United States
by Baker & Taylor Publisher Services